Wallace-Homestead

PRICE GUIDE
TO ANTIQUES
AND PATTERN GLASS

EIGHTH EDITION

p.60

EDITED BY ROBERT W. MILLER

Other books by Robert W. Miller

American Primitives
The Art Glass Basket
Clock Guide Identification with Prices
Clock Guide Identification with Prices, Book II
Fabulous Houston Museum
Mary Gregory and Her Glass
Oriental Primer
Pictorial Guide to Early American Tools and Implements
Wallace-Homestead Flea Market Price Guide
Wallace-Homestead Price Guide to Dolls
Wallace-Homestead Price Guide to Toys

Copyright© 1982
Wallace-Homestead Book Company

ISBN 0-87069-365-4
Library of Congress Catalog No.74-84521

Cover photograph: Perry Struse, West Des Moines, Iowa
Antiques courtesy of: Wilbur and Opal Williams
The China Closet, Engelbert House
1910 Army Post Road Des Moines, Iowa

Other photography: Tom Needham, Panama City Beach, Florida
Marshall Thurman, Knoxville, Tennessee, and
John Shuman III, Pottstown, Pennsylvania

Published by

Wallace-Homestead Book Company
1912 Grand Avenue
Des Moines, Iowa 50309

Contents

Introduction

This Eighth Edition of the WALLACE-HOMESTEAD PRICE GUIDE TO ANTIQUES & PATTERN GLASS is dedicated to the beginning collector and the beginning dealer. We won't tell you that our prices are so up-to-date the ink's still wet, because you're too smart to believe that. However, like prices on everything from automobiles to clothing and food, prices on antiques and collectibles are going out of sight.

We will tell you that this Eighth Edition is a *guide* to help you avoid some of the pitfalls encountered by too many beginners in the world of antiques and collectibles.

Today many people are investment-happy when it comes to antiques. This can be dangerous because if you don't know the market, get ready for the boat ride! Certainly there are many fine investments, but *before* you leap, look around and find out what's going on at the shops, the shows, and the auction houses.

Once again we give you *more* categories, *more* photos, and *more* information. Please compare this Eighth Edition, WALLACE-HOMESTEAD PRICE GUIDE TO ANTIQUES & PATTERN GLASS, to the others *before* you buy any price guide. Buying by mail? Looking for a competent auctioneer? Want to find a reliable person to repair your old clock? Well, as we just said, compare all the price guides, then ask yourself *which* price guide does the most for *you.*

It's all well and good to inundate you with thousands of meaningless prices spewed out of a computer, but aren't you a bit tired of hearing, "Buy ours, we were first in the business"? Anyone knows you're going to buy the price guide that best suits you. That's why we ask you to compare.

Does our split-price system work? It must, everyone else is using it. Are we adding the categories you want to see listed? We must be, the other guides are following our lead. *Guide,* that's the magic word.

We're a guide, no more, no less. And we know we're helping you because our sales have never been better.

What's a good investment in the year to come? Consider fine period English furniture, English carriage clocks, Persian provincial and tribal rugs, Mason's ironstone, 18th century German porcelain, and 18th century Georgian cut glass; also Victorian silver and heavy gold, if gold continues to rise. Be careful about sterling silver. If President Reagan dumps that fifty million ounces on the market, you won't be able to give away sterling. Art Nouveau and Art Deco, both in jewelry and furniture; first edition books and quality Orientals such as Ch'ing porcelain, netsukes, and Japanese prints. As always, if you don't know your antiques, know your antiques dealer.

From where we sit, the next big collecting craze will be American dinnerware. Jewelry continues to bring brisk prices, as do the better pieces of American art glass. And as we've said many, many times, go for quality. Just because it's a bargain is no reason to waste your money. Carry this Eighth Edition with you. Then you'll know what to buy and what to ignore.

We thank you for purchasing what we consider to be the finest price guide in the world. Although every effort has been made to avoid errors, the editor and the publisher cannot be held responsible for errors in typography or in judgment as applied to prices given.

We're always interested in hearing from you, the collector; you, the dealer. Constructive criticism is always welcome as it helps us put together a better price guide. We *do* answer all our mail but be patient, be kind. And be the best-informed in the field of antiques and collectibles by studying this Eighth Edition of the WALLACE-HOMESTEAD PRICE GUIDE TO ANTIQUES & PATTERN GLASS.

How to Buy by Mail

One of the most popular methods of buying and selling antiques is through the U.S. mails. Most antiques publications, whether weekly or monthly, will not knowingly accept advertisements from dishonest people. Unfortunately, some questionable ads slip by the editors, and for that reason we list here some basic rules to follow when you decide to buy or sell by mail.

1. The licensed antiques dealer should guarantee the condition and the authenticity of the merchandise in his ad. This same rule applies to an individual advertising a particular item for sale.

2. When you decide to purchase something that is advertised in one of the many antiques publications, mail your check at once and *always* include a SASE (self-addressed, stamped envelope) in the event the item you order has already been sold. Don't expect the dealer to pay the postage when returning your check. If you especially desire the item, telephone the seller, person-to-person; also, for faster service, send a certified check or a money order. Your personal check may be good locally, but a dealer who doesn't know you has every right to wait until your check clears his bank before mailing you your merchandise.

3. Ask for five-day approval. You won't always get it, but if you do you have the right to return the merchandise if you aren't satisfied.

4. *Unpack Carefully.* Careless unwrapping of merchandise can cost you money, and don't be foolish enough to think you can blame your mistake on the post office. If the post office is responsible, that's one thing—trying to cheat them is a sad mistake.

5. *Pack Carefully.* If you're filling an order, that extra paper and extra time taken can save you lots of grief when the buyer notifies you that your merchandise arrived in a damaged and/or broken condition. If you do receive damaged and/or broken merchandise, save all the wrappings and take the package immediately to your local post office and file a claim. Save the nasty notes and give those responsible time to make good on your purchase.

6. Remember also that buying by mail does *not* include United Parcel Service. Check with the bus lines with respect to saving the wrapping or filing a claim, if you are mailing and/or shipping by bus. Call them and ask what requirements they have for handling your package.

7. Misrepresented merchandise is just that, and you should take every action to get your money back. First, write to the person or persons from whom you made your purchase, sending your letter by Registered Mail, Return Receipt Requested. It will cost you a little more, but you'll know your letter of complaint was received. If your letter fails to get action, check with your local post office to see what, if any, action can be taken. Also, write to the publisher of the publication from whose ad you ordered your merchandise. Most publications are sincere and will honestly try to get your money back. They won't be in business long if they don't.

8. Don't be afraid to order by mail. It's big business and those using the mails to defraud usually end up in court. Reading the advertisement carefully *before* you order can save you a lot of trouble. Buy with confidence and be fair if a disagreement arises between you and the buyer and/or seller. If you're still not satisfied, then follow suggestions in No. 7 above.

How to Buy at Auctions

Whether you're buying at Sotheby Park Bernet, Adam Wecheler & Sons, or Richard A. Bourne Co., to mention just a few of the top auction houses in this country, it doesn't mean a thing unless you understand the chant of the auctioneer.

Few auctioneers' chants are the same. To the uninitiated, it's all a bunch of unintelligible gibberish. Also, the rules of buying vary from state to state, so here are a few basic rules to help you when you attend your first auction:

1. Learn how to bid *before* you bid by listening to the auctioneer's chant for a time, keeping in mind that innocent scratching of your ear or nose or a casual wave to a friend across the aisle may purchase you a genuine toilet seat!

2. You can bid by voice or by the wave of a hand; those known to the auctioneer may bid by a slight nod of the head or some other signal prearranged with the auctioneer. It depends upon the particular auction.

3. Most auction houses will not be responsible for the correctness of description, authenticity, genuineness or condition of the property being sold, so go early and look over the items being offered. When an auctioneer says, "It looks like walnut," he's not saying it *is* walnut. You may be buying a piece of furniture made of poplar. Know what you're buying.

4. The highest bid accepted by the auctioneer is usually the buyer's. If there's a dispute between two bidders, the auctioneer will usually reopen the bidding, but only between disputing bidders. Then, when the hammer falls, the person with the highest bid is the buyer and thereafter the property

is the purchaser's sole risk and responsibility. At most auctions, someone will usually assist you in loading your purchases. Some auction houses will put what you've purchased in a warehouse, at your expense, if you don't claim it within a specified period of time.

5. At an unrestricted sale, or a sale without reserve, the consignors of the items being sold are not supposed to bid. If the consignors bid back their own items, they still pay the full sales commission.

6. Most auctioneers reserve the right to refuse a bid if it is not commensurate with the value of the article or if the next bid is merely a nominal advance over the previous bid. It's the auctioneer's job to get as much as he can for an item, and he's not going to injure the sale by accepting too-low bids.

7. Be knowledgeable from the beginning. Go to the auction in time to get a bidder's number and a good seat. Popular auctioneers with a following will usually fill the house long before the auction begins.

8. Most auction houses will accept your personal check locally, but if you're attending an auction out-of-town, arrange beforehand for credit or take travelers' checks.

There is a National Association of Auctioneers and most states have their own organizations. It's fun to buy by auction and they're becoming more and more popular because of the lure of instant cash to the seller. Most auction houses charge 15 percent of the gross. If you're interested in selling your merchandise by auction, find a reliable firm with which to do business. And, as in any other business transaction, read the contract *before* you sign it and understand what it says *before* you sign it.

How to Buy from Mail Auction Houses

More and more mail auction houses are popping up in the field of antiques and collectibles, and as the rules seem rather confusing to us, we thought we'd list a few and let you judge for yourself.

One firm states that the highest bidder wins at the highest bid sent in. This firm doesn't allow phone calls and there are no reductions given over lower underbidders.

Another mail auction house reduces winning high bids to 10 percent above the second highest bid, except that no bid will be reduced by more than 20 percent, and bids under $5 are not lowered. Phone calls are allowed by this house, and the caller is given the current high bid which, if the caller chooses to overbid, must be topped by a minimum of 10 percent.

Still another firm sells to the highest bidder, except that if more than 15 percent separates the high bid from the next highest, the high bid is reduced by a maximum of 15 percent. During the last two days callers are given the current high bid and are allowed to raise it in 15 percent increments if they have previously bid on the item. Otherwise they must raise by 20 percent.

Sounds like a high stakes crap game at Las Vegas, and as we said, a bit confusing. But mail auction houses are here to stay, so if you're interested in buying antiques and collectibles by this method, learn the rules *before* you bid.

Auction Galleries

Once again we're listing auction galleries, from coast to coast. We're frequently asked, "What do auction galleries have to do with a price guide?" Well, without auction galleries there would be no antiques business, and there certainly would be no price guides.

Here are 38 galleries we're familiar with.

Obviously there are many more. Most are reliable, but some—well, you'll have to be the judge of them.

As always, *before* you sign a contract with any gallery, make sure you thoroughly understand what is meant by "hammer price," "premium charge," etc.

Arizona
Jack Sellner
P.O. Box 1113
Scottsdale, AZ 85251

Arkansas
James E. Wilson & Son
1019 Airport Rd.
Hot Springs, AR 71901

California
Backer's Auction
14100 Paramount Blvd.
Paramount, CA 90723

California Book Auction Galleries
270 McAllister St.
San Francisco, CA 94102

Colorado
Broughton Auction Co.
1645 S. Tejou
Colorado Springs, CO 80906

Wagon Wheel Auctions
Niwot, CO 80544

District of Columbia
C. G. Sloan & Co., Inc.
715 13th St. NW
Washington, DC 20005

Adam A. Weschler & Sons
905 E Street NW
Washington, DC 20004

Florida
Browner Art Co., Ltd.
Margate, FL 33066

Col. Marty Higgenbotham
1702 Edgewood Dr.
Lakeland, FL 33803

Schrader Galleries
211 3d St. S.
St. Petersburg, FL 33701

Urich's Auction Gallery
3628 Washington Ave.
Fort Myers, FL 30901

Georgia
Atlanta Galleries
1405 Spring St. NW
Atlanta, GA 30300

Illinois
Dunning's Auction Service
755 Church Rd.
Elgin, IL 60120

Tom Sapp Auction Co.
Springfield, IL 62700

Stumpf Auction Co.
Mascoutah, IL 62258

Indiana
Kruse Classic Auction Co.
  (antique and classic cars)
Auburn, IN 46706

Lewis & Lambright, Inc.
112 Detroit St.
Lagrange, IN 46761

Iowa
Gene Harris
P. O. Box 294
Marshalltown, IA 50158

Richards Auction Gallery
527 Locust St.
Des Moines, IA 50309

Kansas
Woody Auctions
Douglas, KS 67039

Louisiana
Morton's Auction Exchange
643 Magazine St.
New Orleans, LA 70130

Massachusetts
Richard A. Bourne Co.
Hyannis Port, MA 02647

Robert C. Eldred Co., Inc.
P. O. Box 796
East Dennis, MA 02641

Robert W. Skinner, Inc.
Bolton, MA 01740

Michigan
C. B. Charles Galleries, Inc.
825 Woodward
Pontiac, MI 48053

Minnesota
The Summer Auction Galleries
Owatonna, MN 55060

New Hampshire
Philip E. Fitanides
Hooksett, NH 03106

New York
Christie's USA
502 Park Ave.
New York, NY 10022

William Doyle Galleries
175 E. 87th St.
New York, NY 10028

Sotheby Park Bernet
980 Madison Ave.
New York, NY 10021

Ohio
Paul Aronoff
1117 Vine St.
Cincinnati, OH 45210

Garth's Auctions, Inc.
2690 Stratford Rd.
Delaware, OH 43015

Pennsylvania
Black Bros., Ltd
Carlisle, PA 17013

Tennessee
Clements Antiques
Hixson, TN 37343

Texas
E & M Alexander, Inc.
1285 N. Post Oak Rd.
Houston, TX 77055

Clements Antiques
Forney, TX (Dallas) 75126

Wisconsin
Milwaukee Auction Galleries
5466 N. Port Washington Rd.
Milwaukee, WI 53217

Repairs and Services

When we added this exclusive-to-our-price-guide feature in the Sixth Edition, little did we realize what the response would be. Now, in this Eighth Edition, there are more than 200 places to help you get that music box repaired or find that part for your old telephone, etc.

Always inquire first and *always* enclose a SASE (self-addressed, stamped envelope) for a reply. Some catalogs are free. Some firms do only wholesale business. So be polite, be patient, but *inquire first.*

Escutcheon pulls 13
Escutcheons, brass 13
Eyes, glass (doll, bird, fish, animal) 27

F
Figurine repair 71, 95, 103
Flow Blue matching service 118, 148, 206
Frame repair 20
Furniture restoration 37, 125, 207, 213

G
Gasoline pump globes 149
Genealogical help 24, 57, 60
Glass beveling 150
Glass, custom bent panels 153, 154
Glass domes 14, 155, 156
Glass domes made 9
Glass, gold enamel on 20
Glass, gold leafing on 25
Glass pendalugues 47
Glass prisms 47
Glass repair 46, 130, 151, 152
Glass, serpentine bends on 29
Glass, stained, supplies 31
Glass stoppers—cruets, caster sets 203
Glassmaking 9
Gold leafing 195
Gold plating 157
Gold/silver leafing 189

H
Hall tree hooks 50
Hangers, cup/saucer/plate 14
Hardware, furniture 11, 40, 76, 107
Hardware, hand-forged 58
Haviland china replacement 36, 70, 72, 73, 158, 159, 160
Heisey glass replacement 161
Hummel repair 96, 162, 163, 164

I
Inlay and marquetry 189
Ivory repair 21, 117, 195

J
Jewelry repair 165
Jukebox repair 205

K
Keys, for turn-of-century furniture locks 166

L
Lacquer repair 21
Lamp parts 12, 34, 112, 207
Lamp repair 46, 95, 207
Leather tops, desks 28
Lenox china replacement 118, 119, 120
Locks, desks 13

M
Magazine repair 22
Marble repair, rebuff 189
Mechanical bank repair 86
Mechanical musical instruments, repair/restoration 23, 212
Metal casting service 4
Metal restoration, all types 193
Mirror resilvering 167, 191
Murals, cleaned, restored 53
Music box discs (new) 77, 204
Music box repair 15, 23, 78, 109, 168
Music rolls for grind organs 212

N
Necklace restringing 151, 208
Noritake replacement 90, 169

O
Odors (musty) removed 51
Organs repaired 189

P
Paintings, cleaning, restoring 53, 195
Paleography service 57
Paperweight repair 5
Pattern glass replacement 121, 122
Pearls, knotted and restrung 113
Pedestals, display 14
Pewter repair 46, 190
Phonograph parts 82, 83, 88
Phonograph repair 23, 88, 109
Piano parts 171
Picture frame restoration 170, 195
Pie safe replacement panels 65, 66, 67, 68
Pipes (smoking), restoration 7
Plate racks, multiple 14
Player piano parts 171
Player piano repair 23, 81, 89, 172, 189
Player piano rolls (new) 175
Pool tables refurbished 173
Porcelain repair 16, 21, 46, 211

Suppliers of Repairs and Services

1 B & L Antiquerie
25011 Little Mack
St. Clair Shores, MI 48080

2 Henry F. Witzenberger
15 Po Lane
Hicksville, NY 11801

3 T-K Michael Stained Glass
28200 Florence
St. Clair Shores, MI 48081

4 LEMiniatures
2615 Gravenstein Hwy.
Sebastopol, CA 95472

5 Studio Hannah
Star Route A, Box 93
Flemington, NJ 08822

6 Thompsons
Back Meadows Rd.
Damariscotta, ME 04543

7 Wilson Bergerud
30 Herring St.
Harrington Park, NJ 07640

8 Hector Olszewski
140 W. Houston
New York, NY 10003

9 Globes by Chick
328 Danville Pike
Hillsboro, OH 45133

10 COLONIAL "out-of-print" Book Service
23 E. 4th St.
New York, NY 10003

11 Horton Brasses
   P. O. Box 95
   Cromwell, CT 06416
12 Nowell's Inc.
   P. O. Box 164
   Sausalito, CA 94965
13 Noel Wise Antiques
   6503 St. Claudia Ave.
   Arabi, LA 70032
14 T & B Sales Co.
   P. O. Box 30
   Old Hickory, TN 37138
15 Al Meekins
   P. O. Box 161
   Collingswood, NJ 08108
16 "My Grandfather's Shop" LTD
   940 Sligo Ave.
   Silver Springs, MD 20910
17 Ronald's Woodcarving
   434 W. 4th St.
   W. Islip, NY 11795
18 Morgan, Dept. A03K11
   915 E. Ky.
   Louisville, KY 40204
19 Antique Trunk Supply Co.
   3706 W. 169th St.
   Cleveland, OH 44111
20 J & S Co.
   P. O. Box 4840
   Chattanooga, TN 37405
21 Sierra Studios
   P. O. Box 1005
   Oak Park, IL 60304
22 Paul W. Bowser
   1618 W. Main St.
   New Lebanon, OH 45345
23 Les Gould
   391 Tremont Pl.
   Orange, NJ 07050
24 The Genealogical Helper
   526 N. Main St.
   Logan, UT 84321
25 Mike Wells
   30½ W. Wheelock St.
   Hanover, NH 03755
26 The Bedpost
   Rt. 1, Box 155
   Pen Argyl, PA 18072
27 Schoepfer Eyes
   138 W. 31st St.
   New York, NY 10001

28 Wood & Leather Craft
   Star Route
   Callicoon, NY 12723
29 Same address as #1
30 Constantine
   2050 Eastchester Rd.
   Bronx, NY 10461
31 Whittemore-Durgin
   P. O. Box H2065
   Hanover, NH 02339
32 PECO
   P. O. Box 777
   Smithville, TX 78957
33 Replica Products
   610 57th St.
   Vienna, WV 26105
34 Trans World Trading Co.
   509 S. Cross
   Robinson, IL 62454
35 Appraisers Association of America, Inc.
   60 East 42nd St.
   New York, NY 10017
   (Note: A Membership Directory is available
   at a cost of $3 to persons seeking the serv-
   ices of a professional appraiser.)
36 Mildred E. Webster
   P. O. Box 37114
   Los Angeles, CA 90037
37 Adams Antiques
   426 Main Ave.
   Northport, AL 35476
38 Doll & Craft World
   125 8th St.
   Brooklyn, NY 11215
39 Waymar, Inc.
   6015 S. Lindbergh
   St. Louis, MO 63123
40 Gaston Wood Finishes, Inc.
   3630 E. 10th St.
   Bloomington, IN 47401
41 Seeley's Ceramic Service, Inc.
   9 River St.
   Oneonta, NY 13820
42 Dolls By Rene
   8228 Allport
   Santa Fe Springs, CA 90670
43 Costume Quarterly
   38 Middlesex Dr.
   Brentwood, MO 63144
44 Jeannette Strauss
   3705 Chapel Forge Dr.
   Bowie, MD 20715

45 John J. Mesterhazy
   12917 Westwood Lane
   Omaha, NB 68144
46 Hess Repairs
   200 Park Ave. S.
   New York, NY 10003
47 Williams' Antiques
   Albion, IL 62806
48 BMS Materials
   P. O. Box 222
   Windsor, NY 13865
49 Hardwood Grove Mfg.
   Rt. 2, Box 200
   West Fork, AR 72774
50 Pat & Hanks Antiques
   410 Don Tyler
   Dewey, OK 74029
51 DiPonziano & Assoc.
   P. O. Box 23356
   San Jose, CA 95153
52 Bill E. Berger
   29 E. 12th St.
   New York, NY 10003
53 Museum Services
   P. O. Box 119
   Hingham, MA 02043
54 American Assn. of Conservators
   1250 E. Ridgewood Ave.
   Ridgewood, NJ 07450
55 Graphics International
   P. O. Box 13292, Station E
   Oakland, CA 94661
56 Ms. Micheline Masse
   Stock Market Information Services,
      Inc.
   Montreal, Canada
57 Accelerated Indexing Systems, Inc.
   3346 S. Orchard Dr.
   Bountiful, UT 84010
58 Michael Sissman
   Buttonshop Rd.
   Williamsburg, MA 01096
59 Pandora's Quilt Museum
   2014 Old Philadelphia Pike
   Lancaster, PA 17602
60 Genealogical Bookshelf
   P. O. Box 468
   New York, NY 10028
61 John Crary
   Rt. 1
   Canton, NY 13617

62 W.H.M.
   2686 McAllister
   San Francisco, CA 94118
63 Donna Vernal
   217 E. First
   Waconia, MN 55387
64 Sandy Ritchie
   Rt. 1, Box 17
   Scottsville, VA 24590
65 Clark Mfg. Co.
   Rt. 2
   Raymore, MO 64083
66 Wallin Forge
   Rt. 1, Box 65
   Sparta, KY 41086
67 The Sobys
   P. O. Box 180
   W. Springs, IL 60558
68 Irvin Hoover
   Rt. 1
   Mt. Pleasant Mills, PA 17853
69 The Canery
   250 Brookstown Ave.
   Winston-Salem, NC 27101
70 Haviland Corner Matching Service
   P. O. Box 82
   Belmont, CA 94002
71 Berkley, Inc.
   2011 Hermitage Ave.
   Wheaton, MD 20902
72 Helt's Antiques
   Durhamville, NY 13054
73 Strawflower, Inc.
   801 W. Eldorado
   Decatur, IL 62522
74 House of Antiques
   202 N. 5th St.
   Springfield, IL 62701
75 Helen Lawler
   Rt. 1, Box 334
   Blytheville, AR 72315
76 Antique Hardware Co.
   P. O. Box 877
   Redondo Beach, CA 90277
77 Porter Music Box Co.
   5 Mound St.
   Randolph, VT 05060
78 DB Musical Restorations
   230 Lakeview Ave. NE
   Atlanta, GA 30305

79 The Shade Tree
1318 S. Peoria Ave.
Tulsa, OK 74120

80 Peter Michaels
1922 South Rd.
Baltimore, MD 21209

81 Nicholas Fiscina
20-17 Jackson Ave.
W. Islip, NY 11795

82 Neumann Miller
5482 Lakeview
Yorba Linda, CA 92686

83 Karl Frick
940 Canon Rd.
Santa Barbara, CA 93110

84 Doe's Treasures
P. O. Box 6505
Providence, RI 02940

85 Marleda's
P. O. Box 2308
San Bernadino, CA 92406

86 Bob McCumber
201 Carriage Dr.
Glastonbury, CT 06033

87 Warden's Clock Supply
103 N. Boling
Claremont, OK 70017

88 Musical Americana
354 E. Campbell
Campbell, CA 95008

89 William D. Gilstrap
Rt. 2
Bevier, MO 63532

90 Vintage Patterns II
5304 Thrasher Dr.
Cincinnati, OH 45239

91 McKenzie Art Restoration Studio
2907 E. Monte Vista Dr.
Tucson, AZ

92 Calligraphic Ink
Crystal City Underground
Arlington, VA 22202

93 Emerson Hardwood Co.
2279 NW Front Ave.
Portland, OR 90710

94 Glass Masters Guild
621 6th Ave.
New York, NY 10009

95 Paul Baron Co.
2825 E. College Ave.
Decatur, GA 30030

96 Grady Stewart
2019 Sansom St.
Philadelphia, PA 19103

97 All-Art Restorers
140 W. 57th St.
New York, NY 10019

98 Rikki's Studio
2256 Coral Way
Miami, FL 33145

99 Mr. William and Co.
14 Garfield Pl.
Cincinnati, OH 45202

100 Bostonia Furniture Co.
183 Friend St.
Boston, MA 02114

101 Marcey Medgepeth
Rt. 179
Ringoes, NJ 08551

102 W. B. Lewis
231 Chatham Ave.
Pooler, GA 31322

103 Dorothy Briggs
410 Ethan Allen Ave.
Takoma Park, MD 20012

104 Helen Von Rosenstiel
88 Prospect Park West
Brooklyn, NY 11215

105 Rosemary Evans
9303 McKinney
Loveland, OH 45140

106 Billard's Old Telephones
21710 Regnart Rd.
Cupertino, CA 95014

107 Ritter & Son
P. O. Box 907
Campbell, CA 95008

108 Heritage Clocks of Mass.
P. O. Box 336
Sturbridge, MA 01566

109 Antique Music Box
1015 S. Teljon
Colorado Springs, CO 80906

110 The Broderick Gallery
119 Allandale St.
Jamaica Plain, MA 02130

111 Howard's Stained Glass
2602 S. 11th St.
Gadsden, AL 35901

112 American Lamp
100 Elm Hill Pk.
Nashville, TN 37210

113 Eleanor Sopp
15144 Chamisal
Ballwin, MO 63011

114 The Yankee Drummer
23 Burnham Rd.
Hudson, NH 03051

115 TEC Specialties
P. O. Box 909
Smyrna, GA 30081

116 Modern Technical Tools
Box 681
Hicksville, NY 11801

117 Wedgwood Studio
2522 N. 52nd St.
Phoenix, AZ 85008

118 Elaine L. Mooza
286 Wilson Ave.
Rumford, RI 02916

119 White's
P. O. Box 680
Newberg, OR 97132

120 Jacquelynn's China
4770 N. Oakland Ave.
Milwaukee, WI 53211

121 Oscar Black
1940 Old Taneytown Rd.
Westminster, MD 21157

122 Mrs. Emily Troutman
325 N. 6th St.
Reading, PA 19601

123 Bob Depenbrok
6638 Van Noord Ave.
North Hollywood, CA 91606

124 Pie Galinat
41 Perry St.
New York, NY 10014

125 Stephen W. Weston
Winthrop, ME 04364

126 Sam Robins
8211 Kostner
Skokie, IL 60076

127 James Broaddus
1635 S. 4th
Terre Haute, IN 47802

128 Silver Plated Flatware Matching
Service
142 Hampshire Rd.
Waterloo, IA 50701

129 Zephyr Glassworks
P. O. Box 42
Santa Cruz, CA 95060

130 Ross Jasper
2213 W. 2nd St.
Davenport, IA 52802

131 Best Books
2034 Empire Blvd.
Webster, NY 14560

132 Oak Knoll Books
680 S. Chapel St.
Newark, DE 19713

133 Yankee Peddler Bookshop
94 Mill St.
Pultneyville, NY 14538

134 Bailes
P. O. Box 150
Eureka Springs, AR 72632

135 Ron-Dot Bookfinders
P. O. Box 44
Greensburg, OH 44232

136 Carriage Association of America
P. O. Box 3788
Portland, ME 04103

137 The Fan Man
4606 Travis
Dallas, TX 75205

138 Carolina Caning Supply
P. O. Box 2179
Smithfield, NC 27577

139 Pat's Etcetera Co.
P. O. Box 777
Smithville, TX 78957

140 The Finishing Touch
5636 College Ave.
Oakland, CA 94618

141 Nostalgia
McHenry, IL 60050

142 Berkley, Inc.
2011 Hermitage Ave.
Wheaton, MD 20902

143 Irene Foukes
5170 Kitson
Orchard Lake, MI 48033

144 Mariana Redwine
756 Bluebird Cyn. Dr.
Laguna Beach, CA 92651

145 Char-Mar's
909 N. 7th
Garden City, KS 67846

146 E. Black
6130 SW 12th St.
Miami, FL 33144

147 Busy "B" Antiques
Rt. 1, Box 99
Zumbro Falls, MN 55991

148 Blue Plate Antiques
P. O. Box 124
Sherborn, MA 01770

149 Leslie
1359 Williamsburg
Flint, MI 48507

150 Stained Glass School
1705 S. Pearl
Denver, CO 80210

151 J & L's
1915 Central St.
Evanston, IL 60201

152 R & K Weenike Antiques
Rt. 7
Ottumwa, IA 52501

153 Howard's Stained Glass
2602 S. 11th St.
Gadsden, AL 35901

154 Thomas Malone Studio
12 Ashwood Rd.
Port Washington, NY 11050

155 Family Tree Antiques
P. O. Box 93
Merrick, NY 11566

156 Timesavers
P. O. Box 171
Wheeling, IL 60090

157 Al Bar Wilmette Platers
127 Green Bay Rd.
Wilmette, IL 60091

158 Strawflower, Inc.
801 W. Eldorado
Decatur, IL 62522

159 Helt's Antiques
Durhamville, NY 13054

160 Vera L. Phillips
6427 S. Prince
Littleton, CO 80120

161 Lynne-Art's Glass House
P. O. Box 54-6014
Miami Beach, FL 33154

162 Cordier's Fine Arts
1619 S. La Cienga Blvd.
Los Angeles, CA

163 Daniel Zalles
580 Sutter St.
San Francisco, CA

164 Simms & Associates
18311 SW 95th Ct.
Miami, FL 33157

165 Diamonds by Terry
Burnsville, MI 55337

166 19th Century Co.
P. O. Box 1455
Upland, CA 91786

167 Fagan's
P. O. Box 329
Piedmont, AL 36272

168 DB Musical Restorations
230 Lakview Ave. NE
Atlanta, GA 30305

169 Peggy's Matching Service
P. O. Box 476
Ocala, FL 32670

170 Reed Arts & Crafts
233 W. 5th Ave.
Columbus, OH 43201

171 Inez Pianos, Inc.
2473 Canton Rd.
Marietta, GA 30066

172 Wm. D. Gilstrap
Rt. 2
Bevier, MO 63532

173 American Billiards
Suffern, NY 10901

174 Den of Antiquity
810 Rangeline
Columbus, MO 65201

175 Rand & Upshaw
1425 Miramar
Los Angeles, CA 90026

176 The Sterling Fox
P. O. Box 398
Richmond, KY 40475

177 The Silver Queen
778 N. Indian Rocks Rd.
Belleair Bluffs, FL 33540

178 Senti-Metal Co.
1919 Memory Lane
Columbus, OH 43209

179 Ron Steidinger
Forrest, IL 61741

180 Woodsmith Classics
4021 California Ave.
Carmichael, CA 95608

181 Phoneco
Rt. 2
Galesville, WI 54630

182 Billard's Old Telephones
21710-R Regnart Rd.
Cupertino, CA 95014

183 Paul Jones
429 S. Fredonia
Longview, TX 75601

184 Gary Bradley
Rt 3, Box 606
Corvallis, OR 97330

185 Whittemore-Durgin
P. O. Box H2065
Hanover, MA 02339

186 Triple X Chemical Co.
841 Skokie Highway
Lake Bluff, IL 60044

187 Herbert K. Goodkind
25 Helena Ave.
Larchmont, NY 10538

188 Doe's Treasures
P. O. Box 6505
Providence, RI 02940

189 Kings Mill Services
Highway 64
Wasco, IL

190 Specialized Repair Service
2406 Bryn Mawr
Chicago, IL 60659

191 Squaw Alley
Main and Water Sts.
Naperville, IL 60540

192 Lead 'n Glass
Wheeling, IL 60090

193 Midwest Burnishing
208 E. Main
Round Lake Park, IL 60073

194 The Little Corner
3939 W. Main
McHenry, IL 60050

195 Wiebold, Inc.
413 Terrace Pl.
Terrace Park, OH

196 Mountain Lumber
1327 Carlton Ave.
Charlottesville, VA 22901

197 Leslie Brooks
166-25 Powells Ave.
Beechhurst, NY 11357

198 Layafette
111 Jericho Turnpike
Syosset, NY 11791

199 Robert W. Miller
c/o Wallace-Homestead Book Co.
1912 Grand Ave.
Des Moines, IA 50309

200 Radio Shack
2617 W. 7th St.
Fort Worth, TX 76107

201 Sam Faust
Changewater, NJ 07831

202 Musical Museum
Deansboro, NY 13328

203 Ross's Antiques
Rt. 6
Milford, PA 18337

204 Porter Music Box Co.
Randolph, VT 05060

205 Jukebox Junction
P. O. Box 1081
Des Moines, IA 50311

206 Gloria Kluever
P. O. Box 124
Sherborn, MA 01770

207 John Martin Antiques
Rt. 3
Clarksville, GA 30523

208 J & L's Jewelry
1915 Central St.
Evanston, IL 60201

209 K. Parry
17557 Horace
Granada Hills, CA 91344

210 Slot Machine Repair Service
2404 W. 111th St.
Chicago, IL 60655

211 Mort Jacobs Restorations
231 S. Green St.
Chicago, IL 60607

212 Mechanical Music Center
25 Kings Highway North
Darien, CT 06820

213 Harris Woodcarving
120 E. Main St.
Falconer, NY 14733

Clubs and Publications on Antiques and Collectibles

We hope that you will find this section of the Eighth Edition, WALLACE-HOMESTEAD PRICE GUIDE TO ANTIQUES & PATTERN GLASS, very useful. If you're a collector, it's interesting to know who your fellow collector is *and* if there's a publication or periodical in your field. Your letters tell us that this exclusive feature of our Price Guide is worth the time necessary to identify and print this list of clubs and publications. *Always* correspond *before* sending money. Too many of you don't include a self-addressed, stamped envelope (SASE); then you write and say you didn't receive an answer. Don't expect anyone else to pay your postage. You'll meet a lot of new friends who share your interest in a particular collectible. But, please, don't hold us responsible for any situation arising between you and any of the organizations listed. Want to list your club? Write. We aren't so busy we can't say "thanks" to you who are kind enough to purchase this Eighth Edition of the WALLACE-HOMESTEAD PRICE GUIDE TO ANTIQUES & PATTERN GLASS.

Clubs

Aladdin Lamps
Mystic Light of the Aladdin Knights
c/o J. W. Courter
Simpson, IL 62985

Alice in Wonderland
Lewis Carroll Society of North America
617 Rockford Rd.
Silver Spring, MD 20902

Amusement Parks
National Amusement Park Historical Assn.
P. O. Box 83
Mt. Prospect, IL 60056

Animal Licenses
International Society of Animal License
   Collectors
4420 Wisconsin
Tampa, FL 33616

Antique Auto Racing
Antique Auto Racing Assn.
Rt. 1, Box 116
Ixonia, WI 53036

Antique Automobiles
Antique Automobile Club of America
501 W. Governor Rd.
Hershey, PA 17033

Antiques and Collectibles—free catalog
Wallace-Homestead Book Co.
1912 Grand Ave.
Des Moines, IA 50309

Autograph Collectors
Universal Autograph Collectors Club
P. O. Box 467-WH
Rockville Centre, NY 11571

Banks, Mechanical
Mechanical Bank Collectors of America
P. O. Box 128
Allegan, MI 49010

Barbed Wire
International Barb Wire Historical Society
c/o Jack Glover
Sunset, TX 76270

Beads
The Bead Society of Southern California
P. O. Box 605
Venice, CA 90219

Beer Cans
Beer Can Collectors of America
747 Merus Ct.
Fenton, MO 63026

Bibles
International Society of Bible Collectors
P. O. Box 2485
El Cajon, CA 92021

Bicycle Collectors
Wheelmen
1708 School House Lane
Ambler, PA 19002

Bottle Collecting
Antique Bottle Collecting (British)
Chapel House Farm, Newport Rd.
Albrighton, NR. Wolverhampton
Staffordshire, England

Bottle Collectors
Genesse Valley Bottle Collectors Assn.
P. O. Box 7528
Rochester, NY 14615

Memphis Bottle Collectors Club
1373 Wrenwood St.
Memphis, TN 38122

Pennsylvania Bottle Collectors Assn.
743 Woodberry Rd.
York, PA 17403

Federation of Historical Bottle Clubs
10118 Schuessler
St. Louis, MO 63128

Bottle Openers
Figural Bottle Opener Collectors
P. O. Box 106
Trumbull, CT 06611

Buffalo Bill
Buffalo Bill/Western Americana
P. O. Box 203
Pocahontas, IA 50574

Cabs
American British Cab Society
P. O. Box 904
Stamford, CT 06904

Cambridge Glass
National Cambridge Glass Collectors
P. O. Box 416
Cambridge, OH 43725

Candlewick Crystal
Candlewick Crystal Collectors
2817 Appletree Lane
South Bend, IN 46615

Candy Containers
Collectors of America
P. O. Box 184
Lucerne Mines, PA 15754

Carnival Glass
American Carnival Glass Assn.
P. O. Box 273
Gnadenhutten, OH 44629

International Carnival Glass Assn.
Rt. 1
Mentone, IN 46539

National Carnival Glass Assn.
3142 S. 35th St.
LaCrosse, WI 54601

Carousels
National Carousel Roundtable
448 Riverside Dr.
Honesdale, PA 18431

Carriages, Horse-drawn
The American Driving Society
79 Southgate Ave.
Hastings-on-Hudson, NY 10706

Cars, Professional
The Professional Car Society
12505 Bennett Rd.
Herndon, VA 22070

Chrysler Cars
W.P.C. Club
P. O. Box 4705
N. Hollywood, CA 91607

Cigarette Packs
Cigarette Pack Collectors of America
61 Searle St.
Georgetown, MA 01833

Coin-operated Games
For Amusement Only
1853 Ashby
Berkeley, CA 94703

Coins
American Numismatic Society
617 W. 155th St.
New York, NY 10032

Coins, Etc.
American Numismatic Assn.
P. O. Box 2366
Colorado Springs, CO 80901

"Coke"
The Cola Clan
3965 Pikes Peak
Memphis, TN 38108

Coca-Cola Collectibles
P. O. Box 36M01
Los Angeles, CA 90036

Cookie Cutters
Cookie Cutter Collector's Club
5426 27th St. NW
Washington, DC 20015

Covered Bridge Postcards
Organization for Collectors of Covered
Bridge Postcards
7265 Amanda Northern Rd.
Canal Winchester, OH 43110

Bing Crosby
Bing Crosby Historical Society
P. O. Box 8013
Tacoma, WA 98408

Crosley Cars
Crosley Automobile Club
3323 Eaton Rd.
Williamson, NY 14589

Demography—see **Genealogy**

Dionne Quints
Dionne Quint Collectors
P. O. Box 2527
Woburn, MA 01888

Disneyana
The Mouse Club
13826 Ventura Blvd.
Sherman Oaks, CA 91423

Dolls, Paper
Paperdoll Quarterly (PDQ)
3135 Oakcrest Dr.
Hollywood, CA 90068

Elongated Coins
Elongated Coin Collectors
4872 NW 171st Terrace
Miami, FL 33055

Ford V-8s
Early Ford V-8 Club of America
P. O. Box 2122
San Leandro, CA 94577

Fostoria Glass
Fostoria Glass Society of America
P. O. Box 826
Moundsville, WV 26041

Genealogy
Accelerated Indexing Systems
3346 S. Orchard Dr.
Bountiful, UT 84010

National Genealogical Society
1921 Sunderland Place NW
Washington, DC 20036

Graniteware
American Graniteware Assn.
P. O. Box 605
Downers Grove, IL 60515

Greeting Cards
Prank Mark Society
American Life Foundation
Watkins Glen, NY 14891

Guns
National Rifle Assn.
1600 Rhode Island Ave. NW
Washington, DC 20036

Handbags
The Costume Society of America
c/o The Costume Institute
Metropolitan Museum of Art
New York, NY 10028

Hatpins/Hatpin Holders
International Club, Collectors of Hatpins/
Hatpin Holders
15237 Chanera Ave.
Gardena, CA 90249

Hats—see **Handbags**

Heisey Glass
Heisey Collectors of America
P. O. Box 27
Newark, OH 43055

Hummel
Hummel Collectors Club
P. O. Box 257
Yardley, PA 19067

Goebel (Hummel) Collectors' Club
105 White Plains Rd.
Tarrytown, NY 10591

Infant Feeders
American Collectors of Infant Feeders
16 Algonquin Ave.
Andover, MA 01810

Insulators
National Insulator Assn.
3557 Nicklaus Dr.
Titusville, FL 32780

Yankee Pole Cat Insulator Club
5 Brownstone Rd.
E. Granby, CT 06026

Japanese Swords
Japanese Sword Society, U.S.
5907 Deerwood Dr.
St. Louis, MO 63123

Jazz
New Orleans Jazz Club of California
P. O. Box 1225
Kerrville, TX 78028

Jazz Records
International Assn. of Jazz Record
  Collectors
90 Prince George Dr.
Islongton, Ontario
M9B 2X8, Canada

Jukeboxes
Juke Box Collector
2545 SE 60th Ct.
Des Moines, IA 50317

Jukebox Trader
P. O. Box 1801
Des Moines, IA 50311

Kitchen Equipment
Early American Industries Assn.
P. O. Box 2128
Empire State Plaza Station
Albany, NY 12220

Knives
National Knife Collectors Assn.
P. O. Box 21070
Chattanooga, TN 37421

Lace
International Old Lacers
P. O. Box 1029
Westminster, CO 80030

License Plates
Automobile License Plate Collectors Assn.
P. O. Box 712
Weston, WV 26452

Lithophanes
Lithophane Collectors' Club
Blair Museum of Lithophanes
2032 Robinwood
Toledo, OH 43620

Locks
American Lock Collectors Assn.
14010 Cardwell
Livonia, MI 48154

Marbles
Marble Collectors Society of America
P. O. Box 222
Trumbull, CT 06611

Medals
American Numismatic Assn.
P. O. Box 2366
Colorado Springs, CO 80901

American Numismatic Society
617 W. 155th St.
New York, NY 10032

Medals and Tokens
Token & Medal Society
611 Oakwood Way
El Cajon, CA 92021

Military
American Military Historical Society
1528 El Camino
San Carlos, CA 94070

Milk bottles
MOO
P. O. Box 5456
Newport News, VA 23605

Miniature Figures
Miniature Figure Collectors of America
P. O. Box 1245
North Wales, PA 19454

Model A's
Model A Ford Club of America
250 S. Cypress St.
La Habra, CA 90631

Model A Restorers Club
24712 Michigan Ave.
Dearborn, MI 48124

Model Soldiers
National Capital Military Collectors
P. O. Box 166
Rockville, MD 20850

Miniature Figure Collectors of America
P. O. Box 1245
North Wales, PA 19454

American Model Soldier Society
1528 El Camino
San Carlos, CA 94070

Model T's
Model T Ford Club of America
P. O. Box 7400
Burbank, CA 91510

Motor Bikes
Vintage Motor Bike Club
330 E. North St.
Coldwater, OH 45828

Motorcycles
Antique Motorcycle Club of America
2411 Middle Rd.
Davenport, IA 52803

Movies
Film Collector's World
Rapid City, IL 61278

National Film Society
7800 Couser Dr.
Shawnee Mission, KS 66204

Hollywood Studio Collectors Club
P. O. Box 5815
Sherman Oaks, CA 91403

Old Time Western Film Club
P. O. Box 142
Silver City, NC 27344

Music Boxes
Automatic Musical Instrument Collectors Assn.
State Rd. and Broadview St.
Springfield, PA 19064

Musical Box Society, International
Rt. 3, Box 202
Morgantown, IN 46160

Musical Instruments
American Musical Instrument Society
University of South Dakota, Box 194
Vermillion, SD 57069

Automatic Musical Instrument Collectors Assn. (AMICA)
824 Grove St.
San Francisco, CA 94117

Nautical
National Maritime Historical Society
2 Fulton St.
Brooklyn, NY 11201

Needlework
Collector Circle
1313 S. Killian Dr.
Lake Park, FL 33403

Netsukes
International Netsuke Collectors Society
P. O. Box 10426
Honolulu, HI 96816

Occupied Japan
The Occupied Japan Club
18309 Faysmith
Torrance, CA 90504

Olds, Curved Dash
Curved Dash Oldsmobile Club
3455 Florida Ave.
Minneapolis, MI 55427

Paleography—see Genealogy

Paper/Advertising
National Assn. of Paper & Advertising Collectors
P. O. Box 471
Columbia, PA 17512

Paperweights
Paperweight Collectors' Assn.
P. O. Box 11
Bellaire, TX 77401

Pencils
American Pencil Collectors Society
2501 E. Douglas
Wichita, KS 67211

Society for the Collection of Brand-Name Pencils
4601 W. 101st St.
Oak Lawn, IL 60453

Pens
The Pen Fancier's Club
1169 Overcash Dr.
Dunedin, FL 33528

Pipe Smokers
Universal Coterie of Pipe Smokers
20-37 120th St.
College Point, NY 11356

Pipe Smokes
(This group sends free pipes, tobacco, etc., to our servicemen overseas. You may contribute if you wish.)
National G.I. Pipe Smokes Club of America
1620 W. 11th St.
Brooklyn, NY 11223

Planters Peanuts
Peanut Pal
P. O. Box 4465
Huntsville, AL 35802

Political Items
The Political Collector
444 Lincoln St.
York, PA 17404

American Political Items Collectors
1054 Sharpsburg Dr.
Huntsville, AL 35803

Postcards
Deltiologists of America
3709 Gradyville Rd.
Newton Square, PA 19073

Radios
Antique Wireless Assn.
Main St.
Holcomb, NY 14469

Norman Rockwell
The Rockwell Society of America
P. O. Box BC
Stony Brook, NY 11790

Norman Rockwell Memorial Society
P. O. Box 270328
Tampa, FL 33688

Royal Doulton
Royal Doulton International Collectors Club
U.S. Branch, Box 1815
Somerset, NJ 08873

Sheet Music
National Sheet Music Society
1597 Fair Park Ave.
Los Angeles, CA 90041

Snuff Bottles
International Chinese Snuff Bottle Society
2601 N. Charles St.
Baltimore, MD 21218

Spark Plugs
Spark Plug Collectors of America
P. O. Box 2229
Ann Arbor, MI 48106

Spoons
The Spooner
Rt. 1, Box 61
Shullsburg, WI 53586

American Spoon Collectors
P. O. Box 260
Warrensburg, MO 64093

Stamps
Society of Philatelic Americans
P. O. Box 9041
Wilmington, DE 19809

American Philatelic Society
P. O. Box 800
State College, PA 16801

Steins
Stein Collectors International
P. O. Box 463
Kingston, NJ 08528

Stevengraphs
Stevengraph Collector's Assn.
Daisy Lane
Irvington-on-Hudson, NY 10533

Sugar Packets
Sugar Packet Collectors Club
6826 Home City Ave.
Cincinnati, OH 45233

Tea Leaf (Ironstone)
Tea Leaf Club International
10747 Riverview
Kansas City, KS 66111

Telephones
Antique Telephone Collectors Assn.
614 Main
LaCrosse, KS 67548

Thimbles
Thimble Collectors International
P. O. Box 143
Intervale, NH 03845

Timepieces
National Association of Watch & Clock
    Collectors
Columbia, PA 17512

Tin Containers
Tin Container Collectors Assn.
P. O. Box 4555
Denver, CO 80204

Tokens
Society of Ration Token Collectors
722 W. 5th St.
Guymon, OK 73942

Tokens/Medals
Michigan Token & Medal Society
P. O. Box 1
Tecumseh, MI 49286

Tokens, Tax
American Tax Token Society
P. O. Box 26523
Lakewood, CO 80226

Toothpick Holders
National Toothpick Holder Collectors'
    Society
P. O. Box 246
Sawyer, MI 49125

Toy Trains
The Toy Train Operating Society
25 W. Walnut St., Suite 305
Pasadena, CA 91103

Trucks
American Truck Historical Society
201 Office Park Dr.
Birmingham, AL 35223

Unique/Unusual
The Trivials
603 E. 105th St.
Kansas City, MO 64131

Wallace Nutting
Wallace Nutting Collectors Club
Kampfe Lake, East Shore Dr.
Bloomingdale, NJ 07403

Watch Fobs
International Watch Fob Assn.
5892 Stow Rd.
Hudson, OH 44236

Wedgwood
Wedgwood Society of Philadelphia
246 N. Bowman Ave.
Merion, PA 19066

Wine, French
Vin Mariani Wine Collectors
1724 20th St., NW
Washington, DC 20009

Wizard of Oz
International Wizard of Oz Club
220 N. 11th St.
Escanaba, MI 49829

Woodcarvers
National Woodcarvers' Assn.
718 Fitzwatertown Rd.
Willow Grove, PA 19099

Wooden Money
New York State Wooden Money Society
25 N. Wayne Ave.
West Haverstraw, NY 10993

World's Fair
World's Fair Collectors Society
148 Poplar St.
Garden CIty, NY 11530

Publications

American Collector (general antiques/
   collectibles)
Kermit; TX 79745

American Indian Art Magazine
7333 E. Monterey Way, #5
Scottsdale, AZ 85251

Amusement Review Magazine (slot
   machines)
1853 Asby
Berkeley, CA 94703

Antique Monthly (general antiques)
Tuscaloosa, AL 35401

The Big Reel (movies)
Summerfield, NC 27358

Bottle News
Kermit, TX 79745

Bowers & Ruddy Galleries (coins)
6922 Hollywood Blvd.
Los Angeles, CA 90028

The Citrus Label Society
16633 Ventura Blvd. #1011
Encino, CA 91436

Classic Film/Video Images (movies)
Muscatine, IA 52761

The Coin Slot (antique coin amusements)
P. O. Box 612
Wheatridge, CO 80033

Collectors News (general antiques/
   collectibles)
Grundy, IA 50638

Glass Review Magazine
P. O. Box 542
Marietta, OH 45750

Hobbies Magazine (general antiques/
   collectibles)
1006 S. Michigan
Chicago, IL 60605

The Horn Speaker (radios/phonographs)
P. O. Box 53012
Dallas, TX 75253

The Indian Trader (American Indians)
P. O. Box 31235
Billings, MT 59107

Jerry's Musical News
4624 Woodland Rd.
Edina, MN 55424

Jukebox Collector
2545 SE 60th Ct.
Des Moines, IA 50317

Loose Change Magazine (antique slots)
21176 S. Alameda St.
Long Beach, CA 90810

The Magazine Antiques (general antiques)
551 5th Ave.
New York, NY 10017

MCN Press (military items)
P. O. Box 7582
Tulsa, OK 74105

Mugwumps (musical instruments)
1600 Billman's Lane
Silver Spring, MD 20902

The Old-House Journal (restoration, old
 houses)
69A 7th Ave.
Brooklyn, NY 11217

Old Toy Soldier Newsletter
209 N. Lombard
Oak Park, IL 60302

Spinning Wheel Magazine (general antiques/
 collectibles)
Hanover, PA 17331

Thimbletter
93 Walnut Rd.
Newton Highlands, MA 02161

Appraising, Insuring, and Protecting Your Antiques

Quality antiques are an appreciating investment, and because you should protect any investment, you should have your antiques appraised by a qualified appraiser. I'm a member of the Appraisers Association of America, Inc., 60 East 42nd Street, New York, N. Y. 10017. For $3.00 they will send you a list of all their members, nationwide. Another reputable organization is the American Society of Appraisers, Dulles International Airport, P. O. Box 17265, Washington, D. C. 20041.

Establish the cost *before* you allow an appraisal to be made. You will be quoted either an hourly rate or a flat fee. Keep in mind that there is no such thing as a licensed appraiser. Paying a fee to a city or county for a public service operator's license says absolutely nothing about the appraiser's qualifications. Ask for references. Then check those references before you avail yourself of the appraiser's services. Look for the appraiser who keeps up with current prices of antiques. Spend as much time finding the right appraiser as you did looking for quality antiques.

Because homeowners' and tenants' insurance policies in most states have built-in limits ($100 limit on coins and currency, $500 on jewelry and furs, $1,000 on firearms and related equipment), it's an excellent idea to have your antiques covered on a separate fine arts rider or a personal property floater.

Too many Americans are underinsured. If you think you're underinsured or that your antiques are not adequately covered on your homeowners' or tenants' policy, check with your insurance agent about increasing your coverage. Rates vary from state to state, according to the Insurance Information Institute. Remember, in case of loss, the insurance company can pay you only the amounts stipulated in your policy. In my opinion, insuring your antiques separately is a *very* wise investment. If you have jewelry or furs worth more than the $500 limit, you certainly need further coverage. This obviously holds true for your coins, firearms, silverware, and other collectibles.

The statistics aren't pleasant to think about, but every thirty-four seconds a fire breaks out in a home in America; a theft occurs every twenty seconds. What can you do about it? Well, stop thinking that because the doors and windows are locked, your possessions are safe. They aren't. Locks keep honest people out. What are your options? You could sell your antiques, but then you're right back to square one. Inflation dollars, taxes to be paid.

A lot of people think that if they receive an antique as a gift or inherit one they do not have to pay taxes if and when they sell it. Wrong! You pay capital gains taxes on any profit you make over the original

25

purchase price or its value at the time you received it as a gift or by inheritance.

Some very good advice: Don't get cute with the Internal Revenue Service. You'd be surprised what they know about you, what they have stored in their computer banks. A few years ago I tried to sue the IRS and had a "really big" attorney. He filled me in on the facts of life. Simply stated, he said, "You haven't a chance in court, but you can whisper about them at cocktail parties!"

Always photograph each item. Use a camera with a good lens to get the details. If you're photographing a shiny surface or something behind glass, shoot it at a 45-degree angle. The fine features of a figurine, for instance, will show up better if photographed against a plain wall. Always group small items on a table, rug, or blanket, and get close enough to record good detail. You will not get detail with an inexpensive camera. Nor are instant-type printing cameras recommended for capturing close-up detail.

If you have a fire or a theft, immediately notify the nearest law enforcement agency and your insurance agent. Two few people know about C.I.C. and they should learn about it. C.I.C. stands for Crime Information Center, and 90 to 95 percent of all law enforcement agencies have this facility.

This nationwide system is usually a single computer, dual retriever system; a computer box tied into your state capital and also into the national C.I.C. system in Washington, D.C. If you have a theft of antiques, tell your local, county, or state police what specific items were stolen. They in turn put all pertinent information into the C.I.C. computer. It's recorded at your state capital and in Washington, D.C. But the great

thing about it is that it also goes out to all fifty states. So, if some of your antiques show up in Maine or Texas or Oregon, *every* state knows what's been stolen. The dual response from your state capital and Washington could find your stolen antique instantly.

Security systems are fine if you can afford them. If not, use dead bolt locks—the bolt goes through the panel and cannot be opened with a plastic card or knife. Half the fun of owning antiques used to be displaying them for the benefit of yourself or your friends. If you insist on showing them off in a cabinet or on a table, install a security system. And *always* inform your local law enforcement agency when you're going to be away from home for an extended period.

Keep your small items—valuable coins and stamps—in a safety deposit box. That's like holding hands with a stainless steel female in Des Moines in February, but necessary.

Remember, two people can keep a secret if one of them is dead. You talk and friends who come to visit talk. Unfortunately, we're living with a generation of thieves. Today's burglars skip your $2,000 television-stereo set. They're after portable items such as your sterling silver place settings, your coin collection, your silver candelabra conveniently displayed on the dining room table.

No one can tell you how to avoid being robbed. Keep in mind that professional thieves are looking for antiques, especially the quality kind. It's difficult to outguess them. Just make sure you've taken every sensible precaution to prevent a breakin. With these actions and the security of an adequate insurance schedule, you can enjoy your antiques and collections in your own home with peace of mind for years to come.

Acknowledgments

This Eighth Edition of the WALLACE-HOMESTEAD PRICE GUIDE TO ANTIQUES & PATTERN GLASS is even better than previous editions, thanks to the following dedicated people and organizations:

The Houston Antique Museum, Chattanooga, Tennessee

The McClung Museum, Knoxville, Tennessee

The Bradford Exchange, Chicago, Illinois

Poor Richard's Antiques, Pensacola, Florida

The Franklin Mint, Franklin Center, Pennsylvania

Brown Pelican Antiques, Panama City, Florida

Collector's Haven, Panama City, Florida

Doll & Craft World, Brooklyn, New York

The American Collector, Kermit, Texas

Donn Pearlman, WBBM, Chicago, Illinois

Grace Ellen Dahlburg, Villa Park, Illinois

Jukebox Collector, Des Moines, Iowa

Lamplighter Books, Leon, Iowa

Anita Gold, Chicago Tribune

Jim Frye, WHO Radio, Des Moines, Iowa

Roy Leonard, WGN Radio, Chicago, Illinois

Things II, Denver, Colorado

Joey Rieger, Burnsville, Minnesota

Mrs. Agnes S. DuBosque, Havertown, Pennsylvania

Mrs. Emily S. Troutman, Reading, Pennsylvania

Aunt Annie's Answer, Agency, Iowa

Alan English, Dearborn Heights, Michigan

Stuart Buchanan Antiques, Denver, Colorado

Diamonds by Terry, Burnsville, Minnesota

Granny's Country Cupboard, Oak Creek, Wisconsin

Char-Mars' House of Yesteryear, Garden City, Kansas

American Nostalgia, San Antonio, Texas

The Chicken Coop, Berryville, Arkansas

R & K Weenike Antiques, Ottumwa, Iowa

Powers Happy House Antiques, Garnett, Kansas

Richard B. Draper Antiques, St. Louis, Missouri

Kramer Art Gallery, St. Paul, Minnesota

Frances Edwards Antiques, Algonquin, Illinois

Penny Lane Antiques, Tecumseh, Nebraska

Aronoff Galleries, Cincinnati, Ohio

House of O'Steen, Marianna, Florida

Doll 'N' Craft Works, Lynn Haven, Florida

Farley's Old & Rare Books, Pensacola, Florida

Bottle News, Kermit, Texas

J. M. Antique Sales, Atlanta, Georgia

John III and Susan Shuman, Pottstown, Pennsylvania

Lee Sullivan, Chief of Police, Panama City Beach, Florida

Mary Brubaker, KCCI-TV, Des Moines, Iowa

Judy Simmons, WLIB-FM, New York, New York

Section of General Antiques

ABC (Alphabet) Plates

ABC (Alphabet) Plates

These plates were made for children, late 19th, early 20th century. The alphabet was around the border; the center decorations consisted of proverbs, animals, etc. The plates were made of glass, ceramics, tin, pewter. Now being reproduced in glass.

Ceramic

Aesop's Fables, The Hare and The Tortoise	$ 54- 63
Alphabet on raised rim, Little Boy Blue	29- 36
B is for Billy, 7″	35- 43
Bathing scene at beach	48- 57
Black-faced children, riddle on front (ill.)	46- 55
Brownies, Palmer Cox, 1896	43- 52
Capitol at Washington, 7½″	32- 41
Children in center	28- 36
Clock face center	45- 55
Cricket game, 6½″	49- 57
Crusoe Rescues Friday	70- 78
David and Goliath, 5¼″	34- 43
Dick Whittington and His Cat	31- 40
Dog pulling cart	44- 53
Ducks in center	29- 37
Eagle center, centennial, exposition	115-125
Elephant center	39- 44
Floral center, 6¼″	15- 24
Football center	45- 53
Franklin proverbs (Meakin)	43- 53
Gathering Cotton	62- 72
Girl and boy, 6½″	28- 37

The Graces	54- 63
The Guardian (Meakin)	54- 63
Hen and chicks	28- 36
Horse racing, 7″	34- 43
Hunters and dogs, 7½″	38- 44
Importance of Punctuality, maxim verse	95-108
Little Bo-Peep	52- 59
Little Miss Muffet	38- 45
Mother and daughter, 6½″	38- 44
New Pony (Meakin)	39- 45
Nursery Tales, Cinderella	44- 53
Puss-in-Boots	38- 44
Rabbit, sign language around border	55- 63
Rooster	50- 55
Simple Simon	44- 49
Tired of Play, 6¼″	35- 43

Glass

Child's head, amber, 6¼″	38- 44
Clock, amber, 7¼″	38- 44
Clock, amethyst, 7¼″	60- 69
Daisy, 6¼″	36- 44
Dog's head, blue, 6¼″	38- 44
Ducks, two, amber, 6¼″	38- 44
Elephant center, 6″	32- 41
Hen and chicks, 6¼″	28- 35
Little Bo-Peep	34- 43
Star center	28- 34

Tin

Birds, animals, 8¼″	28- 34
Cock Robin	43- 52
Girl on a swing, 6½″	28- 34
Hey Diddle Diddle, 9¼″	38- 44
Jumbo, 6¼″	33- 42
Liberty, 5½″	55- 64
Mary Had a Little Lamb	43- 52
Numerals, 6½″	34- 43
Tom, Tom, the Piper's Son	39- 44
Victoria-Albert, 5½″	34- 43
Washington bust, 5½″	46- 56

Abacus

Used by the Chinese for centuries, it's simply a counting frame with movable wooden beads. The older ones are collectible today.

Teakwood frame and beads, brass rods	$ 31- 40
Ornate teakwood frame inlaid with mother-of-pearl, beads, brass rods (ill.)	32- 40

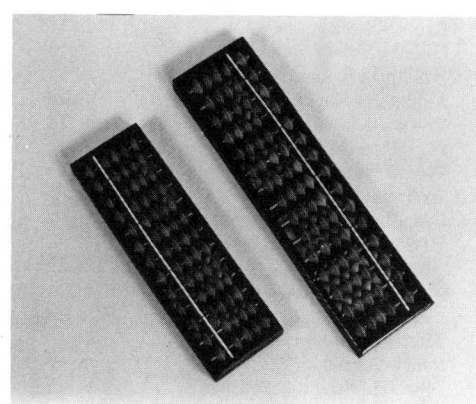

Abacus

Ebony frame and beads, brass
rods (ill.) 30- 39

Adams China

Adams China

William Adams & Sons were famous for
their American scenes on blue and pink china.
The firm was founded in the 1650s at Stoke-
on-Trent, England, and is still in business.
Their Dr. Syntax series is well known.

Bowl, Chinese decor, 11½" dia. . .	$ 54- 63
Cup plate, vegetables, marked	
Adams on bottom	44- 53
Cup/saucer, pink, floral scenes . . .	62- 70
Cup/saucer, Rose pattern, late . . .	62- 71
Dish, vegetable, Schenectady on	
Mohawk River, pink, 10" dia. .	120-128
Plate, bird, by James Audubon,	
black-on-white, 10½" dia.	70- 79
Plate, Columbus landing, blue/	
pink, 9" dia.	85- 95

Plate, garden scene, 9" dia. (ill.) . .	65- 75
Plate, view near Conway, N.H.,	
9" dia.	86- 94
Platter, Lake Champlain, pink,	
14" dia.	122-137
Tureen, soup, farm scene, blue/	
white, ironstone	106-115

Adams Rose Pattern China

Adams Rose Pattern China

Decorated with bright red roses and green
leaves on a white background, made by
various members of the Adams family from
1820 on; still in business. In the early 1900s a
variation of the original was made with a
darker background—almost a dirty white.
This type is worth about one-half the older
type. We'll refer to the newer as Late.
Various marks, all with the word Adams.
Also, after 1891 Made in England was added.
Earlier pieces have only England.

Bowl, 6", early	$144-153
Bowl, 6", late	45- 53
Bowl, 7", late	53- 58
Cracker jar, black basalt, silver	
lid and bail, classical scenes . . .	143-153
Creamer, early	158-170
Creamer, late	84- 94
Cup/saucer, early, scalloped edge	155-170
Cup/saucer, late, plain edge	78- 88
Pitcher, 16" high (ill.)	90- 95
Plate, 7½", early	69- 75
Plate, 7½", late	30- 37
Plate, 8½", early	80- 90
Plate, 8½", late	35- 43
Plate, 9½", early	183-193
Plate, 9½", late	90- 97
Plate, 10", early	192-215
Sugar bowl, early	385-425
Sugar bowl, late	120-145
Teapot, early	485-535
Teapot, late	125-145

Advertising Items

Advertising Items

Chromolithography, the process of printing on tin, and the development of celluloid for buttons and mirrors created a new field for advertisers at the turn of the century. Most items were given away free to customers.

Booklets

Barker's (liniment) "Komic" picture souvenir	$ 5-	7
Hartman Magazine of Health	5-	7
Pe-Ru-Na coloring book	5-	9

Buttons

Campbell Soup, celluloid	6-	8
Cascaret, "All going out—," celluloid	15-	21
Ceresota Flour, celluloid	5-	7
Studebaker, "Used the world over," celluloid	6-	10
Whitehead & Hoag Co., celluloid	5-	8

Clickers

Buster Brown Shoes	6-	9
Dr. Pepper (with celluloid button)	28-	37
H.J. Heinz Co.	5-	8
Hires Root Beer	5-	7
Lava Soap	6-	8

Containers

Adams Spearmint Chewing Gum, tin	24-	30
Lucky Strike cigarette box, tin	7-	10
Roly-Poly Tobacco, tin		350
Weideman Coffee, tin	6-	8
Whitman's candy box, tin (ill.)	10-	15

Metal Signs

Armour Meats, 13"×19"	68-	79
Cherry Sparkle, 6"×13"	14-	23
Dr. Brown's Cel-Ray, 5"×10"	9-	14
Drink Orange Crush, 16"×22"	19-	27
Gillette Safety Razors, 6"×13"	12-	21
Pepsums Stomach Soothers, 5"×9"	15-	22
Sen-Sen Chewing Gum, 6"×6"	34-	41

Mirrors

Ballard's Obelisk (flour)	11-	16
Bell Roasted Coffee	14-	17
Bromo-Seltzer	28-	36
Gillette Safety Razors	12-	16
Holland Furnaces	14-	17
Moller Pianos and Organs	9-	14
Shawmut Rubbers	9-	14
Standard Oil Company	10-	15
Worth Hats	16-	21

Paper Items

Cigar box labels, any make	1-	2
Herrick's Pills and Plasters, wall poster	12-	18
Magazine advertisements, 1920s-1930s	50¢-	75¢
Maltine, bookmark	6-	9
Pearline Pills	4-	6
Piper-Heidsieck notebook	5-	7
RCA fan, cardboard	9-	12
Wrigley's Gum calendar, cardboard, 1927	6-	9
Yellow Kid Ginger Wafers, box labels, ea.	16-	24

Paperweights

Burr & Co., coach builders, glass	14-	22
Crawford Shoes, glass	12-	18
Firestone Tires, glass	12-	20
Plume & Atwood Mfg. Co., glass	12-	18

Postcards

The postcard became legal mailing matter in the 1870s. Every manufacturer in the world used them to advertise products. The value depends on the subject matter.

Agata Glass

Made in 1887 by the New England Glass Company, for less than a year. The glass item to be ornamented was first coated with a metallic stain or mineral color (of color desired) then spattered with alcohol, benzene, or naphtha. When this evaporated, it left a mottled surface on the glassware. Don't confuse the genuine with a marbled ware called Akro Agate.

Bowl, 3" high	$1,750-2,200
Celery vase, pink	1,600-1,800
Cruet, multi-mottling	1,650-1,800
Sugar bowl, blue/green, 4½" high	1,900-2,100
Toothpick holder, four way	850-1,000
Tumbler, pink	800- 950
Vase, lily, 11½"	1,500-1,700

Agate Glass

Eugene Rousseau originated this glass in the 1870s; later it was made by other companies. Gold and other metallic oxides were

Agate Glass

used in the glass batch to achieve the agate effect.

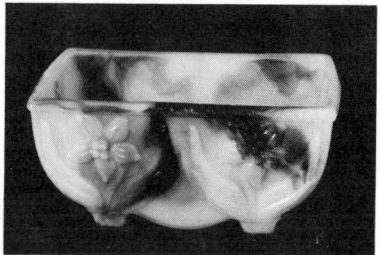

Akro Agate Glass

Akro Agate Glass

The Akro Agate Glass Company didn't get around to making glass until 1932. Before that, in 1911, they were jobbers for a marble company in Ohio. In 1914 they moved to Clarksburg, West Virginia, and made their own marbles. They made various types of glass in several colors until they went out of business in the late 1940s.

Ashtray, leaf-shaped	$ 12-	16
Bowl, green slag	14-	23
Cigarette holder	12-	17
Creamer, 3″ high, blue	14-	23
Dish, shell-shaped, green	9-	15
Match holder, green, white, black	16-	24
Planter, blue/white (ill.)	19-	27
Powder jar, dog, white	29-	37
Tumbler, green/white	16-	22
Vase, blue, 6″ high	17-	22
Vase, green and white	20-	28
Vase, small, orange and white ...	18-	27

Albums

Cherished photographs were kept in ornate albums in the mid-to-late Victorian era.

Albums

Usually velvet-covered with metal hinges.

Average price .... $ 20- 55

Alcohol Collectibles

Alcohol Collectibles

Demon Rum, Carrie Nation — jugs, bottles, advertising material, all are being collected, the older the better.

Bacardi rum, 1-gal., wicker container, 1878, Cuba ......$ 52-	62	
Brown-Forman Distillers decanter w/stopper, late 1800s	58-	67
Cloth tape measure, "No. 7 Gin," late 1800s	7-	10
"Hand" vase, Brown-Forman, Louisville, late 1800s	52-	61
Hanover Rye shot glass (salesman's sample)	18-	26
Jack Daniel advertising folder (ill.)	50¢-	1
Metal serving tray, Hayner's Distillery, 1879	50-	60
Old Crow paper fan, collapsible type	7-	10
Old Tucker decanter, late 1800s .	75-	80
Tin advertising sign, Hampton's Rye, early 1900s	42-	51
Whiskey jug, Doulton, Lambeth, England, 1854 (ill.)	120-130	
Wooden whiskey case, Hanover Rye, Cincinnati, late 1800s ...	40-	48

Alexandrite Glass

Thomas Webb & Sons, England, made this beautiful glass at the beginning of the 20th century. It shades from pale yellow to rose, then to blue. Stevens & Williams, England, also produced it, using the cut-through method to achieve their effect. A ware somewhat similar to the above also was made by Moser of Carlsbad, Czechoslovakia.

Goblet, amethyst, signed
Moser ....$ 170- 185
Match holder, 2½" dia.,
signed Webb 700- 750
Plate, 6", 7" dia., Webb 700- 800
Plate, 8" dia., signed Moser .. 125- 135
Rose bowl, 2" dia., fuchsia,
signed Webb 1,400-1,750
Toothpick holder, ITP, amber,
Webb................. 1,550-1,800
Wine, 3½" high, Webb 240- 250
Wine, 4" high, Stevens &
Williams 240- 260

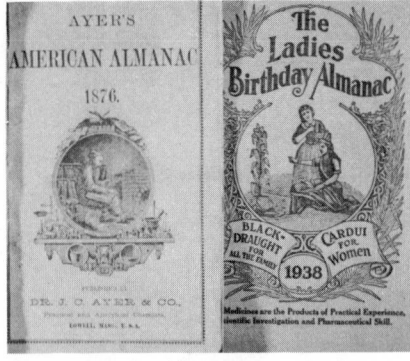

Almanacs

Almanacs

These small booklets forecast the weather as well as predicting many other daily activities.

Ayer's American Almanac, 1876,
published by Dr. J.C. Ayer &
Co. (ill) ....$ 15- 22
Centaur Almanac, 1874,
published by J.B. Rose, New
York 10- 17
Farmer's Almanac, 1849, Boston 14- 20
The Gardener's Almanac, 1952,
by Comstock, Ferre & Co.,
Conn. 16- 24
B.F. Goodrich Farmer's
Handbook and Almanac, 1948 . 5- 7
The Ladies' Birthday Almanac,
1960 (ill.) 5- 8

Leavitt's Farmer's Almanac,
1893, Concord, N.H. 17- 28
Dr. Miles New Weather Almanac
and Hand Book, Miles
Laboratory, 1937 .... 4- 7
Miner's Almanac, 1873,
Pittsburgh 11- 19
Morning, Noon and Night,
1871-2, P.H. Drake & Co's
Plantation Bitters 15- 21
New England Almanack, 1795,
New London, Conn. 28- 35
Old Farmer's Almanac (no "k"),
1868, published by Brewer &
Tileston 11- 17
Old Farmer's Almanac, 1853,
published by Jenks, Hickling
& Swan 25- 34
Pocket Almanac and Account
Book, by Brown's Iron Bitters,
1889 .... 9- 17
Poor Richard's Almanac, 1834,
Tobias Ostrander 23- 35
Rawleigh's Good Health Guide
Almanac Cook Book, 1927 .... 4- 7
Tarrytown Argus Almanac, 1874 10- 16
Vinegar Bitters Almanac, 1879 .. 12- 16
Watkins Almanac and Home
Book, 1939 .... 5- 8
Wright's Pictorial Family
Almanac, 1891 .... 7- 16

Amberina

Amberina

Patented in 1883 for the Libbey brothers and their New England Glass Company, Amberina was made by placing a small amount of gold in a transparent amber glass batch. The article was formed and allowed to cool below a glowing red heat; then specific parts were reheated at the glory hole. This caused the finished product to be shaded

32

Amberina

from amber to ruby red. Genuine Amberina
is scarce today. "ITP" means Inverted
Thumbprint. Lots of repros!

Art glass basket . . . . $	750-	850
Bowl, Diamond Optic, 4¼" dia.	180-	188
Bowl, Diamond Quilted, 4½" dia.	175-	185
Bowl, finger, ruffled, 4" dia. . .	210-	220
Bowl, fluted, applied handles, 4¾" dia.	270-	285
Candlesticks, pair, 14" high . .	210-	240
Caster, pickle, ITP, footed silver plateholder	550-	575
Celery, Daisy & Button, 5" high	310-	320
Celery, Diamond Quilted, 6" high	320-	340
Compote, Diamond Optic, 8" dia.	370-	390
Compote, wafer base, signed Libbey, 8" dia.	400-	425
Creamer, amber handle, 4½" high	240-	260
Creamer, Daisy & Button, 6" high (ill.)	195-	220
Creamer, ITP, clear handle, 4½" high	210-	230
Cruet, Diamond Quilted, c.g. stopper, 6¾" high	300-	320
Cruet, ITP, cut glass stopper, 7" high	240-	255
Cup, punch, Baby ITP	122-	134
Cup, punch, Herringbone, clear handle	148-	159
Cup, punch set 12, all signed Libbey	1,700-	1,950
Cup/saucer, both signed Libbey	180-	195
Decanter, 14½" high, blown glass stopper	450-	575
Decanter, 12½" high, ITP, blown glass stopper	460-	470
Decanter, 12" high, cut glass stopper	482-	510
Mug, amber handle	120-	130
Mug, child's, clear handle	100-	110
Mug, swirled, Diamond, clear handle	150-	165
Parfait, ITP	154-	164
Pitcher, applied, twisted handle, Diamond Optic, 9" high	320-	345
Pitcher, Diamond Quilted, 9¾" high, clear handle	260-	275
Pitcher, milk, ITP, 10" high . .	240-	295
Pitcher, water, applied rope handle, 9" high	460-	520
Pitcher, water, clear handle, fuchsia, 9½" high	240-	260
Plate, 7½" dia.	115-	124
Plate, Diamond Quilted, 7¼" dia.	117-	132
Plate, fluted edge, signed Libbey in pontil	145-	160
Salt, master, 1½" high, Diamond Quilted, ...	140-	152
Salt, master, 1½" high, ruffled edge	135-	150
Salt/pepper shakers, 4" high, pewter tops	225-	240
Salt/pepper shakers, 4½" high, ITP, pewter tops	220-	245
Salt/pepper shakers, 4" high, Expanded Diamond, p. tops	215-	230
Sauce, Daisy & Button, 4¼" dia., expanded diamond . . .	160-	185
Sauce, Diamond Quilted, 4½" dia.	152-	172
Sauce, Diamond Optic, 4½" dia.	130-	158
Sugar bowl, 5" high, double handles, ITP	350-	375
Sugar bowl, 4¾" high, Diamond Quilted	325-	350
Sugar bowl, 4½" high, single handle	325-	350
Sugar bowl, 4½" high, double handles	320-	335
Toothpick holder, Daisy & Button, 3" high	190-	210
Toothpick holder, Diamond Quilted, 3¼" high	192-	220
Toothpick holder, ITP, 3½" high	220-	240
Toothpick holder, trefoil, 3½" high	230-	240
Tumbler, Baby ITP, 3¾" high	98-	120
Tumbler, Diamond Quilted, 4" high	130-	145
Tumbler, enameled flowers, 4¼" high	124-	132

(continued)

Tumbler, Expanded Diamond, 4″ high	107-	125
Tumbler, 4¼″ high	105-	118
Vase, blown, with ribs, applied amber glass rigaree at neck (ill.)	190-	220
Vase, fuchsia, signed Libbey, 10″ high	340-	360
Vase, Hobnail, 7¼″ high	290-	320
Vase, ITP, 9″ high	180-	195
Vase, Jack-in-the-Pulpit, signed Libbey, 14½″ high	430-	500
Vase, lily-shaped, in silver plateholder, 7½″ high	340-	370
Vase, ribbed, 10″ high	340-	380

Amethyst Glass

Amethyst Glass

A dark purple glass. Sandwich made a lot of it after the Civil War.

Barber bottle, castle scene, pewter cap	$ 65-	75
Bowl, finger, rough pontil, 6″ dia.	24-	32
Candleholders, pair, 7″ high	32-	41
Compote, clear stem, 6½″ high	26-	34
Dish, bird decor, 5″ dia.	20-	29
Flask, cornucopia/eagle, rough pontil, one-half pint, 5″ high	162-180	
Lamp, kerosene-type, 8″ high, original brass collar	57-	66
Mug, child's, Little Bo-Peep, 4″ high, handled	41-	50
Paperweight, triangular, floral enamels, 5½″ long (ill.)	22-	31
Pitcher, water, enameled flowers, ferns, 6″ high	39-	47
Plate, 6″ dia., Mary Gregory	100-125	
Sauce, Millersburg, 2½″ deep	37-	40
Vase, enameled flowers, 5″ high, pair	60-	70
Vase, enameled design, possibly Sandwich	71-	80
Vase, etched flowers, 7″ high	44-	52
Wine, bell-shaped, clear stem, 3½″ high, set of 6	52-	61

Amphora

A two-handled Greek vessel for holding wine, oil, etc. Originally made in 720 to 1200 in Rhineland villages as containers for wine which was exported to Britain and certain Baltic countries. What you find today in shops was made by Teplitz in Germany in the late 1800s.

Basket, flowers in relief, 7½″ high, signed	$240-270
Urn, 15″ high, green/gold, blue trim, signed Amphora	280-290
Urn, applied flowers, gold handles, 9″ high	180-185
Vase, applied flowers, gray/white, gold handles, 9″ high	140-160
Vase, brown/green, jewel trim, 11¼″ high	130-140
Vase, floral decor, 8½″ high, signed Amphora with crown	220-250
Vase, gold/green, pink leaf decor, signed Amphora with crown	140-175
Vase, red/white/green, flowers, 10″ high	118-127
Vase, yellow flowers, 7¾″ high, signed	200-220

Andirons

Andirons

Dogs, as they were called in the earlier days, were usually made of wrought iron. Blacksmiths made them to personal order for the housewife. Brass andirons were known in America as early as 1740; even Paul Revere made a few.

Brass, ball top, 19th century, pr.	$325-360
Brass, Georgian, pr., 17″ high	650-750
Brass, poodles, early 19th century, pr.	440-470
Wrought iron, 15″ high, hand-forged, early 19th century, pr.	160-180
Wrought iron, 17″ high, ring top, late 18th century (ill.)	115-128

Animal Collectibles   Animal Dishes (Covered)

Animal Collectibles

Collectors are finding everything from elephant-foot wastebaskets to overstuffed mice.

Brass lion's head door knocker, mid-1800s	$ 160-	180
Plaster lion on teakwood pedestal, 9½" high (ill.)	35-	45
Stuffed mongoose "attacking" stuffed cobra	110-	125
Stuffed moose head	350-	375
Stuffed water buffalo's head, 47" rack	625-	700
Tiger's skin, complete with head and paws, late 1800s	1,500-	1,700
Wastebasket made from elephant's foot, early 20th century	550-	600
Zebra hide, felt-lined	375-	400

Animal Dishes (Covered)

These covered dishes were made in clear, colored, and opal (milk) glass; also of pottery, usually from the Staffordshire District, England. They've been around for over 200 years and have been reproduced in every size and shape without exception. Prices shown are for the old and genuine. One of the finest collections in the United States is at the Houston Museum, Chattanooga, Tennessee.

Camel, 2 humps, white milk glass	$115-130
Cat, white milk glass	120-140
Chick-in-egg-in-sleigh, white milk glass	80- 90
Cow-shape cover, caramel slag (goes over butter)	175-190
Dog, purple slag	150-180
Ducks: clear glass, 6½"	70- 80
frosted glass, 6½"	78- 88
milk glass, white, 5"	94-103
multicolored (ill.)	140-150
Eagle, milk glass	120-130

Fish on skiff, 7" dia., milk glass	70- 80
Hens, colored glass:	
5" and 6", dark amber and light amber	140-149
6½" and 7" dia., frosted	75- 90
Hens, milk glass:	
5", white, Bakewell, Pears cross on bottom, wicker nest	70- 80
5", white with blue head (ill.)	70- 80
7", white, lacy nest	190-220
7", white, lacy nest, caramel, flecked	185-200
Lamb, hexagon base, white	80- 90
Quail, white milk glass	82- 90
Rabbits; milk glass, 5½" same, mule-eared	97-106
Robin on nest, basketweave base, white milk glass	150-170
Swans:	
5", blue	120-130
6", Staffordshire	290-310
7", Sandwich milk glass, pr.	350-400
Turkey, hen, 9", Leeds	320-350

Apostle Pitcher

Apostle Pitchers

Embossed figures of the Apostles set within Gothic window frames were first made at Creussen, Germany, in the 17th century.

                                    (continued)

Daniel Greatbach made one of Parian ware for the American Pottery Company, Jersey City. An Apostle cuspidor was made by the Congress Hill Pottery Company about the same time.

Cuspidor . . . .$ 400- 440
Pitcher, 18th century (ill.) 1,600-1,800
Pitcher, Parian ware,
American 520- 540

Apostle Spoons

Of all spoon designs, this is the most famous. In the 15th and 16th centuries the first ones were made of pewter and silver. At the tip of each spoon was the figure of an Apostle. Twelve Apostles and one spoon of Jesus made a set. Few original sets exist, but many reproductions, adaptations, what-have-you, are on the market today. Reproductions were first made in the 1850s. Careful!

Apothecary Collectibles

Apothecary Collectibles

Apothecary funnel, copper, has
hanging ring, 9″ high . . . .$ 19- 27
Apothecary funnel, glass, 7½″
high 8- 14
Breast pump, has rubber suction
ball, 4″ high 4- 7
Cork press, lever-type, 4 different
sizes, 9″ long 50- 60
Counter scale, 2 large brass pans,
full set of weights 135-145
Display case, tin/wood, 3 drawers 70- 80
Drug mill, looks like small coffee
grinder 52- 61
Hand scale, in wooden box, full
set of weights 38- 50
Hydrometer jar, hand blown,
12″ high 12- 18

Mentholatum lamp, brass, glass
bowl, 6½″ high 14- 24
Mortar and pestle, brass 88-115
Mortar and pestle, porcelain (ill.) . 24- 33
Pill roller, wood, 3″ dia. 18- 24
Sterlizer, tin, looks like a coffee
percolator, 8″ high 21- 30

Appliances

Appliances

Some go back into the early 1800s, such as the wooden clothes wringer. Others came into vogue at the turn of the century, such as the hand-operated vacuum cleaner.

These old appliances are being collected today as decorative items for kitchen, den, whatever.

Clothes wringer, handmade,
early 1800s (ill.) . . . .$ 50- 60
Electric fan, GE, 1915, table
model, still runs 28- 36
Electric iron, early 1900s 17- 22
Vacuum cleaner, hand-operated . 34- 40
Washing machine, hand-
operated, wooden, late 1800s . . 55- 60

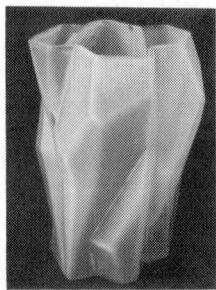

Art Deco

Art Deco

Art Deco or Art Moderne was a style beginning after the Paris Exposition of 1925. It was the first modern design, Lincoln's Zephyr being a classic example. With its contrasting colors and wild lines, it was popular until World War II and is now back in vogue.

Compote, metal/glass, 19″ high . . $130-150
Cup, handled, green/blue,
3½″ high 32- 42

Desk clock, marble and cloisonne, luminous hands	58- 67
Dressing table set, cameo glass, inlaid silver, nudes, 1931	105-115
Elephant head incense burner ...	28- 40
Figurine, ape in "thinking" pose, bronze, 12" high	140-170
Figurine, dancing girl, partially nude, bronze, 10" high	130-140
Figurine, lovers, bronze on marble pedestal, French......	80- 90
Lamp, Dutch silver (pot metal), kneeling black dancer, glass shade	85-105
Lamp, naked man holding nude woman overhead, bronze, glass ball shade	160-170
Mirror, hand, 11" long, nude figure in relief on back	47- 56
Statuette, tubular metals, cubism design, dated 1934 on bottom .	63- 78
Vase, black glass, silver holder, Italian, 14" high	140-160
Vase, blue, geometric design, 16½" high, French (ill.)	92-102
Vase, frosted lion over dead lamb, marble and glass, French 1930s	100-112
Wall plaque, glass and cloisonne, nude figures, 8"×15"	100-112

Art Glass Baskets

During the late 19th and early 20th centuries these beautiful, handmade baskets were always produced by hand and in every type glass. Expensive then, out-of-sight today, the Houston Museum has one of the finest collections in the world. See specific type of glass for prices.

Art Nouveau

Art Nouveau

Rebelling against the accepted forms of art, Art Nouveau was in vogue in the late 1800s, then until just before World War I. Tiffany collectors revived it and today it's highly collectible, in metal, wood, glass. Surface decoration is one of its identifying marks.

Bookends, nudes, sterling silver, pr.	$ 92-120
Bookmark, 2" high	37- 50
Bowl, flower, Galle style, deep cut	140-170
Box, jewelry, footed, sterling silver, 4½" square	70- 90
Brush, sterling silver (ill.)	105-120
Buckle (also brooch), women's profile, silver...............	38- 42
Buttonhook, silver, entwining snake, 8" long..............	29- 39
Buttonhook, sterling silver (ill.) ..	58- 68
Cigarette case, chased copper, birds in relief, enamel-lined ...	95-120
Clock, desk type, nude nymph, in metal case...............	60- 70
Figurine, dancing figure, bronze, 11" high, marble pedestal	140-150

Art Glass Baskets

37

(continued)

Figurine, nude male, Dresden porcelain, 14″ high	180-190
Flask, sterling silver, nude lovers on beach	280-320
Inkwell, devil's tail as penholder, bronze, 2½″ square	60- 90
Lamp, nudes holding 2 glass shades, 14″ high, electrified . . .	250-300
Lamp, young girl holding ciga- rette, cast iron base, 12″ high .	95-125
Match holder (ill.)	40- 50
Pin, angel, brass (ill.)	16- 26
Pin, girl on horseback, brass (ill.) .	21- 31
Pin, profile of lovers, copper- on-brass	29- 37
Spoons, sterling silver, embossed figures, ea.	120-140
Tray, brass, reclining nude on beach, relief, 15″ dia.	95-120
Tray, pin, reclining figures on couch, 14″ dia.	50- 59
Tray, sterling silver, heart- shaped, initialed BHM, fluted rim	140-170
Vase, Amberina-type glass, in holder, 9″ high	60- 70
Vase, pewter, autos racing, 13″ high	120-160
Vase, pottery, flowers and butter- flies in relief, 10″ high	48- 54
Vase, Tiffany type, iridescent, bronze holder, 14″ high	120-140

Audubon Prints

Audubon Prints

Audubon originals, the engravings, are priceless today. The Havell edition, 1827-1838; the "Quadrupeds of America" series in 1844—all highly-collectible today. Many reproductions since 1915. Careful!

All prints listed here are from the Havell and Son Edition, London, completed in 1838.

Plate #	Subject	
4	Purple Finch	$ 925- 975
12	Baltimore Oriole	3,900-4,300
25	Song Sparrow	925- 975
31	White-headed Eagle . .	4,000-4,500
40	American Redstart . . .	925- 950
51	Red-tailed Hawk	2,900-3,200
65	Rathbone Warbler . . .	900- 975
74	Indigo Bird	1,600-1,800
90	Black-and-White Creeper	800- 900
101	Raven	3,200-3,500
115	Wood Pewee	875- 950
133	Black Poll Warbler . . .	975-1,100
139	Field Sparrow	725- 800
148	Pine Swamp Warbler .	825- 875
155	Black-throated Blue Warbler	875- 950
164	Tawny Thrush	1,100-1,200
179	Wood Wren	800- 850
187	Boat-tailed Grackle . .	2,200-2,400
205	Virginia Rail	1,450-1,650
211	Great Blue Heron	3,900-4,200
232	Hooded Merganser . . .	3,000-3,400
265	Puff-breasted Sandpiper	1,100-1,300
287	Ivory Gull	1,700-1,900
311	White Pelican	4,000-4,200
333	Green Heron	2,600-2,800
367	Band-tailed Pigeon . . .	2,000-2,100
382	Sharp-tailed Grouse . .	3,000-3,400
395	Audubon's Warbler . .	1,800-2,000
401	Red-breasted Merganser	3,600-3,800
409	Havell's Tern	1,200-1,400
432	Burrowing Owl	2,200-2,400

All prints listed here are from the Bien Edition, done in 1860 by Julius Bien in New York. All are full-sized plates.

18	Swallow-tailed Hawk .	1,600-1,800
34	Barn Owl	2,300-2,500
57	Great Crested Flycatcher	375- 425
90	Yellow Redpoll	450- 500
124	Lesser Marsh Hen . . .	400- 450
163	Henslow's Bunting . . .	375- 425
189	Song Sparrow	400- 450
226	Fish Crow	1,500-1,650
244	Yellow-breasted Chat .	900- 975
293	Ruffed Grouse	1,800-1,900
358	Glossy Ibis	1,600-1,850
465	Great Auk	1,900-2,200

Austrian, General

Many small potteries produced beautiful porcelain and pottery in Austria during the 19th century. Some were financed by money from America, others manufactured wares

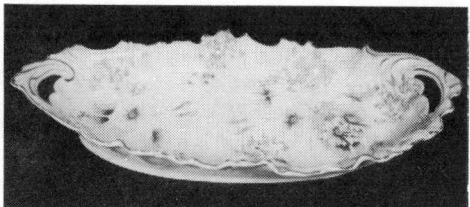

Austrian, General

with American names for export to America only. Carlsbad was the center for many of these firms. Specific firms are listed alphabetically in this Guide.

Tray, flower motif, 8″ long (ill.) .. $35-43
Vase, 10¾″ high, flowers, gilded, handled, Carlsbad 70-88

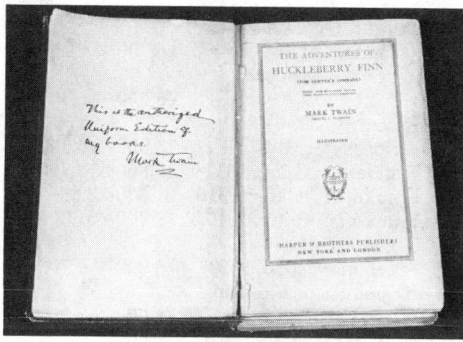

Autographs

Autographs (Philography)

The signatures of known people are always in demand by collectors. Keep in mind that governors, presidents, and the like seldom signed routine documents, leaving this menial task to clerks. Prices quoted here are for genuine signatures only. Holographs are letters written entirely by the hand of the signer of the letter. In the case of presidential letters, these are very valuable. A JFK holograph would bring upwards of $6,000 today.

Arnold, Benedict (patriot/
  traitor, Revolutionary
  War) ....$ 4,300- 4,800
Caruso, Enrico, opera
  star of the 1920s 350- 375
Cody, "Buffalo Bill,"
  program signature ... 50- 60
Coolidge, Calvin, signed
  when campaigning
  through New England 160- 180

Davis, Jefferson, note
  declining invitation to
  supper party 325- 350
Eisenhower, Dwight D.,
  note of thanks during
  World War II 220- 240
Grant, U.S., giving
  Sherman final approval
  to march to the sea ... 7,800+
Grant, Ulysses S., letter
  of regrets for boy killed
  during war 675- 750
Hancock, John, Benedict
  Arnold's commission
  as Major General .... 10,800+
Hitler, Adolph, signed
  document (careful of
  repros here) .... 1,700+
Jackson, Andrew,
  inviting friend to horse
  race at Hermitage,
  Nashville 280- 295
Lincoln, Abraham, note
  to Union General .... 1,400+
Lincoln's Gettysburg
  Address, handwritten
  copy .... 60,000-70,000+
Lincoln, handwritten
  letters, 1846, poems to
  friend.............. 31,000-35,000+
Lipton, Thomas, of tea
  fame, 1713 .... 40- 50
Revere, Paul, handwrit-
  ten signed document . 75,000+
Roosevelt, Franklin,
  presidential station-
  ery, to senator, 1935 .. 190- 210
Roosevelt, Teddy, letter
  of regrets to banquet
  invitation 350- 400
Twain, Mark (if original)
  (ill.) .... 1,000+

Automobiles

Automobiles

In 1947 the Antique Automobile Club of America set up a system whereby buses,

39

(continued)

motorcycles, cars, fire engines, etc., made before 1930 would be classified as authentic antique vehicles. Generally, those cars from 1930 to 1948 are considered Classics. All prices listed here are for autos in restored condition.

Apperson, Jack Rabbit runabout, 1914, 6-cylinder	$27,000-	32,000
Auburn, 4-cylinder touring, 1912	14,000-	18,000
Auburn, touring, 1917	10,500-	11,800
Buick, 2-cylinder, chain drive, 1905	17,500-	19,000
Buick, Model E runabout, 1908	13,800-	16,000
Buick, Model 10 surrey, 1910	22,000-	24,000
Buick, roadster, 1914	15,500-	17,000
Buick, 4-passenger coupe, 1922	9,000-	10,300
Buick, special cabriole, 1936	11,400-	12,400
Cadillac, roadster, 1904	20,000-	21,500
Cadillac, toy tonneau, 1910	26,000-	29,000
Cadillac, V-8, touring, 1916	19,500-	22,000
Cadillac, sport roadster, 1923	23,800-	25,400
Cadillac, Series 61 convertible sedan, 1939	23,700-	25,100
Chalmers, touring car, 1909	19,400-	21,400
Chandler, sport touring, 1921	17,700-	19,200
Chandler, 2-door sedan, 1926	12,300-	13,800
Chevrolet, Baby Grand roadster, 1913	16,000-	17,500
Chevrolet, roadster, 1913	15,700-	16,600
Chevrolet, touring car, 1916	13,400-	15,000
Chevrolet, 490 roadster, 1921	11,400-	13,300
Chevrolet, touring car, 1927	12,700-	14,300
Chevrolet, sport roadster, side mounts, 1929	15,400-	16,800
Chevrolet, standard sedan, 1935	8,900-	9,875
Chevrolet, standard coupe, 1937	6,300-	7,200
Chrysler, 6-cylinder sport phaeton, 1925	16,000-	18,300
Chrysler, Model 60 coupe, Royal 1926	9,200-	10,200
Chrysler, 72 cabriolet, 1928	15,300-	16,700
Chrysler, 6-cylinder coupe, 1934	11,000-	12,500
Cole, 5-passenger, V-8, touring, 1916	12,800-	13,900
Columbia Electric, Victoria, 1904	12,800-	14,200
Columbia Electric, Victoria, 1907	12,800-	14,200
Crane-Simplex, touring car, 1912	44,000-	47,000
Dodge, touring, 1915	9,300-	10,200
Dodge, roadster, 1917	8,200-	9,200
Dodge, touring car, 1922	7,900-	8,700
Dodge, coupe, 1937	10,700-	11,600
Duesenberg, dual cowl phaeton, 1921		125,000+
Duesenberg, phaeton, 1924		140,000+
Durant, 6-cylinder touring, 1923	8,700-	9,450
Essex, 2-door coach, 1921	5,200-	5,700
Essex, Boattail Speedster, 1927	13,600-	14,500
Flanders, touring, 1911	12,800-	13,700
Franklin, roadster, 1910	21,000-	22,500
Franklin, touring, 1917	19,700-	21,600
Graham-Paige, 6-cylinder coupe, 1929	8,900-	9,700
Hispano Suiza, touring car, 1910	37,000-	39,500
Hupmobile, coupe, 1910	9,500-	10,400
Hupmobile, roadster, 1913	11,200-	12,100
Hupmobile, sedan, 1925	7,200-	7,900
International, high wheel auto buggy, 1908	8,900-	9,900
Isotta-Franschini, tourer, 1914	25,500-	26,800
Jordan, Playboy roadster, 1920	15,700-	16,800
Jordan, 8-cylinder sedan, 1927	8,900-	10,000
Lafayette Nash, 2-door sedan, 1936	6,600-	7,500
LaSalle, rumble seat coupe, 1935	13,400-	14,700
LaSalle, opera coupe, side mounts, 1936	11,400-	12,700
Lincoln, LeLand touring, 1922	24,400-	26,100
Lincoln, limousine, 1924	11,200-	12,100
Lincoln-Zephyr, convertible sedan, 1939	20,400-	22,100
Lincoln-Zephyr, convertible coupe, 1941	22,300-	24,000
Locomobile, roadster, 1910	22,400-	24,100

Locomobile, laundelette
coupe, 1915 . . . . 21,000- 22,600
Locomobile, sport
touring, 1922 . . . . 32,000- 34,000
Marmon, speedster,
1911 . . . . 25,300- 26,300
Marmon, Model 34
touring, 1916 . . . . . . 19,400- 21,200
Marmon, Model E 75
touring, 1924 . . . . . . 16,000- 17,800
Marmon, 8-70 convert-
ible coupe, 1931 . . . . 16,400- 17,600
Maxwell, 2-cylinder
roadster, 1903 . . . . . 10,700- 11,600
Maxwell, roadster, 1912 12,500- 13,600
Mercedes, 2-passenger
racer, 4-cylinder, 1908
(ill.) . . . . 145,000+
Mercedes, touring car,
1912 . . . . 57,000- 65,000
Mercer, raceabout, 1913 168,000+
Mercer, sporting, 1915 . 44,000- 49,000
Moon, touring car, 1922 13,000- 13,900
Nash, touring car, 1921 . 12,200- 12,900
Nash, Special 6 sedan,
1926 . . . . 7,900- 8,400
Nash, 400 touring,
1929 . . . . 8,400- 9,100
Oakland, 6-cylinder
touring, 1913 . . . . 21,000- 23,000
Oakland, touring, 1923 . 11,600- 12,400
Oldsmobile, roadster,
1901 . . . . 10,700- 11,600
Oldsmobile, touring,
1918 . . . . 13,400- 14,200
Oldsmobile, V-8 sport
touring, 1928 . . . . 9,200- 9,900
Overland, roadster, 1911 13,200- 14,400
Overland, Model 85
touring, 1917 . . . . 10,300- 11,100
Packard, 4-cylinder
roadster, 1909 . . . . . . 51,000- 55,500
Packard, Twin-Six, 7-
passenger touring,
1915 . . . . 41,000- 44,000
Packard, 7-passenger
limousine, 1922 . . . . . 14,800- 15,900
Packard, 8-cylinder,
120C sedan, 1936 . . . . 13,000- 14,500
Pierce-Arrow, Great
Arrow, 1907 . . . . 49,000- 52,000
Pierce-Arrow, Model 38
touring, 1914 . . . . 51,000- 55,000
Pierce-Arrow, 7-
passenger touring,
1922 . . . . 46,000- 49,000
Rambler, 2-cylinder
touring, 1905 . . . . 14,000- 14,900
Regal, underslung
coupe, 1913 . . . . 22,000- 23,400

Reo, 1-cylinder
runabout, 1904 . . . . . 11,800- 12,800
Reo, 4-cylinder touring,
1910 . . . . 12,800- 14,200
Rolls-Royce, roadster
Silver Ghost, 1910 . . . 160,000-170,000
Rolls-Royce, landaulet,
1914 . . . . 80,000- 84,000
Rolls-Royce, tourer,
1920 . . . . 64,000- 67,000
Rolls-Royce, Model 20
touring, 1923 . . . . . . 43,000+
Sears, motor buggy,
1907 . . . . 9,500- 9,900
Singer, LeMans
roadster, 1933 . . . . . . 9,000- 9,900
Stanley Steamer,
runabout, 1904 . . . . . 25,000- 26,400
Stanley Steamer,
touring car, 1908 . . . . 39,000- 49,000
Stevens-Duryea,
roadster, 1909 . . . . . . 42,400- 44,000
Studebaker, roadster,
1911 . . . . 12,400- 12,750
Studebaker, Model 25
touring, 1913 . . . . . . 15,200- 15,800
Studebaker, doctor's
coupe, 1924 . . . . 9,500- 10,100
Stutz, Bearcat roadster,
1914 . . . . 86,000- 90,000
Stutz, Bearcat
speedster, 1919 . . . . . 47,000+
Stutz, 6-cylinder
touring, 1924 . . . . 27,000+
Thomas, roadster, 1909 . 34,000+
Winton, touring car,
1917 . . . . 39,000- 40,000
Winton, 4-passenger
touring, 1921 . . . . 27,000- 29,000
Winton, 7-passenger
touring, 1923 . . . . 39,000- 41,000

Obviously, there are hundreds of other automobiles. Sorry if we've missed your model.

Automobiliana

From 1900 until 1930 over 1,500 different
makes of automobiles were manufactured in
the United States. Practically every part of
the car is collectible today, especially items
such as radiator caps and emblems, dash-
board clocks, brass head lamps, hubcaps, etc.

Advertisement, Aerocar Motor
Co., "There's No Getting
Away," 1908 . . . . $ 33- 41
Advertisement, Dragon Touring
Car, "The motor that motes,"
1907 . . . . 40- 48

41

(continued)

Automobiliana

Advertisement, Goodrich Safety Tread tires, 1914	20- 30
Advertisement, Metz 22, $475, The Gearless Car, 1913	28- 32
Advertisement, Midland Motor Co., Moline, Ill., 1910	27- 36
Advertisement, Murine (A tonic for the auto eye), 1907	32- 41
Auto Blue Books, 1909 through 1919, ea.	29- 38
Auto Green Books, 1915 through 1926, each	20- 28
Auto Wiring Manual, Abbot-Detroit cars, 1910-1914	47- 52
Book, *Get Out and Get Under,* 1913, illustrated	42- 52
Book, *Salesman's Cadillac,* 1913	51- 60
Book, *The Open Road,* 1914	40- 50
Book, *The Easy Route to California,* 1911	82- 90
Carbide tank for 1909 Ford Model-T	162-170
Carbide tank for 1912 Cadillac	210-240
Dashboard clock for 1914 Pierce Arrow	81- 90
Dashboard clock for 1916 Packard	84- 92
Emblems: average price, each	25- 38

Buick   Cadillac   McFarlan   Stutz
Oakland   Kleiber   DaVis   Overland
Franklin   Essex   DeLage

Bail handle light, brass, 1909 Hupmobile	325-400
Hood ornament, 1930s (ill.)	18- 25
Horn, double twist, brass, bulb-type, 1908 Maxwell	130-140
License plates, enamel-over-metal, 1909-1916, average price	33- 55
Magazine *Car Life,* 1916, 12 issues, all	160-169
Motor meter (forerunner of the speedometer), 1912 Marmon	90-110
Motor meter, 1913 Mercer	130-150
Motor meter, 1914 Columbia	65- 75

Owner's manual, 1908 Rolls Royce	230-270
Owner's manual, 1914 Stutz Bearcat	168-178
Poster, 1913 Auto Show, Chicago, 15"×20", paper	160-190
Radiator cap ornament, knight with lance	79- 87
Radiator cap ornament, Lady Ascot, Rolls Royce, silver, 1911	350-400
Road map showing routes to Chicago from New York City, 1909	70- 80
Sales catalogs, General Motors cars, 1916-1925, all	300-375
Signature of Ramsey E. Olds, creator of the Reo and the Oldsmobile, 1909	31- 40
Spark plug for 1909 Saxon	19- 29
Spark coil for 1910 Model-T; still works	77- 87
Vases, cut glass, used in back seat of 1912 Locomobile limo	94-107
Vases, used in back seat of 1913 Cadillac limousine, pr., cut glass	96-107

Autumn Leaf

Autumn Leaf (Jewel Tea Co.)

The Autumn Leaf line in early years was referred to only as Hall, Jewel or Autumnal design. It wasn't until the 1940s that the pattern was given the name Autumn. In 1960 it got its name Autumn Leaf. Designed by Arden Richards of the Hall China Company, East Liverpool, Ohio, for the Jewel Tea Company in 1933, it quickly became a collectible. At least three other firms used the Autumnal design, but Hall's was then and still is the most famous and most sought after. All pieces listed were made by Hall for the Jewel Tea Company.

Bowls, 6", 6½", 8½", 9"	$ 7- 17
Butter dish, covered, ¼-lb.	28- 35

Butter dish, covered, 1-lb.	70- 83
Cake plate, footed, metal base ...	11- 16
Cake safe	20- 35
Casserole (top is small pie plate) .	22- 28
Clock, electric, 9½" dia.	210-235
Coffee dispenser, 10½" high	32- 40
Cookie jar, covered, tab handles .	37- 44
Custard cup	5- 8
Gravy boat	13- 18
Pitcher, milk, water	11- 19
Platters, 11", 11½", 13" 13½" ..	9- 15
Salt/pepper set (ill.)	13- 16
Tablecloth, 54"×54" and 54"×72"	52- 65
Toaster cover, plastic	11- 15
Vegetable dish, oval	18- 27

Aventurine Glass

This yellowish glass has large numbers of small crystals of copper. It is reasonably collectible, though Fostoria Glass Company, Moundsville, West Virginia, has produced a fair imitation in recent years.

Bowl, ruffled edges, 6" dia. $120-140
Pitcher, clear applied handle, 6" high	138-142
Rose bowl, 3" high	125-136
Vase, flowers, ruffled lip, 11½" high	210-220
Vase, fluted top, 10" high	200-210

Aviation

Aviation

Anything aeronautical from World Wars I and II, Korea, and Vietnam is collectible today. Pilots' wings, charts, emblems, and the aircraft itself from both WWI and WWII—all bring huge prices.

Airmail pilot's chart, Pittsburgh-to-Chicago, 1934 .... $ 68- 85

Arm patches, squadron, 8th Air Force, etc., ea.	2- 3
Leather pilot's helmet, goggles attached, 1930s	40- 45
Leather pilot's jacket, Chinese/ C.B.I. Theater flag on back, WWII	125-150
Pewter mug marked Royal Flying Corps, 1916	100-115
Squadron insignia, taken from old hanger, England, WWI ...	275-300
Sterling silver pilot's wings, WWII	60- 70
Tail insignia, French Spad 13, WWI, 28" high	175-200
Theater poster, "The Dawn Patrol," 1930	45- 55
Wooden propeller, clock in center, WWI	200-225

Baccarat Glass

Baccarat Glass

French, by La Compagnie Des Cristalleries De Baccarat; they also had a factory in Alsace-Lorraine. Factory started in 1765. Famous for their cane and millefiori paperweights, 1860 to 1880. Careful! Excellent fakes are coming into the U.S. Know your dealer if you're after a genuine paperweight.

Bell, clear-cut .... $	45-	55
Bird, frosted, 2-5/8" long	35-	44
Bobeche, crystal, 3½" dia., pr.	40-	48
Bobeche (wax catchers on candlesticks), lacy, pr.	38-	46
Bottle, cologne, cut and polished crystal	36-	44
Bottle, perfume, blue trim, turnstile stopper, pr.	62-	72
Bottle, perfume, cut and polished crystal, 4¼" high .	245-	255
Bottle, perfume, cut glass, 8" high	50-	59

43

(continued)

Bottle, perfume, Paneled Medallions, gold, 6½" high	60-	70
Bowl, cranberry, signed with small "b"	65-	75
Bowl, Rubina, Depose	80-	90
Candleholders, Diamond Point, 7" high, pr.	75-	85
Celery dish, Swirled Rose, signed	40-	50
Chandelier, 12-light, drip pan, amethyst head chain	1,700-1,975	
Compote, clear to yellow, 6½" high	75-	85
Compote, opaque, etched	83-	92
Cup/saucer, demitasse, frosted	45-	53
Decanter, bronze, scroll design, signed	85-	95
Decanter, Rose Tiente	80-	90
Dish, candy, scenic and figural design, 6½" dia.	55-	63
Dish, celery, Rubina, 7" dia.	63-	72
Dish, relish, cranberry, signed	54-	64
Dish, relish, Diamond Point, signed	50-	60
Figurine, nude lady, 9½" high	45-	54
Figurine, whale, 5" wide, signed	43-	52
Goblets, lacy design, c. 1850s, set of 6, all	575-	625
Ice bucket, Pink Swirl	150-	165
Ink stand, script design, signed	90-	100
Inkwell, Diamond Quilt, sterling silver cap, signed	95-	115
Inkwell, hinged lid, frosted	35-	44
Jar, Swirled Rose, silver lid	45-	55
Lamp base, cameo design, flowers	235-	255
Paperweight, Herbert Hoover	83-	93
Paperweight, red/periwinkle, star cut base, 2½" dia., signed, dated "b 1850"	1,800-2,250	
Paperweight, salmon pink, double clematis, 3½" dia., signed, dated "b 1848"	1,975-2,350	
Paperweight, squirrel, signed	57-	66
Pitcher, mold blown, 9¼" high (ill.)	215-	245
Pitcher, Rose Swirl, 4" high	35-	44
Plate, crystal, frosted	45-	54
Plate, Diamond pattern, 6½" dia.	55-	65
Plates, Swirled Rose, set of 6, all	78-	88
Sugar, Diamond Point, signed	73-	83
Tray, Rubina, signed	133-	144
Vase, cameo, roses, 8½" high, signed	245-	265
Vase, Rose Tiente, 9¼" high	175-	185
Vase stick type, cameo, floral decor, 11" high	275-	295

Again, please don't let a bunch of prices lull you into thinking you know genuine Baccarat paperweights. It's one thing to list a hundred or more with prices, but can you tell the old from the new?

Baggage Stickers

Baggage Stickers

Years ago, when it was fun to travel, hotels and steamship lines pasted colorful stickers on your steamer trunks, etc. I'll never forget the Flying Scot and the Orient Express.

Baggage sticker, in good condition	$ 1-	2

Banko Ware

Banko Ware

Some call it Poo Ware and it comes from Korea. It originated in the 1840-1910 period, though Korean potters have been making pottery for centuries. The molded, applied figures around the piece usually tell a story.

Teapot, green ground, applied figures, 6½" high	$250-270	
Vase, red, applied figures, 8" high	88-	98
Vase, red/black glaze, applied figures (ill.), 5½" high	72-	81

Banks, Mechanical

Banks that do something when you insert a coin are called mechanical. Over 300 differ-

Eagle and Eaglets   **Banks, Mechanical**   Always did 'spise a mule

ent kinds were made in this country from the 1870s until the early 1900s. Many reproductions are on the market today, some so good it's difficult to tell the old from the new, especially when the new bank has been "aged" by chipping its paint or fading it with an infrared lamp. Rare banks are expensive, so know your subject before you buy. The asterisk indicates it's being reproduced.

* Acrobat	$1,000-	1,250
Afghanistan	875-	925
* Always did 'spise a mule (ill.)	325-	475
Artillery, 8-sided block house	1,300-	1,550
Atlas	950-	1,100
* Bad accident	540-	570
Bank teller	6,400-	6,600
Baseball player	90-	110
Bowery	7,700-	7,900
Bowing man in cupola	2,300-	2,600
Breadwinner	3,200-	3,450
Butting ram	1,700-	2,000
Cabin	250-	275
* Calamity (football)	2,300-	2,450
Called out	5,400-	5,700
Calumet bank (tin)	160-	170
* Cat and mouse	550-	600
Chandlers bank	370-	390
* Chief Big Moon	525-	550
* Chimpanzee		1,000+
Chinaman in boat		6,400+
Chinaman with queue, tin	1,300-	1,500
Circus	3,500-	3,800
Clever Dick (tin)		1,400+
Clown and dog (tin)		1,900+

* Clown on globe	700-	850
Confectionery store		2,600+
Creedmore	240-	270
Dapper Dan	450-	500
* Darktown Battery	550-	625
Dinah with sleeve	150-	175
Ding Dong Bell (tin)		5,700+
Dog charges boy	475-	575
Dog on turntable	220-	250
Dog, speaking	260-	300
Dog trees cat	11,500-	12,700
* Dog with tray	1,700-	2,000
Donkey	300-	375
* Eagle and eaglets (ill.)	350-	400
Electric safe	450-	500
Elephant, 3 stars	325-	400
* Elephant, Light of Asia	1,500-	1,700
* Elephant wiggles	80-	90
Ferris Wheel		3400+
Football bank	1,300-	1,500
Freedman's bank, desk		17,000+
Frog and serpent (tin)		7,000+
Frog on rock	260-	300
Frog on stump	240-	280
* Gem	270-	310
Giant	5,100-	5,400
* Girl skipping rope		5,000+
Globe on arc	240-	280
Guessing bank	1,900-	2,200
Hall's Excelsior	120-	160
Hall's Lilliput	210-	270
Hen, setting	780-	870
* Hindu with turban	650-	750
* Hold the fort	1,300-	1,500
Home	400-	500
Hoop-la	410-	480
* Humpty-Dumpty	310-	350
* Indian shooting bear	600-	700

(continued)

John Bull's money box		4,800+
* Jolly nigger, butterfly tie	170-	195
(That's the original name.)		
* Jonah and the whale	725-	825
Kiltie bank	825-	925
* Leap frog	725-	800
Liberty Bell	600-	675
Little High Hat	725-	765
* Little Joe	140-	180
Lion and monkeys	400-	475
Magic Safe (tin)	700-	800
* Magician	875-	950
Mammy and child	700-	800
* Mason and hod carrier	775-	800
Merry-Go-Round		7,000+
Mickey Mouse (tin)		2,300+
Mikado	7,400-	7,800
Minstrel, tin	260-	310
* Monkey and organ grinder	250-	350
Monkey and parrot (tin)	300-	365
Mosque	260-	295
Music bank (tin)	1,200-	1,400
National Bank		895+
North Pole	6,200-	6,400
* Owl with book, slot in book	170-	250
* Paddy and his pig	475-	575
Panorama bank	1,450-	1,900
Patronize the blind	1,650-	2,200
* Pegleg beggar	950-	1,200
Picture gallery	1,900-	2,200
Pig in high chair	350-	450
Popeye knockout bank	375-	450
Preacher in pulpit		12,000+
Professor Pugfrog	1,900-	2,200
Pump and bucket	850-	1,100
Punch and Judy (iron and tin)	1,400-	1,700
* Punch and Judy, small or large letters	450-	575
Queen Victoria	5,000-	5,500
Rabbit in cabbage	325-	425
Rabbit, standing, on round base	290-	400
Red Riding Hood		8,600+
Rival	6,400-	6,800
Roller skating rink	4,800-	5,000
Rooster	175-	270
Saluting sailor (tin)	750-	975
Sambo	625-	750
* Santa Claus at chimney	385-	525
Scotsman (tin)	285-	400
Sentry bank (tin)	750-	800
Shoot the chute		5,400+
Signal cabin (tin)	410-	440
Speaking dog	400-	450
* Stump speaker	550-	625
Tabby bank	450-	525
Tammany	130-	185
Tank and cannon bank	375-	450

* Teddy and the bear	475-	550
Tiger (tin)	1,400-	1,700
Time is money	2,000-	2,400
Tower bank	2,700-	2,950
Trick pony	290-	350
Turtle	5,200-	5,700
Uncle Remus	1,500-	1,800
* Uncle Sam	525-	585
Watch bank	585-	695
* William Tell	350-	425
Wimbleton	2,600-	2,800
Windmill (tin)	145-	170
Wireless (tin)	220-	265
Woodpecker	2,000-	2,575

*Being reproduced.

Banks, Still

Banks, Still

These banks don't have any moving parts. Usually cast in the shape of buildings, animal figures, etc., the same advice holds true for these as does for the mechanical. The General Pershing is being heavily reproduced, as are others.

Aunt Jemima with spoon	$ 90-110
Bank building, 5″ high (ill.)	65- 72
Baseball player	90-100
Battleship Maine	150-160
Bird on stump, 4¾″ high	67- 77
Black Beauty	90-100
Blackamoor	80- 90
Boy Scout	84- 93
Buffalo, standing	80- 87
Buster and Tige	180-190
Campbell Kids	250-260
Captain Kidd, 5½″ high	152-170
Cat, sitting	60- 75
Cat with ball, 2½″ high	60- 70
Deer with antlers	68- 78
Dog candy container, 3¾″ high	34- 44
Dog, 5″ long	52- 61
Dog with pack, 3¾″ high	62- 72
Donkey with saddle	140-150

Duck	172-180	Poor tired Tim, tin, 5″ high	62- 70
Elephant on tub, 5¼″ high	70- 80	Prancing horse w/belly band, 4½″ high	54- 63
Elephant with howdah, 4¾″ high	57- 66	Presto #426	61- 70
Empire State Building	70- 80	Radio	68- 75
Feed My Sheep, pot metal, 3″ high	40- 50	Rearing horse, Beauty, 5″ high, on oval base	57- 67
Graf Zeppelin w/wheels, 8″ long	118-128	Red Goose shoes, 3¾″ high	60- 69
Horseshoe	72- 81	Resting camel, 2½″ high	120-130
Humpty Dumpty, tin, 5½″ high	37- 46	F. D. Roosevelt, die cast	46- 55
Indian head, maiden	73- 82	Rooster #187	87- 94
Jumbo savings bank, English, tin, 5¼″ high	32- 41	Shell, WWI	44- 53
Liberty Bell, Carnival glass	50- 60	Soldier, WWI	92-107
Lion, large	90-110	Standing elephant	50- 60
Lion on wheels	98-118	Statue of Liberty	74- 83
Little Daisy	52- 70	Teddy Bear	65- 73
Mailbox, green	45- 53	Thrifty pig	40- 50
Mickey Mouse, aluminum, 8¾″ high	132-150	Tiger	40- 48
Negro mammy	70- 80	Trolley car w/people, 3″ high	120-130
Owl	140-160	Trolley car without people, 3″ high	105-115
Pig with bow tie, 3″ high	72- 82	Turkey	60- 67
		Two kids (goats), 4½″ high	125-140
		Uncle Sam, cash register	72- 82
		Yellow Cab, 4″ high	200+

Banks, Still Photograph: **Louis S. Filles**

Row 1

Taft and Sherman—political	$128-140
Sailor, small, 5½″ high	67- 77
Golliwog (English)	112-120
Santa holding a tree, 5½″ high	92-101
Capitalist	84- 93
Owl on square base	61- 70
Bird on stump	62- 71
Bear stealing pig, 5½″ high	170-190

Row 2

Independence Hall, 9″ high	130-140
Lighthouse	92-115
Panorama	62- 70
Bank building	52- 70

47

(continued)

Banks, Still

Row 3

Liberty Bell on base . . . . $ 69- 82	
Liberty Bell 61- 71	
Independence Hall (3 banks in	
one) 170-190	

Row 4

Bank building, 3½″ high 40- 50	
Bank building, 4½″ high 67- 78	

Bank building, 5½″ high	65- 81
Horse on Tub	73- 82
Small lion	54- 63
Lion on tub	72- 85
Tower bank	45- 56
Bank building, 11″ high	68- 80
Bank building, 7″ high	52- 66

Banks, Still, Pottery

The crudest types were made centuries ago when someone wanted a container in which to bury valuables. They were usually made of fire-hardened clay and they remained popular until replaced by the iron banks in the mid-1800s.

Bear, sitting, 5½″ . . . . $ 47- 56	
Bird 37- 47	
Buffalo 41- 50	
Corn 70- 92	
Gourd 62- 72	
Lion's head 43- 52	
Pig, blue 40- 50	
Teddy Roosevelt 120-140	
Rooster, standing 50- 58	
Tree stump 27- 37	
Zeppelin 60- 70	

Barbed Wire

Barbed Wire

First patented in the late 1800s, there were more than 600 kinds. It had a great effect on the cattle business in the West. It's very collectible today. Rare, one-of-a-kind pieces bring upwards of $100 for 18 inches. Also called devil's rope.

Common variety, 18″ . . . . $ 1- 2

Up to $350 for rare pieces.

Barometers, Chronometers

Used for indicating the weather, barometers go back to the 11th century. A great many of the older ones still work. If you find a Louis XVI, ormolu-mounted, $10,000 is about right!

Banjo, inlaid rosewood, 1860s .	$190-240
Banjo, mahogany, John	
Berwinger	110-130
Banjo shape case, floral	
medallions, mahogany (ill.) . .	140-190
Banjo, silvered dial, rosewood,	
English	320-370
Chronometer, Whyte Thompson & Co., gimbled, double	
cased	1,500+

48

Barometers

Desk style, brass case,
  German 70- 90
Desk style, brass dial, English,
  8" high 40- 55
Hygrometer, thermometer,
  spirit level, Joseph
  Alexander 210-260
Stick type, American,
  mid-19th century 450-525
Stick type, George III, Edin-
  burgh, 40" high, operating .. 310-345
Stick type, ivory register dial,
  rosewood, inlaid, London ... 220-260
Wall, circular, register dial,
  gilt, inlaid rosewood, 45"
  high 370-390

Basalt

Basalt

Wedgwood made this pottery in the late 18th century. It was also made in ancient times and is a black, vitreous pottery, shiny inside, glossy on the outside. It's rather expensive. Look for Wedgwood impressed in the bottom if you want the genuine.

Bowl, 9½" dia., sterling silver
  rim $275-335

Bowl, 12" dia., acanthus decor,
  marked Wedgwood 320-350
Bust, John Dryden, 14" high .. 390-470
Bust, Shakespeare, circa 1800,
  marked Wedgwood 420-480
Candlesticks, 13¼" high, pr. ... 270-310
Chalice, beaded pedestal base,
  marked Wedgwood 250-300
Coffeepot, 9" high 185-220
Creamer, black 87-110
Medallions, 2¼"×2¾",
  marked Wedgwood and
  Bentley, George III and
  Queen Charlotte, pr........ 750+
Pitcher, Flaxman figures in
  relief around base,
  leaves/grapes border at top,
  6¾" high 200-270
Sugar bowl, covered, black ... 240-260
Tea set, sugar, creamer, pot,
  tray, flower motif, all 400-475
Teapot, usual marking, classic
  design (ill.) 250-300

Baseball Cards

Baseball Cards

The first baseball cards were issued in 1886 by Old Judge cigarets. Some of the rarest are Honus Wagner ($1,200+), Eddie Plank ($350-400) and Napoleon Lajoie ($300-350). Other companies, such as Glendale Meats, Signal Oil, and Tip Top Bread, put on these cards on a regional basis at the turn of the century.

Average cost: 50¢ to $1.50 for modern type. For the rare type—what you pay is what it's worth to you.

Basketry

The beautiful and delicate work done by the Indians of our continent is highly col-

49

(continued)

Basketry

lectible today. The Attu, Tlingit, Yokuts, Washo three-rod, Aleutian and Pomo continue to rise in value.

Aleut, yarn used for color pattern, 7½″ high, c. 1900s	$2,250-3,000	
Aleut bottle w/goblet	450-	475
Baskets from Aleutian Islands, sometimes have 40 stitches to the inch— highly collectible	450-	500
Chemehuevi (Southern California), coil, quill design, c. 1930s	550-	600
Eskimo, openwork design, 13″ high, c. late 1800s	325-	350
Eskimo, willow, fern root design, 11″ high, c. 1930s	175-	200
Hopi coil, yucca fiber, deer design, c. 1930s	145-	160
Makah covered box, eagle motif, red/blue (ill.)	250-	275
Moki w/handle and cover, 6½″ high, 3 colors (rare) (ill.)	360-	425
Navajo, tray, wedding type, 15″ dia., willow, c. 1930s	130-	155
Nez Perce Fez, fully beaded, 8¼″ high, c. 1910	900-	975
Pima, olla storage, willow, devil's claw design, c. 1925	110-	145
Pima, coiled bowl, 9″ high, willow, devil's claw design, 1930s	145-	170
San Carlos, tray, 15″ dia., willow, devil's claw design, c. 1920	710-	775
Skokomish, typical rim design of dogs	220-	255
Tlingit rattletop, 4″×5″, c. 1900s	400-	450
Tlingit rattletop, Greek key design, 4″ high, c. 1920s	325-	365

Tsimshian, spruce root w/aniline-dyed design, c. 1920s	135-	160
Walapai, twined, rabbit brush, 8½″ high, aniline dyed, c. 1930s	85-	110
Western Apache, tray, 19″ wide, geometric star design, c. 1920	565-	610
Yavapai, tray, 14½″ dia. willow, typical design, c. 1900s	810-	875
Yokut, bottleneck, yarn and feathers woven into shoulder, c. 1920s	250-	265
Yokut (Tulare), coiled bowl, deer design, 4″ dia., c. 1920s	245-	270

Battersea Enamel

Battersea Enamel

Stephen Janssen made this exquisite enamel work at Battersea, England, for only 5 or 6 years, 1750-1755. Knobs, jewel and patch boxes, lids, etc. A lot was made after 1755 in Staffordshire district, but the true Battersea was made for six years at most. It is reproduced in France today.

Box, angel motif, 2″×3″	$525-600
Box, blue base, "Love Is Eternal"	450-550
Box, 3″×2″, Pixies	500-575
Box, blue/yellow, floral, 4″ square	525-625
Box, green/blue, bird decor, 1½″×2″	460-525
Box, green enamel, white inside, pear shape, 2″×3″	450-525
Box, hunters chasing fox, 2″×4″	375-450
Box, "Love Is Thine," 2¾″×2⅛″	600-650
Box, patch, rose base, white lid, family coat-of-arms	450-570
Box, patch, "Mother" on lid	360-425
Box, 3″×4½″, red/green lid (ill.)	550-700

Bavarian, General

The small firms which produced ceramics

Bavarian, General

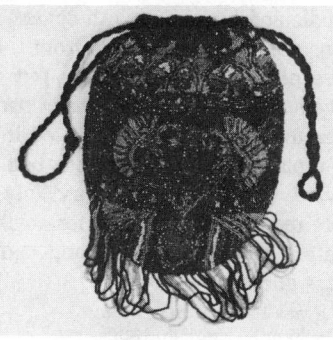

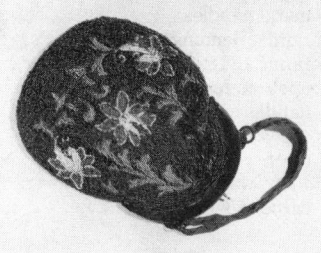

Beaded Bags

in Bavaria have long since disappeared. Who made those pieces you find today, simply marked Bavaria on the bottom? Few records were kept, so we'll probably never know. Look for specific factories listed alphabetically in this Guide.

Berry set, hand-painted flowers, pink, green	$ 38- 50
Bread plate, yellow roses, red border, 11″ long	34- 44
Candy dish, Dresden-type flowers, pink, blue	32- 44
Caster jug, vinegar/oil, red rose, green background	22- 31
Chocolate pot, roses, gilt trim, handled, with lid	47- 53
Hatpin holder, pink and yellow flowers, 8″ high	30- 40
Plate, flowers, garden scene, gilt edge, 7″ dia.	20- 27
Plate, white, gold (center left vacant for amateur painter)	27- 34
Plates, 4 fruit, pastoral scenes, signed PUNCH – Z. S. & Co., Bavaria, 9½″ dia. (ill.), ea.	78- 87
Platter, pink roses around border, 10″ long	40- 50
Powder box, violets in blue and lavender, gilt edge	58- 68
Sugar bowl, multicolored flowers, handled lid	46- 52
Teapot, pink and green floral decorations, 5″ high, lid	30- 40
Vase, gold and red roses, gilt lip, 6½″ high	32- 41

Beaded Bags

They were popular in the early to middle Victorian era.

Beads, tapestry scene, silk lined, silver frame at top with silver chain, late 1800s	$ 29- 38
Black glass beads, silver frame at top with silver chain, late 1800s	32- 40
Cloth, beaded flowers sewn into material, late 1800s (ill.)	14- 21
Garnet beads, opera-type back, snap catch, 5″ wide, mid-1800s	70- 81
Green glass beads, drawstring type, late 1800s	34- 43
Jade-colored glass beads, tortoise-shell frame, shell link handle	40- 50
Red, blue, gold, black, silk cords, peacocks and eyes (ill.)	31- 40
Silk bag, embroidered bead initials, silver frame and chain, late 1800s	32- 42

Bed (and Foot) Warmers

Bed (and Foot) Warmers

The earliest pans had iron handles. Usually what you find in shops today have a wooden

51

(continued)

handle and brass pan with cover. Reproductions are abundant. Coals from the fireplace were placed in the pan and put under the covers to warm the bed. Other bed warmers were made of soapstone, heated in the oven, then placed at the foot of the bed under the covers. The earliest buggy foot warmers were metal with a drawer for coals. Pottery heaters held hot water. Being reproduced in brass and copper.

Brass bed warmer, walnut handle, English, 1800s	$320-350
Buggy-type, moleskin covered metal handles	55- 70
Ceramic, Bennington type	210-260
Ceramic, c. 1890s (ill.)	52- 70
Soapstone foot warmer, bail handle, early 1900s	40- 50
Stoneware, blue/gray, Logan County Pottery Company	57- 68
Tin foot warmer, charcoal drawer, carpet-covered	53- 62

Belleek

Belleek

Made from feldspathic clay in County Fermanagh, Northern Ireland, Belleek was first made in 1857. The most characteristic productions are shell pieces and similar forms, supported by coral branches. Perhaps the loveliest are the openwork basket pieces. A real porcelain, the result of the simple vitrification of feldspar and china clay, it is extremely light and thin with a creamy, ivory surface and an iridescent luster. The typical Belleek mark consists of a hound, harp, tower, and shamrock, with the name Belleek on a ribbon underneath, printed in black, light and dark blue, brown, red, or green. Most original Belleek had this trademark.

Look for marine plants, seashells, dolphins, coral designs, Echinus (sea urchin), Limpet (coneshaped shell of shellfish), Tridacna (clam); also shamrock decorations. A glittering iridescent glaze resembling mother-of-pearl is another way to identify this fine pottery. Made continuously from 1857 to 1941, a black mark was used in conjunction with the hound, harp, etc. Production stopped in 1941, beginning again in 1946, when a green mark was instituted. A Belleek-type was made in America by several factories in the 1880s and 1890s—Ott & Brewer, Trenton, New Jersey, using "O. & B." in a circle; Cook Pottery Company, using "Etruria" and three feathers; Willets Mfg. Co., using a "W" in the form of a snake; The American Art China Works, using "R.E.Co./China/Trenton" as a mark. Lenox, Inc. in Trenton probably made the best of the American Belleek, stopping production just before WWI. Confused? Then, know the genuine *before* you buy!

Animal, dog, black mark, 4½" long	$122-145
Animal, swan, black mark, 3" high	150-185
Basket, openwork, twisted handle, black mark, 8"	174-188
Basket, openwork, woven bottom, black mark, 8½" dia. . .	185-200
Basket, openwork, woven bottom, 10½" dia.	88- 98
Bowl, finger, green mark, 4¾" dia.	75- 84
Bowl, fruit, Lenox, 5½" dia.	66- 75
Bowl, round, openwork, woven bottom, black mark, 7" dia. . . .	240-280
Creamer, Echinus pattern, black mark, 4½" high	72- 81
Creamer, mermaid, black mark, 5" high	67- 77
Creamer, Tridacna pattern, 4¾" high	65- 78
Cup/saucer, Limpet pattern, black mark	140-170
Cup/saucer, Shamrock, green mark	135-160
Cup/saucer, Tridacna pattern, green mark	120-140
Dish, Dolphin pattern, green mark, 5½" dia.	67- 77
Dish, openwork, applied roses, black mark, 5" dia.	68- 78
Hatpin holder, seashells, 6" high, O. & B.	52- 61

Honey jar, beehive shape, green
   mark, 4½" high (ill.) 61- 70
Mug, pink lustre, R.E.A. Co. 44- 52
Mug, Shamrock pattern, green
   mark, 6" high 64- 75
Picture frame, black mark,
   8"×10" 180-192
Pig, sitting, yellow/white, 3" high,
   green mark 62- 64
Pitcher, Limpet pattern, 6¾"
   high, green mark   94-107
Pitcher, monk drinking, W mark .   70- 80
Pitcher, swirling seaweed, black
   mark, 7½" high   90-110
Plate, Limpet, black mark,
   4½" dia. 54- 64
Plate, mermaid, gren mark,
   6" dia. 44- 52
Platter, Shamrock, 11" long,
   green mark 84- 92
Salts, 6 individual, shell and
   coral, black mark, all 110-130
Sugar bowl, Etruria mark, blue/
   white 4¾" high 44- 62
Sugar bowl, Lenox mark, cream/
   white, 5" high 42- 56
Sugar bowl, W mark, blue/green,
   4" high 50- 60
Tea set, mermaid, Lenox mark . . 375-420
Tea set, Neptune, W mark 280-310
Tray, bread, Neptune, green
   mark, 11½" long   90-110
Vase, applied floral, green mark,
   9½" high 140-150
Vase, diamond-faceted tripod,
   dog-paw feet, black mark,
   9" high 260-270
Vase, Etruria mark, blue/yellow,
   flowers, 6½" high 55- 64
Vase, W mark, 8½" high, flower
   pattern   92-102
Vase, W mark, white/yellow,
   floral design, 7" high 68- 78

Bellows

Usually made of wood with leather trim,
they blew air on the smithy's coals or
household fire. Some ornately carved, others
painted. They go back into the dim shadows
of time.

Brass covered wood, leather
   bellows, tavern scene in relief,
   mid-1880s $160-175
Hand-carved, ornate wooden
   bellows, leather good, German,
   dated 1742 162-182
Ornately painted wooden bellows,
   Satan blowing on coals, dated
   1735, East Hampton, Conn. . . 190-220

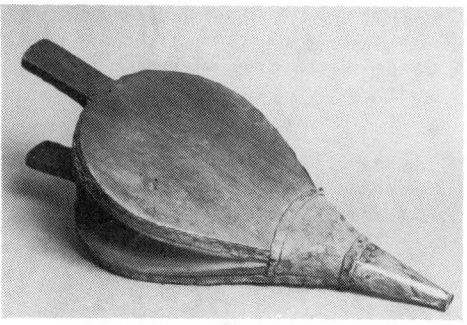

Bellows

Smithy bellows, 5' long, good
   leather, and all parts,
   mid-1800s 162-190
Wood body, leather bellows,
   brass tacks, carved, mid-1800s,
   works   94-110
Wooden bellows, leather good,
   brass tacks (ill.) 70- 80

Bells

Bells

Going back to ancient times, bells have
been made in all sizes and shapes and have
been used for calling to worship, alerting the
town during Indian raids, and, of course, toll-
ing in the New Year. Glass, brass, iron,
wood, paper, just about every material has
been used to make them. Some of the finest
made in this country were and are still being
made at the East Hampton (Conn.) Bell
Factory.

Brass, burnished, 14 on leather
   strap, 1" dia. $140-170
Brass calf bell on leather strap,
   3" dia. 57- 67
Brass, wooden handle, 8½"
   high 50- 60
Chinese brass gong, dragon in
   relief 72- 81

53

(continued)

Cowbell, brass plated, 6″ long,
original clapper 50- 60
Cowbell, leather collar, original
clapper 50- 59
Same, brass 54- 63
Same, copper 50- 60
Dinner chimes, railroad-type,
with mallet 67- 76
Dinner, sterling silver, handle,
4″ long 34- 44
Door, pull type, brass 18- 26
Elephant bell, inlaid enamel,
17″ high   110-125
Farm, cast iron, 26″ dia., goes
on post   375-450
Farm, cast iron 20″ dia. . . . . . .   300+
Hand, brass, 4″ dia. 31- 40
Hand, brass, 7½″ dia.,
12″ high 70- 80
Hand, schoolmaster, brass,
wooden handle, 6″ dia.,
10″ high   120-130
Hand, teacher, brass, 5″ high .   61- 70
India brass (look out for repro-
ductions), 3″ high (ill.), ea. . .   18- 21
Iron church bell, 24″ dia.   550-675
Locomotive, steam whistle
type, brass frame and rack,
16″ dia., 23″ high . . . .   1,200+
Mission bell, Mexican   300-375
Plantation, brass, dated 1877,
8″ high 50- 60
Ship, brass, dated 1858   120-140
Ship, brass, 7″ high   210-230
Sleigh, 20, original leather,
burnished   470-525
Sleigh, 24 on new leather strap,
burnished, graduated sizes .   550-585
Sleigh, 36 on new leather reins,
burnished, small size   370-395
Store, on heavy coiled spring . .   50- 60
Trolley car, 9½″ dia. 80- 88

Bells, Glass

Look out for reproductions from Europe.

Amber, clear handle, 11″ high . . . $135-155
Bristol glass, clear handle   100-125
Burmese, clear handle (rare)   400-440
Carnival, marigold, 8″ high 44- 56
Cranberry, 12″ to top of handle . .   140-170
Cut glass (ill.) 80- 98
Milk glass, 7″ high 85- 94
Nailsea, clear handle   158-180
Ruby glass, red handle 58- 67
Tiffany, clear handle (rare)   350-400
Venetian Latticinio, multicolored,
6″ high   170-190

Bells, Glass

Belt Buckles

Belt Buckles

Made of 14k gold, silver plate, sterling,
engraved, plain. Just about everyone wore a
belt.

14k gold, ornate, inscribed
Lightweight Champion,
1915 . . . .$1,200-1,700
Gold-plated, rodeo type (ill.) . .   58- 67
Ladies' buckle type (ill.) 19- 27
Silver-plated, initialed or plain,
many types 18- 27
Sterling silver, Navy Wings,
St. Christopher's Medal,
World War II 225- 260
Turquoise and silver inlaid,
handmade by Navajos 285- 298

Bennington Pottery

Parian, porcelain, stonewares, Rockingham-
Bennington—all were made at Bennington,
Vermont, from 1793, the first wares being

lead-glazed. The Rockingham-Bennington type ware was also produced by several other Vermont potteries, at Dorset, St. Johnsbury, and Middlebury. Some was also made in Baltimore, Maryland, and today it's difficult to give complete credit to Bennington for everything they made, although certain experts still try to do so.

Bennington type bedpan, mottled brown glaze	$150-180
Bennington type bowl, mottled brown glaze, 7½″ dia.	88- 98
Bennington type bowl, octagonal, 13″ dia.	135-155
Bottle, Coachman, mottled brown glaze, 10½″ high	600+
Bottle, flask-type, mottled brown glaze, 9″ high	160-195
Cake mold, 8¾″ dia.	70- 80
Cake mold, 9½″ dia.	81- 91
Candlesticks, pair, mottled brown glaze, 11″ high	195-225
Churn, mottled brown glaze, wooden lid and dasher	195-300
Creamer, cow, mottled brown glaze	175-210
Cuspidor, enamel, flint, 1849, 7½″ dia.	120-140
Cuspidor, Shell pattern, mottled brown glaze, 8½″ dia.	130-145
Doorknobs, 2 in set, mottled brown glaze, pr.	62- 72
Flask, book-shaped, "Departed Spirits," mottled brown glaze	200-220
Flask, ½-qt., tavern scene, mottled brown glaze	140-160
Foot warmer, holds 1 gal., mottled brown glaze	175-200
Frame, picture, blue/green/brown, flint enamel	197-240
Inkwell, usual color, 4 quill holes, raised design	210-240
Inkwell, dog's head, Rockingham glaze	118-140
Jug, 2-gal., blue/green, flint enamel	90-120
Jug, 1½-gal., mottled brown glaze, 9½″ high	143-168
Mug, birds in relief	70- 80
Mug, frog in bottom	170-190
Mug, Rockingham glaze, 6″ high	110-115
Pitcher, castle scene, 8¾″ high, Rockingham glaze	350-380
Pitcher, Parian ware, paneled vine and flower, rare	600+
Pitcher, tulip and heart, flint enamel, 8¼″ high	140-160

Plates, 8¼″, 9″, 9¼″, 9¾″, mottled brown glaze, av. price, ea.	85-140
Pudding mold, tulip in bottom, Rockingham glaze, 6½″ dia.	120-140
Teapot, 2-qt., mottled brown glaze	117-135
Tobacco jar, covered, 11″ high, mottled brown glaze	210-240
Toby mug, mottled brown glaze, U.S. Pottery Co., c. 1850	140-150
Toby mug, pt., Jolly Good Fellow, 6½″, brown glaze	375-400
Vase, ear-of-corn shaped, 7¼″ high, mottled brown glaze	92-107
Vase, tulip in relief, flint enamel, 7½″ high	240-260

Bennington Pottery

Illustrated Pieces

Top: Hound-handled pitchers (space between head and paws makes it original), ea.	750-900
Bottom: Hound-handled pitcher, "B2" in relief on bottom (rare)	1,600-1,850
Lower left: Zachary Taylor pitcher, Rockingham glaze, 13¼″ high (rare)	3,700+
Lower right: Cow creamer, mottled brown glaze	180-200

Note: The illustrated pieces can be seen at the Houston Museum in Chattanooga, Tenn. Few museums own the Zachary Taylor pitcher.

Bibles

Don't worry too much about finding a King James version or a 15th century Gutenberg

(continued)

Bible

printed before 1456. On the other hand, there are many family Bibles turning up in shops today. Many have their backs broken as this was where money and valuable papers were stored. Did you know the Old Testament contains 39 books, 929 chapters, 23,214 verses, 592,439 words, 2,738,100 letters? The New Testament contains 27 books, 260 chapters, 7,950 verses, 182,253 words and 933,380 letters. Also, the name of Jehovah or Lord occurs 6,855 times in the Old Testament and the word "and" occurs in the Old Testament 35,643 times.

Embossed leather-bound, brass hinge, c. early 1800s (ill.)	$ 90-100
Large, leatherbound, brass hinges, good condition, mid-1800s	75- 90
Miniature, 150 pages, microscopic print	60- 70
Small, carrying size, good condition, mid-1800s	28- 40

Bicycle Ribbons
Photo Courtesy Hake's Americana & Collectibles

The Columbia Road Bicycle

Bicycles

A Frenchman named de Sivrac called it a celerifere as early as 1690; in 1779, Blanchard and Magurier called theirs a velocipede. Later, around 1815, a German baron improved it, calling his a draisine; Curricle, boneshakers, and finally the change from iron to rubber-rimmed wheels. In 1877, the famous English bicycle, Ordinary, showed up in America. Then a man named Pope changed it all with this Columbia high wheeler. When John Dunlap invented the pneumatic tire in 1889, bikers, worldwide, were off and pedaling.

Accessories

Advertising mirror, National Bicycles	$ 42- 52
Advertising mirror, Zimmy Bicycles	40- 50
Advertising charm, brass, Corbin Brake	14- 24
Advertising pin, metal, Spalding	18- 22
Catalogue, Stearns Bicycle, c. 1900	48- 58
Lapel stud, enamel, League of American Wheelmen (L.A.W.), 1898	9- 14
Lapel stud, enamel, Crown Cycles, La Porte, Inc.......	9- 14
Lapel stud, enamel, Alpha Cycle Co., Philadelphia	9- 14
Lapel stud, enamel, L.A.W., Mass. Div., Spring Meet, Boston 1896	9- 14
Lapel stud, enamel, Laclede Mfg. Co. (LaTour), St. Louis	9- 14
Ribbons (ill.), ea.	10- 15
Stickpin, Corbin Brake	11- 16
Stickpin, New Departure Coaster Brake	12- 17
Tray, brass and porcelain, Columbia Bicycles	18- 26

Bicycles

Columbia, ladies' 1896, wood rims, studded tires, works ..	500-600

Columbia, road model (ill.)	1,400+
Columbia, tourist model, 1899, complete, good condition . . .	380-475
Crescent, still works	375-500
Draisine, 1815	3,300+
Iver Johnson, sprocket type, 1915, still works	145-200
Star, 1885	1,400+

Bing and Grondahl

A porcelain factory was established at Copenhagen, Denmark, by Harold Bing in 1853. Famous for their stoneware and earthenware, as well as their porcelain, they achieved fame in the early 1900s for their Christmas plates. See **Christmas Plates.**

Bisque

Bisque

Unglazed china described it perfectly. Fired only a single time to harden to china, the pieces were then decorated with colors. Primarily a product of Europe, it was also made in the U.S. Some of the bisque-type figurines coming in from Japan are of excellent craftsmanship and too many people are being fooled by unscrupulous dealers. Please know your dealer.

Box, candy, rose blossoms, blue/white	$ 37- 45
Candlesticks, bride and groom, 11½" high, pr.	75- 85
Dolls—see **Dolls**	
Figurine, baby in diaper swing . .	28- 37
Figurine, bathing beauty, 9" high	40- 48

Figurine, black baby on potty . . .	38- 45
Figurine, boy and dog, 12" high .	48- 53
Figurine, chicks on nest	40- 45
Figurine, Cupid shooting bow . . .	40- 48
Figurine, Cupid sitting on boy's lap, 8½" high	38- 47
Figurine, dog with puppies	40- 47
Figurine, elephant, on hind legs . .	40- 48
Figurine, elves on mushroom, 6" high	45- 52
Figurine, girl holding kittens	45- 48
Figurine, girl on swing, dog in lap	50- 58
Figurine, kitten with drum	35- 44
Figurine, maiden standing by tree, 9½" high	44- 53
Figurine, monk with beer mug . . .	60- 65
Figurine, nude lady, reclining, 8¼" high	145-165
Figurine, peasant boy, pipe in mouth	47- 54
Figurine, Russian dancer, 7" high	45- 53
Figurine, Santa Claus, 5" high . . .	20- 25
Lamp, cupids, 14" high, no shade	125-146
Match holder, in shape of dog's head	35- 44
Match holder, wall type, boy/girl kissing	35- 43
Match holder, wall type, cherubs .	25- 33
Nodders — see **Nodders**	
Planter, sleigh-shaped	40- 48
Planter, Swiss chalet	44- 53
Slipper, blue/pink, roses	45- 54
Slipper, green/pink, flowers	45- 54
Toothpick holder, fluted edges, pink/brown, 2½" high	28- 33
Toothpick holder, in shape of boy's boot, 2" high	25- 34
Vase, boy with dog, 7¼" high . . .	43- 53
Vase, Cupid, girl lid, 11" high (ill.)	75- 85
Vase, girl in tree, 6¼" high	40- 48
Vase, tree trunk, brown/green, 9" high	45- 53

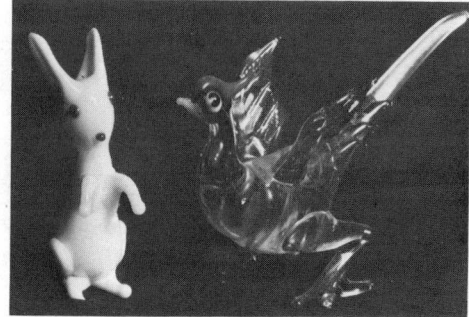

Blown Glass Animals

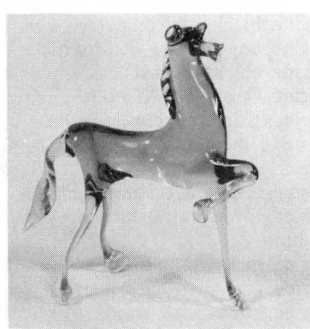

Blown Glass Animals

Blown Glass Animals

These delicate little "creatures" were given away by glassblowers; also sold at expositions, county fairs, etc. Lots of them are around and bring brisk prices when found in perfect condition. Those illustrated are not old. Keep looking.

Boehm Porcelains

Boehm Porcelains

Edward Marshall Boehm made his first pottery figures near Trenton, New Jersey, in 1949. Before he passed away in January of 1969, his beautiful birds, animals, flowers, etc., were known worldwide. Today, many fine museums throughout the world include Mr. Boehm's works as part of their permanent collections. His works bring huge prices, when authenticated, and rightfully so.

Animals
Angus bull, 1950, 5"×8¼" .$	2,400-	2,600
Beagle, 1952, 7"×6¼"	675-	775
Chipmunk, preening, 1959, 3"	1,700-	1,900
Fawn, 1954, 3"×4"	875-	975
Lion cub, 1954, 4½"×5" ..	1,000-	1,300
Raccoons, 1971, 11"×11"×10"	1,700-	1,900
Tiger, 1952, 6"×15"	2,600-	2,800

Birds
American Eagle, large, 1957, 18"×15"	9,500-10,500	
American Eagle, small, 1957, 15"×12"	6,900-	7,400
Blue Grosbeak, 1969, 11"×10"×7"	1,400-	1,700
Bobwhite Quail, pr., 1953, female, 7"; male, 8"	8,300-	8,500
Flicker, 1971, 10½"×9½" (ill.)	2,400-	2,700
Golden Oriental Pheasant, 1954, 6"×21"	32,000-33,500	
Nuthatch, 1963, 11"×16" .	425-	450
Robin, 1964, 13"×8"	5,200-	5,600
Tern, Common, 1968, 16"×12"×14"	6,100-	6,400
Western Meadowlark, 1971, 13"×9"	2,300-	2,500
Young American Eagle, 1969, 9½"×6"×7"	2,200-	2,400

Books
Boehm's Birds, 1960, 8"×10¾"	475-	525
EMB 1913-1969, deluxe edition, 9"×12", 1970...	170-	200

Decorative Pieces
Apollo, 7½"×3½", 1953 ..	775-	850
Choir Boy, 1949, 4½"	350-	425
Cupid with Flute, 1954, 5¼"	600-	675
Mercury, 1953, 7½"×4" ..	700-	800
Pope John XXIII, 1960, 10"	1,600-	1,800
Tulip Pitcher, 1956, 6½" ..	3,200-	3,500
Venus, 1953, 8"	700-	800

Flowers
Daisies, yellow, 1971, 8"×8"×6"	275-	325
Swan centerpiece, 6"×22"×9"	1,850-	2,000

Paintings
Cockatoo and Flowers, 1971, 18½"×15½"	3,700-	4,100
Mockingbirds, pr., 1970, 12"×15"	2,700-	2,950

Plates
European bird plates, set of 8, 10" dia., all	475-	575
Tropical fish plate, 1955, 10" dia.	3,800-	4,000

Bohemian Glass

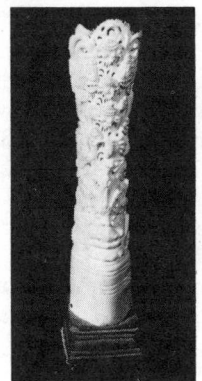

Bone

Bohemian Glass

Ruby-colored, flashed, stained, in blue, yellow, green, other colors; 1870s until early 1900s, most sought after today. Originally made in Bohemia which is now part of Czechoslovakia. Hundreds of reproductions on the market. Careful!

Caster set, 4 bottles, ruby-colored, etched landscapes	$180-200
Compote, red, grapevine motif, 6½" high, covered	135-150
Decanter	70- 82
Decanter, 6 small glasses, deer, forest, etched, yellow	200-220
Goblet, dog chasing deer, etched, yellow	48- 58
Goblet, footed, flower scene, yellow flashed, 7" high	67- 76
Jar, covered, 5½" high (ill.)	68- 78
Lustres, crystal prisms, 15" high, pr.	170-180
Pitcher, deer and castle, 6 tumblers, ruby flashed	110-120
Pitcher, grape pattern, ruby flashed, 12½" high	115-140
Rose petal jar, painted figure, ruby flashed, 8" high	60- 70
Tumbler, deer, etched, green	52- 62
Vase, birds and flowers, red, etched, 11" high	118-125
Vase, deer and castle, blue, 10" high, pr.	94-107
Water set, leaf and grape motif, ruby, etched, 7 pieces	160-170

Bone

So much bone is being sold as ivory, especially the pieces flooding in from the Orient. But because so much of it is around, collectors are buying it. If you're going to spend huge sums for genuine ivory, have a qualified jeweler test it. Sulphuric acid applied to vegetable ivory and others will cause a pink coloring in about 10 minutes. This can be removed by washing with water. The acid has no effect on genuine ivory. **Repeat:** Let an expert do it—any acid is dangerous.

Bone China

This is made from clay with the ashes of bird or small animal bones ground up and combined with the clay to give it added strength.

Bone Dishes

Bone Dishes

In the late 1800s, it was considered fashionable to eat fowl with your fingers. These dishes were held close to the mouth to dispose of the bones and other unedible material. Haviland, Rosenthal, and others made them from the mid-1700s on. Today, people use them for ashtrays. Price depends on who made them.

Book Matches

In the 1850s sheets of thin wooden matches appeared on the market. In 1897, the Diamond Match Company produced them in folder form with advertisements on the outside. Today, millions of advertisers use them to sell their products. Countless thousands of collectors are saving them. Any and all are collectible. If you begin a collection, it's a good idea to remove the matches before putting them in an album.

Common—usually purchased in
  bulk (per thousand) ....$ 10- 16
Early 1900s—usually purchased
  in bulk (per hundred) 19- 26

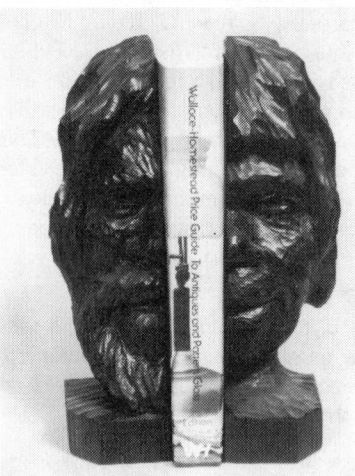

Bookends

Bookends

For years they were considered fashionable. Made from every type of material. All kinds are showing up at shops and shows—from the sublime to the ridiculous.

Bison, 6"×6", late 1800s $180-195
Bronze tigers on marble bases,
  5"×2½", late 1800s 120-140
Cast (pot metal) dog heads,
  4" sq., pre-WWI 30- 45
Copper ships, lead-weighted
  bases, 6"×3¼", 1900s 48- 58
Elephants, rearing, bronze,
  1890s, 8½"×6" 190-210
Indians, brass, on wood base,
  6"×8" 160-170
Ivory elephants, teakwood
  bases, 6" high, 1890s 135-145

Jade Foo dogs, ebony bases,
  5"×3", mid-1800s .... 1,400+
Lincoln, bust, copper, 1880s,
  7"×9½" 178-190
Monkeys at play, carved wood,
  6"×4", early 1900s 42- 52
Owl on limb, brass, 7½"×9" .. 61- 71
Painted iron, flowers 32- 44
Pelicans, carved wood,
  6½"×7" 48- 58
Porcelain, Japan, 5½" high,
  1930s 36- 46
Quartz birds, copper bases,
  4½"×3½", 1900s......... 88- 98
Reclining nudes, brass bases,
  6½"×3", 1900s 100-110
Roosters, painted, on wood
  base, 8"×7" 49- 58
Tigers, bronze, late 1800s,
  6½"×9" 170-180
Wood, carved, Australia (ill.) .. 70- 85

Bookmarks

Used for just that; silk, leather, paper, etc. A "fun" collectible, and there are lots of old ones around. See **Stevengraphs.**

Books

Books

Soft clay cylinders, wax slates, papyrus scrolls, the degreased skins of cows and goats—a few ancient "books," going back before time immemorial. When Gutenberg (or Koster?) invented the printing press, things changed for the better in the book business. If you're looking for out-of-print books, Colonel "out-of-print" Book Service, Inc., 23 E. 4th St., New York, N.Y. 10003, is tops in its field.

Addison, Joseph, *The Free-*
  Holder, London, 1716 ..... $100-125
Ade, George, *Fables in*
  Slang, Chicago, 1900 ...... 42- 52

Agee, James, *Permit Me Voyage*, New Haven, 1934 .. 260-280

Alcott, Louisa M., *Little Men*, Boston 160-180

Alger, Horatio, Jr., *Do and Dare*, Philadelphia, no date (ill.) 30- 38

Alger, Horatio, *Ragged Dick*, Boston, 1868, 1st ed. 600-650

Anderson, H.C., *Tales for Children*, London, 1891 .... 16- 25

Anderson, Sherwood, *Winesburg, Ohio*, New York, 1919 110-125

Anderson, Sherwood, *Perhaps Women*, New York, 1930s .. 80- 90

Arnold, Matthew, *Alaric at Rome*, London, 1893 100-110

Auden, W.H., *Spain*, London, 1937 .... 28- 38

Austen, Jane, *Sense and Sensibility*, London, 1813 (3 vols.) 180-195

Bacon, Francis, *Certaine Considerations*, 1640 ...... 170-190 (Was he Shakespeare's ghost writer?)

Beecher, Henry Ward, *Norwood*, New York, 1874 ..... 62- 80

Beerbohm, Max, *Things Old and New*, London, 1923 .... 50- 60

Bisset, J., *The Orphan Boy*, 1799 .... 30- 40

Buck, Pearl, *Dragon Seed*, 1942, 1st ed., New York 18- 27

Buck, Pearl, *The Good Earth*, New York, 2nd ed. 19- 29

Caldwell, Taylor, *This Side of Innocence*, New York, 1946 . 14- 23

Cather, Willa, *Obscure Destinies*, New York, 1932 .. 60- 70

Clemens, Samuel Langhorne (Mark Twain), *Tom Sawyer*, *The Prince and the Pauper*, *A Connecticut Yankee in King Arthur's Court*—a few of the many books by him. His works bring hundreds of dollars.

Conrad, Joseph, *A Set of Six*, London, 1908 (one of Poland's greatest writers) .. 72- 81

Crane, Stephen, *The Red Badge of Courage*, New York, 1895 .... 66- 76

Crane, Stephen, *The Little Regiment*, New York, 1896 . 62- 72

Cruikshank, George, *The Humorist*, London, 1822 (he illustrated many of Charles Dickens' books) 130-150

DeFoe, Daniel, wrote many books but *The Life and Strange Surprising Adventures of Robinson Crusoe, of New York, Mariner*, printed in London 1719, was his most famous and most valuable. Published in 2 vols., it's a rare, rare find ... 16,000+ (Other books written by DeFoe are *Memoirs of Count Tariff* (350-400), *Advice to the People of Great Britain* (175-200) and *The History of the Wars* (225-275)

Du Maurier, Daphne, *Rebecca*, New York 1938 ... 10- 18

Grey, Zane, *The Lost Wagon Train*, New York, 1936 ..... 14- 18 The greatest western writer of them all.

Hersey, John, *The Wall*, New York, 1950 .... 19- 27

Lindbergh, Charles, *We* (Lindy, a kitten and "The Spirit of St. Louis"—the rest is in the history books), New York, 1927 .... 18- 27

Lindbergh, Anne Morrow, *North to the Orient*, New York, 1935 .... 21- 31

Tarkington, Booth, *Seventeen*, New York, 1916, 1st ed. 19- 27

Trench, P.C., *Tiger Hunting*, London, 1836 160-180

Wescott, David *Harum*, New York, 1898 (movie with Will Rogers) 22- 32

Wouk, Herman, *The Caine Mutiny*, Garden City, 1952 . 17- 29

Obviously, there are millions of old books in every type of shop, at flea markets (see my *Flea Market Price Guide*, $7.95), in attics and basements, etc.

Boot Scrapers

61

Boot Scrapers

Usually set in the brick or cement of the front porch, the sharp blade was used to remove the mud or snow from the soles of the boots. Early 1800s to mid-1900s.

Antique car, brass	$120-140
Bristle brushes in metal frame . . .	48- 60
Cast iron, bristle brush	28- 37
Cast iron, plain, still usable	21- 30
Horseshoes (ill.)	25- 35
Long-backed horse, iron	32- 42
Whale's belly, cast iron (rare)	98-115

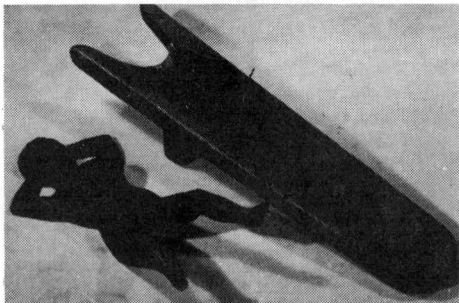

Bootjacks

Bootjacks

Naughtie Nellie and the Beetle are two of the most collectible, though both are being reproduced. They were then and are still being used to remove tight boots. Usually in wood or cast iron.

American bulldog, folding pistol, brass	$ 78- 90
Same, except iron	58- 70
Beetle, brass	92-110
Beetle, harp-shaped, iron	60- 70
Beetle, iron	28- 40
Bull, cast iron	82- 91
Cap pistol, cast iron	44- 51
Cricket, cast iron, 10½"	28- 31
Naughty Nellie, brass	80- 90
Naughty Nellie, cast iron (ill.) . . .	50- 60
Vine, cast iron, 11½"	21- 31
Wood, hand-carved cherry (ill.) . .	38- 48
Wood, hand-carved, lady's leg . . .	40- 47

Being reproduced in Cricket, Naughty Nellie, and Pistol—probably others.

Bottles

Apothecary

Blown, Masson's Guaranteed on label, 14" high	$ 24- 32

Apothecary Bottle

Blown, Self Cure on label, 15" high	22- 30
Blown, squat green, 5" high (ill.)	20- 28
Brown, Extr. Strict on label, ground stopper, 15¼" high . . .	21- 30
Brown, blown, gold label, 8½" high	20- 26
Brown porcelain, label, 7" high . .	18- 27
Bulbous, salesman's sample, fancy base, 11" high	24- 31
Capsicum on porcelain label, blown, 10½" high	20- 24
Clear, blown, stopper, 8" high . . .	18- 22
Clear, blown, Tinc, Orsc on label, 12" high	19- 26

Ardos

Clock	42- 50
Green Duck	41- 48
Rocker	28- 37

Avon Bottle

Avon

Alpine flask, full and boxed	52- 62
Antique telephone, 1969	14- 20
Apothecary jar, 1965	18- 26
Bath, seasons, 1967	8- 12
Bath urn, clear	9- 13
Bath urn, milk glass, 1966	21- 30
Bay rum jug	12- 18

Bay rum keg, 1962	21- 30
Boot, gold top, label	8- 12
Boot, silver top, 1965	9- 14
Bud vase, 1962	14- 21
Bud vase, 1966	11- 20
Bud vase, 1968	14- 19
Candleholder, Christmas, frosted, apple, 1967	12- 18
Candlestick, Christmas, Charisma cologne, 4 oz., red/gold (ill.)	11- 17
Casey's lantern, amber, green, red	16- 30
Christmas ornaments—angel, balls, candle, icicle, sparkler, tree	14- 22
Daylight Shaving Time, 1968-70, 6 oz.	10- 14
Decanter, inkwell, owl	8- 13
Dollars and Scents, 1966	22- 27
Forever Spring, cologne, cream sachet, perfume, powder sachet	12- 20
Gavel, 1967, 6 oz.	17- 23
Gold Cadillac	12- 17
Greek goddess	12- 18
Keynote, label	14- 19
Kitten Little Cologne, 1973	4- 7
Nearness, body powder, toilet water	21- 30
Pony post, short, tall, label	11- 19
Quaintance, cologne, cream lotion, powder sachet, 1949 . . .	54- 63
Quaintance diary, 1949	98-120
Silver stein, 6 oz., 8 oz.	12- 18
Snail, boxed, label	11- 18
Stagecoach embossed, 2 oz., 4 oz.	12- 19
Topaze cream lotion, label	9- 16
Topaze Gem perfume, glass stopper	130-140
Viking horn	21- 31
Warrior head, blue and silver, frosted label	16- 24
Western Choice (steer horns) pr. .	22- 31
Wild Rose, cream lotion, cream sachet, toilet water	22- 30
Windjammer, printed label	9- 18

Ballantine (whiskey)

Duck	24- 32
Fisherman	21- 30
Golf bag	16- 27
Knight, silver	21- 31

Barber (clear, colored or milk glass)

Amber	68- 72
Amethyst	72- 82
Apple green, painted flowers (ill.)	42- 52
Bay rum, amethyst, etched, pewter spout	81- 90
Carnival, marigold, metal stopper	70- 80

Barber Bottles

Cobalt, pewter stopper	62- 71
Cranberry, Mary Gregory figure, pewter stopper	162-180
Cut glass, sterling silver stopper, initialed	77- 87
Hobnail, honey amber, stopper	72- 82
Mary Gregory (ill.)	150-162
Milk glass, octagon base, stopper	68- 78
Sandwich glass, amethyst, silver stopper	150-160
Spanish Lace, blue, stopper . . .	44- 54
Swirled Rib, ITP, amber	78- 88
Tiffany glass, sterling silver stopper, initialed BJM	375-500+

Jim Beam

63

(continued)

Jim Beam

The Jim Beam bottles have created quite a sensation in the bottle field. Several books are available on these highly collectible bottles. The Jim Beams listed here are for identification purposes.

Centennial Series:

Alaska Purchase (1966)	28- 40
Baseball	21- 34
Civil War: North, South, ea.	49- 59
Laramie	18- 27
Preakness	19- 27
St. Louis Arch, 1964	35- 41
Santa Fe, 1960	280+

Customer Specialties:

Cal-Neva	19- 28
First National Bank of Chicago, 1964 (recently counterfeited—be careful)	3,200+
Foremost, black and gold, gray and gold	172-192
Foremost, pink speckled beauty	800+
Harold's Club: 12 bottles made so far, more to come	20-275
Harold's Club, blue slot machine	30- 38
Harold's Club, man in a barrel, No. 1, 1957	540-570
Harold's Club, VIP Executive, 1967, 1968, 1969, 1970, 1971	72-110

Executive Series:

Royal porcelain, 1955	275+
Royal di Monte, 1957	110+
Blue cherub, 1960	120+
Royal rose, 1963	70- 80
Marbled fantasy, 1965	92-108
Prestige, 1967	50- 60
Presidential, 1968	27- 37

Political Series:

Ashtrays, elephant and donkey, all years, pr.	42- 50
Boxers, pr.	50- 60
Clowns, pr.	28- 37

Regal China Series:

Arizona tombstone	31- 40
Black canasta, 1956	27- 37
Broadmoor Hotel	18- 27
Cable car, 1968	19- 28
Grand Canyon, 1969	28- 38
Kentucky Cardinal, 1973 trophy	40- 49
Oatmeal jug	70- 90
Pony Express	20- 28
Scotch bell ringer	28- 38
Thailand	12- 19
Yosemite	17- 27

State Series:

Alaska Star, 1958, 1964, 1965	110-140
Hawaii, 1959, 1967	80- 95
Kentucky Derby, black head, 1967	27- 37
Nebraska	28- 38
North Dakota	120-140
West Virginia Centennial	160-175

Trophy Series:

Dog, 1959	82- 92
Doe, 1963, 1967	55- 65
Fish, 1965	60- 70
Horses, three colors, ea.	50- 60
Ram	220-250
Woodpecker	21- 35

Glass Specialties:

Cannon	24- 34
Cleopatra, rust, 1962	31- 41
Dancing Scot, short, 1963	52- 62
Dancing Scot, tall, 1963	24- 33
Delft blue, Delft rose	20- 30
Mark Antony, 1962	31- 40
Pin: gold top, white top, wooden top	17- 27
Pyrex coffee warmers, 1954, four colors	22- 28
Royal Emperor	20- 30
Royal Reserve	21- 31
Smoked Crystal, 1964	18- 27

Beer

Milk glass, 9″ high	27- 36
Olive green, qt.	10- 18
Red, qt.	15- 19
Schmidt, original label, qt.	19- 26

Bischoff

Bell tower, 1959	50- 60
Boy, Chinese, Spanish	50- 52
Egyptian vase: single, double	50- 60
Fish bottle ashtray	30- 40
Grecian vase, decanter	19- 27
Nigerian mask	30- 40
Red clown	26- 36
Senorita	27- 37

Bitters

From the 1860s until the early 1900s, various concoctions of herbs were mixed with alcohol (sometimes as much as 80%) and peddled as get-wells or feel-betters. More than one gal, fighting Demon Gin, got her pep, probably unknowingly, from sipping her husband's bitters.

Atwood's jaundice, screw top, aqua	38- 49
Brown's iron, honey amber	40- 50
Clark's sherry wine, aqua	120-130
Cole Brothers	38- 47
Electric, embossed	50- 60
Goff's herb, embossed, aqua	29- 39
Pinkerston's Wahoo and Claisaya bitters, amber	60- 67
Prickly ash, qt., amber	81- 92
Tippecanoe, amber	130-142
Willards Golden Seal, aqua	78- 88
Yerba Buena, amber, flask	130-140

Bols

Ballerina	19-	22
Cream de menthe, Delft	26-	36
Dutch: boy, girl	31-	40

Borghini

Dog	24-	33
Ford car, recent, old	16-	22
Horse's head	19-	27
Nubian girl	10-	16
Santa Maria	8-	14

Ezra Brooks

Antique cannon	24-	33
Bucket of blood	27-	36
Cable cars, 3 colors, ea.	19-	28
Churchill bust	18-	27
Clown on drum, short, tall	74-	81
Dueling pistol	19-	27
Grizzly bear	15-	27
Gun series (4)	33-	42
Harold's Club dice	21-	30
Kentucky gentleman	28-	37
Mr. Foremost	30-	40
Oil derrick (gusher)	21-	31
Potbelly stove	19-	27
Queen of hearts	19-	26
Reno arch	14-	19
Trout and fly	19-	26
Wheat shocker, Kansas	27-	36

J.W. Dant

Alamo (black)	20-	28
Bobwhite	32-	42
Crossing the Delaware	19-	27
Field birds (chukar partridge, etc.), ea.	19-	27
Indianapolis 500	30-	31
Patrick Henry	19-	28

George Dickel

Golf club, large	24-	32
Golf club, miniature	9-	16
Powderhorn	19-	27

Doctors

In the late 1800s, many "doctors" promised their products would cure everything from falling hair to falling arches. (Alcohol was the base, and some users touched every one.)

Dr. Baxter's Benevolent Protector, green, pt.	16-	24
Dr. Caldwell's Syrup Pepsin, aqua	16-	25
Dr. Churchill's Hypophosphite Pectoral	14-	28
Dr. Kennedy's Prairie Weed	32-	40
Dr. Kilmer's Swamp Root Kidney Cure	15-	27
Dr. Miles Nervene	15-	23
Dr. Pepper's (indented letters)	14-	22
Dr. Wistar's Balsam	40-	50
Dr. Woods Sarsaparilla and Wild Cherry	82-	96

Figural Bottle

Figurals

Black bear, Smirnoff vodka	21-	31
Brown owl	18-	28
Christmas tree, star stopper		160+
Crying baby, clear, 6½″ high	48-	58
Elephant (used as bank)	12-	20
Face, 12″ high (ill.)	51-	60
Fish, ashtray	29-	39
Guitar, brown	12-	20
Hunter, lady, pr.	36-	44
Lincoln (used as bank)	15-	24
Queen Elizabeth II	19-	27
River Queen boat	19-	28
Violin, blue	54-	62
George Washington bust, miniature	29-	39
Watchtower bell	29-	39

Garnier

Bellows	26-	32
Bullfighter	24-	36
Cardinal	28-	37
Duck	24-	36
Indian	21-	30
Locomotive	26-	34
New Mexico road runner	18-	27
Parrot	34-	42
Pheasant	22-	31
Quail	19-	27
Ship scene	20-	30

Grenadier (Soldiers)

Colonial series, 5 so far, military in nature	27-	34

House of Koshu

Daughter	22-	31
Golden pagoda	18-	27
Pink geisha	60-	69
Princess	19-	27
Two lovers	15-	28
White pagoda	24-	37

65

(continued)

Santa Claus　　　　**Uncle Sam**

Coca-Cola, dated 1909,
  Knoxville, brown 22- 31
Dana's sarsaparilla, Bangor,
  Me., aqua 28- 31
DeWitt's sarsaparilla, aqua . . . 32- 40
Dr. Green's sarsaparilla, clear . 19- 27
Joy's sarsaparilla, aqua 31- 40
Rodway's sarsaparilla, aqua . . 32- 40
Scoville's unembossed, aqua . . 19- 29
Verner's ginger ale, embossed
  seal 18- 27

Whiskey Flask

Whiskey and Other Spirits
Belle of Anderson, milk glass . . 120-140
Binninger's barrel-shaped
  whiskey, amber . . . . 525+
Binninger's peach brandy jug . 310+
Binninger's Regulator, clock
  shape, amber . . . . 570+
E. G. Booz Cabin whiskey — an
  original would be worth upwards of $300, but the 1920s
  reproduction was a perfect
  duplication except the original has a period (.) after the
  word Whiskey on the "roof"
  of the bottle. The 1960s
  reproduction is so obvious it
  should fool no one.
Chestnut Grove whiskey, pt. . . 200-250
Deep Spring, Tenn., whiskey . . 32- 40
Golden Wedding, 1933 . . . . 22- 40
Hart, John and Co., figural,
  amber 39- 49
Hayner Distilling Co., Dayton,
  St. Louis, clear 18- 27
Jo-Jo Monogram, labeled, pt.,
  qt. 70- 80
Lady's Leg, amethyst, green or
  amber 72- 82
Lighthouse figural, C.T.
  Morris, amber, qt. 119-135
Mallard Distilling, Baltimore
  and N.Y.C., violin-shaped . . 38- 48

Miller's Game Cock, Boston . . 19- 27
Jessie Moore's whiskey, amber,
  fifth. 70- 80
Old Charter pure rye 27- 36
Old Gray Mare (ill.), amber . . . 140+
Old Quaker, embossed anchor
  bottom, clear, pt. 50- 60
Paul Jones (printed on bottom),
  amber, pt. 27- 37
Quaker Maid, amber 38- 47
Spring-winter, aqua, ½-pt.
  (ill.) . . . . 220+
Van Denebergh, gin 120-130
Whitney, 1800s (ill.) . . . . 190+

Miscellaneous
Anderson's Dermador 17- 26
Belt buckle, Civil War 14- 20
Binocular shaped, black, qt. . . . 20- 30
Buffalo lithia water 14- 20
Bunker Hill pickles, honey
  amber 32- 41
Burnham's beef wine and iron . 8- 12
Camel saddle, hand-blown 47- 57
Champagne, magnum, green . . 28- 37
Extracts, bottle, blue 14- 22

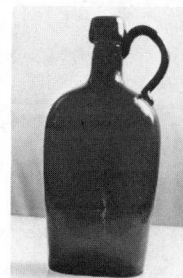

Whiskey Flasks

Whiskey (New)
I.W. Harper/Seagrams

(continued)

Geisha Girl, purple	24-	33
Glover's Imperial mange		
medicine, amber	8-	17
H.J. Heinz, patented 1890	17-	28
Harden's Hand Grenade, star,		
blue, still full	24-	33
Horlick's malted milk, tin lid . .	9-	14
Hudson's Bay, flat, miniature		
(rare)	41-	50
Pickle barrel, emerald green . . .	34-	42

Boy Scout Collectibles

Boy Scout Collectibles

The Boy Scouts of America were incorporated February 8, 1910.

Bugle, brass	$ 38-	52
Old Scout manuals, 1920s and		
1930s	12-	19
Scout and Cub Scout charters		
(ill.)	7-	9
Scoutmaster pins	9-	16
Uniform, complete, 1930s	29-	39

Branding Irons

Used in the West for identifying a rancher's cattle, today they're collectible. Usually twisted iron on a long iron shaft with wooden handle, they were first used in the early 1800s in what is now California. Still being used on cattle and horses today.

Wrought iron, letters "CP" (ill.) . . $ 20- 30

This is an average price, coast-to-coast.

Brass

A yellow alloy, usually consisting of copper and zinc, brass is an easily hammered metal

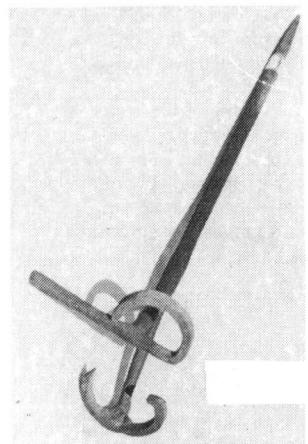

Branding Irons

Brass

which, when polished, takes on a beautiful hue. It's been in use since the days of the early Romans.

Ashtray, 5″ diameter, marked		
India	$ 9-	14
Ashtray, foliage, marked India . .	9-	18
Ashtray/match holder, embossed		
scrolls, dolphins (ill.)	32-	40
Ashtray shaped like lock (ill.)	16-	24
Bookends, rearing horses, 7″		
high, pr.	37-	40
Bowl, 6″ diameter, footed,		
marked India	14-	19
Bowl, 8″ dia., marked China,		
dragon motif	30-	40
Bullet mold, hinged	42-	52
Candlestick, push-up ejector,		
5″ high, pr.	55-	60
Candlesticks, English, marked		
Storrar's, Chester, 10″ high . . .	70-	80
Candlesticks, turned stem,		
8″ high, pr., ...	60-	68
Cigarette box, yellow, green, red		
stones inlaid in lid	21-	31
Coal bucket, iron bail handle	50-	60
Coal hod	112-	114
Coffeepot, 10″ high	28-	32

Dipper, 12½" long	40- 48
Easel, probably held miniature painting, 4½" high	47- 56
Ice tongs, heavy	58- 64
Incense burner, 2-part, marked China	14- 21
Incense burner, w/lid, 4" dia., 1890s	14- 21
Jelly kettle, iron bail handle, 2-gal. capacity	61- 70
Kettles, 6, 8, 10, 12 qts.	60- 70
Keys, assorted sizes, ea.	8- 14
Letter opener, dragon, marked China, 13" long	11- 14
Mortar and pestle, pewter-lined, Russian, Eagle mark	160-170
Pails, 4, 8 qts.	92-107
Paperweight, lion and cubs, 6" dia.	42- 51
Scales, grocery, counter type	78- 90
Sewing bird—see **Sewing Accessories**	
Sewing dog—see **Sewing Accessories**	
Sundial, on 3' high marble base	270+
Tea kettle, 6½" high	80- 90
Tray, flower motif, 7½" dia.	50- 60
Trivet, pierced fretwork, ball feet, 1920s	19- 27
Umbrella stand, flower ring handles	92-101
Whistle, factory, 16" high	140-150

Bread Plates

Bread Plates and Trays

Usually popularizing people, places and things from the mid-1800s on, they were made of glass, china and metal. The U.S. coin plates are considered scarce.

Barley, clear glass	$ 42- 50
Bible	52- 61
Bread Is the Staff of Life, clear glass	44- 53

Bunker Hill Monument	65- 75
Coin, Columbian, gold gilt, clear glass	120-140
Coin, U.S., dollar decoration, frosted glass coins	295-330
Constitution	90-115
Cupid and Venus	48- 56
Dancing Bears	62- 74
Dog Cart	58- 67
Eureka	50- 60
Faith, Hope and Charity, clear glass	77- 86
Frosted Stork	60- 74
Garden of Eden	46- 56
Garfield Drape	64- 72
Give Us This Day Our Daily Bread (ill.)	46- 55
Gladstone	43- 52
Heroes of Bunker Hill	70- 75
Independence Hall	100-115
It Is Pleasant to Labor	56- 63
Last Supper	36- 44
Liberty Bell, blue glass	68- 75
Liberty Bell, 7" × 11"	143-155
Little Miss Muffet	58- 66
Little Red Riding Hood	56- 64
McKinley Memorial, "It Is God's Way," bread platter	64- 74
Nellie Bly (She went around the world in 80 days!)	187-215
Niagara Falls, frosted glass	145-167
Old Statehouse	78- 87
Pacific Fleet	425-450
Philadelphia Centennial, 1876, clear glass	55- 65
Queen Victoria	57- 66
Rock of Ages	74- 84
Sheaf of Wheat	54- 63
Shell and Tassel, oblong, small	67- 75
Shield, star border	87-100
Teddy Roosevelt	97-115
Theodore Roosevelt, clear, frosted	97-116
Virginia Dare (first white baby born in Virginia Colonies)	70- 75
Waste Not, Want Not	57- 63

Brewery Collectibles

Anything to do with breweries, beer halls, and the like is collectible today.

Beer bottle labels, any brand before 1940 (lots of repros here), ea.	50¢ 1
Beer keg paper sign, Cobb & Co's Margate Ale, 8" dia.	$ 7- 10
Calendar plate, Horlacher Beer, 1909, 8¼" dia. (ill.)	60- 70
Cardboard coasters, most brands, pre-World War II, ea.	25¢-50¢

69

(continued)

Brewery Collectibles   Brewery Collectibles

Cardboard sign, bottle-shaped, Schmidt's Beer, 6″×16″	5-	9
Cardboard sign, Cooks Beer, 10″×14″	12-	16
Cardboard sign, Haas Beer, 7″×18″	10-	13
Poster, Silver Springs Brewery, round, 14″ dia., 1910	12-	15
Tin sign, Cook's Goldblum Beer, 14″×28″	32-	40
Tin sign, F.W. Cook Co.	27-	32
Tray, metal, Ballantine's Beer, blue/yellow, 12″ dia. (ill.) . . .	6-	9
Tray, metal, Schmidt's Beer, white/gold/red, 13″ dia. (ill.) . . .	7-	11

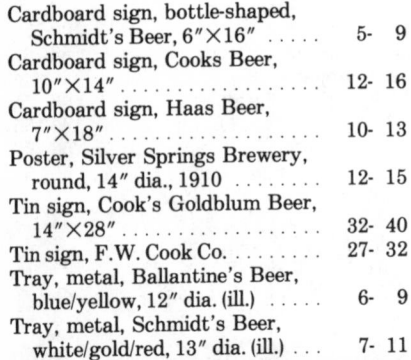

Brides' Baskets

Brides' Baskets

These one-of-a-kind novelties, popular as wedding presents during the mid-1800s until the early 1900s, were made in American and European glass factories. A great many came in a silver or silver-plated basket frame.

Amberina, Quilted Diamond, twisted handle, triple plate frame . . . .$	345-	365
Amethyst, clear ruffled edge, 11½″ dia., quadruple plate frame	190-	215
Cased, apricot, quadruple plate frame, 10″ dia.	185-	195
Cased, pink and white, EPNS, 11¼″ dia. (ill.)	165-	180
Cased, pinks, ruffled edge, EPNS frame, 10″ dia.	165-	175
Cranberry, ITP (Inverted Thumbprint), EPNS frame, 9½″ dia.	175-	185
Cranberry, overlay, ruffled edge, EPNS frame	180-	190
Cranberry, ruffled edge, sterling silver frame, 10″ dia. . .	265-	275
Cranberry to pink, enameled flowers, 11″ dia.	170-	180
Cut, Diamond, Strawberry and Fan, quadruple plate frame, 9¼″ dia.	190-	215
Hobnail, blue/white, EPNS frame, 10¼″ dia.	185-	195
Mt. Washington, Peachblow, ruffled edge, quadruple plate frame, 13″ dia.	1,100-1,275	
New England Peachblow, scalloped edge, quadruple frame, 12½″ dia.	1,000-1,250	
Opaque, blue enameled cherubs, triple plate frame, 9¼″ dia.	175-	185
Pink, swirl designs, EPNS frame, 9½″ dia.	160-	170
Satin glass, ruffled edge, EPNS frame, 10″ dia.	175-	190
Tiffany, gold iridescent, sterling silver frame	975-1,150	

Vasa Murrhina, brown, gold
flecks, triple plate frame,
10¼″ dia. 218- 230
Wheeling Peachblow, quad-
ruple plate frame, 11½″
dia.   1,250-1,400
White, cased blue, clear fluted
edge, EPNS frame, 9½″
dia. 155- 165
Yellow to pink, blue enameled
flowers, EPNS frame, 10½
dia. 160- 175

Bridle Rosettes

Bridle Rosettes

Made of glass, those small buttons were
used to decorate the horse's bridle. They're
being reproduced. The originals are beautiful
when made into pins.

Blue/gray ground, floral, brass . . $ 17- 24
Double heart, brass background .   18- 26
Ducks, grass background (ill.) . . .   22- 31
Eagle and flag, blue background,
brass 18- 24
Flowers, blue/green, birds, brass .   22- 32
Heart design, initials, brass
background 21- 31
Shield and 13 stars, brass
background 27- 31
U.S. Cavalry, brass, pr. 26- 37
Water birds, floral, brass
background 21- 30

Bristol Glass

Bristol, England, became a glass center in
the mid-1700s. Many of the glass vases
attributed to the Amelung Glass Company
and other companies in the U.S. were actually
made at Bristol. One way to identify them is
to hold them to the light—they should look
like an orange forest fire.

Bristol Glass

Apothecary jar, white, green/
white, enameled, cover $100-125
Bottle, dresser, green/gold, blue
enamel trim 60- 70
Bowl, cased blue over white,
scalloped, floral, enameled   115-130
Box, powder, round, dome,
hinged, children and birds,
1840 . . . .   82- 93
Cookie jar, satin finish, floral and
fauna designs   94-104
Epergne, twin tulips, cranberry,
fluted edges   310-330
Hand vase, ruffled top, pink/
clambroth, gilded, frosted 82- 92
Lamp, blue, enameled yellow,
blue, lilies, green leaves   125-135
Lamp, hanging, white, red/yellow
color, floral, brass chain   125-140
Mug, blue, "Love You" 42- 52
Platter, raspberry color, bird-of-
paradise color, matching dish .   40- 50
Rose bowl, blue, frosted, ruffled
lip   97-115
Smokebell, white, applied green
band, crimped rim 32- 50
Toothpick, blue, rectangular
panels 27- 37
Tumbler, white, blue/yellow
enameled flowers 28- 38
Vase, blue/green, enameled birds
and flowers 69- 80
Vase, brown thistle, white satin,
floral enameled decor 78- 88
Vase, castle scene, 10″ high (ill.) .   65- 75
Vase, enameled, blue/yellow,
birds, flowers 84- 92
Vase, insects, flowers, enameled
decor, ruffled lip   172-182

71

(continued)

Britannia Ware

Britannia Ware

In the simplest language, pewter is cast; Britannia is spun. Also, they don't look alike, though the chemical makeup is about the same. If anything it's better than pewter. Usually identified by the small catalog numbers stamped on it. Much of it also has the maker's name. When mass production was started around 1825, the spinning process used less metal and made it harder. Unfortunately, it also brought about poorer designing and less individuality. Consequently, pewter brings higher prices.

Basically, Britannia Ware today brings about 70% of what pewter pieces bring, possibly a little less. See **Pewter.**

British Patent Office Registration Marks

From 1842 until 1883 the wares of many British manufacturers were marked with the following diamond mark, which was an indication that the design was registered with the British Patent Office. The topmost section of the mark indicated the class (in this case IV indicates earthenware and glass). This gave copyright protection for three years. Unfortunately, the manufacturers didn't take too much time incising or imprinting the mark, and a lot of pieces are unreadable.

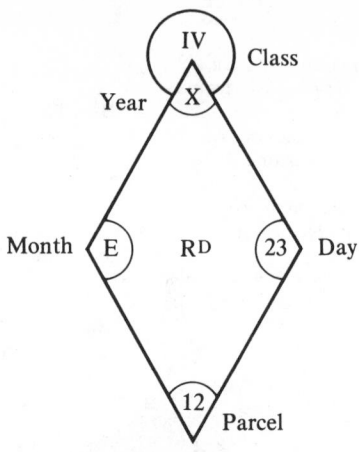

Example of earthenware design registered May 23, 1842

Below is index to letters for each year and month from 1842 to 1867:

YEARS

1842 X, 1843 H, 1844 C, 1845 A, 1846 I, 1847 F, 1848 U, 1849 S, 1850 V, 1851 P, 1852 D, 1853 Y, 1854 J, 1855 E, 1856 L, 1857 K, 1858 B, 1859 M, 1860 Z, 1861 R, 1862 O, 1863 G, 1864 N, 1865 W, 1866 O, 1867 T.

MONTHS

January C, February G, March W, April H, May E, June M, July I, August R, September D, October B, November K, December A.

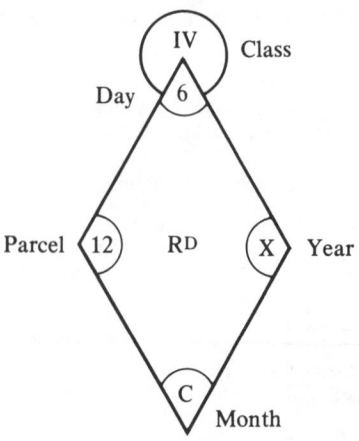

Example of earthenware design registered January 6, 1868

Below is index to letters for each year and month from 1868 to 1883:

YEARS

1868 X, 1869 H, 1870 C, 1871 A, 1872 I, 1873 F, 1874 U, 1875 S, 1876 V, 1877 P, 1878 D, 1879 Y, 1880 J, 1881 E, 1882 L, 1883 K.

MONTHS

January C, February G, March W, April H, May E, June M, July I, August R, September D, October B, November K, December A.

Bronze Figures

Bronze Figures

There are bronze figures and there are "bronze" figures. Too many pot metal fakes are around, so know your bronzes and your dealer. A signed figure is worth more than an unsigned. Don't worry about finding any Frederic Remingtons.

Arab on camel, Austria, 6" high	$ 160-	170
Bird, signed Pautrot	550-	650
Bull, Charolais from Burgundy, signed Rosa Bonheur, 7" high		2,100+
Cossack and girl on horseback, Russia, 11" high, signed Bonoguy	900-	$1,400
Cow, 6" long, signed R. Bonheur	500-	600
Dachshund, 5" high, self-base	100-	175
Deer in forest	95-	120
Elephant, 7" high, signed Fratin	575-	675
Greyhound, signed Mene		800+
Horse, Ch'ing (Manchu Dynasty (ill.)	70-	95
Leopard stalking, 5" high, 12" long	170-	210
Lion roaring, 5" high, 8" long, signed Barye	265-	320
Panther, 7¾" long, signed Bayre	700-	900
Panther crouching, 17" long, signed L. Bureau	195-	220
Pheasant, 7" long, signed Mene		625+
Polar bear stalking seal, Austria, 4" high, 5" long	165-	180
Retriever, signed Mene		950+
Running elephant, 5" high, 7½" long, signed Barye	575-	650
Tiger on marble base, 6" high, 7" long	200-	270
World War I Doughboy, signed Roman Bronze Works (same firm that cast the Frederic Remington bronzes)	160-	185

Keep in mind that if you do find a Frederic Remington bronze (usually a Western scene—bucking horse, Indian shooting a buffalo, etc.) don't sell it. One sold recently for $118,000!

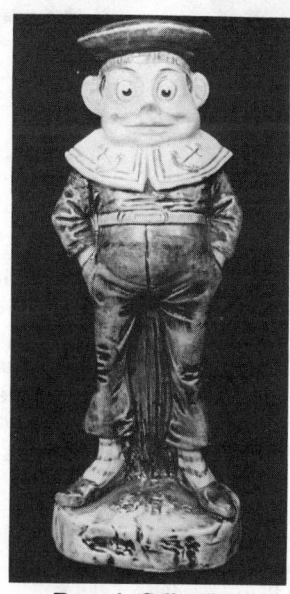

Brownie Collectibles

Brownie Collectibles

Created by Palmer Cox, an artist-author, in 1888, these creatures of fantasy were popular during that period. During the early 1900s they were copied by other artists.

Book, *The Brownies*, Cox	$ 32-	48
Book, *The Brownies, More Nights*	37-	47

73

(continued)

Buffalo Pottery

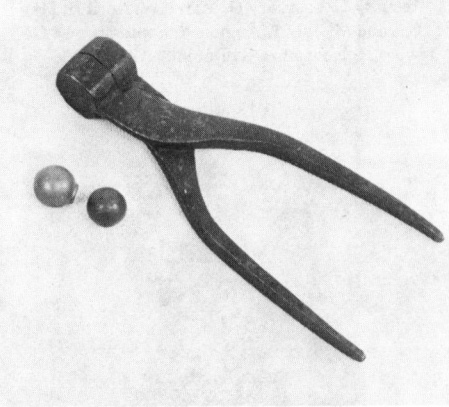

Bullet Molds

Bullet Molds

During the days of the muzzle-loading rifle, hunters, soldiers, frontiersmen molded their own bullets from melted-down lead.

Brass, single, spattered iron, 3"
long . . . .$ 55- 65
Brass, holds 12, 10" long 60- 70
Brass, .41 caliber, holds 4, 6"
long 54- 67
Iron, single, 2" long 38- 50
Iron, single, 4½" long (ill.) 47- 56

Buffalo Pottery

Established in 1901 in Buffalo, New York, the firm supplied pottery for the Larkin Company, which was in the soap business and later developed into a mail order firm specializing in premiums which helped to sell its goods. Best known and the most sought-after is the Deldare ware, first made in 1908. The firm continued until the 1940s. Most Deldare is done in old English tavern and hunting scenes.

Bowl, Deldare, English cricket
matches, 1910 . . . .$ 65- 74
Bowl, floral, 6" dia. 35- 45
Bowl, punch, Deldare, Fallow-
field Hunt, signed J.I.
Streusel 335-360
Candlesticks, Deldare, village
scenes, 9½" high, pr. 175-210
Chamber pot, green, chrysanthe-
mum decor 40- 48
Cinderella pitcher, 9" high 375-410
Creamer, Deldare, village scenes,
1909 . . . . 83- 92

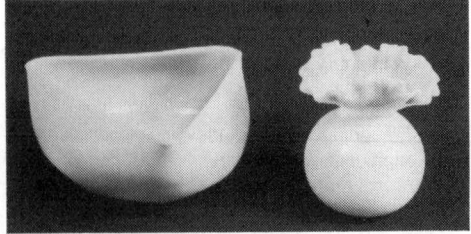

Burmese Glass

Burmese Glass

This translucent, shaded ware, homogeneous in nature, was made at the Mt. Washington Glass Company in the late 1800s. Licensed to produce it in England, Thomas

Webb & Sons called it Queen's Burmese. Burmese was a soft canary yellow shading to flesh pink. Unfortunately it's being reproduced today skillfully enough to fool too many new collectors.

Bell, ivy motif, pink interior $	500+
Biscuit jar, Pairpoint silver frame...............	900-1,200
Bowl, triangular (ill.)......	225- 245
Bride's basket, silver holder, 9" dia........	875- 950
Condiment set, 3 pcs......	500- 550
Epergne, signed Webb	1,800-2,200
Fairy lamp, brass, Clarke holder	800- 900
Glass, juice, satin finish, 4"	150- 172
Paperweight, egg shape ...	570- 625
Pitcher, bright pink-to-yellow, acid, 7" high	1,800-2,200
Queen's Burmese, lamp, pyramid shape, salmon-to-yellow, 3¾" high	400- 475
Queen's Burmese, lamp, same as above, 5¼" high	525- 585
Rose bowl, 4¼" dia.......	480- 525
Salt/pepper shakers, pr., ribbed	400- 450
Toothpick, decorated, signed Webb, 3¾" high .	400- 435
Toothpick, 4-sided, floral design	385- 425
Toothpick, glossy, 5-sided top	300- 375
Tumbler	450- 500
Vase, flared top, petal style, pr.	650- 775
Vase, glossy, signed Webb, 3¼" high (ill.)	225- 250
Vase, lemon to pink, 8½" high	325- 350
Vase, Mt. Washington, acid finish, 8" high	625+
Vase, satin, pink, yellow, signed Webb, 24" high ..	2700+

that was eventually syndicated. Buster Brown and his dog, Tige, appeared on the American market in the form of dolls and other objects. The most famous, of course, were shoes, which are still sold under the Buster Brown name.

Buster and Tige bank, cast iron, 5" high $140-155
Buster "to call dog" whistle.....	14- 19
Button, brass	9- 12
Button pin, Buster and Tige	19- 27
Camera, Ansco, in original box ..	38- 46
Cards, playing, c. 1907	38- 44
Clicker, advertising shoes	10- 13
Comb, brass	12- 14
Cup/saucer, Buster and girl (ill.)..	23- 32
Dish, Buster and girl (ill.)	25- 34
Fork and spoon, silver metal, both	35- 44
Knife, pocket	75- 84
Game, At the Zoo, deck of comic cards	22- 27
Hand puppet, Buster holding Tige, 1906	75- 85
Mirror, advertising	10- 13
Mug, china, gold trim, 3" high ...	55- 65
Pencil, advertising shoes	10- 13
Plaque, advertising	80- 90
Plate, 5" dia................	46- 54
Postcard, Buster at zoo with Tige and girl	8- 10
Scissors	34- 43
Shoe horn, advertising shoes	12- 14
Sign, Buster and Tige, advertising shoes, 21"×25", tin	135-150
Toy, Buster and Tige cart	145-155
Whistle, advertising shoes......	11- 14
Wrapping paper, Buster and girl, poems, complete roll........	15- 19

Buster Brown Collectibles

Buster Brown Collectibles

Dick Outcault created a comic strip in 1902

Busts

Busts

Obviously marble is worth more than plaster, but all are collectible.

Diane, gilded, tinted plaster,
  signed, 15½" high (ill.) . . . . . . $ 80- 90
Venus, plaster, on marble base,
  6" high 58- 70

Butter Molds and Prints

Normally associated with the Pennsylvania Dutch, they were used all over the country in dairying areas. Familiar designs are cow, eagle, heart, dove, swan, star, pineapple, and tulip. Glass molds are rare.

Molds

Acorn and leaf, wood, round . . . . $ 63- 72
Cherries, wood, round 40- 49
Cow design, glass, round (rare) . . 88- 97
Cow design, maple (ill.) 175-190
Cow design, wood, round 47- 55
Eagle, round, maple (ill.) 185-195
Fern design, wood, round 37- 45
Fleur-de-lis, wood 44- 53
Flower design, 4-petal, wood,
  round 46- 55
Pineapple, box-type, maple (ill.) . . 75- 85
Pineapple, wood, round 52- 60
Shamrock, wood, round 56- 65
Shield, flowers, miniature 47- 55
Swan, wood, round, 3½" dia. . . . 74- 83
Tulip design, wood, round 144-153
Wheat sheaf, wood, round 46- 55
Wood, rectangular 23- 32

Prints

Acorn and leaves, wood, round . . 53- 62
Clover design, wood, round 23- 30
Cow design, wood, octagonal 94-103
Cow design, wood, round 22- 30

Dove, wood, round 83- 92
Eagle and Shield, wood, round . . . 128-145
Sheaf of wheat, cherry 66- 75
Swan, maple 77- 85
Tulip design, wood, round 105-115
Wheat pattern, wood, octagonal . 107-115

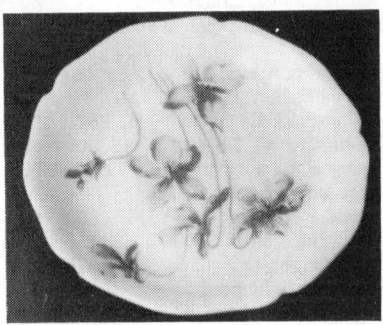

Butter Patties

Butter Patties

There are literally thousands of these around in pressed glass, porcelain (illustrated) and other materials. The nice thing is the still-low price. A friend of mine has more than 4,000 in her private collection. You'd "butter" start collecting yours today.

Button Hooks

What a chore that must have been, putting on and taking off. The gadget used came in many types: silver, gold, platinum, or just plain "hook." Prices paid will depend on whether or not it's marked sterling, 14k gold, or has no mark at all.

Button Hooks

Butter Molds and Prints

Buttons

Buttons

In every shape, in every size, in every material, buttons have been around for thousands of years. Those collectible today are from the mid-Victorian period to the early 1900s.

Carved jade, China . . . . $	14- 19
Cinnabar, carved	8- 11
Ivory, carved rose, flowers	9- 14
Kate Greenaway, children	14- 22
Lady's head, sterling silver	10- 17
Madonna and Child, coin silver . .	15- 23
Touring car, brass, 1904	11- 17
Vermont, military, brass, set of 4	8- 11
White/gold, cloisonne	7- 9

There are millions of styles.

1908, Santa and Holly	62-	70
1909, Omaha, Neb.	22-	29
1911, clothing store, Kansas	19-	27
1912, Heavy Brobst, Nuremberg, Pa. (ill.)	24-	32
1913, flowers, Santa	44-	53
1913, portrait, flowers	19-	27
1916, four-leaf clover, merchant . .	18-	27
1917, sleigh, "Chicago Greets Santa"	51-	60
1918, doughboy, Uncle Sam	29-	32
1919, Betsy Ross and flag	32-	41
1920, Victory decor, merchant . . .	23-	31
1922, fruit, flowers, Newark, N.J.	19-	27
1923, Grant's Tomb	35-	50
1925, horse race, merchant	26-	35
1926, Kentucky Derby, Winner! .	44-	50
1927, merchant, Reading, Pa. . . .	22-	31
1928, rose, trees, merchant	18-	27
1929, car, flags, Indy forever! . . .	60-	70
1966, God Bless Our House	19-	28

Calendars

Calendar Plates

Calendar Plates

Originating in England in the 1880s, they were made in the U.S. from 1905 until the late 1920s. Usually a cheap porcelain, some were made of tin and were intended as giveaways to advertise a merchant's store or product.

1906, girl, tin . . . . $ 29- 37

Calendars

Calendars

The use of calendars goes back to the days of the Romans—probably even beyond. The Gregorian calendar is used by the western world as well as by the Republic of China, South Vietnam, etc. What you find today in shops are from the late 1800s on. Year and condition dictate the price.

1876 Centennial Home Insurance Company, 12 months (ill.) . . . . $	16- 24
1896 Hartford Fire Insurance Co.	6- 11
1896 Root Beer	3- 5
1897 John Hancock	38- 47
1897 Prudential Insurance Co. . .	8- 12
1899 Ayer's Cherry Pectoral	5- 8
1903 Hood's Sarsaparilla (ill.) . . .	26- 34
1904 Dr. Pierce's Cure	35- 42
1904 Nehi	41- 50
1907 Old Forester Whiskey	6- 10
1908 Clarence Brooks & Co.	6- 10
1910 Coca-Cola	118-128
1912 Firestone Tires	31- 40
1914 Coca-Cola	150-170
1915 Ruppert Breweries	28- 37
1916 Coca-Cola	136-144
1920 Coca-Cola	142-150
1932 FDR—Our Man!	32- 41
1934 Coca-Cola	62- 71
1939 Coca-Cola	51- 60
1939 Standard Oil	18- 22

Bird with plumage, executed by C.P. Zaner, Forks, Pa., c. late 1800s (ill.)	$150-175
Deer, executed by William Mills, Watertown, N.Y., c. 1880s	140-150
Eagle, executed by J.M. Schaeffer, Farmersville, Pa., c. late 1880s	175-185
Rooster, executed by Nathanial Borden, Ellenville, N.Y., c. 1850s	160-170
Tiger, executed by Brisbane Wakefield, Portland, Conn., c. 1870	150-160
Whale, executed by Charles Stich, Roxbury, N.Y., c. 1850s .	142-151

Calling Cards

Calling Cards

Not too many years ago, when it was considered fashionable and polite for a gentleman to rise when a lady entered the room, gentlemen had personalized calling cards which were presented to the maid or butler when they called. Today, it's a bit difficult to distinguish one sex from the other and calling cards are collectible, inexpensive and available in most shops.

Average price, in good condition . 50¢-75¢

Calligraphy

Calligraphy

Originally called English round hand, this ornamental pen drawing is derived from the Carolingian minuscule, developed in the late 14th century by Italian scholars intent upon developing a more legible handwriting for manuscripts. It is also called "flourishing."

Cambridge Art Pottery

Made in Cambridge, Ohio, from about 1895 until WWI. It was a brown glazed decorated ware, using a variety of marks such as an acorn, the word Cambridge or Oakwood on the bottom. Vases, when found, bring $135 to $160.

Cambridge Glass

Cambridge Glass

Made in Cambridge, Ohio, by the Cambridge Glass Company, c. 1902, this pressed glass was usually marked with a C in a triangle; after 1906, the word near-cut was used.

Apple Blossom
Amber 3-pc. console set, all ..... $ 45- 55
Caprice Amber
Salt, 3 feet 7- 12
Caprice Blue
Ashtray, 3-part, 6" wide 19- 29
Bowl, 4 feet, 13" dia. 40- 49
Flared bowl, 10½" dia. 30- 38
Handled dish, collar foot,
9½" dia. 25- 34
Relish, 3-part, 7½" dia. 22- 31
Ruffled bowl, 10" dia. 33- 42
Caprice Pink
Candy dish, covered, 3 feet 19- 27
Oval bowl, 4 feet, 11" dia. 18- 27
Chintz Clear
Sandwich server, handled,
10½" dia. 17- 27
Crown Tuscan
Relish, 3-part, 8" dia. 25- 34
Decagon Amber
Bowled, handled, 6" dia., signed
"near-cut" 16- 26
Centerpiece bowl, 12" dia.,
3½" deep 23- 32

Decagon Black
Dish, handled, 6" dia. 12- 19
2-handled plate, hand-painted
flowers, 11" dia. 19- 28
Decagon Cobalt
Ice bucket, scalloped rim,
handled 43- 53
Farber Chrome Amethyst
Compote, 5½" high 19- 29
Creamer, 4" high 10- 16
Sugar bowl, 3" high 10- 18
Farber Chrome Forest Green
Liquor goblet, 4" high 10- 17
Stemmed compote, 5½" high ... 19- 28
Lightening Ebony
Creamer/sugar set, footed, all ... 22- 32
Swan, clear glass bowl, cobalt
head, 10" high (ill.) 34- 44

Cameo Glass

Generally speaking, this was a thin shell of glass with another shell blown into it. Then a design was cut through the outer layer, leaving the inner layer exposed. It also is called cased glass and today is highly collectible. See specific types of cameo glass listed alphabetically in this Guide. LaGras and LeMans are two items being reproduced. Careful, beginners!

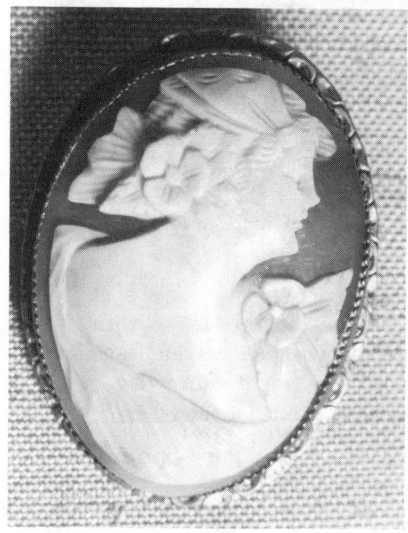

Cameos

Cameos

A small carving in relief on glass, lava, stone, shell, or any other hard substance; usually done on agate or shell because these

(continued)

materials have layers of different colors necessary to the cameoist's work. Cameos were in vogue between 1840 and 1875. Too many repros are on the market today.

Bracelet, seven cameos, classic
figures, silver links $125-135
Brooch, black-white, church, gold
frame 107-115
Brooch, orange-white, lady's
head, gold frame 108-118
Brooch, pink-white, lady's head,
gold frame 121-130
Pin, black-white, woman's profile,
14k gold 170-182
Pin, brown-white, woman and
child, 14k gold 170-180
Ring, girl, pink-white, 14k
mounting 62- 71
Tie pin, man's profile, 14k gold . . 40- 48

Campaign Items

Campaign Items

Since the 1840s, politicians at all levels have advertised themselves with kerchiefs, mugs, plaques, banners, and especially, buttons. All are sought after today.

Bandanna, Teddy Roosevelt's
Campaign Flag, 1912 . . . . $125-140
Mug, "A New Deal With FDR,"
1932, pottery 28- 36
Poster, Hoover's "A Chicken in
Every Pot!", 1928 . . . . 43- 50
Song sheet, Harrison's campaign,
1888 . . . . 26- 35
Stickpin, McKinley's head, gold-
colored, 1896 . . . . 28- 35
Campaign Buttons
Al Smith for President 24- 30

"Bryan & Sewell, Victory 1896" . 33- 38
Davis and Bryan (black and
white) 56- 65
Delegate's button/badge,
National Democratic
Convention, Denver, 1908 . . . . 86- 95
"Dewey-Bricker—NY Young
Republicans" 6- 9
"Down With The Beef Trust"
(Bryan's campaign) 13- 19
"First Voters Taft Club" 10- 17
Gold bug stickpin, McKinley 18- 28
"Harding and Coolidge" 24- 33
"Harding For President" 45- 54
"Home Town Coolidge Club
Plymouth Vermont" 46- 54
"Hoo But Hoover" 52- 61
"I Am A Democrat For Willkie" . . 5- 8
"Labor's Choice—Roosevelt" . . . 16- 24
McKinley-Roosevelt—"A Full
Dinner Pail" 70- 80
"Missouri's Minute Men For
Roosevelt" 30- 37
"My Hat Is In The Ring—T.R." . 17- 26
"OK, America! Play Safe With
Hoover" 44- 52
"Re-Elect Roosevelt" 14- 19
Roosevelt-Fairbanks, G.O.P.,
1904 . . . . 24- 34
"Smith and Robinson" 19- 27
"Support The Coolidge
Administration" 50- 59
Taft and Sherman, flags 24- 34
"The Choice of the People, Wm.
J. Bryan" 24- 33
"The Man of the Hour—
Woodrow Wilson" 115-125
"Watch Willkie Wilt" 7- 10
Wilson—"Stand By The
President" 31- 40

Camphor Glass

Camphor Glass

A cloudy white appearance identifies this glass. After being blown or pressed, it was treated with hydrofluoric acid vapor. Blue camphor glass, attributed to the Sandwich Glass Company of Cape Cod, is extremely rare today.

Art glass basket, yellow flowers, green leaves . . . . $	78-	88
Ashtray, raised flowers	18-	27
Bowl, raised flowers	24-	33
Bowl, rose color, crimped top, 4″ high	30-	38
Box, powder, Cocker Spaniel on lid	18-	27
Cologne bottle, gold gilt, original stopper	31-	40
Compote, open, 6″ tall	32-	41
Compote, yellow, 7½″ tall	31-	40
Creamer, white, flower motif	22-	28
Dish, blue Sandwich glass (authenticated)	220-230	
Jar, powder, pink, silver lid	33-	43
Lamp, miniature, raised flowers .	64-	74
Match holder, pipe shape, souvenir, 1906	31-	38
Plate, 3 kittens	22-	27
Salt/pepper, Three Face, 2¾″ high (ill.) pr.	80-	87
Toothpick holder, shoe shape . . .	32-	41
Tray, oval scalloped border, flowers in relief, 11″ long	27-	36
Vase, light blue, floral motif, 9″ high	34-	43
Vase, loop handles, 6½″ high (ill.)	12-	19
Vase, raised flowers in silver-plated stand	27-	35

Canary Lustreware

Generally attributed to the Staffordshire District, England, early 1880s, the 2 jugs shown are "American"—that is, made to attract the American market. Rare today!

Jug, "Faith and Hope," large . $	975-1,100	
Jug, "Faith and Hope," small	775-	950
Large jug, bright canary-yellow ground, American Eagle, edged and divided into 3 cartouches with silver lustre lines. On each side, large American Eagle, names of 11 states, "Peace, Plenty and Independence" (ill.)	1,250-1,450	
Mug, "Thrift is spending wisely," 2½″ high	410-	485
Small jug, basically same as large jug, "Success to the United States" (ill.) . . . .·. . .	1,100-1,400	

Candelabras

Candlesticks with arms is one way to describe them. The more ornate ones are called candelabrums, usually attached to a vase. Silver, both sterling and plate, brass, base metal, all were used to make the candelabras. Popular in the French and English palaces as far back as the mid-1600s. What you usually find today are early 19th century.

Brass, alabaster urn and base, pr. . . . . $	470-	525
Brass, 12″ high, 8-light, pr. . . .	100-	125

Canary Lustreware

(continued)

Candelabras

Cast pot metal, 17½" high
(ill.), pr. 90- 110
Empire ormolu, 12-light, pr. . . . 1,650-1,750
French ormolu figural, 5-light,
   early 19th century, pr. 575- 650
Gilt metal, George III type,
   cut glass prisms, pr. 650- 725
Sheffield silver (plate),
   English, early 19th century,
   pr. 500- 525
Sterling silver, mid-1800s,
   7-light, pr. 875- 950

Candle Molds

An early American laborsaving device,
they were usually made of tin, sheet iron, or
on occasion, pewter, in connected groups of
slender, tapered tubes. Melted wax was
poured into each tube. Twisted thread acted
as the wick. When the wax cooled or hard-
ened, the mold was dipped in hot water to
release the candles.

Tin, 4 hole . . . . $ 67- 75
Tin, 8 hole 74- 83
Tin, 12 hole (ill.)   94-105
Tin, 18 hole (ill.)   120-130
Pewter, same sizes as above,
   50% higher.
Sheet iron—same prices as tin.

Candlesticks

Shape is important, age-wise. The earliest
were made from solid cast brass or wrought
iron. Hollowstems with the sliding knob to
raise or lower the candle were in use in the
early 1700s; the sheet-iron type, early 1800s.
19th century types were larger and more
ornate.

Beehive, push-up type, bur-
   nished, 9", 10", 11", pr. $140-165
Brass, 1840s, 11" high, pr. (ill.) . . 200-225
Brass, altar type, 22" high 54- 63
Brass, India, 11" high, pr. 42- 52
Brass, twisted stem, 8" high 43- 53
Bull and beehive design, push-up
   type, 7" 52- 61

Candle Molds

82

Candlesticks

Crucifix, pr., Sandwich type	133-139
Glass, dolphin, Sandwich type...	81- 92
Heisey glass, glass prisms, 11½" high, pr.	132-144
Hog scraper, push-up type, base metal, 6" high	100-115
Porcelain, flower motif, pr., 10" high	98-107
Saucer type, push-up snuffer included	61- 69
Winged dragon type, 8½" high, pr....................	57- 67
Wood, turned cherry, 8½" high ..	24- 31
Wood, turned oak, 8" high	22- 32

Candy Containers

These were used for holding tiny pellets of candy and came in the shape of guns, ships, fire engines, cars, boats, etc. Popular at the turn of the century, today they're much sought after. A metal screw cap kept the candy in, though a cork was used on the earlier ones. The Liberty Bell is popular today.

Airplane, tin wings .... $	27- 36
Auto, Pierce Arrow	40- 50
Battleship..................	29- 38
Bear	22- 30
Betty Boop.................	29- 37
Bus, Greyhound	37- 44
Carpet sweeper	31- 40
Chicken-on-nest	16- 25
Dog.......................	14- 22
Donkey pulling barrel	36- 44
Duck, sitting	26- 33
Gun, 4" long	24- 32
House	30- 38
Jeep	16- 27
Lantern, bail, original cap	32- 41
Lantern, tin top	32- 41
Liberty Bell, blue, tin cap	52- 60
Locomotive	41- 50
Moon Mullins	39- 47
Motorboat (ill.)	11- 20
Peter Rabbit................	24- 32
Radio	29- 34
Revolver, clear	33- 42
Scottie dogs, J. Crosetti Co., pr. .	52- 60
Submarine	38- 47
Suitcase	27- 35
Tank......................	19- 27
Telephone	26- 33
Train......................	29- 37
Turkey	28- 34
Van (ill.)	12- 18
Victory bus.................	34- 42
Wheelbarrow	33- 42
Whistle	11- 14

Canine Collectibles

Paintings, lithos, etchings, statuettes: just about anything to do with Fido is becoming collectible.

Bronze wolfhound, 5" high, no signature .... $	45- 55

Candy Containers

(continued)

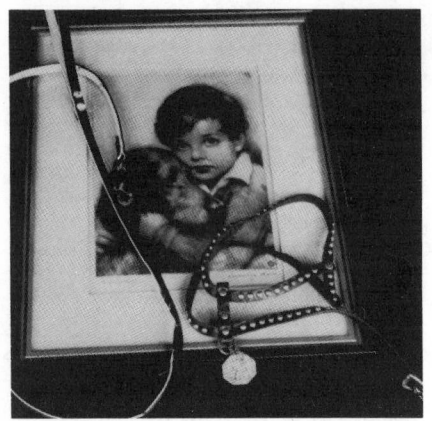

Canine Collectibles

Lithograph, "Grace," copyright
1920, U.S.A., printed in
England 25- 33
Lithograph, "Sympathy," by
J. Knowles Hare, signed and
numbered (ill.) 50- 60
Red Cross harness worn by dogs
in the A.E.F., World War I ... 35- 43

Cans and Containers

Cans and Containers

Biscuit can, English, Old Rover . . $ 11- 20
Biscuit can, Huntley & Palmer,
Churchill 32- 41
Biscuit can, Huntley & Palmer,
George V 38- 46
Candy box, round, w/lid,
decorated (ill.) 7- 11
Cocoa can, Baker's Chocolate,
early 1900s 12- 21
Dan Patch Cut Plug, late 1800s . . 22- 31
Gunpowder can, Winchester
Repeating Arms Co., late 1800s 12- 24
Gunpowder can, American
Powder Mills, late 1800s 36- 45

Hairpin container, Lockford Ltd.,
early 1900s 14- 21
Kitchen cannisters, hand-painted,
tole type, late 1800s, 6 pcs. ... 66- 72
Lard can, Decker & Son, Snow
Brand, late 1800s 18- 25
Milk/cream can, tole type
painting, late 1800s 39- 47
Spark plug box, blue, Benford's
(ill.) 6- 9
Syrup can, Log Cabin, small
type, early 1900s 18- 27
Syrup can, Log Cabin, large
type, early 1900s 26- 31
Tea container, Boswell Ltd.,
japanned finish, late 1800s ... 22- 31
Tea container, Lipton's sailing
yacht label, late 1800s 14- 22
Wax can, antique car label,
polish for 1910 autos 10- 16
Yeast can, Fleischmann's,
early 1900s 10- 15

Canton China

A product of Canton, China, for over two
centuries, it was an inexpensive blue-and-
white, hand-decorated ware made primarily
for export to England and Europe. Those
wares made in the late 1700s and early 1800s
are more collectible than the 20th century
ware.

Bowl, rice, early 1800s .... $ 78- 86
Butter patty, blue 21- 30
Charger, temple scene 115-119
Cup/saucer, blue/white, no handle 40- 50
Dish, shrimp, fish scene 78- 88
Fish bowl, blue/white, on stand,
14" high 410-480
Fish dish, fish shape, blue/white . 42- 52
Ginger jar, blue/white, double
ring, 6" high 44- 52
Lamp, blue/white, shade not
original 58- 67
Leaf, 7" wide (ill.) 72- 81
Milk pitcher, blue/white, mid-
1880s 115-119
Plate, 8" 72- 81
Plate, 9" 74- 81
Plate, blue/white, open lattice
edge, 8¼" diameter 73- 83
Platter, blue/white, cut corners,
late 1700s 210-245
Platter, octagonal, blue/white,
temple scene 170-180
Rose bowl, white poppy
blossoms, cover 40- 48
Soup, blue/white, 8½" dia....... 48- 54

Canton China

Teapot, blue/white, straight spout, late	66- 72
Tile, 5″ square, animal figures . . .	51- 60
Tureen and stand, covered, blue/white	100-115
Warming dish, octagonal, 9″ wide (ill.)	285-310

Capo-di-Monte

Originally made in the factory of the same name in Italy in 1736, since then this ware has been reproduced many times. An N beneath a crown is the usual mark. That made by King Charles of Naples in 1743 is of museum quality and rare. The Doccia factory at Florence has made many reproductions. It's good and fools a lot of people. Just keep in mind that most of the originals are in museums.

Bell, N/Crown mark	$ 85- 95
Box, garden scene, 2½″×3″× 6½″	142-160
Dinner bell, cherubs, blue, Crown mark	110-140
Figurine, boy and girl with cow, N/Crown mark	173-183
Figurine, couple carrying water bucket, Crown mark	150-170
Lamp, swirled green/pink ribbing, usual cherubs	260-280
Plaque, classical figures, 8″×15″ N/Crown mark	425-460

Capo-di-Monte

Plaque, figures in relief depict civilization, 20″ dia. (ill.)	875-950
Stein, drinking scene, blue, Crown mark, 12″ high	650-680
Tea set, teapot, creamer, sugar, unsigned	160-170
Urn, compote type, cherubs, blue, Crown mark	310-340
Urn, 15″ high, cherubs playing, N/Crown mark	200-240
Vase, classical figures, N/Crown mark, 8½″ high	172-181

Card Cases

These were used to hold gentlemen's cards when they went calling during the 17th and 18th centuries. Usually ornate, they were made of gold, silver, ivory, sometimes inlaid with precious stones. See also **Silver**.

14k gold, tiny rubies	$375-450
Ivory, carved, ornate	47- 54
Mother-of-pearl	20- 27
Rosewood, carved, initials	24- 34
Sterling silver, initialed	38- 42
Tortoiseshell	26- 36

Carlsbad

Carlsbad

Wares from Carlsbad were exported to the U.S. in the 19th and 20th centuries. Later, when this area was a part of Czechoslovakia after World War I, some pieces were marked Karlsbad. Wares marked Victoria were made especially for Lazarus and Rosenfeldt, a firm in the U.S. that imported from this European country.

Cracker jar, white luster, pink/green flowers, marked Victoria	$ 44- 53
Pitcher, country scene, twisted snake handle, Karlsbad	75- 85
Plaque, in metal frame (ill.)	38- 45
Plate, cupids, floral border, gold decor, 10″ dia.	38- 48
Plate, pink/green flowers, swirl and flute border, Victoria	38- 47
Platter, apple blossoms in pink, green flower border, Victoria	68- 72
Platter, poppies, birds around border, 12 matching soups, Karlsbad	115-122
Tea set, flowers, birds, fluted border on saucers (set consists of teapot, creamer, sugar, waste pot)	110-122
Tureen, blue/pink roses, floral edge, covered, Karlsbad	51- 60

Carnival Glass (Taffeta)

This originally low priced, iridized glass was made to compete with the expensive Art Glass (Tiffany, Steuben, Durand, Kew Blas, Quezal, etc.) of the early 1900s. It was originally called Taffeta glass and got its present name during the 1920s when circuses and carnivals gave it away as prizes. Grocery stores also gave it away with food purchases. It was dipped in vinegar to iridize it. When the sun came into contact with this "vinegar" glass, it left the glass looking as if it had the measles. Color of individual pieces determines value. Prices range upward from peach (lowest), to marigold to blue, green, or purple, to pastels (any color), to genuine *old* Red Carnival, the most valuable. Being reproduced.

Banana Boat

Floral	$ 42- 52
Grape and Cable, green	170-180
Grape and Cable, marigold	150-160
Peach and Pear, marigold	68- 78
Thistle	84- 93
Wreathed Cherry, purple	140-150
Wreathed Cherry, red	325-350
Wreathed Cherry, white	172-184

Bank

Bell, marigold	28- 37
Owl, marigold	50- 60

Basket

Basketweave, marigold	56- 63
Stippled Rays, 2 handles, purple	39- 47
Tree of Life, marigold	32- 41

Berry Set

Beaded Shell, 6 pcs., purple	260-270
Imperial's Grape, 7 pcs., green	130-140
Three Fruits, N mark, 6 pcs., purple	178-188

Bonbon

Persian Medallion, blue	64- 73
Pond Lily, blue	65- 74
Three Fruits, basketweave, marigold	54- 59

Carnival Glass

Bottles

Barber, marigold	54- 62
Horn of Plenty	51- 61
Raised Grape, purple	240-260
Toilet Water, marigold	53- 61
Whiskey, Golden Wedding, marigold	44- 52
Wine, New England Wine Co., marigold	42- 52

Bowl

Acorn pattern, marigold	51- 60
Apple Blossoms, 5½" dia., purple	58- 68
Berry, Acorn pattern, 7½" dia., blue	44- 52
Berry, Butterfly and Berry, marigold	54- 64
Berry, Lacy Edge, red	142-150
Berry, Peacock at the Fountain, amethyst	134-142
Berry, Vintage Grape, 5½" dia., purple	44- 53
Berry, Water Lily and Cattails, marigold	46- 54
Blackberry Wreath, 9" dia.	61- 70
Bouquet and Lattice, 6½" dia., cereal	30- 40
Candy, Fine Cut and Roses, N mark, purple	67- 76
Captive Rose, 8¾" dia., green	60- 70
Chrysanthemum, footed, 10" dia., blue	78- 87
Dogwood Sprays, marigold	60- 70
Dragon and Lotus, 8" dia.	60- 68
Embossed Grapes, 9½" dia., marigold	54- 63
Embossed Scroll, 8" dia., green	59- 67
Good Luck, 7¼" dia., blue	115-123

Grape and Cable, green	88- 98
Grape and Cable, 6½" dia., marigold	42- 52
Grape and Cable, 7½" dia., purple	60- 70
Grape and Gothic Arches, marigold	39- 47
Heart and Vine, blue	58- 67
Heart and Vine, 8" dia., green	68- 72
Holly, 9" dia., blue	62- 70
Horse's Head Medallion, 6½" dia., marigold	60- 70
Imperial's Cherries, footed, 10" dia., marigold	60- 70
Imperial's Grape, 8¾" dia.	44- 53
Leaf pattern, 5½" dia., marigold	42- 50
Little Flowers, 10½" dia.	69- 78
Louisa, 8¼" dia., amethyst	44- 52
Millersburg's Cherry, marigold	54- 62
Millersburg's Cherry, 7" dia., green	50- 60
Millersburg's Primrose, 9¼" dia.	70- 80
Millersburg's Whirling Leaves, 9½" dia.	78- 88
Pansy Spray, amber	50- 60
Peacock and Dahlia, 7½" dia., marigold	52- 60
Peacock and Grape, 7½" dia., 3" high	52- 62
Peacock and Grape, 9" dia.	145-165
Peacock at the Fountain, 8" dia.	90-130
Persian Medallions, 9" dia., marigold	52- 65
Roses and Ruffles, 8" dia., marigold	48- 57

(continued)

Peacock at the Fountain,
amethyst 150-160
Pineapple, dome foot, marigold   127-136
Singing Birds, marigold   125-145
Stippled Rays, green 62- 71

Cup and Saucer

Bouquet and Lattice, marigold   27- 38
Many Carnival glass patterns,
average 30- 38

Cup, Punch

Acorn Burrs, N mark 39- 51
Buzz Star, marigold 28- 38
Grape and Cable, blue 47- 56
Grape and Cable, N mark,
purple 42- 51
Imperial's Grape, set of 6,
marigold 67- 77
Memphis, amethyst 50- 60
Vintage, marigold 32- 41

Cuspidor

Orange Tree 64- 74

Decanter

Golden Harvest, marigold   92-108
Grape Clusters, stopper,
marigold 72- 85
Imperial's Grape, green   140-160
Imperial's Grape, marigold . . .   82- 93
Octagon, stopper, marigold . . .   83-103

Dish

Berry, Grape and Cable, N
mark 42- 50
Berry, Octagon, marigold 41- 60
Berry, Peacock and Urn, purple   55- 70
Berry, Three Fruits, N mark,
amethyst 52- 62
Candy, Blackberry, 6″ dia., red   131-151
Candy, Fine Cut and Roses,
8″ dia. 72- 81
Candy, Lacy Rim, blue 40- 50
Candy, Millersburg's Holly,
green 71- 81
Candy, Persian Medallion,
marigold 41- 51
Candy, Stippled Rays,
marigold 40- 50
Candy, Wreath of Roses, green   54- 62
Celery, Grape and Cable,
purple   92-102
Celery, Pansy Spray, amber . .   71- 80
Dessert, Fluted Paneled Rays,
N mark 41- 51
Ice Cream, Beaded Cable,
footed, 7½″ dia. 42- 52
Ice Cream, Peacock and Urn,
N mark, blue   112-121
Pickle, Beaded Cable, fluted,
footed, 7¾″ dia. 54- 63
Pickle, Imperial's Pansy,
marigold 44- 54
Pickle, Windmills, green 58- 67
Relish, Grape and Cable, purple   72- 82

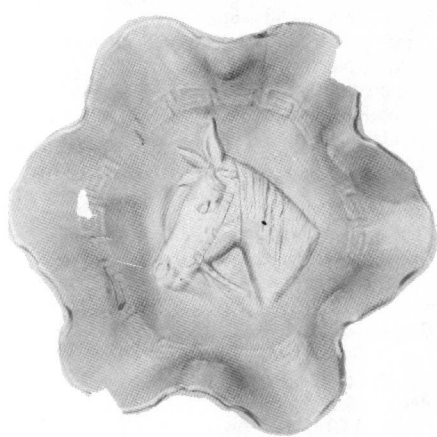

Carnival, Pony

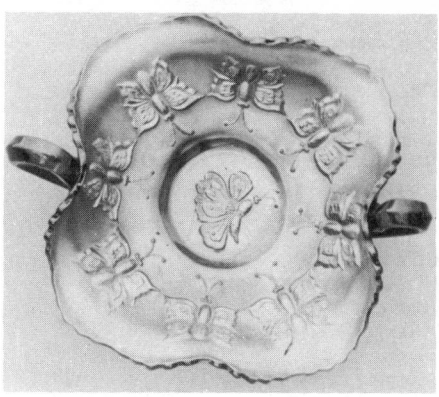

Carnival, Butterflies

Relish, Pansy, marigold 42- 58
Sauce, Acorn Burrs, N mark,
marigold 34- 44
Sauce, Acorn Burrs, purple . . .   50- 60
Sauce, Butterfly and Berry,
marigold 29- 37
Sauce, Fenton's Cherry 39- 51
Sauce, Grape and Gothic
Arches, blue 42- 52
Sauce, Grape and Thumbprint,
N mark, purple 39- 48
Sauce, Lustre Rose, marigold .   27- 39
Sauce, Northwood Flute,
purple 50- 62
Sauce, Panther, ball and claw,
marigold 58- 69
Sauce, Panther, footed, 6″ dia.,
purple 67- 78
Sauce, Peacock at the
Fountain 44- 49
Sauce, Star Medallion 33- 44
Sauce, Stippled Rays, purple . .   50- 62

(continued)

Sauce, Thistle and Thorn,
  marigold 44- 56
Sundae, Northwood's clear
  stem, marigold 51- 62
Vegetable, Bouquet and
  Lattice, marigold 21- 31
Doughnut Stand
  Question Mark, white 74- 84
Epergne
  Four Lilies, marigold   430-450
  Grape pattern, purple   144-156
  Vintage, purple   150-160
Fernery
  Grape Variant, footed, green . .   60- 70
  Lustre Rose, green 70- 80
  Vintage Grape, footed green . .   65- 75
Goblet
  Imperial Grape, 6" high,
    marigold 66- 76
  Wine, Flute, blue 60- 70
  Wine, Orange Tree, blue 62- 72
Hat
  Blackberry, banded 44- 52
  Blackberry, blue 43- 52
  Blackberry, 5", red   140-150
  French Knots 48- 58
Hatpin
  Bumblebee, purple 56- 66
  Butterfly 74- 83
  Flying Bat 57- 66
  Plum and Stem 47- 56
Hatpin Holder
  Grape and Cable, N mark   144-152
  Grape, purple 80- 90
  Orange Tree, marigold   92-107
Insulator
  Corning Pyrex, marigold 44- 53
  Marigold 45- 52
  Marigold, large   96-107
Jar
  Candy, cover, 8" high,
    marigold 37- 46
  Candy, crinkled lid, marigold . .   52- 62
  Cookie, Grape with Thumb-
    print, cover, N mark, white .   875+
  Cookie, Hourglass and Daisy,
    cover, marigold 70- 80
  Cracker, Grape and Cable,
    purple   400-450
  Cracker, Inverted Feather and
    Hobstar, green   230-250
  Pickle, Golden Flowers,
    marigold 37- 47
  Powder, Bambi, marigold 29- 38
  Powder, Orange Tree, cover,
    marigold 70- 80
  Powder, Vintage, cover,
    marigold 70- 79
  Powder, Wreathed Cherries,
    blue 84- 92
  Tobacco, Illinois Daisy,
    marigold   90-102

Lamp
  Metal holder, marigold 67- 77
  Zipper and Loop, 2-burner, 7"
    high, marigold   210-220
Mug
  Fish and Cattail, purple   95-107
  Orange Tree, blue 58- 68
  Robin Red Breast, marigold . .   52- 62
  Singing Birds, marigold 60- 70
  Singing Birds, N mark,
    marigold 70- 80
  Singing Birds, purple 79- 88
  Stork and Rushes, marigold . .   55- 63
  Vintage, marigold 49- 73
Nappie
  Grape and Cable, green   100-112
  Leaf Rays, marigold 54- 62
  Northwood's Butterfly 53- 62
  Question Mark, marigold 37- 47
  Stippled Rays, N mark 52- 61
Pitcher
  Butterfly and Berry, marigold .   140-150
  Diamond Lace, 6 tumblers,
    purple   460-470
  Floral and Grape, 6 tumblers,
    marigold   230-245
  Grape, N mark, 6 tumblers,
    purple . . . .   620+
  Grape and Gothic Arches,
    marigold   135-145
  Imperial's Grape, blue   172-192
  Imperial's Grape, 6 tumblers,
    purple   240-270
  Millersburg's Diamond, green .   140-160
  Nesting Peacock   140-155
  Northwood's Maple Leaf, 6
    tumblers, marigold   270-290
  Peacock at the Fountain, white   510-570
  Poinsettia, marigold 67- 77
  Rose pattern, 8 tumblers   138-146
  Singing Birds, marigold   210-220
  Star Medallion, small, marigold   52- 61
Plate
  Grape and Cable, footed, green   140-160
  Homestead, signed Nu Art,
    marigold . . . .   625+
  Honeycomb, purple 65- 74
  Imperial Jewels, white 71- 80
  Peacock and Urn, white   220-240
  Peacock on the Fence, green . .   190-210
  Strawberry, N mark, green . . .   150-160
  Three Fruits, marigold 70- 80
  Three Fruits, white   170-185
  Vintage, green 88- 98
  Wild Strawberry, N mark,
    green   152-168
Sauceboat
  Fan pattern, purple 86- 95
Shade
  Gas, Mayflower, marigold, pr. .   60- 70
  Light, signed Nu Art,
    marigold, pr. 66- 75

90

Light, quilted, white, pr.	42-	52
Light, white	28-	37

Sherbet

Bouquet and Lattice, pedestal, set of 6, marigold	50-	60
Flute, N mark, green	39-	47
Holly, marigold	32-	42
Iris and Herringbone, marigold	34-	41
Orange Tree, stemmed, marigold	32-	40

Spoonholder

Acorn Burrs	120-130	
Butterfly and Berry, marigold .	55-	61
Hobstar, marigold	41-	50
Kittens, small, marigold	92-101	
Lustre Rose, green	50-	60
Peacock at the Fountain	97-115	

Sugar

Grape and Cable, cover, purple	90-101	
Lustre Flute, handle	56-	66
Lustre Flute, N mark, purple . .	51-	61
Millersburg's Cherry	79-	84
Star and File	50-	61

Swan

Millersburg, purple	175-185	
Pastel blue	61-	71
Pastel green	66-	74

Tray

Butterfly, footed, white	140-150	
Grape, center handles, marigold	70-	80
Pin tray, Grape and Cable, scalloped, marigold	140-150	

Tumbler

Apple Tree, marigold	48-	58
Blueberry, white	62-	70
Butterfly, purple	47-	57
Dandelion, N mark, green	64-	72
Enameled Cherry, blue	38-	48
Grape and Cable, purple	64-	72
Grape and Lattice, white	69-	73

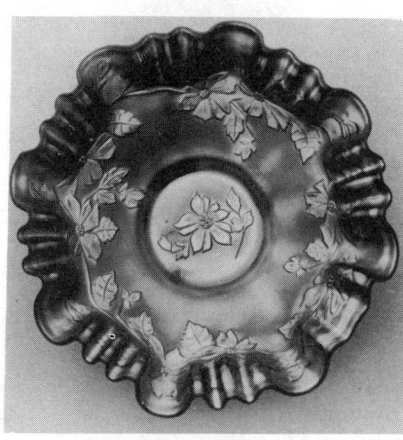

Carnival, Ragged Robin

Grapes, Maple Leaves, N mark, marigold	51-	68
Lattice and Grape, blue	42-	52
Maple Leaf, set of 6, purple . . .	240-260	
Millersburg's Diamond Band, marigold	34-	43
Oriental Poppy, white	118-140	
Peacock at the Fountain, blue .	59-	69
Peacock, N mark, purple	70-	82
Rambler Rose, marigold	38-	40
Singing Birds, N mark, green .	68-	78
Star Medallion, set of 6, marigold	150-160	
Stork and Rushes, blue	52-	62
Vineyard, set of 6, marigold . . .	140-150	
Water Lily and Cattails, N mark	63-	73

Vase

Beaded Bull's Eye, 11″ high, marigold	60-	70
Corn, N mark, green	240-260	
Corn, N mark, marigold	310-340	
Cornucopia, marigold	62-	71
Diamond Point, N mark, 8″ high, purple	55-	65
Feather, green	44-	54
Fine Rib, N mark, marigold . . .	50-	60
Grape, N mark, 16″ high, blue .	69-	78
Knotted Beads, 11″ high, red .	150-160	
Northwood's Drapery, 8¼″ high, amethyst	52-	64
Ripple, 17″ high, marigold	50-	60
Rose Column, green	270-290	

Water Set

Butterfly and Berry, blue	590-770	
God and Home, blue (rare)	3,600+	
Grape and Cable, 7 pcs., purple	470-520	
Peacock at the Fountain, N mark, blue	685+	

Wine

Grape, marigold	44-	53
Iris, set of 6, marigold	48-	60
Octagon, 7 pcs., marigold	250-270	
Orange Tree, green	69-	78
Sailboats, frosted stem, marigold	44-	52

Carousel!

A German, Michael Dentzel, introduced the first carousel to America in 1867. We know the carousel in this country as the merry-go-round, a delightful ride for children of all ages, with a chance of grabbing the brass ring. An American, C.W. Parker, was known as the Amusement King in the late 1880s. Carousel animals that go up and down are known as "jumpers," and Mr.

(continued)

Parker invented and built them. His horses were things of beauty.

Jumper dog, 59″ long, made
by Spillman $1,800-2,200
Jumper dog head, on front of
saddle, jewels, 56″ long
Parker 1,200-1,450
Jumper horse, lion hide
saddle, jewels, made by
Parker, 59″ long 1,300-1,450
Jumper Trojan horse, 60″
long, made by Spillman . . . 1,200-1,400
Jumper zebra, 58″ long, made
by Spillman 1,400-1,600

Caster Sets

Caster Sets

Dating from the early 1700s, caster sets you find in shops today are of the Victorian era—3 to 7 condiment bottles in a metal frame, usually quadruple plate or pewter.
Pickle Caster: see under that listing.

4-bottle, green/clear cut glass,
quadruple plate holder, 7½″
high (ill.) $340-360
4-bottle, quadruple plate frame,
clear glass 160-175
4-bottle, Sheffield silver frame,
Waterford glass, clear 188-200
5-bottle, quadruple plate frame
etched flowers, clear glass 98-108
5-bottle, quadruple plate frame,
amber Daisy and Button 160-180
6-bottle, quadruple plate frame,
clear glass 74- 84
6-bottle, quadruple plate frame,
miniature, clear glass 88-100
6-bottle quadruple plate frame,
Cranberry thumbprint 220-240
6-bottle, quadruple plate frame,
clear glass, patented 1857 170-185
7-bottle, sterling silver frame,
Amberina type 550-600

8-bottle, clear glass, sterling
silver caps 270-290
8-bottle, cut glass, sterling
silver caps 370-390

Catalogs

Catalogs

Every company that could afford to issued a catalog extolling its products. The most collectible today are those that deal with the early automobile industry, jewelry and furniture makers and, of course, the now-expensive original Sears, Roebuck catalog from the early 1900s. Montgomery Ward's also brings brisk prices.

Franklin auto catalog, Syracuse,
N.Y., 1907 . . . . $ 50- 60
Montgomery Ward catalog, early
1900s 160-180
Noritake china catalog, 1964 (ill.) . 1.50- 3
Sears, Roebuck catalog, early
1900s 160-178
Singer sewing machine, parts
catalog, 1920s 9- 17
Spode china catalog, 1964 (ill.) . . . 2- 3

Cauldon China

Cauldon China

This firm didn't make porcelain until the early 1900s. It's very collectible today. English.

Bonbon dish, floral decorations . . $	29-	38
Cup and saucer, Indian Tree pattern	46-	54
Egg cup	18-	27
Ewer, Indian Tree design	41-	50
Flower, "frog," floral decor, 10 holes	28-	37
Plate, hunting scene, 10½" dia. . .	32-	41
Plate, floral decor, roses-in-wreath, 10½" dia.	34-	44
Vase, Indian Tree pattern	50-	60
Vase, round form, roses (ill.)	37-	47

Ceiling Fans

Ceiling Fans

Used in homes and stores after introduction of electricity. Being collected today by decorators and others.

Average price, good condition . . . $180-240
Reproductions available—higher priced.

Celadon

Celadon

This is a rare type of highly fired porcelain from the Sung Dynasty. It's scarce and is only mentioned here because some of it has been brought in from Red China in recent years. It features a glaze that meanders from greens through tones of gray-blue, gray-white, etc. It was also made in Japan and Korea, and undoubtedly military personnel brought home original pieces without knowing their value.

Bowl, diamond shape panels, 11½" dia., Sung Dynasty . . $	2,000+
Bowl, flower leaves, 6¼" dia., late	75- 83
Creamer, blue/white chrysanthemum leaves, late	82- 94
Dish (used as planters), blue/white floral, early 19th century	280-310
Jar, birds in relief, 19th century	190-220
Pitcher, green, flower, decor, "bamboo" handle	330-360
Planter, birds in relief, 19th century	225-260
Plate, scalloped rose pattern, birds, butterflies, enameled (ill.)	160-170
Teapot, floral motif, 6" high . .	95-108
Vase, blue/gray, dragon motif, 9½" high	197-220
Vase, grayish green, blue handles and figures, 16½" high	345-385
Vase, on rosewood stand, bamboo motif, 19th century	365-430

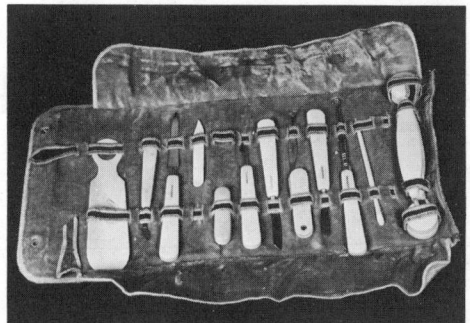

Celluloid

Celluloid ("French Ivory")

Invented by John Hyatt around 1868, celluloid was considered a boon to men who had to wear collars. It was also used for hair-

(continued)

brush backs, combs, etc., but fell from style in the mid-1900s.

Collar box, velvet lined . . . . $	46- 54
Comb, lady's	14- 27
Cream jar w/cover, glass lining, 3″ dia.	19- 27
Dresser set: tray, comb, mirror, hair receiver, powder box, etc. .	73- 82
Dresser tray, 11¼″ long	11- 19
Frame, 6″×9″	25- 36
Glove box, woman on lid	34- 39
Hair receiver and covered powder box	9- 14
Handled cuticle tool	8- 20
Lady's travel kit	31- 40
Manicure set, pink velvet case (ill.)	31- 41
Napkin ring	8- 14
Opener, letter	14- 22
Pansy vase, 6″ high	17- 25
Powder box, w/lid 4½″ dia.	16- 24
Nail buffer, chamois covered, 6″ long	8- 15
Rattle, baby's	14- 23
Shoehorn	7- 16

Centennial Plates

Centennial plates obviously celebrate the 100th anniversary of cities, states, institutions.

Plate, Baltimore & Ohio, 1827-1927, 10″ dia. . . . . $	40- 49
Plate, Civil War, "North-South United," crossed flags, 10½″ dia.	28- 38
Plate, Philadelphia, Declaration of Independence, 1776-1876, 8″ dia.	41- 50
Plate, War of 1812, 9″ dia.	39- 47

Chain Gang Collectibles

Chain Gang Collectibles

In some states these items are still used. Today, collectors are adding them to their collections.

"Arkansas toothpick" leg manacle (ill.) . . . . $	55- 65

Ball and chain with lock (ill.)	78- 80
Handcuffs, with key (ill.)	54- 64
Leg cuffs (manacles)	58- 68

Chalkware

Chalkware

Contrary to popular belief, this was not made by the Dutch Germans in Pennsylvania in the mid-1800s. Italian immigrants in this country, 1820s to the Civil War, made the best—simply, plaster of paris decorated with water colors.

Bank, dog, black, glass eyes . . . . $	40- 48
Bank, rearing horse	18- 27
Bank, turkey, natural colors	48- 58
Betty Boop, 14½″ high	172-181
Bookends, boy and girl reading, pr.	42- 52
Bookends, pirates, painted, pr. . .	47- 51
Cat (ill.)	47- 56
Dog, 11½″ high, early	70- 80
Dove, green/blue wings	190-210
Figurine, bust of Indian	80- 88
Figurine, cat sleeping	60- 68
Owl, 12″ high	170-180
Pigeon, green leaves, red berries .	130-142
Sailor boy, 9″ high	17- 26
Snow White, 12½″ high	31- 41
Squirrel	162-171
Stag, on rectangular plinth	220-230

Cheese Dishes

These wedge-shaped dishes-with-a-cover graced dinner tables for hundreds of years. Every country exported them to America

Cheese Dishes

and you'll find them still fairly inexpensive at shows, shops, and auctions.

Dish, English ironstone, c. 1870 (ill.) . . . . $ 40- 50

Chelsea

Chelsea

This porcelain was made for the fashionable world of London society, from 1745 until 1784 only. Supposedly made to compete with Dresden, it never achieved Dresden's quality. Chelsea can be conveniently divided into four main classes: The first period of the incised triangle and the raised anchor marks, the 1740s; the period of (at first) the raised anchor and the red anchor marks, the 1750s; the period of the gold anchor mark, the 1760s; the Chelsea-Derby period, the 1770s. In 1770 the Chelsea factory was taken over by Derby and the period lasted until 1783. In the 1920s a great number of molds and models of figurines were found at the Spode-Copeland Works and many varied items were reproduced.

Bowl, 6¼″ dia., Red Anchor mark $1,100-1,250
Candlesticks, 11″ high, grape decor, Red Anchor mark, pr. 2,400-2,550
Cups/saucers, demitasse, c. 1770s, set of 6, all 110- 130
Dish, floral design, Gold Anchor mark 65- 75
Dish, Kakiemon decoration, Red Anchor mark 425- 435
Dish, oval, scalloped edge, Red Anchor mark 125- 145
Ewer, floral decor, 10″ high, Red Anchor mark 525- 550
Figurine, girl with lamb, Gold Anchor mark 185- 210
Figurine, dancing couple, Red Anchor mark 1,650-1,750
Figurine, woman with basket, c. 1770s 220- 240
Pitcher, sprig decor, 10½″ high, Gold Anchor mark . . . 350- 375
Plate, fruit decor, 8″ dia., 1770s 47- 57
Plate, hand-painted birds, Gold Anchor mark 345- 365
Plate, sprig decor, Red Anchor mark 850- 975
Sugar and creamer, grape decor, Gold Anchor marks (ill.), ea. 450- 500
Teapot, sprig decor, Gold Anchor mark (ill.) 275- 320

Children's Books

Children's Books

Subject, demand, author, condition—all are important when buying these books that were printed some 100 to 150 years ago.

(continued)

*Adventures of Famous Travellers
in Many Lands,* W.L. Allison,
New York, c. 1880s . . . . $ 16- 26
Baby's Lullaby Book, Charles
Stuart Pratt, Boston, c. 1890s . 28- 36
A Book of Nonsense, Edward
Lear, New York, 1870 . . . . . . 44- 52
The Boys of 1812, Prof. J.
Russell Soley, Boston, 1887 . . . 23- 31
The Christmas Wreath, London,
Pictorial Boards, 1877 . . . . 12- 18
Cinderella, Dean & Son, London,
5 sets, 9 chromolithographed
changes, c. 1880s 55- 65
The Jackdaw of Rheims, Thomas
Ingoldsby, London, Paris, and
New York, color cover, c. 1880s 21- 30
Life and Death of Cock Robin,
Albany, N.Y., c. 1850s 28- 36
Slow and Sure, Horatio Alger (ill.) 5- 18
*The Merry Adventures of Robin
Hood,* Howard Pyle, New York,
1883 . . . . 24- 33
Watt's Songs of Early Religion,
McLoughlin Bros., 1860s 5- 9
Who Was the First Architect?,
The Busy-Bee Series, London,
Edinburgh, and New York,
1877 . . . . 18- 27
Wilson's Larger Speller, Marcius
Wilson, 1864 . . . . 12- 19

Children's Dishes

*Photo courtesy
Hake's Americana & Collectibles*

Children's Dishes

Toward the end of the 19th century the
major glass and pottery firms produced
tablewares specifically made for children.
Little Lamb, Nursery Rhymes, and Bunnykins are just a few of the many pieces made.

Don't confuse a miniature with items
especially made for children.

Berry Sets
Pressed glass, Inverted Straw-
berry, large bowl, clear . . . . . . $ 27- 34
Pressed glass, Lacy Daisy, small
bowl, clear 9- 12
Pressed glass, Nursery Rhymes,
large bowl, milk glass 48- 55
Bowls
Porcelain, French, Limoges, 3"
dia., barnyard scene, set of 6 . . 90-110
Porcelain, "Germany," 5½" dia.,
fishing by the mill, set of 6 90-110
Pottery, Mexican, 5 sizes from
2" to 8", set of 5 . . . . 35- 42
Butter Dishes
Pressed glass, Amazon, clear 29- 34
Pressed glass, Children's
Colonial, clear 20- 25
Pressed glass, Heart Band, clear . 27- 36
Pressed glass, Liberty Bell, clear . 69- 76
Cake Stands
Pressed glass, Beautiful Lady,
clear 24- 29
Pressed glass, Hawaiian Lei, clear 24- 29
Candlesticks
Pressed glass, Swirl, clear, pr. . . . 28- 34
Silver-plated, pr. 22- 27
Canister Set
Tin, kitchen scenes, set of 6 . . . . . 45- 52
Creamers
Pressed glass, Arrowhead-in-Oval 17- 20
Pressed glass, Criss Cross 17- 21
Pressed glass, Jubilee 19- 24
Tin, children playing 7- 9
Cups and Saucers
Felix the Cat, c. 1930 (ill.) 15- 20
Porcelain, French, Limoges,
kitchen scene 17- 20
Porcelain, "Made in Germany,"
Brownies 16- 19
Porcelain, "Made in Japan,"
nursery scene . . . . : 14- 18
Feeding Dishes
Porcelain, Campbell Kids, 7½"
dia., Buffalo pottery 52- 61
Porcelain, French, Limoges, 7½"
dia., Little Bo-Peep 32- 40
Porcelain, "Japan," 7¼" dia.,
little boys at play 29- 36
Feeding Sets
Porcelain, German, Three Bears,
3 pcs. 43- 50
Mugs
Bunnykins, English, 3" high 17- 24
Pottery, Mexican, 4" high 10- 14
Sterling silver, "BH", flowers . . . 45- 55
Plates
Porcelain, 5" dia., Simple Simon . 9- 14

Porcelain, 5¼" dia., Mother Goose center	10- 14
Tin, 5½" dia., Snow White center	15- 22
Tin, 5¼" dia., Little Bo-Peep center	10- 14

Spooner

Porcelain, French, Limoges, flower scene	15- 24

Table Set

Tin, 10 pcs., zoo animals, all	48- 55

Tea Sets

Porcelain, English, c. 1880s, garden scenes, set of 10	60- 68
Porcelain, German, garden scenes, set of 18	85- 95
Porcelain, "Made in Japan," pagoda scenes, set of 15	68- 75
Tin, German, Snow White and Seven Dwarfs, set of 22	110-130

Toilet Sets

Porcelain, German, animal scenes, set of 9	44- 53
Porcelain, "Made in Japan," flower scenes, set of 8	40- 48

Children's Mugs

Children's Mugs

These 19th century items were usually given to children as gifts or as rewards for being good. Leeds, Ironstone, Gaudy Dutch, Liverpool, and Bristol are just a few of the many types made. Highly collectible today.

Boy with farm animals, ironstone $	92-107
Ding Dong Bell, silver plated	40- 50
Franklin maxim, "The way to wealth"	89-100
Glass (ill.), ea.	4- 7
"The house that Jack built"	75- 90
"Long may we live," Canary ware	160-175
"A new carriage for Ann," Canary ware	152-162
"A present for a good boy," Canary ware	160-175

Chocolate Glass

Chocolate Glass

Often referred to as caramel slag, it was made by the Indiana Tumbler and Goblet Company, Greentown, Indiana, and also by Fenton. Popular patterns were Cactus and Leaf Bracket.

Berry bowl, Cactus, 4" dia. . . . . . $	50- 60
Berry set, Leaf Bracket, 6 pieces .	500-600
Compote, jelly, Cactus	128-140
Cracker jar, Cactus	210-225
Creamer, Austrian	92-106
Dish, butter, covered, Leaf Bracket	119-128
Lamp, 7 panel, fancy base and framework	220-230
Mug, Serenade	87- 92
Nappie, handled (ill.)	77- 86
Sugar, Leaf Bracket	84- 93
Tumbler, Cactus	47- 56
Tumbler, 4¾" high (ill.)	54- 63
Tumbler, Sawtooth	54- 62

Chocolate Pot Sets

Chocolate Pot Sets

Just about every porcelain factory in Europe made these sets, popular in the 18th and 19th centuries. See also specific firms elsewhere in the Guide for prices.

Cream flowers, gold decor with 6 cups (ill.)	$140-170

97

(continued)

Lily decor, signed Germany,	
6 cups/saucers	144-153
Oriental decor, Chinese garden	
scene, pot and 6 cups/saucers	142-162
Rose decor, flower trim, signed	
Germany, 6 cups/saucers	140-160
Roses, cream ground, gold decor,	
4 cups/saucers	118-130

Christmas Collectibles/Ornaments

Old-fashioned Christmases are a thing of the past in this country. No stringing of popcorn to drape on the tree, no hiking through the snow to cut down a favorite tree. Older Christmas items are popular collectibles, but if you find old electric Christmas tree lights, be careful. Old wire can cause a fire in a matter of seconds.

Bulbs, Electric

Basket of fruit, green/red	$ 7-	10
Bell	13-	16
Bluebird, milk glass	8-	11
Clock	11-	13
Donald Duck	21-	24
Flower, rose	10-	13
Gingerbread man, brown	8-	11
House, Santa on roof	9-	13
Humpty Dumpty	28-	33
Kayo (comic strip character)	34-	38
Lantern, Japanese	6-	9
Mickey Mouse	9-	23
Minnie Mouse	8-	17
Parrot, milk glass	7-	11
Pinocchio	18-	24
Santa, 5″, 6″, 6½″, 7″	7-	14
Santa, 8″, 8½″, 9″	40-	55
Snowman, 5½″, 6″, 7″	6-	16
Star, various sizes, 3″ to 6″	4-	18

Ornaments

Angel, carved wood, c. 1880s	35-	45
Angel, spun glass wings	7-	9
Beetle	8-	13
Basket of flowers	7-	10
Basket of flowers, carved wood,		
painted, c. 1880s	35-	45
Basket, pressed paper (holds		
candy)	20-	24
Bell, clip-on	6-	9
Bell, pressed paper	13-	17
Bell, red mercury glass	7-	10
Bird, cotton, clip-on	6-	9
Bird, spun glass tail	8-	12
Bugle, clip on	6-	9
Bugs Bunny	18-	24
Church, clip-on	10-	15
Church, mercury glass	7-	10

Christmas Collectibles/Ornaments

Clown head	6-	9
Crane, clip-on	6-	10
Fish, mercury glass	7-	10
Heart, red glass	7-	11
Horse, 5½″, 6½″, 8″	7-	19
Lion's head, pressed paper		
(holds candy)	20-	25
Owl, pressed paper	7-	11
Peacock, clip-on	9-	16
Pear, green glass	6-	9
Pipe, carved wood, painted, c.		
1880s	35-	45
Pipe, painted glass	7-	10
Santa, basket on back (holds		
candy)	33-	43
Santa, mercury glass	8-	13
Santa, open bag, pressed paper		
(ill.)	32-	39
Santa, pressed paper (ill.)	35-	43
Snowman, mercury glass	7-	11
Snowman, pressed paper (holds		
candy), Germany, c. 1900s	95-110	
Star, frosted glass	7-	11
Star, long shaft, for top of tree,		
9½″ overall	25-	33
George Washington, mercury		
glass	33-	43
George Washington, pressed		
paper	40-	50

These are indicative prices. Countless thousands are waiting to adorn your tree.

Christmas Plates

Bing and Grondahl and the Royal Copenhagen factories in Copenhagen, Denmark, make the best-known Christmas plates. Many American firms are now producing a plate.

Christmas Plates

1958	130-140	140-150
1959	165-172	140-150
1960	150-170	150-170
1961	250-280	139-150
1962	73- 83	210-220
1963	110-125	56- 66
1964	84- 92	52- 62
1965	70- 80	50- 60
1966 (ill.)	63- 70	60- 70
1967	61- 70	28- 38
1968	48- 58	25- 34
1969-79	37- 47	23- 33

Year	Frankoma	Bayreuther
1965	200-220	
1966	90-110	
1967	71- 80	98-107
1968	24- 32	37- 46
1970-79	28- 31	36- 43

Year	B&G	RC
1895	$ 3,900+	
1902	340-360	
1903	220-250	
1904	140-160	
1905	138-158	
1906	120-130	
1907	140-155	
1908	90-100	$ 2,300+
1909	115-140	142-153
1910	97-108	119-150
1911	100-108	144-148
1912	96-107	130-140
1913	94-104	138-148
1914	82- 92	130-138
1915	140-155	115-130
1916	98-115	118-132
1917-36	80- 90	95-115
1937	112-118	160-170
1938	122-132	270-280
1939	180-190	250-260
1940	170-178	460-475
1941	320-330	358-378
1942	165-180	420-460
1943	160-170	470-500
1944	105-108	220-238
1945	160-170	400-410
1946	81- 91	210-230
1947	96-115	250-270
1948	61- 65	145-170
1949	68- 78	150-180
1950	97-107	160-170
1951	90-100	300-325
1952	70- 80	140-150
1953	91-101	110-122
1954	80- 90	140-150
1955	95-107	260-270
1956	120-130	160-175
1957	150-160	115-128

Cigar Cutters, Pocket

Cigar Cutters, Pocket

When gentlemen wore vests and watch chains, the pocket-type cigar cutter was one of the attachments. Most were utilitarian but 14k gold and sterling silver models were much in vogue. A quality cigar always has to have the tip snipped off; a 5¢ stinker comes with the hole.

Combination cutter and knife
   blade, 10k gold . . . . $ 44- 53
Combination cutter and watch
   fob, 10k gold 43- 52
Combination cutter and small
   scissors, stainless steel 22- 30
Cutter, stainless steel, Germany
   (ill.) 14- 22
Cutter, embossed, 14k gold 170-190
(Note: It *isn't* the cutter, it's the
   price of the gold.)
Cutter, initialed, sterling silver . . 54- 62

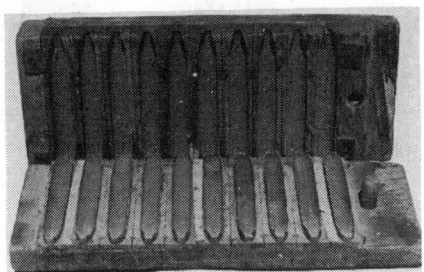

Cigar Molds

Cigar Molds

Used to shape the cigar in the early days, today they make pleasant items to hang in the kitchen or on a den wall.

Cigar molds, base metal, 2 pcs. . . $ 25- 35
Cigar molds, wood, 2 pcs. (ill.) . . . 32- 42
Cigar molds, wood, carved
"Havana's Best" on top lid . . . 44- 53

Cigar Store Figures

Cigar Store Figures

Used in America during the 19th century, almost life-size effigies of Indian braves and squaws were popular decorations outside tobacco shops. Other figures were also used. The practice comes from the Dutch who used this type figure to advertise tobacco in the 1600s. Also used in England in the 1600s.

Indian, 72" high $6,600-6,900
Indian chief, painted, 5'
  high . . . .   6,000+
Indian chief, small 5,700-5,900
Indian chief, wood painted,
  6½" high (R. ill.) 7,700-8,200
Indian chief, wood, painted
  4' high (L. ill.) 6,500-6,800
Indian maiden, 5' high 5,400-5,700
Indian squaw, wood,
  painted, half size 5,300-5,600
Turk, wood, painted 6,600-6,900

Cigarette Pictures

Cigarette Pictures

Pictures of actors, athletes and others were enclosed in packages of cigarettes in 1880s to the 1900s. Strollers Cigarettes was one of the companies that put one of these cards on each pack. Do you remember Ruth Roland, Renee Adoree, Gertrude Olmsted, Alice Terry, Ann Forrest and Hope Hampton?

Depending on celebrity, ea. . . . . .$ 1- 2

Cinnabar

Red lacquer built up slowly with layer after layer is called Cinnabar, the best coming from China in the late 17th century. It's made today any place in the Orient.

Bowl, red-brown, carved . . . .$ 82- 90
Box, red, carving on cover and
  sides, 4"×5" 70- 80
Button, lotus flower design, 4/5"
  dia. 25- 33
Plaque, red, carved, black and
  gold frame, 6"×7½" 44- 53
Snuff bottle, lacquer, floral, birds   130-142
Snuff bottle, red, white, jade top . 180-190
Vase, brass rim, top and bottom,
  pr. 192-199

Cinnabar

Vase, carved flowers on teakwood
   base, 8½" high, pr. (ill.) 360-380
Vase, carved overall floral and
   foliage design 132-141
Vase, trees, mountains, carved,
   8" high 112-121

Civil War Collectibles

Civil War Collectibles

Also called the War Between the States,
depending upon which side you were on. CSA
means Confederate States of America and
GAR means Grand Army of the Republic.
The Blue was the North and the Gray was
the South. "Rebs" were Southerners, those
who rebelled and joined Jeff Davis. "Blue
Bellies" were Union troops, so named
because the dye in their blue uniforms
stained their bellies blue.

Album, regimental photos, 8"×11"	$320-350
Bayonet w/scabbard, CSA	60- 70
Belt buckle, CSA, brass	36- 45
Bowie knife, bone handle, w/scabbard, marked "I*XL" ..	550-650
Bowie knife, ivory handle, w/scabbard, no marking	425-450
Box, cartridges, CSA imprint ...	32- 41
Canteen, cloth-over-wood	80- 90
Cap badge, GAR, enlisted man's .	50- 60
Cartridge pouch, GAR, leather ..	77- 86
Diary, private's account, 150th Regiment	160-180
Discharge paper from 1st Ohio Volunteers, dated June 15, 1863	60- 70
Holster w/belt, Dragoon imprint .	170-180
Horse's bit	24- 27
Knapsack, GAR	48- 57
Leather belt, brass buckle, GAR	51- 61
Naval cutlass, Confederate Navy, 26" serrated edges	195-210
Naval sword, dress, U.S. Navy, 35" long	220-280
Photograph, "Officers of Heavy Artillery" (ill.)	38- 50
Poster, asking recruits to join Glennon's Brigade, GAR	60- 70
Poster offering reward for GAR deserters	61- 71
Saddle bags, CSA, Virginia 1st Cavalry, pr.	260-280
Saddle, McClellan-type, w/saddle bags	245-260
Slave document, 1846, purchase of Becky from Christopher Hutchins by I.W. Rawlings ...	62- 72
Spurs, CSA, officer's	160-180
Telescope, U.S. Navy	250-350

Clambroth Glass

Its gray color, semi-opaque, supplies its
name. Popular during the Victorian era.

Barber bottle, Bay Rum, stopper	$ 23- 32
Candlestick, Sandwich glass, 1850s, 10" high (ill.)	265-280
Cruet, applied blue twisted handle	62- 71
Dish, footed, 8" dia.	28- 34
Egg cup, Diamond Point w/panels	119-122
Goblet, souvenir of Philadelphia, 7" high	28- 37
Toothpick holder, souvenir-type .	19- 28
Tumbler, souvenir-type	31- 40
Tumbler, whiskey	195-210
Vase, fluted top, 8½" high	71- 81

(continued)

Clambroth Glass

Clevenger Glass

Clevenger Glass

During the depression years of the 1930s, this glass was freehand blown—sugar bowls, vases, pitchers; in the 1940s it was mold blown. The Clevenger brothers, Tom, Lorenzo, and Allie, remained in business until the early 1960s. A few years later the shop was reopened and is still in business in Clayton, New Jersey. Early pieces are sought after by serious collectors.

Creamer, amethyst, swirl pattern,
    3½″ high (ill.) $100-110
Pitcher, aqua, expanded diamond
    pattern 105-118
Sugar bowl, amethyst, ribbed,
    3¾″ dia. (ill.) 88- 97

Clews, Ralph and James

Established in Cobridge, England, in 1814, this pottery operated until around 1835 when it was taken over by Wood and Brownfield. Dr. Syntax and the Valentine were two of the most popular subjects. Probably the most popular series was the states.

Creamer, 5½″, eagle on urn $115-122
Cups/saucers, dark blue, Landing
    of Lafayette 122-132
Gravy boat with tray, Landing
    of General Lafayette at Castle
    Gardens, N.Y., August 16,
    1824 260-280
Pitcher, dark blue, 13 original
    states, series, 8″ high 320-340
Plate, 9″ dia., dark blue, states
    series 185-210
Plate, 7¼″ dia., dark blue, Dr.
    Syntax Turned Nurse 235-260
Plate, 10″ dia., dark blue, Dr.
    Syntax and the Bees 220-240
Plate, 10½″ dia., black,
    Pittsburgh, Pa. 180-190
Plate, 9″ dia., Dr. Syntax
    Reading His Tour 240-260

Clocks

For a history of clocks, their current prices and a glossary of terms, see *Clock Guide, Identification with Prices,* Volumes I and II, Wallace-Homestead Book Co., Des Moines, Iowa, $8.95 and $9.95, each. All clocks listed here and many more can be seen there.

American-made, 30-hour, lever
    escapement, metal cased
    clock, time and strike . . . . . $ 150- 175
American-made desk calendar
    clock with alarm, metal case   75- 95
American-made electric table
    clock, carved wood case,
    1920s, time only 48- 58
American-made iron front
    shelf clock, possibly Seth
    Thomas 180- 195
American-made kitchen wall
    clock, 8-day, time only 70- 80
American-made metal cased
    clock, time and alarm 58- 67
American-made miniature
    cottage clock, time and
    alarm 145- 165
American-made Mission-type
    wall clock, green/white glass
    behind pendulum, time only   138- 160
American-made novelty tape
    measure clock, 30-hour 90- 125
American-made sterling silver
    bedside clock, 8-day, time
    and strike 95- 120
Ansonia Brass & Copper Co.,
    Ansonia, Conn., rosewood
    case, sharp Gothic, 8-day,
    time and strike, 1851-1878 .   310- 400
Ansonia Clock Co., brass table
    clock, 8-day, Pat. 1892 . . . .   210- 240

Ansonia Clock Co., bronze
figure mantel clock,
mercury, metal case, open
escapement, time and strike 615- 715
Ansonia Clock Co., Brooklyn,
N.Y., Chrystal Palace clock,
walnut base, mirrored sides,
8-day, time and strike 620- 710
Ansonia Clock Co., Crystal
Regulator, 8-day, time and
strike, mercury pendulum,
open escapement 355- 415
Ansonia Clock Co., Brooklyn,
N.Y., marble mantel clock,
matching candle stands on
either side 410- 500

Ansonia Regulator

Ansonia Clock Co., Regulator
wall clock, oak case, time
only, 1870s (ill.) 270- 345
Ansonia Clock Co., Regulator
wall clock, time and strike,
mahogany veneer 425- 500
Ansonia Clock Co., Brooklyn,
N.Y., round top table clock,
time and strike 140- 160
Ansonia Clock Co., statue
clock, cast metal case,
8-day, time and strike 310- 400
Ansonia Clock Co., walnut
shelf clock, King, 8-day,
time and strike 610- 700
Atkins Clock Co., Bristol,
Conn., miniature Empire
shelf clock, rosewood case,
stenciled tablet, 8-day brass

English Export or German Wall

movement, time, strike and
alarm, 1859-1879 . . . . 560- 650
Bradley & Hubbard Mfg. Co.,
Meriden, Conn., cast iron
case, stenciling with
mother-of-pearl inlay, clock
movement by Ansonia,
1854-1890 . . . . 350- 425
Birge, Mallory & Co., Bristol,
Conn., shelf clock, 8-day,
roller pinion, weight driven,
time and strike 620- 710
Brewster & Ingraham, Bristol,
Conn., walnut Gallery clock,
time only 395- 510
J. C. Brown (Forestville Mfg.
Co.), Bristol, Conn., steeple
fusee, mahogany veneer
with painted tablet, 8-day,
time and strike 395- 475
L. F. & W. W. Carter, Bristol,
Conn., walnut mantel clock,
8-day spring movement
with B. B. Lewis patented
calendar, 1862, time and
strike 1,850-2,500
Chelsea Clock Co., Chelsea,
Mass., wardroom clock,
U.S. Marine Corps on dial,
time only 260- 325
Darch Electric Clock Co.,
Chicago, Ill., flashlight and
alarm clock, 30-hour,
battery operated, Pat. 1910 110- 120

103

(continued)

Davis Clock Co., Columbus,
Miss., column flat top shelf
calendar, rosewood, (move-
made by Gilbert), 8-day,
time and strike 1,400-1,775

Dutch, porcelain hanging wall
clock, time only 80- 110

English carriage clock, brass
case, time and alarm 310- 400

English carriage clock, brass
case, time and strike 230- 275

English export or German
wall clock, box type, solid
oak, time and strike, age
and maker unknown (ill.)... 140- 170

English watchman's clock,
punch type, fusee move-
ment, walnut case 320- 395

Esberger Bros., Jeweler,
Cincinnati, alarm clock
made for their customers .. 70- 85

European case, American
movement wall clock,
walnut case, time and strike 230- 270

Chas. W. Fleichtinger, Sinking
Spring, Pa., oak case,
Victorian kitchen, shelf
calendar clock, 8-day, time
and strike 1,600-1,950

Forestville Clock Manufactory, Bristol, Conn. (one of
J.C. Brown's trade names),
triple-decker, carved top,
walnut case, painted
tablets, 8-day brass move-
ment, 1849-1853 1,150-1,650

French carriage clock, silver
case, repeater with alarm .. 260- 290

French desk clock, brass case
with finials, 8-day, time and
strike 300- 335

French shelf clock, gold gilt
with porcelain dial and cap,
1860-1870 .... 450- 540

French statue clock, brass,
marble, time and strike 375- 500

French statue clock, bronze
figure, porcelain inserts in
cast brass base, time and
strike 520- 600

French statue clock, bronze,
on marble base, time and
strike 550- 650

French statue clock, ormolu,
gilt 475- 565

Galusha Maranville, Winsted,
Conn., octagon drop wall,
calendar, rosewood, time
and strike, Pat. March 5,
1861 1,400-1,800

German game clock, cast
metal, time only 100- 125

German L.F.S. make, oak wall
clock, 8-day, time and
strike, 1890-1900s (ill.) 190- 245

German L.F.S.

German Miniature

German mantel clock, time
and strike 120- 140

German mantel set, 3-pc.,
bisque, time only 165- 200

German miniature carriage
clock, time and strike 155- 210

German, miniature, 8-day,
time and strike, oak case,
1880-1890 (ill.) 140- 180

German shelf clock, time and
strike 165- 210
German wall clock, time only . 140- 155
Gilbert L. Gilbert Clock Co.,
Winsted, Conn., kitchenette
model, light stenciling,
8-day, time only 120- 160
Wm. L. Gilbert Clock Co.,
Winsted, Conn., metal
cased, bronzed, mercury
pendulum, 8-day, time and
strike 340- 385
Wm. L. Gilbert Clock Co.,
Winsted, Conn., miniature
shelf clock, octagon top,
rosewood case, 1866-1871,
time only 165- 230
Wm. L. Gilbert Clock Co.,
Winsted, Conn., oak wall
clock, 8-day, time, strike
and alarm Elipse 440- 515
Gilbert Mfg. Co., rosewood
case, steeple, 30-hour, time
and strike, dated 1868 . . . . 240- 280
Elisha Hotchkiss, Jr., Burlington, Conn., mantel
clock, wooden movement,
30-hour, weight driven, time
and strike 450- 535
Robert H. Ingersoll & Bros.,
Waterbury, Conn., and
Trenton, N.J., alarm clock . 65- 80
E. Ingraham & Co., Bristol,
Conn., Doric rosewood
mantel clock, 8-day, time
and strike, Pat. 1871 . . . . . . 350- 435
E. Ingraham & Co., Bristol,
Conn., night and day alarm
clock 85- 100
Ingraham Clock Co., Bristol,
Conn., oak shelf clock,
8-day, time and strike 175- 250
E. Ingraham & Co., Bristol,
Pa., walnut kitchen clock,
time and strike, 1890-1910 . 340- 375
The Ingraham Co., Bristol,
Conn., kitchen shelf clock,
oak case, time and alarm,
early 1900s (ill.) 190- 240
International Time Recording
Co. (later became part of
IBM) time clock 210- 265
Ithaca Calendar Clock Co.,
Ithaca, N.Y., #3½ walnut
parlor calendar clock, black
dials, etched glass pendu-
lum bob, time and strike . . . 4,700-5,500
Ithaca Calendar Clock Co.,
Ithaca, N.Y., #4½,
Favorite calendar clock,
walnut case, gold letters,
time and strike 2,800-3,450

Ingraham Kitchen (Shelf)

Ithaca Calendar Clock Co.,
Emerald #5, walnut case,
open carving, time and
strike 2,900-3,350
Ithaca Calendar Clock Co., #5
round top, rosewood case,
30-day, time only 2,200-2,775
Ithaca Calendar Clock Co.,
Ithaca, N.Y., #11 octagon,
black walnut calendar clock,
8-day, time, strike and
alarm 1,850-2,650
Ithaca Calendar Clock Co., #9
shelf-cottage clock, per-
petual calendar, time and
strike 1,975-2,600
Ithaca Calendar Clock Co., #10
Farmer's model, perpetual
calendar, time and strike . . 825- 990
Ithaca Calendar Clock Co.,
Bellgrade model, walnut
case, wooden pendulum
hangs in front of calendar
movement, time and strike . 2,250-2,600
Ithaca Calendar Clock Co.,
large Index model, walnut
case, "Index" letters in
gold, made for Lynch
Brothers, 8-day, time and
strike 2,900-3,650
Ithaca Calendar Clock Co.,
small Index model, walnut
case, "Index" letters in
gold, made for Lynch
Brothers, 8-day time and
strike 2,750-3,200

(continued)

Ithaca Calendar Clock Co., Ithaca, N.Y., walnut shelf steeple calendar clock, fretwork under dials, 8-day, time and strike, 1870s 3,000-3,600

Chauncey Ives, Bristol, Conn., Pillar and Scroll clock, wooden movement, mahogany veneer case, painted tablet 2,550-3,000

F. W. Jansen, Chicago, Ill., Nitelite alarm clock 80- 90

C. Jerome, Bristol, Conn., miniature cottage clock, mahogany veneer, time and alarm 185- 235

Jerome & Co. (trade name used by New Haven Clock Co.), Christmas Tree kitchen clock, time and strike 320- 395

Jerome Mfg. Co., New Haven, Conn., mahogany miniature steeple, 30-hour, time and alarm, 1845-1850s 220- 275

F. Kroeber Clock Co., New York City, miniature timepiece 145- 190

R. Lalique (French) table clock, pressed glass case, cut glass dial, battery operated, signed R. Lalique, 1890s 220- 290

Lux Clock Mfg. Co., Waterbury, Conn., Cupid novelty clock, time and strike 160- 190

Lux Clock Mfg. Co., Waterbury, Conn., Show Boat alarm clock; paddle wheel on steamboat revolved with balance wheel, animated dial 75- 110

Mission wall clock, oak case, time only 125- 145

Mission wall clock, time and strike 135- 160

Nicholas Muller's Sons, New York City, flat top black marble mantel clock, outside escapement, time and strike 145- 175

National Watch Co., Elgin, Ill., 8-day car clock 90- 125

New Haven Clock Co., bronze figure mantel clock, 8-day, time and strike 400- 465

New Haven Clock Co., chime mantel clock 160- 180

New Haven Clock Co., New Haven, Conn., small Gothic, mahogany veneer, 30-hour, time and alarm 195- 235

New Haven Clock Co., oak kitchen clock, time, strike and alarm 210- 245

New Haven Clock Co., statue clock, cast metal case, black wood base, open escapement, time and strike 475- 550

New Haven Clock Co., New Haven, Conn., statue-type clock, 8-day, gold dipped, time and strike 185- 250

New Haven Clock Co., walnut shelf clock, 8-day, time and strike 200- 275

New Haven Clock Co., walnut shelf clock, Etna, turned columns, time and strike .. 420- 485

New Haven Clock Co., wood base, brass case, time and intermittent alarm 95- 135

Perry & Shaw, New York City, shelf clock, wooden dial, 30-hour, weight driven, time and strike 260- 320

Daniel Pratt & Co., Reading, Mass., mahogany beehive, 8-day, time and strike, 1832-46 .... 420- 465

Sandoz-Wullie, Swiss, 8-day car clock 85- 120

Sangamo Corp., Springfield, Ill. (subsidiary jointly owned by Hamilton Watch Co. and Sangamo Electric Co.), Sangamo electric clock 185- 215

Sangamo Electric Co., Springfield, Ill., Sangamo electric clock, mahogany case, 11-jewel Illinois watch movement, 1926-1928 ..... 210- 260

Sessions Clock Co., Forestville, Conn., mantel advertising clock, calendar type, originally had Calumet Baking Co. on front 460- 535

Sessions Clock Co., Forestville, Conn., iron front case, brass trim, 8-day, time and strike 140- 170

Sessions Clock Co. (Forestville), Bristol, Conn., oak kitchen clock, Hiawatha, 8-day, time and strike 220- 275

Seth Thomas, black iron front mantel clock, twin marbleized columns on each side, time and strike 225- 275

Seth Thomas, Thomaston, Conn., chronometer lever (ship's type), clock, nickelplated, 15-day 525- 635

Seth Thomas Clock Co.,
Thomaston, Conn., column
gold leaf and gilt columns,
painted tablets, Empire
style, 8-day brass move-
ment, Pat. 1867, time and
strike 900- 975

Seth Thomas cottage clock,
rosewood case, 8-day, strike
and alarm 325- 380

Seth Thomas, parlor #1,
calendar clock, model #1,
mahogany veneer, 8-day,
time and strike   950-1,400

Seth Thomas, Eclipse walnut
kitchen clock, 8-day, time,
strike and alarm 425- 500

Seth Thomas electric chime
clock 115- 140

Seth Thomas, Thomaston,
Conn., engine room clock,
8-day, brass, Pat. April 16,
1878, time only 625- 700

Seth Thomas Clock Co.,
Fashion calendar clock,
Model #5, long pendulum,
made for Dixie Calendar
Clock Co.   3,100-3,550

Seth Thomas, Fashion, model
#2, walnut veneer, made for
Southern Calendar Clock
Co., St. Louis, Mo., 8-day,
time and strike   3,300-3,800

Seth Thomas, Fashion, model
#4, walnut case, made for
Southern Calendar Clock
Co., St. Louis, Mo., Fashion
in gold letters on door,
8-day, time and strike   3,300-3,750

Seth Thomas, Thomaston,
Conn., long alarm, metal
case, 8-day, time and alarm   170- 210

Seth Thomas, oak wall clock,
Regulator, #1, weight
driven, time only   1,300-1,500

Seth Thomas, oak case,
chimes and strikes on bells,
8-day, 1918 . . . .   175- 225

Seth Thomas Clock Co., reproduction Pillar and Scroll,
walnut case, brass 8-day
movement, 1929-1934, time
and strike 220- 250

Seth Thomas Clock Co.,
Plymouth Hollow, Conn.,
rosewood case, hexagon
columns, stenciled tablets,
8-day weight movement,
time and strike 510- 580

Seth Thomas, round top shelf
clock with full pillars, 8-day,
time, strike and alarm 300- 375

Seth Thomas Clock Co.,
Plymouth Hollow, Conn.,
shelf clock, calendar, rosewood case, hexagon
columns, stenciled tablet,
8-day weight movement,
time and strike   2,700-3,000

Seth Thomas Standard OG,
mahogany veneer, 30-hour,
time and strike 425- 525

Seth Thomas Clock Co.,
walnut calendar clock,
parlor #5, 8-day, time and
strike   1,800-2,450

Seth Thomas and Sons,
Thomaston, Conn., walnut
shelf clock, with fretwork,
time, strike and alarm 340- 400

United Electric Co., Brooklyn,
N.Y., FDR—The Man of the
Hour clock, animated dial,
bartender's arm shakes
drink, 30-hour, time and
alarm 175- 200

United Electric Co. Brooklyn,
N.Y., FDR—The Man of the
Hour clock, plain dial, 30-
hour, time and alarm 150- 170

Vienna Regulator wall clock,
baby 2-weight, time and
strike 620- 695

Waltham Watch & Clock Co.,
Waltham, Mass., 8-day car
clock 90- 110

Waterbury Clock Co., Waterbury, Conn., calendar #43,
walnut clock, 8-day, 1860s,
time and strike   1,800-2,450

Waterbury Clock Co., carriage
clock, 8-day, strike and
repeat 265- 320

Waterbury Clock Co., metal
cased, bronze figure mantel
clock, time and strike 300- 385

Waterbury Clock Co., metal
cased mantel clock, outside
escapement, time and strike   175- 210

Waterbury Clock Co., Waterbury, Conn., miniature OG,
mahogany veneer, gold-
leafed inner frame, 30-hour,
time and strike 260- 310

Waterbury Clock Co., miniature schoolhouse clock,
time only 210- 270

(continued)

Waterbury Clock Co., oak
kitchen clock with barom-
eter and thermometer, time
and strike   300-   400
Waterbury Clock Co.,
Waterbury, Conn., shelf
clock, open pendulum, time
and strike   170-   220
Waterbury Clock Co., Water-
bury, Conn., walnut kitchen
clock, time, strike and alarm   250-   310
Waterbury Clock Co., walnut
shelf clock, 8-day, time and
strike, mercury pendulum .   325-   400
Waterbury Clock Co., walnut
shelf clock, 8-day, time and
strike   270-   345
Waterbury Clock Co., Water-
bury, Conn., walnut shelf
clock, 8-day, time and strike   225-   275
Waterbury Clock Co., walnut
shelf clock, time and strike .   210-   260
E. N. Welch, chestnut shelf
clock, Coghland, time,
strike and alarm, 1864-1903   325-   400
E. N. Welch (Forestville),
Bristol, Conn., La Reine,
1-day desk clock, lever
escapement, brass plated,
Pat. Sept. 17, Oct. 11, 1878 .   165-   210
E. N. Welch, Bristol, Conn.,
paperweight clock, octagon
lever, duplex movement,
emerald green glass case,
30-hour   350-   425
E. N. Welch, pressed oak
shelf clock, Robert E. Lee,
time and strike, 1864-1903 .   475-   555
E. N. Welch, shelf clock,
mahogany veneer, painted
tablet, 8-day, time and
strike   220-   270
E. N. Welch Mfg. Co., Bristol,
Conn., small cast iron valise
clock, 30-hour   75-   90
E. N. Welch Mfg. Co., Forest-
ville, Conn., walnut kitchen
clock, time and strike, 1864-
1903   275-   320
E. N. Welch, Bristol, Conn.,
walnut shelf clock, full, open
columns, time and strike . .   475-   560
Welch, Spring & Co., Bristol,
Conn., Lucca shelf clock,
rosewood case, 8-day, time
and strike   360-   425
Welch, Spring & Co., Bristol,
Conn., Patti movement,
rosewood case, 8-day, time
and strike, 1870   600-   675

Welch, Spring & Co., Bristol,
Conn., wall clock, rosewood
case, painted tablet, time
only   475-   560
Western Clock Mfg. Co.,
Westclox alarm clock   50-   60
Western Clock Co., La Salle,
Ill., Westclox alarm,
30-hour   40-   50
Western Clock Co., Westclox,
Baby Ben alarm   30-   38
Western Clock Co., Westclox,
Big Ben alarm   42-   55
Western Clock Mfg. Co., inter-
mediate Big Ben alarm
clock   35-   45
Western Clock Co., Westclox
miniature alarm   33-   43
Western Clock Mfg. Co.,
La Salle, Ill., Waralarm,
made during World War II .   63-   73
Western Clock Mfg. Co.,
Waralarm clock   35-   45
Western Clock Co., La Salle,
Ill., Westclox ironclad
alarm clock   33-   42

Cloisonne Enamel

Cloisonne Enamel

Developed during the 19th century, glass
enamel was applied between small ribbon-like
pieces of metal on a metal base. Supposedly
from Japan, most of what is found in shops
today is European and brought into the U.S.
between 1870 and 1900.

Ashtray, dragon motif, China,
3½" dia. . . . . $ 23-   31

Ashtray, enameled, matchbox
holder attached, China,
5" dia. . . . .　30-　35
Bowl, brown ground, multi-
colored floral design, chop
mark . . . .　78-　86
Bowl, green/red, China, 4" dia.　38-　43
Box, black ground, yellow/
green/red, dragon, 3"
square, early . . . .　40-　48
Candlesticks, black/blue/
green, dragon motif, 11"
high, pr. . . . .　120- 130
Clock w/two yellow urns, other
colors include blue, pink,
green, clock 11" to top of
finial . . . .　2,350-2,475
Decanter, usual color . . . .　38-　43
Desk blotter, blue/green, roll
type, China . . . .　30-　37
Dish, floral design, Oriental
motif, chop mark . . . .　45-　54
Dish, yellow, dragon, 5" dia.,
China . . . .　50-　55
Ginger jar, blue ground, red
flowers, cover, chop mark . .　120- 135
Incense burner, Foo Dog, 10"
high, China . . . .　50-　59
Napkin ring, blue ground,
birds, China . . . .　25-　30
Pitcher, black ground, butter-
flies, birds, floral, chop
mark . . . .　165- 175
Plate, blue, flowers, 11" dia.,
China . . . .　48-　55
Plate, Japanese, blue/red/
green, 6½" dia., chop mark .　68-　78
Snuff bottle, blue ground,
Buddhist emblems, stopper,
chop mark . . . .　150- 165
Teapot, brown ground,
flowers, 7" high, chop mark　100- 120
Teapot, yellow ground, cane
handle, chop mark . . . .　75-　85
Tray, Japanese, morning
glories, fruit, bamboo
pattern, brass rim, 12" dia.,
China . . . .　235- 250
Urn, Japanese, covered,
bronze finial, floral design,
2½" high, 2¼" dia., China .　65-　75
Vase, beige ground, turquoise/
gold, dragons, 11" high
(ill.) . . . .　155- 165
Vase, blue ground, butterflies,
chop mark . . . .　175- 185

Clothing

Old frock tailcoats and dresses of the same

Clothing

period are in demand today. Most of what
you find in attics and shops is from the late
1800s and early 1900s. World War I uniforms are much in demand. Nazi uniforms
are becoming collectible.

Coat, coonskin, 1920s $325-350
Dress, homespun, early 1800s . . .　32- 41
Gowns, silk, velvet, lace, puffed
sleeves . . . .　40- 50
Neckpieces, fox or mink, foot
snaps . . . .　27- 37
Top hat, black silk, collapsible
type, Brooks Bros. (ill.) . . . .　42- 52
Swallowtail coat, velvet lapels,
early 1900s . . . .　69- 78

Coal Hods

Lugging coal from out-of-doors was a pain
in the 1800s, but at least the hods were
decorative. Usually black with bright flowers
and birds, the coal hod stood out in every
room.

Stamped iron, black, removable
liner, flowers/birds, claw feet . . $ 75- 92
Tin/copper, painted with remov-
able liner, flower motif, 17½"
high . . . .　75- 95
These are average prices.

Coalport

The factory operated at Coalport, England,
from the late 1700s until 1926, since then at
Stoke-on-Trent, making bone china.

Bowl, fruit, blue fluted and
ruffled sides, castle scene . . . . . $ 75- 85

(continued)

Chocolate pot, Indian Tree, rose/
green foliage, 6 cups and
saucers 170-180
Cup/saucer, black/orange floral
on white 24- 32
Cup/saucer, Indian Tree 34- 42
Dish, floral decor, 1820, 9¼"
square 92-107
Letter holder, 1820, rose/green . . 160-170
Mug, leaf design, white, 4½" high 80- 90
Pitcher, Indian Tree, 5" high 77- 87
Plate, Indian Tree, scalloped,
7½", set of 6 . . . . 77- 84
Platter, Indian Tree, 13" 60- 69
Salt/pepper, Indian Tree, beehive
shape, pr. 47- 54
Tea service, blue banding, gilt,
pink blossoms, approximately
30 pcs. 440-480
Trivet, Indian Tree 48- 57
Vase, 6", cobalt, gold trim,
handled 110-130

Coat of Arms

Coats of Arms

Mentioned here because too many firms,
both in America and in Europe, guarantee to
trace your family's heritage. The New
England Register's Roll of Arms is a reliable
firm. Too many firms are not reliable, are in
business only to get your money. Many
families can be traced, but it's expensive and
if you're a Miller, Johnson, Smith, or Jones,
save your money. If you don't know where
your family came from, read Darwin's
Theory. See **Genealogy.**

Coca-Cola Collectibles

Coca-Cola Collectibles

Anything with "Coke" or "Coca-Cola" on it
is highly sought after today. The prices are
high, too.

Ashtrays, all sizes, all years, ea. . . . . $	9-	65
Bingo board, 1930s	14-	20
Binoculars, 1910	150-	160
Blotter, 1930	6-	10
Blotters, 1900s-1920s, ea.	17-	55
Book, *Know Your War Planes,* 1943	30-	40
Book, *Pause for Living,* 1960s	8-	13
Bottle openers, 1910-20s, ea. . .	29-	40
Buddy Lee doll, deliveryman, 1928, 12½" high	153-	170
Calendar, 1975	3-	5
Calendars, 1900-08, complete .	625-	675
Calendars, 1909-15, complete .	460-	525
Carrying tray, 1915	75-	90
Case, miniature, 28 bottles, gold finish	36-	45
Case, wooden, 24 bottles, c. 1920	10-	15
Cigarette case, 50th anniversary, 1936	140-	160
"Coke Can" radio, 1971	36-	45
Comb, "Drink Coca-Cola 5¢" .	22-	27
Coupons, good for one free bottle of Coca-Cola, 1900 . .	116-	128
Coupons, same deal, 1920s . . .	45-	58
Cribbage board, 1930	34-	44
Dominoes, 1940	25-	37
Glass, drinking, 1900	180-	187
Glass, drinking, 1905 (ill.)	155-	180
Glass, drinking, 1921	45-	58
Glass, drinking, 1930s, pewter	58-	67
Glass holder, 1901 (ill.)	300-	325

110

Key fob, bulldogs, 1½"×1", metal, 1925	98-	115
Key fob, 1½" dia., celluloid, 1900	279-	299
Key fob, oval, 1¾"×1¼", 1906	253-	268
Knife, switchblade type, 1909	80-	95
Leaded glass globe, hanging type, late 1920s	3,300-3,600	
Mechanical pencil, 1930	33-	43
Menus, 1900-05, "Hilda Clark," ea.	162-	176
Milk glass shade, dome light, 10" dia., 1920s	415-	445
Miniature plastic bottle and case, 1970	14-	19
Mirror, "Girl in bonnet," 1914	140-	160
Needle cases (held sewing needles), 1920s, ea.	44-	54
Night light, "Courtesy of your C-C Bottler," 1945	12-	19
Pencil sharpeners, 1930s-60s, ea.	14-	34
Playing cards, 1909-27, ea. deck	65-	75
Playing cards, 1930-40s, ea. deck	21-	34
Postcard, "Coca-Cola Delivery Truck," 1915	70-	85
Pretzel dish, "Coke" bottles for legs, 1936	51-	60
Radio, shaped like drink box, 1949	169-	174
Radio, shaped like "Coke" bottle, 24" high, 1930	285-	298
Seltzer bottles, 1900-20s, ea. .	58-	70
Sheet music, "Old Folks at Home," "The Palms," "Rock Me to Sleep, Mother," "Juanita," "My Old Kentucky Home," ea. .	130-	145
Sign, 8" dia., glass, 1915	95-	125
Sign, 30"×7¾", tin, in shape of arrow, 1927	98-	130
Sign, tin, 15"×18½", "Hilda Clark," 1904	1,575-1,700	
Syrup bottles, 1910-20s, ea. . .	150-	175
Take home carton, late 1930s .	35-	45
Toy drink dispenser, 1960 . . .	98-	115
Toy stove, electrified, 1938 . . .	175-	190
Thermometers, 1930-50s, ea. .	44-	53
Thimble, aluminum, 1920	36-	43
Tray, "bottle," 9¾" dia., 1900	865-	945
Tray, girl in yellow bathing suit, 1937	45-	53
Tray, 8½"×19½", "Elaine," 1917	120-	138
Tray, oval, "Hilda Clark," 18½"×15", 1904	965-1,250	
Tray, 10" dia., "Vienna Art," 1905	168-	183

Tray, 10½"×13¼", farm boy w/dog, 1931	78-	92

Coffee Grinders

Coffee Grinders

This product was made for the wall, the lap and the table, of glass, metal, or wood. When ready-made coffee came on the market in the 1920s, out went the grinder. The large wheel types are in demand today.

Arcade, iron and glass	$ 47-	56
Box type, Stobridge	68-	75
Dovetail, Arcade Manufacturing Co., wood and iron	60-	70
Drawer, wooden base	60-	69
Glass container, iron, Enterprise	34-	42
Iron base, patented July 12, 1898, Enterprise	152-162	
Iron, early	60-	70
Lap type, cherry box, brass crank (ill.)	75-	85
Lap type, metal, 7½" high, 6" wide	60-	70
Lap type, wooden, iron dome top	62-	72
Lap type, handled, cherry (ill.) . . .	77-	87
Pewter bin, dovetailed, brass knob, signed W. W. Weaver . . .	93-106	
Store type, signed Enterprise Manufacturing Co., 1873, 12" high	94-103	
Table model, drawer, iron and wood, 6½" high	200-240	
Turn crank, drawer, iron	70-	80
Two wheels, red, Cole Manufacturing Co., Philadelphia	550-675	

Repros all over the place!

Coins, American

The gold and silver market is still fluctuating badly and it's having the usual effect on collectible coins. The best way to protect yourself is to do business with a reliable

111

(continued)

Coins, American

dealer. Remember, the bullion prices of gold and silver dictate the value here.

Kennedy half dollar, 1964 (ill.) . . . $ 6- 8
Large copper cent, 1851 (ill.) 6- 9
$10 gold piece, Liberty Head,
1907 (ill.) 360-400
$5 gold piece, Liberty Head, 1883,
(ill.) 190-225

Coins, Elongated, Rolled Out

Earlier ones were rolled out or pressed by hand. The Franklin Institute in the 1930s had a machine that, for 10¢, would deliver a coin with your choice of The Lord's Prayer or St. Christopher Protect Us on it. How many pennies were elongated or rolled out is unknown.

Lord's Prayer on copper penny . . $ 6- 10
St. Christopher Protect Us 6- 10

Coins, Foreign

Consult a reliable coin dealer and study your catalogs. Generally speaking, unless the coins are silver or gold, they have no real value.

Top Row
Commemorative, 400th anniver-
sary, William Shakespeare's
birth, 1964, silver (ill.) . . . . $ 15- 19
Thaler, Maria Theresa, reeled
edge, silver (ill.) 14- 20
Commemorative, 175th anniver-
sary, Wolfgang Mozart,
1751-1931, Austria (ill.) 35- 43
Bottom Row
Peso, Mexican, 1964, silver (ill.) . . 1.50- 2
Ireland, silver, 1966 (ill.) 10- 14

Coins, Elongated, Rolled Out

Coins, Foreign

Coin Spot Glass

Collar Boxes

Coin Spot Glass

Opalescent spots in the glass that look like coins. Light blue, clear, cranberry, amethyst. In mid-1800s, many firms made it.

Bowl, ruffled edges, 6" dia.	$ 32- 42
Bride's basket, opalescent spots .	180-200
Cruet, light blue	79- 88
Pitcher and 6 glasses, blue and white (pitcher, ill.)	230-240
Shade, light blue, 8¼" high	90-120
Shade, white, ruffled, 6½" high ..	42- 50
Sugar shaker, cranberry, opalescent spots	61- 70
Syrup, cranberry, handled, pewter cap	68- 78
Tumbler, light blue...........	32- 41
Tumbler, red with opalescent spots....................	66- 76
Tumbler, amethyst with opalescent spots ....:	65- 75
Vase, amethyst, 7½" high	84- 93
Vase, cranberry with opalescent spots....................	120-140

Collar Boxes

Few things were more uncomfortable in "the good old days" than collars. When they weren't being worn, they were stored in these boxes which are now collectible.

Camel back hinged box, 6½" wide, 5" high (ill.)	$ 17- 26
Imitation seal grained leather, 5⅜" high, 6¼" dia.	16- 25
Horseshoe novelty shape, transparent celluloid, 6¾" high	19- 27

Square shape, tinted celluloid, cover embellished with gilt, 2 compartments within, satin lined, 6⅞" overall 24- 34

Collectors' Plates

Workmanship, who made it, the artwork itself, how many in the "limited" edition? Those are the important things to know **before** you buy and/or invest in collectors' plates. Less than 10,000 in a limited edition would be a good buy. Always check the hallmark on the underside.

American Crystal

1969—Astronaut ....$	36-	44
1970—Christmas	38-	47
1971—Christmas	30-	40
1971—Mother's Day	29-	38

American Sterling

1971—Christmas Customs .	29-	38
1971—Mother's Day	28-	37
1971—12 Days of Christmas	28-	36

Anri (Italy)

1971—Birthday	59-	69
1971—Christmas	132-	140
1971—Plaque, carved	55-	64
1972—Father's Day	52-	61
1972—Mother's Day	50-	60
1974—Mother's Day	70-	80

August, Wendell

1972—Columbus, pewter ..	80-	90
Sterling silver	362-	374
1972—Kennedy, pewter ...	64-	72
Sterling silver	290-	310

(continued)

1972—Pilgrim, pewter	54-	64
Sterling silver	290-	310

Bareuther (Bavaria)

1968—Christmas	41-	50
1969—Christmas	32-	41
1969—Mother's Day......	62-	70
1969—Father's Day	64-	74
1970—Christmas	28-	34
1971—Mother's/Father's ..	22-	31
1972—Mother's/Father's ..	28-	29
1973—Christmas	31-	40

Belleek (Ireland)

1970—Christmas, Castle Caldwell	126-	132
1971—Christmas, Celtic Cross	50-	60
1972—Christmas, Flights of the Earls	58-	67

Berlin (Germany)

1970—Christmas	144-	152
1971—Christmas	37-	45
1971—Christmas stein	38-	47
1971—Father's Day	29-	38
1971—Mother's Day......	31-	40
1972—Olympic	27-	37
1974—Christmas	42-	50

Bing & Grondahl (also see Christmas Plates)

1969—Poster Plaque	19-	27
1969—Mother's Day......	355-	400
1970—Jubilee	52-	61
1971—Jubilee	58-	67
1971—Mother's Day......	26-	35
1972—Mother's Day......	28-	32

Boehm (U.S.A.)

1972—Mute Swans.......	475-	525
1973—Eaglet	240-	260

Burgues (limited edition)

Carolina wren w/dogwood .	1,000+
Chipmunk w/fly amanita ..	500+
Golden-wing warbler on nest	1,700+
White-throated sparrow ...	1,150+

Cartier

1972—Annual Cathedral plate	88-	97

Castle

1970—Fountainbleu	34-	43
1971—Fountainbleu	38-	47

Church

1968—Christmas	28-	37
1969—Christmas	26-	36
1970—Christmas	21-	31

Cybis (limited edition)

Chinese goddess	1,700-2,100
Clematis w/house wren	2,100+
Hamlet	2,100+
Hiawatha	1,750+
Limnettes—Wonderful Seasons, set of 4	700- 850
Minnehaha	1,900-2,200

Nashua	3,100+
Sacagawea	4,200+
Stallion	700- 800
Tranquility Base	2,200+

Cybis (non-limited edition)

Buffalo	59-	67
Bunny	38-	46
Colts	340-	360
Deer mouse	92-	106
Eskimo child's head	200-	240
First Flight	60-	64
Heidi	150-	162
Madonna 5"	62-	72
Madonna with bird	184-	195
Magnolia...............	240-	270
Mushroom	260-	280
Owl	50-	60
Pandora	128-	137
Pinto colt	192-	200
Wood wren w/dogwood....	170-	180

Dali, Salvador

1971—Lincoln Mint	160-	170

Daum (France)

1972—Four Seasons, set of 4		675+
Bach & Beethoven, pr.	140-	180

Delft, Blue

1969—First Men around Moon................	39-	48
1969—First Men on Moon .	41-	50
1970—Christmas	19-	27
1970—Mother's Day......	15-	24
1970—Pilgrim Fathers	18-	27
1971—Mother's Day......	15-	24
1971—Father's Day	20-	27
1972—Father's Day	19-	28

Delft, Royal (Holland)

1971—Mother's Day......	68-	78
1972—Commemorative, Apollo 8..............	27-	36

Donaldo

1968—John F. Kennedy ...	31-	41

Doughty

1972—Birds	425-	475
1973—Birds	385-	420

Ellard

1970—Thanksgiving, first edition	40-	50
1971—Thanksgiving, Home in the New World	30-	40

Fenton

1970—Christmas, Little Brown Church.........	21-	30
1970—Christmas, marble ..	22-	31
1970—Glass Blower	19-	27
1970—Mother's Day	24-	33
1971—Printer	18-	27
1971—Valentine	24-	35
1972-3—Mother's Day	21-	30

114

Collectors' Plates   Photo Courtesy Franklin Mint

Franklin Mint (sterling silver)

1970—Rockwell Annual . . .	670-	770
1971—Rockwell Christmas Annual	375-	475
1972—Cardinal	195-	220
1972—Rockwell Christmas (ill.)	240-	250
1973—Easter, The Resurrection, 22k		4,600+

Frankoma

1965—Good Will Towards Men	240-	270
1966—Bethlehem Shepherds	81-	90
1967—Gifts for Christ Child	70-	80
1968—Flight Into Egypt . .	24-	32
1969—Cherokee alphabet plate	10-	13
1969—Laid in a Manger . . .	12-	18
1969—Oklahoma plate	11-	21
1969—VIP bottle vase	38-	47
1973—Bicentennial	18-	27

Fuerstenberg

1971—Christmas, Rabbits .	25-	32
1972—Easter, Chicks	24-	33
1972—Mother's Day	26-	35
1973—Mother's Day	21-	30

Gorham

1971—Rockwell, 4 seasons (4 plates)	165-	270
1972—Rockwell, 4 seasons (4 plates)	150-	198
First Edition—Rockwell, butter girl	97-	106

Granget (limited edition)

Bobwhite quail	3,400-3,900
Canada geese	4,200-4,500
Great blue heron	8,400-8,700
Hairy woodpecker	3,000-3,300
Mallards	2,900-3,300
Mourning doves	1,800-2,100
Pintails	3,400-3,700
Ring-necked pheasants	5,800+
Screech owl	3,200-3,400
Woodcocks	1,500-1,700

115

(continued)

Granget (non-limited edition)

1972—Christmas, European glaze, finish	60-	68
1973—Spring	85-	94

Haviland (France)

Abraham Lincoln	105-	108
Martha Washington	42-	51
1970—Christmas, partridge		125+
1971—Dancing angels	27-	37
1971—Partridge	41-	50
1971—Rutherford B. Hayes		120+
1971—President Grant	122-	131
1971—President Lincoln	140-	160
1971—Unicorn tapestry	140-	150
1972—Unicorn tapestry	97-	107
1974-5-6—Independence series	70-	80

Hummel, Berta

1971—Christmas, angel		1,700+
1972—Mother's Day, Hooky	120-	130

Hutchenreuther

Dancing girls (white)	170-	180
Geese in flight	340-	360
Peacock	132-	141
Pheasants	162-	178
Song birds of America, set of 2	190-	220
Stag and dog (color)	220-	240

Imperial

1969—America the Beautiful, red Carnival	38-	46
1970—America the Beautiful, green Carnival	40-	50
1970—Christmas, Carnival	20-	30
1971—Christmas, Carnival	27-	36
1971—Christmas, Doeskin	29-	37
1971—Coin plate, Crystal	30-	40

Ispanky (limited edition)

The Hunt (decorated)		2,700+
Jessamy	525-	625
King Arthur	370-	420
Morning	560-	640
Orchids	1,400-	1,800
Owl	850-	975

Ispanky (non-limited edition)

Elizabeth	175-	186
Huck Finn	150-	160
Peter Pan	149-	160
Prudence	150-	160

Israel

1967—Tower of David	24-	32
1967—Wailing Wall	24-	33
1968—Masada	22-	31
1969—Rachel's Tomb	17-	27
1970—Lake of Galilee	18-	28
1973—Acre	19-	27

Jensen, Svend

1970—Mother's Day	78-	88
1971—Mother's Day	80-	90

Collectors' Plates

Kaiser (Bavaria)

1970—Passion Play	24-	33
1970—Royal Horse Show	29-	38
1970—Christmas, first edition	44-	52
1971—Christmas	27-	36
1971—Mother's Day, first edition	34-	43
1972—Mother's Day	21-	30
1973—Yacht, "Cetonia"	74-	81

Kirk

1972—Thanksgiving	128-	140
1972—Washington	150-	180
1972—Mother's Day	162-	180
1973—Christmas	174-	185
1973—Mother's Day	140-	165

Lalique (France)

1965—Crystal		1,785+
1965—Annual		2,250+
1967—Annual	170-	190
1968—Annual	120-	135
1969—Annual	110-	120
1970—Annual	90-	100
1971—Annual	75-	85
1972—Annual	72-	82
1973—Annual	78-	88

Lincoln Mint (sterling silver)

1971—Dali, Don Quixote	250-	300
1972—Dali, Dionysus	185-	240
1972—Easter, Dali, gold-on-silver	178-	245
1972—Madonna Della, sterling	250-	300

Lindner, Doris (limited edition)

Aberdeen Angus	770-	840
Charolais bull	840-	865
Dairy Shorthorn	950-	1,200
Hereford bull	800-	900

116

Jersey bull	825-	925
Jersey cow	800-	900
Quarter horse	915-	925
Shire stallion	1,900+	

Lladro (Spain)

1971—Christmas	52-	61
1971—Mother's Day	120-	130
1972—Mother's Day	50-	60
1973-74—Mother's Day	72-	81

Marmot

1970—Christmas, Polar Bear	60-	70
1970—Father's Day, Stag	28-	38
1970—Stag Plaque	34-	42
1971—Christmas, Buffalo	27-	36
1971—Father's Day, Horse	20-	30
1971—President Washington	34-	40
1972—Mother's Day, Seals	24-	33
1973—Christmas, Snowman	40-	55
1974—Mother's Day	40-	54

Moser (Czechoslovakia)

1970—Annual	440-	510
1971—Mother's Day, Peacocks	260-	310
1972—Annual	140-	170
1972—Mother's Day, Butterflies	140-	150
1973—Mother's Day, Squirrels	125-	170

Noritake

1970—Easter Egg, first edition	42-	52
1971—Easter Egg	24-	33
1972—Easter Egg	21-	31
1973—Valentine Heart, first edition	40-	50

Orrefors

1970—Notre Dame Cathedral	80-	90
1971—Westminster Abbey	75-	85
1972-73—Mother's Day	69-	74
1973—Annual	74-	84

Pickard

1971—Game Birds, pr.	450-	550
1972—Truman plate	72-	90
1973—Lincoln	62-	80

Porsgrund

1968—Christmas, church scene	105-	130
1969—Christmas	28-	39
1970—Castle, Hamlet's	19-	29
1970—Christmas	22-	31
1970—Deluxe Christmas	74-	83
1970—Jubilee	28-	38
1970—Mug	19-	27
1971—Christmas	24-	33
1971—Father's Day	19-	27
1971—Mother's Day	19-	26
1972—Easter	18-	27

Reed & Barton

1970—Christmas	350-	450
1971—Christmas	160-	170
1972—Silver & copper annual	110-	150
1972—Audubon plate, Sandpiper, silver & copper	160-	190
1973—Russell's Free Trapper	140-	158

Rorstrand

1968—Christmas	54-	63
1969—Christmas	22-	32
1970—Christmas	24-	32
1971—Christmas	21-	31
1971—Father's Day	27-	37
1971—Mother's Day	22-	31
1972—Mother's Day	31-	40
1973—Father's Day	24-	33

Rosenthal

1967—Christmas	125-	135
1971-3—Winblad Christmas	210-	280

Roskilde

1968—Church	31-	40
1969—Church	19-	27
1970—Christmas	22-	31
1971-2-3—Church	27-	37

Royal Copenhagen, RC (see Christmas Plates)

1969—Apollo II	54-	63
1969—Mermaid Summer	41-	50
1971—Mother's Day	120-	130
1971—Statue of Liberty	42-	52
1972—Mother's Day	44-	52
1972—Olympic	50-	60
1973—Mother's Day	40-	48

Royale

1971—Mother's Day	25-	29
1971—Father's Day	50-	60
1972—Mother's Day	29-	38
1972—Father's Day	29-	37
1972—Christmas	30-	40
1972—Game plate	240-	270
1972—Crystal annual	350-	400
1973—Christmas	40-	50

St. Amand

1970—First edition	27-	44
1971—Second edition	20-	30
1971—Christmas	24-	33

Santa Clara

1970—Christmas	24-	32
1971—Mother's Day	27-	37
1972—Christmas	24-	32
1972—Mother's Day	31-	40

Schumann

1970—Beethoven	24-	32
1971—Christmas (Azburg)	26-	37
1972-3 Christmas	28-	38

Seven Seas

1969—Astronaut	24-	33
1970—Christmas, New World	29-	34

117

(continued)

1970—Mother's Day	26-	35
1970—History	38-	47
1971—Christmas Carol	31-	40
1971—Mother's Day	28-	37
1972-3—Mother's Day	30-	40

Spode

1970—Christmas	49-	52
1970—Annual	47-	56
1970—Charles Dickens	120-	130
1970—Winston Churchill bust	150-	172
1971—Christmas	38-	47

Stanek

1968—First Moon Landing		1,900+
1972—Columbus		1,000-1,200

Tirschenreuth

1969—Christmas	34-	42
1970—Christmas	28-	37
1971—Christmas	24-	33
1972-3—Christmas	24-	29

Val St. Lambert

1968—Rembrandt & Rubens, pr.	97-	106
1969—Pilgrims plate	170-	185
1969—Van Dyck and Van Gogh	72-	82
1970—Old Masters (set of 2)	67-	77
1970—Pilgrim Fathers	66-	74
1970—Rembrandt Crystal	68-	72
1970—Rubens Crystal	48-	58
1970—Van Dyck Crystal	52-	61
1970—Zodiac	180-	220
1971—Washington	310-	340

Veneto Flair

1970—Madonna	750-	875
1971—Elephant	325-	400
1971—Three Kings	370-	410
1971—Wildlife, Stag	460-	575
1972—Last Supper, set of 5		1,950+
1972—Mother's Day	180-	196
1974—Cat	82-	92

Vernonware

1971—Christmas, Poppytrail	45-	54
1972—Christmas, Poppytrail	41-	51
1973—Christmas	37-	47

Washington Mint

1972—Mint Picasso	140-	150
1972—Mint Sawyer	142-	152

Wedgwood

1969—Astronaut (Apollo II)	183-	194
1969—Christmas	170-	182
1970—Christmas	58-	62
1971—Calendar plate	32-	50
1971—Christmas, Piccadilly Circus	54-	70
1971—Mother's Day	48-	62
1973—Christmas	61-	71

Wyeth, Andrew

1971—The Kuerner Farm	78-	90
1971—Royal Tettau Pope Paul VI	110-	120
1972—Fourth of July annual	192-	240

Combs

Combs

Usually made of tortoiseshell, though some were made of silver, ivory or bone. They go back to the 16th century. Those you find in shops today cost from $5 to $13.

Average price	$ 10-	20
Barette, carved (ill.)	11-	20
Ivory, inlaid, imitation diamonds	14-	29
Sterling silver, ornately carved	24-	36
Tortoiseshell, carved (ill.)	14-	18
Tortoiseshell, ornately carved	17-	27

Comic Books

Would you believe that a 10¢ comic book from the 1920s today may be worth over $150? Volume I, No. 1, has a lot to do with the value. Big Little Books, early comic pages from newspapers, etc., are all collectible. "G-VG" means "Good-Very Good."

A-1 Comics, Issue #5, Masquerader, G-VG	$ 3-	4
A-1 Comics, Issue #14, Tim Holt #1, Mint	22-	27
A-1 Comics, Issue #45, American Air Forces, Mint	2.50-	4
Action Comics, Issue #3, Superman, Mint	775-	820
Action Comics, Issue #10, Superman cover, G-VG	450-	475
Adventures into Horror, Issue #1, Mint	3-	4.50
Adventures into Terror, Issue #4, G-VG	2-	3
Air Fighters Comics, Vol. 1, Issue #1, Mint	120-	135
Al Capp's Shmoo, Issue #3, Mint	8-	9

Al Capp's Shmoo, Issue #5,
G-VG 4- 5
All Great Crime Stories, 1949
(one shot), Mint 8- 10
All-Star Comics, Issue #2,
Green Lantern, Johnny
Thunder, Mint 220- 240
All-Star Comics, Issue #5, first
appearance of Hawkgirl,
Mint 175- 200
All-Winners, Issue #2,
Destroyer & The Whizzer,
G-VG 85- 97
Amazing Adventures, Issue
#1, Mint............... 9- 12
Atomic Comics, Issue #3,
Mint 4.50- 6
Banner Comics, Issue #3,
Captain Courageous begins,
Mint 80- 95
Baseball Comics, Issue #1,
Mint 13- 17
Batman, Issue #1, Batman
origin retold, Mint 1,550-1,700
Batman, Issues #17-25, G-VG,
ea. 28- 35
Behind Prison Bars, Issue
#1, Mint............... 6- 8
Big Chief Wahoo, Issues #3-6,
G-VG, ea. 6- 9
Bill Barnes, America's Air
Ace, Issues #7-12, G-VG, ea. 3- 6
Black and White, Issue #1,
Dick Tracy, Mint 185- 210
Black and White, Issue #3,
Lone Ranger, Mint 57- 65
Blackhawk, Issues #119-160,
G-VG, ea. .... .95- 1.50
Buck Rogers, Issue #1, all
Sunday strip reprints, Mint 160- 173
Buck Rogers in the 25th
Century, Issue #1, Mint ... 3- 5
Comic Comics, Issues #2-10,
G-VG, ea. 2.50- 4
The Comics Magazine, Issues
#2-5, Mint, ea. 28- 36
Comics on Parade, Tarzan by
Hal Foster, Issue #1, Mint . 135- 150
Comics on Parade, #30-104,
Mint, ea. 7- 10
Green Hornet Comics, Issues
#2-3, Mint, ea. 55- 65
Ha Ha Comics, Issues #7-99,
G-VG, ea. .... .75- 1
Jeep Comics, Issue #3, G-VG . 2- 3
Jingle Jangle Comics, Issues
#2-10, Mint, ea. 14- 19
Joe Louis, Issues #1-2, Mint .. 5.50- 9
Lorna the Jungle Girl, Issues
#2-26, G-VG, ea. 3- 6

Oakey Doakes, Issue #1 (one
shot), Mint 36- 44
Our Flag Comics, Issues #3-5,
Mint 4- 8
Science Comics (1st series),
Issues #2-8, Mint, ea. 44- 53
Science Comics (2nd series),
Issues #1-5, Mint, ea. 4- 7
Sky Blazers, Issue #2, G-VG . 7- 9
Son of Sinbad (Kubert cover),
Issue #1, Mint........... 11- 16
Super Duper, Issue #9, Mint . 11- 15

Big Little Books
Air Fighters of America,
G-VG 8- 11
Alley Oop and Dinny, Mint .. 19- 25
Andy Panda, Mint 32- 40
Bambi, G-VG 14- 18
Bambi, Mint 22- 30
Betty Boop and Snow White,
Mint 14- 19
Billy the Kid, Mint 11- 14
Blondie (any one of 15 books),
G-VG to Mint, ea......... 7- 14
Bringing Up Father, Mint ... 26- 34
Buck Jones (any one of 12
books), G-VG to Mint 13.50- 20
Buck Jones in Night Riders,
Mint 37- 45
Buck Rogers (any one of 22
books), G-VG to Mint 23- 38
Buck Rogers in the City of
Floating Globes, Mint 80- 95
Bugs Bunny (any of many
books), G-VG to Mint 9- 16
G-Man and the Gun Runners,
G-VG 16- 24
Gene Autry (any one of many
books), G-VG to Mint 11- 19
Gene Autry in Gunsmoke,
Mint 33- 41
Gunsmoke, G-VG 3.75- 5
Jackie Cooper in Gangster's
Boy, G-VG 9- 14
Joe Louis, the Brown Bomber,
Mint 22- 30
Ken Maynard (any of 5 books),
G-VG to Mint 11- 19
Little Orphan Annie (any of
many books), G-VG to Mint 14- 24
Little Orphan Annie, Under
the Big Top, Mint 33- 42
Lone Ranger (any of many
books), G-VG to Mint 14- 27
Mickey Mouse (any of many
books), G-VG to Mint 14- 26
Pilot Pete and His Dive
Bomber, G-VG 4.75- 6

119

(continued)

Popeye (any of many books),
G-VG to Mint   11-   18
Robinson Crusoe, G-VG   9-   15
Silly Symphonies, Mint   33-   42
Smilin' Jack (any one of many
books), G-VG to Mint   13-   27
Tom Mix, Riding Avenger,
G-VG   22-   37
Wally Homestead and His
Devil Printers, Mint   12-   18

Commemorative Medals

Commemorative Glasses

Commemorative Glasses

Any event, such as the 100th anniversary of the Winchester rifle, is likely to be commemorated in glasses, wristwatches, plaques, and the like. Because they're fragile, glasses that last over the years eventually bring high prices.

Presidents glasses, 1930s, set
of 12 . . . .$ 32-   41
Winchester-Western glasses,
set of 6 (ill.)   18-   27
World's Fair (1939) glasses, set
of 12   48-   58

Commemorative Mugs

of famous buildings, too, such as the one shown in this illustration. It's now the Museum of Yesterday's Toys, 52 St. George Street, St. Augustine, Florida. Visit the toy museum.

Commemorative Medals

More and more collectors are seeking out commemorative medals, made to celebrate a particular event or individual. They were made of cast metal, sterling silver, 14k gold, and bronze. The illustration here, The American Doughboy, was made by M. Lordonnois in 1919 and is bronze. Prices vary according to artist and type of metal used.

Compasses

Commemorative Mugs

Just about every event is celebrated; a lot

Compasses

Instruments for indicating direction; those

with a magnetic needle swinging freely on a pivot and pointing to the magnetic north are highly sought after.

Boy Scout compass in canvas
case, 1920s . . . . $ 18- 23
Engineer's compass in mahogany
box, signed "W. & L.E. Gurley,
Troy, N.Y.," "E" and "W"
backward (ill.) 140-200
Ship's compass, in original box,
WWI destroyer 310-370

Confederate Provisional Stamps and Envelopes

June 1, 1861, the South stopped using stamps made by the federal government. The Confederacy set up provisional post offices throughout the South. Today, a stamp and/or envelope from one of these offices, dated October 14 (the first day the proper Confederate stamps were available for use), or after, would be worth a considerable amount. Some stamps from the following offices range in value from $1,200 to $16,000. A stamp's value depends on its rarity, condition, etc. Consequently, we give you only the locations of some of the Confederate post offices. If you think you have a rarity, check with a reputable stamp dealer.

Athens, Georgia
Autaugaville, Alabama
Baton Rouge, Louisiana
Beaumont, Texas
Bridgeville, Alabama
Danville and Emory, Virginia
Franklin, and Lenoir, North Carolina
Goliad, Texas, and Gonzales, Texas
Helena, Texas
Knoxville, Tennessee
Macon, Georgia
Spartanburg, South Carolina
Uniontown, Alabama

Not all are mentioned. There are probably 25 more. Any Southern stamp dated between June 1 and October 14, 1861, should be checked.

Construction Collectibles

Anything to do with the early days of building is collectible today.

Audels Masons and Builders
(set of 4), copyright 1924 (ill.) . . $ 9- 13
Blueprints of old buildings 7- 10
Early handmade level, late 1800s 21- 30

Construction Collectibles

Old brass door plates and
doorknobs, ea. 15- 21

Cookbooks

Cookbooks

These gourmet's delights, especially those printed in the early 1900s, are collectible today. Who can ever forget Fannie Farmer's candies and her cookbooks? Condition and age establish the price.

Average price, in good condition . $ 4- 11
Common Sense in The House-
hold, 1900, Scribner's (ill.) 4- 7
The Herbalistic Almanac, 1950
(ill.) 4- 7

Cookie Molds

Hand-carved, these have been around for centuries. Most European countries export them into U.S. antiques shops. Those from Holland are particularly collectible. They make great wall decorations!

Depending on age and condition . $ 31- 40

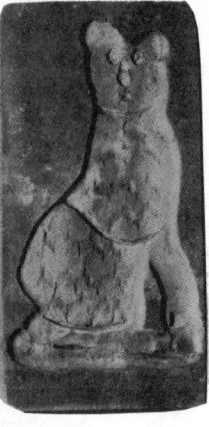

Cookie Molds

Cooking Items

Cooking Items

Apple roaster, tin, late 18th
   century $110-125
Bird roaster, stamped, soldered
   tin, 12″ wide, early 19th
   century 50- 60
Bread pans, black sheet iron, 4
   sizes from 5″ to 12″ wide, all . . 50- 60
Chafing dish, copper, Sterno
   burner, 1920s (ill.) 60- 77
Cylinder churn, cedar, galvanized
   iron hoops, c. 1895 . . . . 62- 72
Dough mixer/kneader, tin, cast
   iron, c. 1880s 40- 49
Egg beater (or mixer), blue glass,
   cast iron, tin, crank-type
   beater 31- 42
Fish boiler, pieced tin, 20″ wide,
   has fish rack and cover, c. 1890 51- 60
Jelly bag strainer, wire, cloth,
   fastens on bowl, c. 1930s 22- 31

Omelette pan, polished iron,
   c. 1870s 25- 34
Pea sheller, galvanized iron, 9″
   long, "Acme Pea Sheller Co" . . 27- 37
Peach parer, cast iron, 10″ long,
   crank type 27- 36
Potato slicer, iron, wood, c. 1870s 31- 40
Sausage stuffer, tin, wood, 2
   handles, 21″ long, c. 1870s 22- 32

Coors Pottery

In 1910, the Coors Porcelain Company began manufacturing pottery in Golden, Colorado, but what is found in shops today is the pottery and dinnerware made in the 1930s. There were about 35 vase styles and 4 lines of earthenware dishes. The pottery has a satiny texture; most pieces have a matt finish. Some colors are Delft blue, white, yellow, turquoise, brown-beige, peach-beige, pastel aqua and lilac pink.

Ashtray, white, "Coors" in
   center, raised signature . . . . . . $ 12- 19
Casserole, white 17- 27
Cookie jar, covered, Rosebud
   pattern, ink stamp "Coors
   USA" 17- 27
Honey pot, lilac pink, two-
   handled, ink stamp mark 24- 33
Jug, water, Rosebud pattern,
   turquoise, 7″ high, ink stamp
   mark 28- 37
Mortar and pestle, 1¾″ and 3″
   high, ink stamp "Coors
   Porcelain" 16- 27
Salt/peppers, Rosebud pattern,
   ink stamp mark "Coors USA" . 24- 33
Vase, rope-handled, 8″ high,
   turquoise liner, 8″ high 28- 38
Vase, white, 6″ high, turquoise
   liner, ink stamp mark 24- 33
Vase, yellow, rope-handled, 12″
   high, ink stamp mark 28- 37

Copeland-Spode China

Joseph Spode, 1770, Staffordshire, England, later taken over by W. T. Copeland and Sons who marked their wares "Late Spode." Delft, Salt Glaze and Jasperware were a few of the many items made, including porcelain figurines and fine dinner services. Copeland and Garrett came along later to continue the line.

Copeland-Spode China

Chocolate pot, Indian Tree,
  6 cups and scalloped saucers .. $160-190
Creamer, shell shaped, c. 1860 ... 108-119
Ewer, heavy beading, leaves,
  ring handle with mask, 1870 .. 110-122
Gravy boat, heron, palm tree,
  gilded grape leaves, 1847 .....   62- 75
Jug, Jasper ground, applied
  grapevine and drinking scene . 151-166
Pickle, pink, embossed hunting
  scene, silver fork, 1897 ....   58- 68
Pitcher, blue/white, raised fig-
  ures, cherubs, floral decor   94-107
Plate, bird's nest, butterfly
  rushes, daisies 42- 52
Plate, castle scene, blue/white,
  (ill.) 55- 70
Plate, plover, blue/white 54- 63
Sugar bowl, shell-shaped, c. 1860. 107-118
Teapot, Jasper ground, grape-
  vine, 6¼" high 140-150
Teapot, white, birds, bamboo
  in relief, pewter lid, 1875 127-130
Tureen, cream ground, storks,
  palm trees, ladle and tray 84- 94

Copper

One of the world's most important metals,
it's been used for centuries in every shape,
size and object. Wire, cooking utensils,
jewelry, weathervanes, you-name-it.

Apple butter kettle, dovetail
  bottom, mid-1800s, 25" dia. $ 425- 475
Basket, Art Nouveau, cherubs
  in relief, 13" high 72- 82

Copper

Copper

Basket, double handle,
  hammered bottom, 1920s,
  10" dia. 40- 49
Candy kettle, mid-1800s,
  19" dia. 190- 225
Chafing dish, complete, 1920s 105- 115
Coachman's horn, 38" long,
  pewter mouthpiece,
  mid-1800s 125- 140
Coffee set, French, 4-pc.,
  1890s, all 125- 135
Cover pan, zinc handles,
  1900s 45- 55
Desk set, 5-pc.—inkwell,
  blotter holder, letter holder,
  pen(s) holder, tray, 1920,
  all 120- 130
Dippers, many types, all ages,
  average price 22- 85

123

(continued)

Foot warmer, brass bail handle, early 1800s	67-	77
Milk pail, iron handle, late 1800s	92-	110
Planters, set of 6, brass handles, pre-WWI, all	80-	90
Plaque, hand-tooled, Vikings-in-ship, 3″×7″, dated 1905	65-	75
Samovar, brass-footed, 15″ high	245-	265
Teapot, 9″ high (ill.)	40-	49
Umbrella stand, brass bottom, tooled scenes of flowers, 1900s	125-	140
Vase, pewter base, tulip lip, 14″ high, 1900s	55-	65
Vase, silver inlay of butter-flies, flowers, 9½″ high, 1900s	100-	115
Wash boiler w/lid, burnished, early 1900s	130-	145
Weathervane, American eagle, complete, mid-1800s	1,900-2,200	
Weathervane, racing sulky, complete, after Civil War	2,100-2,300	

Copper Lustre

Copper Lustre

The use of a copper compound in the glaze resulted in a metallic, copperlike surface. Made in the Staffordshire District, England, in the early 1800s. Most of what you find to-day was imported into the U.S. between 1835 and the late 1800s. Reproductions since the 1920s have caused this ware to fall from popularity. The new is heavier and much thicker than the old.

Bowl, floral on green bands	$ 75-	87
Bowl, dark green, raised red roses, 4″ dia.	65-	75
Chalice, beaded border, enameled floral decor, 4½″ high	68-	78
Compote, royal blue band, 3 raised groups, girl, cat, 1820	74-	90
Creamer, 3″ high	27-	36

Flowerpot, beaded border, enameled decor, 4½″ high	215-240
Goblet, pink and white floral, green leaves	91-107
Mug, blue band, greyhound, cow in relief, 3″ high	82- 91
Mustache cup and saucer, left-hand, 3 brothers, ship	94-108
Pitcher, blue band with pink roses, 6″ high	110-114
Pitcher, bulbous, up-down ridges, Hawkes spout, 6″ high	110-118
Pitcher, Wedgwood, brown, Fallow Deer, 4″ high (ill.)	77- 86
Salt, master, blue band, em-bossed pink roses, footed	41- 50
Sugar bowl, blue band, beaded, raised floral, children, footed	54- 64
Teapot, floral and leaf design, 6½″ high	172-183
Toby jug, early, high relief on hat and cheeks	300-380

Coral

Coral

This hard substance made up of the skeletons of certain marine animals has been around for years and it gets more collectible every day. The rarest is the black and when carved into delicate statues brings upward of $10,000. Beads, brooches, necklaces, ear-rings, carvings—just a few of the many objects made from coral. The pink coral, carved Chinese maiden illustrated is valued at $950-1,400. Be careful of colored plastic that fools too many beginning collectors.

Coralene

Coralene

Glass with applied glass beading that looks like natural coral. Made at the New England Glass Company in the late 1800s, it's highly collectible today. Don't be fooled by the cheap type sold in stores during the same period. Rub the surface; if the beads come off, it's junk.

Pitcher, birds and leaves	$425-470
Pitcher, ribbed, green opalescent, bird and flowers, 7½" high, signed Webb (ill.)	500-520
Toothpick, satin glass, silvered, cased	350-385
Tumbler, graduated pink, cased, gold branches, 5" high	240-270
Tumbler, Seaweed pattern on yellow cased glass	248-270
Tumbler, white satin, brown oak leaves, Mt. Washington Glass Co.	260-280
Vase, blue/white, cream casing, yellow seaweed branches, 8½" high	274-284
Vase, coral branch beading, off-white casing, 4½" high	410-450
Vase, pink overlay, ruffled top	400-470
Vase, red beads, garnet gems	400-475
Vase, satin, yellow and white, wheat sheaf, 5" high (ill.)	330-370
Vase, yellow coral branch beading, white casing, 5½" high	420-430

Poor imitations now available.

Coronation Collectibles

After a coronation, items in china and glass appeared on the English market. Tin candy

Coronation Collectibles

and cracker boxes are especially collectible today. Elizabeth II paperweights are considered prizes today by those who seek out coronation items.

Beaker, Edward VII, 1902, Royal Doulton	$ 40-	48
Brandy snifter, King Edward VIII, coat of arms	29-	39
Cup, Garter emblem, 5" high	37-	47
Cup, King Edward VII	26-	36
Cup/saucer, Mary/George V (ill.)	27-	37
Globe, Edward VIII, porcelain	29-	39
Handkerchief, Elizabeth II, 1953	8-	12
Humidor, Queen Elizabeth II, 1953, silver plate	32-	42
Mug, George V and Mary, 1911, portraits, 3" high	41-	50
Paperweight, QE II, 1953, St. Louis	270-310	
Plaque, Edward VII, Alexandra, 1902, Royal Doulton	81-	89
Plate, bread, George VI, 1937	29-	38
Plate, Edward VII, 1902	31-	40
Spoon, George VI, 1911, demitasse	19-	27
Teapot, Elizabeth II, 1953, gold portrait, crest	37-	46
Toby mug, George V, Queen Mary, 1910, hand-painted, 6"	40-	46
Tray, QE II, 1953	11-	21
Tumbler, Elizabeth II, blue	27-	36

Cosmos Glass

See **Pattern Glass Section**.

Coverlets

Quilt, Log Cabin pattern,
 patches, wool and cotton,
 75" 145-155
Robe, blue silk, gold thread,
 gold birds, China 240-260
Rug, needlework, England,
 85"×41" 370-420
Sampler, alphabet, animals,
 child's age, dated 1828 . . . . 80- 95
Shawl, black silk, embroidered,
 Spanish, 5' square 72- 92
Spread, Statue of Liberty,
 100"×85" 400-500
Tablecloth, homespun, cream
 color, crocheted edge,
 68"×64" 70- 82

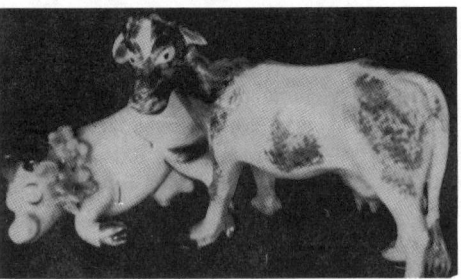

Cows and Bulls

Coverlets

Made during the 18th and 19th centuries, they were the original do-it-yourself item. Women sheared the sheep, carded the wool, dyed it to the desired color, spun it on a wheel, wove it on a loom. There are four kinds of coverlets, each popular for a short time only: Double-woven, Jacquard, Summer/winter, Oversheet. Prices vary as to condition, location, and collector. See **Quilts.**

Bedspread, Popcorn pattern,
 crocheted, 90"×100" $310-350
Bedspread, "United We
 Stand," Alcott . . . . 1,400+
Bonnet, hoop, 1790s 250-270
Carpet, oblong panels, needle-
 work, 175"×90" 300-345
Coverlet, blue/white, double-
 bed size, handloomed, 1840s
 (ill.) 210-240
Dresser scarf, Battenberg, 4½"
 long, 16" wide 44- 54
Jacquard, signed, red, eagle
 motif 280-295
Jacquard, unsigned, red, eagles
 at corners 240-270
Lap robe, sleigh, horse head de-
 sign, woolen, 50"×60" 141-151

Cows and Bulls

This is a don't-ask-me-why category, but for some reason, especially in the dairy regions of Illinois and Wisconsin, collectors are going "ape" for anything that has to do with a cow—and that's no bull!

Brass cow, marked Old Nell . . . . . $ 10- 19
Oil painting of cow, Sheffield
 Farms, early 1900s 97-140
Reclining cow (ill.), not old 8- 14
Staffordshire cow (ill.), 1800s 58- 67

Cracker Jars

These are kissin' cousins to the cookie jar. In continuous use for the past 150 years, they come in pottery, wood, glass. Some had silver-plated lids.

Acid finish with enameling,
 Britannia handle and lid $120-130
Bristol glass with enameled
 flowers/butterflies 88-110
China, blue/green, floral decor (ill.) 57- 67
Limoges, shell design, gold trim . 60- 70

Cracker Jars

Satin glass, frosted, bead and
grape design 200-218

Bowl, Mt. Washington, gold
 iridescence, enameled lobster
 decor, 5½" high $140-185
Bowl, white, blue dots, 8" dia.
 (ill.) 270-290
Lemonade set, blue, 8 pcs. 70- 78
Pickle jar, hourglass shape, silver
 plated 60- 70
Pitcher, applied reeded handle,
 clear 54- 62
Sugar bowl, pink, enamel floral,
 silver cover 54- 62
Sweetmeat jar, sapphire blue,
 red strawberries, amber edge . . 400-430
Toothpick holder, marine green . .   37- 46
Toothpick holder, hat, green 37- 47
Vase, applied blue glass buttons,
 12½" high 39- 48
Vase, Chinese decor, floral,
 13½" high 115-124
Vase, cranberry, 6½" high 74- 82
Vase, iridescent, signed
 Imperial . . . ., 131-140

Crackle (Craquelle) Glass

Cranberry Glass

Crackle (Craquelle) Glass

Invented by the Venetians in the 16th century, it was made by plunging hot glass into cold water, then reheating and reblowing it. This process produced the crackled effect. It's also called frosted and iced glass. Some of the finest was made at Sandwich; also at Hobbs, Brockunier and Company, Wheeling, West Virginia, in the late 1800s. Being reproduced by Pilgrim Glass Corporation.

Cranberry Glass

Gold was added to the glass batch, which was then blown or molded. When reheated at a low temperature, the cranberry shade developed. It also was called Ruby glass. In later years, copper was substituted, creating a harsh amber-red tint. There are many Cranberry pieces represented in this Guide. Here are a few. Oh, those repros!

Bottle, barber, green/white
 flowers, 8" high . . . . $ 51- 67

(continued)

Bowl, finger, Inverted Thumb-
print (ITP), 5" dia. 90-108
Bowl, rose, pleated and fluted
top, 4¾" dia. 91-115
Box, blue decorated flowers,
4½" square 50- 60
Candlesticks, twisted stem, 10¼"
high, pr 121-131
Compote, clear pedestal base,
6¼" high 105-121
Creamer, fluted lip, clear
handle, 3½" high 50- 59
Cruet, ITP, 8" high (ill.) 95-110
Knife rest, ball ends are cut,
3¼" wide 70- 80
Rose bowl, ribbed, applied clear
rigaree, snail feet, berry prunts,
signed Webb, 5" high 345-365
Wine set, 11" high decanter,
10" wide tray, 6 glasses 160-180

Crazing

This word is included in this Guide because
it confuses so many people. It's simply a fine
network of cracks or fissures in the glaze
caused by the unequal shrinkage of the body
and glaze during the cooling. It does not
mean the piece is cracked and/or damaged.
Some pottery factories deliberately "crazed"
certain pieces. Rookwood Pottery Company
was one.

Creamware

See **Queensware**.

Crest China

Crest China

An inexpensive "fairing" (small souvenir)
china made in England and the U.S. during
the late 19th century—usually found in
mugs, toothpick holders, shoes, or pin trays.

Creamer, miniature, green crown
emblem, 2¼" high (ill.) . . . . $ 18- 25

Figurine, "The first to rise," man
in bed, nightcap, Germany 40- 45
Mug, "Sip Slowly," 5½" high . . . 32- 42
Pin tray, floral design, France,
1880s 14- 19
Powder box, "Love's light never
dims," Germany, 1887 . . . . 30- 35
Shoe, applied flowers 15- 18
Toothpick holder, "Take one,"
Germany, 1890s 14- 18

Cros

Henry Cros revived the 17th century
method of molding glass objects from pate de
verre, "paste of glass." The Egyptians
developed the technique hundreds of years
before. Cros made large panels in relief from
1840 to 1907, successfully making pate de
verre in 1884. It's scarce but still found occasionally in Europe and in American shops
that specialize in imports.

Crown Derby

Crown Derby

An earlier factory of the same name
operated in the early 1800s, but what we
know as Crown Derby today was made in
England in the late 1870s until the late 1880s.

Coffeepot, Oriental decor, brown
floral . . . . $ 86- 95
Creamer, flowers, oriental-type,
Crown mark 31- 42
Cup/saucer, white/blue, floral
decor 65- 80
Ewer, turquoise ground, raised
gold floral decor, 9" 130-165
Figurine, seated lady, white
ground, 6½" high 95-109
Plate, dark blue/white, rust
panels, 9" dia. 40- 60
Plate, flower border, 8½" dia. . . . 52- 70
Toothpick, white ground, flowers 44- 54
Vase, red/gold, 6" high 88- 98

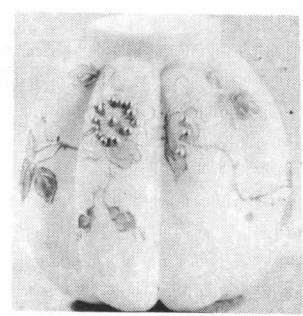

Crown Milano

Crown Milano

This fine glass was made in the late 19th century by the Mt. Washington Glass Company. It is often decorated with flowers and leaves overlaid with gold and silver. Quite a few pieces were marked with the letters C.M. in the pontil.

Bride's basket, enameled
pansy decor, tricorn,
signed . . . . $ 2,500+
Bowl, melon rib, floral
decor, 4½" 475- 575
Bowl, tan, flowers, pewter
top and handles 440- 470
Cookie jar, signed   950-1,100
Cracker jar, apricot, apple
blossom limbs and
flowers, signed 650- 750
Cracker jar, jeweled,
mottled background,
applied gold threading,
signed MT. W.G. Co.,
c. 1890 (ill.) 1,450-1,600
Cracker jar, pansy, signed .   700- 800
Cracker jar, quadruple plate
rim and lid, pansy decor,
signed, c. 1894 (ill.) 670- 800
Humidor, cream ground,
pansies, silver-plated lid,
signed M.W. 750- 850
Jewel box, original lining,
Mt. Washington Glass
Co. 560- 650
Shade, floral, gold, Burmese
coloring 560- 585
Sugar bowl, covered, melon
rib, floral decor 420- 435
Sugar shaker, Mt.
Washington, pewter top .   410- 430
Tumbler, gold decor, signed
Crown 435- 510
Vase, cream ground, apple
blossoms, signed, 6½"
high 920- 970

Vase, white satin ground,
pink shading, pansies,
6" high 915- 980
Vase, yellow to peach
ground, Mt. Washington
Glass Co.   925-1,000

Cruets

Cruets

These came in all sizes and usually were made of pressed or blown glass. The more expensive were cut. Every glass company made them, from the late 1700s on. Reproductions galore.

Amber, clear handle . . . . $ 49- 56
Beveled Star, amber, clear
stopper 38- 47
Blue, amber stopper and handle,
8" high 72- 81
Bohemian glass, deer scene 30- 40
Cobalt overlay cut to clear, Rose
pattern 82- 92
Cranberry, enameled lilies of
the valley (ill.) 80- 88
Cranberry, ITP, clear stopper . . .   94-108
Cut glass, signed Hawkes 112-130
Depression glass, American
Sweetheart 27- 37
Emerald green ground, white
enamel lily of the valley 67- 77
Frosted glass, green enamel
decor, 7½" high 44- 53
Green cut to clear (ill.) 100-125
Green ground, white and gold
enamel, floral 57- 64
Mary Gregory glass, boy with
hoop, blue/white 100-125
Millefiori, canes, yellow/white,
blue, cut glass stopper 210-240
Opalescent, Stars and Stripes
(ill.)   92-109
Paneled Thistle, prism stoppers .   48- 57
Peachblow, Wheeling, yellow,
amber handle and stopper 670-750
Pink swirl, blown 73- 82

(continued)

Rayed Star base, notched handle,
cut glass, 7½" 42- 51
Spatter glass, clear stopper 58- 67
Strawberry, Hobnail, clear
applied handle and stopper . . . 37- 46
Tiffany, blue, ribbed, signed 310-340
Vasa Murrhina, clear stopper . . . 78- 84
Vaseline to pink, Hobnail, 7"
high 54- 63
Venetian glass, blue swirl 58- 67
Waterford, new mark 67- 77
Zipper edge on ribs and handles,
5½" high 34- 43

Cuff Links

Cuff Links

Came the first double cuff on the sleeve of a shirt or blouse, the type where the cuff turned back on itself and was fastened with a link, came the first cuff links. They were made of inexpensive metal on up to platinum, solid gold, sterling silver, inlaid with diamonds and emeralds. The earlier types are collectible today.

Artist's palette cuff links, 1900s,
pr. . . . . $ 10- 15
Imitation jewels cuff links,
1900s, pr. 8- 12
14k gold, inlaid with emeralds,
1930s, pr. 650-750
Brass, army coat buttons made
into cuff links (ill.), pr. 21- 27

Cup Plates

During the mid-1800s, gentlemen drank their tea or coffee from the saucer. The plates that held the cup while he was slurping are collectible today, both in glass and in china. Sandwich made the most beautiful glass ones. They should ring when plinked. Reproductions were made in glass by Westmore-

Cup Plates

land Glass Company in the 1930s. They don't ring. Still being made.

Beaded hearts, Midwest, glass . . $ 34- 42
Benjamin Franklin, clear glass . . 36- 45
Blue/white, Clews china, 1819 . . . 37- 47
Brown, eagle and floral border,
boat center, Clews, 1825 . . . . . 33- 42
Bunker Hill, Sandwich 41- 50
Dark blue, scenic views, Clews
1822, pr. 57- 67
Heart center, 13 hearts, clear
glass 24- 32
Henry Clay, clear glass 27- 37
Log cabin, clear glass 135-140
Sailing ship, men in rowboat, ship
border, brown, Staffordshire . . 24- 33
Sandwich, clear glass, 3⁵/₁₆" dia.,
eagle looking left 61- 70
Sandwich, clear glass, 3½"
dia., Henry Clay, star under
bust 50- 60
Sandwich, clear glass, 3⁷/₁₆" dia.,
U.S. Constitution 57- 67
Valentine, blue 132-141
Wedding Day, 3 weeks after
(reverse faces) 22- 32

Currier and Ives

Nathaniel Currier worked for himself in 1834. In 1857, James Ives joined him in the firm that was to become one of the world's greatest producers of inexpensive lithographs. Scenic, political, disaster, nautical, sporting scenes, horses, animals, biblical scenes; no subject was ignored. Original C & I prints show up under magnification as a series of short lines; reproductions show up as a series of small dots. C & I prints were made in three sizes: small folio, 7.8"X12.8";

Currier and Ives

medium folio, 13″×20″; large folio, 18″×27″. Do beware of insurance company calendar prints and all those reproductions. C & I went out of business in 1907.

American Farm Scenes, #1, "Spring," large folio	$ 600-	650
American Farm Scenes, #2, "Summer," large folio	460-	480
American Farm Scenes, #3, "Autumn," large folio	455-	485
American Farm Scenes, #4, "Winter," large folio	1,800-	2,300
"American Girl," 1871, small folio	90-	128
"Arkansas Traveler," 1870, small	105-	140
"Autumn Fruits," small, medium	120-	130
"The Bad Husband," 1870, small	90-	140
"Battle of Gettysburg, Pa.," 1863, large	240-	265
"Beach Snipe Shooting," 1869, medium	580-	625
"The Beautiful Persian" (ill.)	62-	80
"Belle of the Winter," medium	275-	360
"The Best Horse," small	130-	144
"The Bible and Temperance," N. Currier, small	182-	192
"A Black Squall," 1879, small	44-	52
"The Boatswain," N. Currier, small	98-	107
"Bombardment of Fort Sumter," small	140-	150
"Boy and Dog," small	135-	150
"Brigham Young," medium	120-	140
"California Gold," N. Currier, small	570-	640
"Canvasbacks," small	190-	220
"A Champion Race," 1889, small	310-	360
"Champions of the Union," large	180-	190
"The City of Boston," 1873, large	470-	510
"City of New York," N. Currier, 1844, small	400-	420
"City of New York," N. Currier, 1855, large		1,700+
"Clipper Ship *Flying Cloud,*" N. Currier, 1853, large		6,300+
"Dartmouth College," small		1,600+
"The Death Shot," small	165-	180
"A Fair Start," small	88-	98
"Farmyard Pets," small	130-	150
"Feast of Roses," 1873, small	132-	142
"Flying Fish," 1879, small	160-	180
"The Game Cock," N. Currier, small	220-	240
"General Grant," medium, large	90-	150
"General Robert E. Lee," small	92-	120
"General Tom Thumb's Marriage," 1863, small	115-	127
"Going It Blind," N. Currier, small	90-	110
"The Golden Morning," small	145-	165
"The Grand Drive, Central Park, New York," 1869, large		2,100+
"Grant in Peace," small	90-	115
"Great Exhibition of 1860," small	120-	140
"Hanover," 1887, small	140-	160
"Highland Fling," 1876, medium	125-	160
"Horace Greeley," medium	115-	135
"The Hunter's Dog," N. Currier, small	210-	240
"In the Harbor," small	260-	300
"Indian Buffalo Hunt," medium		550+
"Iroquois," 1882, large	600-	710
"The Jockey's Dream," 1880, small	100-	130
"Jolly Young Ducks," 1866, small	81-	91
"Quail," 1865, small		290+
"Rail Shooting," small		1,450+
"Reading the Scriptures," N. Currier, small	64-	73
"A Run of Luck," 1871, small	90-	110
"Rush for the Pole," 1887, small	140-	150

(continued)

"St. Lawrence," small	140-	165
"Santa Claus," 1882, small .	130-	160
"The Season of Joy," 1872, small	82-	92
"The Shoemaker," small . .	97-	108
"Starting Out on His Mettle," 1876, small	140-	160
"View on the Rondout," small, medium	185-	210
"Warming Up," 1884, small	125-	160
"The Water Jump," 1884, small	350-	400
"Wood Ducks," small	180-	210
"A Wreath of Flowers," small	125-	150

Cuspidors

and cigars, every hotel lobby, barbershop, and beer parlor had at least one. They were also called spittoons.

Brass, 10″ dia.	$ 70- 85
Glass, patent January 8, 1898 . . .	62- 80
Rockingham pottery	150-170
Rockwood, 11″ dia., 1914	195-240
Silver-plated, hotel-type	60- 75
Porcelainized metal, 2 pcs.	24- 33

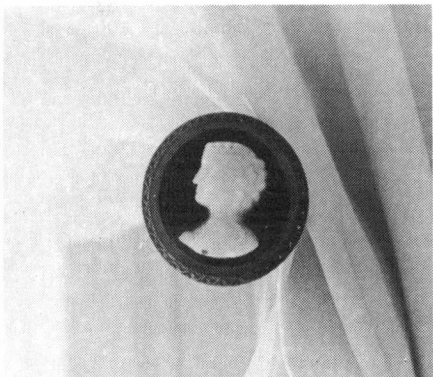

Curtain Tiebacks

Curtain Tiebacks

During the Victorian era, the day of floor-to-ceiling drapes, usually velvet, these tiebacks were used to hold the drapes open during the day. Sandwich Glass tiebacks are very rare today. Made of brass, cast iron, inlaid with porcelain medallions (illustrated), sometimes just a velvet cord with tassels.

Brass, stamped design, pr.	$ 32- 41
Medallion type, brass framing (ill.), pr.	58- 68
Sandwich Glass (authentic), star-petal design, pr.	98-125
Sandwich type, blue or other colors, pr.	42- 52
Porcelain head, iron spike, screw-type, pr.	27- 37

Cuspidors

Usually made of brass, the early ones were made of pottery, also glass. When it was fashionable to chew tobacco, before cigarettes

Custard Glass

Custard Glass

See **Pattern Glass** section for specific items and prices. Look out for reproductions.

Banana boat, Louis XV, 5″ high (ill.)	$165-188

Cut Glass

The "brilliant period" of this glass ranges, generally, from 1880 until 1915. How do you tell if it is cut or pressed? (1) **Ring.** Cut glass will ring like a bell when tapped lightly. (2) **Sparkle.** When held to the light, you can notice the refractions made by the cutting. Pressing destroys this quality. (3) **Sharpness.** If the edges are sharp, the glass is cut; smooth edges denote pressed glass. (4)

132

Weight. Cut glass, because of a high lead content, is usually heavy. Cut and engraved glass are done on a wheel. Etched glass is not a type of cut glass—it's made by the application of a corroding acid. Cut glass is always hand-blown or blown-molded, never pressed. Since there are thousands of reproduction pieces on the market today, don't assume that (1) through (4) above distinguish the old from the new. Study, learn by feeling, but know from whom you buy.

Cut Glass Basket

Baskets
Cornflowers, handled, 13½" high (ill.) .... $	260-	275
Harvard pattern, intaglio floral, 12" high	200-	235
Pinwheel pattern, 7" high ..	140-	155

Bowls
Etched flowers, signed Clarke, 9" dia.	250-	265
Flowers, deep cut, signed Irving, 8" dia. (ill.)	160-	170
Green cut-to-clear, signed Dorflinger, 5" high (ill.) ..	325-	345
Hobstar, Pinwheel pattern, 8" dia.	160-	170
Russian pattern, panels of fans	120-	135

Boxes
Cigarette, signed Hawkes, late	65-	75
Collar, mirror inside for m'lady, silver bindings ..	180-	195
Dresser, silver rim, 5¾" dia. (ill.)	175-	195
Dresser, Venetian pattern, silver trim	128-	137

Cut Glass Bowl

Butter Dishes
Hobstar, Strawberry, Diamond Point and Fan, signed Hawkes	275-	285
Pinwheel and Fan, cut knob finial	120-	135
Rosette flowers, cut knob finial	100-	118

Celery Dishes
Florence pattern, boat type, signed Libbey	275-	300
Grecian pattern, signed Hawkes	195-	210
Strawberry, Diamond and Fan, boat type, signed Hawkes	200-	235

Cut Glass Bowl

Champagne Tubs
Basketweave............	200-	225
Chrysanthemum, jug, 2 qt., no stopper, signed Hawkes	190-	220

Cut Glass Box

133

(continued)

Chandeliers

Empire Ormolu, 19th
century . . . .   3,700+

Five branch, cut glass
hurricane globes   . . . .   2,700+

Gas fixture type, clear and
frosted glass, mid-1800s . 1,000-2,000

Hanging lantern with
smoke bell, early 1800s . . 1,400-1,600

Cheese Dishes

Diamonds, fans, sterling
silver dome 375- 400

Hobstar, 5" high, cut knob
finial 295- 325

Mitre Star, varied pattern,
7½" high 375- 400

Compotes

Flowers, 7¼" high, signed
Hawkes, sits on plate of
same design, 16½" dia.   850- 900

Isabella, 7" high, short
stem, square top 180- 200

Seashells, 6" high, short
stem, signed Clark 235- 255

Creamers

Flower design, 2¾" high   140- 155

Harvard pattern, jug,
straight-sided, fluted top   75- 85

Hobstar 78- 87

Pinwheel 67- 77

Cruets

Corinthian, 4-oz. oil, vinegar
to match, both 130- 145

Harvard, 8-oz., signed
J. Hoare 165- 175

Prism, 4, 5, 6-oz., short-
stemmed, signed Libbey,
ea. 155- 167

Decanters

Bull's Eye, pt., qt., 1½-qt.,
ea. 220- 245

Corinthian, pt. and qt., long
necks, some handled, ea. .   225- 235

4 sherry glasses, match
Mitre Star decanter
all 75- 85

Diamond Point, 12¼" high

. . . .   155- 170

Mitre Star, 10½" high   300- 315

Ewer

Victorian cut, 14" high,
quadruple plate
"Cherub" handle   . . .   265- 280

Fruit Bowls

Corinthian, 20-point
Hobstar base 230- 245

Hobstars, ribbon cut 125- 140

Sunburst, prism, cane
ribbons 125- 140

Humidor

Deep cut, sterling silver lid,
6½" 450- 500

Cut Glass Punch Bowl

Cut Glass Pitcher

Ice Tubs

Corinthian, 5¾" dia. 150- 165

Florence, 9" dia. 160- 170

Hobstar and Diamond cut,
5½" dia. 155- 165

Inkwells

Pinwheel, sterling silver lid   57- 65

Swirl Rib, brass lid 45- 53

Knife Rests

Finecut shaft, frosted
knobs, 3" long 50- 55

Prism, Star cut ends, 6"
long 65- 75

Zipper, squared ends, 3"
long 45- 53

Lamp

Box Diamond, 17" high   475- 500

Pitchers

Brilliant cut, 6½" high,
signed Hawkes (ill.) 240- 255

Florence, miniature, 6" high   125- 135

Hobstar, Thumbprint
handle, 10" high 225- 235

Pinwheel, tankard type . . .   220- 245

134

Punch Bowl		
Mitre Star, Leaf Fan, 11″ high, base separate (ill.)	1,450-1,550	
Sugar Bowl		
Flower design, 2¾″ high	130-	140
Toothpick Holders		
Diamond and Fan	55-	67
Fluted sides, prism base	60-	70
Pinwheel	55-	65
Tumblers		
Block, Star bottom	55-	65
Diamond and Fan	45-	53
Middlesex, signed Hawkes, late	68-	78
Vases		
Brunswick, V-shape, 12″ high, signed Hawkes	275-	300
Harvard, frosted flower decor, 13″ high	260-	275
Heavy cut, 16″ high, signed Hawkes	750-	800
Intaglio flowers, signed Sinclair, 14″ high	475-	500

Cut Glass Trademarks

Early American Period, 1771-1830
Middle Period, 1830-1880
Brilliant Period, 1880-1905

Most signed cut glass that one finds today is from the Brilliant Period. There were over a thousand cutting shops during this 25-year period. They did not make glass but bought their blanks from firms such as Libbey, Pairpoint, C. Dorflinger & Sons, Gillinder & Sons, T.G. Hawkes Glass Co., United States Glass Co., H.C. Fry Glass Co., and Corning Glass Co. "Signatures" were acid-etched on the bottom, inside the bottom, or on handles. Look carefully—signed pieces bring 40% to 50% more than unsigned. Here are a few trademarks used during the Brilliant Period.

1. T. B. Clark & Co., Honesdale, Pa. (1886)
2. C. E. Wheelock & Co., Peoria, Ill. (1893)
3. H. P. Sinclaire & Co., Corning, N.Y. (1890s)
4. Tuthill Glass Co., Middletown, N.Y. (1890s)
5. H. C. Fry Glass Co., Rochester, Pa. (1900s)
6. C. Dorflinger & Sons, Inc., White Mills, Pa.
7. J. D. Bergen Co., Meriden, Conn.
8. Lotus Cut Glass Co., Barnesville, Ohio (1911)
9. Richard Murr, San Francisco, Cal. (1905)
10. H. Perilstein, Philadelphia, Pa. (1906)
11. T. B. Clark & Co., Sellyville, Pa. (1898)
12. Phoenix Glass Co., Monaca and Pittsburgh, Pa. (1881)
13. Corning Glass Works, Corning, N.Y. (1904)
14. Corning Glass Works, Corning, N.Y. (1904)
15. Corning Glass Works, Corning, N.Y. (1909)
16. Corona Cut Glass Co., Toledo, Ohio (1906)
17. L. Straus & Sons, New York, N.Y. (1894)
18. Thatcher Bros., Fairhaven, Mass. (1894)
19. C. Dorflinger & Sons, White Mills, Pa. (1892)
20. C. Dorflinger & Sons, White Mills, Pa. (1892)
21. O.F. Egginton Co., Corning, N.Y. (1899)
22. T.G. Hawkes & Co., Corning, N.Y. (1890)
23. T.G. Hawkes & Co., Corning, N.Y. (1890)
24. T.G. Hawkes & Co., Corning, N.Y. (1902)
25. J. Hoare & Co., Corning, N.Y. (1895)
26. Libbey Glass Co., Toledo, Ohio (1895)

135

(continued)

27. Libbey Glass Co., Toledo, Ohio (1896)
28. Libbey Glass Co., Toledo, Ohio (1901)
29. Libbey Glass Co., Toledo, Ohio (1901)

Cut Velvet Glass

Cut Velvet Glass

Satin glass that shows the design in high relief with the white lining showing where the pattern was cut is called Cut Velvet. It was sometimes found with diamond quilting but usually ribbed. The Mt. Washington Glass Company and the Phoenix Glass Works in Pennsylvania made a great deal of it in the late 1800s. Repros, repros!

Bowl, blue, fluted lip, 8″ high $240-270
Bowl, Diamond Quilted, deep
    rose, 6″ dia. 233-243
Creamer, fluted top, white lining,
    ribbed yellow, signed Mt.
    Washington Glass Co. 230-250
Pitcher, deep rose, Diamond-
    Quilted, applied handle,
    Phoenix Glass 162-170
Tumbler, blue, ribbed, glossy,
    7″ high 148-160
Tumbler, honeycomb, pink,
    Diamond Quilted, 6½″ high,
    Phoenix 210-230
Vase, blue, Diamond Quilted, 10″
    high 220-240
Vase, pink/white casing, slender
    neck, 7½″ high (ill.) 247-260
Vase, yellow and white Diamond
    Quilted, 6″ high 172-182

Czechoslovakia

Daguerreotypes

Czechoslovakia

This country claimed its independence from Austria-Hungary after World War I. Most pieces are marked "Czechoslovakia" though some are artist/maker marked, indicating they were made before the country became independent. Most of what you find are in the $8 to $30 range.

> Vase, handled, stenciled design under glaze, signed Erphila Art Pottery on paper label, 7" high (ill.) . . . . $ 24- 32

Da Latte

Another of the cameo types, it was usually opaque and was made by Andre De Latte in Nancy, France, in the 1920s. Light fixtures were also made there, but De Latte is best remembered for his cameo glass.

> Box, 3½" high, 4" square, pink ground, cut blue flowers, signed $450-525
> Vase, aqua ground, birds, flowers, blue/green decor, signed, 8¾" high 475-490
> Vase, blue ground, purple iris decor, signed, 9½" high 480-540
> Vase, gold/red ground, yellow/ pink floral, signed, 11½" high . 500-515
> Vase, opaque ground, handled, river scene, 14" high 320-360
> Vase, pink with mottled blue ground, lavender-pink floral, signed 340-360
> Vase, yellow, trees, deer, brown background, signed, 8½" high . 450-480

Daguerreotypes

The method is named for the Frenchman who discovered it—Louis Jacques Mande Daguerre—in 1837. He covered a bright copper plate with silver salts, then placed it between two pieces of glass to protect it. When exposed to light, the silver compound produced a picture. Civil War scenes are collectible and rare.

> Civil War soldier, Union Army
> (ill.) . . . . $ 58- 68
> Daguerreotypes without case . . . 3- 4
> Eagle on American Flag 31- 41
> Girl with dog 27- 37
> Volunteer fireman, Ambrotype* . 52- 62
> Wedding photo 24- 34

*Ambrotypes are photographs on glass.

Daguerreotype Cases

Daguerreotype Cases

Littlefield, Parsons and Company patented these cases on October 14, 1856. When you find them with the daguerreotypes missing, they make fine holders for your favorite photos.

> Average price . . . . $ 9- 16

D'argental

Another of the cameo-type glasses produced in the last part of the 19th century, it was named for its originator who lived in France. Somewhat similar to Galle and Lalique. Scarce.

Bowl, yellow matte, red roses,
leaves, carved, 6" high, signed . $410-450
Bowl, red matte, blue/white
flowers, carved cameo, 8½"
high 450-500
Vase, blue morning glories, yellow
ground, cameo, 8" high 410-460
Vase, frosted blue ground, brown
and rust leaves, signed, 6"
high 420-445
Vase, 3-layer, amber-rose ground,
signed, 7" high 510-560

Darning Eggs

In Grandmother's day, this was a very important item in the sewing basket. They're collectible, especially those with sterling silver and 14k gold handles. What you pay depends on condition, etc.

Darning Eggs   **Daum Nancy**

Daum Nancy

Auguste and Antonin Daum made and signed this beautiful cameo-type glass in the late 1800s. They also made fine enameled glass. Both are hard to find today.

Bottle, acid cut ground, man
and windmill, enameled,
stopper . . . . $ 475- 550
Bowl, blue iris cut through,
floral, 8" high, signed 670- 740
Bowl, fruit decor, blue
ground. 310- 340
Box, carved blue crocus, blue-
green ground, lid, signed . . 440- 480

Compote, amethyst, footed,
8½" high, signed 235- 260
Compote, blue and brown
ground, sprigs, leaves,
footed, 8" 420- 450
Jar, floral scene cut through,
acid finish, signed 420- 480
Lamp, enameled leaf decor,
mottled floral background,
signed 1,400-1,600
Pitcher, frosted green, floral,
9½" high, signed 450- 500
Plate, turned up sides, yellow/
orange 368- 425
Rose bowl, green, blue cut
through, 3½" high 320- 370
Tumbler, barrel shape, gold
ground, flowers, 5" high . . . 400- 500
Tumbler, white ground,
shaded red, blue, green,
signed 475- 525
Vase, birds in trees, green/
blue/brown/red, 8" high,
signed 640- 720
Vase, enamel, floral, medal-
lion, 4½" high, signed 450- 500
Vase, flowers, 28" high 1,700-1,900
Vase, mottled orange, yellow,
6½" high, signed 410- 430
Vase, satin, orange/green,
enameled pseudo-cameo
technique, 8¾" high (ill.) . . . 240- 265
Vase, serpentine shape, floral,
brown/green/blue, 7¼"
high, signed 510- 530
Vase, summer scene, 10" high,
signed 445- 485
Vase, winter scene, 9" high,
signed 470- 525

Davenport China

Davenport China

Made by John Davenport at Lonport, England, late 1700s, this china is light in weight, cream colored, and has a soft, velvety texture. It's marked with the name Davenport above an impressed anchor. The factory closed in the late 1800s.

Creamer, bulbous white with deep blue decor	$ 96-107
Cup/saucer, Derby colors, 1810	70- 85
Dish in plated holder, Imari colors, 1875	95-115
Dish, vegetable, Berry pattern, impressed signature and anchor	49- 61
Ewer, white, blue marbling, 1815	128-140
Jug, bright blue decorations, 1800	182-197
Platter, blue/white Oriental, reticulated border, anchor mark	99-120
Tea set (teapot, covered sugar), Spring pattern in red/green, anchor	240-270
Teapot, pink lustre decorations	240-260
Trivet, blue/red decor, no mark	97-108
Urn, blue/gold on white, 6″ high (ill.)	230-260

De Vez

De Vez

This glass was made in Pantin, France, and was similar in style to that made by Marinot, Rousseau, and others. It is another of the cameo types, late 1800s, and is scarce today.

Atomizer, birds, brown/yellow, 6″ high, signed	$450-500
Bowl, 3″ high, 5″ dia., flowers/birds	270-290
Bowl, 4″ high, 4½″ dia., scenic, blue/green, signed	370-380
Vase, acid cut, harbor scene, 8½″ high, signed	640-685
Vase, scenic, satin ground, signed, 8½″ high	510-620
Vase, 7″ high, river scene, mountains, signed	420-440
Vase, 7½″ high, house/trees, pink, green, signed	400-450
Vase, translucent ground, castle scene, signed, 10″ high	510-620
Vase, 11″ high, scenic, blue/red iridescent, signed	385-410

Vase, 14″ high, clouds, blue/green ground, signed	500-520

DeVilbiss

DeVilbiss

Steuben made both atomizers and cologne sets for this company. All pieces are signed DeVILBISS.

Atomizer, black satin glass, orange enamel floral, brass fittings, 5½″ high (ill.)	$ 42- 52
Atomizer, blue opalescent, 6″ high	34- 44
Atomizer, gold/amber, 4¼″ high	38- 48
Atomizer, orange/gold, brass fittings, 5½″ high (ill.)	37- 47
Atomizer, white opalescent, 5¾″ high	30- 40
Cologne, orange/gold, brass fittings, 4½″ high (ill.)	40- 47
Cologne, white opalescent, 5½″ high	29- 38

Decanters

Decanters

Used mainly by taprooms and inns to store their wines and liquors, they became stylish in homes in the mid-1700s. This first were crude in shape and material; later they were

139

(continued)

made of cut glass, Amberina, even Tiffany glass.

Amber, Inverted Thumbprint, stopper, pedestal foot .... $ 60- 70
Brown, blown, fluted sides, clear stopper, attributed to Sandwich, 1850s, 14" high 120-140
Clear, gold leaf design, 12" high (ill.) 220-260
Clear, hand-painted eagles, dated 1779, blown, clear stoppers, pair 650-725
Clear, 4-part, stoppers, Sandwich type, late 1800s, France, 12½" high 120-130
Clear, signed Libbey, silver overlay, Riverboat type 170-190
Cobalt, swirled body, clear stopper, pontil mark, mid-1800s 150-160
½ pint, 3-mold (McKearin G 111-14) 170-190
Engraved glass, floral/Cupid designs in silver base, 6½" high, pr. 460-500

Decoys

Decoys

Prices for these have gone sky-high. The prices given are for decoys in good condition, taking age and wear into account.

Black Duck, by Gus Wilson . . $ 140- 150
Black Duck, by Thomas Fitzpatrick, Delanco, N.J. 145- 160
Black Duck, by Wild-fowler Decoys, Inc., Old Saybrook, Conn. 75- 85
Black Duck, by Mason's, Premier grade 165- 180
Brant, by Mason's, Challenge grade 180- 195
Buffleheads, drake and hen, by Doug Jester, pr. 220- 235
Canvasback Drake, made of balsa, by the Ward Brothers, Crisfield, Md. Both Stephen W. (1895-1976) and

his brother, Lemeul T., Jr. (1896-), are world-famous for their birds 550- 600
Canvasbacks, balsa, drake and hen, Ward Brothers, pr. 1,400-1,500
Cape Cod Black Duck 75- 85
Chesapeake Bay Coot, by Madison R. Mitchell, Havre de Grace, Md. 100- 120
Coot, by Singing River Decoy Co., New Orleans, La., pre-1940 .... 65- 75
Coot, by Benjamin J. Schmidt, Centerline, Mich. 165- 180
Coot, maker unknown, initials "D.G." carved in bottom .. 55- 65
Coot, by Xavier Bourg, Larose, La. 140- 155
Gadwall Drake, by John English; repainted by Robert White 450- 500
Goldeneyes, drake and hen, by Madison R. Mitchell, pr. ... 300- 325
Life-sized Great Horned Owl, by C. Victor Bracher, c. 1943 .... 400- 425
Mallard Drake, by Harry Fennimore, Bordentown, N.J. 177- 186
Mallard Hen, by the Jester family, Chincoteague, Va... 85- 95
Old Squaw Drake, by Milton Crowley, South Addison, Me., c. 1920s 80- 90
Old Squaw Drake, by Norris E. Pratt 80- 90
Red-Breasted Merganser, by Gus Wilson, Casco Bay, Me. 225- 250
Red-Breasted Merganser, by Harry V. Shourds 255- 270
Red-Breasted Merganser Drake, by Hurley Conklin . 165- 180
Red-Breasted Merganser Drake, by Frank Dobbins, Jonesport, Me. 90- 100
Redhead Hen, by H. Keyes Chadwick; carved in 1949 when he was 80 .... 255- 280
Scaup Drake, hollow-carved by Harry V. Shourds 165- 175
Scaup Hen, hollow-carved by Capt. Jess Birdsall, Barnegat, N.J. 60- 70
Sleeping Canvasback Hen, by J. Corbin ("Corb") Reed, 1962 .... 220- 245
White-Winged Scoter, by Warren Wass, Cape Split, Me., c. 1905 .... 60- 70

Dedham Pottery

Dedham Pottery

Alexander Robertson founded this company in Chelsea, Massachusetts, in the late 1860s. He changed its name from Chelsea Pottery to Chelsea Ceramic Art Works in 1872, and finally to Dedham Pottery around 1894. They specialized in crackleware in blue and high-fired colored pieces. The rabbit motif is what you see the most of on Dedham pottery. Most collectible today.

Bowl and plate, rabbits, signed	$123-140
Bowl, mushrooms, Chelsea Pottery mark	75- 85
Candlesticks, rabbits, signed, pr.	170-190
Chocolate pot, rabbits, signed	160-170
Creamer, elephants, 4½" high	155-175
Creamer, rabbit, 3¾" high	120-140
Creamer, rabbit, 6¼" high	133-143
Cup/saucer, rabbits, elephant, polar bear	120-140
Dish, elephants, Chelsea Pottery mark	80- 90
Egg cup, rabbits	150-160
Mayonnaise bowl, rabbits, 6¼" dia.	98-107
Mug, handled, rabbit border, 5½" high	200-220
Mug, handled, water lily, large	88- 94
Plate, duck, 10" dia.	130-140
Plate, rabbit, 8"	110-121
Plate, rabbit, 10" (ill.)	72- 81
Plate, swan, 8½" dia.	172-182
Plate, turkey, 8"	120-130
Platter, rabbit border	190-230
Salt/pepper shakers, rabbit, pr.	160-180
Sauce dish, rabbits	70- 82
Saucer, water lily, 4" dia.	54- 63
Sugar bowl, lid, 3"	160-170
Tile, 6" square, horse chestnut	92-102
Tray, elephant border, 7¼" long	260-280
Vase, blue over green, 4½" high	500-550

Vase, charcoal gray, raised floral decor, 6" high	90- 98

Dejeuner Set

A porcelain tray, teapot, cream jug, sugar bowl and one or two cups with spoons. A set for one was called Solitaire; for two, Tete-a-tete. Usually made of soft paste porcelain, they were popular in the early 1800s until just before the turn of the century.

Deldare

See **Buffalo Pottery**.

Delft

Delft

Earthenware with a blue decoration on a white background. Tin compound was used to produce the glaze and a number of companies made it at Delft, Holland, at the beginning of the 17th century. It was also made in England. Most of what you find in shops today is from the late 1800s until World War I. Now being reproduced.

Ashtray, windmill scene	$ 30- 38
Bottle, blue/white, 9½" high, 1740s	225-245
Bottle, Dutch girl with dogcart, windmill scene	47- 57
Clock, Dutch scene, 8-day German movement	170-180
Coffee grinder, wall type, typical	92-102
Cow, 6" long, signed Delft	75- 85
Creamer, flowers, Holland, 2¾" high	16- 20

141

(continued)

Creamer, sleeping cow, Germany,
1890 .... 50- 60
Cup/saucer, floral, Holland, 2"
high 12- 17
Cup/saucer, windmill scene 12- 18
Figurine, Dutch, girl and boy,
pr. 50- 60
Inkwell, stand, metal cap, blue/
white, no mark 40- 50
Jar, lid, Dutch boy, 13" high 270-281
Plaque, sailing scene, 18th
century, 14½" high 288-292
Plate, blue, Dutch canal in winter,
13½" dia. 50- 60
Stein, drinking scene along canal,
dated 1723, 11" high, pewter
cap 342-362
Tray, water scene, blue/white,
12" wide 160-185
Vase, blue/white, scrolls, lovers,
16" high, pr. 270-285
Vase, windmill, Holland, 7½"
high (ill.) 110-120
Wine bottle, Holland, Dutch boy,
7½" high 44- 53

Demography
See **Genealogy.**

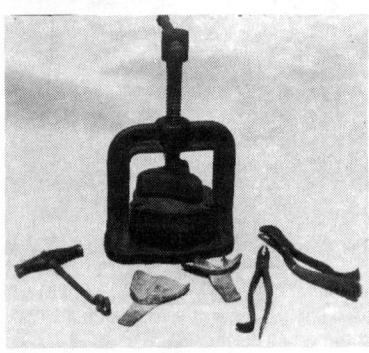

Dental Collectibles

Dental Collectibles

If you think going to the dentist today isn't
fun, you should note what our grandparents
went through. Old dental tools, tooth pullers,
and the like are being collected today.

Cast iron mold for making false
teeth, late 1800s (ill.) .... $ 47- 56
Dentist's cabinet, glass doors,
wooden drawers, early 1900s .. 74- 86
Dentist's chair, felt covered, tilt-
back type, late 1800s 140-170
Dentist's drill, foot-powered type,
late 1800s 70- 80

Hook-type tooth puller, mid-
1800s (ill.) 22- 31
Plier-type tooth puller, late 1800s
(ill.) 18- 27

Depression Glass, Miss America

Depression Glass

The glass is confusing because collectors
and those compiling books about it have
given names to patterns unnamed by the
makers. It was made during the depression
years of the late 1920s and early 1930s and
was considered inexpensive tableware. Hocking, Westmoreland Glass Company, and the
Indiana Glass Company were three of many
firms making it. Pink, green, milk-white, and
amber were just a few of the colors.

Bowl
American Sweetheart, cereal,
pink .... $ 10- 17
Horseshoe, berry, 9" dia., topaz .. 21- 39
Normandie, berry, 8½" dia.,
green 17- 27
Patrician, berry, 8½" dia., green . 14- 23
Petal Swirl, console, footed, 10½"
dia., teal 26- 34
Poppy, vegetable 19- 28
Royal Lace, fruit, 3 legs, 10" dia.,
green 26- 34
Sandwich, console, 9" dia. 20- 27
Sharon (Cabbage Rose), cereal,
pink 14- 25
Windsor Diamond, berry, 8⅜"
dia., pink 14- 23
Butter Dish, Covered
Cherry Blossom, pink 48- 57
Floral, green 42- 52
Lace Edge (Open Lace), pink 31- 41
Windsor Diamond, green 32- 42
Candleholder
Madrid, pink, pr. 19- 27

Petal Swirl, double branch, teal,
pr. 21- 32

Child's Set
Cherry Blossom, 14 pcs., Delfite .   170-180
Cherry Blossom, 14 pcs., pink . . .   140-162

Cookie Jar
Cameo.   21- 28
Princess, pink 19- 27
Royal Lace, glass cover, cobalt . .   62- 72

Creamer and Sugar
Cameo.   17- 26
Madrid, blue 31- 40
Petalware, monax or cremax 14- 22
Princess, topaz 19- 27

Cup and Saucer
Adam (Adams) 10- 14
American Sweetheart, monax . . .   13- 22
American Sweetheart, pink 9- 18
Cameo.   10- 17
Cherry Blossom 12- 24
Dogwood (Wild Rose), thin, pink .   12- 23
Horseshoe, pink 11- 22
Madrid 10- 20
Mayfair (Open Rose), blue 30- 34
Miss America, pink (ill.) 14- 23
Moderntone, cobalt 9- 18
Petalware, pink or crystal 9- 20
Princess, topaz 10- 19
Ribbon Candy, crystal 10- 20
Rosemary (Dutch Rose), pink . . .   9- 17
Royal Lace, cobalt 22- 31
Royal Lace, crystal 9- 27

Decanter
Cameo, 10" high 38- 47
Mayfair, drop stopper 42- 50

Pitcher
Adam, 8" high 40- 50
Doric and Pansy, footed, 7½"
high, teal. 60- 70
Floral, footed cone, 32 oz., 8"
high 21- 30
Horseshoe, footed, ½ gal., green .   52- 61
Miss America, 65 oz., 7¾" high,
pink 42- 52
Patrician, 67 oz., 8½" high,
amber 40- 50
Sharon (Cabbage Rose), 80 oz.,
green.   125-145

Plate
Adam, cake server 14- 26
Adam, dinner 9- 20
American Sweetheart, dinner,
monax 10- 22
American Sweetheart, salad, 8"
dia., cherry red (ill.)   90-100
Cameo, dinner 8- 19
Cherry Blossom, dinner 9- 17
Christmas Candy, dinner, teal . . .   8- 18
Cloverleaf, salad, 8" dia. 9- 19
Cloverleaf, salad, 8" dia., ebony . .   17- 26

Depression Glass, American Sweetheart

Dogwood, dinner, pink 12- 21
Floral, salad, 8" dia. 9- 18
Florentine, dinner, hexagonal . . .   9- 20
Florentine, dinner, round 8- 18
Lace Edge, salad, 8³⁄₈" dia. 9- 20
Madrid, divided grill 9- 19
Mayfair, cake, footed, 10" dia.,
green or pink 17- 26
Miss America, salad, 8½" dia.,
green.   10- 26
Moderntone, cake, 10⁵⁄₈" dia.,
cobalt 14- 24
Normandie, divided grill, 11" dia.,
pink 8- 27
Petal Swirl, serving or cake, teal .   16- 25
Princess, dinner, topaz 9- 17
Rosemary, dinner, green 9- 18
Sandwich, dinner, 10½" dia. 10- 17
Sandwich, footed salver 16- 25
Sandwich, dinner, 12" dia. 9- 20

Platter
Cameo.   17- 27
Doric, oval, 12" 10- 20
Miss America, oval, 12", crystal .   12- 24
Petalware, oval, 13", cremax 22- 34

Salt and Pepper Shakers
Cameo, footed, 4" high, pr. 32- 44
Cube, pink 17- 27
Miss America, footed, pink, pr. . .   23- 34
Moderntone, footed, 4½" high,
cobalt, pr. 28- 37
Sandwich, pr. 24- 35
Windsor Diamond, pr. 26- 36

Tumbler
American Sweetheart, table,
9 oz., pink 18- 26
Cameo, footed cone, 9 oz., green .   10- 20
Cherry Blossom, cone, round
foot, 9 oz., Delfite 24- 33
Doric and Pansy, table, 9 oz.,
teal 17- 22

143

(continued)

Floral, footed cone, 7 oz., 4¾″ high	9- 17
Mayfair, 9 oz., pink	9- 18
Patrician, 9 oz.	10- 19
Royal Ruby, table, 9 oz.	9- 19

Desk Sets

Desk Sets

Every type, from the lowliest to the most expensive, was in vogue until the invention of the ink-filled pen.

Brass desk set, French, mid-1800s, signed M. Bounel	$ 450-	525
Desk set, brass, cut glass ink-wells, early 1900s	97-	108
Desk set, iron, 2 inkwells, footed, mid-1800s	54-	64
Paperweight type, pelican, signed Davesen (ill.)	74-	83
Tiffany desk set, 5 pieces, signed Tiffany Studios, bronze/glass	900-1,400	
Tiffany desk set, 6 pieces, Spider Web, signed and numbered	1,400-1,600	

Disneyana Collectibles

Disneyana Collectibles

Mickey Mouse watches are out of sight, pricewise. Anything having to do with the early days of Disney is highly collectible today. Look out for reproductions!

Bugs Bunny mug, plastic	$ 9-	16
Davey Crockett pocket knife	17-	28
Donald Duck bank, plastic	42-	52
Donald Duck watch, Ingersoll, 1939, marked WDP (ill.)	200-240	
Dopey figurine, chalkware, 4″ high	24-	37
Dumbo creamer	19-	27
Mickey and Minnie Mouse figurines, painted, ea.	52-	61
Mickey Mouse alphabet bowl, cereal premium	41-	52
Mickey Mouse clock, Ingersoll, 1930s	400+	
Mickey Mouse dishes, child's service for 6, Japan	92-104	
Mickey Mouse watch, Ingersoll, metal band, running condition	247-262	
Pluto mug, Japan	38-	47
Pluto pencil sharpener	9-	18
Snow White and 7 Dwarfs cottage cheese glass, milk company premium, set	120-145	
Snow White fork	24-	32
Snow White watch, running condition	110-124	

Documents

Old deeds, land grants, marriage certificates, all are collectible and bringing good prices. A land grant dated later than 1836 isn't too valuable as presidents were given secretaries about that time and the secretary signed for the president. Fun to collect and getting more valuable every day.

Average price, common variety	$ 4-	10

Doll Furniture and Accessories

Bed, complete with spread, blue finish	$ 30-	35
Bedroom set, 5-pc.: bed, tin washstand, table, 2 chairs, oak, 1″ scale, all	130-145	
Birdcage with bird	35-	44
Bird's-eye maple bed, 4″×21″, slats, handmade quilt	210-225	
Bookcases, balsa wood, pr.	18-	24
Booth table, 3 pcs., all	19-	27

Doll Furniture

Brass bed, 4"×19", springs, pad, spread, all	185-195
Candelabra, pot metal, 2" high	9- 15
Chair, ladderback, 4" high	14- 23
Chair, wicker rocker, 2½" high	18- 25
Cradle, hand-carved, 12"×16"	37- 45
Cradle, hand-carved, walnut, 13½" high to hood, pre-Civil War	95-115
Desk, dropfront, matching chair, both	28- 36
Desk, wooden, brass pulls, 6¼" high (ill.)	65- 75
Fireplace tools with stand, 6 pcs., all	9- 14
Knives and forks, service for 12, complete, all	35- 45
Living room suite, 6 pcs., complete, all	48- 57
Stove, 4-burner, 4" high	20- 25
Trunk for doll clothes	65- 75
Wicker porch set, 4 pcs.: swing, settee, 2 chairs, all	105-115

Dolls

This category is one of the most popular and getting more expensive every day. Just know your dolls or get a book and study.

All Bisque

American, all painted bisque, marked STORY BOOK DOLL USA 11; mohair wig, painted features, jointed at hips and shoulders, 5" tall ...$	55-	70
American, Nancy Ann Story Book Christening Baby, all painted bisque, marked STORY BOOK		
DOLL USA 2; molded/painted hair and features, jointed baby body. All original, 3½" tall	58-	72
American, Nancy Ann Story Book Doll, all painted bisque, marked STORY BOOK DOLL USA; mohair wig, molded/painted features, shoes and socks, jointed at shoulders, 5¼" tall	59-	69
Austria and Germany, all stone bisque, marked C.D. Kenny Co. (ink stamp); molded/painted hair, features, and clothes; jointed at hips and shoulders, 4" tall	70-	80
French (?), all bisque, socket head, marked 2; mohair wig, glass sleep eyes, closed mouth, jointed at hips and shoulders, molded/painted shoes and black stockings, 8" tall	460-	520
French type, all bisque, swivel head, marked 16/0; human hair wig, paperweight eyes, closed mouth, jointed shoulders and hips, molded/painted shoes and socks, 7" tall	410-	465
French type, all bisque, clothes sewed on; mohair wig, glass inset eyes, closed mouth; jointed shoulders and hips, molded/painted shoes and socks. All original, 4" tall	365-	425
French type, all bisque, marked 13 on head and body; socket head, mohair wig, glass inset eyes, closed mouth; molded/painted shoes with heels and long black stockings, 5" tall	255-	275
German, all bisque, swivel head, marked 4; mohair wig, glass inset eyes, closed mouth; jointed shoulders and hips, molded/painted shoes and socks, 9" tall	425-	485
German, all bisque, unmarked; molded/painted hair, features, and		

(continued)

clothes; jointed at hips
and shoulders, 6″ tall ... 275- 350
German, all bisque, un-
marked; molded/painted
hair, features, and
clothes, 2½″ tall 185- 250
German, all bisque, marked
Germany; molded/
painted hair, features,
and clothes, 2¼″ tall.... 210- 265
German, all bisque, marked
Germany 4325; molded/
painted hair, features,
and clothes, 2″ and 3″
tall, ea................ 220- 265
German, all bisque, marked
Germany; molded/
painted hair, features,
and clothes, 2¼″ tall,
ea. 210- 265
German, Andy Gump, all
bisque nodder, marked
ANDY GUMP Germany;
molded/painted features,
hat, and clothes; swivel/
nodding head, 4″ tall ... 290- 355
German Nodder, all bisque,
marked Germany;
molded/painted hair,
features, bonnet, purse,
clothes, and shoes, 3″
tall 200- 255
German, Nodder, all bisque,
marked Germany;
molded/painted hair,
features, hat, clothes,
shoes and socks; swivel/
nodding head, 3″ tall ... 195- 255
German Rachel, all bisque
nodder, marked
RACHEL Germany;
molded/painted face,
features, arms, hat, and
clothes; swivel/nodding
head, 3½″ tall 220- 265

Celluloid Dolls
Best & Co., all celluloid,
marked BEST U.S.A.,;
molded hair, features and
body, 3″ tall 48- 60
Buschow & Beck (?), celluloid, swivel head, molded/
painted hair, inset glass
eyes, closed mouth; celluloid jointed body marked
(a helmet) Minerva. 18½″
tall 195- 245
Buschow & Beck (?), celluloid shoulder-head,
marked (a helmet) Ger-

many To2 8ct; molded/
painted hair, inset glass
eyes, closed mouth; cloth
body with celluloid
hands, 10½″ tall 92- 108
Company unidentified, all
celluloid, marked patent
No. 12574 No. 12575;
molded/painted features,
legs push into body,
squeaker, 5″ tall 67- 80
Company unidentified, all
celluloid, jointed at hips
and shoulders, molded/
painted features and
clothes. Marked
JAPAN, 3″ tall 35- 45
Company unidentified, all
celluloid baby; jointed at
hips and shoulders,
molded/painted hair,
painted eyes, closed
mouth. Body marked
CVO (superimposed
in a circle) U.S.A. 7″ long 62- 75
Company unidentified, celluloid head, hands, and
feet, molded/painted fea-
tures; cloth body stuffed
with excelsior. Marked
JAPAN, 8″ tall 55- 65
Company unidentified, celluloid shoulder-head,
marked Made in France;
molded/painted hair,
inset celluloid eyes, open/
closed mouth; all cloth
body, 15½″ tall 170- 210
Rheinsche Gummi, celluloid
shoulder head marked
turtle in a diamond;
human hair wig, inset
glass eyes, open mouth,
cloth body with celluloid
arms. All original
Swedish costume, 11″
tall, pr............... 330- 370
Unmarked, all celluloid,
molded/painted features
and clothes, jointed at
shoulders, 6″ tall 57- 67
Unmarked, "Carnival Doll,"
all celluloid; molded/
painted hair, features,
shoes and socks; jointed
at shoulders, 12″ tall.... 65- 80

China Frozen Charlottes, Frozen Charlies
Charlotte in a tub, pink
china with molded/

146

painted features in white
china tub, 1¼″ and 2″ .. 195- 230
Frozen Charlotte, unglazed,
molded hair and features
with painted eyebrows,
3″ tall 68- 85
Frozen Charlotte, unglazed,
mohair wig, painted fea-
tures, 3¼″ tall........ 70- 85
Frozen Charlotte, white
china, mohair wig,
painted features, 4″ tall . 75- 95
Frozen Charlotte, white
china, molded/painted
hair (1850s type) and
features, 4¼″ tall 75- 95
Frozen Charlotte, white
china, molded/painted
hair (1850s type) and features, 5½″ tall........ 85- 110
Frozen Charlotte, white
china, molded/painted
hair (1850s type) and features, gold lustre shoes,
2″ tall 58- 72
Frozen Charlottes; three
black Charlottes are un-
glazed with molded hair
and features; white Char-
lotte is white china with
painted hair and features.
1″ down to ½″ tall, ea. .. 42- 60
Frozen Charlie, flesh tint
face; molded/painted boy
style hair, molded eye-
lids, painted features,
white china body, 11½″
tall.................. 350- 395
Frozen Charlie, all over
flesh tint; molded/
painted boy style hair,
painted features, 14″
tall.................. 395- 440
Frozen Charlie, flesh tint
face; molded/painted boy
style hair, painted fea-
tures, white china body,
15½″ tall............ 420- 465
Frozen Charlie, flesh tint
face; molded/painted boy
style hair, painted fea-
tures, blue tie, white
china body, 16½″ tall ... 460- 520
Frozen Charlie, flesh tint
face; molded/painted boy
style hair, painted fea-
tures, white china body,
16½″ tall............ 510- 575

China Head Dolls
1830s Biedermeier type,

china-shoulder-head;
human hair wig, blue
painted eyes; cloth body
with china arms and legs,
19″ tall 2,650-3,108
1830s Biedermeier type,
china-shoulder-head;
human hair wig, blue
painted eyes, cloth body
with china arms, 24″ tall. 3,300+
1830s Biedermeier type,
china-shoulder-head; wig
missing, blue painted
eyes, cloth body and
china arms and legs, 9″
tall, ea............... 1,375-1,650
1830s Biedermeier type,
china-shoulder-head;
light creamy tint; mohair
wig, blue painted eyes,
cloth body with china
arms and legs, 18″ tall .. 2,400-2,800
1830s Biedermeier type,
china-shoulder-head,
light flesh tint; human
hair wig, blue painted
eyes, cloth body with
china arms and legs,
15½″ tall............ 2,500-2,900
1840s type, china-shoulder-
head, pink tint; brown
painted eyes, cloth body
with kid arms, 27″ tall .. 2,400-2,700
1840s type, china-shoulder-
head, slight pink tint;
blue painted eyes, cloth
body with kid arms,
23½″ tall............ 1,700-2,000
1840s type, china-shoulder-
head, pink tint; blue
painted eyes, cloth body
with china arms and legs,
17½″ tall............ 1,500-1,800
1840s type, china-shoulder-
head; brown painted
eyes, cloth body with kid
arms, individually
stitched/wired fingers,
14″ tall 1,575-1,800
1840s type, china-shoulder-
head, pink tint; blue
painted eyes, cloth body
with china arms and legs,
14″ tall 1,750-2,000
1850s type, Jenny Lind,
china-shoulder-head,
creamy tint; brown
painted eyes, cloth body
with kid hands and feet,
16″ tall 2,400-2,750

147

(continued)

Marotte (doll on stick), bisque flange head, marked 3200 AM. Music box plays when doll is twirled, 14" tall.....................$425-600

Pinocchio, composition swivel head, molded/painted hair, features, clothes. Marked DIS. and ©Walt Disney. Made by Ideal Novelty & Toy Co., 11" tall........................$135-165

Bisque socket head, marked C. M. Bergmann-Simon & Halbig 8½. Tiny red 18 on forehead, human hair wig, sleep eyes, open mouth, wood and composition body, 21" tall. $375-475

Byle-Low bisque swivel head, marked Copr. BY GRACE S. PUTNAM. Made in Germany, molded-painted hair, glass sleep eyes, closed mouth, cloth body, celluloid hands, 14" tall. $510-530.

1850-60s type, china-shoulder-head; blue painted eyes, cloth body with china arms and legs, 4¼" tall 250- 320

1850-60s type, china-shoulder-head, flesh tint; brown painted eyes, molded lids, lower lashes, exposed ears, cloth body with china hands on kid arms, 20" tall 2,950-3,100

1850-60s type, china-shoulder-head, creamy tint; brown painted eyes, molded lids, lower lashes, smiling mouth, cloth body with kid arms, 27½" tall 4,400-4,800

1850-60s type, china-shoulder-head, marked 1845 (in black under-glaze) on lower part of back left shoulder; light flesh tint, blue painted eyes, cloth body with kid arms and feet, 25½" tall 3,100-3,600

1850-60s type, Jenny Lind, china-shoulder-head; blue painted eyes, molded lids; cloth body marked Patd. Dec. 15, 1885; china arms, Philip Goldsmith body, 22" tall 3,450-3,700

China, Heads Only

Doll Head, 1850-60s type, creamy china, 3" tall, 2½" tall, ea. 160- 185

Doll Head, 1850-60s type, 2½" tall 110- 140

Doll Head, 1850-60s type, turned head, 6" tall, ea. . . 255- 275

Doll Head, 1880s type, 3" tall, 4" tall, 2½" tall, ea. . 130- 155

Doll Head, 1880s type, china-shoulder-head, white china, blue painted eyes, 4½" tall 155- 175

Doll Head, 1880s type, china-shoulder-head, white china, blue painted eyes, 3½" tall 150- 170

Doll Head, 1880s type, china-shoulder-head, white china, blue painted eyes, 2" tall 135- 155

Cloth Dolls

Chase, Martha J., boy, cloth stockinet head; molded, oil painted hair and features, molded ears, early pink sateen covered cloth body with oil painted stockinet arms and legs, 18½" tall 300- 380

Chase, Martha J., baby, cloth stockinet head; molded, oil painted hair and features, molded ears, sateen covered cloth body with oil painted stockinet arms and legs, 26" tall 230- 260

Chase (?) (similar to Martha Chase except a finer finish), cloth stockinet head; mohair wig, molded, oil painted features, molded ears, sateen body with oil painted stockinet arms and legs, 20½" tall 240- 280

Chase, Martha J., toddler, cloth stockinet head; molded, oil painted hair and features, molded ears, sateen covered cloth body with oil painted stockinet arms and legs, 16½" tall 245- 295

Kamkins, molded cloth head; mohair wig, oil painted features, all cloth body, jointed at hips and shoulders, 21" tall 320- 355

Kruger, R. G., dwarfs, molded mask face with painted features, velveteen body; tag reads AUTHENTIC WALT DISNEY CHARAC-TER, exclusive with R. G. KRUGER New York. 12" tall, ea. 95- 135

Lenci, molded felt head, mohair wig, painted eyes; felt, straw-stuffed body, jointed at hips and shoulders. All original. Boy marked #300J, girl's tag missing, 18" tall 320- 370

Lenci, all felt, swivel head; yarn-like hair sewed into felt in rows, molded/painted features with side glancing eyes; body jointed shoulders and hips. Paper tags on dress, MODELLO DEPOSITATO LENCI

149

(continued)

TORINO made in Italy.
19″ tall 350- 410

Lenci, molded felt head, mohair wig, felt, straw-stuffed body, jointed at hips and shoulders. All original including tags. Marked boy #300/10, girl #300/34, 18″ tall, ea. 360- 425

Lenci, troubadour and dancer, all felt, swivel head; molded/painted hair and features, body jointed shoulders and hips, stitched knee. Paper tag says LENCI di E. SCAVINI Made In Italy N 161. All original, 25″ tall, ea............... 400- 425

Lenci, flapper, molded felt head, painted eyes; felt, straw-stuffed body, joint-ed at hips and shoulders. Original costume, 25″ tall................ 350- 395

Unmarked, all printed cloth boy with printed clothes. Box in hip pocket marked QUAKER CRACKELS, 15″ tall 132- 150

Unmarked, all printed cloth doll, 11″ tall.......... 70- 80

Unmarked, all printed cloth doll with printed clothes. Marked on body, My Name is Miss Flaked Rice, 25½″ tall 130- 140

Unmarked, early molded cloth head, molded/painted hair (1840s type), painted eyes, all cloth body, 21″ tall 360- 425

Unmarked, German peasant girl, cloth head; molded/oil painted features, cloth body. All originals, 12″ tall 185- 210

Unmarked, molded cloth head covered with silk stockinet, mohair wig, painted eyes, cloth body with mache hands, 26″ tall, pr.............. 450- 530

Unmarked, Orphan Annie, all cloth doll with painted features, mohair wig. All original, 16½″ tall..... 130- 145

Walker, Izannah, molded cloth shoulder-head, oil painted hair and features, all cloth body with oil painted hands, 16½″ tall................. 1,950-2,350

Wellings, Norah, Jack Tar, felt head, molded/painted features, all cloth body; marked on foot, Made in England by Norah Well-ings, 10½″ tall 33- 45

Composition Dolls

Alexander Doll Co., compo swivel head, marked MADAME ALEXAN-DER SONJA HENIE; mohair wig, glasslike eyes, open mouth; compo jointed body, 17½″ tall.. 140- 165

Alexander Doll Co., compo swivel head, marked PRINCESS ELIZA-BETH ALEXANDER DOLL CO.; mohair wig, glasslike sleep eyes, open mouth, compo jointed body, 17″ tall ... 170- 200

Alexander Doll Co., compo flange head, marked MADAME ALEXAN-DER; molded/painted hair, glasslike sleep eyes, open mouth; cloth body with compo arms and legs. All original, 24″ tall.................. 185- 215

Alexander Doll Co., compo swivel head, marked MADAME ALEXAN-DER SONJA HENIE; mohair wig, glasslike sleep eyes, open mouth, compo jointed body, 21″ tall.................. 190- 220

Alexander, Madame, all compo, swivel head, marked X (in a circle); human hair wig, plastic sleep eyes, open mouth; body marked 13, jointed shoulders and hips, 13″ tall.................. 135- 170

Alexander, Madame, "Dionne Quints," all compo, swivel head, marked DIONNE ALEXANDER; molded/painted hair, plastic sleep eyes, open/closed mouth; jointed baby body marked MADAME ALEXANDER. All original, mint condition, 10″ long, 9½″ head cir-cumference, set 850- 925

Alexander, Madame,
"Sonja Henie" all compo,
swivel head, marked
MADAME ALEXAN-
DER SONJA HENIE;
mohair wig, plastic sleep
eyes, open mouth, body
jointed shoulders and
hips, 18″ tall 140- 165

Foreign, in Native Costume
Haiti, black woman, all
painted wood, jointed at
hips and shoulders, 9″
tall.................. 54- 63
Hungary, boy has mache
head, molded/painted
hair and features; girl has
silky, fine, thread-type
hair, molded/painted fea-
tures; both have all cloth
bodies with stitched
fingers; oilcloth shoes on
boy, woolen shoes on girl.
All original, 9″ tall, ea. .. 40- 50
India, dancer; all cloth,
thread-type hair, molded/
painted features; painted/
stitched fingers and toes.
All original, 12″ tall 56- 66
Ireland, Nu-Art-Dolls,
marked Georgene Novel-
ties, Inc., U.S.A.; all
cloth, yarn-type hair,
molded/painted features.
All original, 14″ tall, pr. . 58- 70
Italy, musician; cloth head,
silky threadlike hair,
molded/painted features,
hard plastic unjointed
body. Original clothes
with paper tag, 6″ tall ... 40- 50
Italy, cloth head, fine,
thread-type hair, molded/
painted features; cloth
body with plastic hands.
All original, 8″ tall 38- 50
Japan, crawling baby,
mache bobbing head,
human hair wig, inset
glass eyes, closed mouth;
cardboard body with
mache arms and legs, 8″
long 85- 100
Japan, geisha girl, mache
head, human hair wig,
inset glass eyes, closed
mouth; cloth/cardboard
body with mache hands
and feet, 8¼″ tall 42- 55

French Bisque, Children
Gaultier (probably), bisque
socket head marked F. G.
inside scroll; human hair
wig, paperweight eyes,
closed mouth; mache/
wood jointed body,
23″ tall 2,100-2,450
Gaultier & Fils (probably),
bisque socket head
marked F6G; human hair
wig, paperweight eyes,
closed mouth; mache/
wood jointed body, 15″
tall 1,600-1,975
Gaultier & Fils (?), Bapteme
or Christening doll,
bisque socket head
marked F. G. (in a scroll)
6; human hair wig, paper-
weight eyes, closed
mouth; mache torso and
arms jointed at shoul-
ders, bisque hands;
mache lower portion con-
tainer for sweetmeats.
"Paul" ink-stamped on
bib, 12″ tall 1,100-1,400
Gesland, bisque swivel
head marked F 5 G;
mohair wig (probably
original), paperweight
eyes, closed mouth;
stockinette covered body,
mark stamped on back,
(first words or letters not
readable). F. GESLAND
Brevette S.G.D.G. 5 Rue
Berange PARIS; wood
shoulderplate, arms and
legs jointed, 17″ tall 1,900-2,200
Jullien, Jr., bisque socket
head marked JULLIEN
12 human hair wig,
paperweight eyes, closed
mouth; mache wood
jointed body, 30″ tall ... 1,900-2,250
Jullien Jr., bisque socket
head marked JULLIEN
8 importe; human hair
wig, glass sleep eyes,
open mouth; mache/wood
jointed body marked
with paper label, BEBE
L'UNIVERSEL INCAS-
SABLE; mama-papa pull
cords, 23″ tall 725- 850
Jumeau, bisque socket head
marked DEPOSE TETE
JUMEAU Bte S.G.D.-G.
15; human hair wig,

(continued)

paperweight eyes, closed mouth, applied pierced ears; mache/wood jointed body marked BEBE JUMEAU Diplome d'Honneur, 33″ tall 3,400-3,700

Jumeau, bisque socket head marked DEPOSE TETE JUMEAU Bte S.G.D.-G. 6 (red check marks); human hair wig, paperweight eyes, closed mouth; mache/wood jointed body marked JUMEAU MEDAILLE D'OR PARIS; mamapapa pull cords, 16″ tall . 1,600-1,800

Jumeau, bisque socket head marked Depose TETE JUMEAU Bte SGDG; human hair wig, inset paperweight eyes, closed mouth; mache/wood jointed body marked JUMEAU MEDAILLE D'OR PARIS, 19½″ tall 1,900-2,250

Jumeau, bisque socket head marked DEPOSE TETE JUMEAU Bte S.G.D.-G. 6; (red check marks); human hair wig, paperweight eyes, closed mouth; mache/wood jointed body marked BEBE JUMEAU Depose d'Honneur, 15″ tall 1,600-1,850

Jumeau, bisque socket head marked 1907 16; human hair wig, paperweight eyes, open mouth; mache/wood jointed body, 33″ tall 1,200-1,400

Jumeau, bisque socket head marked Depose TETE JUMEAU Bte SGDG; human hair wig, inset paperweight eyes, closed mouth; mache/wood jointed body marked JUMEAU MEDAILLE D'OR PARIS, 18½″ tall 2,650-3,200

Jumeau, bisque socket head marked DEPOSE TETE JUMEAU Bte S.G.D.-G. 2 H8; human hair wig, paperweight eyes, closed

mouth; mache/wood jointed body, 11″ tall, RARE SIZE 1,400-1,700

Jumeau, bisque socket head marked TETE JUMEAU 8; human hair wig, paperweight eyes, open mouth; mache/wood jointed body marked BEBE JUMEAU Diplome d'Honneur; has mamapapa pull cords, walking mechanism, 17″ tall 2,800-3,200

Jumeau, Portrait, pale bisque socket head, unmarked; human hair wig, inset paperweight eyes, closed mouth; mache/wood jointed body marked JUMEAU MEDAILLE D'OR PARIS, 16″ tall 1,600-2,000

Kammer & Reinhart, Character, bisque socket head marked 11 K (star) R SIMON HALBIG 115/A; mohair wig, glass sleep eyes, closed pouty mouth; mache/wood jointed body. 12½″ tall 1,800-2,200

Steiner, Jules Nicholas, "Phenix," bisque socket head marked five pointed star 92; human hair wig, paperweight eyes, closed mouth; mache/wood jointed body; mama-papa pull cords, 22″ tall 2,300-2,500

Steiner, Jules Nicholas, bisque socket head marked STEINER Bte S.G.D.G. Sie C 3 BOURGOIN Jne; human hair wig, wire handle at crown of head behind ear opens and closes the glass eyes; closed mouth; mache/wood jointed body, 20″ tall 2,700-3,100

Tiburee, Alexandre Celestin, Bebe Mothereau, bisque socket head marked B.M.; human hair wig, paperweight eyes, closed mouth; mache/wood jointed body, 23″ tall . . . 2,500-2,700

Unmarked, Bru type, bisque swivel head on

bisque shoulder plate;
mohair wig, glass sleep
eyes, open/closed mouth
with five molded teeth;
kid body with bisque
arms, 19½" tall 2,100-2,400

French Bisque, Fashion

Gaultier (probably), French
Fashion, bisque swivel
head; mohair wig, paper-
weight eyes, closed
mouth; bisque shoulder
plate marked F.G.; kid
gusseted adult body with
individually wired and
stitched fingers, 12½"
tall 1,600-1,900

Jumeau, bisque socket head
marked X over 7; human
hair wig, paperweight
eyes, open mouth; mache/
wood jointed adult body
marked BEBE
JUMEAU Diplome
d'Honneur, 22" tall 900-1,100

Rohmer, untinted Parian
type bisque swivel head;
mohair wig, paperweight
eyes, closed mouth;
bisque shoulder plate and
arms; kid/wood body and
legs, marked on stomach
MME ROHMER
BREVETE S.G.D.G.
PARIS (in an oval);
typical two eyelet
holes below the mark,
jointed shoulders and
hips, 16" tall . . . .   3500+

Unmarked, French Fashion,
bisque socket head;
human hair wig, paper-
weight eyes, closed
mouth; adult kid body,
fingers individually wired
and stitched, bisque
shoulder plate, 33" tall . .   3,000+

Unmarked, French Fashion,
Parian quality bisque
shoulder head; mohair
wig, paperweight eyes,
closed mouth, head bent
forward looking down;
kid body, individually
wired and stitched
fingers, 15" tall 900-1,100

German Bisque, Babies

Bahr & Proschild, bisque
socket head marked 604
(over) 5; mohair wig,

glass sleep eyes, open
mouth; mache jointed
baby body. 13" long, 11"
head circumference 365- 450

Borgfeldt, Geo., & Co.,
Character, bisque
socket head marked G
326 B A 3 M.D.R.G.M.
259; molded/painted hair,
glass sleep eyes, open
mouth; mache jointed
baby body, 14" long, 9½"
head circumference 400- 475

Company unidentified,
Character, breather
baby, bisque socket head
marked Made in Ger-
many 100/12; human hair
wig, glass sleep eyes,
open nostrils, open
mouth, oscillating
tongue; mache/wood
jointed baby body. 23"
long, 15" head circumfer-
ence 575- 650

Gans, Otto, bisque socket
head marked OTTO
GANS Germany 975 A.
11. M.; human hair wig,
glass sleep eyes, open
mouth; mache/wood
jointed baby body. 22"
long, 14" head circumfer-
ence 450- 515

Heubach, Ernst, bisque
socket head marked
Heubach Kopplesdorf
300 19/0 Germany;
mohair wig, glass sleep
eyes, open mouth; mache
jointed baby body, 7"
long, 5½" head circum-
ference 220- 260

Heubach, Ernst, Character,
bisque socket head
marked HEUBACH-
KOPPELSDORF 300 •
3 Germany; human hair
wig, glass sleep eyes,
open mouth; mache/wood
jointed baby body, 18"
long, 13" head circumfer-
ence 320- 360

Heubach, Ernst, Character,
bisque socket head
marked HEUBACH-
KOPPELSDORF 300
7/0 Germany; human
hair wig, glass sleep eyes,
open mouth; mache/wood
jointed baby body. 12½"

(continued)

long, 9½" head circumference 340- 380

Kestner, J. D., Jr., Hilda, Character, bisque socket head marked Made in F Germany 10 237 J D K Jr. 1914 c (in circle) Hilda Gesgesh N. 1070; mohair wig, glass sleep eyes, open mouth; mache/wood jointed baby body. 12" long, 10" head circumference 700- 755

Kestner, J. D., Jr., Character, bisque socket head marked J. D. K. Made in 17 Germany; molded/painted hair, glass sleep eyes, open mouth; mache/wood jointed baby body. 22" long, 16" head circumference 625- 715

Kestner, J. D., Jr., Character, bisque socket head marked J. D. K. Made in Germany; painted hair, glass sleep eyes, open mouth; mache jointed baby body. 14½" long, 11" head circumference . 295- 350

Kestner, J. D., Jr., Character, bisque socket head marked Made in Germany 152 4; mohair wig, glass sleep eyes, open mouth; mache jointed baby body. 12" long, 10" head circumference 360- 450

Kley & Hahn, Character, bisque socket head marked K & H (in a streamer) Germany 167-15; human hair wig, glass sleep eyes, open mouth; mache/wood jointed baby body. 26" long, 17" head circumference 720- 840

Marseille, Armand, bisque socket head marked Germany 341/3K. A.M.; painted hair, glass sleep eyes, closed mouth; mache jointed baby body. 9" long, 7½" head circumference 320- 385

Marseille, Armand, bisque flange head marked A.M. Germany 347-19; painted hair, glass sleep eyes, closed mouth; cloth body

with bisque (replacement) hands. 13" long, 9" head circumference 295- 375

Marseille, Armand, brown bisque socket head marked ARMAND MARSEILLE Germany 990 A 7/0 M; human hair wig, glass sleep eyes, open mouth; brown mache/wood jointed baby body. 11" long, 7½" head circumference 360- 420

German Bisque, Children
Company unidentified, Dollar Princess bisque socket head marked THE DOLLAR PRINCESS 62 SPECIAL made in Germany; mohair wig, glass sleep eyes, open mouth; mache/wood jointed body, 25" tall 280- 320

Goebel, William, bisque socket head marked W.G. (intertwined) 120 3 Germany (in a rectangle); human hair wig, glass sleep eyes, open mouth; mache/wood jointed body, 16" tall 265- 295

Handwerck, Heinrich, bisque socket head marked 109-11 Germany Handwerck 2½; mohair wig, glass sleep eyes, open mouth; mache/wood jointed body. Original costume, 21" tall 360- 420

Handwerck, Heinrich, bisque socket head marked 11½" 99 DEP HANDWERCK 3; human hair wig, glass sleep eyes, open mouth; mache/wood jointed body, 21" tall 370- 410

Handwerck, Heinrich, bisque shoulder head marked Hch 3/0 H. Germany; human hair wig, glass inset eyes, open mouth; kid body with bisque arms, 19" tall 295- 320

Handwerck, Max, bisque socket head marked 30 H (K over 3 inside the H); human hair wig, glass inset eyes, open mouth; mache/wood jointed body, 24½" tall 325- 360

Marseille, Armand, bisque
socket head marked
ARMAND MAR-
SEILLE Germany 390
A. 6 M.; human hair wig,
glass sleep eyes, open
mouth; mache/wood
jointed body, 23″ tall ... 355- 420
Marseille, Armand, Char-
acter, bisque socket
head marked ARMAND
MARSEILLE 971 Ger-
many A 3 M; human hair
wig, glass inset eyes,
open mouth; mache/wood
jointed body, 17″ tall ... 1,600-1,900
Marseille, Armand, "Flora-
dora," bisque shoulder
head marked FLORA-
DORA A.M.-6-DRP
made in Germany;
mohair wig, glass inset
eyes, fur eyebrows in-
serted in slits in bisque,
open mouth; kid body,
bisque hands, 24″ tall ... 320- 370
Mon Tresor, bisque socket
head marked MON
TRESOR Germany 10;
human hair wig, glass
inset eyes, open mouth;
mache/wood jointed
body, 23″ tall 525- 600
Recknagel, Th., bisque
socket head marked R/A
DEP 12/0; solid dome,
mohair wig, glass inset
eyes, open mouth; mache
body, jointed shoulders
and hips, painted shoes
and socks, 8″ tall 185- 250
Recknagel, Th., bisque
socket head marked 1909
D E P R 2 A; mohair wig,
glass sleep eyes, open
mouth; cardboard body
with mache arms and
legs. Original costume,
18″ tall 140- 185
Schmidt, Paul, bisque
shoulder head marked
Germany P. Sch 1899 6;
human hair wig, glass
inset eyes, open mouth;
kid gusseted body,
bisque hands, 22″ tall ... 360- 420
Simon & Halbig, bisque
socket head marked S H
1078; human hair wig,
glass sleep eyes, open

mouth; mache/wood
jointed body, 26″ tall ... 510- 620
Simon & Halbig, bisque
socket head marked 12
SH 1039 D E P; human
hair wig, glass sleep eyes,
open mouth; mache/wood
jointed body, 24″ tall ... 550- 640
Simon & Halbig, bisque
shoulder head marked 10
SH 8; human hair wig
stationary glass eyes,
open mouth; kid/cloth
body with bisque arms,
17″ tall 520- 610

German Bisque, Naughty Nudies
Bisque girl, Heubach figurine, unmarked; molded/
painted hair, features,
and clothes; intaglio eyes.
12½″ tall .... 1,600+
Bisque girl, mohair wig,
molded/painted features,
molded white slippers;
marked 400 L, 5″ long .. 160- 195
Bisque girl, mohair wig,
molded/painted features,
molded blue slippers,
marked 405 J, 6″ long ... 220- 245
Bisque girl with kitten, unmarked; molded/painted
hair, features and
clothes, 5″ long 200- 300
Bisque nude girl, marked
40V; mohair wig, molded/
painted features, molded
pink slippers, 3½″ tall .. 190- 240
Bisque nude girl, marked
405R; silk net over
mohair wig, molded/
painted features, molded
pink slippers, 4″ tall 180- 220
Bisque nude girl, marked
2829 Germany; molded/
painted hair, features,
cap and slippers (rust), 3″
long 140- 170
Bisque nude girl, marked
2829 Germany; molded/
painted hair, features,
cap and slippers (blue), 3″
long 115- 140

Mechanical Dolls
Lanternier, A & Cie, walking doll with spring windup cart; bisque swivel
head marked MON
CHERI PARIS 03 on
bisque shoulder plate;

(continued)

human hair wig, inset
pupil-less glass eyes,
open/closed mouth with
molded teeth; cloth body
with bisque arms and
metal jointed legs, 10½"
tall 2,750-3,700

Limoges peasant cart, key
windup boy pulls girl in
cart (she shakes bell on
stick); girl has bisque
socket head marked S &
H Germany, mohair wig,
inset glass eyes, closed
mouth, mache body with
bisque arms; boy has
bisque socket head
marked Germany S & H
Simon Halbig. All origi-
nal, 12" tall 2,450-2,650

Unmarked mechanical
mache head, human hair
wig, glass eyes, closed
mouth; brass body with
mache arms, legs and
violin; mechanism in
body connected to music
box. When wound, head
turns, eyes roll, arm with
bow moves as if playing;
music box plays three
melodies, 18" tall
(overall) 1,800-2,350

Wolf, Louis & Company,
mechanical, bisque
socket head marked L.
W. & CO. 12 11/0; mohair
wig, glass inset eyes,
open mouth; mache body,
jointed shoulders and
hips with wind key;
wooden rocker rocked by
flip lever. 10" tall
(overall) 1,100-1,400

Metal Dolls
Heller, Alfred, metal
shoulder head marked
DIANA DEP (in a
square); molded/painted
hair, painted eyes, closed
mouth; cloth body with
bisque arms, 12½" tall . . 100- 140

Juno (head only), metal
shoulder head marked
JUNO; molded/painted
hair and features, 6"
tall 95- 130

Juno, metal shoulder head
marked JUNO; molded/
painted hair, painted

eyes, closed mouth; kid
body with bisque arms,
16½" tall 140- 160

Juno (head only), metal
shoulder head marked
JUNO; wig missing,
glass sleep eyes, open
mouth, 6" tall 95- 125

Minerva, metal shoulder
head marked MINERVA
Germany; molded/paint-
ed hair, painted eyes,
closed mouth; all cloth
body, 10" tall 90- 120

Miscellaneous Materials
Plaster-Bisque, flange head
with molded/painted hair
and features; all cloth
body. Original clothes,
5¼" tall   38-   50

Plaster-Bisque, swivel head
marked 463 17/0; mohair
topknot, inset pupil-less,
glass googlie eyes, open
mouth, brass rings in
nose and ears and around
neck; mache body jointed
at hips and shoulders.
Original grass skirt, 7"
long 230- 260

Plaster-Bisque, swivel head
with molded/painted hair
and features; body same
material, jointed at hips
and shoulders, 7" tall . . .   72-   85

Plaster, W.P.A. Project
Dolls, molded plaster
heads, mohair wig, paint-
ed features; cotton
wound, wire armature
bodies with plaster arms
and legs. All original,
9½", 15½", 16", group . . 300- 340

Porcelain Mickey Mouse, all
porcelain with molded/
painted features and
clothes; paper sticker, C
(in circle) 1960 WALT
DISNEY PRODUCTS,
INC.   80-   90

Rawhide, African (?), jointed at hips and shoulders,
molded asphalt hair,
inset bead eyes, brass
ring in nostril. Primitive
museum piece, 8" tall . . . 310- 350

Rawhide, Darrow's Raw-
hide Head, molded/paint-
ed features and hair, 6¼"
tall 290- 325

Rawhide, Darrow's Rawhide Head, molded/painted features and hair, 4½″ tall 255- 270

Soap, Shirley Temple, all soap, unmarked; molded/painted hair and features; molded arms, legs and dress, 5½″ tall 25- 32

Terra-Cotta shoulder head, unmarked; molded/painted hair with ribbon and bow, molded/painted features; new cloth body with bisque arms and legs, 13″ tall 205- 228

Pincushion Dolls

China Pincushion marked 6102 Germany; molded/painted hair with ribbon, features, and clothes, 2¾″ tall 85- 96

China Pincushion marked 74500 Made in Germany; molded/painted hair, features, and clothes, 4″ tall 86- 96

China Pincushion marked 5230 Germany; molded/painted hair, features, and clothes, 3″ tall 78- 88

China Pincushion, unmarked; molded/painted hair and features, 6″ tall 80- 90

China Pincushion marked Germany; molded/painted spit-curls, features, and collar, 1¾″ tall 98- 107

China Pincushion marked Germany 2352; molded/painted hair, features, bonnet, and clothes, 3¾″ tall 98- 115

China Pincushion marked 5468; molded/painted hair with ribbon/flowers and features, 2″ tall 80- 90

China Pincushion marked 6233 Germany; molded/painted hair with comb, features, and clothes, 3″ tall 84- 93

Plastic and Vinyl Dolls

Alexander, Madame, Cissette, all hard plastic swivel head, synthetic wig, plastic sleep eyes, closed mouth; body marked MME. ALEXANDER; jointed shoulders/hips above knee, 9″ tall 70- 82

Alexander, Madame, Elise, all hard plastic except soft vinyl over-sleeved arms, swivel head marked ALEXANDER; synthetic wig, plastic sleep eyes, closed mouth; body marked MME. ALEXANDER; jointed shoulders, elbows, hips, knees, and ankles. All original, 16″ tall 120- 140

Alexander, Madame, hard plastic swivel head, unmarked; synthetic wig, plastic sleep eyes, closed mouth; hard plastic body, jointed at hips and shoulders, walking legs, turns head, 14½″ tall 92- 115

Alexander, Madame, Jacqueline, vinyl swivel head marked ALEXANDER Co. 1961, rooted hair, plastic sleep eyes, closed mouth; vinyl body, jointed at hips and shoulders, 21″ tall 180- 220

Alexander, Madame, Kathy, all soft vinyl, swivel head marked MME 1958 ALEXANDER; molded/painted hair, plastic sleep eyes, closed mouth, nursing hole; jointed baby body. All original. 16″ long, 11½″ head circumference 95- 115

Alexander, Madame, Little Genius, hard plastic swivel head; synthetic wig, plastic sleep eyes, open mouth/nurser; soft vinyl jointed baby body. All original with paper tag and dress label— LITTLE GENIUS by Madame Alexander, 7″ long 44- 53

Alexander, Madame, Little Granny, soft vinyl swivel head marked ALEXANDER 1965; synthetic rooted hair, plastic sleep eyes, closed mouth; soft

(continued)

vinyl arms, hard vinyl torso and legs, jointed shoulders and hips. All original, 13″ tall 45- 55

Alexander, Madame, Little Mary Sunshine, soft vinyl swivel head marked ALEXANDER 1961; synthetic rooted hair, plastic sleep eyes, open/closed mouth; soft vinyl arms, hard vinyl torso and legs, jointed shoulders and hips. All original, 14″ tall 52- 61

Alexander, Madame, Madame Doll, soft vinyl swivel head marked ALEXANDER 1965; rooted synthetic hair, plastic sleep eyes, closed mouth; hard vinyl body, jointed shoulders, hips and knees. All original, 14″ tall 48- 56

American Character Doll Co., Tiny Tears, hard plastic swivel head marked AMERICAN CHARACTER DOLL PAT. NO. 2.675.644; synthetic hair rooted in skull cap, plastic sleep eyes, open/closed mouth with nursing hole; all rubber jointed baby body. 15½″ long, 13″ head circumference 92- 107

Company unidentified, all latex compo, swivel head marked STEHA (in an elongated diamond) DRP 839466; synthetic wig, flirting sleep eyes, closed mouth; jointed body and voice box, 21″ tall 70- 80

Company unidentified, all hollow rubber with molded/painted hair, features, and clothes. Marked Made in France (in a circle), 9½″ tall 24- 32

Sieberling Latex, Dopey, all latex marked DOPEY (on hat) c (in circle) WALT DISNEY SEIBERLING LATEX MADE IN AKRON, O. U.S.A. (marked on back), 5½″ tall 37- 47

Sun Rubber Co., all hollow rubber with molded/painted hair, features, and clothes. Marked Ruth E. Newton The Sun Rubber Co., 8½″ tall 18- 27

Unmarked, Early American rubber doll (possibly gutta percha mixture), rubber shoulder head; molded/painted hair, painted eyes, closed mouth; cloth body with leather arms, 18″ tall . . . 280- 310

Wax Dolls

Unmarked, French novelty, poured wax baby head, arms, and legs, painted features; mache egg. All original, 5¼″ tall 445- 505

Unmarked novelty doll-candy container, poured wax head; inset glass eyes, birdlike fur body with metal feet; head comes off to open container, 5″ tall 130- 150

Unmarked, solid wax shoulder, head and arms (head and arms molded in one piece); mohair wig, inset pupil-less eyes, closed mouth; cloth body with solid wax legs. All original, 9″ long 185- 205

Unmarked, wax-over-mache head; mohair wig inserted in slot in head, inset pupil-less glass eyes, closed mouth; cloth, straw-stuffed body with kid arms, 15″ tall 285- 325

Unmarked, wax-over-mache head; molded hair and ribbon, inset pupil-less glass eyes, closed mouth; cloth, straw-stuffed body with mache arms, 15″ tall 260- 280

Unmarked, wax-over-mache head; molded hair and ribbon, inset pupil-less glass eyes, closed mouth; cloth, straw-stuffed body with mache arms, molded/painted mache legs, 17½″ tall 255- 270

Unmarked, wax-over-mache head; mohair wig in original setting, glass sleep eyes, closed mouth, pierced ears; cloth, straw-stuffed body with wax-over-mache arms; mache legs with molded/painted shoes. Mint condition, 17½" tall 265- 285

Wooden Dolls

Schoenhut, Albert, wood swivel head; mohair wig, decal eyes, open/closed mouth; wood body with metal spring joints marked SCHOENHUT DOLL Pat. Jan. 17'11 U.S.A. and Foreign Countries, boy, 19½" tall 500- 550

Schoenhut, Albert, wood swivel head; mohair wig, decal eyes, open/closed mouth; wood body with metal spring joints; marked SCHOENHUT DOLL Pat. Jan 17'11, U.S.A. and Foreign Countries, girl, 19½" tall 495- 545

Schoenhut, Albert, wood swivel head; mohair wig, painted intaglio eyes, closed mouth; wood body with metal spring joints marked SCHOENHUT DOLL Pat Jan. 17'11, U.S.A. and Foreign Countries, boy, 19" tall . .   365- 420

Schoenhut, Albert, wood swivel head; mohair wig, painted eyes, open/closed mouth; wood body with metal spring joints marked SCHOENHUT DOLL Pat. Jan. 17'11, U.S.A. and Foreign Countries, girl, 16" tall . .   460- 510

Schoenhut, Albert, Character Toddler, wood swivel head; mohair wig, painted eyes, closed mouth; wood body with metal spring joints marked SCHOENHUT DOLL Pat. Jan. 17'11, U.S.A. and Foreign Countries, 16½" tall 365- 420

Unmarked, Chinese man, wooden head; carved/painted features, painted black hair with human hair pigtail in back, cloth body. All original, 8½" tall 110- 125

Unmarked Early Peg-Wooden, all wood; gesso/painted hair and features with tuck comb; peg-jointed at hips, shoulders, elbows, and knees, 2¼" tall 245- 265

Unmarked, Early Peg-Wooden, all wood, gesso/painted hair and features with tuck comb; peg-jointed at hips, shoulders, elbows, and knees, 3" tall 325- 365

Door Knockers

Door Knockers

These have been around for hundreds of years and are made of wood, metal, even glass. Iron and brass were the most popular, in animal heads and other forms.

Brass, American Eagle, 1800s (ill.) $280-360
Brass, dog's head, 7" high, old . . .   62- 70
Brass, fox head, 8" high 60- 70
Brass, hand holding ball 70- 88
Brass, horse's head, flowing mane, dated 1845   150-175
Brass, jaguar growling, 8" high . .   70- 80
Brass, lion with ring in mouth, French, 1800s   140-160
Grecian bust, head only, bronze, 4½" high 70- 90
Iron, cat's head, smiling, 4" high 34- 47
Iron, gloved hand 50- 60
Iron, hand, fist-shaped, 8" high, old 32- 44
Iron, hammer 39- 47
Iron, horseshoe 40- 50

(continued)

Iron, horseshoe hitting hammer head, 1930s	40-	49
Iron, spur hits metal block on wooden board	44-	54
Pewter (?), hand holding ball, 1920s	32-	44
Spur	40-	50

Doorstops

Doorstops

Made of many materials. Metal stops in the shapes of animals or buildings were used for propping open doors. Particularly popular in the 1920s.

Cottage, iron, 5¾″ high	$ 30-	40
Dogs: Airedale, Bulldog, Chow, German Shepherd, etc.	42-	47
Fala, FDR on side, 10″ high (ill.)	43-	52
Flower basket, cast iron	21-	30
Flowerpot, cast iron, enameled, 7¼″ high	24-	34
Frog, iron, webbed feet, 15″ high	32-	41
Horse pulling cart, iron, 6½″ high	29-	37
Horse, rearing, lead base, 1930s	32-	42
Lady, cast iron, enameled	19-	27
Lion, painted, 15″ high	32-	41
Parrot, red/yellow/green, 10″ high	37-	46
Polo player on horse, 9″ high	29-	37
Rabbit, iron, 11″ high	41-	50
Ship, Mayflower, cast iron	42-	52
Sunbonnet girl, 6½″ high	34-	40
Squirrel, iron, 11″ high	40-	50
Wagon train, horse, 10″ high	39-	50
Wolf, on leash, iron	34-	42

Dorflinger Glass

Christian Dorflinger founded his first fac-

Dorflinger Glass

tory at White Mills, Pennsylvania, in 1865, having come from Alsace, France, in 1846 to learn the American glass trade. He also operated a factory in Brooklyn, New York, from 1852 until the late 1880s when J. S. Hibbler took over all the firm's interests. The Kalana Lyly pattern shown here is but one of the many fine examples of glass made by one of the greatest glassmakers in the world. It's of interest to know that Mr. Dorflinger brought the great Nicholas Lutz to America in 1860.

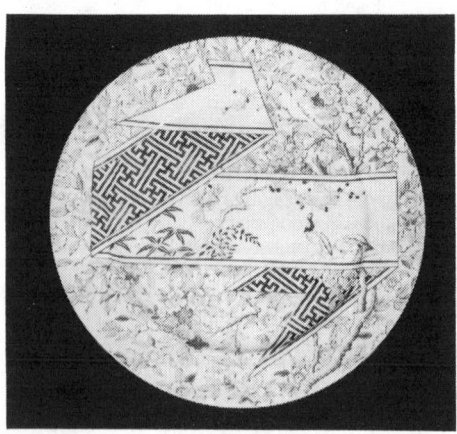

Doulton Pottery

Doulton Pottery

In the mid-1850s Henry Doulton's partner, John Watts, retired and Mr. Doulton continued the firm as Doulton and Company. From the 1850s until just before 1900, his wares were marked Doulton Lambeth. After 1901, Royal was added to the firm's name,

160

without the Lambeth. See **Royal Doulton** in this Guide. Salt-glazed stoneware was just one of the many fine types of pottery made at Doulton.

Biscuit, jar, 1880s	$170-190
Bowl, flowers, gold trim, artist-signed	92-107
Ewer, blue scrolling, floral decor, 9" high	54- 62
Ink bottle, slipware finish	33- 42
Mug, probably for ale, tan/brown, artist Hannah Barlow	67- 70
Mustard pot, blues, brown, 1883	81- 90
Pitcher, hunting scenes, tan/brown	72- 81
Pitcher, Columbian Exposition, 1893	120-130
Plate, Dickensware, Tom Pinch	62- 72
Plate, Melrose, 9" dia.	41- 51
Plate, tavern scene, artist M. Aitken, 9" dia.	60- 70
Plate, varicolored flowers, 1884, 10" dia. (ill.)	40- 48
Tray, Dickensware, signed Noke	110-120
Vase, hunting scene, 1870s . . .	72- 81
Vase, multicolored, 8" high . . .	67- 77
Whiskey jug, marked JRD and Fine Old Scotch Whiskey . . .	155+

Dresden China

Dresden China

In the early 1700s, Johann Bottger produced the first porcelain in Europe that was considered quality. His factory was at the Royal Saxon Porcelain Works at Meissen, Germany. His work was finely decorated in exquisite shapes, often with raised enamel

flowers. The famous crossed swords in blue are known throughout the world. Unfortunately the factory is now behind the Iron Curtain. Most of the Dresden in the U.S. was brought in by importers in the late 19th century.

Basket, floral decor, twisted handle, 7" high	$ 110-	120
Bowl, flowers, hand-painted, gold trim, 10" . .	94-	107
Box, open latticework, silver mounts	370-	410
Candelabra, 6-candle, 22" high, boy/girl, blue ground, flowers, pr.		1,250+
Candleholder, pink-applied roses, 14" high	97-	109
Chocolate pot, cobalt, gold border, miniature roses . .		250+
Compote, reticulated, 11" high, pr.		475+
Cup/saucer, floral designs overall	99-	120
Figurines, cupids, ladies, 8¼" high (ill.), pr.	1,200-1,500	
Lamp, applied flowers, square base, early	370-	420
Plate, deep, ribbed, blue/yellow decor, signed Villeroy and Boch	90-	110
Plate, pink floral decor, 9" dia., reticulated border . .	50-	60
Plate, reticulated border, cherubs	74-	83
Tea caddy, flowers/roses, gold, blue Crown under glaze	92-	130
Teapot, roses with thorns, leaves, gold, blue Crown .	160-	180
Urn, battle scene, 16" high, pr., old mark	145-	160
Vase, floral decor, white ground, 8"	220-	245
Vase, painted birds, signed, 6" high	170-	190
Vase, portrait of gentleman, overlay gold decor, 10" high	185-	220

Durand Art Glass

Resembling Tiffany in some respects, Durand was made by the Vineland Flint Glass Works in Vineland, New Jersey, around 1924. Victor Durand, founder, put paper labels on some pieces while others were signed with a V in the pontil. Victor Durand,

(continued)

Durand Art Glass

Dye Cabinets

Jr., ran the factory until his untimely death in 1931. The factory was then taken over by Kimble. See **Kimble Glass.**

Bowl, blue, label, signed $420-450
Bowl, gold iridescent, signed
  "V" 210-250
Candleholders, gold lustre, opal
  and gold, 6" high, signed 230-250
Compote, blue feather pattern,
  amber base, 7" high 470-500
Decanter, blue, iridescent, signed,
  8" high 375-410
Lamp, green, pulled feather
  design, gold threading, bronze
  cherub base, electrified (ill.) . . . 260-270
Perfume bottle, orange iridescent,
  signed DeVilbiss 150-170
Plate, cobalt, Peacock Feather
  pattern, cut flowers, 8"
  dia. 310-330
Rose bowl, green/gold, original
  paper label 170-190
Shade, gas, white ground, gold/
  green, calcite interior 135-150
Vase, blue iridescent, orange trim,
  8½" high 342-420
Vase, blue, white, swirls from top
  to bottom, 9" high 310-340
Vase, green, gold, rose iridescent
  threading, signed 340-390
Vase, orange, iridescent, blue
  highlights, 8½" high 365-420
Vase, peach iridescent, beehive
  shape, 7½" high 520-545
Wine glass, blue, white loops,
  vaseline stem 150-170

Dye Cabinets

These were found in country stores in the late 1800s. They held the many colors of powdered dyes (to be mixed with water) the housewife needed to dye her cloth for dresses, tablecloths, etc.

Dye cabinet, cherry, good portrait
  on front $325-357
Dye cabinet, poplar, family scene
  on front 270-290
Dye cabinet, walnut, hand-
  painted flowers 290-310

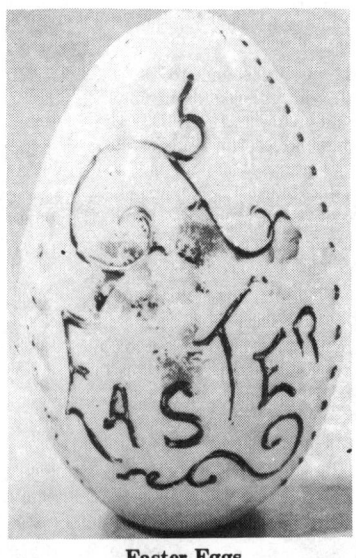

Easter Eggs

Easter Eggs

Usually of blown glass, they were favorites with the children in the mid-1800s. The same type is used to attract hens to a nest. The older types were hand painted, professionally or otherwise.

Easter egg, 4" high, handblown
  (ill.) . . . . $ 42- 50

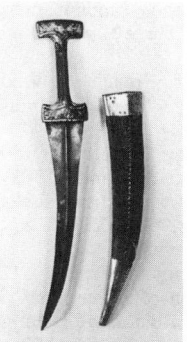

Edged Weapons

Edged Weapons

"On guard!" Two words that brought fear to more than one man. Any and all are collectible and going up in price every day.

American Indian pipe
  tomahawk, c. 1780, 19"
  overall \$950-1,200
American Revolution
  horseman's saber, 36", s.e.
  blade 650- 700
Arabian chieftain's Jambiya
  dagger w/sheath, 9½" d.e.
  blade 115- 135
Australian knuckle-duster
  fighting knife, WWII, 6½"
  long 155- 170
Austrian officer's sword
  w/sheath, WWI, 29" s.e.
  blade 170- 195
British artillery, short sword,
  c. 1810, brass hilt, 22" long .. 250- 275
British general officer's
  sword, silver hilt, c. 1825 975-1,100
British naval boarding ax,
  c. 1840-1860, 21" handle,
  10" iron head 300- 340
British naval officer's sword,
  c. 1790, 30" straight s.e.
  blade 255- 275
British prison guard's sword,
  c. 1850, 22" curved s.e.
  blade 125- 135
British trench knife, WWI,
  marked Robbins-Dudley,
  4¼" long 200- 225
Ghurka knife (Kukri), WWII,
  9" incurved blade, has 2
  miniature knives in leather-
  covered wooden case 55- 65

Indo-Persian fighting knife,
  c. 1820, 9" d.e. reverse
  curved blade 90- 110
Italian cup hilt rapier, 17th
  century, 34" long d.e. blade .. 265- 300
"Khyber" knife and sheath,
  pearl handled, 11" long 165- 190
Knights of Columbus
  ceremonial sword, made by
  Pettis & Ranken, Troy,
  N.Y., c. 1925, 29" long 95- 115
Revolutionary naval cutlass,
  28" straight s.e. blade 345- 365
Special Civil War contract
  cavalry saber and scabbard,
  marked Tiffany & Co., 36"
  curved s.e. blade 385- 450
U.S. Civil War saber bayonet,
  probably for Merrill Navy
  rifle.................... 165- 185

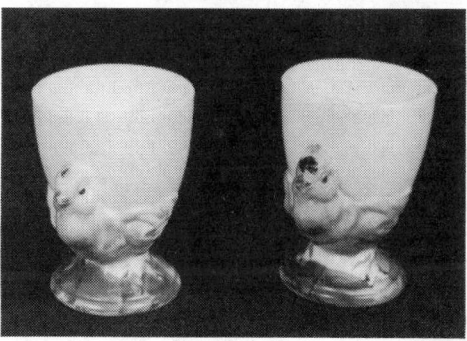

Egg Cups

Egg Cups

Found in the tombs of the Egyptian kings, they were in use in Asia more than 4,000 years ago. You'll find them in sterling silver, brass, glass, pewter, porcelain, even hand-carved wood.

Two egg cups, early 20th
  century, porcelain, ea. ....$ 8- 10

End-of-Day Glass

See **Spatter Glass.**

Engravings, Etchings

If horseracing once was considered the sport of kings, this category is fast becoming a collectible of millionaires. The prices being realized at the better auctions are staggering. This is a "for reference only" category.

Marius A.J. Bauer, contemporary Dutch etcher, b. 1867, "Entrance to a Mosque," etching, signed proof.

(continued)

"Night in Ely Cathedral"

"Portrait of Jan Asselyn"

Nicholas Bazin, French, c. 1636-1706, "Marie Therese, Queen of France," line engraving.

Jacques Firmin Beauvarlet, French, 1731-1797, "Pierre Mignard," line engraving.

Frank W. Benson, American, b. Salem, Mass., 1862, "The Punter," etching, proof, signed in pencil.

Arthur Brisco, English marine painter-etcher, "Three Bargers," etcher, proof, signed in ink.

Felix Buhot, French, b. Valognes, 1847, "La Place Breda," etching, signed in the plate.

David Young Cameron, painter-etcher, b. Glasgow, Scotland, 1865, "Hotel de Sens," etching, proof signed in pencil.

C. Chartran, "Leo XIII," etching, signed proof on vellum.

A.G.L. Desnoyers, France, 1779-1857, "St. Catherine of Alexander," line engraving, proof before all letters.

Albrecht Durer, 1471-1528, Germany, "Apollo and Diana," engraving, signed in the plate.

Cornelius Dusart, Dutch, 1660-1704, "The Violin Player," etching, signed in the plate.

Kerry Eby, American, 1890s, "Spring Freshets," etchong.

Jean Louis Forain, French painter, etcher, lithographer, 1852-1931, "Lourdes—La Paralytique," etching, signed in pencil.

G. Garavaglia, "La Madonna Della Seggiola," line engraving, proof before letters.

Axel Herman Haig, Sweden, 1835-1921, "Burgos Cathedral: Interior," etching, signed proof.

Childe Hassam, American painter-etcher, b. 1859, "Walt Whitman's House," etching, proof, signed in pencil.

Philipp Kilian, German engraver, 1628-93, "Damian Hartard," line engraving.

Alphonse Legros, French etcher, 1837-1911, "Le Refectoire," etching, proof, in the second state.

James McBey, 1883-1959, "Night in Ely Cathedral," etching, signed in ink (ill.).

Rembrandt Van Rijn, Dutch painter-etcher, "Portrait of Jan Asselyn," etching, signed in the plate (ill.).

Pieter Van Schuppen, 1627-1702, "Louis, Dauphin de France," line engraving, dated 1684.

Levon West, "Blizzard Coming," etching, proof, signed in pencil.

Epergnes

These elaborate table centerpieces, designed to hold sweetmeats, fruits, or with

Epergnes

Eskimo Art

Eskimo Art

vases to hold flowers, were in vogue in the early and mid-1800s. Many were attributed to the Sandwich Glass Company, Sandwich, Massachusetts, but as many come from Europe and few were signed. It's another case of knowing your dealer.

Blue, crimped top, bowl with
  trimming $265-370
Cranberry, crimped top and
  lower bowl, 3 lily vases, 20″
  high   320-360
Crystal/blue, opalescent, 4 lilies,
  25″ high overall   190-240
Rose/pink, upper and lower
  edges ruffled, 4 lilies, 27″ high .   270-285
Ruffled bowl, 3 lilies, silver
  frame, 12½″ high   270-283
Sandwich Glass overshot, mid-
  1800s (ill.)   620-770
Silver plate, 11″ high, 4 lilies   175-195
Single lily, sterling silver base,
  12″ high   370-420
White satin glass, silver-plated
  standard, 3 glass lilies, 22″
  high   220-245

Eskimo Art

These natives of Canada, the Aleutian Islands, Alaska, Greenland, and Siberia have carved items from walrus tusks, whales' teeth, and wood. Their basketry is world-famous. The most sought after work today was made in the mid-1800s, although much of

what you find in antiques shops was made to be sold at the trading posts.

Arctic fox, carved from walrus
  tusk, 1¼″×5¼″, c. 1930s $160-180
Basket, rye grass, yarn woven in,
  11″ high, c. 1900   90-130
Basket, utility type, designs
  aniline dyed, 7½″ high, c. 1930   28- 37
Cribbage board, in shape of seal,
  12½″ long, c. 1880s   265-310
Dominoes, complete set in box,
  c. 1930s   125-150
Eskimo, soapstone with ivory
  spears, 7″ high, c. 1900s (ill.) . .   250-275
Fish dish, wooden, 6½″×8″,
  c. 1930s   90-110
Fish spear (called a leister),
  carved from walrus ivory   165-200
Mask, carved cedar, 10½″×7½″,
  c. 1880s   650-750

(continued)

Mortar, wooden, for grinding
tobacco, 4½"×8½", c. early
1800s 90-135
Snow goggles, wooden, leather
thongs, c. 1900s 45- 65
Trinket box, carved from walrus
tusk, late 1880s (ill.) 275-325

European Art Glass

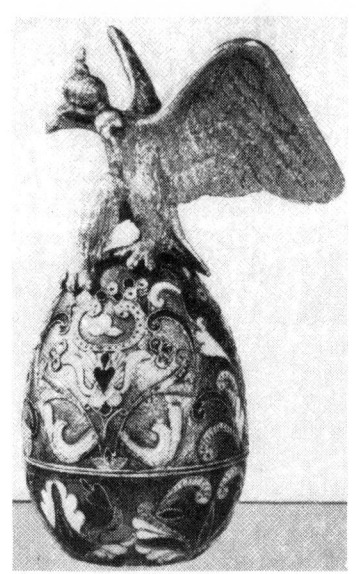

Faberge

European Art Glass

The uninformed collector buys this type of glass too often as Tiffany or Steuben on the basis that it's guaranteed. Many producers of good art glass didn't sign their pieces, thus creating more confusion. If the piece isn't signed, you should demand and get a written receipt when you buy. The American market was flooded with European art glass in the late 1800s. Just know from whom you're buying.

Bowl, 8" dia., green (ill.) .... $ 35- 45
Vase, blue, pink/blue flowers,
6" high 36- 47
Vase, green, yellow flowers, 8"
high 34- 44
Vase, orange, castle scene,
fluted top, 7½" high 38- 47
Vase, ruffled lip, fine enameling, pink liner, 6" high 70- 80
Vase, white satin glass, yellow
liner, clear frosted feet, 4¾"
high 125-140

Faberge

Peter Carl Faberge was jeweler to the Russian Imperial Court from the early 1870s until 1914. One of the largest collections in the world is the Matilda Geddings Gray Foundation Collection.

Ashtray, Art Nouveau, silver,
1900...................$ 695- 775
Bell push, in form of jade
elephant, ruby eyes, 2" high 3,550-3,675
Cigarette case, rectangular,
silver gilt, green moss
agate, with cabochon ruby
thumbpiece 3,400-3,550
Clock, gilded silver, gold
overlay, translucent
enamel, 1914 3,400-3,650
Figure, Atlas, gilded, silver
mounted 3,750-3,875
Icon, Our Lady of the Sign ... 3,600-3,750
Inkwell, hollowed-out cube of
onyx mounted in silver,
photograph of the
Czarevitch on front, 3½"
high 2,450-2,600
Letter opener, silver, gold,
diamond knob, 12" long ... 2,300-2,450
Penholder, silver 1,700-1,850
Shade, candle, silver-mounted,
1900................... 1,100-1,250

The illustrated Imperial Easter egg is similar to one that was presented to Czarina Marie Feodorovna by her husband, Czar Alexander III, around 1893. It's considered priceless today.

Faience

A tin glaze earthenware, this "soft" pottery achieves its opaqueness by being treated

Faience

with tin oxide. Delft and Majolica are made by the same process.

Bottle, white ground, flower
motif, 7½" high $160-190
Dish, blue/white, Oriental, pr. . . . 145-170
Inkwell, French, yellow glaze,
signed VP (Veuve Perrin) (ill.) . 160-180
Jar, blue/white, landscape,
handles, Italy, 18" high, pr. . . . 210-245
Jug, tulip, roses, tin glaze,
enamel, 1780s 132-150
Plate, floral, insects, Armorial,
Italy, pr. 172-181
Plate, tin glaze, red/blue, French,
1765 121-140
Platter, Delft type, 18" ×15" 170-180
Teapot, 11" high, signed 270-290
Tureen, lettuce decor, French,
1770, pr. 420-445
Vase, 12" high, tin glaze, signed . 78- 92

Fairy Lamps

Fairy Lamps

Candle-burning night lamps consisting of two parts, base and shade, were first made by the Samuel Clarke Company, England, in the mid-1850s. Phoenix Glass Company, Monaca, Pennsylvania, was granted the exclusive right to make them in the U.S. Came electricity, out went the light in the fairy lamp. Lazarus and Rosenfeld, New York City, imported thousands of them from

Bohemia in the 1880s. Made in every type of glass, from cheap to Tiffany and Amberina.

Amber Swirl and Cut pattern
base, acorn shade, signed
Clarke $140-160
Blue base, bulbous shade, raised
floral decor, signed Clarke 195-240
Bisque, Cocker 143-167
Camphor top, clear bottom,
blown glass wick holder 222-250
Cranberry glass shade, hobnail
base, signed Clarke 210-240
Green satin, ribbed, signed
Clarke 110-150
Green/white, swirls, thorn decor . 102-140
Lithophane, child scene, white
porcelain base, signed Clarke . . 375-400
Millefiori shade, glass base 220-250
Pink quilted satin glass, signed
Clarke 140-170
Rose satin top, Diamond pattern,
clear base, signed Clarke 188-225
Satin glass, pink/blue 265-295
White, pink stripes 160-175
Yellow satin glass shade, ribbed
pattern base, signed Clarke . . . 125-160

Fans

Fans

During the Victorian era young ladies gave many signals with the fan. One gesture could mean "Leave me alone!"; another, "Mother's watching!" Fans were made of every type of material. Paper and ivory seemed to be the most popular. Who invented the first fan is unknown.

Advertising, Cafe Brightwood,
Kingston, N.Y., 1908, paper . . $ 8- 12
Black lace sticks, floral on black
satin, opens to 22" 50- 60
Black lacquer, silver flower
painting on back, 21" 51- 70
Celluloid frame, white, carved
flower, 7" long 32- 41

(continued)

Engraved and painted,
blossoms, butterflies, 22" 37- 47
Floral, vocalist, buildings,
flowers, 24" 27- 37
Ivory splats, chiffon, sequins,
9" long 40- 50
Lace, sandalwood, painted, 8" ... 42- 51
Paper and wood, matadors, bull
fight, 18" long 15- 24
Paper, Japanese (ill.), ea. 6- 8
Silk, black/green, 13" long 50- 60
Tortoiseshell ribs, ostrich
plumes, 9" long 70- 78
Turkey feathers, hand-painted,
1870s opens to 19" 73- 81
White lacquer, silver-plated
handle, 1900s, opens to 22" ... 42- 52

Feather Work

Cut into the shape of flower petals and leaves, usually painted or dyed, this work is mainly found in a glass box-in-frame.

Bouquet of blue and green
flowers, glass and frame in
good condition ....$ 38- 52
Pansies, blue, yellow, green glass
and frame in good condition... 40- 50
Roses, pink, yellow glass and
frame in good condition 47- 54

Fiesta Ware

Fiesta Ware

Homer and Shakespear Laughlin founded the Homer Laughlin China Company in East Liverpool, Ohio, in 1871. At one time it was the world's largest single pottery plant. In March, 1937, Fiesta Ware was patented in red, blue, yellow, and green. Fiesta was a first in commercial pottery. Red was the

most difficult color to control. A redesign took place in 1969 and the ware was discontinued in 1973. Most pieces are incised "FIESTA." Red pieces bring 45 to 80 percent more than other colors.

Bowls, nested, 11½", 10", 8"
6", green, all ....$ 27- 36
Carafe, 3-pt., green 29- 37
Casserole, covered, blue 47- 52
Casserole, in metal holder,
yellow 55- 65
Chop plate, 15" dia., green 18- 27
Chop plate, 13" dia., yellow 16- 26
Coffeepot, regular 41- 50
Creamer, stick handle, blue 9- 14
Mustard jar, yellow 20- 27
Marmalade jar, blue 27- 37
Marmalade jar in metal holder,
green.................... 42- 52
Plate, 12" dia., yellow (ill.) 11- 17
Tea cup, blue 4- 7

Finger Bowls

Finger Bowls

Always accompanied by a matching underplate, these small receptacles for cleansing the fingers after eating were made of a variety of glassware.

Amber, ITP ....$ 42- 50
Apple green, Depression glass
type 16- 24
Bohemian glass, blue, deer scene . 51- 60
Cobalt 41- 50
Cranberry, Lutz-type threading . 78- 86
Green, fluted lip 37- 45
Moser glass, green/blue 44- 53
Mother-of-Pearl, Diamond
Quilted satin glass (ill.) 300-375
New England Peachblow, satin
finish (ill.) 525-575
Pink, Depression glass type..... 15- 21
Threaded glass, pink/blue 37- 44
Tortoise glass, enameled florals
(ill.) 325-360

Fire Fighting Collectibles

Another of the Americana series that's now

Firefighting Collectibles

highly sought after. Call it a fire sale if you will, but the amounts being paid certainly aren't fire sale prices.

Bell, hand-cranked, East Hampton Bell Factory	$150-170
Fire bucket, Elmira, Engine 3	280-340
Fire bucket, English, London Fire, paint worn thin	240-270
Fire bucket, Scarsdale's Finest	300-370
Fire lantern, Dietz King, brass	75- 90
Helmet, brass eagle finial, English, c. 1870	240-280
Helmet, leather, Philadelphia, c. 1860s	275-340
Hose nozzle, brass, 14¾" long, c. 1890	99-140
Parade belt, lettered P.R. Abbit	75- 87
Presentation shield, Tannersville, N.Y.	1300+
Silver-plated engine lamp, King Neptune	1300+
Speaking trumpet, brass, names of volunteers engraved on lip	420-550
Speaking trumpet, silver plate, dated 1872	350-450
Speaking trumpet, sterling silver, Boston 1872	510-570
Wooden chest, fire rescue scene painted on front	1400+

Firemarks

Firemarks

Associated Firemen's Insurance of Baltimore, Md., issued in 1848.

Citizen's Fire, Marine and Life Insurance Co., Wheeling W. Va., 1856.

City Insurance Company of Cincinnati, Ohio, about 1846.

Clay Fire and Marine Insurance Co., Newport, Ky., 1789.

Firemen's Insurance Co. of Pittsburgh, Pa., about 1851.

Franklin Insurance Co., St. Louis, Mo., 1855 (ill.)

Home Insurance Co., New Haven, Conn., 1859.

Insurance Co. of Florida, Jacksonville, Fla., 1841.

Insurance Co. of North America, extremely rare in copper, eagle rising from cloud.

Western Mutual Fire and Marine Insurance Co., St. Louis, Mo., 1857.

Each of these firemarks is worth at least $300 or more, some as much as $2,700.

Firemen's parade belts, various sizes and colors	$125-180

If you're into fire fighting paraphernalia, visit the Home Insurance Co. Museum, 15th floor, 59 Maiden Lane, New York City, or the American Museum of Fire Fighting, Fireman's Home, Hudson, N.Y. There are other museums, of course, but these two, in particular, are great.

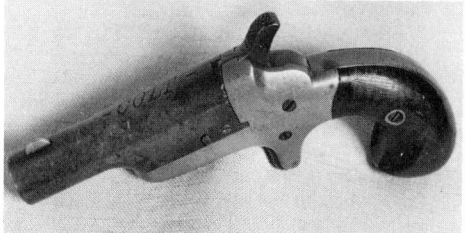

Firearms

Firearms

This is a highly collectible (and expensive) category. Skillful repros are flooding the market, so do business with reliable people, please. Abbreviations used are as follows: cal—caliber; revol—revolver; CW—Civil War; perc—percussion; FL—flintlock; BL—breechloading; PG—pistol grip; SS—single shot; bbl—barrel; mkd—marked; oct—octagonal; SA—single action; DA—double action. Please Note: Federal Firearms Regulations: All firearms made in or before 1898 have been exempted from federal firearms regulations

169

(continued)

which means that unless your state or town has a special law preventing your purchase of such a gun, they can be freely sent and purchased interstate and mail order. On those guns made after 1898, there is a prohibition for sales to anyone except a federally licensed dealer. The federal law does not conflict or cancel any existing state or local laws that might be in effect in your area; hence, although weapons prior to 1898 are exempt under federal law, it is still necessary for you to sign a statement regarding permits or other requirements in your own local area if applicable. Don't get cute with the regulations. You're a candidate for a prison term if you do.

American Hand Guns:

Allen & Thurber 6-shot .31 cal perc Pepperbox, mkd Young & Smith—New York—Allen's Patent ...$	375-	450
Allen & Wheelock 5-shot .31 cal perc DA revol, 4″ oct bbl............	475-	550
American perc pocket (or belt size) pistol, c. 1840-50, carved stock, silver, gold inlay, 4″ large round bbl.................	2,000-	2,300
Cased Colt DA 1878 Frontier Model revol....	900-	975
Colt .36 cal 5-shot perc Pocket Model of Naval caliber	625-	695
Colt #3 Derringer .41 rim-fire...................	575-	650
Colt .44 cal perc Army revol	635-	675
Colt 5-shot .31 cal perc revol, 4″ oct bbl, 2-line N.Y. address	900-	1,350
Colt Open Top 7-shot .22 cal spur trigger revol ...	300-	375
Colt SA Frontier revol, 44/40 cal, mkd on side Colt Frontier Six Shooter	875-	950
Colt 3rd model .44 cal perc Dragoon revol, 8″ bbl	5,400-	5,650
Colt 5-shot .31 cal perc revol, 4″ bbl	365-	445
Colt .36 cal perc Navy revol	1,000-	1,225
Cooper .36 cal perc Navy DA revol, 4″ oct bbl, Frankford, Philadelphia address	775-	860
CW Rogers & Spencer .44 cal perc Army revol	1,100-	1,350
Derringer pistol, 2¾″ fluted bbl swivels, mkd Double Header—E.S. Renwick Manuf'r—New York—Pat. June 21, 1864	5,300-	5,575
FL martial pistol.........	1,100-	1,250
.41 cal rim-fire Derringer, mkd XL Derringer, spur trigger	265-	300
Harpers Ferry FL martial pistol, mkd Harpers Ferry 1807	2,650-	2,775
H. Aston .54 cal martial pistol, 1848	520-	545
James Warner 6-shot .31 cal perc pocket revol, 2½″ round bbl.................	285-	335
Manhattan Arms Co. perc SS .31 cal, mkd Hero, 14″ round bbl	245-	280
Merwin & Bray Firearms Co., N.Y., 5-shot, .30 cal cup-primed revol, 3½″ cot/ribbed bbl	465-	520
Metropolitan .36 cal perc CW revol, fashioned after an 1851 Colt	1,550-	1,700
Remington Beals .36 cal perc Navy revol	465-	495
Savage .36 cal CW perc ring trigger Navy revol..	425-	455
Sharps 4-bbl .22 rim-fire Pepperbox............	465-	535
6-shot perc .31 cal Pepperbox, 4½″ ribbed bbls, mkd S. Baylis—1853 along rib, etc.	2,300-	2,550
6-shot .31 cal perc revol, made by Wm. Marston, New York, mkd The Union Arms Co., known as 7th model, 5¼″ bbl...	575-	625
Smith & Wesson Model L 1, 2nd, 3rd issue 7-shot .22 rim-fire revol, ea.	1,250-	1,450
(Called Ladysmiths because the gay gals in the West carried them in their garters. Wesson was highly religious—when he learned of this, he stopped making this pistol, making it highly collectible today.)		
Spalding & Fisher dbl bbl (side-by-side) perc belt size pistol, .36 cal 5″ bbls, single trigger..........	395-	435
Starr SA .44 cal CW perc Army revol, 8″ bbl	1,550-	1,675

.22 cal rim-fire Derringer/
pocket pistol, mkd
Lombard & Co., Spring-
field, Mass. 375- 435

.35 cal perc pistol, mkd
Bacon & Co., Norwich,
Ct., oct/rnd bbl, 4″ long . 245- 285

.31 cal perc Pepperbox,
6-shot, mkd Allen &
Thurber, Norwich, Ct.,
3¼″ bbls 520- 555

U.S. Navy Boxlock perc
pistol, mkd Ames-
Springfield—U.S.N.—
1845 on lock 725- 775

American Shoulder Guns

Ballard sporting rifle, combination .44 rim-fire and
perc, 27½″ rnd bbl 585- 675

Boy's Cadet size perc military musket, 1840-1860,
45″ overall. 565- 635

British cavalry officer's FL
pistol, c. 1760-1775, .69
cal 1,650- 1,875

British Modified Pattern of
1796 FL cavalry pistol,
.76 cal, 9″ bbl, mkgs of
17th Light Dragoons . . . 565- 645

British naval officer's FL
holster pistol, c. 1800,
.52 cal 785- 865

British perc holster pistol,
c. 1830-1840, 8″ oct. bbl,
14″ overall, mkd with
American eagle and
patriotic motifs 4,450- 4,650

Burnside CW perc BL
carbine 445- 495

Colt's Patent-Hartford
1863 CW .58 cal perc
musket 1,500- 1,700

Committee of Safety
FL Revolutionary
musket, 41″ bbl 2,250- 2,450

CW repeating .50 cal rim-
fire carbine, 30″ bbl, mkd
Triplett & Scott 595- 675

Evans sporting rifle, .44 cal,
30″ rnd bbl 675- 770

FL cavalry carbine, .64 cal,
Brown Bess type lock,
20″ bbl 625- 675

FL Kentucky-style rifle, .54
cal, 36″ oct bbl, mkd
Derringer Phila 3,750- 3,900

Henry lever action repeating .44 rim-fire, Ser. No.
7055 . . . . 3,200- 3,500

Kentucky full stock perc

rifle, c. 1830, .38 cal, 41″
oct bbl 2,400- 2,650

Maine or Massachusetts
half stock Kentucky style
sporting rifle, c. 1820,
31½″ oct bbl, .64 cal,
mkd Leland 875- 975

Parker DB 10 gauge
hammerless shotgun,
"D" grade, 29″ bbls 375- 450

Plains-type rifle, .41 cal,
32″ oct bbl, mkd J.H.
Johnston—Great
Western Gun Works,
Pittsburg, Pa. 435- 495

1797 State of Pennsylvania
Contract FL musket,
mkd Miles/CP 2,250- 2,450

Sharps New Model 1859,
.52 cal perc carbine, used
by cavalry in CW 525- 595

Spencer CW cavalry
carbine, .50 cal rim-fire,
22″ bbl 650- 725

Spencer CW 7-shot repeat-
ing carbine, .52 cal rim-
fire, 22″ bbl 575- 675

Springfield 1873 rifle, 45/70
cal 450- 500

U.S. FL common rifle, mkd
U.S.—N. Starr—Midd'n
—1826 . . . . 2,300- 2,450

U.S. FL musket, mkd
Harpers Ferry—1831 . . . 1,375- 1,485

U.S. Mississippi rifle, .54
cal, mkd E. Whitney—
U.S.—1848 . . . . 575- 675

U.S. Springfield trap-door
45/70 cal rifle, dated 1890 425- 475

Winchester Hotchkiss 3rd
model, 45/70 cal. 1,350- 1,550

Winchester saddle ring
carbine, 38/40 cal, 20″
bbl 300- 375

Foreign Hand Guns

Belgian perc belt pistol,
6½″ oct bbl, .52 cal 950- 1,050

British cavalry officer's FL
pistol, c. 1760-1775, .69
cal 1,650- 1,875

British Modified Pattern of
1796 FL cavalry pistol,
.76 cal, 9″ bbl, mkgs of
the 17th Light Dragoons 550- 650

British naval officer's FL
holster pistol, c. 1800, .52
cal 750- 850

British naval officer's FL
pistol, c. 1790, 9″ brass
oct bbl 875- 975

171

(continued)

British perc holster pistol,
c. 1830-1840, 8″ oct bbl,
14″ overall, mkd with
American and patriotic
motifs 4,100- 4,475

Dutch over/under pistol,
c. 1650, .46 cal, 13¾″
oct bbls 10,500-10,750

English combination FL
pistol and sword, mkd
Clarke—London, .50 cal,
3″ rnd screw bbl, 29½″
overall 2,500- 2,650

English FL Dragoon pistol,
Queen Anne period, 18″
overall, 11″ rnd bbl, c.
1700-1710 .... 2,300- 2,475

European martial FL pistol,
c. 1840, .65 cal, 10″ rnd
bbl................. 400- 475

European perc pistol, c.
1840, 9″ rnd bbl, 15½″
overall, .67 cal 625- 695

FL boxlock English pocket
pistol, c. 1790, .41 cal,
mkd Brasher—London,
2½″ rnd screw bbl 365- 465

French boxlock FL holster
pistol, c. 1760, .38 cal,
6″ overall............ 325- 385

German FL holster pistol,
c. 1680, 21″ overall, mkd
Herman Ghiot, 13½″
rnd bbl.............. 3,200- 3,450

Italian FL holster pistol,
c. 1720, 16″ overall, 9½″
rnd bbl.............. 3,400- 3,575

Match pair, cased English
perc dueling pistols,
.44 cal, 16″ overall, 10″
oct bbls, mkd J. Purdey
—Oxford St.—Gun Mfr—
London 7,500- 8,450

Mid-Eastern FL holster
pistol, c. 1750, .60 cal,
19½″ overall 4,550- 4,750

Miniature blunderbuss-
pistol, FL, mid-Eastern,
c. 1750, 11¾″ overall,
5½″ oct/rnd blunderbuss
bbl................. 475- 600

Miniature FL pistol, c.
1720, 4¾″ overall, .28 cal,
mkd Claude Niquet A
Liege 2,750- 2,900

Scottish Highland and
military style, 18th
century, FL belt pistol,
type used in Colonial
America, .62 cal 950- 1,275

Spanish Miquelet belt
pistol, c. 1810, 5½″
oct/rnd bbl............ 695- 795

Foreign Shoulder Guns

Ancient matchlock wall
gun, India, 8″ overall, 18
lbs., early 18th century
(or earlier) 525- 675

Ancient North African
(Berber) Snaphauce
camel gun, 5′3″ overall,
49″ oct/rnd bbl 400- 450

Austrian perc .58 cal rifle,
issued to U.S. troops at
beginning of CW, 37″ bbl 550- 650

British Enfield .577 cal perc
musket, mkd 1858—
Tower with crown over
"VR"................ 750- 975

British FL swivel blunderbuss, 24″ brass bbl,
muzzle, 3″ dia., 22 lbs.,
41″ overall............ 1,450- 1,700

British officer's FL fusil or
full stock fowling piece,
c. 1790, 38″ oct/rnd bbl .. 645- 750

British 10 gauge side
hammer dbl bbl shotgun,
30″ bbls.............. 275- 315

CW British Enfield .577 cal
perc rifle musket, mkd
Barnett—London Tower 455- 515

Dutch FL military rifle,
used during American
Revolution, 36″ oct/rnd
bbl, .67 cal mkd Thone &
Zoon—Amsterdam 1,650- 1,875

Dutch FL officer's fusil, 36″
bbl, .70 cal 950- 1,100

English perc dbl bbl side-
by-side shotgun, c. 1850,
28″ bbls, 14 gauge 395- 475

French/Belgian DeLvigne
.69 cal perc musket,
imported for CW use by
Union Army, 40″ bbl ... 550- 650

French Charleville FL
musket, 1763, CP mkgs . 2,475- 2,675

French FL musket, used by
American in Revolution-
ary War 1,600- 1,850

French FL musket, mkd
Charlottesville on lock,
American Revolutionary
War 1,000- 1,275

German/Dutch FL musket,
43″ bbl, type used in
American Revolution ... 825- 900

German FL musket, 17th
century, military, 42″

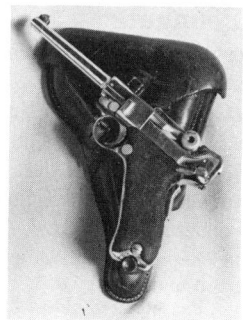

Firearms

oct/rnd bbl, .80 cal, mkd Leopold I of Wiemer-Neustadt	2,350-	2,600
Italian FL full stock fowling piece, c. 1750, 5' overall, .67 cal, mkd P. Bonafino	3,200-	3,425
Italian Vetterli bolt action rifle	170-	195
Japanese matchlock musket, 42" oct bbl, .64 cal	575-	650
Japanese matchlock musket, 40" oct bbl, .57 cal	575-	665
Japanese pill-lock short hand cannon or carbine, 41" overall, 9 lbs., quite ancient	550-	600
2nd model British Brown Bess FL musket, 42" bbl, used during French-Indian and Revolutionary Wars	2,200-	2,450

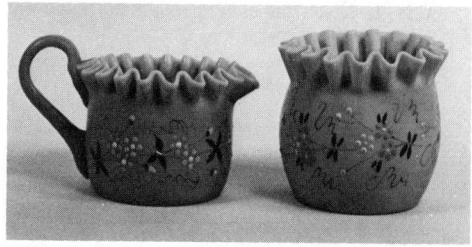

Fireglow

Fireglow

When held to a light this glass, attributed to the Mt. Washington Glass Company, shows a fiery opalescence. It was made during the 1890s.

Creamer, ruffled top, pink/blue flowers (ill.)	$ 76- 92

Sugar bowl, ruffled top, pink/blue flowers (ill.)	74-	91
Vase, autumn leaves, 7½" high	120-	140
Vase, Bristol style, child's face, button feet	160-	170
Vase, brown/blue leaves, 7" high	132-	142

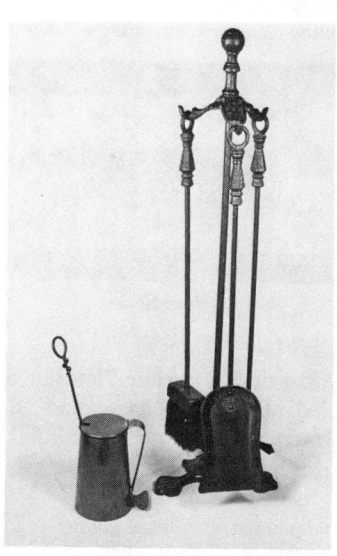

Fireplace Accessories

Fireplace Accessories

Our ancestors depended on the fireplace for warmth and a place to cook their food. The tools they used are collectible today. Brass and copper pieces are especially desirable; andirons (fire dogs), coal hods and fenders are among the most desired. See also **Andirons, Bellows.**

Coal box, English, tooled brass	$130-150
Fender, brass, English, mid-1800s	400-475
Fender, brass, fan-type mid-1800s	565-650
Fire tending tools in rack, brass, mid-1800s, 4 pieces (ill.)	180-210
Grate, iron, on legs	80- 90
Lighter, Cape Cod (ill.)	30- 40
Screen, hinged type, English	130-150
Screen, solid iron type used in summer to cover fireplace	87- 97
Tools: shovel, poker, brush, in brass stand	64- 76

Fischer China

The firm was founded by Moritz Fischer in Herend, Hungary, in 1839. It was still operating in the 20th century just before World War II.

(continued)

Egg cup, gilt trim $140-160
Figurine, sitting dog, white . . .   60- 70
Vase, embossed flowers, reticu-
   lated handles, 12" high 360-380
Vase, medallion front and back,
   yellow scrolls, hunting decor   365+
Vase, pink/beige/green, 12½"
   high 320-340

Fish Sets

Fish Sets

In vogue during the late Victorian era, they
consisted of a large platter and 12 plates.
Each piece was decorated with a fish. Haviland, Rosenthal, and most other china companies made these sets.

Hand-painted, embossed gold,
   sauceboat, 12 plates, blue/
   green $172-190
Haviland, green/pink flowers,
   fish in pond, 16 pcs., in
   leatherette case 345-380
Limoges, enameled branches,
   hand-painted, 23" long (ill.) .   375+
Limoges, seashells and fish,
   platter and 6 plates 142-156
Platter, 12 plates, painted
   trout, bass, perch, carp, pike 220-240
Porcelain, seashells, lily pads,
   frogs, signed Germany, 12
   pcs. 260-275
Roses/vines, hand-painted,
   Austria, 8 pcs., 1908 180-210

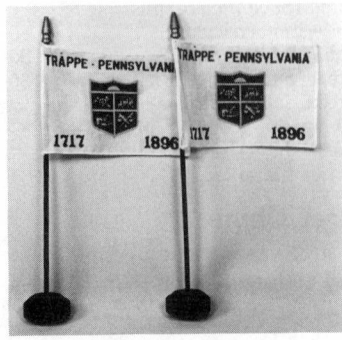

Flags, Pennants

Flags, Pennants

Old Glory! All types are collectible, the
older the better. On June 14, 1777, the
American Congress resolved that the flag of
the thirteen United States be thirteen stripes,
alternating red and white; that the union be
thirteen stars, white in a blue field, represent-
ing a new constellation.

Flags, 11" high, commemorate
   the 179th anniversary of
   Trappe, Pa., home of oldest unrestored Lutheran church in
   America (ill.) . . . . $ 27- 36

Flasks

Flasks

Chestnut, ½ pt., red brown,
   c. 1830s $250-280
Cut glass, sterling silver caps . . .   57- 67
Glass, ½ pt., pewter cup fits over
   bottom, 1930s 34- 44
Grain, pt., aqua, maker unknown,
   c. 1850s 170-200
Hip type, ½ pt., sterling silver,
   1920s 50- 60
Ribbed, ½ pt., yellow amber,
   c. 1840s 190-210
Sterling silver, monk, 4½" high
   (ill.) 175-225
"Success To The Railroad," pt.,
   olive green, large eagle on
   reverse side, made by Kensing-
   ton Glass Works, Philadelphia,
   c. 1830 320-340
Violin, ½ pt., aqua, c. 1850s 130-140
Walking stick, ¼-pt. capacity,
   glass rod fits inside, silver cap . 140-150
Washington and Taylor, qt.,
   aqua 220-230

Florentine Art "Cameo"

Made in Bohemia, this glass has a satin glass body and is heavily decorated with enamel. Some think it's cameo glass but it isn't. Late 18th, 19th century.

Vase, blue satin glass, white
flowers, 8" high .... $ 82- 92
Vase, green satin glass, butterflies and flowers, 8½" high ... 75- 87
Whiskey glass, blue satin glass,
castle scene, set of 6 240-270

Flow Blue

Flow Blue

China on which the color ran during the firing is called Flow Blue. Made at Staffordshire and other potteries, it was popular during the early and mid-1800s. Highly collectible today.

Bone dish, Johnson .... $ 16- 27
Bone dish, Ormonde (Meakin) ... 28- 37
Bowl, soup, Rose pattern, 8" 16- 24
Butter dish, Gridley 92-107
Butter pat, bluebirds 16- 27
Cake stand, flower decor, 13"
high 118-129
Chocolate pot, blue/gold,
LaBelle .... 95+
Compote, floral decoration,
molded leaf handles, cover 62- 73
Creamer, Haddon 62- 74
Creamer, Alfred Meakin, 4½"
high 52- 61
Cup/saucer, demitasse, Lorne ... 42- 52
Dish, vegetable, open, 12½"
dia. 51- 60
Gravy boat, boat scene,
Ovando 31- 41
Gravy boat, Paisley 49- 58
Jar, biscuit, barrel shape, elks,
1890 mark 59- 67

Pitcher and bowl, gilt, La
Belle 140-152
Pitcher, gravy, Lonial 31- 40
Plate, Castro pattern, 14" dia. ... 34- 43
Plate, flowers/leaves, cobalt,
11" dia. (ill.) 41- 50
Platter, Blue Danube, oval
10¼" dia. 50- 60
Platter, Jenny Lind, 11" long ... 78- 87
Platter, scalloped edge, Krona,
Wood and Sons 64- 73
Ring tree 32- 41
Sauce, Touraine, Alcock 22- 31
Syrup, dark blue, pewter cap 40- 50
Teapot, Touraine, Alcock 150-160
Tureen, vegetable, Touraine 80- 90

Fluting Irons

Fluting Irons

Made of iron or brass, they rolled pleats in petticoats and cuffs. Early 1800s to early 1900s.

Fluting iron, marked Geneva,
roller type (ill.) .... $ 67- 72
Iron handled tube, 3-legged
stand, early 52- 61

Flytraps

Flytraps

Popular in the mid-1800s, some were crude affairs made of wood or metal. The collectible

175

(continued)

type is made of glass. The top was removable so one could put in sugar water to attract the flies.

Blue, Sandwich-type glass, beehive shape, mid-1800s (ill.) $270-320
Cranberry, other colors, same type as above 185-200
Metal, box type, late 1800s 70- 79
Wood, box type, late 1800s 33- 41

Folk Art, American

Folk Art, American

Folk painting is the product of one untrained in art; the effort of the painter to depict or portray scenes, persons or objects of interest to them. A lack of perspective, depth, and proportion, are a few of the chief characteristics of folk painting in America. Once again, prices change too quickly to give you an honest cost. A John Brewster, Jr., recently sold for $67,000; a J. Bradley, $43,000; a Nathaniel F. Wales, $12,000. Folk Art, American, is here to stay.

"Brothers," done in crayon, Connecticut, c. 1860, 8"×11"
"The Country Church," c. 1855, 7"×11"
"Farm in West Cornwall, Connecticut," 1895, 8½"×18"
"Farm Scene," signed J.F. Gilman, dated 1871, charcoal, 19"×27"
"Fort Plain, New York," c. 1850, 23"×34"
"Home for Thanksgiving," New York State, c. 1850, 25"×30"
"Hunters," c. 1870, 14"×22"
"Landscape with Sawmill," G. Marston, 1863, 22"×30"
"The Mansion," charcoal c. 1850, 15"×23"
"Mississippi Farm by a River," c. 1875, 22"×27"
"Morning Chores in New Hampshire," c. 1840, 30"×36"

"Train on a Bridge," painted on tin, c. 1840, 10"×14"
"The Village Banker's Home in Winter" (ill.), c. 1870, 22"×27"
"Village Lake with Indians," c. 1850, 17"×23"
"Young Lady on a Balcony" c. 1820, 20"×36"

Much of this type of Americana is around. A lot of fakes are around also, so challenge the auctioneer if you don't think he's right (he probably is), question the antiques dealer, and know from whom you buy.

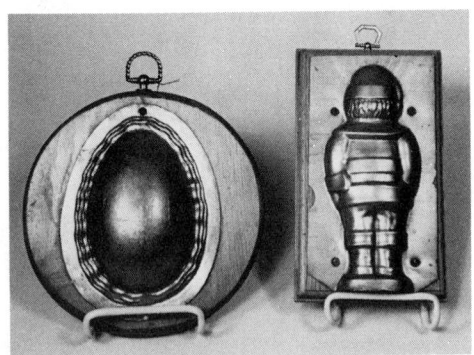

Food, Candy Molds

Food, Candy Molds

Food molds are usually made of ironstone or metal, tin and pewter. Candy molds are usually made of metal.

Bride and Groom .... $ 60- 72
Calf's head jelly mold, ironstone, rabbit 42- 51
Candy, Easter egg, mounted on wood (ill.) 18- 27
Candy, pewter, turkey, 4" 34- 44
Candy, Santa Claus, mounted on wood (ill.) 16- 26
Candy, tin, rabbit 40- 50
Gelatine mold, ironstone, boar's head 52- 62
Heart and Cupid 44- 52
Hobby horse 50- 60
Pudding mold, ironstone, ear of corn 54- 63
Relish mold, tin 32- 41
Rooster 32- 41

Foot Warmers

Some were made of soapstone, some were hollow pieces of pottery into which hot water was poured. Others were crude wood/tin affairs. All had the same purpose.

Foot Warmers

Glazed blue/white pottery,
hollow, marked Alcove Ohio,
12″ wide . . . . $ 70- 77
Soapstone, 12″×10″, with wire
handle 40- 48
Tin, carpet-covered, held char-
coal, used in early autos 50- 60
Walnut, 4 pillars, punched tin
hearts. 6″ high (ill.) 110-122

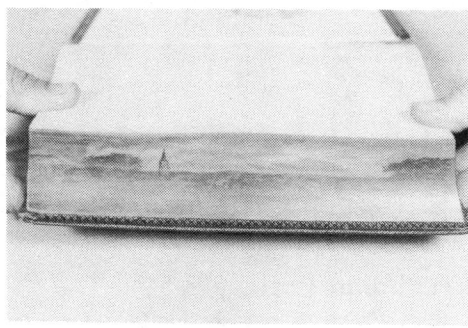

Fore-Edge Paintings

Fore-Edge Paintings

Few people other than those who collect
rare books know about this subject. Look for
a book with pages gilded on the edges, then
gently push the pages back. If there is in-
deed a fore-edge painting, you'll see it. Price
depends on the subject, the painter, if a first
edition, etc.

Painting of Buffalo, N.Y.; book
about Erie Canal (ill.) $375-450

Foreign Legion Items

The French Foreign Legion, based in North
Africa, was the most famous of volunteer
military units. Now things related to the
Foreign Legion are becoming collectible.

Foreign Legion Items

Cap badges, French Foreign
Legion, pre-World War I, ea. . . $ 24- 33
Discharge papers, pre-World
War II 27- 40
Toothpick holder, paste porcelain,
late 1800s (ill.) 37- 46

Fostoria Glass

Fostoria Glass

Originally manufactured in Fostoria, Ohio,
in 1887, the factory was moved a few years
later to Moundsville, Virginia, where it continues to make a quality glassware. Discontinued patterns and early 20th century pieces
are what collectors and dealers look for. Most
pieces you find are in the $8, $20, and $65
range. It's lovely glass to collect, and here
are a few of the many patterns: American,
Baroque, Beverly, Amber and Green; Fairfax
Ebony, Green, Pink, Rose, Topaz; Lafayette

177

(continued)

Clear; Mayfair Amber, Ebony, Green, Pink, Rose, Optic Rose, Pink, Clear. Enjoy collecting a lovely glass!

Bowl, pink opalescent	$ 34- 44
Bookends, dog heads, pr.	47- 56
Candleholders, Baroque, w/prisms, pr.	69- 78
Candleholders, Topaz, 2-light, pr.	64- 72
Cruet, Optic Rose, 5" high	28- 37
Figurine, duck, Beverly	24- 33
Mugs, fish-shaped	12- 17
Platter, Ebony, open handles	32- 40
Vase, clear pedestal base, acid etched acorns and oak leaves (ill.)	67- 72

Francesware

Pitcher, blown, 4 mold, amber stained top, frosted hobnail body, 8" high (ill.)	260-280
Sauce, 4½" square, hobnail	31- 40
Tumbler, typical	51- 60
Water set, 6 pieces, frosted, amber tops, all	415-470

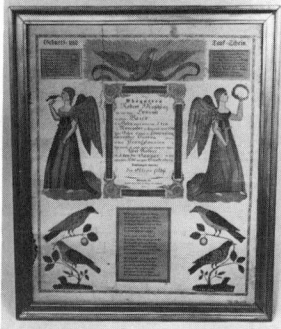

Frakturs

Frakturs

Simply put, a fraktur is a birth certificate that is ornately decorated. They were popular in the Pennsylvania German area in the early to late 1800s.

Birth certificate, framed, signed W. Grofs, 1861. Printed in Allentown, Pa., 16"×19", hand-colored birds, angels, and an American eagle (ill.) .... $ 90-120

Francesware

Frosted with stained amber rims or tops, this glass made by Hobbs, Brockunier and Company was both pressed and blown-molded in the 1880s. A real collector's item today. Don't confuse the name with Francis Ware, which was japanned tinware made and decorated by Henry and Tom Francis in Philadelphia around 1830.

Bowl, clear, 7" square	$ 64- 73
Match holder, frosted, amber top	72- 82

Frankoma Pottery

Frankoma Pottery

John Frank began the pottery firm in Sapulpa, Oklahoma, in 1933. He combined his chemical knowledge with the pottery making traditions of the Indians of the Southwest. The mottled lines result from the use of colored earthenware clays. The pacing leopard was the original trademark, but it was discontinued because of difficulty encountered reproducing it in soft clay. "FRANKOMA" is the mark used today. In 1965 they began making commemorative Christmas plates.

Bowl, 11" dia., mottled hues of brown and yellow, Leopard mark	$ 49- 58
Christmas plate, "Laid in a Manger," 1969	27- 36
Christmas plate, "Gifts for the Christ Child," 1967	57- 60
Cookie jar, mottled blue, FRANKOMA mark	41- 50

Cup/saucer, mottled brown and
yellow, FRANKOMA mark
(ill.) 24- 33
Vase, 11″ high, brown/green,
Leopard mark   110-121
Vase, 6″ high, blue/brown,
FRANKOMA mark 19- 27

Fraternal Order Collectibles

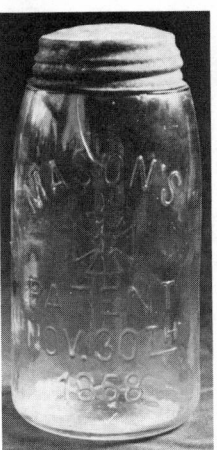

Fruit Jars

Fraternal Order Collectibles

Elk, Moose, Lion, Eagle, Mason, Odd
Fellow—all are fraternal organizations. What
they wore or carried during the 18th and 19th
centuries is collectible today.

A.O.F. parasol, 1908 convention . $ 39- 47
BPOE ashtray, Cincinnati, 1904,
Rookwood pottery (rare) 58- 70
BPOE handled mug, elk and
clock 32- 42
F.O.E., watch fob 27- 36
Knights of Columbus match safe   28- 37
Masonic jug, Canary ware,
English   310-328
Masonic shaving mug 31- 40
Odd Fellow's jug, pink lustre,
English, rare   325-350
Plate, Masonic, 10¼″ dia. (ill.) . . .   17- 26
Shrine goblet, Washington, D.C.,
1902, red flashed glass 29- 38
Shrine, Omaha, 1918, mug 28- 30

Freehand Ware

This was made by Imperial Glass Company, Bellaire, Ohio, in the 1920s and is mentioned here because, as a lustred art glass,
people are confusing it with late Carnival.
They're also confusing it with Imperial's Imperial Jewel, which is an onionskin type of
glass. Also being collected as Carnival.

Fruit Jars

In one word—Mason—John Landis Mason,
that is. A tinsmith by trade, at the age of 26,
in his shop in New York City, he designed his
now-famous wide-mouth jar, the Mason's
Pat. Nov. 30th 1858. He also invented the tin
screw-on lids to fit the jars he farmed out to
the various glassmakers in the area. **Important:** This explains why there are so many
names on his jars, but always with Mason's
name blown into the glass. Many pioneer
firms are still in the business, such as Drey,
Ball, Kerr, and Boyd. Mason's "Black" glass
jars are priceless today.

Atlas, Cloverleaf, pt. or qt. . . . . . . $ 19- 27
Atlas, E-Z Seal, amber, qt. 31- 41
Ball, Ideal, ¼ pt., ½ pt., clear or
green (ill.) 18- 29
Banner, patented February 9,
1864, aqua 36- 47
Clark's Peerless, pt. or qt. 27- 37
Crown emblem, ½ gal., amber . . .   40- 50
Eureka, qt., clear 32- 40
Gem, qt., clear 15- 26
Globe, pt., amber 68- 78
Hazel preserve, Atlas lightning
seal, qt., aqua 19- 29
Lightning, qt., amber 42- 51
Mason, Maltese Cross emblem,
patented November 30, 1858,
½ gal., amber 54- 62
Mason's 1872, patented, qt.,
aqua 32- 41
Smalley self sealer, qt.,
amethyst 32- 41
Victory, qt. or ½ gal., clear 18- 28
Woodbury, qt., aqua 34- 42
Mason's Pat. Nov. 30th 1858
(ill.) 55- 64

Fry Glass

Fulper

Fry Glass

Made by H.C. Fry Company, Rochester, Pennsylvania, 1900 to 1929. Fine cut glass for the first 15 years, then Foval glass was introduced after 1925. Some pieces are marked Fry. Gold was used in the batch to make Foval. Collectors are just beginning to appreciate Fry glass. Usually a combination of two colors in pastel shades of greens, pinks, blues. Foval is also known as Pearl Art.

Bowl, black, clear bell stem, 6″ tall, marked Fry, dated	$190-240
Candlesticks, blue trim, 13″ high, Foval	360-420
Cologne bottle, clear, green stopper, signed Fry	125-140
Creamer, opalescent, green trim under tray, signed	180-197
Cup and saucer, Foval, 2½″ high (ill.)	82- 94
Custard cup, ovenware, 1919	42- 51
Epergne, intaglio cut, signed	190-220
Foval, barber bottle, milky white, fiery opalescent	74- 83
Foval, candlestick, blue/white, 10″ high	192-199
Foval coffeepot, opalescent, white handle, 10″ high	295-330
Foval, compote, cream color base, blue standard, 9¼″ dia.	140-170
Foval, cup/saucer, blue jade handle	92-102
Foval, pitcher, yellow iridescent, cobalt handle, 6 tumblers	220-240
Pitcher, craquelle, applied blue handle	110-140
Pitcher, opalescent blue stripes over blue crystal, 4 tumblers	320-345
Sugar bowl, covered	240-260
Toothpick, ruffled, applied blue crystal handles	72- 81
Vase, craquelle, blue application	92-107
Vase, cream, cobalt handles, 7½″ high	170-190

Fulper

The Fulper Pottery Company in Flemington, New Jersey, made this pottery in the mid-1880s. It was never the quality of Rookwood or Weller. They also made all-bisque dolls. The firm operates under the name of Stangl Pottery today.

Bookends, dogs, pr., 6½″ high	$ 47- 57
Compote, base is 3 dragons, blue/green	170-180
Jardiniere, multicolor, 8″ high	92-100
Jug, brown, Philadelphia, 1926, 6″ high	68- 78
Lamp base, bright blue, reticulated base	94-103
Lamp, mushroom shade, 17″ high	138-160
Vase, blue glaze, 9″ high	57- 67
Vase, green matte finish, signed, 6¼″ high	67- 72
Vase, poppies, 12″ high	78- 88
Vase, 7″ high, brown/blue glaze, Fulper (ill.)	75- 92
Vase, tortoiseshell, 13″ high, signed	62- 72

Funeral Collectibles

Like it or not, collectors are avidly seeking things relating to funerals.

Embalming tools, early 1900, set of 12	$ 58-	70
Glass coffin, 2 pcs., late 1880s (rare)	450-	525
Hand-carved walnut coffin, 1850s (ill.)	400-	500
Horse-drawn hearse, belveled glass windows, original lamps and fixtures		7,800+

Furniture, American

The prices quoted here have to be very general as antique furniture prices are climb-

Funeral Collectibles

ing steadily, day by day. The better auction galleries are getting unbelievable prices for Chippendale, Queen Anne, Hepplewhite—both American and English—and there's no end in sight. Just know what you're doing, or pay a member of the Appraisers Association of America to assist you.

Pilgrim style, 1650-1690
William and Mary style, 1690-1720
Queen Anne style, 1720-1750
Chippendale style, 1750-1775
Shaker, 1776-1900
Hepplewhite style, 1785-1800
Duncan Phyfe, 1795-1847
Sheraton style, 1800-1820
American Empire style, 1820-1840
Rococo style, 1840s to 1860s
Gothic style, 1840-1865
Belter furniture, 1844-1863
Cottage furniture, 1850-1880
Spool-turned style, 1850-1880
Renaissance style, 1860-1875
Louis XVI style, 1865-1875
Eastlake style, 1870-1880
New England style, 17th to mid-19th centuries
Pennsylvania Dutch, 18th and 19th centuries

Armchairs

Bentwood, c. 1860, caned, set of 6 . . . . $	280-	300
Ladder-back, maple, rush seat, c. 1840, set of 4 . .	435-	475
Ladder-back, sausage turned, old green paint, rush seat	160-	175
Ladder-back, Shaker style, 4-slat, New England, rush seat . . .	285-	320

Massachusetts, c. 1730s .	395-	435
Medallion back, open arms, oak, uphol-stered, c. 1890s	100-	125
Platform type, open arms, curved wooden frame, upholstered . . .	185-	225
Windsor, comb-back, ser-pentine crest rail	1,800-	1,975
Beds		
Brass, double size, swell-foot end, c. 1880s	975-	1,100
Brass plated, double size, bow-foot end, c. 1890s .	575-	625
Cabinet mantel type, elm, beveled mirror, c. 1890s	325-	360
Child's, iron, white enamel, drop sides, c. 1890s	225-	245
Half tester, walnut, re-cessed veneer panels, c. 1850	1,900-	2,250
Jenny Lind spool, double size	400-	450
Oak, double, raised panel-ing, head-and-foot-board, c. 1890s	245-	275
Oak, twin, carved, head-and-footboard, c. 1890s	190-	235
Rope, high posts, cherry, corn-shuck mattress, c. 1820	895-	975
Spool, low posts, triangu-lar headboard, c. 1855 .	600-	675
Walnut, single, molded foot and head rail, carved crest, c. 1850 . .	395-	475

(continued)

Benches

Church pew, pine, unre-
stored, New England,
c. 1850s, 10' long 725- 765
Cobbler's, complete with
all tools, original condi-
tion, c. 1840 . . . . 575- 675
Deacon's, original dark
finish, 10' long, New
Hampshire, c. 1820s . . 775- 850
Deacon's, spindle back,
8-leg, Connecticut,
c. 1830 . . . . 875- 900
Mammy rocker, remova-
ble guard rail, sten-
ciled, c. 1840 . . . . 1,100- 1,250
Mammy rocker, wooden
cog to operate butter
churn, etc., c. 1840 . . . 1,350- 1,450
Porch, poplar, heeled
through seat, solid
back 145- 165

Bookcases

Globe Werneke type, 5-
section, oak, top and
base, all 225- 245
Library type, 6' wide,
4 adjustable shelves,
3 glass doors 465- 500
Oak, 5 adjustable
shelves, open lattice-
work in top, glass
door 265- 300
Oak, 6 shelves, glass
doors, c. 1880s 195- 235
Rosewood, wall type, 3
shelves, c. 1840s 275- 350

Bureaus

Bowfront, maple, carved
pulls, 4-drawer, c.
1860 . . . . 575- 675
Cottage, 4-drawer, pine . 250- 325
Hepplewhite, pine,
bracket feet, 4-drawer . 675- 725

Chairs

Arm, Eastlake, open
arms, open-crested
back, 1875 . . . . 175- 225
Arm, open arms, button-
tufted upholstery, wal-
nut, incised lines 275- 300
Corner, walnut, burl
veneer panels, c.
1850s 325- 365
Eastlake, side, machine
lines and carving, up-
holstered, c. 1870s . . . 185- 220
Gentleman's, applied
veneer panels, button
tufting, c. 1855 . . . . . . 385- 410

Gentleman's, oval back,
finger roll, open arms,
c. 1860 . . . . 365- 400
Lady's, carved crest, bal-
loon back, finger roll,
c. 1845 . . . . 345- 365
Lady's, spoon back,
carved crest, uphol-
stered, c. 1855 . . . . 355- 385
Mahogany, veneered
back, inlaid, c. 1890 . . . 145- 175
Morris, reclining, brass
rod at back, loose cush-
ions, c. 1890 . . . . 235- 365
Parlor, made of rattan,
shellac finish, c. 1890s 140- 160
Parlor, spring seat,
upholstered, oak,
mahogany finish, c.
1890s 135- 150
Parlor, made of reed,
shellac finish, c. 1890s 140- 155
Reading, lady's parlor,
full twist spindles, oak,
c. 1890s 175-200
Reading, large arm, oak,
spoke back, silk
damask seat, c. 1890s . 175- 195
Rocking, rectangular
caned back, applied
burl veneer, c. 1860 . . . 185- 200
Roman, birch, curved
seat, open arms, silk
damask seat, c. 1895 . . 145- 165

Furniture, American

182

Rocking, swan neck
arms, caned back and
seat, c. 1850   195-   235
Side, cane seat, maple,
vase back   145-   165
Side, carved cresting,
oval back, walnut,
needlepoint uphol-
stery   210-   235
Side, demi-arms, burl
veneer panels, machine
lines and carving   210-   235
Side, Hitchcock type,
rush seat, 33″ high
(ill.)   150-   175
Side, molded and pierced
back piece supported
by turned columns . . .   245-   265
Turkish, leather, oak
frame, steel springs,
moss/hair filled   175-   200
Windsor, arrowback,
writing arm, unre-
stored   290-   345
Windsor, comb-back, c.
1835 . . . .   1,800- 1,950
Windsor, lady's birdcage,
original black paint . . .   195-   245
Windsor, side, butterfly
back, saddle seat,
signed E.P. Rose   . . .   350-   395
Chaise Longues
Cherry frame, fully up-
holstered, incised lines,
Eastlake style   450-   500
Fully upholstered, maple
legs, loose cushion,
c. 1870s   425-   475

Louis XV style, finger
roll, tufted back 900- 1,250
Chests
Apothecary, oak, 60-
drawer, porcelain
knobs, c. 1840   875-   975
Blanket, bracket feet,
poplar, black brush
and comb decoration
(ill.)   375-   450
Blanket, cherry, dovetail,
rattail hinges, c.
1730s 1,350- 1,450
Blanket, Pennsylvania
Dutch, green, dull red
trim 1,900- 2,200
Blanket, pine, strap
hinges, 2 drawers in
base, c. 1830   850-   950
Chippendale, bowfront,
cherry, 6-drawer,
c. 1760 . . . .   5,100- 5,400
Chippendale type,
mahogany, ogee feet,
6-drawer   625-   665
Dower, Pennsylvania,
painted and decorated
pine, hinged top,
animals, fowls, c.
1773, 19¾″ high, 50½″
long (ill.) 3,900- 4,300
Dower, Pennsylvania
Dutch, painted green/
red w/flowers on front .   3,600- 3,750

Furniture, American

183

(continued)

Furniture, American

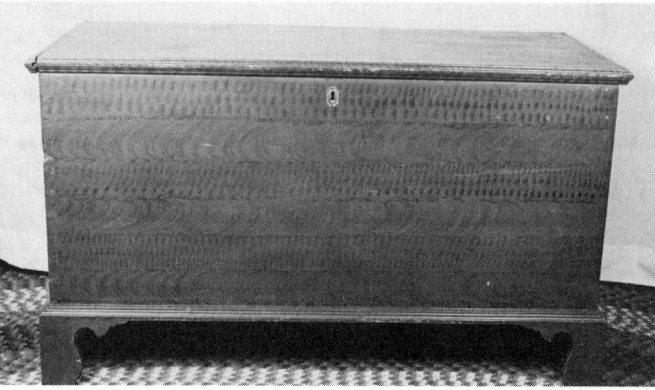

Furniture, American

Dower, Pennsylvania
  Dutch, tulip decor,
  original paint, c. 1810 . . 3,900- 4,350
Hepplewhite, pine, 4-
  drawer, veneered
  mahogany front, c.
  1790 . . . . 975- 1,200

China Cabinets
Corner, swell front, 4
  adjustable shelves,
  oak, c. 1890s 450- 475
Mahogany, carved crest,
  beveled glass on 3
  sides, 5 adjustable
  shelves 525- 575
Oak, glass on 3 sides,
  mirror on top, lattice-
  work in door, c. 1890 . . 450- 475
Oak, spiral fluted pillars,
  beveled glass on 3
  sides, c. 1890s 550- 600
Oak, swell-shaped glass
  in ends, carved feet, 4
  adjustable shelves . . . 600- 650

Cradles
Hooded, hickory, hand
  holes, c. 1820s 425- 450
Hooded, pine, c. 1830s . . 350- 400
Open, walnut, spindle
  construction, c. 1850s . 345- 365
Rocker type, cutout
  hearts, maple (ill.) 375- 400
Rocker type, slat deco-
  rated, cherry, c. 1830 . 345- 385
Round rails, square
  posts, knob finials,
  walnut, c. 1840 . . . . . . 295- 365

Cupboards
Corner, cherry, 2 doors
  above and below, 1
  drawer, c. 1830 . . . . . . 3,100- 3,350

Corner, maple, solid
  doors above and below,
  scroll top, c. 1850 . . . . 2,750- 3,000
Corner, poplar and pine
  paneled doors, c. early
  1800s, 6' 7" high . . 1,900+
Corner, poplar, glass
  doors above, solid
  below, original paint,
  c. 1840s 1,600- 1,800
Dutch, cherry, glass
  doors above, solid
  below, chamfered
  corners, solid ends,
  wooden knobs, c.
  1760s 4,400- 4,750
Hanging, pine, single
  glass door, 3 shelves,
  c. 1830s 495- 545
Linen, Pennsylvania,
  original green paint,
  solid doors, c. 1830 . . . 1,600- 1,875
Open, glass doors above,
  solid below, 3 drawers
  in middle, c. 1850 . . . . 2,400- 2,575

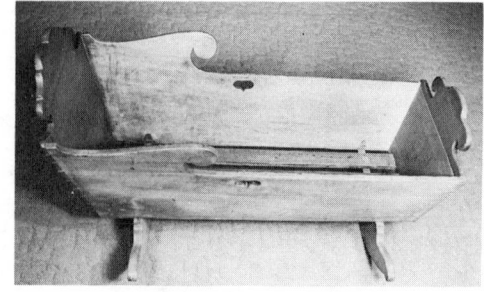

Furniture, American

184

Open, recessed top, glass
doors above, solid
below, carved pulls,
c. 1840 . . . .   1,300- 1,475
Pantry, Pennsylvania
Dutch, red/green,
white flower decor,
c. 1740 . . . .   2,500- 2,700
Pewter, painted pine,
New England, 6
shelves, solid doors
below, c. 1750s 2,500- 2,650
Pewter, pine, hutch top,
3 shelves, solid doors
below, 2 drawers,
c. 1830 . . . .   2,300- 2,450
Pie safe, pine, pierced
geometric tin panels   500-   525

Desks
Bureau, fall front secre-
tary drawer, carved
pulls on 3 drawers,
c. 1860s   650-   725
Butler's, walnut, c. 1850 . 2,350- 2,450
Chippendale, shell-carved
mahogany yoke-front,
gadrooned base, New
England, 18th century,
42¾" high, 41¼" wide
(ill.) . . . .   32,000+
Chippendale style,
cherry, slant-front,
Oxbow, Block and Fan
interior, original pulls,
ball/claw feet, c. 1750 . 3,400- 3,600
Chippendale style,
mahogany slant-front,
Colonial, 38" high,
36½" wide (ill.) 4,650- 4,900

Furniture, American

Cylinder front, walnut,
veneered cylinder
panel, machine lines
and carving, spindled
gallery, 3 drawers
below, c. 1840s 2,300- 2,450
Drop front, table type,
walnut, beaded mold-
ing, c. 1850s   725-   825
Hepplewhite, mahogany,
slant-front, original
bail handle pulls, c.
1790 . . . .   3,500- 3,750
Lady's, pine, 4 drawers
below writing surface,
c. 1820   695-   750
Lady's, walnut, 3
drawers below writing
surface, c. 1850   650-   700
Lap, mahogany, brass
trim overall, ink bot-
tles, etc., c. 1840   300-   325
Plantation, walnut, glass
doors above lift-top
writing surface, c.
1830s 1,850- 1,995
Rolltop, oak, c. 1880s . . .   900- 1,200
Rolltop, oak, miniature,
child's, c. 1890s   450-   500
Rolltop, walnut, c.
1860s 1,800- 2,450
Schoolmaster's, mahog-
any, bookcase top,
burned legs, c. 1830s . .   475-   575
Schoolmaster's, oak,
cubbyholes below gal-
lery rail, c. 1850   400-   450
Schoolmaster's, walnut,
turned legs, single
drawer below, c. 1840 .   575-   650
Dough Troughs
Chestnut, lid, turned
legs, dovetailed box,
c. 1860   450-   575
Pine, squared tapered
legs, original red paint,
c. 1840s   600-   675
Pine, turned legs, dove-
tailed box, grained
finish, c. 1840s   495-   575
Poplar, dovetailed box,
on box frame, c. 1830 .   450-   485
Dressers
Dressing case, marble
top, burl stiles, mirror
frame, applied molding
around lower drawers,
c. 1830   760-   855
Marble top, molded burl
veneer panels on
drawers, c. 1840   525-   575

185

(continued)

Furniture, American

Marble top, projecting
front ring, molding on
drawers, original pulls,
c. 1860   585-   675
Marble top, swing mirror,
2 boxes, applied mold-
ing on drawers, c.
1840s   675-   785
Oak, beveled mirror, 4-
drawer, c. 1870   250-   285
Oak, German beveled
mirror, 2 small, 2 large
drawers, c. 1895   190-   225
Oak, lyre frame mirror,
2 small, 2 large
drawers, applied mold-
ing on mirror frame
and drawer fronts,
brass-plated pulls,
c. 1890   190-   245
Oak, 4-drawer, wooden
pulls, c. 1870   195-   245
Oak, 6-drawer, spindled
gallery on top, brass
pulls, c. 1860s   275-   315
Pine, 3-drawer, New En-
gland, c. 1790 . . . . . .   2,000- 2,250
Wooden top, burl veneer
panels on drawers,
teardrop pulls, c.
1850   575-   610
Wooden top, maple swing
mirror, 2 hanky boxes,
marble insert, c. 1850 .   675-   775

Dry Sinks

Cherry, splashboard
back, single door
below, c. 1850   675-   775
Pine, high back, candle
drawer, single door
below, c. 1840   550-   625
Pine, lift top, 2 drawers
below, c. 1850   495-   550
Pine, single door below,
c. 1830   550-   595

Footstools

Mahogany frame and
legs, upholstered, late
1800s   195-   225
Mahogany veneer, cabri-
ole legs, needlepoint
cover, c. 1870s   265-   300
Maple, carved legs, c.
1840   195-   245
Scroll type, Louis XV,
velvet upholstery, c.
1860   425-   565
Walnut, beaded edge,
upholstered, bun feet,
c. 1860   195-   245

Hall Trees

Oak, French beveled
mirror, 6 iron hat
holders, double um-
brella holders, c. 1880 .   325-   395
Oak, German beveled
mirror, 6 double hooks,
iron, umbrella holder,
seat w/lid, c. 1870s . . .   300-   325
Walnut, burl veneer
raised panels, molded,
incised pediments,
double umbrella
holders, pierced back,
marble shelf over
drawer, c. 1840 . . . . . .   975- 1,300
Walnut, German beveled
mirror, veneer raised
panels, brass double
hat hooks, marble shelf
over drawer, carved
applied ornaments,
c. 1840s 950- 1,250

Hat Racks

Accordion type, 7
wooden pegs, porcelain
tips, chestnut, c. 1860 .   125-   140
Accordion type, 13
wooden pegs, porcelain
tips, walnut, c. 1850 . .   100-   135
Walnut, molded frame, 8
wooden pegs, c. 1850 .   175-   200

Love Seats

Hepplewhite, walnut,
carved mirror back,
c. 1790 . . . .   1,200- 1,300

Medallion back, walnut
frame, upholstered,
Louis XV style 975- 1,350
Serpentine back, walnut
frame, upholstered, c.
1850s   765-   850
Victorian, mirror back,
New England, pine-
apple upholstery, c.
1850 . . . .   975- 1,350
Wooden framed back,
applied burl veneer
panels, incised lines,
c. 1830s 975- 1,250

Lowboys
Mahogany, drake feet,
Pennsylvania, 18th
century, 32″ high,
34½″ long 3,600- 4,200

Magazine Racks
Oak, spindle construc-
tion, c. 1890s   75-   95
Wall type, reticulated,
chestnut, c. 1880   125-   145
Wall type, walnut, East-
lake style, c. 1875   115-   135

Mirrors
Courting, walnut,
11″×15½″, c. 1800 . . .   775-   850
Mahogany, scrolled crest,
floor type, c. 1870   300-   355
Shaving, 2-drawer, wal-
nut, c. 1850   275-   325
Sheraton, maple frame,
carved, 21″×29″,
c. 1790   450-   550
Wall, Chippendale,
carved and parcel-
gilded, walnut (ill.) 4,300- 4,550
Wall, curly maple, New
England, c. 1830   375-   450

Secretaries
American Empire,
mahogany veneer,
bookcase top, c. 1830 .   1,200- 1,450
Block front, mahogany,
Massachusetts, all
original, c. 1750 . . . . . .   50,000+
Chippendale, Philadel-
phia, cherry, slant-
front, c. 1765 . . . .   50,000+
Sheraton, mahogany,
original pulls, c. 1815 .   3,200- 3,450
Tambour, mahogany,
late 18th century,
bureaulike base, 4
graduated drawers,
French splayed
bracket feet, 2
diamond-glazed doors
above 3,400- 3,600

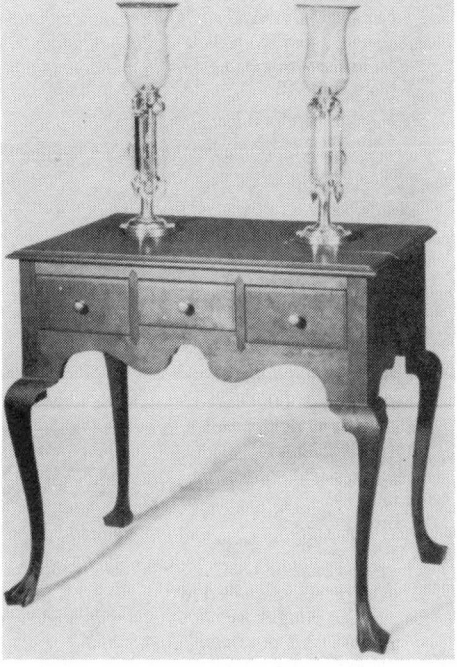

Furniture, American

187

(continued)

Sideboards

American Empire, pie-
crust molding, cherry
top, mahogany, c.
1830s 1,800- 1,975

Butler's, bird's-eye
maple, New England,
c. 1800 . . . .   3,100- 3,350

Hepplewhite, breakfront,
butler's, mahogany . . .   6,500- 6,900

Marble top, molded
drawers, veneer
panels, chamfered
corner stiles w/applied
molding, projecting
front, c. 1840 . . . .   1,900- 2,350

Sheraton, mahogany,
4 doors, 3 drawers,
c. 1810 . . . .   4,900- 5,450

Sofas

Belter, laminated rose-
wood, ornately carved
back, c. 1840   11,000-12,600

Double arch, molded
frame, button-tufted
upholstery, c. 1850 . . .   1,300- 1,450

Finger roll back, tufted
upholstery, walnut
frame, c. 1860 . . . .   1,150- 1,350

Serpentine back, walnut
frame, Louis XV style   975- 1,250

Wicker, 5 feet wide   195-   245

Stands

Lamp, marble recessed in
molded rim, walnut,
tripod base, c. 1859 . . .   265-   335

Lamp, marble recessed in
molded rim, cherry,
carved bird ornament,
tripod base, c. 1840 . . .   325-   385

Night, curly maple, 2-
drawer, turned legs,
28″ high (ill.)   385-   450

Night, 2-drawer, porce-
lain knobs, turned legs,
walnut, c. 1850   285-   375

Parlor, marble top,
squared corners, in-
cised lines, c. 1855   285-   335

Parlor, rectangular
marble top, veneer
frieze, machine lines,
c. 1850   375-   450

Parlor, round wooden
top, walnut, tripod
base, c. 1860   195-   285

Tables

Banquet, walnut drop-
leaf, 91″ long, c. 1840 .   2,900- 3,500

Butterfly, dropleaf,
cherry, c. 1750s 995- 1,350

Card, Hepplewhite,
cherry, c. 1790 . . . .   1,400- 1,700

Card, Sheraton, inlaid
mahogany, serpentine-
front, Boston, c. 1800
(ill.) 2,400- 2,650

Chippendale, card,
lunetted corners, c.
1770   19,000-23,000

Chippendale, piecrust tilt
top, birdcage, carved
base, claw feet   . . .   1,650- 1,850

Console, maple, lift top,
1-drawer, c. 1820s   850-   925

Dining, rectangular,
dropleaf, cherry, c.
1840   795-   850

Dining, round extension
w/5 leaves, cherry, c.
1830s 2,350- 2,650
Dining, round extension
w/3 leaves, walnut,
turned legs, c. 1850 . . .   800- 895
Dining, square extension
w/4 leaves, pedestal
base, c. 1860 . . . .   700- 800
Kitchen, chestnut, rec-
tangular top, turned
legs, c. 1860s 400- 475
Kitchen, pine, dropleaf,
drawer at one end,
c. 1840s 550- 595
Library, lower shelf,
1-drawer, c. 1870s 245- 265
Library, poplar frame,
mahogany veneer top,
rectangular top 165- 185
Parlor, mahogany,
French legs, c. 1890s . .   145- 175
Parlor, oak, half shelf,
rectangular top, c.
1895 . . . .   175- 195
Round, 48″ dia., pedestal,
lion's paw feet, tiger
oak, c. 1890 . . . .   550- 650
Round, oak, 54″ dia.,
pedestal, square feet,
3 extra leaves 450- 500
Round, oak, 36″ dia.,
round base, lion's paw
feet, 2 extra leaves,
c. 1890s 475- 550
Tavern, cherry, round,
single drawer, c. 1830 .   850- 900
Tavern, maple, single
drawer, turned legs, c.
mid-1800s 775- 895
Tea, tray-top type, Chip-
pendale, carved
mahogany, claw-and-
ball feet, New York,
18th century (ill.) 2,800- 3,450

Washstands
Commode, marble top
and splashboard, burl
veneer panels on 3
drawers, molded pilas-
ters, projection front,
c. 1840 . . . .   575- 625
Commode, marble top
and splashboard, sin-
gle drawer, 2 doors
below 475- 525
Maple, 1 drawer, towel
racks at each end,
c. 1870 . . . .   250- 275
Oak, single drawer, slop

jar compartment,
brass-plated handles . .   225- 275
Oak, 3 drawers, slop jar
compartment, c.
1890s 195- 245
Pine, towel bars, opening
for basin, 1 drawer
below, c. 1850 . . . .   295- 450

Whatnots
Corner, on cupboard
base, 3 graduated
shelves w/fretted
backs, c. 1860 . . . .   460- 525
Corner, walnut, 5 gradu-
ated shelves, turned
finials, c. 1850 . . . .   475- 525
Hanging, glass doors
above, 2 drawers
below, applied molding
at top 295- 350
Hanging, walnut, leaf
carved, 4 graduated
shelves, c. 1850 . . . . . .   395- 450
Side, 5 graduated
shelves, walnut,
turned finials, c. 1860 .   425- 475

Furniture, English

The demand for the genuine far exceeds the
genuine. Prices are staggering—and going,
going h-i-g-h-e-r! The prices listed here are
already out-of-date.

William and Mary style, 1689-1702
Queen Anne style, 1702-1714
Early Georgian style, 1702-1745
Chippendale style, 1745-1765
Adam style, 1765-1790
Hepplewhite style, 1780-1800
Sheraton style, 1790-1810
Regency style, 1793-1820

Beds
Adam style walnut and
damask bedstead
w/round fluted pillar
legs . . . .$ 1,700- 1,975
Chippendale style carved
mahogany 4-post canopy
w/acanthus carved flar-
ing tester and shaggy
claw feet 6,100- 6,400

Cabinets
Chippendale style, book,
mahogany, 2 paneled
cupboard doors, bracket
feet 5,900- 6,400
Early Georgian breakfront,
carved and inlaid mahog-
any, plinth base 7,100- 7,500

(continued)

Hepplewhite, bowfront, on
stand, inlaid mahogany,
in 2 sections, round
tapered legs 7,500- 7,975
Regency style, breakfront,
4 glazed doors, cupboard
below 5,500- 5,800
Sheraton style, carved and
inlaid, butler's china,
w/secretary drawer,
double doors, single-
shelved cupboard 7,400- 7,750

Furniture, English

Chairs
Adam-Hepplewhite, painted
and gilded, tapered legs. 2,450- 2,700
Chippendale style wing, on
mahogany molded square
legs 6,600- 6,900
Early Georgian, damask
upholstery, walnut, pad
feet 3,600- 4,200
Gilded, decorated, inlaid
M.O.P., papier-mache,
c. 1860 (ill.) 186- 245
Hepplewhite style, dining,
leather seat, balloon
back, set of 4 .... 3,700- 4,650
Queen Anne style, corner,
slip seat, shell-carved
front legs 3,000- 3,500
Queen Anne style, dining,
solid and burl walnut,
fiddle-shaped seat, leaf-
carved cabriole legs 2,900- 3,200
Regency style, library, rosewood, leather upholstery,
reeded seat rails, incur-
vate legs 2,900- 3,350
Sheraton style painted and
decorated armchair,
shield-shaped back
w/square tapering

splayed legs, crewel
embroidery 2,800- 3,700
William and Mary style,
side, walnut, needlepoint
seat and back 1,900- 2,300

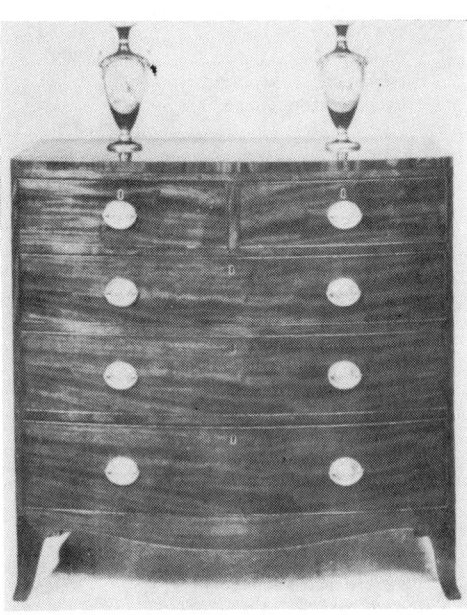

Furniture, English

Chests of Drawers
Early Georgian mule type,
mahogany, on ogival
scrolled bracket feet 4,800- 5,700
Hepplewhite, inlaid mahog-
any, serpentine front,
valance apron continuing
to splayed feet 4,000- 4,550
Hepplewhite, mahogany,
bowfront, splayed
bracket feet 4,200- 4,550
Queen Anne, inlaid burl
elm and walnut 5,400- 5,700
Sheraton, inlaid mahogany
bowfront, c. 1800, 41½"
high, 41" wide (ill.) 4,200- 4,500
William and Mary style, on
bun feet 3,800- 4,200
Chest-on-Chests
Chippendale, mahogany,
scrolled bracket feet 22,000-24,500
Queen Anne style, black
and gold, 3 drawers
below, 6 above, resting on
cabriole legs, club feet ... 11,700-12,650

Furniture, English	Furniture, English

Desks

Early Georgian, walnut and mahogany, counting-house type 3,600- 3,975

Queen Anne, slant-front, inlaid walnut, cartouche-shaped brasses and bail handles, molded base w/bracket feet 6,800- 7,400

Sheraton, carved mahogany cylinder, pullout slide, tapering legs, castered, c. 1800, 41½" high, 46" long (ill.) 6,800- 7,450

Sheraton style, inlaid mahogany and leather kidney-shaped pedestal desk, kneehole style 8,500- 9,300

Writing, Georgian, mahogany double-sided pedestal type, red leather top, 18th century, 30½" high, 54" wide (ill.) 3,900- 4,450

Love Seats

Early Georgian, walnut, loose seat cushion, acanthus-carved cabriole legs, claw-and-ball feet . . 6,100- 6,450

Secretaries

Early Georgian, cabinet type, inlaid walnut and burl walnut, 2 mirrored doors, bracket feet 14,800-15,750

Queen Anne, bookcase type, inlaid burl walnut, slant-front, double doors above, bracketed feet . . . 19,700-22,600

Settees

Queen Anne, 2-chair back, walnut, slipseat, slight cabriole legs, pad feet . . . 6,200- 6,500

William and Mary, walnut, needlepoint covering, loose seat 5,400- 5,650

Sideboards

Hepplewhite, small bow-front, inlaid mahogany, tapering legs w/string lines, spade feet 8,300-10,600

Regency style pedestal sideboard, inlaid mahogany and satinwood, valanced gallery, on quadrangular pedestals, each w/shallow drawer and cupboard, short saber feet 8,500- 9,900

Sheraton style bowfront, inlaid mahogany and burl wood, bottle drawers, etc., square tapering legs inlaid w/panels of burl wood 8,600- 9,900

Stools

Early Georgian, mahogany and damask, fireside type, cabriole legs, club feet 2,200- 2,500

Queen Anne, w/valanced frame and cabriole legs, club feet 3,100- 3,500

Tables

Breakfast, Sheraton, mahogany, late 18th century, 28½" high, 50½" long 3,400- 3,700

Chippendale mahogany octagonal tripod, tilting top, tilting on a "bird-cage" support, whorled feet 4,300- 4,700

(continued)

Chippendale, side, mahogany and inlaid satinwood, on square tapered legs w/ormolu toes 4,600- 5,500

Early Georgian 3-pedestal hunt table, mahogany, splayed tripods ending in snake feet 5,400- 5,900

Hepplewhite style, card, cabriole legs crested w/shell motifs, slightly scrolled toes 3,400- 3,650

Library, extension, drop leaf, mahogany, carved base, claw feet 1,700- 1,975

Sheraton style, inlaid satinwood, sewing, octagonal top, 2 drawers, sewing bag, tapered square legs . 2,600- 2,875

Sheraton style, mahogany tilting-top breakfast, top on 4 reeded splayed supports terminating in conforming brass toe caps . . 3,300- 3,650

Wine Cooler Stands

Adam style, mahogany, 2 brass handles, zinc-lined . 1,900- 2,350

Early Georgian, mahogany, brass lion masks, loose ring handles 2,350- 2,650

Regency style, mahogany, fluted lower border and square supports 2,250- 2,450

Furniture, French

Following its American and English neighbors, quality French furniture has gone out of sight, pricewise. Too much reproduction of the Louis XV and Louis XVI will eventually bring down the price of the original.

Louis XIV style, 1643-1715
Regence style, 1715-1723
Louis XV style, 1715-1774
Louis XVI style, 1774-1792
Directoire style, 1793-1804
Empire style, 1804-1814
French Provincial, made in provinces

Beds

Directoire style, alcove type, carved fluted posts . . . . $ 2,450- 2,700

Directoire style, day type, loose cushion and bolster 2,500- 2,700

Chairs

Directoire style, armchair, painted, upholstered loose cushion . . 1,800- 2,200

Directoire style, ladderback, rush seat, fruitwood, tapered legs . . . 2,200- 2,500

Empire style, salon type . 1,300- 1,450

Louis XV style, carved beechwood, sage green satin, balloon-back, closed arms, loose seat cushion (ill.) 3,200- 3,450

Louis XV style, carved beechwood, striped green satin, modified wing back, set of 6 (ill.), all 4,300- 4,700

Louis XV style, walnut, dining, silk damask upholstery, cartouche-shaped molded back, cabriole legs 3,400- 3,700

Louis XV style, wide armchair on cabriole supports, sides, back and loose cushion in floral damask upholstery 3,400- 3,900

Louis XVI style, armchair, carved and painted, loose cushion . 2,400- 2,850

Regence style, caned armchair, carved beechwood, silk damask seat, X-scroll stretcher, loose cushion 2,300- 2,900

Chaise Longues

Louis XV style, walnut, canted back, molded rails, cabriole legs, upholstered 4,300- 4,650

Cabinets

Louis XV style, inlaid mahogany, inset w/Sevres porcelain plaques, oblong top, cabriole legs w/shelf stretcher and shaped front 11,750-13,400

Louis XV style, serpentine-front encoignure, inlaid tulipwood and kingwood, marble top, 2 doors, cabriole feet . . 7,600- 8,800

Louis XVI upright type, inlaid w/tulipwood and kingwood, marble plateau 5,750- 6,900

Candlestands

Louis XVI telescopic, w/round statuary marble top, on arched tripod w/slender shoe feet 2,500- 2,750

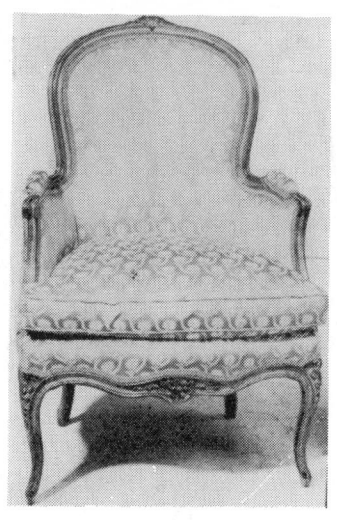

Furniture, French

Furniture, French

Chests

Louis XVI style, com-
mode w/oblong marble
top, foliated cabriole
legs 4,200- 4,600

Regence, serpentine com-
mode, inlaid woods,
marble, 4-drawer 4,600- 5,500

Regence, walnut com-
mode, marble top,
4-drawer 4,000- 4,650

Desks

Directoire style, boudoir,
writing, mahogany,
rectangular 2-tier
stand; rear supports
enclose a rising silk
screen 4,500- 4,875

Directoire style, fall-
front, mahogany, 4
long drawers on square
tapered supports,
plinth feet .... 14,000+

Empire style, Bonheur-
du-jour (lady's desk),
ormolu mounts,
mahogany 7,500- 9,000

Louis XIV Boulle ebony
and brass marquetry,
7 small drawers, 32"
high, 44½" long (ill.) .. 6,700- 7,500

Louis XV style, Bureau
Plat, painted and
decorated, serpentine-
contoured top, 3 work-
ing drawers, the
reverse w/mock

drawers, angular
cabriole legs .... 14,000+

Louis XVI style, brass-
mounted Acajou
Bureau a Cylindre
w/marble plateau,
fluted tapering legs ... 5,000- 5,400

Provincial, Louis XV
style, slant-front,
oblong top, whorl feet . 5,400- 5,800

Mirrors

Empire style, cheval
glass, mahogany,
frame richly inlaid,
ormolu candelabras,
urn mountings 3,600- 4,300

Louis XVI style, carved
and gilded, wall type,
upright frame w/pan-
eled borders around
mirror, arched cresting
outlined w/carved leaf
scrolls 3,600- 4,400

Secretaries

Louis XVI style, brass-
mounted Acajou secre-
tary w/marble top,
metal gallery, 2 glazed
doors, on square taper-
ing feet 5,800- 6,750

Sideboards

Louis XV style, buffet-
verrier, inlaid fruit-
wood and ash, super-
structure has 4 open
tiers, cabriole legs 6,400- 6,900

(continued)

Galle Cameo Glass

Furniture, French

Louis XV style, buffet
base, carved walnut,
oblong top, 2 frieze
drawers and 2 fielded
cupboard doors, squat
cabriole legs 9,100-10,000

Tables

Directoire style, mahog-
any tric-trac w/remov-
able oblong top on
square, tapering legs . 4,700- 5,450

Empire style, wall,
mahogany, w/marble
top, figural supports,
mirror panel 5,450- 5,650

Louis XV inlaid tulip-
wood and amaranth
tric-trac table w/oblong
reversible top, back-
gammon well, on angu-
lar cabriole legs 7,900- 8,650

Louis XV small writing
type, oval top, tapered
angular cabriole legs .. 8,700- 9,500

Louis XVI brass-
mounted Acajou
Bouillotte table
w/drum top and
pierced gallery, 2 small
drawers, on fluted
tapering legs 5,800- 6,450

Louis XVI carved and
gilded petite console
w/marble top, a guil-
loche-carved elongated
S-scroll support...... 6,500- 7,000

Louis XVI mahogany
extension dining table,
on square tapering
legs 6,000- 6,450

Louis XVI walnut library
type, oblong top pan-
eled in leather 4,900- 5,450

Galle Cameo Glass

Establishing his first factory at Nancy,
France, in 1883, Emile Galle developed a
fine cameo glass. Because so many assis-
tants made Galle glass, it is impossible to
know for sure which pieces Emile actually
made. After his death in 1904 a star (★)
was put in front of "Galle." This was done
only for a short time, and today Star Galle
is also quite collectible. All pieces were
signed.

Atomizer, brown/green,
frosted ground.........$ 285- 375
Bowl, blue, floral, scenic
lake and boats, 6″ high,
signed .... 725+
Bowl, purple on frost,
flowers, 5″ signed .... 900+
Box, covered, 6″ dia.,
signed .... 450+
Chandelier, 15″ high, floral
glass prisms, signed .... 2,200+
Cruet, thistles, maroon,
beige/pink, applied han-
dle, signed .... 550+
Inkstand, faience, 14″ long,
signed 550- 670
Jardiniere, yellow/black,
acid etched, 8½″ high .... 2,400+
Lamp, glass, table, 23″
high, signed .... 1,400+
Pitcher, 9″ high, signed 675- 875
Rose bowl, flowers/birds,
Star Galle 725- 900
Tumbler, vaseline color,
gold/enamel border, 6″
high, signed 300- 395
Urn, cherries/birds, acid
etched, Star Galle .... 2,400+
Vase, apricot/green, acid
clear, 7″ high (ill.) .... 450+

Vase, bird scene, blue/ yellow/white, 7¼" high . . .	475-	625
Vase, dark green, red ground, Star signature . . .		625+
Vase, lotus blossoms, yel- low/pink/white, 5½" high, signed		600+
Vase, miniature, frosted, mauve to clear, floral, Star Galle (ill.)	270-	293
Vase, water lilies, blue/yel- low/green, 6½" high, signed	585-	710

Game Plates

Game Plates

Plates decorated with fish, animals or birds fall into this category. They usually came in sets, 12 plates and a serving platter. Popular during the 1800s, most were made in Europe. Globe China Company in Ohio also made them in the late 1800s. Repros!

Bass on fly lure	$ 92-	110
Birds in flight, blue/gold back- ground, France, 8½" dia.	50-	60
Buck and doe, forest scene in vari- ous colors, 9" dia.	44-	56
Deer, Buffalo Pottery	50-	60
Deer grazing, Bavaria, 7½" dia. .	30-	40
Grouse, gold rim, Germany 11½" dia.	54-	66
Mallard duck, gold border, Staf- fordshire china, 7" dia.	52-	70
Pheasant, blue/gold background .	60-	70
Pheasants, signed Crown of Gold	27-	36
Quail, gold rim, pierced for han- dling	60-	75
Turkey, hunter, multicolors, Globe, 8" dia.	24-	33

Turkey on platter	36-	47
Wild boar in woods, Austria, 8" dia.	41-	50
Woodcock, 8" dia. (ill.)	17-	27

Games

Games

Salem, Massachusetts, calls itself the "game capital of the world." Sailors who returned to its port brought home games like parcheesi and chess from the Orient. A form of backgammon goes back to 3000 B.C. "The games people play" is more than just a song.

Alley Oop	$ 16-	21
Authors, c. 1912	14-	23
Checkered Game of Life	40-	50
Fibber McGee	20-	30
Fish Pond (ill.)	51-	60
Italian chess board, inlaid with ivory, mid-1880s, all pieces hand-carved	700-	900
Numerica, Parker Bros., 1895 . . .	14-	19
Old Maid and Old Bachelor (or Beaux and Belles)	51-	61
Pollyanna	14-	22
Ring My Nose, 1925	21-	30
Sambo Target	32-	42
The United States Game, Parker Bros.	60-	70

Garden Furniture

Most of what you find today in the better antiques shops is from the mid-to-late Victorian era up until World War I.

Armchairs, white-painted wrought iron, set of 6	$500-575
Center table, painted cast iron and white tile	250-275
Easy chairs, white-painted rat- tan, set of 4	280-310
Fountain figure, terra-cotta, winged Cupid, 31" high	350-375
Jardinieres, ochre-painted, set of 4	275-325
Occasional table, green-painted wrought iron, inlaid marble top	375-425

(continued)

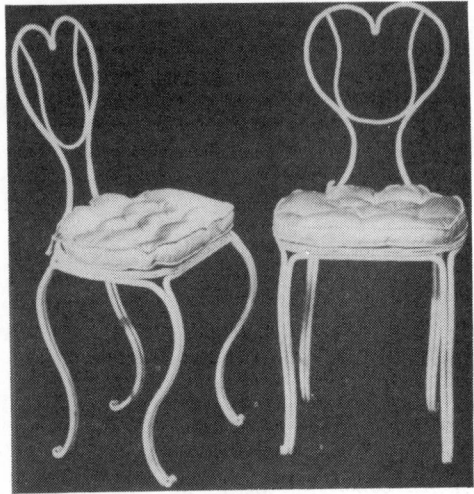

Garden Furniture

Side chairs, white-painted
  wrought iron, set of 6 (ill.) 480-525
Terrace chairs, white-painted
  wrought iron, set of 6 525-575
Terrace table, rattan, 27½" high . 300-350

Gaudy Dutch

This highly-decorated lightweight china was made around 1825 in the Staffordshire District in England, reputedly for the Pennsylvania Dutch trade in the York, Lancaster, and Philadelphia areas. Today, the general collector confuses it with Gaudy Ironstone. The latter was made at a much later date and was marked. Gaudy Dutch was not. Some examples are impressed "Wood" and "Riley."

Bowl, King's Rose, 14" dia. $200-250
Creamer, Dove pattern, 3½"
  high (ill.) 250-270
Cup/saucer, handleless, signed,
  1856 210-230

Cup/saucer, Single Rose (ill.) . . . .   260+
Pitcher, Carnation pattern, 6"
  high 375-440
Plate, Dove pattern, 9¾" dia. . . .   625+
Plate, Urn pattern, 7¼" dia.
  (ill.) . . . .   250+
Teapot, footed Daisy and Chain
  pattern 178-198
Toddy, Carnation pattern 380-450
Waste bowl, Carnation pattern . .   88-110

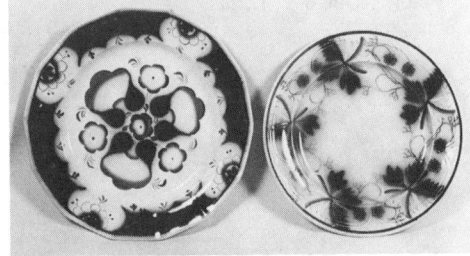

Gaudy Ironstone

Gaudy Ironstone

This was created in the early 1850s to stimulate more interest in the plain white ironstone. Decorated to some extent in the style of Japanese Imari, it is sometimes confused with Gaudy Dutch, but it really looks more like Gaudy Welsh. It never achieved popularity and was discontinued after a few years.

Cup/saucer, cobalt, orange/blue
  flowers $167-187
Gravy boat and dish, red/blue/
  green, floral decor 67- 79
Pitcher, blue/orange/green, 6"
  high 161-172
Plate, Pinwheel design, cobalt/
  burnt orange (ill.)   92-110
Plate, dinner, dark blue, 9¼"
  dia. 70- 80

Gaudy Dutch

Plate, Blackberry/Leaf design,
 cobalt, impressed WALLEY
 (ill.) 92-115
Platter, floral, signed Copeland,
 10½″ dia. 172-184

Gaudy Welsh

Gaudy Welsh

Made after 1850, this type of chinaware is cruder than Gaudy Dutch. Its bluish-purple coloring is one of its characteristics. General collectors confuse it with late Imari.

Cracker jar $115-135
Creamer, Daisy and Chain
 pattern 70- 82
Creamer, Oyster pattern,
 signed Allerton's (ill.) 60- 70
Cup/saucer, Tulip pattern (ill.) . . . 81- 91
Cup/saucer, Tulip pattern, no
 handle 52- 61
Ewer, Tulip pattern, 4″ high 64- 73
Mug, handled, Urn or Vase
 pattern 54- 63
Pitcher, blue/red, reptile handle . . 92+
Pitcher, Oyster pattern 80- 90
Plate, Strawberry pattern, 8¼″
 dia. 105-120
Platter, Wagon Wheel pattern . . . 115+
Tea set, complete 24 piece,
 Tulip pattern 710-810
Teapot, Strawberry pattern 195-226
Sugar bowl, covered, Daisy and
 Chain pattern 130-147

Genealogy

A recorded history from one ancestor to another; demography—the science of vital statistics; paleography—the study of describing or deciphering ancient writings. Look in the Clubs and Publications section for places to write, etc. Since our Bicentennial, more and more people are interested in their family backgrounds. The book, *Roots*, is just one example.

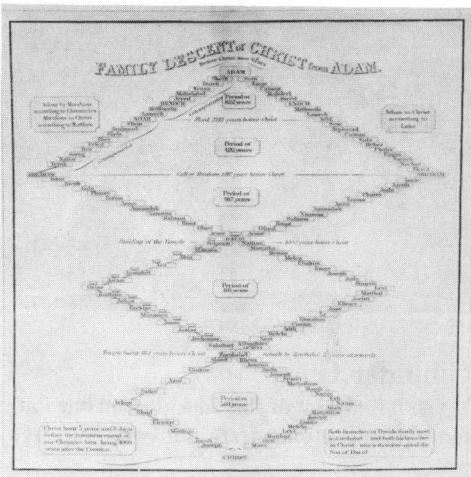

Genealogy

Gibson Girl Plates

Gibson Girl Plates

The eminent American artist, Charles Dana Gibson, produced a series of 24 drawings titled "The Widow and Her Friends." The Royal Doulton Works, Lambeth, England, reproduced the drawings on plates in the early 1900s.

"Failing to Find Rest, She
 Returns Home" . . . . $ 78- 88
"Miss Babbles Brings a Copy"
 (ill.) 78- 88
"Mrs. Diggs Is Alarmed" 78- 88
"She Finds That Exercise" (ill.) . . 78- 88
"She Goes as Juliet" 78- 88
"She Is Disturbed by a Vision" . . 78- 88
"She Looks for Relief" 78- 88
"They All Go Skating" 78- 88
These are indicative prices.

197

Gillinder Glass

Gillinder Glass

You'll find a lot of this fine glass in our Pattern Glass Section. Here are two indicative pieces.

Candlesticks, pr., white milk
   glass, crucifixes, 6-sided bases,
   9½" high (ill.) . . . . $ 97-106
Goblets, pr., 3-part mold, 1876
   Centennial, 6½" high (ill.) 62- 73

Girandoles

Girandoles

These are mantel garnitures, and a set consists of a centerpiece with a 3-branch candelabrum and 2 sidepieces for holding single candles. The bases were usually made of marble or alabaster and the main body cast in brass. Cut prisms, 4 to 6 inches long, hung from the tops of the 3 pieces. They were expensive when they were in vogue, early 1800s to mid-1800s.

Gold leaf, marble base, prisms,
   girl and boy, birds, 16" high,
   pr. $400-500
Indian, full figure, spear, 3
   branches 580-625
Man and woman in European
   attire, double handle, brass,
   prisms, pr. 470-520
3-piece set, 2-step marble and
   brass bases, star-cut prisms . .   500+
3 ornate brass arms, glass
   prisms, girl and boy on
   marble base, pr . . . .   500+

Glass Mugs

Also see specific type and make in **Pattern Glass Section**.

Hobnail, blue (ill.) . . . . $ 17- 26
Little Orphan Annie mug 38- 47
Mephistopheles, blue opalescent,
   3¼" high (ill.) 46- 56
Mug, lemonade, cranberry (ill.) . . 54- 62
Postum mug, 1930s 28- 37
Shirley Temple, 3¾" high 21- 31
Sterner's Clothing Store mug,
   1920s 19- 27
Stump glass mug 27- 36

Glass Types
Cased Glass

Glass with layers of different colors—one color actually encases another. Usually two colors are used, three sometimes found. Four to five are rare.

Flashed and Overlay Glass

A gather of glass of one color is covered while hot with a thin layer of another color. This double gather is achieved by dipping the

Glass Mugs

first quickly into the hot metal of the other. It's then worked out on a metal slab and blown, as if it were one piece; the thin layer being on the outside.

Luster-Stained Glass

A luster stain is applied much like varnish on the inside or the outside of the glass. After it's "painted," the glass is heated in the kiln to fix the color. Copper luster stains the outside red; green, blue, yellow or purple are also used. This is a cheap imitation of cased glass.

Gold

Gold

Too few people know anything about this metal. The weight (karat) of the gold is important. 24k is pure gold. One karat is 1/24 part of pure gold. 20k gold is 20 parts pure gold, 4 parts alloy. Cheap jewelry is usually mounted in 10k or 12k settings. Expensive jewelry is usually mounted in at least 18k settings, the other 6 parts being an alloy to harden the setting, as gold is a soft metal. Examples of various types are listed below. Originally, "pure" meant unalloyed metal; "standard," 11/12 fine, or 11 parts pure gold, 1 part alloy. The world's going crazy goldwise.

Gold Alloys

English gold: 75% gold, 12½% silver, 12½% copper.

Green gold: 60% gold, 40% silver.
Roman gold: 10 parts fine gold,
　3 parts silver, 7 parts copper,
　4 parts guinea alloy.

White gold: the basis of all white gold alloys is a fine grade of German silver with a high percentage of nickel. Can be made in any karat weight.

Blue gold: used in place of platinum, 18 parts gold, 6 parts iron.

18k gold for rings, watch cases, etc.: 19½ grains fine gold, 3 grains fine copper, 1½ grains fine silver.

Incan God (ill.), 23k gold	$750-850
California 25¢ pieces, 14k gold (ill.), ea.	150-200

Know what you're doing, especially if you're buying gold outside the United States. Always buy from the stores, banks, etc., controlled by the government of that particular nation. Gold-plated lead coins are literally a dime a dozen, valuewise.

Goofus Glass

Goofus Glass

This is pressed glass painted by spraying before firing. What you find today usually has the paint chipped off in places.

Bowl, brown, red flowers, 10" dia.	$ 30-	40
Bowl, Dogwood pattern, 8" dia.	34-	47
Compote, red, gold over green, open, 7" high	20-	36
Dish, ruffled, gold, shaded red, blues, 10" dia.	34-	42
Jar, pickle, flowers, red/gold, 20" high	27-	36
Lamp base, green, red, gold	36-	42
Plate, cake, red/gold, 8" dia.	9-	14
Plate, ruffled edges, gold/red, 10" dia. (ill.)	21-	30
Vase, grapes, 8" high	16-	27
Vase, poppy, opalescent, 8" high	28-	39
Vase, rose, 7" high	29-	37

Goss-on-Trent

Goss-on-Trent

Considered a fairing, these ivory-tinted porcelain pieces were made in the 19th century by William Goss at Stoke-on-Trent, England. Other factories imitated his wares.

Cup/saucer, Shakespeare crest	$ 14-	20
Elephant	21-	30
Hen-on-nest	19-	27
Pitcher, flowers, 4" high (ill.)	23-	31
Plates, 4" and 6" dia.	16-	27
Vase, horseshoe, 3-leaf clover, 4" high	22-	31

Gouda Pottery

Gouda Pottery

The land of the cheese—since the early 1700s the area around Gouda, Holland, has also been known as a pottery center. Clay pipes were one of the first products made. Art Nouveau type pottery came in around 1910. What we find today came from the 1910-1920 period.

Bowl, green/blue/yellow	$ 60-	70
Candlesticks, floral pattern, 5½" high, pr.	80-	90

Compote, yellow/green, 11" high	75-	85
Decanter, blue decoration on gray, 6" high (ill.)	60-	67
Jug, matt finish, signed Canada	110-	121
Pitcher, orange/green/black, 6½" high	130-	150
Plate, green/yellow pears, striped border, 6½" dia.	40-	50
Tobacco jar, scroll/leaf decor, 7" high	152-	170
Vase, multicolored glaze, 8" high, paper label	92-	107

Granite Ware

This is a thick, heavy clay ware that too many people confuse with ironstone. Granite Ware was a product of the 1850s and was mass-produced for the people who couldn't afford anything better. It fell from grace in the late 1880s when the vogue shifted to European porcelains, Haviland in particular.

Graniteware

Graniteware

The speckled glaze that looks like granite gives this metalware its name. Popular in the early 1900s, today it's collectible for decorative purposes. Blue or gray, with mottled backgrounds. Being reproduced.

Cream can, blue/gray	$ 42-	51
Coffeepot, gray/blue, 9" high, lid (ill.)	40-	50
Hanging shelf, gray/blue, 16" wide	50-	60
Lunch pail, gray/blue	40-	50
Strainer, brown/white	34-	44
Teapot, blue/gray, lid, 6" high	33-	46
Washbasin, white inside, blue/white outside	45-	55

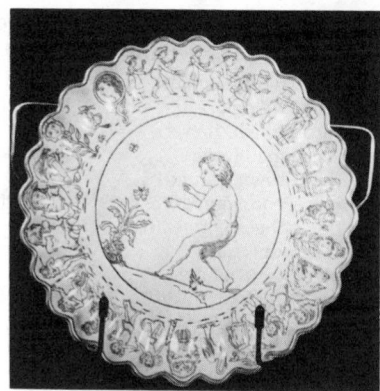

Greenaway, Kate

Greenaway, Kate

Daughter of an artist, she was born in England in 1846. As a young lady she illustrated Christmas cards, later doing many books. English and German potteries used her illustrations of children on their wares.

Buttons, brass, for child's
dress, set of 6 .... $ 97-108
Coffeepot, children under tree,
5½" high 120-140
Cup/saucer, children playing
with dog 42- 52
Fairy lamp, girl, Parian, 6"
high .... 150+
Matchholder, boy, bisque 70- 80
Mug, pink, children playing 70- 80
Plate, 2 girls playing ball, 5"
dia. 66- 75
Plate, Copeland China, 8¼"
dia. (ill.) 72- 81
Salt/pepper, pr. in wicker
basket 81- 90
Teapot, children on cover and
pot, 6" high............... 61- 72
Tray, boy with hoop, girls
playing, silver frame 150-160

Greentown Glass

Made by the Indiana Tumbler and Goblet Company, Greentown, Indiana, around 1894, one of the items sought today is "Fighting Cocks" on a blue basketweave base. See specific types in **Pattern Glass Section.**

Gunderson Peachblow

The Gunderson Glass Company, successors to the Pairpoint Company, which was formerly the Mt. Washington Glass Com-

Gunderson Peachblow

pany, all at New Bedford, Massachusetts, made this "new" Peachblow from 1952 until 1957. It was not as well colored as the earlier Peachblows and was heavier.

Cup/saucer, reeded, opal handle .. $130-150
Decanter 230-240
Goblet...................... 180-200
Pitcher, water 240-260
Toothpick, pink/white, 2½" high
(ill.) 72- 82
Toothpick holder, 1¾" high 120-130
Tumbler 120-140
Vase 240-272

Hair Work

In the late 1850s, *Godey's Lady's Book* printed directions for hair work, followed in 1864 by *Peterson's Magazine.* The craze lasted from then until the end of the 1800s. Brooches, lockets, woven chains, everything that could be made with human hair (also, cow's hair, though no one admitted to that), was produced. Most articles were made by braiding and interlacing hair over hollow forms. Hair wreaths, bouquets, and the like were made and framed for hanging on the wall. They're being collected today.

Bouquet of flowers, brown/black
6" high, in open frame .... $ 20- 32
Wreath, brown/black, 10" dia.,
under glass in frame 26- 36

Hampshire Pottery

James Scollay Taft founded the firm in Keene, New Hampshire, in 1871. Flowerpots were the first items made. Around 1878 the firm produced pottery with a majolica finish, then a Royal Worcester type finish. Various marks were used, some of which were im-

(continued)

pressed on the base, while others were stamped on in color. "J.S.T. & Co., Keene, N.H." and "Hampshire Pottery" were just two of more than six marks used. Shapes and colors are similar to Majolica and Rookwood.

Bowl, fruit, Royal Worcester
  finish, 13½" long, signed $195-245
Bowl, 6" high, matt green, leaf
  motif, signed Hampshire
  Pottery 75- 90
Chocolate pot, creamware,
  goldenrod decoration, 9" high,
  signed J. S. Taft, Hampshire
  Pottery 135-165
Chocolate pot, dark green glaze,
  embossed panel design, 9½"
  high 95-120
Mug, Mt. Monadnock, tan, 4½"
  high, signed Hampshire
  Pottery 83- 95
Pitcher, beige glaze, embossed
  blackberries, both sides, 4¼"
  high 75- 85
Pitcher, souvenir type, Lake
  Sunapee, 6½" high 80- 90
Stein, Royal Worcester finish,
  brown/green trim, impressed
  Hampshire, 6" high 195-235
Stein, white, glazed, straight
  handle, signed J.S.T. & Co.,
  Keene, N.H., 5½" high 75- 85
Teapot, dark green, highly glazed,
  twig handle and finial, impressed Hampshire Pottery,
  5" high 70- 85
Teapot, green, ribbed design, wire
  handle, 3¾" high 75- 85
Vase, matt green glaze,
  embossed tulip design,
  impressed Hampshire, also M
  in circle, 8" high 70- 80
Vase, two-handled, mottled matt
  blue finish, 5" high, impressed
  Hampshire 75- 85

Handbags, Ladies'

Some of the late Victorian bags are quite ornate. Some of the metal frames, clasps, and chains were 14k gold, others silver plate. Age and condition dictate price.

Rhinestone covered, silver chain . $ 17- 27
Victorian type, blue velvet, silver
  plate fixtures 18- 27

Handel

This firm manufactured lamps, shades, other items such as tobacco jars, in Meriden, Connecticut, late 1890s until World War II.

Bowl, cased, brass collar,
  signed, 6¼" dia. $110- 130
Box, verde finish, flowers
  inside, signed Runge 260- 294
Humidor, brown ground,
  Arabic scene, signed 360- 390
Humidor, tobacco, green/red
  ground, hunter and dog .... 340+
Jar, cookie, blue/white,
  flower, transfer 340- 380
Jar, tobacco, bird dogs,
  brass trim, signed 350- 395
Lamp, blue, Arabic scene, 3
  lights, 19" high .... 1,875+
Lamp, desk, green art glass,
  gold feather (Quezal?)
  overlay, signed 850-1,100
Lamp, lily pond, frogs,
  green/white shade, 3-
  light, 22" high 975-1,400
Shade, yellow/opalescent
  green, floral designs,
  signed, 13" dia. 950-1,200
Vase, trees, signed and
  numbered, 8" high 240- 280

Hand-painted China

Hand-painted China

This is mentioned because there are so many questionable pieces around today. Haviland specialized in selling white blank pieces to amateur painters, as did other companies. Just because it says Haviland on the back doesn't mean it was painted by their artists.

Plate, floral motif, 8" dia., signed
  "Rudolstadt" (ill.)........... $ 62- 70
Plate, floral motif, 8½" dia.,
  signed "Bach and Beyer"
  (ill.) 54- 64

Hardware

Porcelain and brass doorknobs, keyhole

Hardware

plates, hinges, doorbells—anything to do with old hardware is being collected.

Keyhole plate (ill.)	$ 15- 20
Knob, fleur-de-lis (ill.)	22- 32
Hinges, brass, 8″ long, pr.	65- 80

Hatpins and Hatpin Holders

Hatpin Holders

Made of every type of material but usually glass, they were plain, decorated, even cut. Popular during the mid-1800s, they make fine flower holders.

Blue/gold, birds, flowers, gilt edge, Austria	$ 32- 42
Carnival glass, Marigold, trunk-shaped, N in bottom	52- 61
Fastened to porcelain tray, ring tree each side, Austria	33- 42

Flowers and birds, gilt, Bavaria	21- 31
Sterling silver, initialed, signed Tiffany and Company on side	97-108
Tiffany glass, probably part of dresser set	120-140
White ground, blue/green/purple, Iris decor	30- 40

Hatpins

Originally designed to hold m'lady's hat in place, some had a metal shaft 12 inches long. Usually they had an ornamental "jewel" on the end. They went out of style right after World War I when the gals started wearing smaller hats.

Abalone, 10k shaft, 10″ long	$ 10- 16
Blue/white porcelain button, 11″ shaft	14- 27
Butterfly, rhinestones, 11″ shaft	16- 24
14k gold knob, 2 initials, 10½″ shaft	24- 37
Jade button in 14k gold setting, 11″ shaft	27- 37
Kitten, 10k shaft 11″ long	12- 21
Porcelain, flowers, 11″ shaft	19- 28
Sterling silver flower, 11″ shaft, Tiffany jewelry, flower-shape	84- 93

Haviland China

Haviland China

This is the most complicated china in the world today. Many people were involved, both here and abroad. Suffice it to say, the first factory was started in Limoges, France, in 1842, by David Haviland, an American importer. He called his firm Haviland and Company. If you're a serious collector, you

(continued)

already know these facts. If you're just beginning, buy a book and study.

Bone dish, Ranson pattern, set of 6	$ 60-	70
Bone dish, white	19-	27
Bowl, berry, blueberries, gold lip	50-	60
Bowl, Miramar pattern, 9″ dia.	34-	42
Bowl, salad, strawberries, flowers, gold rim	44-	52
Box, jewel, pink moss roses, blue-velvet lined, hinged lid	50-	60
Butter chip, pink/blue flowers, set of 6	27-	36
Butter dish w/lid, green/yellow roses	81-	91
Cake plate, Clemonceaux pattern, 9″ high on standard	42-	50
Candlesticks, pr., green/yellow, gold trim, 12½″ high	64-	74
Celery vase, purple flowers, gold, open handles	44-	52
Chocolate pot, blue/yellow flowers, gold trim	81-	91
Coffeepot, yellow/roses, signed C.F.H. (Charles Field Haviland china, not by Theodore or David)	52-	62
Creamer and sugar, lily-of-the-valley motif, blue trim, gold rim	74-	83
Cup/saucer, demitasse, spring flowers, blue/pink ground	32-	40
Decanter, signed H & Co., Limoges, floral decor	60-	70
Dinner set, service for 8, Autumn Leaf	950-1,100	
Mug, shaving, apple blossoms, initials LBJ	42-	52
Pitcher, grapes on vine, gold handle, signed, 10″ high	70-	80
Plate, dinner, 9¾″ dia., signed Theodore Haviland Limoges (ill.)	31-	40
Plate, bread and butter, autumn leaves, gold rim	32-	42
Plate, oyster, 8½″ dia., signed H & Co., Limoges	31-	40
Platter, pink roses, gold border blue background	42-	51
Powder box, white/roses, signed H & Co., Limoges	61-	70
Toothpick holder, pinched side, Aurene color, 3″ high	32-	42
Tray, dresser, floral background, rose/pink border	37-	47
Tureen, vegetable, morning glories, hand-painted, cover	90-	110

Heisey Glass

Heisey Glass

From 1895 until 1954 some of the finest glass in the world was produced by this firm at Newark, Ohio. It was made in clear and in colors. Imperial Glass Company, Bellaire, Ohio, purchased many of the Heisey molds and is reproducing Heisey today sometimes without the Heisey trademark—an "H" inside a diamond. Paper labels were also used. See specific patterns in **Pattern Glass Section.**

Bowl, oceanic, clear, 12″ dia.	$ 40-	50
Bowl, signed, 9″ dia.	38-	47
Crystolite, clear punch cup	9-	14
Diamond Optic, pink, mustard jar w/lid & spoon, 3½″ high	21-	30
Empress, pink, dolphin-footed, 3-handled sugar	18-	27
Express, clear, footed sugar, 3″ high	15-	27
Express, pink, dolphin, footed creamer	19-	27
Express, pink, footed sugar	19-	27
Flat Panel #352, clear, 2-qt. jar, covered, used for tobacco, lid impressed "Benson & Hedges NY Pat Dec 25 03," 6½″ dia.	78-	88
Goblet, Puritan, 4⅜″ high, signed	24-	32
Narrow Flute, clear, footed creamer, 3¼″ high	19-	27
Oceanic (Orchid Etch), clear, crimped bowl, 12″ dia., unsigned	40-	50
Pillows, clear, footed mint tray, 6½″ dia.	39-	47
Pitcher, 8″ high, signed (ill.)	60-	70
Ridgeleigh, clear, cigarette box w/lid, 4″ long	26-	36
Sherbet, Greek Key, clear, 4½ oz.	16-	24
Thumbprint and Panel, clear, ice pitcher	74-	83
Twist, emerald, flared 4-footed bowl, 12″ dia.	44-	52

Heisey Glass Animals

Some were made in the 1930s but the most famous were designed by Royal Hickman who worked for the Haeger Pottery Company. All were pressed in a mold. Some animals were marked with the Diamond H. Some were even marked twice, while others weren't marked at all. Most were made in crystal but some were made in deep amber, honey amber, and cobalt (blue). Some were frosted completely, others only partially. In 1962, Imperial Glass Company, which had purchased Heisey's molds in 1958, reproduced certain animals. Not all the reproductions are marked with the Diamond H. Those listed here have never been reproduced.

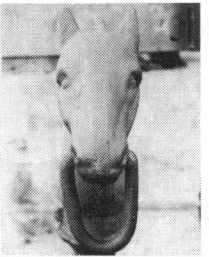
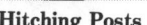

Hitching Posts   Holly Amber Glass

Chick, 1″ high	$ 48- 60
Ducklings, floating or standing, 2¼″ and 2⅝″ high	50- 58
Elephant, 4½″ and 5⅞″ high	75- 84
Fish bookend, 6⅝″ high	91-110
Gazelle, 11″ high	88- 97
Giraffe, 11″ high	80- 88
Rooster, 5⅝″ high	80- 90
Rooster vase, 6½″ high	80- 87
Tropical fish piece, 12″ high	100-115

Others were goose (wings down), Clydesdale horses, filly horse (head forward), same (head backward), show horse, horse head bookends, rearing horse bookends, piglets, bunnies, rabbit, cygnet, sparrow. Reproduced items, 1962-1968, were bull, hen, fighting rooster, dogs (Airedale, Scotty), donkey, ducks (3 mallards), medium elephant, geese (wings up, wings half-way), horses (flying mare, plug horse, ponies), pheasant, pigeon, rabbit, rabbit paperweight, and swan.

Hitching Posts

Used for years to keep the horse from wandering while its master visited or shopped. The Jockey is the most famous, also the one being reproduced the most.

Chimney sweeper, 32″ high	$140-170
Hitching block, iron marked "Foundry, Toledo, 1885" (the portable kind you hitched to bridle)	44- 50
Hitching post, black bear on hind legs, ring in paw, 36″ high, European	370-410
Hitching post, Negro boy in jockey's clothing, ring in hand, 27″ high	300-360
Horse's head (ill.)	150-180

Holly Amber Glass

See **Pattern Glass Section**. Mentioned here because it's so rare some classify it as art glass. It isn't.

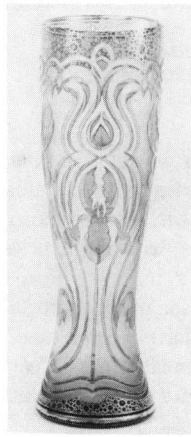

Honesdale Glass

Honesdale Glass

The factory that made this glass was originally established to decorate glass for Christian Dorflinger in White Mill, Pennsylvania, during the mid-1800s. The factory was purchased in 1916 by C.F. Prosch. He made one of the poorest imitations of cameo glass ever seen.

Cameo vase, blue ground, red/ yellow rose blossoms, 10½″ high, signed	$240-290
Cameo vase, clear ground, green grapes, blue base, 12¾″ high, signed	215-225
Cameo vase, frosted iridescent, green/yellow flowers, 12″ high	140-170
Vase, acid cut, blue/gold, frosted, signed, 7″ high (ill.)	200-260

(continued)

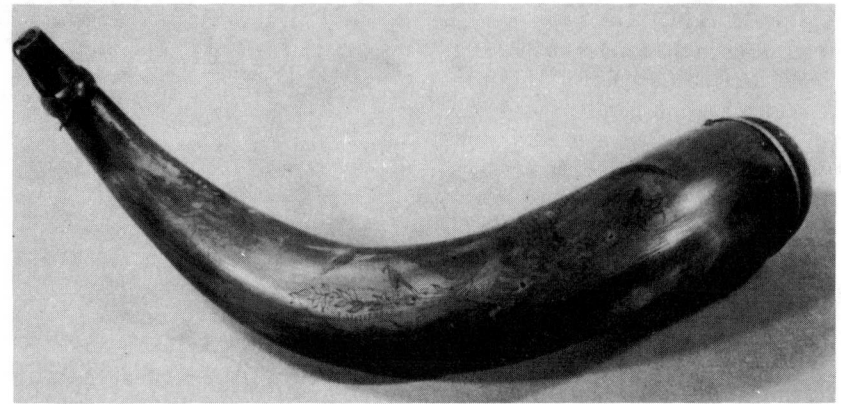

Horn

Vase, Art Nouveau, floral decor,
yellow-to-green, 11¼" high,
signed 160-180
Vase, iridescent, blue/green
enameled flowers, 10" high . . .   80- 90

Horn

Horns from various animals have been
used for centuries to hold liquids, gunpowder,
food, you-name-it. Powder horns dating back
into the 1800s bring high prices today. To
bend the calf's horn, an iron ring was fastened at the base of the skull. It didn't hurt!
Texas Longhorn cattle had magnificent
horns, some measuring 7 feet across! See
also **Powder Horns and Flasks.**

Hunting horn (ill.) . . . . $ 62- 72
Napkin ring 16- 20
Snuffbox, mid-1800s, American .   40- 47
Texas Longhorns, velvet in
center, ready for mounting . . . 100-109
Tumbler 16- 24

Hot Plates

Hot Plates

Used to hold hot dishes, plates, etc.; just
about everyone made them.

Hull Pottery

Hull Pottery

This pottery was made in 1903 by Acme
Pottery Co. at Crooksville, Ohio. Hull Pottery Co. took over and made art pottery from
1917 until 1950.

Basket, Ebb Tide, dark red,
15½" . . . . $ 27- 37
Basket, green to blue, handled . . .   32- 42
Bowl, green to pin, 9" high 21- 31
Candleholder, Blossomflite,
handled, rose 12- 23
Pitcher, brown/pink, handled
(ill.) 30- 40
Planter, green/pink flowers, 8"
high 17- 27

Plate, ovenproof, light green, mottled edge, 10½″ dia.	10-	16
Planter, dog, cream, paper label, 8″ high	16-	27
Planter, ducks, green/yellow, 6½″ high	14-	23
Salt/peppers, Red Riding Hood, 3″ high	16-	24
Vase, tulips, red to blue, 7¼″ high	21-	32
Vase, 2 handles, blue/pink, 6½″ high	23-	34
Vase, 2 handles, light green, 6″ high	22-	34
Vase, yellow to blue, flowers, 8½″ high	21-	31

"Feeding Time"

Hummel Trademarks

TMK-1	**TMK-2**
Crown Mark	Full Bee Mark

1935-1948	1950*-1959

TMK-3	**TMK-4**
Stylized Bee Mark	Three Line Mark

© by
W. Goebel
W. Germany

1960*-1965	1966*-1971

TMK-5	**TMK-6**
VEE/G Mark	G Mark

1972*-1979	1979-

*Dates are approximate—earlier documented examples are known.

Hummel Items

Sister Maria Innocentia, born Berta Hummel in Massing, Germany, loved children, and her sketches, first sold in the 1930s, attracted the attention of the Goebel porcelain factory in Rodental, a small town near Coburg, in Bavaria. Authentic pieces bear both "M.I. Hummel" and the Goebel mark. Look out for Japanese fakes.

Ashtrays

Happy Pastime (TMK-1)	$200-	210
Singing Lesson (TMK-2)	130-	140

Bells

Let's Sing (TMK-5)	100-	125
Farewell (TMK-5)	50-	60
Thoughtful (TMK-5)	60-	70

Bookends

Book Worm (Crown), pr.	550-	600

Candleholders

Angel Trio (TMK-1), set	180-	200
Candlelight (TMK-1)		550+

Figurines

Apple Tree Boy (Crown)	160-	180
Apple Tree Girl (Crown)	130-	150
Bird Duet (Crown)	240-	300
Eventide (Crown)	300-	360
Feeding Time (TMK-4) (ill.)	70-	90
Happy Pastime (Crown)	240-	250
Let's Sing (Crown)	270-	300
Letter to Santa (TMK-4)	175-	200
Mail Is Here (TMK-2)	450-	500
She Loves Me (Crown)	230-	250

Madonnas

Flower Madonna, 11½″ (TMK-1)		500+
Madonna with Halo (TMK-3)		50+

Music Boxes

Little Band (TMK-5)	160-	200

207

(continued)

Nativity Sets
Small (TMK-4) 650- 700
Large (TMK-4) . . . .   900+
Plaques
Ba-Bee Rings (TMK-2), pr. . . . .   160+
Merry Wanderer (TMK-3) 100- 110
Annual Plates
1971 Heavenly Angel 800-1,000
1973 Globe Trotter 120- 140
1974 Goose Girl 75-   80
1975 Ride into Christmas 55-   60
1977 Apple Tree Boy 60-   65
1979 Singing Lesson 80-   90

Imari

Imari

A gaudy decorated type of chinaware imported into this country mainly from Japan in the last part of the 19th century. The original was made in Japan as early as 1600. During the 19th century, imitations were made in England. It's being reproduced today but it shouldn't fool anyone.

Bowl, blue/white, orange
flowers, 7", not old $270- 310
Bowl, cobalt, scalloped rim,
6½" dia.   54-   64
Bowl, panels alternating
blue and orange, 10" dia.,
Japanese 250- 270
Creamer, orange/blue, old,
not Japanese   75-   90
Cup/saucer, handles, usual
colors, Japanese, 19th
century   70-   80
Dish, blue/white, fish shape,
8½" long   82-   92
Jar, ginger, orange/blue,
original wood stopper, 6"
high, Japanese 150- 170
Jardiniere, plum trees, 14"
high . . . .   1,700+
Pitcher, Staffordshire,
usual Oriental colors,
1880s, 9" high 170- 190
Plate, green/red/blue, tan-
gerine panels, 8½" dia.
(ill.)   80-   90
Platter, blue, red, cobalt
design, Oriental signa-
ture, old 175- 190
Platter, landscape, dragons,
temple, 14" dia., old 170- 182
Teapot, peacocks, prunus,
blue/red, w/domed lid 84-   94
Vase, 4 panels, flowers, 7½"
high 172- 182

Icons

Icons

These are religious mementos, usually paintings with a brass encasement. Dating from the time of Christianity on, what you find in shops today are usually from the mid-1800s on. A triptych is just a 3-panel icon.

Brass, Greek, on wooden
panel, 17th century,
13"×16" $650- 750
Brass, Greek saints, enamel
background, 6"×6½" dia. . . 420- 440
Brass, Eastern Orthodox
church scene of Jesus,
5"×7½" . . . .   1,100+
Bronze, Russian Orthodox
church scene, 18th cen-
tury, 14"×18" 725- 815
Painting on wood, brass en-
casement missing,
5½"×7" (ill.) 175- 200
Triptych, cathedral scene,
Russian, 17th century,
ornate, 16" high . . . .   1,600+
Triptych, 3-panel, Jesus and
Mary scene, 18th century,
15" high 625- 640

India Brass

India Brass

Most of what you find in shops today was either brought home by soldiers serving in the China-Burma-India Theater during World War II or is brand new. It is usually stamped "India" on the bottom. It was tooled brass, the items often being made from U.S. Army artillery shells. A form of enamel was rubbed into the tool crevices.

Dinner gong (ill.) . . . . $	21-	31
Ewer, handled, 13" high with 6 cups to match	30-	40
Incense burner, hanging type . . .	22-	32
Kettle, matching tray	30-	40
Lamp, hanging-type, electrified . .	50-	60
Teapot, 11½" high, World War II	24-	37
Vase, 8" high	34-	44
Vase, 14" high, on teakwood stand	33-	42

Indian (American) Artifacts

Indian (American) Artifacts

Indian (American) Artifacts

Even with all the fakes flooding the market, this is a hot collectible, nationwide. Just know your Indians!

Apache Indian cradle board, c. 1860, 36" overall . . . . . . $	465-	510
Arrowheads, common type, ea.	.75-	2
Beaded belt, 42" long	120-	135
Beaded pouch, Oklahoma Indian	240-	265
Boots, buckskin, coin buttons	110-	135
Bow, wooden, Plains Indians, 47" long	55-	65
Breechcloth, Navajo, beaded, buckskin	260-	285
Chief's wearing blanket, Three Hills Reservation, gray/ white	875-	975
Eastern Woodlands all beaded cap, possibly Iroquois, c. 1840	435-	475
Fighting ax, Mohawk, 8" overall	125-	145
Halberd type spike-tomahawk, New England, c. 1720s, 7" overall	275-	310
Hatchet, Western Plains, c. 1870s, 5" overall	135-	160
Low bowl, pottery, Hopi, cream yellow slip, black/ orange designs, 8" dia. (ill.) .	115-	140

(continued)

Moccasins, Arapaho, deerskin, beaded	90-	110
Painting, "Ignacio," signed Chas. Craig, 1889 (ill.)	2,600-3,000	
Peace pipe, clay, Sioux	195-	235
Pipe, tomahawk, handmade pottery bowl, 9" long	260-	280
Purse, Sioux, beaded, deerskin, 4"×7"	110-	135
Sioux bear claw necklace, c. 1850s, about 9½", 21 claws	1,300-1,400	
Spike-tomahawk, Eastern Woodlands, c. 1750s, 8" overall	395-	425
Tomahawk, original handle and rawhide	85-	100
Trade beads, glass, amber, blue	135-	155
Vest, buckskin, beaded, tassels, Hopi	625-	675
War bonnet, eagle feathers, heavily beaded, Plains Indians	1,600-1,850	
War club, Comanche	75-	90
Western Plains pipe-tomahawk, c. 1870s, 6½" overall	270-	300
Zia bowl, pottery, white slip, black/red design, 8" high (ill.)	140-	165

Indian Tree Pattern

Indian Tree Pattern

This pattern was popular from the 1850s until just before World War I. It takes its name from an Oriental, not an Indian, shrub. The colors were very soft—blue, pink, green— and it was made by various potters in England: Minton, Cauldron, Maddox, to mention a few. Also see specific firms.

Berry set, Maddox, bowl, 10" dia., 6 sauces, 5" dia.	$155-177	
Butter dish, covered, Burgess & Leigh	69-	78
Cake stand, Maddox	70-	80
Compote, Copeland, 8" high	44-	53
Creamer	51-	61
Plates, Cauldon, 9", 10", 11" dia.	31-	40
Plate, Noritake, 10" dia. (ill.)	24-	32
Salt/pepper shakers, Minton, pr.	54-	62
Sugar bowl, covered	53-	67
Sugar bowl, covered, Minton	50-	60
Teapot, 6 matching cups/saucers	160-180	
Vase, Cauldon, 8" high	71-	81
Vegetable dish, 10" dia.	47-	57

Inkwells and Bottles

Inkwells and Bottles

These containers for holding ink usually were made of glass and have been around for centuries. Ink was made from chimney soot, dried berries, dried blood. The ballpoint pen rang the death knell for inkwells.

Blue, iridescent, pewter lid, Steuben type	$ 51-	62
Brass, crab, glass liner	70-	80
Brass, glass liner, alabaster base	34-	52
Cloisonne, 2 inkwells, on marble base	87-	97
Covered container, 2 lovebirds, footed iron stand, 4" high	40-	50
Cranberry, bronze, marked Germany 1875 on bottom	65-	78
Crystal, two glass-lined, tray, footed	47-	57
Cut, embossed silver hinged top, 3½" high	34-	44
Elk, 2 inkwells and rack (ill.)	110-127	
Green alabaster, dome top, square base	42-	52

Ink stand, French porcelain, blue/
green/orange enamels, c. 1910,
3½" high 54- 64
Iron inkstand, horse, brass cap,
penholder on horse's back 42- 52
Milk glass, two cats, iron base ... 130-142
Ormolu, cherubs, red/gray marble
base, ormolu feet, France 170-190
Pen rack, iron and glass, dated
1877 .... 32- 47
Pewter, holes for quill pens,
England, 3" high 39- 52
Porcelain, flowers/cupids, 3 ink-
wells, on wood base 200-240
Red glass, round base, brass tray,
2 penholders 40- 57
School desk, black bakelite cap .. 24- 34
Swirl design, star base, brass
cover, footed.............. 40- 48

Hemingray, No. 14, vaseline 58- 68
Hemingray, No. 19, (ill.) .. 50- 60
Hemingray, No. 19, clear 12- 19
Knowles, No. 2, cable, green 20- 30
Locke, No. 21, green 41- 50
Lynchburg, No. 31 .... 12- 21
Maydwell, No. 20, milk glass 19- 27
McLaughlin No. 16, emerald
green 9- 15
Muncie, large, with stand....... 64- 73
No. 63, Carnival glass, Pyrex 31- 40
Opaline, No. E14-B 90-110
Peru-K. C. G. Company 51- 61
Postal beehive, pink 19- 28
San Francisco, pony, aqua 16- 27
W. E. Manufacturing Company,
aqua, Patented December 19,
1871 .... 24- 34
Whitall Tatum Company, No. 1,
purple 18- 27

Insulators

Insulators

Little did they think that when they strung
telephone and telegraph wires from coast to
coast, those glass insulators would create
such a furor in the antique business today.
Books, clubs, magazines, all having to do
with the insulator, are in great demand.

Armstrong, dome No. 2 .... $ 24- 32
B. T. C., Canada, ice blue 34- 40
Barclay, patent spiral groove ... 19- 27
Brookfield, green, 1865 .... 12- 18
C. C. T. and Company 31- 40
California, baby signal, smoky .. 18- 27
California, signal, gray 19- 29
Diamond pony, olive green 17- 26
Gayner, No. 48-400, aqua 18- 27
Green pottery 21- 30
H. G. Company, aqua, standard
signal, double petticoat 17- 26
Hawley, Pa., aqua, beehive 21- 30
Hemingray, double petticoat
beehive, aqua 21- 30

Invalid Feeders

Invalid Feeders

During the 18th and 19th centuries many
potteries in the Staffordshire District in
England made these feeders. Adams, Clews,
Jackson, Mayer, Ridgway, and Stevenson—
these are just a few of the many. Don't confuse with a Scuttle mug.

Invalid feeder (ill.), mid-1800s
possibly Clews .... $ 91-107
Invalid feeder, J. and J. Jackson,
1830s 80- 92
Invalid feeder, Ralph Stevenson,
early 1800s, marked R.S.W.... 82- 92

Iowa City Glass

The Iowa City Flint Glass Manufacturing
Company was incorporated in April of 1880.
Iowa City factory was its general name. It is
difficult to positively identify this glass, and
the workmanship is on the crude side. Most
pieces are quite thick, with mold lines much
in evidence. Animal/bird motifs were very
popular. Figures were often combined with

(continued)

Iowa City Glass

mottoes such as "Be Gentle" (with lamb); "Be True" (with dog), etc.

Animal-motto plates, each	$ 40-	50
Compote, etched birds, flowers, 6" high (ill.)	52-	61
Creamer, Alhambra design	34-	43
Goblet, deer motif	37-	47
Mug, dog motif	44-	52
Platter, beehive motif, oval-and-bar border	58-	72
Platter, Elaine, oval-and-bar border	61-	72
Spooner, open handles	32-	42

Iron

Iron

Without it there would be no United States as we know it today. It rusts if not painted, but is durable and long-lasting, and helped to build our nation.

Andiron, girl/boy motif, 14" shank	$ 47-	57
Anvil, blacksmith's size		1,100+
Apple peeler	34-	43
Bank, Battleship Oregon (still type)	47-	57
Bookends, horses, pr.	24-	33
Bootjack, beetle, 10"	21-	31
Buggy step (makes nice towel holder in kitchen)	17-	26
Candle trimmer, patented 1854	42-	51
Cherry pitter	34-	44
Doorstop, flower basket	20-	27
Figurine, boy with flower, garden, 26" high	62-	72
Footscraper, Dachshund, 15" long	37-	46
Grinder, for counter or table use	27-	36
Harpoon, toggle hook, original	170-	180
Ice tongs	29-	39
Ladle, long handle, 13"	27-	37
Mold, rabbit, 2-part, hinged, for ice cream	42-	51
Nutcracker, dog's tail closes jaw to crack nut	37-	46
Rack, hat, coat, 6 hooks, 28" wide	34-	47
Sadiron	24-	33
Sadiron, French, mid-1800s	38-	47
Stove, potbelly, old, ornate	87-	97
Stove, Sears, miniature, 8½" high (ill.)	27-	37
Tongs, ironworker or blacksmith	38-	47

Irons

Irons

Being reproduced but still collectible. Children's sizes very popular.

Asbestos "Tourist Iron"	$ 24-	32
Children's flat iron (ill.)	27-	37
Cross Hatch, original	31-	40
Curled handle, original	19-	28
Nickel-plated iron (ill.)	16-	27
Rope handle, old variation	17-	26

Ironstone

Ironstone

Ironstone is an earthenware made from slag from the steel mills, with clay. Durable, it was first patented in 1813 by C. H. Mason. Later, many English firms made it, Meakin being famous for its lightweight ware. Other firms making it were Edwards, Johnson Brothers, Clemenston, Burgess, Podmore and Walker, Meller and Taylor, Wilkinson.

Bone dish, wheat motif	$ 19- 27
Bowl, covered, 6½″ high, Meakin	32- 42
Bowl, sugar, floral decor, gold lustre designs, Edwards	40- 50
Coffeepot, Burslem, opaque granite china, 11″ high	168-200
Dish, relish, oblong, 6″ dia., Johnson Brothers	27- 42
Dish, vegetable, covered, Clemenston	32- 50
Gravy boat, Cable decoration . . .	17- 26
Jug, red/blue, English, 7½″ high .	70- 80
Mold, pudding, flower designs inside, Wilkinson	34- 44
Pickle dish, flower/birds, Meakin	24- 33
Pitcher, lustre decorations, Walley	60- 70
Pitcher, white/blue, Meakin, 9½″ high	31- 42
Plate, blue/white decor, Podmore and Walker	40- 50
Platter, Oriental pattern, 14″ long, Clemenston	37- 50
Saucer, Tea Leaf, 4½″ dia. (ill.) . .	15- 26
Shaving mug, white, Alcock	32- 40
Soup tureen w/ladle	72- 80
Sugar bowl, blue/tan, wood	44- 52
Teapot, lustre decorations, Meakin	70- 81
Vase, Oriental decor, 8″ high	53- 63
Vase, red/blue, Mason, 8½″ high	54- 63

Ivory

Ivory

For centuries the Chinese were experts at carving it, and genuine pieces bring high prices today. Look for the grain. What's now being carved in the Orient is made from the bones of horses and cows. It's easy to age new ivory: Soak in vinegar, wrap in burlap, bury in the backyard for a few months. Watch out for those netsukes coming in from Japan. And, remember where you buried it!

Bottle, snuff, carved	$160-180
Box, hand-painted miniatures on lid, pink/white, 3″ square . .	120-140
Chess set, carved from elephant's tusk, Chinese, 18th century	1,400+
Doctor's doll, nude, reclining Oriental, 9″ long (ill.) . . . . (In China until early 1900s doctors could not touch a female patient—she pointed to the doll to show where she had pain.)	295-360
Figurine, carved, boy playing with dog, 5″ high	70- 80
King holding Kuei with both hands, 14″ high	520-640
Letter opener, carved, 9″ long . . .	27- 36
Napkin ring, carved, pair	35- 42
Statue, Shou Lao, China, 37″ high	1,800+
Tusk, 35″ long, carved, 9 figures, dragon, lion, elephant heads . .	2,700+
Vase, dragons, lotus decor, 7″ high	180-210

Ivory, Miniatures

"The smaller the better!" This was the motto of the skilled ivory carver. A betel nut from India, the size of a small pea, contains no less than 15 perfectly carved elephants. You find these miniatures in shops today and they're fun to collect.

Elephant, 3″ high (ill.)	$ 74- 83
Mouse, ¾″ high	19- 27
Pendant, sun motif, 2½″ across (ill.)	41- 50

213

(continued)

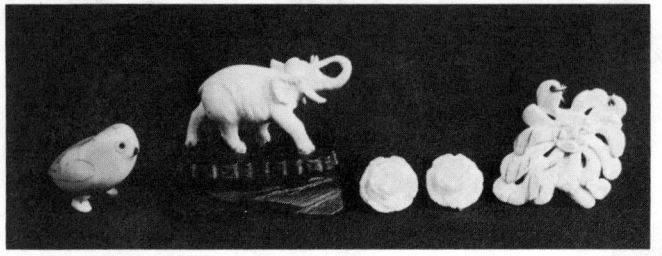

Ivory, Miniatures

Jackfield Pottery

Ptarmigan, 1½″ high (ill.)	51- 60
Rose earrings (ill.)	32- 42

Jackfield Pottery

Sometimes decorated with scrolls and flowers, this red-bodied pottery in relief is covered with a thick black glaze. It differs from basalt and should confuse no one. Jackfield originated in England in the early 17th century. Most of what you find in shops today was made in the 19th century.

Coffeepot, 9″ high	$140-160
Creamer, cow	100-120
Creamer, fluted, gold enameling, 7″ high	90-110
Dogs, black, 10″ high, pr.	91-107
Figurine, rooster, black, England, 12″ high	94-107
Jug, green/black, gold leaf, England, 9″ high	84- 93
Pitcher, molasses/black ground, 8″ high (ill.)	112-116
Sugar bowl, handleless, enameled birds	82- 92
Syrup, pewter lid, enameled flowers	94-107
Teapot, black, medallion decor . .	86- 94
Vase, enamel decor, square base, 11″ high	105-112

Jack-in-the-Pulpit Vases

In vogue around the turn of the century, they were made in all colors and resembled their namesake.

Bowl, rose/amber, paneled glass applied	$ 69- 80
Vase, Amberina, 8″ high	230-260
Vase, blue/pink body, 5″ high . . .	38- 47
Vase, Cranberry, clear, star base, 11″ high	72- 82
Vase, milk glass, blue, 8½″ high	40- 50
Vase, opalescent, white, 6½″ high	81- 92

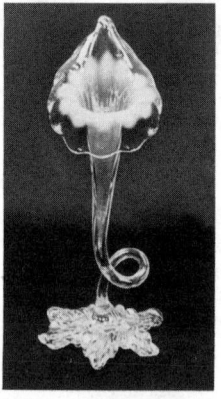

Jack-in-the-Pulpit Vases

Vase, Peachblow, Sandwich	375+
Vase, Quezal, 10″ high, signed . . .	250+
Vase, Rubina, Hobnail pattern, 11″ high	76- 85
Vase, twisted column, vaseline, 9½″ high (ill.)	80- 90
Vase, white/purple slag	37- 48
Vase, vaseline, opalescent, 7½″ high	90-108

Jackson, J and J

Around 1831 this firm made many American views of the states, such as Pennsylvania, Ohio, Connecticut and Massachusetts. Their factory was in Burslem, England, at a pottery formerly owned by the Wedgwoods. The Jacksons closed down around 1843.

Cup plate, 4½″, For Conanicut, R.I.	$158+
Plate, 9″, Baltimore Monument	160+
Plate, soup, 10½″, City Hall, New York	160+
Platter, 11″, New Haven, Conn. . . .	170+
Soup tureen, 13″, Schenectady on the Mohawk River	185+

214

Jade

Jade

Usually associated with China, this cool, green, semiprecious stone has been around for years. Don't worry about finding any from the Ch'ien Lung dynasty or even finding an Imperial jade ring. But there are many interesting pieces in shops today. Know your dealer. It doesn't mean it's jade just because it feels cool against your face. So does an ice cube! Much alabaster passes for the real thing. Know!

Ashtray, 3″ dia. $130-148
Bottle, snuff, black/green,
  2¼″ high 360-387
Box, light green-to-white,
  average color 290-320
Butterfly, carved, white/green . . . 170+
Cordial, green, set of 6 270-295
Figurine, dragon, trees,
  brown/green 275-295
Foo Dog on teakwood base . . . . . 3,400+
Grapes, bunch, 5″ 180-220
Incense burner, Foo Dog,
  5½″ high . . . . 525+
Letter opener, 8¼″ long 120-130
Netsuke, dragons, 1¼″ 90-120
Pendant, white/green, 2½″ 80- 87
Sword ornament, dragon,
  white/green 140-150
Thumb ring 105-121
Vase, carved, trees, flowers,
  9½″ high . . . . 1,400+

Vase, green, carved birds,
  teakwood stand, late 1800s . . . 285-340
Vase (rare), black, 8″ high (ill.) . . . 11,000+

Japanese War Items

Japanese War Items

Anything to do with wars is collectible. Japanese military items are no exception. Most are from World War II.

Cigarette pack, "From Island
  of Attu, May 13, 1943" (ill.) $ 7- 12
Dagger, worn by Japanese
  officer, sharkskin handle . . 85- 120
Helmet, pith style, cork lined
  (ill.) 42- 52
Japanese battle flag, white
  with red ball, 14″×19″ 90- 105
Mine detector in mahogany
  box 122- 142
Pilot's helmet, name on peak . 50- 60
Samurai sword, military issue 122- 140
Samurai sword, name on
  blade, sharkskin hilt 1,100-1,400
Wind indicator, used on air-
  craft carrier (ill.) 67- 80

Jasperware

See **Wedgwood**.

Jewel Boxes

Popular in the late 1800s until the early 1900s. They were usually made of pot metal, then quadruple-plated, silver-plated or dipped in a cheap gold solution. Then they were stuffed with cotton, which was covered with velvet. Also made of wood, ivory, etc.

Gilded metal, Art Nouveau, pink
  lining (ill.) . . . . $ 44- 52
Gold-plated, blue velvet lining . . . 27- 37

(continued)

Jewel Boxes

Quadruple-plated, velvet lined, on lid "Where's My"	27- 36
Silver-plated, velvet-lined, footed	27- 32
Sterling silver, velvet, initialed BHM	85-150
Velvet ring box, 2″ square (ill.) . . .	9- 18
Walnut box w/drawer, primitive (ill.)	60- 67
Wood, inlaid rosewood, tufted velvet lining, lock and key, French, mid-1800s	120-140

Jewelry

Jewelry

In a word, antique jewelry is being bought to wear; expensive antique jewelry is being bought as an investment. See **Gold**. Always get a receipt and know from whom you purchase. Obviously, you can't get a receipt from the Czar, but Cartier's will oblige if you purchase the Czar Alexander II of Russia necklace, consisting of emeralds and pearls, priced modestly at $1,250,000 or higher. Stop in during your lunch hour. Since the days of the Egyptians, women (and now men) have been fascinated by jewelry of all kinds. The age, content of gold or platinum, carat of the stone, quality—all enter into the price. Be careful!

Beads, agates, orange/white, graduated sizes, silver-plated clasp	$ 45-	53
Beads, amber, graduated sizes, 32″ overall, 14k clasp	115-	130
Beads, Art Deco, sterling silver, "lady" pendant, 19″ overall	55-	63
Beads, coral, hand-carved, graduated sizes, 27″ overall, 14k clasp	48-	53
Beads, coral, 6-strand, hand-carved, sterling silver clasp	350-	400
Bracelet, Art Nouveau, emeralds alternating with real pearls, 14k chain, 2 clasps	875-	950
Bracelet, baby, gold-filled, secret joint	28-	37
Bracelet, 14k gold, hand-engraved, secret joint, safety chain	525-	575
Bracelet, 14k gold, 1 diamond, ½c, 6 genuine sapphires . . .	1,400-1,650	
Bracelet, 18k solid gold, hand-engraved	665-	710
Bracelet, 10k solid gold, machine-turned	65-	75
Bracelet, platinum, 36 cut diamonds, 35 sapphires, all genuine	875-	925
Bracelet, watch chain type, 18k gold (ill.)	450-	500
Brooch, black mourning type, 6 styles, ea.	45-	55
Brooch, Bohemian garnets, 3 styles, ea.	70-	80
Brooch, brown/white cameo, 14k frame	360-	380
Brooch, Bull's Helmet cameo, 14k gold frame	435-	455
Brooch, 14k gold, carnelian shell cameo	395-	430

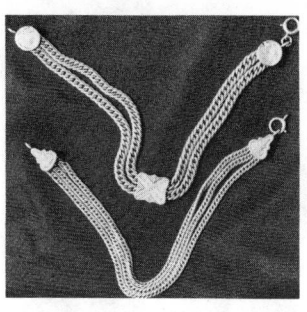

Jewelry

Jewelry

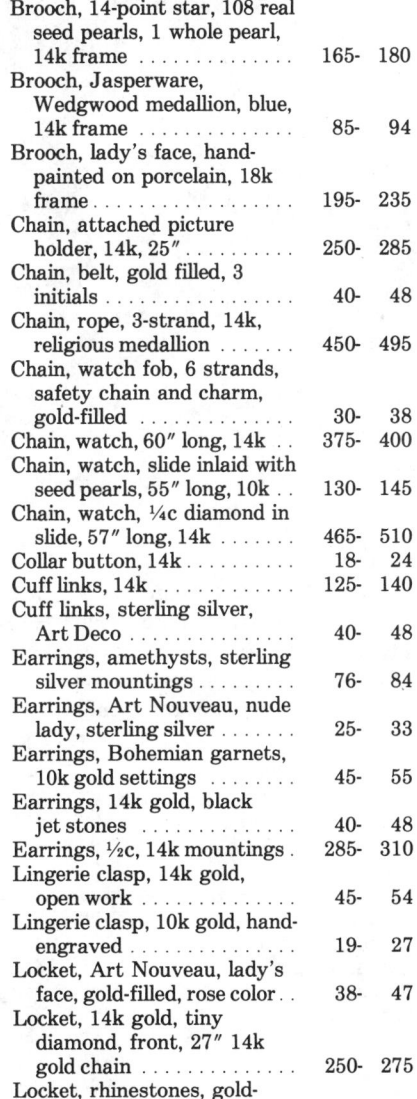

Brooch, 14-point star, 108 real seed pearls, 1 whole pearl, 14k frame	165-	180
Brooch, Jasperware, Wedgwood medallion, blue, 14k frame	85-	94
Brooch, lady's face, hand-painted on porcelain, 18k frame	195-	235
Chain, attached picture holder, 14k, 25″	250-	285
Chain, belt, gold filled, 3 initials	40-	48
Chain, rope, 3-strand, 14k, religious medallion	450-	495
Chain, watch fob, 6 strands, safety chain and charm, gold-filled	30-	38
Chain, watch, 60″ long, 14k	375-	400
Chain, watch, slide inlaid with seed pearls, 55″ long, 10k	130-	145
Chain, watch, ¼c diamond in slide, 57″ long, 14k	465-	510
Collar button, 14k	18-	24
Cuff links, 14k	125-	140
Cuff links, sterling silver, Art Deco	40-	48
Earrings, amethysts, sterling silver mountings	76-	84
Earrings, Art Nouveau, nude lady, sterling silver	25-	33
Earrings, Bohemian garnets, 10k gold settings	45-	55
Earrings, 14k gold, black jet stones	40-	48
Earrings, ½c, 14k mountings	285-	310
Lingerie clasp, 14k gold, open work	45-	54
Lingerie clasp, 10k gold, hand-engraved	19-	27
Locket, Art Nouveau, lady's face, gold-filled, rose color	38-	47
Locket, 14k gold, tiny diamond, front, 27″ 14k gold chain	250-	275
Locket, rhinestones, gold-filled	24-	33

Locket, sterling silver, hand-engraved, 26″ sterling silver chain	48-	54
Lorgnette, sterling silver, 45″ chain	325-	340
Necklace, 14k gold chain, 2c Australian opal	325-	350
Necklace, green jade, 43 beads, graduated sizes, 14k gold clasp	450-	500
Necklace, platinum chain, 2c diamond pendant, Victorian	575-	620
Pin, Art Deco, sterling silver, 2″ long	65-	75
Pin, bar type, chip diamonds in silver-plated frame	25-	33
Pin, 18k gold in shape of leaf, w/diamonds and pearls (ill.)	350-	400
Ring, amethyst, 4 stones, 2½c ea., 18k white gold setting (ill.)	550-	585
Ring, black onyx, 1 small diamond, 18k gold setting	110-	130
Ring, child's, ¼c diamond, 14k gold setting	75-	90
Ring, coat-of-arms crest, 18k gold	750-	850
Ring, green emerald, 4c, 18k gold setting	1,700-	1,900
Ring, pink shell cameo, sterling silver setting	45-	53
Ring, sardonyx, 14k setting	95-	110
Ring, 6-star black sapphire, 38c, 18k gold setting (ill.)	1,400-	1,550
Ring, topaz, 4c, 10k setting	55-	65
Ring, yellow sapphire, 62c, 18k gold setting (ill.)	1,975-	2,250
Ring, zircon, 2c, 10k gold setting	70-	80

Jewelry Store Collectibles

By the turn of the century every jewelry store gave away attractive colored cards extolling its products.

Average price, good condition ...75¢-$1.50

Jewelry Store Collectibles

Jugtown Pottery

Jugtown Pottery

In 1922 this pottery company began operations in Jugtown, North Carolina. Jacques and Juliana Busbee were the founders and Ben Owens worked with them until the early 1960s. Orange was a favorite color as was a Chinese blue glaze. The pottery was also made in a plain gray salt glaze with dark blue designs and in vibrant colors as described. Most pieces are "Jugtown Ware" impressed.

Bowl, Oriental motif, green/gray glaze, 5" dia. (ill.) . . . . $ 20-	28
Creamer, russet color, clear glaze, 3¾" high (ill.) 22-	31
(These two pieces were made and signed by Ben Owens.)	
Candleholder, handle loop, orange, 7" dia. 40-	50
Pitcher, green/blue, 6½" high . . . 42-	60
Pitcher, orange, 7¾" high 34-	50
Planter, blue/red, mottled, 6" high 42-	52

Sugar bowl, covered	35-	45
Vase, green/brown, 6" high	32-	42
Vase, orange, 4" high	31-	41
Vase, rose/green, 8" high	41-	49

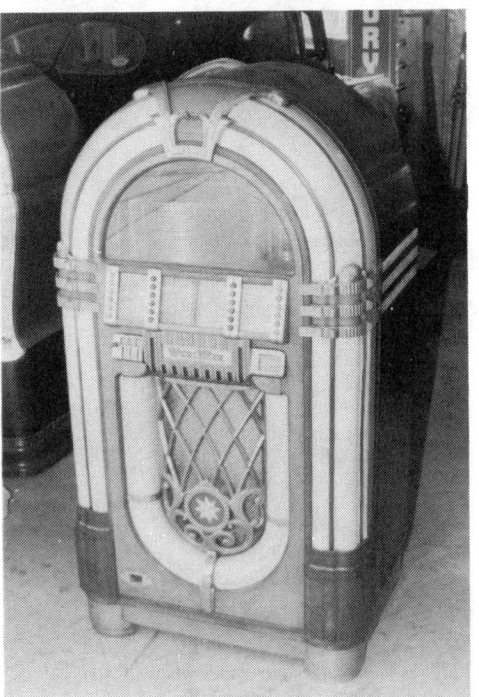

Jukeboxes

Jukeboxes

The meaning of the original word, "jook," was a roadhouse where naughty ladies of the night held forth. Anyone who grew up in the 1920s and 1930s remembers the nickel jukeboxes. "Juke box Saturday night!" The prices listed are for boxes in average good unrestored condition.

Rock-Ola, #1422 . . . . $	875-	950
Rock-Ola, #1426	875-	950
Rock-Ola, #1428	800-	875
Seeburg, #146	285-	325
Seeburg, #147	285-	325
Seeburg, #148	285-	325
Seeburg, A model	350-	425
Seeburg, B model	285-	325
Seeburg, C model	475-	550
Wurlitzer, #1100	900-	975
Wurlitzer, #1080	1,950-2,250
Wurlitzer, #1015 (ill.)	1,800-1,950
Wurlitzer, #950	5,500-6,000+
Wurlitzer, #850	3,400-3,600

Wurlitzer, #780 1,750-1,950
Wurlitzer, #750 1,250-1,450
Wurlitzer, #700 . . . .   700- 800
Wurlitzer, #600 . . . .   575- 675
Wurlitzer, "Victory" 3,400-3,650

KPM

KPM

This mark was used at Meissen for two years, c. 1723. In the 1830s it was adopted by the Royal Factory in Berlin. Ten years later the Prussian eagle was added to the letters. Other factories adopted the KPM letters in the late 19th century. There is no proof that the factory using KPM was sanctioned by the royal families still ruling in Germany at that time. There's obvious confusion about the late KPM and eagle today. Scarce, but know what you're finding.

Bowl, raised flowers inside,
  blue, 8" dia. . . . . $ 57- 62
Chocolate pot, Silesia, Onion
  pattern 62- 70
Creamer, sugar, violets, green/
  pink ground, ea. 58- 68
Cup/saucer, demitasse, white
  ground, pink roses, 1830s 54- 60
Dish, raised leaves, cover, oval,
  10" dia. 52- 62
Figurine, boy with goat, 9" high .   82- 90
Picture, porcelain, family scene,
  15"×20" 525-600
Plaque, cupids, pink/blues,
  6"×8" . . . .   1,800+
Plaque, 5½"×6¾", musicians . . .   325+
Plate, cake, tulips, reticulated
  handles, rims, 9" dia. 60- 70
Plate, gypsy boy, 10" dia. 70- 80
Teapot, creamer, sugar, tray,
  cups/saucers, flowers/
  butterflies 420-470
Vase, cherries and apples, 9½"
  high 210-240

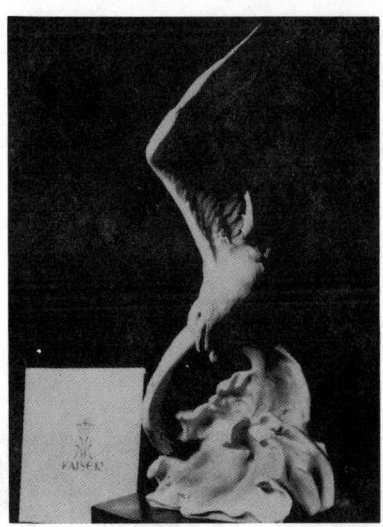

Kaiser Porcelain

Kaiser Porcelain

Bavaria, since 1872. Not antique but highly collectible today. Cybis and Ispanky porcelains are also collectible. Prices listed are for Kaiser.

Flying Heron . . . . $ 75- 85
Goose Girl 130-150
Humming Bird 145-170
Kingfisher, limit 2,000 260-290
Pheasant, limit 1,500 300-370
Pigeon group, limit 2,000 180-190
Sea Gull (ill.), limit 1,000 . . . . 2,000+

Kelva
See **Wavecrest.**

Keramo Porcelain

Keramo Porcelain

This was from Karlovy Vary, the world-

                              (continued)

famous spa in Carlsbad, Czechoslovakia. The illustrated spa glass (porcelain) was filled with the health-giving waters, which were sipped through the top of the handle as illustrated here.

Keramo spa sipper (ill.) . . . . $ 34- 43
Porcelain bottle to take home a
    sample for friends 32- 41
Souvenir plate marked Karlovy
    Vary, 1925 . . . . 26- 35

Kew Blas Glass

Kew Blas Glass

Made at the Union Glass Works, Somerville, Massachusetts, in the 1890s, it was an iridescent glassware contemporary with Tiffany, Durand, Quezal, Steuben, and others. The name is not taken from Walter Blake's last name though he did work at the factory. Sometimes signed Kew Blas on the bottom, otherwise difficult to distinguish from other glasses named here.

Bowl, gold iridescent, signed
    "Kew Blas A 500," 15″ dia.
    (ill.) $295-335
Bowl, rose, gold iridescent/green
    decor, Zipper pattern 275-300
Candlesticks, gold swirled,
    signed, 9″ high, pr. 450-500
Creamer, Zipper pattern, 2½″
    high 225-260
Plate, iridescent, blue, 6½″ dia. . . . 240-260
Tumbler, blue iridescent, signed,
    3½″ high 170-185
Tumbler, gold iridescent, signed,
    4″ high 155-170
Vase, gold iridescent, signed,
    5½″ high 400-450
Vase, green/brown iridescent,
    signed, 9½″ high 485-535
Vase, pink/purple iridescent,
    signed, 8″ high 475-500

Wine, gold iridescent, signed,
    4¾″ high 135-155

Kewpies

Kewpies

Rose O'Neill drew pictures of these pixielike figures for the *Ladies Home Journal* in the early 1900s. Around 1911 Kewpie dolls began to appear on the American market. The bisque dolls came from Germany, but the most common were the ones made of celluloid. Being reproduced.

Bank, glass, tin lid . . . . $ 89- 99
Bowl, cereal, 6″ dia. 120-140
Candy container, 1915 92-107
Creamer, Kewpies playing in
    yard 97-120
Cup/saucer, Germany, pink
    lustre trim 90-110
Dish, feeding 42- 52
Doll, bisque, Japan, 4″ 40- 50
Doll, bisque, signed Rose
    O'Neill 110-120
Doll, composition, Rose O'Neill
    label, 12½″ 70- 80
Doll, dressed, celluloid mark,
    2½″ high 18- 27
Figurine, seated figure, 3″ high . . 183+
Ice cream mold, hinged, pewter . . 38- 50
Ice cream tray, signed Rose
    O'Neill 51- 60
Lamp, chalkware, fringe shade . . 50- 62
Pitcher, 4 action Kewpies,
    Royal Rudolstadt 270-280
Plate, Royal Rudolstadt,
    signed Rose O'Neill 40- 50
Postcard, Christmas, "We love
    you" 12- 18
Powder jar, signed 92-107
Teapot, creamer, sugar, signed
    Rose O'Neill, porcelain 130-140
Thimble 12- 21
Toothpick, "Thinker," 5½″
    high 68- 74
Tray, Kewpies picking berries,
    signed 245-252
Vase, handled, Kewpies
    playing, signed 132-140

Keys

Keys

Shown here because there are thousands of different kinds. The old Spanish dungeon keys are quite collectible. Keys are a fun item to collect and decorate with. Too many to give specific prices.

Average price	$1-	2
Brass, early 1800s	6-	9
Folding type, nickel-plated	5-	7
Iron, jail type, large	7-	10

Kimble Glass

Kimble Glass

In the late 1800s, Colonel Ewan Kimble operated a factory at Vineland, New Jersey, for a relatively short time. The factory also operated jointly as Kimble and Durand. Not too much is known about this glass, but it is considered scarce today. After Durand's death in 1931, the factory was taken over by Kimble and today is part of Owens-Illinois. It is **not** spelled Kimball!

Bowl, Cluthra in white, rose, 4" high	$220-255
Candlesticks, blue/green, iridized, 14" high, pr.	350-400
Vase, blue, white inside, scalloped, curved top, 7" high	110-125
Vase, Cluthra, blue/gray spirals, yellow iridescent, 6" high	265-270

Vase, Cluthra, orange/white bubbles, dark handles, 11" high, signed "K-20144-11, Dec-7" (ill.) 282-295

King's Rose Pattern

King's Rose Pattern

Produced in the Staffordshire District, England, around 1820 to 1830, it's a soft-paste porcelain made especially for the Pennsylvania Dutch trade. The enamel decorations are usually in warm yellows, greens, pinks, and dark reds. Sometimes the colors flake off with use. It was good porcelain.

Coffeepot, 10¾" high	$ 1,100+
Cup/saucer, large size, King's Rose	240-255
Cup/saucer, regular size	200-225
Cup/saucer, regular size	190-218
Plate, dinner, divided border, 9" dia.	140-160
Plate, dinner (ill.)	195-220
Plate, toddy	160-175

Kitchen Gadgets

Some good, some bad, but all getting more expensive. Buy it if you like it, but keep in mind that, like so many other "collectibles," a lot are being skillfully reproduced. If you're collecting things to do with the kitchen, you should purchase the Third Edition of my *Wallace-Homestead Flea Market Price Guide.* Hundreds of items are listed and priced.

Aluminum pans, set of 6, wooden handles, all	$ 40- 48

221

(continued)

Knives

Knives

Remember Grandfather's advice, "Always cut away from your thumb!" All kinds of knives are collectible today, especially unusual pocket types.

Masonic, 14k gold, ornate enamel and initials	42- 52
Pocket, Hopalong Cassidy, 3-blade	33- 42
Pocket type, company advertising, fits on key chain, 2″ long	31- 40
Remington, Babe Ruth emblem 2-blade, bone handle	96-109
Remington, hunting type, 9″ blade, leather case	80- 90
Remington, pocket, 2-blade	40- 50
Remington, R333, Boy Scout insignia, stag handle	114-130
Sterling silver penknife, 2-blade nail cleaner	44- 53
Winchester, Hawk bill, 1-blade, wood handle	74- 83
Winchester, pocket type, 3-blade, leather punch	62- 72
Winchester, 2-blade	70- 80

Kutani

Kutani

Kutani is one of the most famous names in china and pottery in the world, its manufacture dating back to the 1550s. The artists who paint this magnificent ware are referred to in Japan as human treasures. Most of what you find in shops today is fairly new and varies in price according to size. Usually, each Kutani vase comes in a wooden box with the artist's signature on the outside of the box.

Prices vary between $25 and $200 for 20th century Kutani.

Vase, 9″ high, new (ill.)	$140-165

La Verre Francais Cameo Glass

This was one of the Cameo types exported in bulk by France to New York around the turn of the century. Various stores sold it until it lost popularity around World War I.

Bowl, blue/orange, flowers, signed, 11″ dia.	$540-600
Lamp, tortoiseshell color, signed	850+
Planter, yellow/orange, Art Deco, 7″ high	260-280
Vase, blue/orange, berries on yellow ground	360-410
Vase, flying birds, blue/yellow/orange, signed Charder	385-420
Vase, frosted yellow ground, cut blue/orange, signed	440-480
Vase, tortoiseshell color, orange/blue, signed	420-450

Lace

Lace

There's considerable interest in French crocheted filet, Irish crochet from the 1840s, applique from about 1850. Tatting with small bobbins was popular in the 1870s. Today doll collectors search out the old lace for decorating dresses. European in nature, wherever it's found collectors are buying it, by the piece or by the box.

Lacquer (see Cinnabar)

This is an Oriental form of art. Layer upon layer of lacquer was applied to the item, then designs were cut into the lacquer layers or painted on in typical Oriental style.

Bowl, floral designs, painted	$ 52- 62
Box, carved fish designs in red/black, footed	52- 62
Fireplace screen, carved in lithoplane style	101-118

223

(continued)

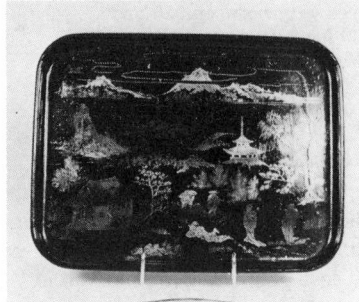

Lacquer

Jewelry box, 6-drawer, painted
   designs 120-130
Sewing box, black, gold dragon
   designs, painted 68- 78
Tea caddy, 2 compartments,
   pewter lids 110-120
Tray, black, gilded Oriental
   decor, 12¼″ wide (ill.) 42- 57

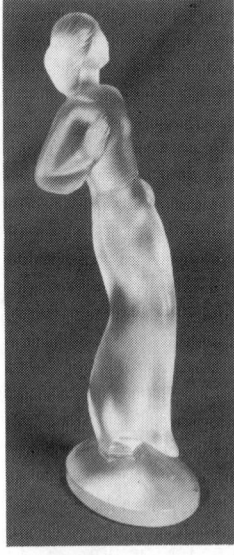

Lalique Glass

Lalique Glass

Rene Lalique made this fine art glass in France at the turn of the century. He was an associate of Emile Galle, and their works are similar in many respects. A combination of blowing, pressing, frosting, and cutting achieved the excellent effect Lalique gave to his glass. "New" Lalique is being made in France today. All listed pieces are signed "R. Lalique."

Bottle, frosted background,
   dancing ladies, 6″ high $325-355
Bottle, heart-shaped, butterflies,
   4½″ high 95-115
Bottle, perfume, frosted, clear
   tulips, 6¼″ high 95-115
Bottle, perfume, lotus blossom
   shape, stopper 95-115
Bottle, perfume, plunger type,
   frosted ladies, 14″ high 125-145
Bowl, fish, shellfish, shell feet,
   France 295-325
Clock, frosted lovebirds, cut glass
   dial, 10″ high 325-375
Covered box, deep gray tone,
   scarabs in relief, 2½″×3½″ . . . 345-495
Cup/saucer, leaves, flowers, cut
   pattern 80- 95
Decanter, clear body, frosted
   neck, stopper, 9″ high 385-475
Dish, frosted swan on saucer vase   95-110
Figurine, lady, 7½″ high (ill.) 85-110
Jar, powder, clear/frosted thorns,
   4¼″ high 155-175
Knife rest, crystal center, frosted
   knobs 75- 90
Plate, annual, 1966, 1967,
   1968, ea. 355-375
Salt, frosted birds, 2″ high 45- 55
Toothpick, frosted cherubs, 2½″
   high 55- 69
Vase, frosted, dancing nudes,
   footed, 10″ high 200-225
Vase, frosted grape pattern,
   10″ high 160-185
Vase, lotus blossoms, protruding
   petals, 11″ high 190-225

Laminated Glass

Tiffany and Quezal both made this type of glass in the early 1900s. It was a multi-colored opaque glass and hard to make. It's relatively scarce, but a real plum when found.

Lamps

Art Deco lamp, clowns playing,
   green glass shade, 14½″
   high . . . . $ 71- 90
Art Deco lamp, reclining nudes
   on base, glass globe, 12″
   high 80- 92
Art Nouveau lamp, ballet
   dancer, blue metal shade,
   14″ high 240-260
Alcohol lamp, glass cover,
   4″ high 26- 36
Auto lamp, brass kerosene
   type 110-120

Gone With the Wind Lamp

Iron Betty Lamp

Banquet lamp, brass base, porcelain shade	170-180
Betty lamp, iron, early 1800s (ill.)	240-260
Betty lamp, iron, 4″ long, spike hanger (ill.)	140-152
Bicycle lamp, carbide, 3″ high, magnifying lens, 4½″ high	52- 64
Bracket lamp, mercury reflector	42- 60
Brass lamp, Rayo-type, frosted shade, 9″ high	78- 90
Bristol glass type, blown olive green font, blue base, 11″ high (ill.)	92-112
Camphene lamp, double brass burners, pewter base	97-108
Carbide miner's cap lamp, chrome reflector	40- 50
Carriage lamp, bail handle, clamp slot on side, kerosene	70- 90
Chandelier lamp, brass, china shade, pull-down type, 1860s	290-320
Clear glass lamp, 9″ high	31- 41
Coach lamp, brass, glass, 3 sides, kerosene	62- 72

Cobalt (blue) lamp, 7½″ high, kerosene	70- 80
Fairy lamp—see **Fairy Lamps**	
Flint glass lamp, whale oil type, early 1800s	70- 80
Floor lamp, triangular base, green shade, Tiffany type (not signed)	110-125
Gone With the Wind lamp, brass fittings, cast iron base, 23½″ high (ill.)	360-380
Gone With the Wind lamp, green ground, pink/yellow flowers	260-285
Gone With the Wind lamp, hand-painted "cows grazing," brass base	300-380
Gone With the Wind lamp, red satin shade and base	270-290
Hand lamp, Coolidge Drape shade, 9½″ high, clear	110-125
Kitchen lamp, white shade, brass font, 1880s	80- 90
Log cabin lamp, clear glass	115-130
Millefiori, 1880s, 12½″ high, base and shade both millefiori (ill.)	240-270
Oil lamp, Sandwich, Heart & Waffle, mid-1850s(ill.)	180-200
Piano lamp, floor type, marble top, porcelain-painted shade	230-255
Satin glass lamp, brass/wood base	220-260
Pulpit lamp, spring base, copper, 12″ high	70- 80
Student lamp, single, milk white shade, brass	270-280
Student lamp, double, green shade, brass	650+

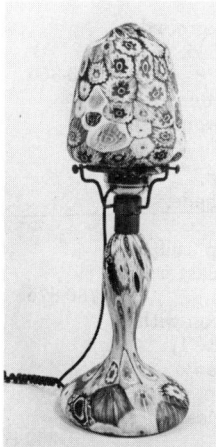

Millefiori Lamp   **Bristol Glass Type Lamp**

(continued)

Lamps

Tiffany-type Lamp

Table lamp, green/blue ground,
flower decor, electrified,
1890s 310-360

Tiffany floor lamp, shade
signed LCT, 6' 6", bronze (see
Tiffany)

Tiffany-type table lamp,
caramel slag glass shade,
brass base .... 485+

Tiffany-type table lamp, tulips/
leaves glass, gilded cast iron
finial, 24½" high (ill.) 750-875

Tiffany table lamp, green with
red flowers, signed LCT,
16½" high (See **Tiffany**)

Tiffany-type table lamp, metal
base, caramel slag glass
shade, 16½" high .... 350+

Wall lamp, iron ring type,
pressed glass bowl, white
shade, 1880s 74- 83

Wall lamp, tin bonnet 70- 80

Alladin

This is one of the most popular lamps ever
made. The Mantle Lamp Company of
America, Inc., was founded in Chicago in
1908. These lamps are still being made in
Nashville, Tenn. All lamps are priced
with complete burners and shades.

Practicus table lamp $240-260
Model No. 1 table lamp 138-158
Model No. 1 parlor lamp....... 260-275
Model No. 2 table lamp 187-210
Model No. 2 parlor lamp....... 225-240
Model No. 3 table lamp 140-160
Model No. 3 parlor lamp....... 245-265
Model No. 4 table lamp 140-155
Model No. 5 table lamp 144-153
Model No. 10 table lamp 290-320
Model No. 1241 variegated
(two-tone) tan crystal vase
lamp, 12" tall 110-122
Model No. 1242 Bengal red
crystal vase lamp, 12" tall 240-270
Model 1233 blue Venetian Art
Craft crystal vase lamp,
10¼" tall 130-145
Model 1247 red venetian Art-
Craft crystal vase lamp,
10¼" tall 210-240
Style 99, Venetian, clear,
Model A table lamp, 1932 340-370
Style 101, Venetian, green,
Model A table lamp, 1932 160-170
Style B-110, Cathedral, white
moonstone, Model B table
lamp 185-220
Style B-100, Corinthian, clear
crystal, Model B table lamp ... 80- 90
Style B-82, Beehive, amber
crystal, light, Model B
table lamp 92-101
Style B-82, Beehive, amber
crystal, dark, Model B
table lamp............... 160-180
Style B-86, Quilt, green
moonstone, Model B table
lamp 160-180
Style B-39, Washington Drape
(round base), clear crystal,
Model B 88-108
Style B-62, Short Lincoln
Drape, ruby crystal, Model
B table lamp 450-510
Style B-76, Tall Lincoln Drape,

cobalt crystal, Model B table lamp (lamps with scallop design on the foot are worth much more) 450-510
Style B-25, Victoria, decorated china, Model B table lamp . . 350-390
Caboose lamp, Model B w/shade 162-182
Caboose wall bracket lamp, alacite font 110-130
Floor lamp, Model No. 12, w/shade, 1254 series 120-140
Floor lamp, Model B, brass, w/shade 250-270
Hanging lamp, Practicus, w/shade 240-260
Hanging lamp, Model No. 2 w/shade 270-290
Hanging lamp, Model No. 3, double chandelier . . . . 785+

Lamps, Miniature

Originally known as night lamps, today we call them miniature lamps. Every company made them in blown, blown-molded, pressed, every color, every price range. Most are collectible.

Blue glass, Inverted Thumbprint, 6½" high . . . . $ 97-109
Brass banquet lamp, purple shade, 8" high 84- 93
Brass cabin lamp, 7" high 61- 74
Brass, saucer type, 4½" high with chimney, patented 1873 52- 70
Bristol glass, pink, chimney-type shade 78- 84

Bristol glass, white, blue decor, 8" high 76- 87
Cased glass, red over milk glass, matching half shade . . 120-135
Clear glass, umbrella shade, flower decor 52- 72
Cobalt Little Duchess, 7½" high 62- 72
Cosmos glass, white shade, 7½" high 320-360
Cranberry Beaded Swirl, 8" high 98-108
Cranberry, handled, 5½" high . 99-112
End-of-Day (Spatter Glass), 7" high 97-108
Gold Eagle, orange body, gold trim (ill.) 140-165
Milk glass, Columbus bust base (ill.) 170-180
Milk glass, hand-painted, 5½" high 37- 47
Milk glass, pink slag, Swan, shade, rare (ill.) . . . . 870+
Mt. Washington glass, blue flower decor, 7½" high 270-300
Satin glass, blue, matching ball shade 115-120
Satin glass, green 8" high 100-109
Satin glass, pink, 8" high 120-130
Satin glass, pink with flowers, frosted shade, 7" high (ill.) 110-120
Satin glass, red, 6½" high 110-120
Satin glass, white/pink diamond quilt, 7" high 130-140
Tiffany miniature mushroom lamp with shade, green/white, original bulb signed Edison Mazda; lamp signed

Lamps, Miniature

(continued)

LCT, 8″ high (rare) . . . .   2,700+
Tulip lamp, flowers in green,
   8½″ high . . . .   135+

Lanterns

Lanterns

From the earliest pine splints during Colonial times to the first electrical types, 1870 on, lanterns have been made in every size and shape to fit a particular need. Good repros are appearing at shows.

Buggy lantern, red bull's eye
   reflector . . . . $ 92-107
Candle lantern, tin and glass,
   early 1800s 46- 56
Candle lantern, tin, folding
   type 60- 70
Candle lantern, tin, 12″ high 70- 80
Carriage lanterns, beveled
   glass, red reflectors, pr.   280-328
Miner's lantern, iron, patented
   snuffer marked Hailwood 51- 67
Paul Revere type, pierced tin 72- 81
Police lantern, kerosene, bull's-
   eye lens, tin, 1880s 55- 65
Porch lantern, electrified 34- 44
Railroad lantern, hooded,
   inspector's 51- 61
Railroad lantern, red, squat
   globe, marked Southern RR . .   42- 52
Ship's lantern, captain's,
   copper reflector . . . .   225+
Ship's lantern, red globe, brass
   frame, 20″ high   475-560
Skater's lantern, brass, with
   wire, kerosene (ill.) 70- 80
Skater's lantern, silver-plated,
   mid-1800s, chain, kerosene . . .   50- 60
Skater's lantern, tin, wire
   handle (ill.) 52- 62
Whale oil lantern, tapered glass
   globe, tin, early 1800s   120-150

Lap Desks

Lap Desks

When one had to travel in the early days, one took a portable desk along. Usually it was made of wood, contained ink, quills, sealing wax. Most of the ink in powder form—when mixed with water, it did the trick.

Rosewood, English, 18th century,
   complete $170-190
Rosewood veneer box, brass
   hinges, 4 compartments,
   12″ across (ill.)   160-180
Walnut, English, hidden com-
   partment under pen tray,
   1800s   210-220

Latticinio

Latticinio

Made by an ancient technique lost in time, this glass was produced by various glass houses in the mid-to-late 1800s. Uninformed collectors confuse it with Lutz-type glass. Latticinio's crossed, cruved lines beneath the decoration give it a peppermint cane effect. Actually it's a filigree glassware, first devel-

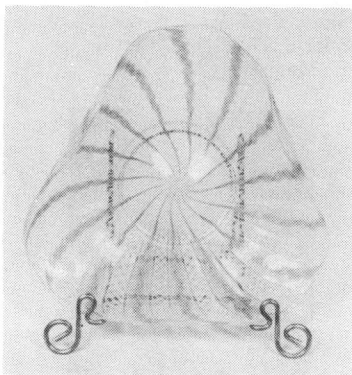

Latticinio

Leather Items

oped in the first or second century, B.C. Don't worry about finding any piece this old. Most of what you find in shops today is in the $55-70 range. If it proves to be old, you've found a bargain. If not, you haven't paid attention when we say, "Know your antiques or know your antiques dealer!" Being reproduced—from the island of Murano, near Venice, Italy.

Plates, typical design, twisted
    threads, gold/white (ill.), ea. . . . . $ 64- 76

Leather Items

Cowhide has been used for just about everything: postcards, shoes, hats, dresses, pants—you name it! Now collectors are quietly buying things made from cowhide. The bola illustrated is still used by cowboys in South America. When released, three balls wrap it around the legs (or feet) of the cow or horse.

Lavender Pots

Leeds Ware

Lavender Pots

The dried flowers, leaves, and stalks of a European flower akin to the mint family, when dried, were used to fill sachets, perfume clothes and linens. The crushed plant was kept in a lavender pot, made by most European porcelain firms during the 1800s and until World War I.

Haviland lavender pot, rose
    petals, pink border, 2 lids . . . . . $ 62- 72
Royal Worcester lavender pot,
    2 lids, (ill.) 68- 74

Leeds Ware

Begun in Yorkshire, England, about 1758, this was a fine grade of creamware that competed with Wedgwood. A few years later reticulated and punched wares were made, with few pieces ever marked. Extremely rare and collectible today.

Bowl, blue/white, twisted
    handles . . . . $ 54- 64
Cream pitcher, yellow/blue/
    green, 4½" high   150-160

229

(continued)

Cup/saucer, handleless, floral
decor 82- 92
Jug, creamware, 1780, flowers
in red   150-162
Mug, Chinese decor, early 18th
century   110-127
Pitcher, farmer's coat-of-arms
(rare) . . . .   1,000+
Pitcher, flower decor, 6" high
(ill).   190-220
Plate, blue edge, marked, 12"
dia. 82- 94
Plate, creamware, openwork,
marked, 9" dia. 74- 88
Platter, cream, shell pattern,
16½" wide   155-162
Sugar bowl w/lid, yellow/green,
4½" high   92-109
Teapot, red/green, shell pattern
in body, 7½" high   230-250
Tureen, white body, blue decor,
22" high, lid   230-255

Legal Documents

Legal Documents

Old handwritten deeds and wills, especially those from England with the magnificent red wax seals and ribbons, are all being sought after today.

Aetna fire insurance policy, 1875,
$300, on white paper . . . .$ 8- 13
English land deed on heavy
parchment with ornate wax
seal, early 1800s 50- 60
Framed cemetery plot receipt,
"Woodlawn, Bronx, NY," 1892   12- 16
Handwritten deed, dated 1878
(ill.) 5- 9
Mortgage deed, Norfolk, N.Y.,
1858, handwritten 10- 16
Quitclaim deed, 1849, Hunter,
N.Y., handwritten 12- 18

Warranty deed, Westchester
County, N.Y., 1866, "Certifi-
cate Magistracy" 14- 19

LeGras

LeGras

This gentleman was known for his unusually imaginative glassware and bottles. He discontinued operations just before World War I. His scenic reproductions, also made in his factory at Saint-Dennis, were considered masterpieces. Being reproduced.

Bowl, beige, brown, green-
cased, signed 4½" high . . . . . .$ 525+
Bowl, rose, enameled spring
scene, scalloped top, 7½"
high   190-240
Lamp, green, orange, trees,
electrified, signed, 7¼" high
(ill.)   480-580
Vase, Art Deco, autumn
leaves, 8½" high   340-370
Vase, brown, orange leaves,
enameled, 16" high   350-385
Vase, cameo, cut back foliage,
green/blue, signed   485-650
Vase, cameo, green, yellow,
cobalt, acid cut to clear, 13" . . .   625+
Vase, cameo white apple
blossoms, green back-
ground, 8½" high   380-397

Lenox

This firm started business in 1906 in Trenton, New Jersey. Among other wares, it made a good Belleek type.

Ashtray, shell-shaped . . . .$ 12- 21

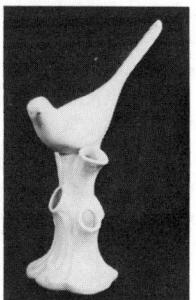

Lenox

Atomizer, perfume, penguin
  shape, 4″ high 42- 52
Bottle, woman's head shape,
  Hattie Carnegie cosmetics 70- 80
Bowl, oval, cream, gilt edge 58- 68
Candy box, cream, gold edge 70- 80
Coffee service, Ming pattern,
  pot and bowl, large creamer . . .   81- 90
Cup/saucer, Ming pattern 24- 33
Jar, mustard, green, silver
  overlay, lid 38- 47
Mug, gold scene, pr. (rare)   130-140
Plate, Ming pattern, 8¼″ dia. . . .   44+
Salt, swan-shape, master and 4
  small, set 52- 63
Tray, pin, gold band, 6″ dia. 29- 32
Vase, Art Nouveau, 6½″ high,
  green, gold gilt 82- 92
Vase, bird-shaped flower 10″
  high (ill.) 42- 52

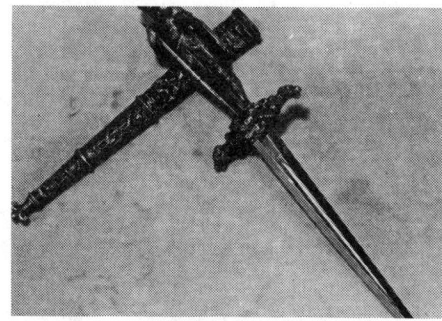

Letter Openers

Letter Openers

Made of bone, ivory, gold, silver, brass, wood, this item has been used for hundreds of years.

Alabaster, carved Chinese
  designs, 8″ long . . . . $ 19- 27
Brass, ornate case, African
  figure, late 1800s (ill.) 50- 60

Gold, 14k, castle scene, French,
  dated 1834, 7½″ long   428-487
Ivory, carved figures on handle,
  early 1800s 42- 52
Silver-plated, souvenir of Phila-
  delphia Centennial, 1876 . . . . .   32- 43
Sterling silver, marked Tiffany,
  6½″ long   310-340
Wood, many types, souvenir, etc.   29- 37

License Plates

License Plates

Since the early 1900s these have been collectible. The early plates, porcelain-on-metal, bring brisk prices today. All plates are in demand, from the 1900s until World War II.

Porcelain, on metal, Pennsyl-
  vania, 1907 . . . . $ 40- 50
Tin, any state, 1900 to 1915 . . . . .   19- 28
Tin, any state, 1920s to 1940s . . .   12- 20
1950s on 1-1.50

Lighter-than-Air

Lighter-than-Air

When Count Ferdinand von Zeppelin developed a dirigible airship around 1900, man had another way to fly through the heavens. Used by our own Navy during the 1930s (see ill.), who can forget that fateful day

231

(continued)

at the Lakehurst Naval Air Station in New Jersey, when the across-the-Atlantic Graf Zeppelin exploded and burned? Menus, air schedules, postcards, sheet music—all collectible.

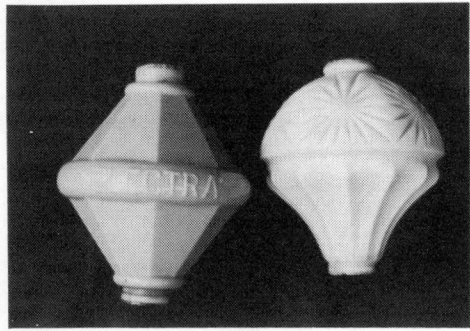

Lightning-Rod Balls

Lightning-Rod Balls

They were supposed to keep the house or barn from being struck by lightning, but they didn't. They appeared in the 1840s—glass, opaque, mirrored, or translucent. A hole at either end allowed one to be slipped over a lightning rod. The usual sizes are 3½" to 4½" in diameter. Green and orange, also ruby, are considered rare colors; white and blue, fairly common.

Ball, blue milk glass . . . . $	9-	12
Ball, Electra, white, made in Albany, N.Y. (ill.)	8-	11
Ball, gold-toned mercury glass . .	15-	22
Ball, Hawkeye, white (ill.)	8-	11
Ball, W.C. Shinn, clear	8-	11

Limoges Porcelain

Limoges Porcelain

Limoges, France, is a village, not a maker

of porcelain. The uninformed buyer purchases this as a particular brand. Haviland (see **Haviland**) was the most famous maker in this village. Other makers at Limoges were Ahrenfeldt and Son, A. Lanternier, R. Delinieres and Cie., Bernardaud and Cie., P.H. Leonard, Fontanille and Marraud, Raynaud and Cie., Union Limousine. These are but a few and prices are dependent on maker, year, type.

Atomizer, pearl lustre, hand-painted flowers . . . . $	34-	44
Bowl, fruit decoration, 9" dia. . . .	38-	50
Bowl, orange poppies, 10" dia. . . .	34-	50
Box, enamel, farm scene	54-	64
Box, pill, floral scene, hinged 2½" square	52-	62
Butter pat, green floral, gold trim	12-	19
Candlesticks, pair, blue with white violets, 8½" high	70-	78
Chocolate set, pot and 8 cups/saucers, floral background, pink/white	108-128	
Creamer, flowers, pink/green	21-	31
Cup/saucer, daisies, blue border .	30-	40
Cup/saucer, yellow and pink roses, gold trim	24-	27
Dish, bone, floral design, green/pink, set of 6	54-	63
Fish set, yellow platter, different fish on each of 8 plates, set	200-209	
Mug, hand-painted, gold handle, drinking scene, 8" high	64-	73
Pitcher, cider, yellow/green flowers, gold handle, 14" high .	73-	82
Pitcher, tankard, grapes, green background, 12½" high	72-	82
Plate, cake, pink roses, gold border, set of 8	74-	83
Plate, gold border, gold horse chestnuts, leaves outlined in gold, 9" dia.	52-	70
Plate, dinner, gold band, roses in center, set of 12	170-190	
Platter, green/blue floral design, gold border, 16" dia. (ill.)	60-	70
Tray, celery, blue and yellow, reticulated border 5½"×12" . .	60-	70
Tureen, soup, handles, yellow roses inside pink roses outside, 15" dia.	72-	82
Vase, pink poppies, black background, 11" high	64-	74

Lindbergh

Lucky Lindy, The Spirit of St. Loius—Captain Charles Lindbergh left Roosevelt

Lindbergh

Field on Long Island, N.Y., at 7:52 a.m. (DST), May 20, 1927. With only a tiny kitten to keep him company, he flew nonstop across the Atlantic, arriving in Paris, France, at 5:17 p.m. (DST), on May 21, 1927. One of our great nation's greatest heroes, his contributions to world aviation were many. Anything to do with Lindy is collectible today, including the tragic kidnapping of his infant son.

Lithograph Stones

Lithograph Stones

Too many people confuse lithographing with etching. Lithographs, a form of early American art, were drawn on blocks of stone with a greasy crayon, then transferred to the paper by pressure of a press. These stones are hard to find but a plum when you find one.

Lithographs

Currier and Ives made them famous; other firms also. Most American lithographs weren't marked with the year and copyright until after 1848. Have fun, there are lots around. Just know your dealer.

"The Marquis de Sade Suite,"
  signed twice and dated by
  Salvador Dali, 1968, 58/160
  (ill.) $450-485

Lithographs

Lithophanes

Lithophanes

Highly translucent porcelains with impressed designs are formed by the difference in the thickness of the plaque. Thin parts let a lot of light through; thicker parts are usually shadows. First made in Berlin, Germany, around 1825, later other factories in France and England made them. Rarely signed. Extremely fragile. Highly collectible.

Candle shield, 3 scenes, ornate
  wooden frame $180-220
Candle shield, woman seated,
  knitting, metal stand and
  frame 245-278
Farm family, 5"×7", metal
  frame and stand 170-185
Hanging type, boy/girl in
  doorway, 6¼"×4½" (ill.) 110-120
Mother, child, puppy, 6"×5" 170-190
Mug, lithophane bottom, German
  soldier, WWI, 9½" high 140-152

(continued)

Plaque, forest scene, 4"×5" 170-180
Plaque, lovers in boat, village
   scene, 4"×5" 160-170
Shade, leaded panels, children
   scenes, 4"×4" 300-385
Tea warmer, 4 German scenes,
   converted burner 220-250

Liverpool Pottery

Liverpool Pottery

Various potteries made this ware from the mid-1700s to the mid-1800s. From about 1788 to 1820 the leading pottery, Sadler and Green, decorated its wares with line drawings, usually in black and white or cream colored. The decorations were often designed for the American colonies, with famous people, eagles, and scenes from everyday life. Scarce.

Bowl, covered, blue/white
   Herculaneum $170-180
Creamer, strawberry lustre 150-160
Creamer, white/black transfer,
   Temperance 172-195
Cup/saucer, black transfer,
   castle scene, handleless 105-140
Cup/saucer, 1800, black
   transfer 120-130
Jug, George Washington, ship,
   10" high (ill.) 520-545
Pitcher, large, English farm
   scene (ill.) .... 500+
Plate, black, English ship 180-198
Plate, blue Chinese decor,
   1780s 155-185
Tea set, teapot, sugar and
   creamer, Queen Anne shape,
   strawberry lustre 465-545

Lobmeyer Glass

Ludwig Lobmeyer opened his factory in Zlatno, Hungary, in the 1870s. He made the first commercial iridescent glass of the 19th

Lobmeyer Glass

century. No two pieces are alike in color. Typical pieces are in fine, clear glass, with transparent enamel washes, and/or flashed with red and yellow.

Candlesticks, gold rimmed, birds/
   flowers, pr. .... $ 62- 70
Cups/saucers, demitasse,
   transparent washes in floral
   patterns, flint glass, ground
   pontils, 2" high (ill.), set 60- 70
Vase, gilded, black enameling,
   chinoiserie decor 181-191

Lockets

These small hinged cases of silver, gold, or other metal, for holding a lock of hair or a photograph of a loved one, usually worn suspended from a necklace, have been collectible for years. The gold ones, often studded with diamonds, that hung from a man's watch chain are especially valuable.

Gold locket, studded with
   diamonds, late 1800s, 14k $395-450
Silver-plated locket, 1930s 16- 27

Locks and Keys

Locks and Keys

Here's a delightful hobby. These have been used to protect everything from a cabin door to the entrance of Louis XIV's castle.

234

They come in all sizes and shapes. Locks with keys bring more than just plain locks. Yale, Sargeant, Keen Kutter—just a few of the famous lockmakers.

Lock, brass, "Quality—Six
Lever" (ill.) $22-30
Lock, brass, with key, early 1800s .. 60-70
Lock, brass, with key, late 1800s ... 24-34
Lock, iron, with key, jailhouse
type 72-82
Lock, N.Y. Central Railroad, with
keyhole guard................ 40-48
Lock, padlock type, Baltimore &
Ohio RR 44-52
Lock, padlock type, late 1800s 21-30
Lock, wood, with wood key, early
1800s 60-70

Loetz Glass

Loetz Glass

Similar in appearance to Tiffany glass and made about the same time, it was produced in Austria and was considered a fine quality iridescent glass. The factory was also noted for its superior cameo effects produced on cased glassware. Sometimes marked Loetz in the pontil.

Atomizer, orange, cameo, cut,
5¾" high $210-240
Bowl, green shading to gold,
pinched sides 300-400
Bowl, ribbed with iridescence,
folded down lip, green iridescent threading, 4½" high (ill.) . 240-270
Inkwell, green, iridescent
purple/white in base, signed ... 225-260
Lamp, mushroom shade, tur-
quoise iridescent, 20" high 295-380
Paperweight, blue, feather
design, signed.............. 248-300
Rose bowl, Art Deco, amber,
iridescent, 4½" high......... 250-275
Tumbler, gold iridescent speck-
ling, 3" high 94-108
Vase, blue iridescent, gold/pink
threads, flower-form, signed .. 310+

Vase, iridescent, turquoise, 9½"
high, signed 320-385
Vase, rose, copper, green 300-365

Lotus Ware

Lotus Ware

Knowles, Taylor and Knowles Pottery Company, East Liverpool, Ohio, made this fine and delicate porcelain of warm whites and glossy greens in the late 1800s, and only for 10 years. First marks were KTK on the bottom; later they put the firm's name in a circle enclosing a crescent and star. Scarce.

Berry set, 3 pieces .... $ 400+
Bowl, green/gold, cream ground,
KTK mark 145-185
Bowl, roses, turquoise medal-
lions, signed KTK (ill.) 370-420
Creamer, pink flowers, fish-
scales, signed 210-260
Creamer, white, classic shape,
KTK (ill.) 198-240
Pitcher, fishnet, enameled
flowers, 4¼" high.......... 440-480
Tea set, green/gold or cream, all .. 450+
Vase, pink/blue floral, gold
handles, signed KTK 600-675
Vase, roses, fishscales, signed
8" high 255-285

Lowestoft Porcelain

Lowestoft Porcelain

Made at Suffolk, England, from about 1757 to the early 1800s; it is also claimed that the porcelain pieces were imported from China

235

(continued)

and only decorated in England. If this is so, it should be designated as Chinese porcelain.

Basket, blue decoration, floral, 9″ dia.	$260-285
Bowl, pink/yellow florals, medallions, front and back, 10″ dia.	370-420
Coffeepot, lighthouse, gold trim, initial A	260-282
Cup/saucer, demitasse	99-112
Cup/saucer, Horn-of-Plenty, demitasse	99-130
Cup/saucer, rose decor (ill.)	70- 80
Platter, blue decoration, 12″ dia.	160-180
Teapot, floral, Famille Rose pattern, 6½″ high	370-420

Lustre Art Glass

Lustre Art Glass

Conrad Vahlsing made this glass in the 1920s. He was a son-in-law of Martin Bach, Sr., who made the famous Quezal glass. Vahlsing's glass is most collectible today. Specific prices would be the same as Quezal. See **Quezal.**

Lustres

Lustres

These vaselike vessels with hanging prisms were decorative devices for holding candles and were intended as mantel and tabletop pieces. They were made of every type of glass. Usually the glass was Bristol or Bristol type, in every color.

Blue/white enamel floral, cut glass prisms, 10″, pr.	$320-370
Bohemian glass, one row crystal prisms, 1890, 14″ tall	340-370
Bristol, blue ground, yellow/green decor, 11″ high, pr.	326-360
Cranberry, gold enameled decor, cut glass prisms, 14″ high, pr.	500+
Enameled decor, gold, ruby, single row of prisms	370-395
Green, medallion, flowers, prisms, 12″ high, pr.	440-490
White-cut-to-cranberry, prisms, pr.	420+

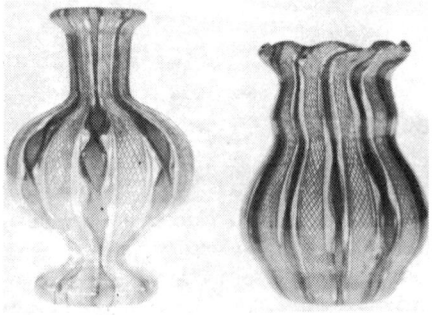

Lutz-type Glass

Lutz-type Glass

Nicholas Lutz came from St. Louis, France, in 1860 to work for Dorflinger at White Mills, Pennsylvania. It's really impossible to distinguish his articles of glass from those of other capable glassworkers of the same period. He also worked at Sandwich.

Basket, threaded, ruffled, 6¼″ dia.	$ 92-107
Bowl, berry, threaded, ruffled and crimped	120-140
Bowl, finger, apricot color	150-170
Compote, spiral striped, blue/white, 13½″ high	520+
Cup/saucer, demitasse, Latticinio, pink/white	170-192
Dish, bonbon, swirled candy cane, red/blue	165-190

Ewer, spiral striped, blue/
  white, applied pedestal 320-348
Pitcher, blue/gold threading,
  13½″ high 390-440
Plate, pale blue, gold twisted
  thread, pink ground 125-145
Tumbler, blue/gold, white,
  striped, flared lip 170-190
Vase, white clear, blue threads,
  4″ (ill.) 210-245
Vase, white diagonal threads,
  7½″ high 195-240
Vase, white frosted, embossed
  cranberry threads, 4″ high
  (ill.) . . . . 240+

Lycett

The Lycett family decorated china for four generations. They came from England to the U.S. in the 19th century. President Lincoln commissioned them to decorate the dinner service for his second inauguration. Their formula for gold decoration was secret and has never been copied.

Maastricht Ware

Maastricht Ware

This is a Dutch product made in Holland from the 1830s until the end of the 19th century. The English taught the Dutch how to make it. Petrus Regout and Company are again making this fine product. The sphynx with the firm's name is on all pieces.

Breakfast set, cup/saucer, plate,
  dike scene, all . . . . $ 40- 52
Cup/saucer, orange/black, dike
  scene 44- 52
Dish, blue/orange, deep, 9″ dia. . . 40- 50
Plate, blue, castle scene, signed
  Regout Company 41- 52
Plate, flow blue, 8½″ dia., pr. 34- 44
Plate, Liberation 54- 62

Platter, red/green flowers, yellow
  ground, 12½″ long 42- 52
Tea tile, Oriental scene, Regout
  Company 29- 38
Tureen, large, white, includes
  ladle 54- 63

Magazines

Magazines

Antique Magazine, April 1927 . . . $ 13- 18
The Art Journal of America, 18
  issues, 1875-1876, large engrav-
  ing in each issue, all 135-145
Colliers, 1939-1949 . . . . 70- 80
The Cottage Hearth, Feb. 1883 . . 12- 19
Country Gentleman, 1919-1926,
  all 62- 72
The Delineator, Oct. 1895, illus-
  trations colored w/crayon 7- 12
Godey's Lady's Book, 1840s,
  7 color plates 40- 47
Good Housekeeping, 1924-1940,
  all 145-170
House Beautiful, 1920-1925, all . . 62- 72
Ladies Home Journal, 1915
  through 1925, all 80- 90
The Ladies World, 1914-1919 . . . . 60- 70
Life, 1915-1919, all 68- 80
Life (ill.) 6- 9
McCall's Magazine, 1920s 1.50- 2
McClures, Nov. 1904 . . . . 8- 12
Needlecraft Magazine, Sept.
  1923 . . . . 9- 15
The New Yorker, 1932-1942, all . . 110-120
Peterson's, 1867, 12 color plates . 37- 48
Pictorial Review, 1921 through
  1924, all 32- 42

(continued)

The Red Book, Jan. 1906 . . . .   8- 12
Theater Magazine, 1911-1915,
  all 78- 88
The Travel Companion, 3 issues,
  all 14- 28
The Youth's Companion, 1922, 6
  issues, all 42- 52

Generally, magazines are priced, depending on the year, condition, etc., at $2 to $5. If you're lucky, you'll find a Frank Leslie leather-bound with color fashion plates, $55-$70.

Magic Lanterns

These were the forerunners of home movie machines. They operated on kerosene or candles and probably caused more than one fire in their day. Most came from Germany during the late 1800s until the early 1900s.

8-slide candle, reflector, lens . . . . $ 60- 70
11-slide, kerosene, reflector, lens,
  tin 80- 87
5-slide, candle, tin, lens 62- 72
24-slide, electrified, 1920s 80- 90
Average price, each slide 3- 6

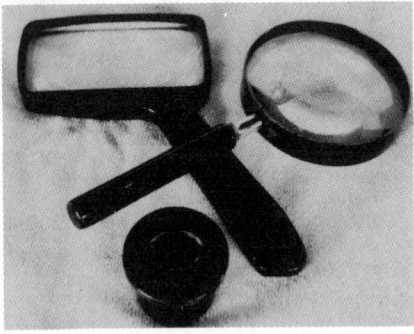

Magnifying Collectibles

Magnifying Collectibles

Old microscopes, magnifying glasses, and the like are all collectible today. If the lens is pre-World War I German, it's even more valuable. Check with a doctor friend or ask the hospitals where they trade their older models for the newer type microscopes.

Majolica

This is a soft pottery or faience covered with a glossy coating turned opaque by treating it with tin oxide. It was made as early as the 12th century, later in most European

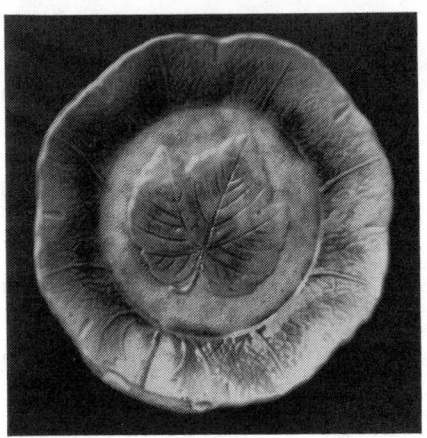

Majolica

countries. Most of what you find today is from the mid-1800s. Griffin, Smith and Hill made it in the U.S. in the late 1800s and A & P stores gave it away as premiums at that time. They called it Etruscan and it was marked GSH in script on the bottom.

Cake stand, sunflowers,
  American, GSH . . . . $ 82- 92
Compote, sunflowers, American,
  GSH 74- 83
Creamer, green/yellow, lovebirds,
  pink lining 84- 98
Cup/saucer, cobalt/yellow, brown
  ground, handleless 88- 92
Cuspidor, blue ground, fruit
  decor, 6½" high 70- 80
Dish, leaf, Etruscan mark,
  American, GSH 60- 70
Figurine, girl and boy playing,
  8" high, pr.   108-118
Humidor, Turk, 7" high   90-100
Jar, tobacco, floral decor, pink/
  green, pipe on lid, 6" high 75- 85
Jardiniere, flower design, stand,
  28" high   112-118
Jug, blue ground, dog, children,
  pewter lid, 7½" high 57- 67
Match holder, Negro boy, 6½"
  high   135-145
Pitcher, child with dog, 7" high . .   40- 50
Pitcher, fern pattern 48- 58
Plate, leaf pattern (ill.) 58- 65
Plate, shell/seaweed, Etruscan
  Majolica, 7" dia.   97-107
Platter, leaf decor, 12" long 62- 72
Spooner, shelf/seaweed, pink/
  green glazes. Etruscan
  Majolica   97-120

Sugar, cauliflower cover,
    Etruscan, GSH, American 52- 62
Syrup, pewter top 37- 47
Tea set, teapot, sugar, creamer,
    sunflowers, brown ground 220-230
Teapot, shell/seaweed, pink/
    green glazes, 6″ high 195-220
Toothpick, 3-handle, brown/
    green 37- 46
Vase, two monkeys, green
    ground 88- 92

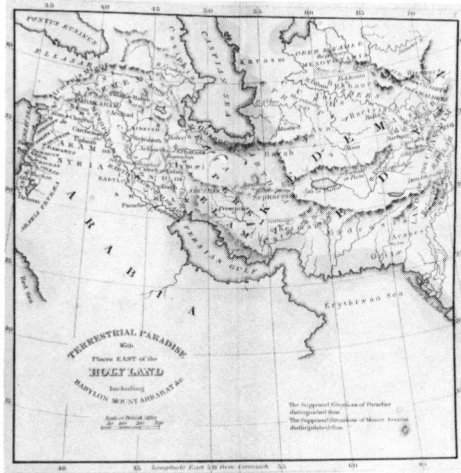

Maps

Maps

The older the better. A lot of guessing went into making maps many years ago. Today, examples of these maps are highly collectible.

Africa $35-50
Arkansas, double folio, color,
    Bradley's Atlas, 1886,
    22″×15″ 19-29
Balkan States, L.L. Poates
    Engraving Co., 1921,
    9¼″×11¼″ 9-14
Central America, color,
    Worldwide Encyclopedia,
    10¼″×7½″ 7-12
Florida/N. & S. Car./Ala. by
    George F. Cram, Chicago,
    1889 17-26
France, color, 1873, 8¾×5⅝″ 15-19
Holland and Belgium, color,
    9″×11¾″ 15-23
Holy Land, from Bible Atlas,
    published by Newton Case,
    1832 (ill.) 11-18
State maps of Arizona, Wyoming/

Idaho, North Dakota, Louisiana, Iowa/Minnesota, New
Jersey, by C.S. Hammond &
Co., New York, 1914,
10½″×13″, ea. 8-11

Marble

Marble

This is a hard, crystalline or granular metamorphic limestone, white or variously colored, sometimes streaked. It will take a high polish. Don't confuse it with alabaster.

Chinese coolie, contemporary,
    6¾″ high (ill.) .... $. 34- 43
Collie dog, 9″ long 26- 36
Elephant bookends, 7½″ high,
    pr. 32- 42
Lion-on-pedestal, 8″ high 31- 41
Mother cat with kittens, 7″ long . 38- 47
Penguin bookends, 6″ high, pr. .. 35- 46
Rooster, 4½″ high 19- 27
Tiger, 8″ high 31- 40
Urn, flower motif, 12½″ high 38- 48
Vase, fluted lip, 11″ high 30- 40

Marble Glass

This was an addled or opaque glass. Usually worked on a blower's pipe, it was then sprinkled with pulverized, colored glass flux. When reheated, it was finished in the regular way. It was made by various firms in England around 1893. Collectible today.

Marblehead Pottery

It could be called "therapy" pottery as it was first made by convalescing patients in a sanitarium at Marblehead, Massachusetts, in 1904. About three years later a plant was

(continued)

established, and although Herbert J. Hall, M.D., is credited with its founding, Arthur E. Baggs was responsible for the actual production. Most pieces are marked with an incised sailing ship and MP, although others have the initials A.B. incised. Paper labels were also used. Matt-glazed and tin-enameled faience were two of the several finishes used. The plant closed in 1936 and Mr. Baggs took a position at Ohio State University.

Bowl, 3½" dia., blue glaze	$ 39- 99
Tile, blue, sailing ship signature, 4¾" square	150-168
Vase, bulbous, matt green ground, brown/yellow/black, 7" high	100-109
Vase, matt gray, "tree" design, 12½" high	81- 90
Vase, medium green matt ground, geometric design, 3½" high	64- 72
Vase, mirror blue ground, high glaze, 5½" high, ship signature	69- 79

Marbles

Marbles

Glass companies in Pennsylvania and Ohio made the large glass marbles used by boys at the turn of the century. Some had colored stripes while others had animals inside. The larger are more collectible than the smaller.

Agate, black/white, ½" dia.	$ 18-	25
Agate, brown/white, ⅞" dia.	19-	27
Agate, green/white, ¾" dia.	16-	24
Bennington, mottled or fancy, 1¼" dia.	3-	6
China, bull's-eye, ⅝" dia.	7-	11
China, leaves, ½" dia.	9-	14
China, leaves, ⅞" dia.	9-	14
Goldstone, ⅝" dia.	27-	36
Kayo (comic strip), black/white	29-	35
Limestone, ⅝" dia.	4-	8
Multicolored swirl (ill.)	10-	16
Sandy (comic strip), blue/white	29-	35
Sulphide, baby (all positions)	98-112	

Sulphide, boar	88-110
Sulphide, boy on stump	105-116
Sulphide, cat, lying down	98-112
Sulphide, cat, sitting	86- 95
Sulphide, cow, grazing	94-115
Sulphide, frog	110-116
Sulphide, girl and dog	106-113
Sulphide, goat	77- 86
Sulphide, lamb (ill.)	73- 83
Sulphide, owl, wings spread	128-135
Sulphide, ram	76- 85
Sulphide, rooster, running	74- 83
Sulphide, rooster, standing	57- 65
Swirls, Latticinio, onionskin, ea.	48- 56

Mary Gregory

Mary Gregory

We know that she did exist and that she did work for the Boston & Sandwich Glass Company on Cape Cod. Obviously, she didn't decorate all those pieces attributed to her. She never tinted her fingers and/or costumes. They were always white. Look for children, 5 to 12. Tinted figures must be called Mary Gregory type and were made in Europe in the mid-1880s. No collector should buy this glass as original before talking to an expert. Lots of repros.

Barber bottle, blue, boy playing with kite, all white figure	$185-	220
Biscuit jar, girl on swing, all white figure, blue glass	150-	170
Jewel box, black, girl in tree, all white figure	158-	178
Lamp, black, girl on the tree limb, all white figure	400-	475
Mug, cranberry, girl jumping rope, all white figure	165-	180

Perfume, cranberry, ITP, girl on swing, all white	158- 172
Pitcher, cranberry, boy with hoop, all white figure	270- 298
Pitcher, 6 tumblers, cranberry, ITP, girl and boy in tree, all white figure	300- 380
Rose bowl, girl, all white figure	165- 180
Tumble-up (carafe with tumbler), boy, all white figure	265-300
Vase, clear, girl rolling hoop, all white figure	120- 135
Vase, girl on swing, all white figure	360- 380
Vase, green, boy with butterfly net, all white figure	90- 108
Vase, ruby, boy holding horn, ITP, 9″ high (ill.)	800-1,100

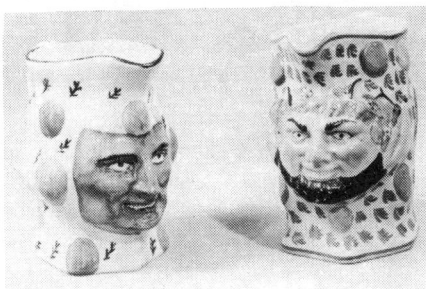

Mask Jugs

Mask Jugs

These are old English Lustre pottery types. Many firms made them in the late 1700s and early 1800s, Leeds Pottery, also Thomas Harley at Longton. They're scarce today. Though hard to find, a few are still around, especially in American shops specializing in English imports.

Masks

Witch doctors and devil's brew! Hand-carved wooden masks come from every country in the world. Most of the old ones are in museums, but lately good examples of the art have been showing up in antiques shops. Mentioned here because people are beginning to collect them as antiques. Good haunting!

Masonic Items

These were commemorative or souvenir pieces, usually made of red/clear glass, though some were made of metal and/or pottery. Late 1800s until World War I.

Champagne glass, Minneapolis, Minn., 1905	$ 27- 37
Cup, loving, 3-handle, Solomon's Lodge, Philadelphia, 1910	58- 68
Cup, Syria temple, 1905	44- 52
Goblet, clear, Syria Temple, Lexington, Ky., 1908	21- 31
Goblet, Syria Temple, 1909	54- 62
Jar, tobacco, emblem on lid, signed, dated, Royal Bayreuth	122-150
Mold, ice cream	27- 37
Mug, Lulu Temple, 1906	34- 44
Plate, Albany, N.Y., 1914	34- 42
Plate, Philadelphia, 1911, 9″ dia. .	32- 40
Spoon, Islam Temple, San Francisco, 1902	19- 27

Mason's Patent Ironstone

Mason's Patent Ironstone

The Mason family first started making porcelain in 1802. It was 1813 before they made Ironstone, when Charles J. Mason took out his famous Ironstone patent. It was in a sense porcelain, as described in the patent. In reality it was a heavy, hard, opaque earthenware. G.M. and C.J. Mason, 1813-1829, was the first mark used; then C.J. Mason and Company, 1829-1844; and C.J. Mason, 1845-1848. The firm went bankrupt in 1848. Ashworth and Brothers, Hanley, England, produces a Mason-type ware today.

Bowl, red scene, early mark . . . . . $	55- 63
Butter dish, Chinese decor	70- 79
Creamer, Chinese decor, 1819-1844 mark, 5½″ high	71- 81
Creamer, miniature, red flowers, blue underglaze (ill.) 2¾″ high .	80- 90

(continued)

Jug, Chinese decor, 6¼″ high,
early mark 54- 63
Pickle dish, Oriental pattern 30- 40
Pin tray, Oriental scene, 1829-
1844 mark, 6″ long 49- 60
Plate, American naval scene,
early mark 77- 86
Plate, Oriental pattern, 1829-
1844 mark 47- 56
Platter, Japanese scene, 14″
long 46- 53
Teapot, red flowers, blue under-
glaze, 8½″ high 54- 64
Tureen, red/blue flowers 68- 70

Match Holders

Match Holders

In the days of Lucifers or "house burners" (sulphur-headed matches), match holders were in vogue and were used to hold matches on the wall or the table. Used from mid-1800s until early 1930s. Many repros.

Bird, 4½″ high, iron . . . . $ 35- 45
Boots, china, green/yellow, 4½″
high 32- 41
Bulldog's head, porcelain,
Austria 34- 42
Butterfly, milk glass, 5″ high . . . 36- 46
Cast iron, c. 1880s 22- 30
Charlie Chaplin, clear glass (rare) . 71- 80
Cricket, brass, hinged lid 38- 46
Dog, stump holds matches, iron . 28- 37
Elephant, clear glass 31- 40
Flower basket, iron 30- 40
Grape leaf, 3″ high, milk glass . . . 31- 40
Indian head, 6″ high, hangs on
wall, milk glass 45- 54
Jenny Lind, clear glass 61- 70
Man with cane by tree stump,
china, Germany 23- 33
"Matches" hangs on wall, tin,
5½″ high (ill.) 22- 31
Rooster, hand-painted, Austria,
china 32- 39

Two-compartment w/striker, tin,
hanging type, 5″ high (ill.) 16- 27

Match Safes

Match Safes

They did just that—kept the matches safe when in one's pocket. Usually metal with a snap lid or cap, they were inexpensive when purchased. See **Silver.**

Brass, bulldog, hinged . . . . $ 49- 58
Flower/leaves, Germany 14- 19
Papier-mache, painted figures . . . 18- 26
Philadelphia Centennial, silver,
3″ high, hinged 47- 54
Sterling silver, 3″ high (ill.) 52- 61
Sterling silver, whiskey adver-
tisement, bottle-shaped 32- 41
Tin, many types, average 12- 19

Mayer, T.J. and J., Pottery

Mayer, T.J. and J., Pottery

The year 1829 was the beginning of this

242

fine china company. The coats-of-arms of the 13 original states are especially collectible. Stoke, Staffordshire, England.

Bowl, scalloped and embossed
 rim, 10½", Arms of Maryland . $740-790
Cup plate, 4½", South Carolina . . 220-260
Plate, 8¾", Arms of Rhode
 Island 275-370
Platter, 19", New Jersey 720-775
Soup plate, 9½"-10", New York . 160-175
Vegetable dish, 8",
 Massachusetts 720-780

McCoy Pottery

McCoy Pottery

This pottery has been made in Roseville, Ohio, since 1910. In 1967 the firm was acquired by the Mt. Clemens (Michigan) Pottery Co. Early pieces are now becoming collectible.

Blossomtime 700 Line
Jardiniere, ivory, sq., 4" tall . . . . . $ 15- 24
Planter, ivory 17- 26
Vase, ivory, McCoy, 6¼" 11- 15
Vase, yellow, concave sides, 8" . . 16- 21
Butterfly Line
Planter, rose (leaf relief only), 8" . 10- 19
Spoon rest, green, NM USA 15- 22
Cookie Jars
Bear #22 . . . . 53- 62
Black antique stove 29- 38
Blue windmill 19- 27
Have a Happy Day (smile) 32- 41
Honey bear 29- 38
Mr. and Mrs. Owl 40- 50
Rocking horse 42- 51
Flowerpots
Dark green Double Beetle band . . 14- 22
Green basketweave #2, 3¼" 10- 16
Green, long leaves and dots, 3½"
 dia.×3½" tall, NM 12- 19

Green, long leaves, two, 3 3¾"
 dia., 2¾" tall, NW 12- 17
Orange Double Beetle band, 5" . . 14- 19
Springwood Line
Bowl, 4-ftd., pink, 6⅝" dia.,
 McCoy USA 11 20
Jardiniere, pink, 5⅜", McCoy
 USA 18- 23
Vase, green, round bottom, sq.
 top, 7¼", McCoy USA 11- 19
Swirl Line
Planter, orchid, ftd., 7" long,
 McCoy USA 8- 11
Vase, orchid, ftd., 7" tall, McCoy
 USA 9- 15
Tea Set Items
Creamer, pink/turquoise, matt,
 McCoy 8- 11
Leaf creamer, 2-tone green, #108
 (ill.) 10- 19
Pinecone green/brown, 3-pc.,
 McCoy 40- 48
Pinecone green creamer 13- 19
Pinecone green teapot and lid . . . 21- 30
Pinecone teapot, no lid, light
 crazing in and out 19- 27
Tea set, 3-pc., green/brown 40- 48
Teapot lid, as above 10- 17
Vases
Butterfly vase, 7", McCoy 15- 21
Cornucopia, cream, light crazing,
 7", McCoy 17- 27
Dark green vase, ftd., 10-sided,
 7¼"×4½", McCoy USA 15- 19
Flowers and Leaf Blades, green,
 handled, 8" 14- 22
Handled, ftd. vase, turquoise,
 Stylized Leaf and Twig, 9" . . . 16- 22
S&H/Peppers, pr. 14- 19
Swan vase, pink, 9", McCoy 15- 23

McKinley Act, 1891

Required that the name of the country of origin appear on all imports into the U.S.A.

Medals, U.S. and Foreign

Ever since the handmade silver medal was given by Congress to the three men responsible for the capture of a British officer connected with Benedict Arnold, the U.S. has been giving out medals for just about everything. The British, French, Italians, and Germans are also "medal happy." It should be noted that any medal made of sterling silver has gone up in value, just for the silver content.

(continued)

Medals, U.S. and Foreign

Medical Items

Old instruments, bottles, prescriptions, books—all are of special interest today, especially to one allied with the field of medicine.

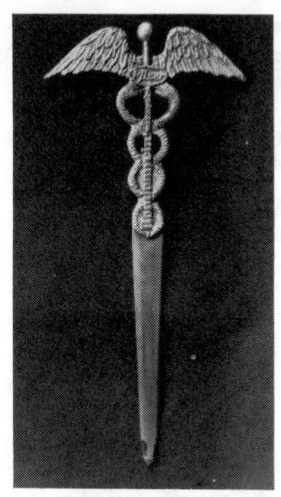

Medical Items

Meissen, Onion Pattern

Meissen

See **Dresden China.**

Meissen, Onion Pattern

Originally known as Bulb pattern, it's more commonly called Onion pattern today. A whiteware with cobat decorations, it was made in the latter part of the 19th century. Reproductions from Europe are causing havoc for the uninformed collector.

Baby feeder, 6¾″ long (ill.)	$ 26-	34
Bowl, 6″ dia.	43-	51
Bowls, 7″, 8″ square, pierced edges	60-	70
Breadboard	34-	42
Butter dish, covered	115-	140
Candleholders, 4¼″ high (ill.), pr.	57-	64
Creamer, individual and porridge, 3½″ to 5½″ high	50-	60
Cheese dish, covered	130-	138
Cup/saucer, coffee (ill.)	27-	37
Cup/saucer, demitasse	32-	41
Cup/saucer, tea	27-	36
Egg cup	22-	30
Plate, 8″ dia.	32-	41
Plate, chop, 14″ long	94-	103
Plate, soup, 9″ dia.	42-	50
Platter, 12″ long	105-	114
Rolling pin	51-	60
Salt, master, footed 3¼″ dia.	60-	70
Sauce, 4¾″ dia.	21-	31
Teapot with matching tile	140-	148
Tureen, soup, Crossed Swords	169-	178
Vase, scroll feet, 6½″ high	64-	73
Vegetable dish, covered, 10″ square	132-	141

Many other pieces made in the Onion pattern.

Mercury Glass

Silver nitrate was sloshed around inside double-walled objects of glass, then the entrance hole was sealed. As air seeped in, the

Mercury Glass

"mercury" flaked off, leaving an unpleasant-looking object. Made in England and the U.S., late 1800s.

Bowl, gilt interior, 5″ high	$ 50-	60
Bowl, 6″ dia.	52-	60
Bowl, 6″ dia., painted flowers, 6″ high	64-	72
Candleholder, signed Perdue, 8″ high	40-	49
Creamer, clear handle, quadruple plate spout, 8½″ high (ill.)	79-	89
Dish, sweetmeats, sectioned	19-	28
Ornament, Christmas, grapes, 2½″ dia.	10-	17
Pitcher, clear handle, 12½″ high	90-	100
Salt, footed	37-	46
Spooner	57-	67
Sugar shaker, metal cup	58-	68
Tieback, curtain, flower decor, pr.	34-	42
Vase, blue/clear, painted flowers on front, 8″ high, pr.	47-	56
Vase, floral bands, castle scene painted on front, 9½″ high pr.	77-	86
Wig stand, pedestal base, 10″ high (ill.)	88-	94

Mettlach

Jean Francois Boch founded the Mettlach

245

(continued)

Mettlach

pottery in 1809 in an old abbey named Abbey Mediolacum ("Between the Lakes") from which the name Mettlach was derived. In 1841, the Nicholas Villeroy family joined the Boch family. V & B developed the technique of overglaze painting—firing a particular piece at 2400 degrees, then low firing other colors at lower temperatures; thus allowing the use of many colors and holding the same true color in stein after stein. V & B introduced many other techniques, pioneering the way for many of the world's famous potters. The main factory at Mettlach burned in 1921 and was never rebuilt. All attempts at reproducing this great pottery have failed; what is on the market today should fool absolutely no one. The Black Forest stein is considered the choicest collector's item, bringing over $5,000 when found and authenticated. Baskets, beakers, bowls, flagons, jugs, mugs, pitchers, plaques, tumblers, and urns were also made, but the stein made V & B world-famous. Serious Mettlach collectors collect by the number. Stein Collectors International is a great club to join. See **Clubs to Join.**

Plaques

#1044—a large series—
most plaques with this
number sell . . . . $ 275- 325
#1384 . . . . 875- 950
#1920 . . . . 750- 850
#2195 . . . . 720- 800

#2442, 2443, 2445, ea. 760- 830
#3131 . . . . 210- 220
#3163, 3164, ea. 820- 900
#7025, signed "Stahl" . . . . . 3,450+
#7040, 7041, 7043, 7045, ea. 2,300-2,700
#7066 . . . . 450- 550

Steins

#368, ½ L (liter—1.0567
liquid quarts) 425- 500
#406, ½ L 320- 350
#485, 1 L 375- 400
#675, ¼ L 180- 210
#675, ½ L 260- 280
#1052, ½ L 450- 495
#1069 . . . . 725- 800
#1095, ½ L 310- 370
#1100, ¼ L 295- 328
#1104, 1½ L 325- 365
#1157, 1 L 420- 440
#1164, ½ L 420- 470
#1266, ½ L 160- 175
#1286, 5½" high (V & B) . . . 420- 480
#1498, 5 L 2,800-3,200
#1526—a large series —
½, 1, 3 L 240- 450
#1536, ½ L 400- 450
#1655, ½ L 510- 550
#1786, 1 L 1,000-1,100
#1863, ½ L 540- 585
#1909, 3/10 L 165- 195
#1932, ½ L 575- 685
#1941, 3 L 1,900-2,400
#2027, ½ L 575- 625
#2035, ½ L 490- 580
#2044, ½ L 480- 540
#2086, ½ L 320- 385
#2089, ½ L 510- 585
#2122, 5 L 2,800-3,000
#2181, ¼ L 245- 285
#2184, 3/10 L 500- 540
#2391, ½ L 455- 520
#2479, ½ L 720- 800
#2500, ½ L 700- 800
#2556, 1 L 475- 525
#2582, ½ L 465- 525
#2768, ½ L 435- 485
#2802, ½ L 1,700-1,950
#2878, 1 L 600- 700
#2912, ½ L 350- 420
#2938, 1 L 560- 640
#2950, ½ L 585- 700
#2958, 3 L 1,400-1,600
#3091, ½ L 520- 600
#3099, 5 L 5,700-6,800
#3168, ½ L 520- 620

Obviously, hundreds and hundreds more. You're mixing with the professionals when you collect Mettlach steins, so read up and save up.

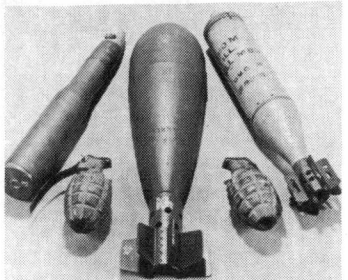

Military Collectibles

Military Collectibles

Items from the Revolutionary War on have long been collectible. Nazi items are now collectible, as will be items from the Korean and Vietnam conflicts. Also, see **Japanese War Items** and **Nazi War Items**.

Armband, English firefighter, World War II	$ 18- 27
Bayonet and scabbard for Enfield rifle, World War II	42- 52
Bayonet with leather sheath, Civil War, Union Army	60- 70
Belt buckle, brass CSA	41- 50
Canteen, clay (throwaway type), Union Army stamp, brown	98-130
Canteen, U.S. Cavalry, Civil War	85- 95
Flag, Union Jack, English, World War I, 40″×28″	48- 60
Helmet, English, World War I	38- 49
Helmet, English, World War II	32- 41
Saddle, McClellan type, Union Army, Civil War	140-170

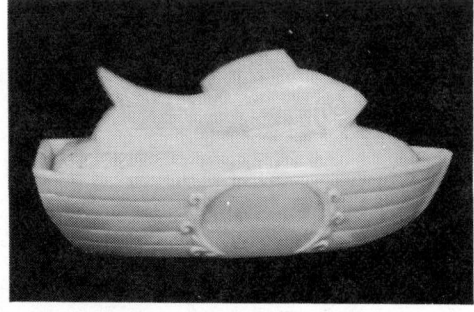

Milk Glass

Milk Glass

See **Pattern Glass Section** for specific pieces and prices. Prices for a few selected items are given here.

Battleship Maine, white milk glass	$130-150

Milk Glass

Dolphin condiment dish, opalescent, 3¾″ high, scroll beadwork	74- 83
Drum and cannon, covered dish	84-100
Eagle on nest, "The American Hen," covered dish, white opalescence, 4½″ high	89- 94
Fish, covered dish (ill.)	75- 85
Hand and dove, covered dish	87-110
Uncle Sam, covered dish	100-120

A huge collection of milk glass can be seen at the Houston Museum, Chattanooga, Tenn. Reproductions have ruined this as a serious collector's item.

Millefiori Glass

Millefiori Glass

This ornamental glass was made by fusing together slender canes or rods of glass, then cutting across them in small sections. These sections then were imbedded in the glass object being made. Lots of companies made it, here and abroad, mid-1800s on. General collectors will have a difficult time telling the old from the new. The paperweights are especially hard to distinguish. Watch out! Still being made on the island of Murano, Italy.

Basket, blues/greens, small	$175-200
Bowl, 2 handles, 2″ high	125-142
Box, covered, 3″ high	180-195
Chocolate pot, 9″ high, no cups	175-185

247

(continued)

Creamer, red flower spray,
striped handle 182-192
Cup/saucer, demitasse 172-182
Cruet, cut glass stopper, 6" high . 360-390
Inkwell, paperweight base 250-300
Goblet, clear stem 185-210
Globe, lamp, 4" dia. 175-190
Lamp, has matching shade, 14"
high 240-260
Rose bowl, fluted lip, 6½" high . . 140-150
Salt, open, master, 6 small 310-370
Tumbler, 4" high (ill.) 92-107
Vase, 4" high 140-155
Vase, 4" high, scalloped top 155-170
Vases, handled (ill.), ea. 85- 95

Minton

Miniatures

Miniatures

In the mid-1800s salesmen carried miniatures of their products: furniture, carriages,
any bulky item. Anything miniature is collectible today: dollhouse furniture, pressed
glass dollhouse dishes, and other items.

Bowl, blue porcelain, 1½" dia. . . . $ 24- 33
Bucket, pressed glass, metal bail
handle, 2" high 20- 31
Candlestick, brass, 1½" high, pr.   22- 31
Coal hod, brass 25- 35
Cowbell, brass, 7/8" 32- 40
Flatiron, on trivet (rare), 2½"
long 49- 60
Furniture, cabinet, rosewood,
German, 19th century 100-120
Jug, water, brass, ¾" high 19- 27
Kettle, handle, brass, 1½" high . . 17- 26
Lamp, clear, Thistle Panel, with
chimney, 3½" high 37- 46
Toby jug (ill.) 6- 9

MINTON
YEARLY MARKS

Impressed in the clay to show year of manufactu
42—1942 inclusive. The figures 43 etc. have been us
1943 onwards.

Minton Yearly Marks

Minton

This factory, established in England
around 1793, continues today under the same
name. Early pieces were incised with the
firm's name and are highly collectible now.
Their Yearly Marks are shown here.

Bowl and pitcher, blue, leaves,
flowers, marked $300-350

Bowl, lapis blue, wild vines/
   leaves, 9" dia. 146-157
Butter dish, covered, floral motif . 140-160
Chocolate pot, white, etched/gold
   trim, marked 160-180
Compote, enameled roses, signed,
   8" high 165-190
Cup/saucer, demitasse, blue decor
   panels in gold rims 92-102
Egg cup, floral motif 29- 38
Jug, blue/white Jasper, 4½" high . 70- 80
Pitcher, water, grapes, gold
   decor, 11" high, marked 162-172
Plate, Tree of Life pattern, 6½"
   dia. (ill.) 54- 63
Teapot, sugar, creamer, white/
   gold trim, red roses, marked . . 125-145
Tile, blue/white, 6" sq. 48- 58
Vase, birds and flowers, 7½"
   high 170-185
Vase, brown/green/turquoise,
   10" high 220-240
Vase, farm scene, blue, 5½"
   high, impressed mark 230-240

Mug, large, blue and gray bands,
   seaweed design, 6" high (ill.) . . 190-220
Mug, multicolored, 3¾" high (ill.) 180-197
Mug, red ground, black/blue/
   cream mottling, green-
   threaded top 185-200
Mug, Tree pattern, 5" high 185-200
Mug, white ground, blue bands,
   5" high 210-225
Pitcher, syrup, ferns/leaves,
   8½" high 285-300
Pitcher, water, tan/black/white,
   4" high 270-310
Salt shaker, earthworm design . . 92-107
Sugar bowl, trees, green band,
   5½" high 270-295

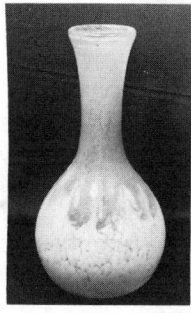

Monart Glass

Monart Glass

This glass was made in Scotland after World War I. Its style is considered Art Deco. Small pieces of embedded colored glass show through the heavy body.

Bowl, 4" dia., pink/blue/green,
   dark green swirls $110-145
Vase, 5½" high, red to mottled
   brown, green rim 148-178
Vase, 10¾" high, Cluthra type,
   green to mottled light blue,
   ground pontil (ill.) 450-500

Mont Joy

This is cameo and enameled glass made at Pantin, France, by the same firm that produced De Vez.

Bowl, frosted body with
   enameled flowers, signed,
   3¾" dia. $270-320
Rose bowl, ruffled lip, cameo cut
   back, enameled lavender
   violets, gold leaves, 5" high,
   signed Mont Joy (ill.) 180-195
Vase, bud, carved, red poppies,
   purple ground, 20" high 370-400

Mocha Ware

Mocha Ware

Similar to Leeds Ware, Mocha is usually cream colored and decorated with seaweed, worms, or other such "lovely" items, in various colors on bands of blue, tan, red. It was first made in Tunstall, England, in the late 1700s to the 1800s by William Adams, later by his son. Apparently it was never marked.

Bowl, earthworm, blue/red,
   7" dia. $235-265
Bowl, seaweed band, blue,
   8½" dia. 400-450
Bowl, tan/blue/white, feather
   bands, 5" wide 272-292
Chamber pot, creamware, blue/
   green, brown bands 300-340
Dish, master salt, green bands,
   leaf handle 170-178
Jug, seawed design, 5" high 200-220

249

(continued)

Vase, enameled iris, buds, gold
leaves, acid-etched ground,
6" high 280-320
Vase, flowers, gilded, frosted
green, signed, 11" high 485-515
Vase, mottled orange/black
ground, signed, 11½" high ... 345-410

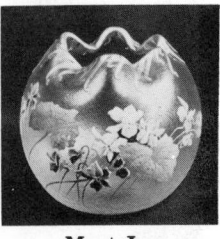

Mont Joy

Moorcroft Pottery

Moorcroft Pottery

This is a modern English pottery which, for
some unexplainable reason, is highly collectible. Factory established in 1913 by William
Moorcroft at Cobridge. Script signature.

Ashtray, red/yellow flowers,
script signature ....$ 34- 43
Basket, metal holder, 6" dia.,
green flowers 70- 80
Bowl, blue/white decor, fruit 64- 73
Bowl, pewter foot, 6¼" dia., fruit
decor, lavender/yellow/red/
green (ill.) 62- 72
Box, covered, orange/maroon,
4½" dia. 70- 80
Compote, green ground, purple
flowers, 4½" high 70- 78
Cup/saucer, fruit decor green
script 59- 68
Inkwell, blue background,
signed 77- 79
Tea set: pot, sugar bowl,
creamer, blue ground. All have
pewter lids 260-285
Vase, bud, light/dark green,
trees, 8" high, script signature 210-220

Moriage

Not a specific company but a definition
that applies to Japanese ceramics that have
applied clay (slip) decorations. This type of
decoration has been used for more than 200
years and is quite predominant on export
wares produced since the Nippon era
(1891-1921). Designs include lacy effects,
border trimmings, birds, animals, floral

decor, and landscapes. The most popular is
the jewel-eyed slip trailed dragon. Workmanship dictates the value.

Cup/saucer, butterflies, green
M in wreath, Nippon ....$ 47- 58
Hatpin holder, 6" high, floral
panels 50- 60
Pitcher, 12½" high, jewel-eyed
dragon 230-240
Plate, 8" dia., green/yellow
flowers 60- 67
Teapot, dragon motif, Blue
Maple Leaf, Nippon 82- 91
Vase, flowers, gold trim, 10½"
high, green M in wreath,
Nippon 160-175
Vase, 14½" high, jewel-eyed
dragon, green M in wreath 260-290
Vase, peacock, floral decor,
11½" high, Double T
Diamond mark .... 200+

Mortars and Pestles

Mortars and Pestles

The Egyptians used a crude form to grind
sacred potions. Usually made of brass or a
hardwood such as lignum vitae or bird's-eye
maple, larger ones served for grinding grain,
smaller ones for pulverizing salt, spices, and
drugs.

Brass, early 1800s (ill.) ....$ 88-115
Iron, late 19th century 55- 63
Ironstone bowl (mortar), wooden
pestle, mid-1800s 70- 80
Wood, bird's-eye maple, early ... 74- 82

Moser Glass

This Art Nouveau glass as well as other
types, some highly enameled, was made by
Ludvig Moser at his factory in Carlsbad,

Moser Glass

Austria, at the turn of the century. Most collectible today.

Bottle, perfume, blue cut to clear,
7¼" high, signed $140-160
Bowl, vintage decor, cranberry,
footed, 7", signed 88- 97
Candlesticks, Alexandrite, cube
type, signed, 10", pr. 280-310
Compote, amethyst, gold border,
7" high 265-285
Compote, cranberry, cut overlay,
signed, 9" high 220-250
Cruet, amethyst to clear,
mushroom stopper, gold band,
5" high 120-135
Decanter, panel cut, signed 122-130
Dresser set, 2 perfumes, hair
holder, tray, jewel box, gold
enameled, all pieces signed 460-495
Goblet, cobalt, jeweled/enameled,
signed 240-265
Jar, tobacco, panels/florals,
leaves, rayed star base 110-140
Toothpick, clear, crystal 70- 78
Vase, amber, gold band of
Amazon women and centaurs,
gold stripes, signed Moser
Karlsbad (ill.) 245-275
Vase, amethyst, clear/intaglio cut
floral, 11" high 385-420
Vase, clear to yellow, top to
bottom decor 140-150
Vase, opalescent blue and white,
enameled leaves and insects,
applied red cherries, 6½" high
(ill.) 525-575

Moss Agate Glass

This is a form of crackled glass and was created by Frederick Carder when he worked for Stevens and Williams in England in the late 1890s. Slightly yellow and very heavy, the orange, yellow, white, and black-colored glass, crushed into a powder and sprinkled on the object while still hot, gave texture to the glass and at the same time created the natural color of moss agate. Rare.

Moss Rose Pattern China

Moss Rose Pattern China

In the mid-1800s, the English potters used this garden flower to decorate certain wares. It was used on ironstone ware for almost 50 years.

Bone dishes, set of 6, all . . . . $ 88- 95
Box, covered, rectangular,
2½"×6" 27- 35
Coffeepot, Johnson Bros., 8½"
high 70- 78
Creamer, 4½" high 34- 42
Cup/saucer, Haviland 32- 40
Cup/saucer, Meakin 23- 30
Dresser set, 4 covered boxes, pr.
candlesticks, pin tray, large
tray, all 145-150
Dresser set, 3 covered boxes,
candlestick, large tray 110-120
Pitcher, Bavaria, 8½" high 42- 50
Pitcher, Haviland, 8" high 58- 62
Pitcher, Ironstone, 9¼" high 47- 53
Plate, Bavaria, 7" dia. 23- 31
Plate, cake, pierced handles,
8¼" dia. 19- 25
Plate, Johnson Bros., 5½" dia. . .   14- 19
Platter, 14"×19", Meakin 45- 53
Platter, 13½"×18¼", American-
made 34- 42
Saucedish, Johnson Bros. 28- 37

251

(continued)

Shaving mug, Austria	32- 41
Shaving mug, Johnson Bros.	31- 40
Sugar bowl, Ironstone	41- 50
Tea set: teapot, sugar, creamer, 8 cups/saucers, tray, all	215-230
Teapot, American-made	35- 41
Teapot, Meakin, 7¾″ high	55- 62
Water set: large bowl, large pitcher, small pitcher, soap dish, toothbrush holder, slop jar, chamber pot (thunder mug), all	550-600

Mother-of-Pearl

Mother-of-Pearl

This beautiful material comes from the abalone, the pearl oyster, and other marine shells. The hard, pearly internal layer is used in the arts and in the making of pearl buttons.

Checkerboard, inlaid abalone, 16″ square	$ 55- 65
Dresser set: brush, comb, hair holder, nail buffer, all	95-110
Frame, sterling silver trim, 11″✕9½″	40- 50
Knife set, 8 pcs., sterling silver trim, all	120-135
Madonna, 6″ high (ill.)	45- 55
Pen, 14k gold nib	10- 14

Motorcycles

The Indian 'cycle once had a self-starter— a Hendee Special; before that, a hand crank. Remember "Cannonball" Baker? He made a fortune in the early days riding motorcycles across the U.S.A., attempting to set records. In 1911, in England the front wheel brake was first introduced—a Wilkinson. Old motorcycles are highly collectible.

1905 Clement (French), running condition, 4-cylinder	$1,700-2,350
1908 Hendee (later, Indian), still runs	3,300-3,800
1909 N.S.U., 7 H.P., poor condition	1,450-1,850
1910 Excelsior Auto-Cycle, excellent condition	2,200-2,700
1911 Henderson, 4-cylinder, good condition	3,600-4,400
1911 Thor, poor condition	1,650-2,250
1912 Emblem, needs work	1,400-2,200
1912 Marvel, good condition	1,700-2,400
1912 Pierce, 4-cylinder, running	1,900-2,700
1913 Merkel, runs	1,600-2,400
1914 Harley-Davidson, good condition	2,700-3,400
1914 Yale, 2-cylinder, poor running condition	1,700-2,400
1922 Cleveland, modified for racing, good condition	1,800-2,700
1923 Evans Power-Cycle, running	1,600-2,300

Mt. Washington Peachblow

Mt. Washington Peachblow

New Bedford, Massachusetts, 1886. It shades from rose color at top to pale blue in lower portion. Don't buy it if you don't know it. Too many repros.

Basket, bride's, 10½″✕ 4¼″, in quadruple-plated frame	$ 650- 725

Biscuit jar, cameo, sterling silver ring, lid, bail	875- 925
Biscuit jar, enameled decor, sterling silver ring, lid, bail	625- 670
Bowl, bride's, footed, glossy finish, 6½" dia.	400- 475
Bowl, finger, fluted edge, acid finish	375- 425
Bowl, rose, fluted lip, 4¼" high, acid finish	375- 425
Butter dish, glossy finish, ITP, glossy finish	1,300-1,375
Creamer, acid finish, applied "rope" handle, 4¼" high	850- 900
Cruet, blown glass stopper, ITP, 6" high (scarce)	2,700+
Cup, punch	425- 455
Cup/saucer, glossy finish . .	575- 610
Darner, pear-shaped, glossy finish	270- 300
Decanter, ITP, 8½" high . .	1,900-2,350
Muffineer, triple-plated cap, 5¼" high	800- 875
Pitcher, applied clear handle, ITP, 9¼" high . .	1,400-1,575
Pitcher, decorated with flowers, acid finish, James Montgomery's poem on side (ill.)	1,700-1,900
Plate, acid finish, 5½" dia. .	225- 260
Plates, set of 6, 5" dia., all	1,300-1,450
Salt/pepper shakers, tomato-shaped, floral decor, pr.	485- 550
Toothpick holder, glossy finish, 4¾" high	400- 425
Toothpick holder, glossy finish, ITP	435- 465
Tumbler, water, glossy finish, ITP	485- 535
Tumbler, whiskey, glossy finish	460- 510

Movie Photos

Shirley Mason, Mabel Normand, Gloria Joy, Hale Hamilton—who remembers them? All were movie stars in their own right. Anyway, photos of movie stars are collectible, especially from the early days—the type given away by drugstores, music stores, etc.

Average price . . . . $	2- 3
If signed (and authenticated)	15- 22
Dedicated to a person	9- 16

Muffineers

Muffineers

Usually made of glass or silver, these containers were used for sifting sugar or cinnamon on muffins. Much larger than a salt shaker, they were popular in England in the late 1800s.

China, cobalt, floral decor, 5¼" high . . . . $	34- 42
China, green/gold, decorated, silver cap	32- 41
Cranberry glass, 5" high	78- 89
Glass, cut, clear, sterling silver top, 7¼" high	72- 81
Opalescent, lid, 6" high (ill.)	34- 41
Porcelain, silver cap, England, Meakin	32- 42
Spanish Lace, raspberry/satin, plated cap, 6" high	70- 80
Sterling silver, 6" high, beaded, 3 curved feet	49- 52

Mugs, Porcelain

Mugs, Porcelain

Used for ale, whisky, tea, every English

(continued)

porcelain firm made them, also other European firms. See specific types for prices.

Mug, pink, red leaves . . . . $ 22- 31

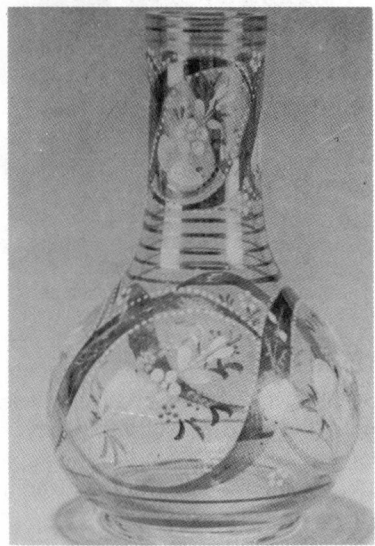

Muller Freres

Muller Freres

The Muller brothers made a fine grade of glass, including cameo, at Luneville and then at Crois Mare, France, from early 1900s until World War II.

Cameo vase, acid cut and
  enamel scenes in brown/yellow/
  lavender, 4" high, signed $425-485
Cameo vase, birds, enameled,
  multicolored, signed 475-540
Lamp, hanging, Art Deco,
  wrought iron frame 525-600
Lamp, table, 2 hanging shades,
  cameo cut leaves 850-925
Vase, ringed neck, enameled,
  flower decor (ill.) 240-260

Music Boxes

The Swiss and Germans were skilled makers of music boxes. Many European countries produced them but the movements usually came from Switzerland. Made from the 17th century on.

Artison disc organ . . . .$ 1,375- 1,550
Birdcage type, bird moves
  and sings 600   675
Bremond, 6" cylinder 1,900- 2,350

Music Boxes

Capital style A "Cuff" box,
  w/6 "cuffs", c. 1896 . . . . . 4,200- 4,450
Columbia, 6 selections   875   975
Coset Calliope, manual, 45
  pipes, brass 12,600-13,500
Dawkins, 6 tunes, 6"
  cylinders 2,400- 2,750
Double comb, Polyphon,
  coin-operated 2,575- 2,950
Kalliope disc box, 7 discs . . 2,450- 2,650
Lochmann, winding rod,
  gold leaf decor, 21½"
  disc 3,500- 3,750
Mandolin, cylinder, No. Co
  12 . . . . 1,400- 1,675
Orchestral cylinder w/drum
  and 5 bells, plays 12
  tunes 2,400- 2,575
Paillard piccolo zither, 2
  combs, plays 12 tunes . . . 2,500- 2,700
Regina, automatic, No. 33,
  12 39" dia. discs 6,200- 6,475
Regina coin-operated, 12
  records 4,750- 4,975
Rivenc interchangeable
  cylinder box, plays 8
  tunes on 1 cylinder 2,000- 2,350
Seeburg, Style K, piano,
  mandolin, xylophone,
  nickelodeon, 62" high . . . 5,875- 6,350
Stella upright disc box, 10
  bells, coin-operated 7,700- 7,975
Swiss, 9-bell cylinder 1,900- 2,175
Swiss, 4-tune, 5" cylinders,
  double comb 1,975- 2,400
Swiss, 8-tune cylinder, bells,
  c. 1900 . . . . 3,000- 3,650
Swiss, 8-tune cylinder,
  outside crank, 2 extra
  cylinders 2,200- 2,450
Swiss, 10-tune cylinder,
  bells 3,350- 3,500

Swiss, 12-tune cylinder, 5 bells	4,300- 4,575
Swiss, wooden grained case, plays 10 hymns, 22" across (ill.)	1,200- 1,650
Symphonion disc box, 22 discs	4,300- 4,600
Symphonion, 5 bells	4,700- 5,200
Symphonion, single comb ..	1,650- 1,900
Universal cylinder box, 10 cylinders, Pat. 1891	3,000- 3,375

Music Stands

Music Stands

Just that—a rack on legs to hold sheet music. They've been around for years and collectors use them to hold the family Bible or dictionary.

Ornate ironwork, cherry board, 1890s (ill.) ....\$	98-135
Ornate ironwork, double board, poplar, 1890s	98-145

Musical Instruments

Accordion, Adolphus Special...............\$	110-	145
Accordion, Concertone, 10 keys, enameled, mahogany finish	100-	130
Accordion, Kalbe Imperial, twin bellows, nickel-plated clasps and keys, 2 stops, 2 sets of reeds ..	395-	450

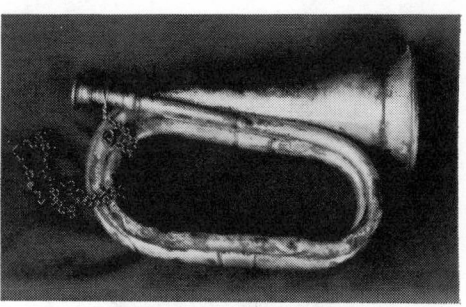

Musical Instruments

Accordion Pitzschier, mahogany panels, 19 nickel keys, made in Germany, sold in U.S., c. 1890s	550-	625
Bagpipes, Scotland, mid-1800s	2,200-2,600	
Bagpipes, Scotland, pre-WWI	675-	775
Banjo, calfskin head, 25 nickel-plated brackets, maple neck, fingerboard inlaid with M.O.P., c. 1890s	365-	450
Banjo, maple shell, nickel band, 6 screw brackets, 11" calfskin head, c. 1890s	185-	225
Banjo, shell covered in calfskin, hardwood neck, 40", c. 1860	395-	475
Bugle, artillery, brass, c. 1890	120-	155
Bugle, Boy Scout, brass, c. 1920 (ill.)	40-	40
Bugle, Civil War	285-	375
Bugle, officer's, nickel-plated, c. 1890	125-	145
Castinets, Mexican, c. 1920	35-	45
Castinets, Spanish, c. 1890s	75-	90
Cello, American-made, sold by Sears, c. 1910	350-	410
Cello, American-made, 4-string bass, c. 1890s ...	650-	750
Cello, ¾ size, 4 strings, iron head, c. 1890s, American-made	775-	845
Clarinet, Laube style, A, low pitch, c. 1890	325-	350
Clarinet, Laube style, B-flat, low pitch, 1900s ..	225-	245
Clarinet, Laube style, C, low pitch, c. 1890s	245-	265
Concertina, French, c. 1850s	395-	445

(continued)

Musical Instruments

Concertina, mahogany, 20 keys, English, bone buttons, c. 1880	275-	325
Cornet, Artists', B-flat, nickel-plated, c. 1890s ...	285-	325
Cornet, Concertone, 1 water key, M.O.P. buttons, silver-plated mouthpiece, brass, c. 1900	145-	185
Cornet, Dupont, C, polished brass, M.O.P. buttons, c. 1890	195-	245
Cymbals, American, 10", 11", 12", 12½", 13", leather handles, c. 1890s, ea.	90-	145
Cymbals, English, c. 1850s .	175-	200
Cymbals, French, c. 1890s .	140-	165
Drum, Acme Professional bass, 24" dia., 26" dia., 28" dia., 30" dia., c. 1890s	180-	225
Drum, Acme Professional bass, 14" dia., 16" dia., c. 1890s	165-	185
Drum, band instrument, American, c. 1860s	850-	950
Drum, Revolutionary War field type, American	1,600-1,750	
Drum, toy, tin, twisted rope strap, painted, c. 1880s ..	139-	159
Flute, American, 8-keyed, c. 1900	110-	125
Flute, French, 1-keyed, c. 1850s, ivory (rare)	4,000+	
Flute, Italian, c. 1880s	2,300-2,395	
Flute, ivory, 4-keyed, c. 1850s	1,800-1,975	
Guitar, American, Civil War	2,200-2,450	
Guitar, American, The Acme, c. 1895	150-	165
Guitar, Spanish, c. 1750s ..	12,000+	
Guitar, The Kenmore, c. 1900s	155-	175
Guitar, The Richard, concert size, c. 1900	260-	300
Harmonica, Doerful's International, celluloid, 10 double holes, 40 reeds ...	50-	60
Harmonica, Duss Band Tremelo, 3-in-1, 32 double holes, etc.	22-	32
Harmonica, Hohner, concert, c. 1890s, 20 double holes, 80 reeds	195-	245
Harp, English, maple base, 5' 7", c. 1850s	975-1,400	
Harp, Italian, carved rosewood, 5' 6", c. mid-1700s	5,700-6,200	
Jews' Harp, 2", 2¼", 2½", 2¾", 3¼", 3½" frame, c. 1900s, ea.	8-	24
Lap harp, late 1890s (ill.) ...	225-	245
Lute, Flemish, c. 1750	1,110-1,440	
Lute, French, early 17th century	13,000+	
Lute, Spanish, c. early 17th century	11,000+	
Mandolin, American, rosewood, c. 1860s	160-	210
Mandolin, English, late 17th century	10,000+	
Mandolin, French, early 17th century	15,000+	
Mandolin, French, c. 1790s .	1,900-2,400	
Oboe, English, c. 1890s	3,300-3,500	
Oboe, German, c. 1890s ...	4,400-4,650	
Saxophone, Bantone, bell front, 3 valves, upright bell	975-1,300	
Saxophone, DuPont, alto, bell front, polished brass	165-	235
Saxophone, DuPont, B-flat tenor, B-flat baritone, polished brass	255-	285
Saxophone, Tourville & Co., alto, silver, polished	175-	215
Trombone, DuPont, B-flat, baritone valve, polished brass	295-	365
Trombone, DuPont, B-flat, tenor valve, E-flat alto slide, brass	495-	565
Trumpet, Concertone, B-flat, 1 water key, brass	155-	175
Trumpet, Holton, B-flat. "The King," lacquer bore	265-	345

Mustache Cups

Mustache Cups

They were popular in the 1800s. The partition in the cup supposedly kept the beverage from running down grandfather's vest. The majority were made in Germany using the transfer method—a method similar to our decals of today. Left-handed cups are rare. Lots of repros here.

Cup, blue floral, "Love Is Eternal" in gold	$ 47-	57
Cup, brown matt glaze, left-handed, 1890s	66-	74
Cup, diamond/shell pattern (ill.)	38-	45
Cup, gold band	30-	40
Cup, horses	18-	27
Cup, lavender, flower decor, man's name in gold	52-	61
Cup, "Love the Giver," blue/yellow background	52-	70
Cup, "Papa" in gold	60-	70
Cup, pink/orange, "WJM" in gold	52-	64
Cup/saucer, beaded leaf cluster, gold initials	59-	68
Cup/saucer, blue, white, scrolled medallions, Germany	54-	63
Cup/saucer, bright blue/green, gold initials, 1860s	52-	61
Cup/saucer, floral spray, German inscription, gold letters	47-	57
Cup/saucer, quadruple plate, revised initials, birds	57-	67

Nailsea Glass

This glass was produced at Nailsea, England, beginning in 1788. The loops and swirlings of the colored glass, combined with clear or opal glass, identify it. The more common color combinations are red/white and green/white. More repros!

Nailsea Glass

Atomizer, clear, white loops, 7¼" high	$120-140
Bottle, blue, white looping, blown stopper, 11¼" high with stopper	175-190
Carafe, matching late, dark blue/white typical looping	140-160
Cookie jar, blue loopings, Britannia lid and bale, 6½" high	150-165
Caster set, 4 bottles, blue/white loopings, cut stoppers	160-178
Cruet, blue, white loops, 6¼" high	180-200
Cruet, dark red, white loopings, blown stopper, 6½" high	71- 82
Cup/saucer, blue swirl, 19th century	58- 68
Epergne, flower base, blue/white loopings around base, brass fittings	240-270
Fairy lamp, satin to clear, signed Clarke in base	270-295
Flask, red swirls, 5½" high, no cap	160-180
Gas shade, white loopings, 3" filter	82- 92
Pitcher, blue, white loops, clear handle, 10½" high	300-340
Rolling pin, cranberry swirl, 16" long	252-272
Rose bowl, blue looping, 4" dia.	180-200
Tumbler, white/blue loops	77- 87
Vase, green satin, fluted top, 19th century	140-160
Vase, white with blue loopings, black handles and base, 9½" high (ill.)	110-125

Nakara

See **Wavecrest.**

Napkin Rings

These were in vogue for less than 50 years,

(continued)

Napkin Rings

beginning in the late 1870s. They were made of every type of material, including cut glass. Most common are those from pot metal or quadruple plate.

Cherubs, silver plate, Derby Silver Co.	$ 35- 42
Child's name engraved around chicks scratching, silver	40- 47
Porcelain, hand-painted, flowers and bees, Germany	28- 37
Silver plate, boy fishing on rock	40- 47
Silver plate, boy with hoop	37- 46
Silver plate, butterfly (ill.)	40- 48
Silver plate, cherub, child's initials	27- 36
Silver plate, fireman's helmet, Pairpoint	72- 81
Silver plate, large boot	32- 41
Silver plate, rooster (ill.)	32- 41
Silver plate, souvenir, Niagara Falls	38- 47
Silver plate, wild boar, barrel type, Pairpoint	70- 80
Sterling silver, dog chasing cat, initialed	172-188
Sterling silver, Georgie, beaded edge	170-180
Sterling silver, owl on branch, child's name	160-170

Nash Glass

Nash Glass

A former employee of the Tiffany Glass Company, Douglas Nash purchased Tiffany's Long Island factory around 1929. His glass was flamboyant in color and most of it was signed Nash on the bottom.

Bowl, gold, stretched edge, 8" dia. signed	$370-410
Candlestick, gold, water base, 5" high	140-150
Decanter, pair, green/shaded gold, 15" high	345-395
Plate, chintz, alternating greens and pinks, signed Nash, 6¾" dia. (ill.)	140-170
Plate, yellow, orange chintz, signed, 8" dia.	170-180
Vase, chintz/orange decor, 7½" high, signed	350-385
Vase, flower form, ruffled top, pedestal base, peacock blue, 5½" high (ill.)	440-480
Vase, green, fluted top, 8½" high, signed	540-620
Vase, iridescent, gold, impressed veins circling vase, 6" high, signed	570-595
Vase, Tiffany blue, 8" high, signed	375-420

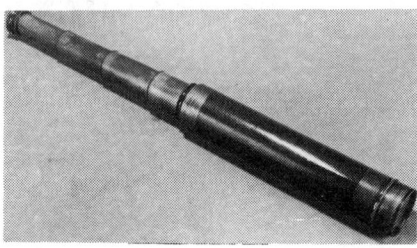

Nautical

Nautical

"Where away?" was the cry from the deck when a sailor in the crow's nest spotted a whale, an enemy ship or land. The English and the Germans made the best telescopes, from the early 1700s on. A real gem when found in original condition.

Telescopes

Ship captain's, 13" when closed; 2 large sections, opened to 30"	$ 350- 420
Ship captain's, c. 1820, wooden barrel, brass mounts, 35" overall, marked "Gardner & Sons-Glasgow-Day or Night"	320- 385
Ship captain's, 36" overall, original leather covering, c. 1850	295- 500

258

Ship captain's, made by a woman, Janet Taylor-Minories, London 420- 520
Ship captain's, walnut tube, brass, 26″ overall (ill.) 265- 320

Other Nautical Items

Blubber or "boat" spade, 17″ overall 170- 185
British East Indiaman's logbook, 9½″×15″, 1799-1802 . . . . 620- 700
The British Mariner's Directory & Guide to the Trade & Navigation of the Indian & China Seas, by Elmore, 342 pages 435- 500
British midshipman's journal, 1929-1932, 8″×13″ 300- 345
Clipper Ship card, 3½″×6½″, colorful, used to advertise for cargo 280- 320
Copper ship's oil lamp, 18″ high, oil font intact 240- 270
Greener percussion, muzzle-loading harpoon gun, English 1,700-2,100
Harpoon for Greener gun, c. 1850, 51″ overall, iron shaft 310- 340
History of Nantucket by Obed Macy, Mansfield, Mass., 1880, 313 pages 62- 72
"Lead," used for determining depth of water, 30″ overall, in pin box 220- 240
Letter from Commodore Perry to his wife, handwritten, 4 pages, 1852 . . . . 320- 370
Logbook from the ship *Urchin,* 10½″×12½″, 1838-1839 . . . . 450- 575
Notes on torpedo fuses, by a Lt. Converse, U.S.A., 1875, published by U.S. Torpedo Station, Newport, R.I., 31 pages 78- 98
Ordnance Instructions for the U.S. Navy, Navy Dept., Washington, 1866 . . . . 87- 97
Sailing ship's stick-type barometer, on gimbal mount, English, 1820 1,350-1,700
Sailor's valentine, octagon-shaped, hinged case, seashells, etc. 470- 500
Ship captain's telescope, 30″ overall, covered with leather, twined rope 300- 350
Ship's boat horn, 16″ overall . 240- 270
Ship's medicine chest, c. 1830, mahogany, 8″×10″×9″, c. 1840s 550- 650

Ship's running lights, pair, brass, 14″ high, 1930s 410- 440
Ship's sextant, brass, 9″ wide, 8½″ high, 6 swivel filters, etc. 680- 780
U.S. Navy ship's Battle-rattle used to sound General Quarters 380- 410
Whale-killing lance, c. 1840s, 59″ overall 320- 345
Whaling bomb lance gun, c. 1860s, breech-loading, American 1,600-1,800

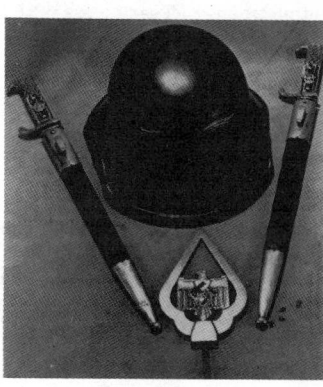

Nazi Items

Nazi Items

Hitler may have lost the war but collectors of his military items are growing every day. They are so popular, in fact, that reproductions are beginning to appear on the market.

Afrika Corps Service Medal . . . . . $ 70- 85
Armband, German Armed Forces ("Deutsch Wehrmacht"), black/yellow 45- 55
Armband, H.J. (Hitler Youth), bevo weave 54- 65
Army mess kit 60- 74
Bayonet, Nazi police eagle's head, bone-type grips (ill.) 140-165
Bayonet, police, eagle's head, etc. (ill.) 110-155
Belt buckle, swastika insignia . . . 78- 95
Dagger, Army, w/eagle and swastika cross guard 220-260
Dagger, carried by the Brown Shirts, wood grips, eagle, etc. . 200-245
Dagger, Hitler Youth, "Blut Und Ehre" on blade 275-300
Dagger, Luftwaffe, 1937 model, flying eagle on cross guard . . . 255-285
Doll, Storm Trooper, 11″ high, painted composition head 170-195
Flag, 4′×7′, swastika and German Cross 115-135

259

(continued)

Helmet, Afrika Corps, tan	
camouflage	210-245
Helmet, Luftschultz w/wings (ill.)	68- 78
Helmet, Nazi police, chin strap,	
etc.	165-190
Helmet, "R.L.B." (Air Defense	
League), parade type	310-345
Iron Cross, 2nd class	50- 65
"Kreta" cuff title—awarded to	
participants in battle for Crete	210-245
Luftwaffe badge, pilot, marked	
"Imme"	310-345
Luftwaffe badge, "Webr.	
Schneider A wien"	385-535
Mountain troops rucksack	67- 77
Peaked cap, Army infantry	
officer, silver cord, red piping	230-250
Peaked cap, Artillery officer,	
silver cord, red piping	230-250
Peaked cap, Luftwaffe officer	210-235
Peaked cap, Navy captain, gold	
bullion wreath	265-295
Photograph of Hitler and friends,	
signed by Hitler	195-295
Pith helmet, Afrika Corps, green	
felt body, both metal badges	95-115
Tunic, Luftwaffe, officer's	
summer white, complete	510-545
Uniform, chaplain's Reichswehr	
tunic	335-355
Uniform, medical officer's	275-310
Uniform, Panzer Grenadier	245-275

Needlework

Patterns were first engraved and hand-painted on paper; later they were stamped in color on canvas. If done in wool stitches this was called Berlin work. In addition to personal items, popular patterns were done in the form of bookmarks, mottos such as Home Sweet Home, Welcome, and religious sentiments. *Godey's* was just one of many magazines that printed patterns for this type of work.

Daily, "God Is Good," early 19th	
century	$ 34- 44
Handkerchief flowers, blue/gold,	
19th century (frame not	
included)	38- 48
Sampler, "Friends Forever,"	
early 19th century	61- 72
Scarf, flowers, 36" long	27- 37

Netsukes

Usually carved of ivory, they're used as fasteners, such as buttons for garments. The

Netsukes

old are highly collectible and they're being skillfully reproduced in Japan. Careful! It's pronounced "Netski."

Apple vendor, woman	$ 65- 85
Boar	70- 84
Cat	55- 65
Child with dog	67- 77
Crab, stained dark brown (soak-	
ing in strong tea achieves this)	78- 90
Devil's mask	65- 75
Dog playing with fish	78- 90
Elephant, two blind men	100-115
Frogs on lily pad	78- 90
Happy/sad face (head revolves)	95-110
Hare on tortoise's back	67- 77
Houseboat	89-100
Kabuki player	67- 80
Man carrying basket of fish	75- 85
Man carrying boat net	68- 78
Man carrying bundle of straw	68- 78
Man carrying donkey	105-118
Man holding tortoise	68- 78
Mouse, stained brown	65- 75
Owl	69- 85
Pearl diver	60- 70
Reaper	68- 83
Running boar	70- 85
Smiling man with bread	70- 80
Sumo wrestlers (look out for	
repros)	70- 80
Tiger	74- 86
Two women, one holding fish	70- 80

New England Peachblow

Also called Wild Rose, it shades from rose at top to white in lower portion. Edward Libbey patented it in 1886 under the Wild Rose name. Being reproduced.

Bottle, perfume, 4" high	$ 560- 585
Bowl, bride's, acid finish	395- 420
Bowl, finger, fluted lip, 4½"	
dia.	245- 270

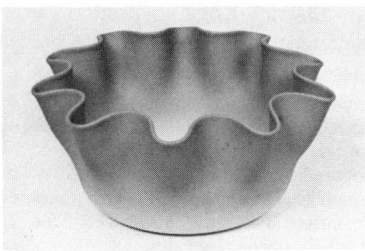

New England Peachblow

Bowl, finger, satin finish,
5" dia. (ill.) 585- 600
Bowl, rose, crimped top 645- 675
Bowl, tricornered, 5¼" dia. . . 380- 420
Butter dish, glossy finish 1,350-1,500
Creamer, applied clear handle,
4½" high 920- 970
Creamer, applied reeded
handle, 4¼" high 900- 965
Cruet, clear stopper 875- 935
Cup, punch 365- 410
Darner, apple, acid finish 300- 320
Darner, pear, glossy finish . . . 310- 345
Decanter, blown glass
stopper, applied reeded
handle, 9½" high 2,475-2,550
Lamp base, font only, glossy
finish 650- 725
Pitcher, applied clear handle,
glossy finish, 10¼" high . . . 1,600-1,675
Pitcher, applied twisted
"rope" handle, satin finish,
11" high 1,500-1,600
Salt/peppers, triple-plated
caps, acid finish, pr. 485- 535
Shade, lamp, 10½" dia. 585- 610
Sugar bowl, applied clear
handles, 4½" high 625- 655
Toothpick holder, 3½" high . . 370- 400
Tumbler, glossy finish, 5"
high 460- 485
Vase, crimped top, satin
finish, 6¾" high 750- 775
Vase, fluted lip, acid finish,
7½" high 765- 820

New Martinsville "Peachblow"

New Martinsville "Peachblow"

Its factory name was Muranese. Made at the New Martinsville, West Virginia, factory in the late 1800s and until 1907, Joseph Webb of the famous Sturbridge, England, family invented it. It got its name "Peachblow" in the early 1940s when antiques dealers tried to unload large amounts of it, following the success story of the famous Wheeling Peachblow (see). It is good glass but doesn't remotely compare to any of the three famous Peachblows—Mt. Washington, New England, and Wheeling.

Bowl, fluted edges, 8½" dia.,
Sunburst $170-185
Bride's basket w/frame, 6" dia.,
Sunglow 173-185
Bride's basket w/frame, 8" dia.,
Sunburst 190-215
Bride's basket w/frame, 10" dia.,
Sunburst 195-220
Lamp shade, Frosted Salmon,
3½" high 110-120
Large berry bowl, Sunburst (ill.) . 175-190
Small berry bowl, Sunglow 133-145
Sugar shaker, original cap,
Sunrise 100-115
Syrup jug, metal cap, 6" high . . . 110-120
Vase, floral panels, fluted lip,
Salmon, 8" high 140-155
Vase, ruffled lip, Sunray, 7½"
high 152-170

Newcomb Pottery

It was opened in 1896 by Ellsworth and William Woodward as a workshop extension of the art school of Sophie Newcomb Memorial College for Women, New Orleans. By 1897 it was producing on a large scale. Most of the pottery was turned on the wheel by Joseph Fortune Meyer. It's highly collectible today.

Bowl, blue/green/pink tie-vine
motif, matt glaze, Newcomb . . $135-160
Bowl 3⅞" high, blue/green/pink
yellow narcissus motif 200-240
Bowl, plain glaze, undecorated,
2⅛" high, Newcomb mark 130-160
Bowl-vase, 4¾" high, blue/
green, Spanish bayonet motif,
matt glaze, decorator Julia
Michel 210-270
Inkstand, with liner and lid,
blue/green/brown, glossy
glaze, decorator Joseph Meyer 90-120

(continued)

Newcomb Pottery

Mug, florals, blue underglaze,
    signed Joseph Meyer   785-970
Pot, Ali Baba type, plain
    green semi-matt, 3⅛" high . . .   95-120
Vase, green/blue, oak tree motif,
    matt glaze, 5¼" high 200-250
Vase, misty blue, massed flowers,
    blue/yellow 340-390
Vase, 7¾" high, blue/green con-
    ventionalized motif, glossy
    glaze (ill.) 195-240

Newhall China

Newhall China

Some say this was the first true English
china. It was made at Newhall in the Staffordshire District, England, around 1781. At
first they specialized in hard-paste porcelain,
later they produced bone china.

Creamer, enameled flowers, 4"
    high (ill.) $132-142
Creamer, Pink Lustre
    decorations   95-107
Cup/saucer, Blossom Band decor   66- 69
Mug, Oriental scene, 3" high 69- 78
Plate, rose decor, 7¼" dia.,
    early 74- 82
Plate, rose decor, 8" dia. 77- 87
Sugar bowl, Pink Lustre
    decorations 130-148
Teapot, creamer, sugar, Oriental
    decor 196-207
Teapot, Oriental decor, 7½" high   210-240

Newspapers

Newspapers

Some are highly sought after, while others
are fodder for the recycling machines. Age,
condition, information given—all dictate the
price.

Harper's Weekly, New York,
    July 15, 1871 (ill.) $3-6
The Stars and Stripes, France,
    August 9, 1918 (ill.)   3-5

Niloak Pottery

This multicolored pottery was made at
Benton, Arkansas, in the late 19th century
until 1946. Glazed on the inside, it had a dull
finish on the outside. Most desirable colors
are rust and chocolate brown. "Niloak" is
always stamped in bottom. Beginning to be
collectible. These are indicative prices.

Bowl w/flower frog . . . . $ 55- 64
Bud vase, 8" high 48- 58
Candlesticks, 7½" high, pr.   88-100
Chamber stick, 5" high 50- 60

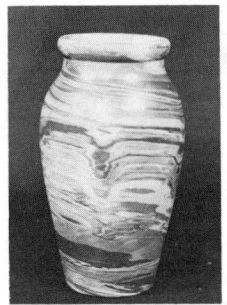

Niloak Pottery

Cigarette box	30-	38
Elephant, 1″ high	57-	65
Humidor, 6½″ high	78-	90
Jigger, 2¼″ high	28-	35
Match holder, 1½″ high	30-	35
Tile, 4½″ square	37-	45
Vase, brown/tan/yellow, 6½″ high, the usual colors (ill.)	34-	43
Vase, 6½″ high	33-	44
Vase, 9″ high	47-	55

Nippon

Nippon

Hand-decorated, generally it's defined as porcelain made in Japan between 1891 and 1921 for export. It was **not** a specific type of porcelain. The name used on the back of each piece denoted the country of origin. After 1891 the U.S. required that imported items from all foreign countries be marked with the name of the exporting country. Nippon is the Japanese word for Japan, but in 1921 the U.S.A. stated that the word Nippon was no longer acceptable as a country of origin marking. Thus ended the Nippon era.

Ashtray, Persian design, signed	$ 40-	48
Ashtray, scenic, Green Wreath mark	35-	44
Basket, landscape scene, Green Wreath mark, 6¼″ high	65-	74
Basket, windmill scene, Maple Leaf mark, 7″ high	72-	80
Biscuit jar, forget-me-nots, gold trim, 7½″ high	85-	94
Bowl, blue/pink flowers, gold medallion center, 6¼″	45-	53
Bowl, handled, gilt flowers, ivory ground (ill.)	23-	32
Bowl, pink apple blossoms, bluebird on branch, signed	37-	44
Bowl, rope handles, farm scene, Green Wreath mark, 5¼″	30-	37
Box, covered, harbor scene, beaded edges, Noritake RC mark	65-	74
Box, covered, 2 lovers, Noritake-Nippon mark	75-	84
Cake set, roses/birds, 7 pcs., Green Wreath mark, all	110-120
Candleholder, twisted vines, 8″ high	40-	48
Candlesticks, blue, gold trim, 7¼″ high, pr.	72-	80
Candlesticks, gray/red, floral scene, 8″ high, Noritake "M" in Wreath, pr.	85-	94
Chocolate set, bluebirds in tree, gold trim, Green Wreath mark	100-108
Chocolate pot, floral scene, gold beading, 10½″ high	105-110
Choclate set, gold floral scenes, 11 pcs., all	80-	90
Chocolate pot, sailboats on lake, 11″ high	110-125
Condiment set, salt/peppers, toothpick holder, mustard jar, floral scenes, all	58-	65
Condiment set, usual pieces, gold dragon motif, all	75-	85
Cookie jar, bluebirds on nest, Noritake-Nippon mark	105-110
Cookie jar, large bird in flight, 8″ high	90-110
Cracker jar, gold flowers, RC Nippon mark	135-140
Cracker jar, raised enamel dragon, 7½″ high	130-140
Creamer, pink flowers	14-	22
Cup/saucer, cobalt, gold trim, Green M mark	19-	26
Cup/saucer, pink flowers, signed	22-	31
Cup/saucer, wild roses, gold handle, Nippon, hand-painted	21-	28
Dish, cobalt, gold trim around rim, 6½″ dia.	18-	26
Dish, handled, gold flowers, 5″ dia.	12-	17
Dresser set, pink flowers, green/white borders, all	120-130

(continued)

Ewer, farm scene, gold overlay,
12" high, "M" in Wreath
Nippon 140-150

Ewer, gold overlay, blue handles,
10" high 135-144

Figurine, fisherman, 5½" high,
signed 40- 48

Figurine, pony at fence, 6¼"
high, Green Wreath mark 43- 52

Figurine, rearing horse, 6" high,
signed 44- 52

Hatpin holder, gold dragon, blue
ground, 6" high 29- 37

Hatpin holder, twining vines,
gold/red, signed, 5½" high 28- 35

Humidor, bluebirds in tree, red
trim, 7" high 115-124

Humidor, fishermen with nets,
6¼" high, Green Wreath mark 85- 95

Humidor, Indian on horse, 7"
high, signed 120-130

Lemonade set, pitcher, 8 mugs,
floral scenes, all 155-163

Lemonade set, pitcher, 6 mugs,
sailboat at sunset, all 140-150

Match holder, green/red, gold
trim, 2½" high 23- 31

Mug, blue flowers on gold ground,
5¾" high, signed 44- 52

Mug, gold twisted handle, dragon
motif, 6" high, signed 45- 55

Mug, green floral scene, gold
handle, 6¼" high, Green
Wreath mark 52- 58

Mustache cup, Indian with pipe,
signed 130-140

Mustard pot, gold flowers, blue
ground, RC Nippon mark 30- 38

Mustard pot, red roses, green
trim, signed 32- 40

Nut set, dragons, blue ground,
bowl, 5 dishes, all 65- 74

Pitcher, floral scene, 13¼" high .. 62- 70

Pitcher, hand-painted roses, gold
handle, 11½" high 65- 73

Pitcher, sunset on lake, 15" high . 61- 70

Planter, owl in flight, 7" high,
signed 85- 92

Plaque, rearing horses, "M" in
Wreath Nippon mark 95-105

Plaque, sailboat at sunset, 9¼"
dia. 65- 74

Plate, boat scene, blue, red trim,
6" dia., signed 40- 48

Plate, sailboat on pond, open
handles, 6¼" dia. 38- 44

Plates, open handles, pink roses,
gold borders, 6, all 120-130

Platter, Phoenix, gold border,
11" dia. 75- 84

Salt/pepper, blue flowers, gold
trim, pr. 18- 24

Salt/pepper, green ground, gold
dots, pr. 16- 24

Sugar bowl, bluebird in tree,
signed 27- 35

Sugar bowl, yellow roses, Green
Wreath mark 28- 36

Tankard, bear on stump, 11½"
high 130-140

Tankard, Indian on horse, 12"
high, RC Nippon mark 140-152

Tea set, gold dragons, blue
ground, 17 pieces 147-155

Tea set, red/yellow flowers, 13
pieces, all 132-140

Teapot, garden scene, 8" high,
Green Wreath mark 32- 38

Teapot, hand-painted roses, gold
trim, 7" high, signed 28- 36

Teapot, lake scene, gold trim,
7¾" high 31- 38

Tray, dragon motif, 8½" high ... 44- 52

Tray, farm scene, gold trim, 9"
dia. 52- 58

Vase, Art Nouveau scene, gold
handles, 9¼" high 46- 55

Vase, bathing scene, beaded
handles, 8" high 40- 47

Vase, twisted vines, red ground,
11" high 55- 62

Nodding Figures

Nodding Figures

Sometimes called pagods these porcelain figures have heads and hands that are attached to the body with wires. Any movement causes the figure to move up and down. 18th and 19th centuries, considered quite collectible today.

Bird in tree, trunk sways, bisque . $ 48- 60

Boy holding dog, dog's head
moves, porcelain, 18th century   60- 74

Chinese boy in rickshaw, head
and hands move, bisque type . .   62- 72

Farm couple, green/yellow/
orange, 6¾" high (ill.) 71- 81

Girl and boy kissing, heads nod,
porcelain 34- 42

Hindu, turbaned, holding basket,
snake moves too, bisque 58- 67

Old lady in chair, sleeping head
nods, bisque 38- 42

Noritake China

Noritake China

Produced by the Nihon Toki Kaisha firm in Nagoya, Japan, after 1904, for export only. Azalea is the best-known pattern. It was given away as a premium by the Larkin Tea and Coffee Company in the early 1900s. More Noritake is on the market than any other mark. Look for Noritake Nippon, Noritake M in Wreath Nippon, and Noritake RC Nippon marks. They're the earliest. Modern Noritake is marked Noritake China, Japan, with the familiar "M" in the wreath above.

Basket, Azalea pattern, 5" long . . $ 89-106

Berry set, 6-pc., floral scene,
Green M in Wreath mark, set .   74- 88

Berry set, 7-pc., Azalea pattern,
all   84-100

Bowl, Azalea pattern, 10½" dia. .   32- 42

Cake plate, Azalea pattern,
7" dia. 58- 68

Celery dish, Azalea pattern,
12¼" long 41- 51

Celery dish, crimson roses, 9"
long, RC mark 29- 37

Compote, Azalea pattern,
6½" dia. 52- 61

Creamer, Azalea pattern,
4½" high 30- 40

Cup/saucer, Sedalia pattern, set
of 12, Green M mark, all 80- 90

Cup/saucer, Swans, gold rim,
RC mark 18- 27

Chocolate set: pot, 8 cups, floral
scenes, Green M mark, all . . .   77- 86

Condiment set, Azalea pattern,
6-pc. 47- 57

Dish, Azalea pattern, sauce type .   9- 14

Dresser set, 7-pc., blue flowers,
gold border, new mark, all 61- 70

Egg cup, Azalea pattern 29- 40

Figurine, boy fishing, green/
yellow, RC mark, 6" high 52- 62

Mayonnaise set, 3-pc., Azalea
pattern, all   105-118

Plates, Azalea pattern, 7", 8½",
9¾" dia. 10- 19

Platter, Azalea pattern, 14" long .   42- 52

Salt/pepper, Azalea pattern, pr. . .   24- 32

Salt/pepper, owl motif, Green M
mark, pr.   27- 37

Shallow bowl, cherry blossom
scene, 3-handled, Green M
mark 37- 47

Tea set, garden scene, varied
colors, RC mark 55- 65

Tea set, 17-pc., floral scenes,
gold rims, Green M mark, all . .   130-160

Tile, Azalea pattern 34- 42

Tobacco jar, horse's head, blue/
red, Green M mark 58- 68

Vase, Azalea pattern, 8¾" high . .   79- 90

Vase, floral scenes, 7¼" high (ill.)   32- 42

Vase, salmon/pink, 8" high 37- 47

Nudes

Those that adorned the walls of the western saloons are priceless today. These 19th century "streakers" are most collectible if and when you can find them. Obviously, an oil painting would be worth more than a lithograph unless the fame of the artist or the nude entered into it.

Nutcrackers

Teeth, stones, factory-made devices—they were all used for opening nuts. A popular type in the early 1900s was an animal whose tail opened its mouth, into which the nut was inserted.

(continued)

Nutcrackers

Alligator, brass, 13″ long . . . . $	58-	67
Bear's head, wood, 8″ long	55-	64
Cat, seated, iron, 11″ high, tail opens mouth	31-	39
Dog, iron, 11″ long, same operation (ill.)	34-	44
Dragon, brass	52-	61
Squirrel, brass, 8½″ long, same operation	42-	52
Tiger, bronze	67-	77
Turtle, iron 8½″ long, same operation	34-	44
Wolf's head, iron, marked Renz, 9″ high, same operation	38-	49

Occupied Japan Items

Occupied Japan Items

The United States occupied Japan for 7 years, from August, 1945, until April, 1952. "Made in Occupied Japan" and "Occupied Japan" are the most common marks found on items manufactured for export during that 7-year period.

Animals

Dog, 4½″ long . . . . $	9-	12
Easter rabbit pulling egg, 4″ long	6-	9
Frog playing drum, 2½″ high . . .	6-	10
Monkey playing violin, 3¼″ high	6-	10
Mother and baby swan, 2″ wide .	5-	8

Ashtrays

Cherubs	6-	9
Dog and fire hydrant, 4″ high . . .	6-	9
Elf sitting on leaf, 4″ wide	9-	13
Frog with open mouth, 3½″ high	6-	10

Bisque

Boy with dog, 6″ high	12-	18
Bud vase, 6″ high	12-	16
Colonial couple, pr.	23-	30
Cupids on pedestals, pr., 7½″ high	18-	26
Peasant couple, 5½″ high, pr. . . .	23-	30

Cups/Saucers

Black, Trimont china	14-	17
Blue Willow style	14-	17
Grey, Orion china	14-	17
Green, Trimont china	14-	17
White bone	14-	18

Figurines

Court jester, 6½″ high	10-	14
Dancers, 1930s style, 2¼″ high, pr.	18-	23
Farm couple, 7″ high	17-	23
Fisherman and mate, 5″ high, pr.	28-	36
Shelf sitter, 3″ high	8-	12
Warrior, 5″ high	12-	16

Figurines, Children

Boy, Hummel type, 5½″ high, "American Children, I bring you greetings," on bottom	45-	55
Boy playing horn, 3½″ high	9-	12
Girl, Hummel type, 5½″ high, same inscription on bottom (The Hummel types are good enough to fool many collectors of the real thing)	45-	55
Peasant girl with lamb, 5″ high . .	12-	16
Pigeon-toed girl, 4½″ high	10-	14

Glassware and Lacquerware

Coasters, lacquerware, set of 6 . .	30-	38
Cracker server, scalloped edges, w/glass cheese dip dish and lacquer lid, 13½″ dia.	44-	53
Lighthouse, battery-operated, souvenir of Coney Island	28-	36
Niagara Falls hanging plate, lacquerware	14-	19

Planters

Angel pulling cart, 4″ wide	12-	15
Donald Duck and basket, 2″ wide	15-	23
Donkey and packs, 3″ wide	12-	16
Elf and basket, 5¾″ wide	17-	23
Owl on limb, 3½″ wide	12-	15
Panda climbing tree, 4″ wide	9-	14

Salt/Pepper Shakers

Chicken in nest, 3-pc., all	12- 18
Dog and chair, 2-pc.	16- 24
Elephants, 1-pc.	9- 13
Mexican boys, pr.	12- 16
Roses with butterflies, 3-pc., all . .	10- 15

Toby Mugs

Captain Patches, 2¾″ high	14- 19
Devil's face, 2″ high (rare)	24- 33
Gent and dogs, 7″ high	44- 53
Jail bailiff, 7″ high	44- 53
Street peddler, 7″ high	44- 53

Toothpicks

Cowboy, 4¼″ high	17- 24
Pixie, 3″ high	12- 17
Satsuma, vase type, 2¼″, 2½″, 11″ high, ea.	10- 15

Vases

Angel, bud type, 2¾″ high	6- 9
Boy blowing horn, 2″ high	6- 9
Girl on stump, 3″ high	12- 16
Miniature (ill.)	8- 12

Office Equipment

Old adding machines are collectible, as are old typewriters, such as the early Hammond or Blickensderfer. Any piece of mechanical office equipment from the early 1900s on is collectible today.

Adding machine, hand-operated, early 1900s	\$ 52- 62
Blickensderfer typewriter, late 1800s	68- 78
Hammond typewriter, wood case, late 1800s	74- 85
Typewriter, 1910s-1920s, still works	62- 72

Ohr Pottery

George E. Ohr made his pottery at Biloxi, Mississippi, from 1883 until just after World War I. It was made from local clay and fired at low temperature. An extremely thin pottery, a contorted shape was one of its characteristics as were the many glaze colors Ohr used. Some referred to him as the mad potter of Biloxi but few denied his genius. He signed his pieces "G.E. Ohr, Biloxi" and "Geo. E. Ohr, Biloxi, Mississippi" in block letters or "G.E. Ohr" in script.

Bowl, folded lip, dark green/ brown glaze, 2″ high	\$ 70- 90
Bowl, one side folded halfway over, mustard glaze, 2¾″ high .	68- 78
Candlestick, dark maroon, rough texture (ill.)	170-190
Candlestick, handled, mottled green glaze, 3¾″ high	108-128
Mug, handleless, dark brown glaze, 3¾″ high	150-190
Mug, puzzle, green glaze, decorated handle, pierced sides, 3½″ high	175-185
Pitcher, folded neck, blood red glaze, 6½″ high	350-425
Teapot, applied snake, pink "raku" glaze, 5¼″ high	500-600
Vase, dark brown glaze, 2½″ high	85-140
Vase, folded neck, dark lead glaze, 4¾″ high	98-140
Vase, folded waist, green speckled glaze, 2½″ high	140-170
Vase, 4-petal top, pinched, pewter-gunmetal bowl (ill.)	240-280
Vase, pinched sides, ruffled edge, 3¾″ high	190-225
Vase, squat, matt pewter finish, dented side (ill.)	240-270

Ohr Pottery

Old Hall Porcelain

Old Hall Porcelain

Originally from Job Meigh and Son, Old Hall Works, Hanley, England, 1790. Name changed to Old Hall Earthenware Company in 1861; changed again in 1887 to Old Hall Porcelain Works. The firm ceased production in 1902. It was an opaque earthenware of the Staffordshire type. Generally, Staffordshire-type earthenware pieces are in the same price range as Old Hall. See specific Staffordshire types for prices. An indicative piece is shown.

Pitcher, cream brown transfer
leaves and flowers, 4″ high,
signed "Old Hall Earthenware
Co." (ill.) . . . . $ 39- 49

Old Ivory China

Old Ivory China

The ground color of this ware gives it its name. Made in Silesia, Germany, in the last part of the 1800s, the marked pieces bear the crown Silesia mark, and/or pattern stock numbers.

Berry bowl, numbered . . . . $ 50- 60

Berry set, bowl and 6 small
  bowls 300-370
Cake plate, Silesia, open handles,
  numbered 74- 90
Cake plate, 10″ dia., numbered . . 79- 90
Celery bowl, Silesia, numbered . . 54- 64
Chocolate pot, peach color/rose,
  numbered 190-240
Comb and brush tray, pattern
  #16, 11½″ 55- 67
Creamer and sugar, numbered . . . 82-100
Cup/saucer, numbered, orange
  poppies, green leaves 54- 65
Platter, peach color, numbered
  (ill.) 135-150
Relish, dish, numbered 44- 54
Saucedish, numbered, 5″ dia. 37- 47
Teapot, floral, peach, numbered . 190-220
Toothpick, numbered, 2″ high . . . 72- 84
Tray, numbered, Silesia, 2″ 63- 74

Old Paris China

Old Paris China

During the 18th and 19th centuries a number of pottery and porcelain factories were located in Paris. The better products were known as Old Paris, although few pieces were ever marked as such.

Cake plate, white, gold trim . . . . . $ 59- 70
Compote, 5¼″ high (ill.) 61- 70
Creamer, numbered, white, gold
  trim 44- 54
Cup/saucer, white, gold trim 80- 90
Figurines, children with pets,
  pastel colored, pr. 140-160
Pitcher, water, white, gold trim . . 107-122
Plates, fruit, floral decor, 10″ dia. 57- 68
Tea set, pot, creamer, sugar,
  flower motif, gold trim 325-355
Teapot, white with gold trim 98-118
Vases, handled, gold trim, early
  1850s, pr. 365-395

Old Sleepy Eye Collectibles

In 1906 the Western Stoneware Company

of Monmouth, Illinois, was formed to produce "premium" pottery for Sleepy Eye Milling Company in Sleepy Eye, Minnesota. The town and the mill were named for a Sioux Indian. His likeness, in profile, is on most of the pottery you find today. Other premiums were also given away by the mill. All are highly sought after now. The pottery is being reproduced in mugs, sugar bowls, small pitchers, salt/pepper shakers, and steins. Other reproductions are a glass jar, a large tumbler, a small advertising mirror, and the paper barrel labels. Be careful.

Advertising cards, 10 in set,
  5½"×9", all $380-490
Advertising postcards, 9 in set,
  3⅜"×5½", all 360-450
Cookbook, Old Sleepy Eye on
  cover 90-125
Cookbook, shaped like the end of
  a bread loaf 95-130
Letter opener, bronze 85- 95
Paperweight bust, bronze 130-145
Pitcher, blue-on-gray, 4" high . . . 135-155
Pitcher, blue-on-white, 4" high . . 85- 95
Pitcher, green 130-140
Stein, blue-on-gray, 7" high 270-285
Stein, yellow, 7¼" high 270-285
Vase, blue-on-gray 325-345
Vase, multicolor, bullrushes, 8¼"
  high 165-175

Onyx Glass

Onyx Glass

Characterized by its raised, 8-petal and leaf design, this decorative glass was made in 1889 by Dalzell, Gilmore and Leighton Company, Findlay, Ohio. It was only made for six months. Colors were silver, amber, orange, raspberry, orchid, and purple. Considered scarce today, it was referred to as Oriental Ware by the people who made it.

Cream pitcher, silver $320-380
Lamp, 2-post base, silver 700-825
Salt shaker, amber 120-140
Sugar bowl, covered 328-390
Syrup, silver floral design, silver-
  plated cap, 6¾" high, applied
  opalescent handle (ill.) 320-410
Tumbler, raspberry 220-270

Opalescent Glass

Opalescent Glass

Clear or colored with a milky white opalescence, it's usually blown or mold blown. Seldom were pieces made as a set. It was made by Sandwich in their early days. Many other comanies also made it, and many other pieces were made. Check various art glass sections and specific companies in **Pattern Glass Section**, this Price Guide.

Vase, white opalescent-to-clear,
  tree bark design, 11" high (ill.) . $ 50- 60
Vase, yellow opalescent with
  Spanish Lace design, frilled
  top, 6½" high (ill.) 79- 92

Opaline Glass

This glass looks like the opal when held to a light—milky iridescence with a fiery orange background. Don't confuse it with the cheaper milk glass, also made in the late 1800s. Being reproduced.

Barber bottle, 11" high . . . . $ 58- 69
Bowl, birds, cherries, 10" dia. . . . 40- 50
Box, blue, pink/white flowers,
  hinged top 60- 70
Butter pats, rose, beaded, set
  of 6 . . . . 41- 51
Inkwell, blue, silver deposit,
  gold, fluted 68- 78

269

(continued)

Lamp, apple green, 13½" high
  overall, French   95-107
Match holder, pipe-shaped,
  souvenir 19- 27
Perfume, opaque white/gold
  enamel, 1850s, England   130-160
Sugar bowl, rose/opaque white,
  covered, 4" high 72- 82
Tumbler, raised rose/flower
  pattern 70- 80
Vase, blue overlay, pink ground,
  6½" high   96-108
Vase, gray, classic lines, ruffled
  top, 4½" high   140-150
Vase, rose, floral, leaves, rose
  motif, 5½" high   107-117

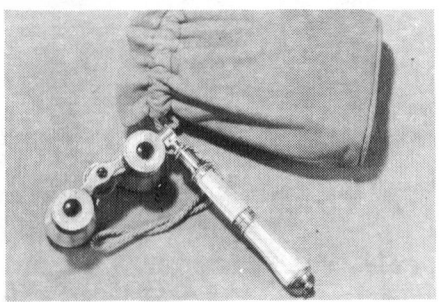

Opera Glasses

Opera Glasses

Simply, these are small binocular telescopes, used at the opera, theater, etc. From the plainest type to the glasses illustrated here, they came in all sizes and shapes. The French and Germans made the best. Some were inlaid with precious gems. They're turning up in shops today as old estates are emptying their attics and basements.

American, leather covered, in
  leather case, Bosch and Lomb,
  1900s . . . .$ 40- 50
French, mother-of-pearl inlaid,
  early 1900s, removable handle
  (ill.) 62- 72
German, polished brass, Zeiss-
  Ikon lenses, velvet case, early
  1900s 57- 67

Optical Items

Optical Items

During the 1800s peddlers traveled from farm to farm selling spectacles. Our ancestors bought the pair they could see best with, a far cry from the practices in optometry today.

Brass frames, adjustable in
  leather case (ill.) . . . .$ 34- 43
14k gold frames, adjustable,
  in leather case 70- 80
Metal frames, bifocals pasted on .   37- 47
Metal frames, no case 18- 27

Organs

Organs

No Victorian parlor was complete without an organ. The cheaper models were made of oak, while cherry, walnut and maple were used in the more expensive models. Most piano tuners can repair the bellows and broken pedal straps. Tuning the pitch keys requires only a musical ear and a wire coat hanger. Type of wood, age, and condition dictate the price.

Acme Queen parlor model, 5
  octaves, 11 stops, 2 octave
  coupler . . . .$ 850- 950
Bilhorn telescope organ,
  portable 350- 425
Chestnut, complete with
  adjustable 3-legged stool,
  c. 1860   975-1,300
The Grand Sterling, walnut,
  c. 1880s (ill.)   975-1,400
Happy Home, oak, c. 1904 . . .   750- 850
Home Favorite piano-organ,
  made for Sears, Roebuck,
  c. 1903 . . . .   775- 875
Oak, swing-out candleholders,
  display rack, c. 1880s 850- 975

Oriental Rugs, Others

These beautiful rugs came into vogue in this country during the late Victorian era. The best were made in Persia (now Iran). Bokhara, Kurd, Cabistan, Sarouk—these are famous names when one discusses the better rugs. Some have over 800 knots per square inch. Some of the new Oriental rugs can fool the less knowledgeable buyer. A little dirt can make them look very old!

Ardebil, 5½'×3½'	$1,200-1,300
Bakhshaish Herati carpet, rose leaves, 16' 9"×17' 3", c. 1789	4,500-4,800
Bessarabian carpet, bouquets of roses, 10' 7"×9' 4"	3,500-3,850
Chinese, 4'×2'	800- 875
Chinese, 5'×3'	725- 825
Chinese bird rug, midnight blue ground, peonies, 7' 3"×4' 8", c. Tao Kuang	3,600-3,800
Chinese carpet, apricot field, birds, 10' 11" square, c. Late Ch'ien Lung	3,975-4,500
Chinese rug, tawny rose field, peonies, 8' 11"×6' 1", c. Ch'ien Lung	3,800-4,500
Daghestan prayer rug, 5' 11"×5' 3", c. 1918	2,400-2,650
Fachralo Kazak prayer rug, 4' 8"×3' 5", c. 1916	3,900-4,600
Fereghan carpet, 26'×19', green/blue field, allover trellis of blossoms, etc., c. 1730	4,500-4,800
Hamadan Sehna carpet, 18'× 10', trellised Herati pattern	3,600-3,900
Kashan prayer rug, 4½'×7', c. 1830	2,300-2,750
Kashan prayer rug, 4½'×7'	2,800-3,800
Kashan prayer rug, silk, 6' 5" ×4' 1", c. 1880	3,100-3,500
Kum, 7'×4½'	2,600-2,900
Kum, mosaic, 7'×5'	2,500-2,900
Kum, mosaic, 6'×4¼'	2,200-2,500
Nain, 8'×5'	5,300-5,600
Samarkand, sea green field, fawn medallion, pink/fawn borders, 6'×5'	3,700-4,500
Sarouk hall runner, 13'×3'	3,100-3,400
Sarouk hall runner, 13½'×4'	3,500-3,700
Sarouk hall runner, 17'×3'	3,600-3,800
Turkish Bergama prayer rug, 3' 10"×3' 6", c. 1800s	4,900-5,500

Overlay Glass

Too much of this type of glass is attributed

Overlay Glass

to the Sandwich Glass Company. Most of what you find today is from the Stourbridge District in England, mid-1800s. Reproductions that should fool no one are sold in this country by a St. Louis, Missouri, firm.

Basket, opalescent, thorn handle, yellow feet, green leaves, amethyst stems (ill.)	$375-425
Ewer, lavender, white opalescent design, pink flowers (ill.)	280-310
Ewer, serrated top, blue to white, pink/yellow/blue flowers, amber handle, Mt. Washington (ill.)	330-420
Genuine Sandwich pieces start at	300-350
Stourbridge-type pieces, slightly less	250-300

Owens Pottery

Owens Pottery

The J.B. Owens Pottery Company produced this pottery in Ohio from the mid-1800s until 1933. It is comparable to Roseville and Weller.

Candleholder, Utopian, berry/leaf decor, brown glaze	$ 64- 74
Letter holder, floral decor, 3½" high	39- 48

271

(continued)

Mug, Utopian, fruit on vine,
5½" high 99-109
Pitcher, flowers, green leaves,
green ground, 10" high 84- 93
Pitcher, orange/brown/yellow
floral leaves, Utopian 102-116
Pitcher, tankard-type, berries/
leaves, artist-signed 82- 92
Vase, green leaves, green-to-pink
flowers, 5½" high 91-102
Vase, Lincoln, brown, tan, identical to an earlier Weller vase
(ill.) 79- 87
Vase, Utopian, orange pansies,
6" high 70- 80
Vase, Utopian, pansy decor,
6½" high 72- 81

Paintings

Oil paintings, water colors, and pastels
from the 17th, 18th, and 19th centuries,
American or European, are highly collectible.
American folk art is especially popular.

"The Ambush," signed F.
Remington, gouache
monotone .... $9,000+
"Autumn in the Catskills,"
signed Thomas Cole, oil,
c. 1817 .... 775- 850
"Autumn Landscape,"
signed Guy C. Wiggins,
oil, c. 1910 .... 535- 625
"Coast Scene," unsigned,
possibly Ben Foster,
c. 1890, oil 475- 525
"A Country Stream," signed
Henry Pember Smith, oil,
c. 1875 .... 675- 775
"Fighting Meat," signed
C. M. Russell w/buffalo
skull remarque 3,500-3,800
"Forest Opening," signed
Roswell Morse Shurtleff,
oil, c. 1879 .... 650- 700
"Italian Landscape," attributed to Richard Wilson,
R.A., c. 1750 .... 675- 750
"Ocean Wave at Twilight,"
signed A. Eugenie,
pastel 125- 175
"An Old Courtyard,"
signed Mark Anthony,
oil, c. 1855 .... 850- 975
"Seashore in Algiers,"
signed Frederic A. Bridg-
man, oil, c. 1912 .... 675- 750
"Smiling Countryside,"
signed W. H. Hilliard, oil,
c. 19th century 750- 825

American Folk Paintings
"Civil War Generals," un-
signed, oil, c. 1865 925-1,000
"The Dayan Family,"
signed H. Pudor, oil,
c. 1858 .... 775- 850
"Gentlemen at a Fireplace,"
signed W. Twatman, oil,
c. 1843 .... 800- 900
"Landscape with Sawmill,"
signed G. Marston, oil,
c. 1863 .... 600- 700
"Mill by a Stream," signed
Virtue Howard, oil, c. 1853 . 550- 650
"Thompson's Mill, Bowery
Bay, Astoria," signed E.
Doolittle, oil, c. 1877 ...... 565- 625
"Village Election," un-
signed, c. 1860, oil 900- 975
"Wife of a New England
Sea Captain," signed
William LaFarge, oil,
c. 1860 .... 675- 750

Paintings, Miniature

Paintings, Miniature

These were usually painted on ivory; children and women in small oval metal or ivory
frames. This type of painting has been done
for centuries.

Children in garden, hand-
painted, ivory frame,
1800s $190- 260
Court lady, plumes in hair,
signed, in ivory frame 240- 270
Duchess of Devonshire,
hand-painted on ivory,
ivory frame 290- 350
Gentleman, American,
1860s, hand-painted,
ivory frame 280- 350
Lady, pink dress, pearls,
signed Davis, ivory
frame 300- 400
Man, ivory frame, signed
James Peale, 2" .... 2,900+
Officer, Continental Army,
1775, ivory frame 220- 260

Pairpoint

Pairpoint

Successor to the Mt. Washington Glass Company, from 1880, these people made silver and silver-plated wares, in addition to good blown glass objects such as candlesticks.

Barber bottle, chased silver, plated, signed	$170-185
Bell, cut crystal, 5½" high	58- 67
Box, hinged silver inlay top, cut glass	140-160
Candlesticks, wheel cut, silver leaves base, pr.	200-220
Caster set in silver frame, handled, 11" high	130-140
Centerpiece, footed bowl, flint, 5¼" high, 12¼" dia. (ill.)	170-190
Compote, Old Colony pattern, 10" high	210-230
Cracker jar, grape decor, blue, shell feet	240-260
Decanter, orange, ribbed inside, 5" high	92-107
Lamp, blown red flowers, signed base, 14" high overall	600-700
Mustache cup and saucer	150-160
Paperweight, blue center, bubble design, 3¼" dia.	800-885
Perfume, paperweight base, flower finial on stopper, pr. . . .	375-450
Pitcher, cut crystal, 11½" high . .	160-190
Plate, flowers/birds, 10" dia.	72- 92
Vase, overlay, cobalt, 6½" high . .	70- 80

Paisley Shawls

The Scots at Paisley, Scotland, 1800 to 1860, made a lovely imitation of the Kashmir (India) shawls.

According to condition, average prices today are:	$110-160

Paleography.
See Genealogy.

Paper Money, American

Paper Money, American

Front (obverse), back (reverse), Star Notes, COPE, Demand Notes, California Gold Bank Notes. If any of these words confuse you, you shouldn't be spending a lot of money for old paper money. Learn before you buy. Also, know what "Unc," "Extra Fine," "Very Fine," "Fine," "Good," and "ADP" (average dealer prices) mean in terms of quality, especially if you're buying by mail.

Paper Money, Foreign

Paper Money, Foreign

Seek out a reliable dealer if you don't know what you're doing. It is impossible to list what's collectible except in a publication that specializes in currency.

Paperweights

These small objects of glass were used to hold down paper on desks and tables. The Baccarats, Clichys, Gillilands, and Millefioris bring tremendous prices today when found and authenticated. Scuffing a new one on

273

(continued)

Paperweights

cement or with sandpaper doesn't mean it's old. Look out for repros!

Baccarat, faceted white
dahlia, 2½″ dia. $3,400-3,750
Baccarat "flower" doorknobs,
2½″ dia., pr. 8,200-9,400
Baccarat, flowers, salmon/
pink/white rose, 2½″ dia. . . . 3,350-3,550
Baccarat, Liberty Bell,
contemporary 255- 265
Baccarat, millefiori, w/4 con-
centric rings of multicolor
canes, 2½″ dia. 3,400-3,650
Baccarat, periwinkle bouquet,
3″ dia. 4,800-5,750
Baccarat, single rose, 2⅝″
dia. 3,375-3,550
Bohemian "Apple," speckled
w/gilded "jewels," 3½″
dia. 275- 345
Bristol, engraved lacy filigree,
5-rosetted cluster, 3¼″
dia. 745- 835
Brooklyn, millefiori, base cut
in the form of a star, 3½″
dia. 575- 650
Clichy, millefiori, marked with
"c" beneath, 2½″ dia. 3,100-3,500
Dorflinger, open flower
design 165- 195
Glass, cardboard photo (ill.) . . 15- 20
Jersey, lily, on stand, yellow/
rose flower, 9½″ high 775- 850
Millville, rose, half-open, green
leaves, 4″ dia. 575- 650
New England sulphide por-
trait, w/portraits of Victoria
and Albert, cameo profile,
2⅝″ dia. 750- 800
Pairpoint, air bubbles, not
signed 170- 185

St. Louis, fruits/pears/
cherries, 3⅛″ dia. 2,300-2,450
Sandwich, poinsettia, salmon/
pink petals, green leaves,
2⅝″ dia. 500- 550
Scottish, millefiori, by Pierre
Ysart, hexagonal blossoms
w/maker's initials, 3″ dia. . . 475- 550
Somverville, Five Little Pigs,
on a grassy mound, 5″ dia. . . 1,750-1,975
Val Saint Lambert, thin over-
lay, faceted and cut, 2½″
dia. 1,450-1,600
Whitefriars, millefiori, on
amber gold ground, 2⅜″
dia., c. 1848 . . . . 200- 275
Zanesville, millefiori, 2⅝″
dia. 725- 825

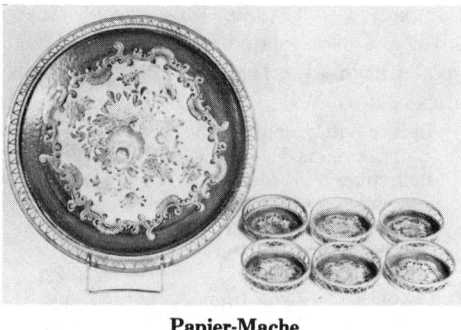

Papier-Mache

Papier-Mache

Chewed paper is a better word for it. Paper is soaked in water, ground up, molded into forms, japanned and dried at a high heat, around 300 degrees. The finished product is extremely tough and durable. A lot of so-called Chippendale trays were made by this method, then decorated.

Basket, MOP inlay, butterflies/
flowers, 11″ dia. $135-145
Box, pearl inlay, 4″ square 37- 47
Box, snuff, pewter inlay in top,
hinged 31- 41
Easter egg, red, chick and
mama 32- 42
Figurine, bird, glass eyes, 4″
high 32- 42
Inkstand, birds, floral leaves, 3″
square 35- 65
Inkwell, MOP inlay, 8½″ wide . . . 58- 68
Lap desk, black, brass fittings,
MOP floral decor 160-170
Lap desk, pearl inlay, floral decor,
slant-top cover 70- 80

274

Stationery rack, Oriental gilt, 7″ wide	60- 70
Tray, gold Chinese decor	31- 40
Tray, Japanese, embossed and painted, 12″ dia., with 6 coasters (ill.)	22- 32
Tray, lacquered, black ground, birds, flowers	180-190
Wine tray, recesses for decanters, pearl inlay	130-140

Pitcher, Niagara Falls design, U.S. Pottery Co.	580-620
Plaque, Greek goddess, floral border, 11″ square	180-190
Sugar bowl, pond lily	106-122
Tray, Bennington type	95-108
Tumbler, classic figures, 4¼″ high	44- 54
Vase, blue/white, Bennington type	130-140
Vase, corn decor, 6½″ high	150-170

Parian Ware

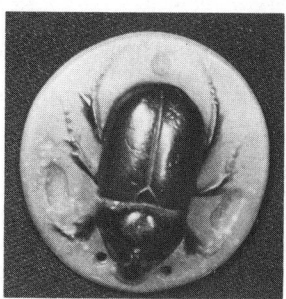

Pâte de Verre

Parian Ware

First made by Copeland in England in 1842, by Fenton at Bennington, Vermont, in 1847, and by the United States Pottery Company, same town, 1853-1858. It was also made by Morrison and Carr, New York City, and by the Southern Porcelain Company, Kaolin, South Carolina. The best American made is attributed to Fenton and U.S. Pottery Company.

Bowl, lilies, 5″ dia. . . . . $	60- 70
Box, embossed flowers, white, cover, 3½″ dia.	73- 83
Bust of Dante, 5″ high	90-110
Bust of Dickens, 6¼″ high	85- 95
Bust of Shakespeare, 8″ high	98-107
Candleholder, Cupid, grapes, tinted leaves, 7″ high	110-125
Creamer, miniature, wheat sheafs, blue-tint	80- 90
Cup/saucer, pond lily	70- 80
Ewer, ring handle, Copeland, 1850s, 8″ high	140-150
Figure, bust of Venus, signed, 9″ high	99-109
Figure, dog chewing bone	70- 80
Pitcher, calla lilies and basket-weave design, 10″ high (ill.) . . .	295-340
Pitcher, hanging game, 10″ high, (ill.)	275-320
Pitcher, lavender, white, babes in woods	140-160

Pâte de Verre

Translated, Pate de Verre means paste of glass. This is a molded glass which is formed from ground lead glass. The resulting powder or crystals are made into a paste by a complicated formula. The glass paste is then molded, fired, and carved. As early as 1400 B.C. this formula was known and the French seem to have revived it, with the Daum brothers leading the way. It's been discovered as a medium for sculpting by contemporary artists in the past few years.

Atomizer, blue/brown, pine cones . . . . $	790- 860
Bowl, cream/yellow, orange sunflowers, signed A. Walter, Nancy	475- 540
Figurine, monkey reading book, signed	950-1,100
Lamp, leaves/berries, gold/white, 5″ high, signed A. Walter, Nancy	1,200-1,400
Medallion, scarab beetle, sienna coloration, 2¾″ dia. (ill.)	350- 420
Pendant, brown/black beetle on gray ground, signed A. Walter, Nancy	300- 370

Pâte Sur Pâte

This means paste on paste. Its wares were

275

(continued)

designs in relief, this being achieved by adding layer on layer of thin pottery paste to the design. Solon was the most famous of the Frenchmen making it, but the best known comes from the Minton factory in England. An original, signed M. Solon, would be quite valuable today.

Bowl, cameo center, seraph,
  green ground, Germany $195- 240
Candy dish, handles, pedestal,
  signed, 5″ high 900-1,200
Picture, cherubs, black/blue/
  white, velvet mat framed ... 460- 560
Plaque, muse, blue ground,
  signed, 4″×8″ 380- 440
Plate, blue/gold/white, classical figures, 9″ dia......... 150- 195
Plate, blue/white medallions,
  gold edge, signed, 9″ dia. ... 280- 330
Vase, light green ground,
  white flowers, signed 9″
  high 310- 360
Vase, white/blue medallions,
  green floral, signed Birk,
  7″ high 500- 575

Mr. Peanut alarm clock 18- 26
Mr. Peanut ashtray, gold 23- 32
Mr. Peanut ashtray, silver, anni-
  versary issue, 1906-1956 .... 45- 54
Mr. Peanut "Bic" lighter 16- 24
Mr. Peanut drink stirrers, 6 in
  set, all 1.50- 3
Mr. Peanut jointed wooden doll
  (rare) 125-140
Mr. Peanut measuring spoon.... 1.50- 2
Mr. Peanut peanut butter
  spreader 1.50- 2
Mr. Peanut serving spoon 1.50- 2
Mr. Peanut tin store sign,
  14″×20″ 17- 35
Mr. Peanut watch 18- 25
Planters nut chopper, fits 8-oz.
  Planters cans 11- 17
Planters paintbook, presidents
  of U.S.................... 11- 14
Planter Peanut belt buckle 6- 9
Planters Peanut greeting card ... 11- 14
Planters Peanut lapel pin 11- 15
Planters Peanut wall clock (rare) . 140-160
Planters ski cap 5- 8
Planters 12-month coloring book . 11- 15

Peanut Collectibles
Photo courtesy Planters Peanuts

Peanut Collectibles

It all began in 1906, in Wilkes-Barre, Pennsylvania, when Amedeo Obici and Mario Peruzzi decided to go into the peanut business. But it wasn't until 1916, when a local schoolboy drew "Mister Peanuts," that the world suddenly became aware of goobers and how great they tasted.

Barrel jar, glass, peanut finial on
  8″ lid (ill.) $225-265

Peking Glass

Peking Glass

Chinese cameo glass, 18th and 19th centuries. Scarce today. Some of the finest comes from the Ch'ing Dynasty (Tung Chih period, 1862-1874).

Beaker, bronze-form, painted
  enamel figures........... $ 600- 670

Bowl, blue, blown, 4½" dia.	1,300-1,600	
Box, green, enamel, lid inlaid with pearl	670-	770
Plate, jade green, 9" dia.	700-	800
Snuff bottle, amber color, quartz stopper	700-	800
Snuff bottle, black/white	610-	730
Tumbler, gray/green, 4¼" high	385-	450
Vase, cameo yellow raised floral decor, 4½" high	585-	675
Vase, white ground, carved red flowers, 8½" high, on box stand	590-	670

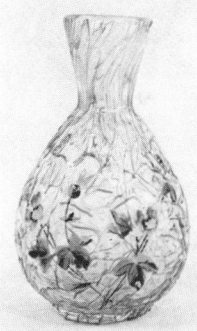

Peloton Glass

Peloton Glass

This glass was first made in Bohemia in 1880. Small threads of colored glass were rolled into the surface as the hot glass was removed from the furnace. Sometimes the pieces were dipped in an acid bath to give them a satin finish. Another item being reproduced.

Cracker jar, pink/red, blue ground, silver lid	$ 85-110
Cruet, multicolors on clear overshot	370-410
Pitcher, pink/blue, enameled decor, white opaque filaments	140-160
Pitcher, pink and blue threads, clear background, pink handle	150-170
Rose bowl, pink/blue miniature (rare)	240-260
Tumbler, blue filaments, 6" high	120-140
Vase, green red, yellow threads, ruffled lip, 5" high	160-180
Vase, miniature, pink threads on clear glass, enameled white flowers, 4" high, green leaves (ill.)	180-220

Pennsylvania Dutch Items

Pennsylvania Dutch Items

The Lord's hand helped these gracious people and today many of us are fortunate to know them and to appreciate their work.

Cabbage slicer, 22" long	$ 72-	82
Chest, miniature, handmade lock, domed lid, russet background, yellow borders, yellow tulips, 8¼" wide (ill.)	500-	545
Coverlet, blue/green/red/white, "Mount Joy, Lancaster County"	1,400-1,700	
Jewel chest, Dutch graining, "Corelia Brunning" on lid	275-	320
Whatnot, hanging type, green ground, red decorations, 11½" high (ill.)	160-	180

Perfume Bottles

277

(continued)

Perfume Bottles

These have been around for centuries in all sizes and shapes. Made of glass, silver, pure gold, carved from jade, inlaid with precious stones, even "Avon calling!"

Chinese jade, dragon motif, mid-1800s	$ 90-100
Cut glass, sterling silver cap with applicator attached, early 1900s	88- 98
DeVilbiss (see) atomizer, iridescent, gold trim, flower motif . .	82- 92
English lavender bottle	9- 12
Moser (see) perfume bottle, multicolored enamel, Czechoslovakia, 6½" high	180-200
St. Louis, paper label, acid etched, 10¾" high (ill.)	200-225
Tiffany glass, signed LCT Favrile	180-195

Peters and Reed Pottery

Though established by John Peters and Adam Reed in 1898, it wasn't until 1912, when Moss Aztec was developed, that the first of the art lines was introduced. Other art lines were Pereco, Landsun, Chromal, Persian, and Montene. These finishes were semimatt in various colors, blended colors, designs, and iridescent variegated finishes.

Frog, Landsun, 4" long	$ 14- 24
Pitcher, Cavalier design, 7½" high	140-185
Pitcher, wreath design, 11" high .	95-109
Vase, Chromal, Art Deco scene, blue/green, 4¾" high	87- 96
Vase, Moss Aztec, leaf design, 13" high	71- 81
Vase, Pereco, teal blue on Landsun blank, 9½" high	61- 71

Pewter

An alloy of tin with lead, brass or copper, Colonial pieces are rare because the early settlers were not permitted to bring much of the raw material with them when they settled in America. Also, many pieces were melted down to make bullets during our Revolution. Pieces marked pewter generally were made after WWI. Older pieces have English or American touchmarks. **Never** polish old pewter.

Ale cup w/handle, touchmark D.L.	$ 300- 375

Pewter

Baptismal bowl, 6" dia.	275-	300
Cake basket on pierced foot, swinging handle, 10"×3" . .	340-	390
Candlesticks, American, 12" high, pr.	265-	310
Candlesticks, plain w/beaded edge, 9" high, pr.	265-	300
Coffee pot, Dunham, 12" high	145-	165
Compote, marked Pewter, 5" high	74-	85
Creamer, footed, 4" high	100-	125
Cup, American, c. 1840s	195-	235
Dinner plates, English, 18th century, 9", touchmark of Thomas Swanson, set of 6, all	3,300-3,500	
Egg cup, blue glass lining, on round foot, 2"×2"	135-	165
Flower holder, marked D. Barnes	68-	85
Fruit bowl, pedestal, 9" dia. . .	110-	135
Gravy boat	120-	145
Inkwell, 8" dia.	110-	130
Jug, ½-pt., Irish, touchmark Austen & Son, Cork, 5" high	180-	210
Lamp, saucer base, handle, 4" high	145-	175
Mold, candy, elephant	48-	65
Mug, 1-pt., plain loop handle, made by Lane of Peckham .	900-	975
Napkin ring, c. 1890s	22-	29
Peg lamp, American, 4½" high	185-	210
Pitcher, water, Rockford, 19th century	65-	80
Plate, 8" dia. (ill.)	195-	215
Porridge bowl, flat bottom, 6" dia.	260-	275

Porringer, English, 18th century, touchmark W.B. 675- 800
Queen Anne teapot, 9", touchmark of Jas. Dixon 1,400-1,675
Relish holder, 6" high 495- 555
Syrup pitcher, 5½" high 245- 265
Tankard, hinged lid, touchmarks, dated 1901 .... 115- 145
Tankard, 6-qt., center rib, handle, 9" high 325- 375
Teapot, acorn finial, Boardman, 8" high 235- 265
Tray, English touchmarks, 8" high, c. 1880s 165- 180
Tray, hunting scene, 16" wide.................. 145- 180
Vase, Kiberty & Co., 7½" high 125- 145
Water pitcher, strainer at spout, 11" high 395- 440
Whale oil lamp w/bull's-eye shade, 8" high, touchmark of R. Gleason............ 2,175-2,375
Wine cooler, English, 18th century, 8" high, reeded rings on the base, 11" dia. at top.................. 2,300-2,450

Phoenix Glass

Phoenix Glass

This firm, located in Beaver County, Pennsylvania, made a fabricated Pearl Satin glass in the late 1800s. It also produced other glass, some rather good for the period. Don't confuse it with Lalique.

Basket, dogwood, 5" wide ..... $ 58- 68
Bowl, girl in bathing suit, satin finish, pink/green 133-152
Box, covered, green, floral decor, 6" square 72- 82
Candlestick, blue, swirl stem, 4½" high 34- 42
Ginger jar, birds, cover, 9½" high 80- 90
Lamp, fruit decor, brown leaves, vines 120-140

Plate, cherry, 4" dia. 64- 72
Teapot, gold/wine color, 7" high . 50- 60
Vase, blue ground, birds in flight, 8" high (ill.) 90-115
Vase, pillow, white geese in relief on blue ground, 8½" high 110-148
Vase, pinecone decor, purple, 7" high 84- 92
Vase, pink ground, sculptured trumpet vines, original label .. 93-107
Vase, yellow ground, dancing girls, blue/ivory 99-109

Phonographs

Thomas Edison invented the phonograph in 1877 and for years it was known as the "talking machine." Many firms manufactured their own versions. Old Edisons are particularly collectible today.

Columbia AG Grand........$1,400-1,475
Columbia BI 335- 365
Columbia BK, 14" brass belled horn................... 285- 325
Columbia, cylinder 420- 450
Columbia Grafonala, 1911, Regent model 285- 325
Columbia Gramaphone, 1886, 12 cylinders............. 625- 675
Columbia Grand Graphophone, 1905 .... 190- 245
Columbia, keywind 385- 440
Edison Amberola 290- 345
Edison, inside horn, Amberola, 30 cylinder records 325- 365
Edison Maroon Gem, original K reproducer............ 635- 685
Edison, Model C, 12 cylinder records 475- 525
Edison Suitcase Home 345- 375
Gem Graphophone Talking Machine, 1902........... 185- 265
Grand Peerless Talking Machine, 24 cylinder records 465- 535
Graphophone Grand, 1903 ... 270- 310
Modernola, walnut case, complete with lampshade 1,150-1,300
Regina Graphophone, disc-type, 1902 .... 240- 280
Sear's Cecelian, 1924 .... 220- 245
Victor, Gold Medal, 1905, dog trademark............... 285- 455
Victor, Model E., horn, table model.................. 235- 265
Victor, Model VV-IV, oak case, 1906 .... 285- 345
Victor, Royal, 1905, "dog" ... 410- 445

279

(continued)

Victrola, VV-S-215 (Thompson
neutrodyne radio on left
side) 375- 445
Vitanola, 1925 . . . . 245- 285

Phonograph Records

The 78 rpm market generally breaks down
into four major groups: Popular—dance
bands, combos, instrumental units; Classical
—the "straights," strictly defined, operatic
companies; Jazz-Blues—intimate, one-to-one,
a small club, etc.; Country-Western—collect
anything you can get your hands on. H-O-T!
Ajax, Banner, Blue Disc, Brunswick, Capitol,
Comet, Decca, Emerson, HMV (His Master's
Voice), Melotone, Oriole, Regal, Varsity, and
Victor are a few of the many record companies who, struggling and failing, brought
music to what it is today.

Andrews Sisters, "Bei Mir Bist
Du Schoen," 1937 . . . . $ 4- 6
Andrews Sisters, "Beer Barrel
Polka," 1939 . . . . 2- 3
Armstrong, Louis, "Heebie
Jeebies," 1926 36-45
Bailey, Mildred, "Washboard
Blues," 1938 . . . . 4- 5
Berigan, Bunny, "I Can't Get
Started," 1937 . . . . 7- 9
Blake, Eubie, "Baltimore Buzz,"
1921 11-14
Carter, Benny, "Swing It," 1933 . . . 5- 7
Dorsey, Tommy, "Song of India,"
1937 . . . . 3- 5
Garland, Judy, "Over the Rain-
bow," 1939 . . . . 4- 6
Herman, Woody, "Woodchop-
per's Ball," 1939 . . . . 4- 6
McKinney's Cotton Pickers,
"Cherry," 1928 . . . . 6- 8
Savitt, Jan, "720 in the Books,"
1939 . . . . 4- 6
Venuti, Joe, "Weary River,"
1929 8-10
Webb, Chick, "I Can't Dance,"
1934 . . . . 5- 7
Williams, Clarence, "Weary
Blues," 1923 . . . . 6- 9
Wilson, Teddy, "Rosetta," 1935 . . . 7- 9

Photography

Mathew B. Brady, best known for his
photographs of Lincoln and the Civil War,
created the public's interest in photography.
Today, millions enjoy this fascinating hobby

Photography

Adlake Repeater 4"×5" plate,
made by Adams & West-
lake Co., Chicago, Ill. . . . . . $ 70- 85
Adox 35mm, made by Adox
Kamerawerk, Wiesbaden,
Germany, c. 1930s 30- 40
Amerex 16mm subminiature,
made in Occupied Japan,
1948 . . . . 19- 25
Anscoset 35mm rangefinder,
made by Ansco 95- 115
Buster Brown box, made by
Ansco 14- 18
Buster Brown folding,
No. 2A 13- 18
Cadet Model B2 box, made by
Ansco 6- 9
Climax Detective, made by
E. & H.T. Anthony, c. late
1890s 1,200-1,450
Climax Enlarging, made by
E. & H.T. Anthony, c. late
1890s 165- 170
Dollar Box, 1910, made by
Ansco 22- 33
Hawkeye Junior box camera
for rollfilm or 4"×5" plates,
c. late 1890s 93- 103
Klimax 5"×7" folding plate,
c. 1912, made by Butcher &
Sons, London, England . . . 50- 60
Kodak, Autographic Special
No. 2C, c. 1920s 48- 58
Kodak, Brownie No. 1 box, for
117 film, c. 1900 . . . . 285- 300
Kodak, Brownie No. 3 box, for
124 film, c. 1905-34 . . . . 12- 19
Kodak No. 3, 118 film,
c. 1915-26 . . . . 25- 30
Kodak No. 3A folding pocket
camera (ill.) 100- 115
Leica B "Compur" model
35mm viewfinder, dial-set,
c. 1927 3,500-3,700
Leica C 35mm viewfinder 290- 320
Leica G, 5/50mm, c. late
1930s 135- 150

Lumiere Sinox folding, for
rollfilm, made by Lumiere &
Co., Lyon, France   16-   19
Mason Harvard all-metal
pinhold camera for plates,
c. 1890 . . . .   165- 180
Mendel Detective, for plates,
high-speed lens 150- 165
Mikut Color, for 3 color
separation negatives on 1
plate, c. 1930s 325- 360
Nettel Deckrullo, for 9×12cm
plates, c. 1919   55-   65
Plaubel Makina III folding,
c. 1930 . . . .   160- 175
QRS Kamra, bakelite box, for
35mm film, late 1920s   45-   55
Ray box, for 30½″×30½″
plates   65-   75
Reflex folding focal, for plates,
postcard size, c. 1912 . . . . .   140- 160
Rex magazine, for 4″×5″
plates, c. late 1890s 120- 140
Scovill folding view, for
5″×8″ plates, Waterbury
lens, c. late 1880s 180- 200
Seneca box, for 4″×5″ plates .   25-   30
Trio No. 1A folding, for 120
film   20-   25
Univex plastic box, for No. 00
film, model A, c. 1936   14-   17
Vive No. 1 box, for plates,
c. 1890s, made by Vive
Camera Co.   85-   95
Vokar I rangefinder, for 35mm
film, c. 1940 . . . .   93- 103
Welta folding, for 35mm film,
c. 1930   30-   38
Wirgin Stereo, for 35mm film,
Steinheil Cassar lenses   60-   68

Piano Rolls

Piano Rolls

Now that player pianos are making a comeback, here's a simplified guide to tell you
which piano rolls work on which type player
piano and/or organ.

281

Average price, in working condition . . $6-8
(Certain AMPICO rolls bring $45
or more.)
Piano Roll Guide
A roll—basic coin piano roll of nickelodeon
industry.
G roll—later 4X rolls. Keyboard style L, G,
KT, KT special.
H roll—Styles J, H and most Seeburg
photoplayers.
MSR roll—Styles MO, celeste and most
Seeburg photoplayers, interchangeable
with H rolls.
HO roll—used on small pipe organs.
XP roll—used on style X expression piano,
also style Phono-Grand.

Pianos

Pianos

Maker, condition, year made—these dictate
price.

American Home upright,
maple, full size,
c. 1903 . . . . $ 350- 475
Baldwin Baby Grand, c.
late 1890s 550- 675
Beckwith Cabinet Grand,
upright, c. 1890s 1,250-1,400
Broadwood Grand 2,850-3,400
Chickering Ampico-A
Grand 5,100-5,350
Cranisch & Bach, rose-
wood, c. 1890s 4,500-4,750
Emerson Oak Grand 5,200-5,350
Kimball Grand 4,100-4,350
Schiller, c. 1890s,
upright 1,450-1,600
Sears, Roebuck Home
Favorite, mahogany,
c. 1890s 750- 875

(continued)

Steinway & Sons Grand,
7' rosewood case,
c. 1876 . . . . 14,000+

Steinway & Sons Grand,
inlaid satinwood/
mahogany w/Wedg-
wood porcelain
medallions (ill.) 7,400-8,400

Pianos, Seeburg

From 1907 to 1927, J.P. Seeburg's company manufactured thousands of nickelodeon pianos, orchestrions, and other automatic musical devices such as the Phono-Grand, a combination phonograph and compact piano. The Rudolph Wurlitzer Company was Seeburg's chief rival. Most of the rolls for the above instruments were cut by the Clark Orchestra Roll Company, DeKalb, Illinois, or the Automatic Music Roll Company, a Seeburg subsidiary. Other excellent arrangements can be found on Capitol and Columbia rolls.

Pickard

Wilder Pickard founded his company in Illinois around 1894. They're still in business. Once buying their pottery blanks from other firms, they now make their own.

Bowl, flowers and leaves, gold,
signed . . . . $ 78- 90

Bowl, fruit, leaves, gold fluted
top, 8" high. 62- 75

Box, powder, with lid, Art Deco
flowers, gold/black/cream,
signed 110-185

Candlesticks, etched gold, 4"
high, pr. 65- 78

Chocolate pot, pearlized ground,
white, orchids, green leaves . . . 210-280

Compote, violet/gold, artist
signed, 8" high 175-240

Creamer and sugar, forest scene,
gold handles and rim, pr. 90-115

Dish, open handles, 8" dia. 28- 32

Pitcher, cider, gold color, blue
trim. 58- 70

Pitcher, orange poppies, signed
Fuchs 56- 75

Plate, gold center, flowers,
signed, 7" dia. 22- 36

Relish dish, pink/blue, floral,
signed 26- 37

Salt/pepper, pr., all gold, 4"
high 32- 40

Teapot, gold colors, 5" high,
cover 58- 68

Tray, garden scene, signed E.
Challinor. 350-400

Vase, floral, gold, signed,
12" high 67- 77

Vase, peacock, multicolored,
paper label, signed E.
Challinor. 525-700

Vase, scenic, signed Marke 80- 92

Pickle Casters

Pickle Casters

Consisting of a glass jar sitting in a metal frame, with tongs and/or fork, usually made of quadruple plate, sometimes sterling silver. Considered a novelty of the late 1800s, they were more decorative than functional. Also see **Pattern Glass Section** for specific patterns.

Amber, Cane pattern $170-190

Amberina, ITP, spoonholder and
tongs 425-480

Amethyst, enameled flowers 250-300

Birds/flowers, enameled, blue/
white, silver fork, frame 110-130

Blue looping, white threaded
glass, silver fork, frame 99-107

Blue/white, Spanish Lace, silver
fork, frame 95-120

Chain and Shield pattern, silver
fork, frame 70- 80

Clear, Cane (ill.). 80- 90

Cranberry, silver fork, frame 140-155

Cranberry, ITP, silver fork, frame 220-240

Cupid and Psyche, silver fork,
frame 140-155

Daisy and Button, amber, silver
  fork frame 108-127
Dark green glass, Thistle pattern
  down side, silver fork, frame . . 110-125
Fine Cut pattern, clear, silver
  fork, frame, footed 140-175
Herringbone pattern, green,
  silver fork, tongs, frame 130-148

Picture Frames

Picture Frames

There are so many composition frames around today that a word of caution is necessary. Never clean gold gilt or gold leaf with water—**always** use alcohol. It won't dissolve the gold and/or plaster of paris molding. Use spackle to fill in broken areas, using fingernail cleaning tools to finish the design just before the spackle is hard. Then regilt. If too shiny, use cigarette ash moistened with water to dull the gold finish.

Black, gold leaf liner, 16"×26",
  c. 1875 . . . .$175-195
Black/gold leaf, open network
  cylinder composition,
  18"×26" 190-220
Gold leaf, 9"×16", c. 1880s 150-175
Oak, gold liner, 14"×17",
  c. 1860s 120-135
Oak, silver liner, 8"×10",
  c. 1880s 100-120
Oval, applied composition pieces,
  16"×20", c. 1890 120-130
Oval, applied gold composition
  pieces, 10"×12", c. 1870s 115-128
Oval, simulated wood grain,
  14"×18", c. 1900 85-100

Oval, walnut, 9"×12", c. 1880s . . 120-130
Simulated wood grain, burnished
  gold liner, 10"×14", c. 1870s
  (ill.) 115-120
Toned wood, cylinder composi-
  tion, 16"×20", c. 1860s 145-155
Tortoise, gold gilt liner, 10"×12",
  c. 1860s 155-170
Walnut cross, carved leaf corners,
  burnished gold liner 75- 85
4-frame, 10"×12", gold gilt,
  c. 1870s 115-130
4-frame, 20"×24", gold leaf,
  c. 1887 135-140
3-frame, 16"×20", walnut outer
  frame, gold composition liner,
  c. 1890s 115-130

Pigeon's Blood Glass

Pigeon's Blood Glass

This red glass was made near the end of the 1800s. Today, some dealers sell any dark red glass as Pigeon's Blood. The original is an orange-red.

Bottle, cologne, 5" high $185-240
Bowl, beaded top, fluted sides,
  9" dia. 170-210
Butter dish, covered, 8" wide 195-240
Candlesticks, footed, twisted
  stem, 9¼" high, pr. 180-240
Candy dish, overlay, 8" dia. 72- 90
Caster set, 5-bottle, silver caps . . 240-280
Child's mug, "For a Good Boy,"
  5½" high, handled 92-128
Compote, 7" high 192-240
Compote, scalloped edge, 8" high 195-260
Creamer, metal top, clear applied
  handle 160-185
Pitcher, clear applied handle,
  11" high 265-290
Salt, hexagonal, red/orange (ill.) . . 30- 40
Syrup jug, metal top 160-185
Tumbler, 4½" high 82- 92
Vase, pedestal base, scalloped
  edge, 8½" high 135-145

(continued)

Vase, pink/white flowers, green
leaves, 12½" high 460-560
Vase, slender neck, flat base,
enameled, 7" high, France 180-190

Pincushions

Pincushions

In every shape, made from every material, they were used for just that—pins. Later they held safety pins. They were popular during the 19th century when young ladies stayed home and sewed.

Average price $6-12

Pink Lustre China

Pink Lustre China

Made in the Staffordshire District, England, in the early 1800s, it gets its name from pink decorations used on the ware. Houses and fernlike trees were popular decorations. It is comparatively scarce today.

Biscuit barrel, 5½" high, houses/
trees $160-170
Bowl, houses/trees, 4" dia.   90-110
Bowl, trees, 6¼" dia.   90-100

Box, covered, 2½"×2¼"×3¾" .   95-110
Butter dish, covered, houses/
trees 85- 93
Cup (handless)/saucer, floral
pattern (ill.) 58- 67
Cup/saucer, schoolhouse pattern .   58- 67
Mug, child's house/trees, c. 1850,
3½" high 77- 85
Pitcher, floral pattern, 8¼" high . 130-140
Pitcher, house/trees, 7½" high . . 130-140
Plate, child with lamb, 7¾" dia. . .   53- 61
Plate, floral pattern, 8¼" dia. . . .   53- 61
Plate, floral pattern, 7½" dia.
(ill.) 53- 61
Plate, houses/trees, 8" dia. 53- 61
Slipper, souvenir, Chicago
World's Fair 30- 38
Sugar bowl, floral pattern 82- 91
Sugar bowl, houses/trees 123-132
Teapot, floral pattern, 6½" high . 122-130
Teapot, houses/trees, 6¼" high . . 122-130

Pink Slag

This rare glass is surrounded in mystery as to where it was made and by whom. Possibly Challinor, Taylor and Company made some at Tarentum, Pennsylvania. They made the purple (marble) glass. Miniature lamps in the shape of swans bring huge prices today. Also see **Pattern Glass Section.**

Berry bowl, 6½" dia. $690- 780
Butter dish, covered, 6" dia. . . .   1,000+
Creamer, 3½" high, handled . . .   600- 700
Lamp, miniature, in shape
of swan (one at Houston
Museum) 925- 985
Punch cup 500- 600
Sugar bowl, covered, 4" high . .   725- 760
Tumbler, ITP or Inverted
Feather and Fan, 4" high . . .   440- 485

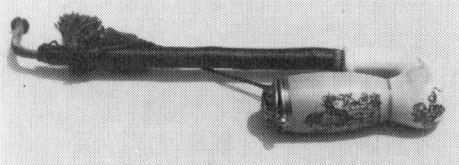

Pipes

Pipes

Pipe bowls were carved from briar roots, meerschaum, or molded in porcelain and clay. When or who lit up the first one is lost to history.

Beethoven, briar, carved . . . . $ 62- 70
Briar, carved, sea captain 62- 72

Deer's head carved into bowl,
curved 10" stem 95-115
Elk's head bowl, B.P.O.E. and
date, straight 6" stem 68- 79
Face of monk in bowl, curved 7"
stem, clay 51- 60
Lion devouring prey, curved
stem, 11", briar 75- 85
Meerschaum, deer pursued by
dog, 9" curved stem 54- 64
Meerschaum, horse's head, trees,
9½" curved stem 70- 80
Opium pipe, Chinese figures, 14"
long, old 77- 86
Panther's head, glass eyes, 10"
straight stem 54- 64
Porcelain bowl, painted decor
(ill.) 52- 62
Satyr, briar, carved 61- 70

Blue basketweave, 10" high 65- 75
Clear glass, shades to blue/green
at top, blown, 11" high 110-122
Cut, Strawberry and Fan, clear
applied handle, signed Libbey . 182-196
Daisy and Button, V ornament,
12½" high 120-140
End-of-Day (Spatter glass), multi-
colored, 9½" high 108-121
Pomona first grind, 7½" high . . . 675-750
Royal Vienna, painting of church,
village background, 9" high . . . 153-164
Sapphire blue, clear applied
handle, blown, 8" high 110-130

Pisgah Forest Pottery

Pisgah Forest Pottery

Walter B. Stephen founded this firm near Mt. Pisgah, North Carolina, in 1914. With his mother he produced a pâte-sur-pâte decorating technique, using as themes American scenes such as log cabins, buffalos, and covered wagons. Stephens also developed a high gloss glaze in several colors. He passed away in 1961, but the pottery is still in operation. Early pieces would be quite collectible today.

Vase, 5½" high, crackle glaze,
turquoise color, pink lined (ill.) . $ 49- 70

Pitchers, Glass

Every company made them in every size and shape. The Houston Museum's collection of over 15,000 pitchers is said to be the largest in the world. Any challengers? Also see **Pattern Glass Section.**

Amethyst, clear applied handle,
9" high . . . . $ 60- 70

Plated Amberina

Plated Amberina

This extremely rare art glass was made by the New England Glass Company in 1886. Opalescent glass was plated with a gold-ruby mixture, then reheated to develop a deeper color of certain portions which would then blend into the lighter part of the glass. Being reproduced.

Bowl, 8" dia., 4" high . . . . $6,800+
Cup, punch . . . . 3,800+
Pitcher, 7" high (ill.) . . . . 5,600+
Syrup jug . . . . 5,000+
Tumbler . . . . 3,400+
Vase, 6½" high, in silver holder . . . . 6,400+

These and others can be seen at the Houston Museum.

Playing Cards

The decks you find in shops today are usually from the past 75 years. Index numbers in the corners were used after 1877. The decks of European cards, before 1850, are rare and hard to find.

(continued)

Playing Cards

Advertising type, Louisville and
  Nashville R.R. . . . . $ 6-11
Advertising type, 20th Century
  Limited, seal unbroken 7- 9
French, early 1800s (ill.) 24-33
Marilyn Monroe, different poses,
  2 decks in illustrated box 60-70
Russian, early 1800s (ill.) 27-37
Shirley Temple, seal unbroken   9-12
World's Fair, New York, 1939 11-20

Pomona Glass

Pomona Glass

Joseph Locke invented it in 1884, first producing it at the New England Glass Company. It's a frosted ground on clear glass and decorated with mineral stains. Two types were made—first and second grind. First grind was etched by acid; second grind, the cheaper of the two methods, consisted of rolling the glass piece in particles of acid-resisting materials which were picked up by it. The piece was then etched. It's always blown. Don't confuse it with Midwest

Pomona, a pressed glass in which you can see the mold lines.

Bowl, second grind, amber,
  4½″ dia. $140-160
Box, cornflower design, first
  grind 158-168
Celery vase, amber flashed, first
  grind 455-525
Creamer, cornflower motif,
  second grind 150-170
Cruet, first grind, applied foot,
  cornflower decor, 7″ high (ill.) . 300-350
Cup, punch, first grind, diamond
  quilted, 2¼″ high (ill.) 195-240
Cup/saucer, diamond-quilted
  pattern, second grind 110-130
Pitcher, blue, floral designs,
  pebbled surface, first grind . . . 575-650
Tray, cornflower, first grind,
  12″ long 272-350
Tumbler, oak leaf, second grind,
  4″ high 180-220
Vase, amber flashed, second
  grind, 3½″ high 210-260
Vase, amber flashed, second
  grind, 3½″ high 210-260

Pontil Mark

So many people ask, "What is a pontil mark?" It is simply the scar left on the bottom of a piece of blown glass where the pontil rod has been broken off. The pontil rod was used to hold the glassware during its manufacture. Pontil marks are either jagged or ground smooth. Smooth globs of glass sometimes have been put on the bottom by manufacturers of new glass to make you think it's old and blown. Careful!

Porcelains, Miniature

Porcelains, Miniature

It was popular in the 18th and 19th cen-

286

turies to paint faces on tiny pieces of porcelain which were then put in lockets or inside watches. Church scenes and landscapes were also popular.

French, church scene, 1″×1½″,
  18th century $110-150
French, little boy, 1½″×2″ (ill.) . . 135-160
American, 19th century (ill. far
  right), Miss Lillian Russell 150-190

Porto Bello Ware

Porto Bello Ware

Made at Portobello Pottery, Midlothian, Scotland, late 18th century to commemorate Admiral Vernon's victory over the Spanish at Puerto Bello, Panama, on November 23, 1739. Usually it is a brownish-red pottery, glazed, with figures of ships, fortifications or other scenes. Designs on the first pieces made were in white. It remained popular until the 1860s and can be found in shops today.

Bowl, 4″ dia. $180-220
Jug, 7″ high 250-270
Pitcher, large (ill.) 250-310
Pitcher, small 235-275
Plate, English coat-of-arms, 7″
  dia. 170-190
Platter, view of Puerto Bello,
  11½″ long 145-180
Tray, octagonal, signed 300-390
Probably many other pieces.

Portrait Plates

Considered fashionable in the late 1800s, these plates featured portraits, usually female, and were produced commercially for several years.

Blonde woman, copyright, 1909,
  11″ dia. . . . . $ 40- 50
Garfield, 13 stars around border,
  10″ dia. 37- 46

Girl's head, date 1884, France,
  10″ dia. 40- 49
His Majesty, Meakin, 11″ dia. . . . 40- 50
Lady's bust, blue, pink flowers,
  8″ dia. 41- 50
Abraham Lincoln and wife, 10″
  dia. 95-107
Louis XV, Sevres, 10″ dia.,
  blue/gold trim 150-170
Man holding bird, forest scene,
  8″ dia. 42- 52
Peasant girl in wheatfield, 10″
  dia. 50- 59
Queen Elizabeth II, Johnson
  Brothers, 10½″ dia. 50- 62
Three ladies at fountain,
  Germany, 11″ dia. 40- 52
George/Martha Washington,
  reticulated edges, Germany, 8″
  dia. 67- 77
Martha Washington, white
  ground, pink roses, Germany . 51- 60

Postcards

Postcards

Originating in Austria in 1869, the penny postcard's popularity has grown steadily over the years. Some things to consider when buying postcards for a collection or for resale are subject, color and detail, condition; also, has it been cancelled. Cancellation marks are important because of the reproductions flooding the market in recent years. Whether you buy postcards in bulk or individually, collecting them can be a rewarding hobby. Prices range from 10¢ to $50, depending, of course, on value. Average price, 25¢.

Pot Lids

The Pratt Works at Fenton, England, made most of them. Used for holding shaving soaps, hair oil, etc., they were popular in

(continued)

Pot Lids

the mid-to-late 1800s. Designs were placed under the glaze by a multicolor transfer method similar to decals of today.

Checker Game	$ 95-107
Contrast	95-109
Garibaldi	94-104
Hide and Seek	92-103
Lovers on the Bridge	92-107
Low Life	98-106
A Pair	84-100
Racing Scene	99-110
The Shrimpers	82- 92
Village Wedding	92-107
Warming at the Fire	92-107

Pottery, Early American

Pottery, Early American

During the 1800s and 1900s, a great deal of homemade pottery was made in this country. What Ma needed in the kitchen, Pa made in his crude kiln.

Bowl, milk, red clay, 10″ dia.	$ 50- 60
Crocks	
2-gal., gray, blue flowers, no lid ..	68- 79
3-gal., Pennsylvania redware, no lid	75- 85

5-gal., gray, blue lettering, lid ...	75- 85
16-gal., gray, stenciled name, no lid	140-160
Foot warmer, marked "Logan Cnty., Ohio," blue/gray, with wooden stopper	88- 97
Jugs	
1-gal., druggist, brown, handled (ill.)	54- 62
2-gal., for "moonshine," cob stop.	50- 60
5-gal., tan/brown, stenciled name.	69- 78
Pitcher, tanware, 5½″-6½″ high .	127-134
Saltbox, hanging type, Logan County, Ohio, blue/gray, wooden lid	38- 48
Tray, red clay, crude handles, dated 1854	58- 68

Powder Horns and Flasks

Powder Horns and Flasks

With the invention of the muzzle-loader rifle and pistol, these items were a necessity. From the crudest type, a cow's horn, to the ornately engraved brass and copper models, all are most collectible today.

Brass and pewter, 8½″ long, c. 1830	$100-125
Brass, fluted sides, patent dispenser, c. early 1800s	155-170
Brass, hunter and dog, patent dispenser, 5″ long	165-180
Brass, 6″ long, hanging game on both sides (ill.)	85-195
Brass, small, 4½″ long, type found in cased Colts	145-170
Calf's horn, wooden plug type, early 1800s, hand-carved	70- 80
Carved powder horn, New Hampshire, 14″ long, c. 1846	365-400
Civil War, CSA, base metal, 8″ long	75- 85

(continued)

lockwise, from top: Covered tureen with ladle, $295-310. Butter chip, $12-14. Coffee cup
60-70. Cup plate, $45-55. Mush bowl, $45-55. Large plate, $24-26. Covered brush holder,
145-155. Egg cup, $200+ (rare). Bread or service tray, $50-60. Covered vegetable,
135-145. Coffeepot, $145-155. Milk pitcher, $135-145. Chocolate cup, $225+ (rare).

hotograph from *Grandma's Tea Leaf Ironstone* by Annise Doring Heaivilin.

Top row: Teapot, $30-33. Cup, $5-6. Coffeepot, $20-23. Cup, $3-4. Pekin teapot, $43-46
Measure, $11-13. Milk kettle, $23-26. Teapot, $22-24. Coffeepot, $36-38. *Second row:* Egg
pan, $11-13. Cuspidor, $43-47. Sugar bowl, $34-36. Coffeepot, $11-13. Funnel, $11-13. Cof
feepot, $16-19. Teakettle, $24-26. Pitcher, $11-13. Pie plate, $5-7. Egg cup, gold trim
$14-16. *Third row:* Covered kettle, $24-26. Churn, $140-160. Spoon, $5-7. Pekin teapot
$26-28. Roaster, $24-26, Pie plate, $8-10. Coffeepot, $34-36. "Reed" oval roaster, $15-17
Photograph from *Graniteware Collectors' Guide with Prices* by Vernagene Vogelzang and
Evelyn Welch.

o row: Two-toned coffeepot, $21-23. Brown teapot, $11-13. Pekin teapot, $21-23. White teapot, -46. Green teapot, $5-7. Green percolator, $24-26. Green percolator, side handle, $14-16. Yellow and ite teapot, $34-36. Yellow coffeepot, $9-11. Brown coffeepot, $14-16. Brown teapot, nickel lid, $36-38. *ond Row:* Black and white cake pan, $5-7. Brown and white pan, $14-15. Orange and white ashtray, -13. Floral soup plate, $8-10. Green Chrysolite tea steeper, $36-38. Shaded green coffeepot, $14-16. wn teapot, $16-18. Green pie plate, $8-10. *Third row:* Brown dipper, $11-13. Orange dipper, Poland, 7. Yellow skimmer, Poland, $5-7. Brown and white sugar bowl, $46-48. Yellow bowl, $5-7. Dark green per, $7-9. Metallic green platter, $14-16. Brown funnel, $6-8. "Corona" fruit design plate, $7-9. xican cup, $3-4. Platter, $7-9. Red, white tray, $24-26. Brown, white kettle, $34-36.

otograph from *Graniteware Collectors' Guide with Prices* by Vernagene Vogelzang and elyn Welch.

Book Worm, Hum. 8, $80-100.

Large Nativity Set, Hum. 260, $2,200-2,800.

Photographs from *Hummel Art II* by John F. Hotchkiss.

She Loves Me, She Loves Me Not,
Hum. 174, $65-80.

Let's Sing, Hum. 110/0, $50-75.

Doll Mother, Hum. 67, $90-110.

Apple Tree Girl, Hum. 141,
$100-120.

Photographs from *Hummel Art II* by John F. Hotchkiss.

Walnut bureau washstand with splash back, towel bars, projection front, round knobs, chamfer stiles, plank sides, 37″×15½″×35″, $375-450. Symphonian mahogany veneered music box, $2,500-2,700.

Photograph from *Victorian Furniture Styles and Prices, Book II* by Robert and Harriet Swedberg.

Eastlake walnut parlor table, burl veneer, 30″×21½″×28″, $275-325.

Pair of walnut gentleman's chairs, tufted backs, cabriole legs, flower crests, 38½″ high, each, $475-525.

Photographs from *Victorian Furniture Styles and Prices, Book II* by Robert and Harriett Swedberg.

Assorted thimbles with animal, bird, fish and fowl motifs in a variety of materials. *Top row:* Reindeer, $110-120. *Third row:* Seagull, Denmark, $16-22. *Fourth row:* Sinclair Oil advertising plastic, $2-5.

Photograph from *Thimble Americana* by Myrtle Lundquist.

Bald Kestner Hilda, 16″ tall, D. Kay
Crow collection, $1,400-1,600.

All bisque, 9″ tall, marked "164/13,"
stationary glass eyes, jointed limbs,
D. Kay Crow collection, $275-325.

Heubach baby, 6″ tall,
marked "HEU" in a square,
all original, D. Kay Crow collection, $225-240.

Photographs from
*Herron's Price Guide to
Dolls and Paper Dolls*
by R. Lane Herron.

An array of miscellaneous kitchen gadgets ranging in price from $1-15.

Photograph from *Kitchens and Gadgets in the American Home, 1920-1950* by Jane H. Celehar.

Left to right: Green-handled beater and pitcher set, $9-18. Revolving cookie cutter, $5-8.50. Cream and egg whip, $6.50-15. Bottle and jar opener, $2-3.50. Bottle, can, jar opener, $3.50-6.

Photograph from *Kitchens and Gadgets in the American Home, 1920-1950* by Jane H. Celehar.

1 Eli Terry, Jr., Terryville, Conn., 1837, mahogany mantel clock, 30-hour, brass works, double door, $620-710. 2 Seth Thomas, Plymouth Hollow, Conn., mahogany mantel clock, 8-day, wooden works, double door, $450-575. 3 Ansonia Clock Co., 1880, walnut teardrop shelf clock, time and strike, $365-450. 4 French-style metal case clock, 8-day, time and strike, $165-225. 5 Welch, Spring & Co., Forestville, Conn., Pat. 1868, rosewood, round top, full pillars, 8-day time and strike, $195-240.

Photograph from *Clock Guide Identification with Prices* by Robert W. Miller.

1 Eldridge G. Atkins, Bristol, Conn., 1838-1842, mahogany, 30-hour, wooden movement, $560-665.   2 John Berge, Bristol, Conn., 1830-1860, triple decker, 8-day,
weight driven, brass movement, $725-850.   3 Ansonia Clock Co., "Trianon,"
bronze finish, porcelain insert, 8-day, time and strike, $260-325.   4 New Haven
Clock Co., mirrored sides, walnut shelf clock, $295-345.   5 Ansonia Clock Co.,
bronze, figure of Newton, visible escapement, 8-day time and strike, $380-425.

Photograph from *Clock Guide Identification with Prices* by Robert W. Miller.

301

An array of signed American majolica from the 1880s. *Top row:* Griffen, Smith & Company Etruscan Shell and Seaweed centerpiece, $285-310. *Second row:* Etruscan Ball Players Cider Jug, $400-450. Hummingbird plate from the Eureka Pottery Company, Trenton, N.J., $65-85. Clifton Decor vase by the Chesapeake Pottery Company, $60-75. *Third row:* Fern pattern jug from the Etruscan potters, $115-140. Small Sunflower jug, Etruscan, $125-150. Lettuce Leaf plate by Wannopee Pottery Company, New Milford, Conn., $35-45. Fish pattern bouquet holder by George Morley, $75-90. Etruscan Sunflower underplate, $65-85. Avalon Faience vase by Chesapeake Pottery Company, $40-60. *Bottom row:* Shell and Seaweed lidded butter keeper by Griffen, Smith & Company, $300-350. Leaf pattern tray by the Tenuous Pottery Company, $30-40. Etruscan-made Shell and Seaweed cigar box, $300-350. Prices for all American majolica pictured are based on rarity, color, artistry of workmanship, and are for pieces in perfect condition.

Photograph from *American Majolica, 1850-1900* by M. Charles Rebert.

American majolica pieces in Shell and Seaweed pattern. *Top row:* cake stand, $285-310. Saucedish, $45-65. Array of plates, each, $75-125. Teacup and saucer, $100-125. Shell-shaped, footed ice cream dish, $45-65. Centerpiece, $285-310. *Bottom row:* cider jug, $165-195. Waste bowl, $95-120. Spooner, $90-110. Large serving platter, $195-225. Coffeepot, crooked spout, $195-225. Three butter pats, each $45-60. Lidded sugar, $165-195. Creamer, $100-125. Jug, $145-165. All pieces in perfect condition.

Photograph from *American Majolica, 1850-1900* by M. Charles Rebert.

Very rare ice water jar, applied handles, brush decorated design in cobalt, impressed Red Wing Stoneware Company on lower front, $2,000-2,250.

Photograph from *The Clay Giants, Book 2* by Lyndon C. Viel.

Civil War, pewter, brass cap and
   tip, 7½" long, marked U.S. ...   70- 80
Copper, eagle, dated 1804, 7"
   long   150-170
Cow's horn, 8" long, brass cap
   and tip, c. 1845 ....   65- 73
Cow's horn, scrimshaw-carved
   eagle and name, signed
   Herman B. Seaborn, c. 1840
   (ill.)   175-225
Japanese flask, for matchlock
   musket, 8" long, c. 1780   115-140
Leather flask, brass trimmings,
   9" long, c. 1845 ....   60- 69
Persian flask, brass, 10¼" long,
   c. mid-18th century   124-144
Pistol, Colt's patent, 4½" long,
   brass, zinc, c. 1855   125-145
Pistol, 3½" long, brass, c. 1835 ..   74- 92

Pomade jar, signed, 3" high   90-110
Snuff jar, blue/tan/black, animal
   scene 42- 51
Sugar, matches creamer above ..   145-160
Teapot, large, Greek maidens,
   6" to spout (ill.)   220-270
Teapot, pastoral scenes, 7" to
   spout   240-270
Urn, hunt scene, 4½" high   90-110
Vase, red/black, deer in forest,
   8" high   120-140

Pre-Columbian Artifacts

Pratt Ware

Pratt Ware

The Fenton factory in the Staffordshire District, England, made this pottery from 1775 to 1805. Raised figures and decorations highly colored in green, purple, black, and orange are qualities of Pratt. Transfer pictures were also used. See **Pot Lids.**

Box, green/purple, naval battle,
   covered .... $ 87- 97
Candelholder, black/orange, pr.,
   11" high 80- 92
Compote, church scene, 4" high ..   168-188
Creamer, gray/green, cottage
   scene, 4" high   142-162
Cup/saucer, scenic transfer 50- 60
Pitcher, Doves of Peace, 5" high,
   purple/orange/green   285-300
Plate, fuchsia/purple/green, 10"
   dia. 74- 82
Plate, horse race, blue, gold trim,
   9" dia. 80- 90

Pre-Columbian Artifacts

So many fakes are on the market, it's difficult to give you a fair price. If interested in this type of art, **Know Your Dealer**—even that is no guarantee. We mention the subject here because so much of it is flooding American and European markets. Watch it, senor! **Yes,** the illustration is a fake.

Burial figures, male or female,
   solid, from western Mexico,
   3" to 6" tall, ea. .... $ 60- 70
Colima figure, female, 5½"
   high   100-120
Clay heads, male or female,
   from Vera Cruz—Huastec
   culture, ea. 12- 19
Religious figures, Huastec
   (figures were broken as part
   of the religious rite), 2" to
   6" tall, ea. 11- 22
Stone carved figure,
   1500-5000 B.C. (ill.)   800-1,000
Vicus pitcher, dog head, 8½"
   oval   750-850

Presidential Collectibles

Presidential Collectibles

These are items such as autographs or menus from the White House. Matchbooks marked "Stolen from the White House" were presidential favorites. Also photos, lithographs, anything having to do with United States presidents.

Fountain pen marked FDR, used
  to sign Congressional bill, 1936 $ 47- 56
Lithograph, Jefferson Davis,
  ɔresident of Confederate
  S⁺ates (ill.). 42- 52
Matchbooks, presidential seal or
  "stolen" type 8- 12
"Peanut" card, Carter campaign,
  1976 . . . . 2- 3
Photo of Harry Truman, signed . 78- 88
Senate restaurant menu, LBJ
  scribbled on front 21- 31

Primitives

Primitives

If you like primitives, buy *American Primitives* by Robert W. Miller, Wallace-Homestead Book Co., Des Moines, Iowa 50309, or from your local bookstore.

Adjustable candleholder, tin,
  1840s, 6″ high. . . . . $ 64- 74
Andirons, brass, ball type,
  1840s 240-270
Andirons, claw feet, hand-forged
  1840s 140-160
Battling stick, used for washing
  clothes, early 1800s 50- 60
Bed warmer, copper, maple
  handle, 1830s 240-260
Beeswax mold, used to make
  blocks of beeswax, 2-pc.,
  1820s 110-130
Bellows, wood, leather, crude,
  1820s 68- 78
Betty lamp, wrought iron, twisted
  rod on hook, 1820s 265-310
Block plane, #4 size, maple,
  Kingston, N.Y., 1840 . . . . 60- 70
Branding iron, initials, "T.Y."
  mid-1800s 88- 99
Brass kettle, 6-gal., w/iron bail
  handle, 1840s 315-345
Broad ax, mid-1800s 295-340
Broom press, used to make crude
  brooms, early 1800s 68- 78
Buttress, used for trimming
  hooves of oxen, early 1800s . . . 67- 77
Cabbage cutter, 1830s (ill.) 44- 54
Cabbage cutter, early 19th
  century (ill.) 52- 62
Candle mold, tin, 12-tube,
  15″ high, 1830s. 125-145
Cane or sorghum cutter,
  wooden handle, mid-1800s 97-109
Cherry pitter, cast iron, 1860s . . . 70- 80
Closed scorp, used to carve dough
  bowls, 1820s (ill.) 48- 57
Cobbler's clamp, maple, 2-pc.,
  mid-1800s 160-180
Cooper's ax, mid-1800s 245-180
Corn grater, early 1800s 39- 47
Cornhusker, wooden w/leather
  thumb holder, mid-1800s 29- 38
Cowbell, copper, 8″ high,
  mid-1800s 42- 52
Cowbell, tin, 4″ high, 1840s 44- 52
Double Cruise (Phoebe lamp),
  mid-1700s 220-270
Dough bowl, carved from
  buckeye wood, 1820s, 18″ long 94-109
Fence stretcher, iron, mid-1800s . 78- 87
Flail, used to separate wheat
  from chaff, 2-pc., wooden 62- 74

Flambeau or flaming torch, used
to light the way when checking
railroad engines at night,
mid-1800s 115-130

Froe, used to make wooden
shingles, early 1800s 78- 88

Goat yoke, bent hickory,
mid-1800s 82- 91

Grinding stone made from
sandstone, 19″ dia., early 1800s   81- 91

Hand adze, early 1800s 81- 90

Hand-carved pulley block,
early 1800s   89-110

Handmade mousetrap, twisted
wire, mid-1800s, 10½″ long . . .   59- 68

Hetchel, used to remove flax
husk, early 19th century 52- 70

Hitching block, cast iron,
c. 1850s, buggy type 59- 68

"Hog scraper" candlestick,
5″ high, early 1800s 78- 90

Horse bit, 1830s (ill.) 18- 27

Horse collar made from corn-
husks, late 1700s 62- 71

Ice chisel, used to cut ice from
frozen lakes and ponds, 1840s . 120-130

Ice tongs, iron, late 1800s 81- 92

Kettle, dovetail bottom, iron bail
handle, 1830s, 26″ dia. 470-540

Maple chopping block, on legs,
mid-1800s 350-380

Maple rolling pin, early 1800s . . .   50- 60

Meal scoop, mid-1800s 51- 61

Meal sifter, used to remove lumps
from flour, 1840s 58- 68

Meat scale, brass, 1860s 160-180

Nutmeg grater, tin, wall-type,
late 1800s 36- 45

Peavey, complete with wooden
handle, 1850s 152-171

Pie crimper, double wheel,
early 1800s 52- 62

Roll, "devil's wire" (barbed wire),
1860s, per ft. 1- 2

"Rope key" ("rope jack"), used to
tighten ropes on rope bed, 1780   46- 55

School bell, brass, wooden handle,
7″ high, original clapper, 1830 . 120-145

Shoulder yoke, for carrying milk
pails, etc., 1840s 108-120

Sled auger, used for boring holes
in beams, c. 1820s 64- 72

Sleigh bells, string of 24 on
original leather, East Hampton
Bell Manufactory, 1840s 270-295

Sleigh bells, string of 30, 1850s . . 190-240

Spanner wrenches, hand-forged,
1840s, ea. 9- 13

Spoke shave, mid-1800s 44- 53

Spud, used for peeling bark from
trees or logs, early 1800s 70- 80

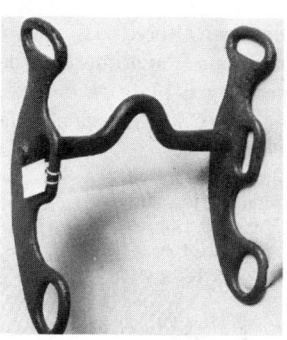

Primitives

String holder, iron, "Beehive"
type, 1840s 52- 61

Tavern candle chandelier, tin/
wood, 1840s 470-540

Three part boot last, hand-carved
maple, mid-1800s 105-111

Tin grain scoop, 9½″ long, 1830s .   42- 49

Tooth puller, hand-forged,
early 1800s 40- 48

Turkey feather duster, late 1800s   39- 48

Waffle iron, Heart pattern, iron,
2-pc., 1840s 90- 97

Winnowing tray, woven from oak
strips, early 1800s 74- 82

Wooden butter churn, complete
with lid and dasher 310-360

Wooden lemon squeezer, 2-part,
1820s 32- 40

Wooden mortar and pestle,
maple, early 1800s 112-150

Wooden washboard, hand-carved,
mid-1800s 29- 39

Wrought iron barn hinges,
early 1800s, pr. 110-125

Prints

Prints

Signed; signed and numbered; signed,
numbered and remarqued; limited edition
—all these affect the value, assuming the

(continued)

print has not been altered to fit a frame and is in good condition. Remarques are the artist's marks placed on a plate or on the original painting, such as C.M. Russell's buffalo skull.

John James Audubon, the original edition engraved by Havell & Son called "The Birds of America"; there were 435 plates in all:	
Plate #6, Hen Turkey . . . $	7,400 +
Plate #14, Prairie Warbler	1,400 +
Plate #27, Red-Headed Woodpecker	3,000 +
Plate #82, Whip-Poor-Will	2,600-3,000 +
Plate #158, American Swift	985-1,400
"The Battle of Lake Erie," line engraving, drawn by Sully, engraved by Murray, Draper, Fairman & Co., published in Philadelphia	370- 410
"Battle of New Orleans," print, aquatint by Debucourt, litho by Case & Green, 1815	182- 192
"Bonaparte in Trouble," line engraving, A. Doolittle	170- 200
"Chesapeake and Shannan," colored aquatint, painted by Robert Dodd, published in August 1813	220- 290
"Fishing Along the Seine," pencil, lithograph, signed Charles Mondin	67- 80
"Le Serapis et le Bon-Homme Richard," line engraving, without artist's or engraver's name, framed	170- 190
"The Mediator and Alexander," line engraving, colored, Robert Dodd, published in London, 1783, by John Harris	295- 380
"Naval Battles of the Civil War," 4 lithographs, C & I	1,100-1,400

Of the different series—The Havell Prints; The Brien Edition; The Octavo Edition; The Audubon Quadrupeds; Audubon Prints on Fabric—the Octavo Edition is the most valuable.

"The Bathers," by Winslow Homer, 1872, wood engraving	175- 240
"Gathering Berries," by Winslow Homer, 1874, wood engraving	145- 180
"High Tide," by Winslow Homer, 1871, wood engraving	150- 180

If you're interested in buying and/or selling old prints, first establish contacts with reputable dealers who specialize in old prints. Also, read the periodicals that specialize in this field.

American Artist, 1 Astor Plaza, New York, N.Y. 10036

Art Investment Report, 54 Wall St., New York, N.Y. 10005

Print Trader, 6762 79 St., Middle Village, N.Y. 11379

The illustrated print, "General Washington," a mezzotint, was published in 1785 in London. It is considered exceptionally rare.

Other things to remember: If marked "Published According to Act of Parliament," it's English, after 1735. If marked "Entered According to Act of Congress in the year —," it's American, after 1802. The first copyright laws passed by our government were in May, 1790.

Puppets

Puppets

Probably Punch and Judy are the most famous. Whatever, they've been around for centuries. The papier-mache types are showing up at shows and auctions.

Charlie McCarthy, hand type . . . $	22- 32
Elvis, hand type	20- 25
Indonesian, stick type (ill.)	45- 55
Punch and Judy, hand types, ea. .	35- 45

Quartz

Quartz

Figure, Kuan Yin, holding
  lotus blossom, 5½" high . . . $ 52-   62
Figurine, elephant group,
  trunks up, 4" to 7" high . . .   140-   180
Figurine, tiger, green, 7" high,
  teakwood base   160-   180
Snuff bottle, blossoms and
  leaves, carved, 3½" high,
  ivory stopper   84-   93
Vase, dancing figures,
  22¾" high (ill.)   600-   650
Vase, dragons, birds, fruit
  motif, teakwood stand,
  8" high   270-   300
Vase, fruit scene, rose-colored,
  13" high   140-   160

Queen's Burmese

See **Burmese Glass.**

Queen's Rose

Queen's Rose

English, soft-paste porcelain, maker
unknown, probably early 1800s.

Creamer . . . . $ 79-100

Cup and saucer   95-150
Sugar bowl, covered   88-140
Teapot (ill.)   140-170

Queensware

A cream-colored earthenware developed by
Josiah Wedgwood about 1765. Many potteries have copied it.

Quezal Glass

Quezal Glass

Martin Bach, Sr., made this glass from
1901 to 1920. Formerly associated with Tiffany, Bach somewhat copied his former
employer's work. Most pieces are signed
Quezal. His son-in-law, Conrad Vahlsing,
opened a shop after Bach's death, calling his
wares Lustre Art Glass, which is also collectible today.

Bowl, ruffled top, signed,
  4" high $370-   410
Candlesticks, pr., blue
  iridescence   820-   915
Compote, blue iridescence,
  8½" high   470-   525
Finger bowl, gold iridescent,
  ribbed, signed, 4" dia.   160-   180
Goblet, footed, iridescent
  gold, signed, 5½" high   180-   200
Lamp, hanging, 4 iridescent
  shades, brass fixtures   720-   850
Lampshade, iridescent gold,
  feather design, signed,
  5" high (ill.)   170-   190
Nut dish, blue/rose, iridescent
  bronze, signed, 2½" dia.   140-   150
Perfume bottle, gold, signed,
  8" high   280-   310
Plate, blue iridescent, 11½" dia.   600-   670
Rose bowl, gold, purple/red
  iridescent, signed   270-   310
Salt, master and 6 individual,
  ribbed, iridescent gold,
  all signed   360-   385

(continued)

Toothpick holder, iridescent
gold, Feather design,
signed, 3″ high............ 94- 120
Vase, Feather pattern, red/
purple, swirled base, 10″
high, signed 900-1,100
Vase, Feather pattern,
white/green/gold, signed,
9″ high................. 1,100+
Vase, green/gold feathers,
white opalescent ground,
8″ high................. 875- 990
Vase, peacock, blue, signed 745- 855
Vase, silver overlay, irides-
cent, signed, 9½″ high...... 1,450+
Vase, trumpet, iridescent
gold, signed, 8½″ high 500- 575

Dutch Tulip 150-170
Fanny's Fan 250-275
Festoon..................... 145-175
Flying Dutchman............. 185-220
Golgotha 250-300
Henry of the West 275-325
Jacob's Ladder 175-225
Lost Ship 155-180
Melon Patch 175-220
Nine-Patch 185-235
Old Maid's Ramble........... 350-400
Pierrot's Pom-Pom 245-275
Puss in the Corner 355-410
Rambling Rose 195-230
Rocky Glen 195-235
Setting Sun 240-270
Storm at Sea................ 235-270
Swing in the Center 275-320
Tangled Tares 225-275
Texas Tears 275-355
Tic-Tac-Toe................. 100-130
Tippecanoe and Tyler Too 475-560
Tobacco Leaf 260-310
Travel Star 175-220
Turkey Tracks 160-195
Underground Railroad 450-550
Wagon Tracks 240-330
Water Wheel 140-160
Wild Goose Chase 175-245
Yankee Puzzle 195-230
Young Man's Fancy........... 200-240
Zigzag..................... 185-235

Quilts

Quilts

Most pieced quilts are formed by simple arrangements of diamonds, squares, right-
angled triangles, stitched into a geometric
design. Many are more than 150 years old.
Today, all old quilts are collectible. Crib
quilts are especially sought after. Some of
the more popular patterns are Aeroplane,
Basket, Flowerpot, Variable Star, Pansy,
Fool's Puzzle, Log Cabin (I and II), Tennessee Tulip—to mention a few. Be prepared to
pay anywhere from $50 to $600, depending
on condition and scarcity. See **Coverlets.**
Does yours need repairs? See "Quilts,
Repair" in **Repairs and Services.**

Arkansas Traveler ....$ 80- 90
Autumn Leaf 110-140
Bear's Paw 140-165
Blazing Sun 130-170
Brown Goose 235-280
Caesar's Crown 125-140
Cats and Mice............... 165-190
Double Irish Chain 235-265

Quimper

Made in Finistere, France, from the end of
the 17th century, its early products were in
the style of Rouen. Pierre-Paul Caussy
worked the factory from 1743 until 1782
when it was acquired by Antoine de la
Hubaudiere. The Breton figures and floral
sprays which most people recognize today as
Quimper were originated by Julies Henriot
who, more than likely, copied them from a
potter named Fougeray. The familiar "HB"
mark is that of Hubaudiere.

Ashtray, bone, dish-shaped,
Breton figures, 6″ dia. ....$ 27- 37
Bowl, signed, 6″ dia............ 29- 39
Butter pat, set of 6, peasants in
field...................... 46- 55
Coffeepot, Breton figures, 11″
high, signed 39- 48

Quimper

Cup/saucer, flower and leaf	27-	36
Dish, flower motif, miniature, salesman's sample (ill.)	8-	12
Flower holder, birds, flowers, 7″ high, signed	51-	60
Knife rest, women, flowers	37-	42
Mug	27-	37
Pitcher, milk, signed	42-	51
Plate, flowers, peasant woman, signed Henri Quimper, 8″ dia. (ill.)	32-	42
Platter, peasant man, 12½″ long	68-	78
Porringer, 2 handles, peasants, signed	42-	51
Salt, peasants, oval	27-	36
Salts, flower motif (ill.), ea.	24-	33
Teapot, 2-cup size, Breton peasants, signed Henri Quimper	84-	92
Tray, man, woman in field, signed, 10″ long	70-	80
Vase, peasant man, flowers, 6½″ high	42-	52

Crosley, #5-38, 1926	225-	250
Crosley, "Radak HR," 1922	275-	320
Freed-Eiseman, #FE-15, 1924	225-	250
Kellog, "One Tube," 1922	115-	135
Magnavox, #TRF-5, 1925	245-	265
Mission Bell, "Mantle," 1930	225-	250
Q.T., Radio, "Little Giant," 1925	200-	225
RCA, "Radioal Senior," 1923	175-	200
Stromberg-Carlson, "Treasure Chest," 1928 (ill.)	275-	300
Western Air Patrol, #100, 1926	160-	175
Wurlitzer, #9A, 1929	165-	190
Zenith, "Super Portable," 1924	475-	500
Zenith, #40A, 1929	140-	165

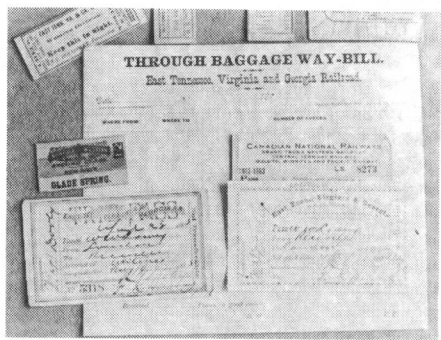

Railroad Collectibles

Radios

Guglielmo Marconi and Heinrich Rudolph Hertz get much credit for having invented the radio. But it took a lot of different men and a lot of time. Joseph Henry would get my vote. No matter, the influence of radio on the world is known and obvious. Those wireless sets of the 1920s are now highly sought after.

Acme Apparatus, "Acmephone," 1924	$110-	135
Ajax, crystal set, 1924	80-	95
Atwater Kent, #5, 1921	975-	1,300
Atwater Kent, #10 (kit)	425-	475
Blue Seal, "Cincodyne," 1925	350-	400

Railroad Collectibles

Anything to do with the Iron Horse is sought after today. Railroad silver, really just a silver-soldered product—lots of it made by Reed and Barton—is especially collectible.

(continued)

Attendants and waiters badges, most lines, ea. . . . . $	5- 10
Bonds, all railroads issued them, average price	6- 15
Breast badges, ea.	10- 14
Caboose lamp	45- 55
Cab badges, any railroad, average price, ea.	16- 24
Conductor's ticket punch, American brand	9- 15
Creamer, Southern RR	35- 44
Cuspidor, porcelainized, Maine Central	20- 24
Hand lantern, clear, Rock Island Line (ill.)	38- 46
Hand lantern, red, Southern Pacific	40- 48
Inspector's lantern, Bangor & Aroostock	75- 85
Journal box oil can, N.Y.N.H. & H.	30- 35
Knife, fork, spoon, napkin holder, Louisville & Southern R.R. . . .	43- 52
Menu holder, Rock Island Line R.R.	20- 24
Passes: issued to conductors, officers of the company, average	6- 10
Postcards, depicting various R.R. scenes, ea.	50¢-75¢
Pullman step	55- 65
Railroad employees' collar insignia, ea.	5- 10
Railway Express sign, 18"×18", reversible	35- 40
Tamping bar, 16 to 25 lbs.	12- 19
Track maul, 5 to 10 lbs.	14- 17
Tickets: Norfolk and Western, E. Tennessee, Virginia and Georgia R.R. (ill.), average price, ea.	4- 8
Timetables, most railroads, c. 1900s, average price, ea.	2- 3

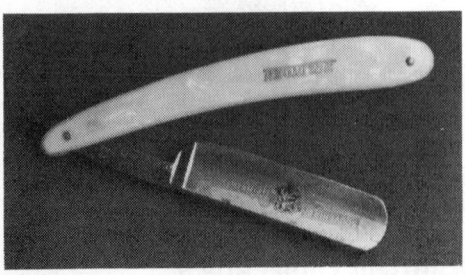

Razors

Razors

For years, Grandfather Pushbutton took his life in hand every time he shaved. Sailors prided themselves on being able to shave with a straight razor while the ship rolled from side to side. King Gillette ended it all when he invented the safety razor. The old straight razors are collectible and bringing good prices, depending on age and condition.

Ivory handled, polished Sheffield steel, original case . . . . $	32- 40
King razor	11- 20
Others, average price	10- 18
Safety razors, early 1900s, average	4- 7
Solingar (ill.)	20- 30

Reading Artistic Glass Works

Reading Artistic Glass Works

Founded by Lewis Kremp in Reading, Berks County, Pennsylvania, the firm operated from 1884 to 1886. The usual objects were made, including spittoons and whimsical canes. Opalescent colors included violet, canary, green, pink, white, and sapphire. Flint colors included green, light blue, amber, gold, and white. Specialty types had either mottling, overshot or craquelle finishes. Beginning to show up in shops in the Northeast.

Pitcher, 9½" high, pink with white mottling, thumbprint design, unusual 2-pc. opalescent, reeded handle (ill.)	$260-275
Vase, 14" high, baluster shape, black, applied neck ring (ill.) . . .	240-260
Vase, 14" high, baluster shape, frilled top, black with white mottling (ill.)	259-272

Red Wing Pottery

1878-1967. Produced art pottery in the 1920s; Red Wing, Minnesota. Comparable to Roseville, and Weller. Usually marked "Red

Wing USA" or "Red Wing Pottery, Inc." or "RW USA."

Bowl, deco relief, 8½" dia., marked Red Wing Pottery, Inc.	$ 24- 32
Bowl, white/brown trim, 8" dia.	14- 23
Candlestick, red maroon, 3" high, signed	10- 18
Cookie jar, Dutch scene, RW USA	29- 38
Cornucopia vase, ribbed and scalloped, 7¾" long, RW USA	18- 27
Creamer, waffle weave, 5⅜" high, RW USA	11- 18
Crock, blue/gray, 7½" high	39- 49
Marmalade jar w/lid, Red Wing USA	10- 16
Pitcher, ice guard, green swirled design, 7" high, marked Red Wing	40- 50
Vase, brown, mottled, Redwing USA	22- 32
Vase, chartreuse, flowers, bird of paradise, Red Wing USA B2000	28- 38
Vase, leaf-shaped, 9" high, blue/pink, Red Wing USA 1239	26- 35
Vase, white, flowers in relief, green, RW USA	23- 32
Vase, white, 7½" high, Red Wing, USA, Pat. Pending	14- 27

Redware

Redware

This is an unglazed red pottery, often with applied relief motifs, a Staffordshire type. Few pieces were signed with maker's name. Most of what you find today was made after 1850.

Pudding mold, swirl design	$ 85- 95
Teapot, dragon design (ill.)	93-109
Teapot, Oriental decor	100-120

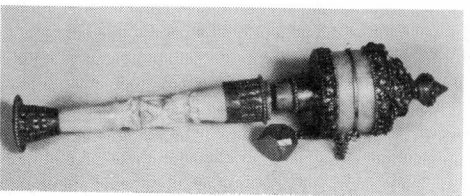

Religious Items

Religious Items

Bibles, figurines, and rosaries are just a few of the many things used for worship. The King James version of the Bible, dated 1658, is at the Houston Museum. The Staffordshire figurines of Ira Sankey, a great song leader and composer, and Dwight L. Moody, are considered scarce and highly collectible.

Bible, King James version	$ 5,800+
Bible, leather-covered, brass locks, mid-1800s	85- 97
Cross, ivory, on chain, hand-carved	44- 53
Hymnals, any denomination, good condition	5- 8
Pews from old churches, ea.	260-300
Prayer wheel, Tibet (ill.)	200-240
Staffordshire figurines, Sankey and Moody, ea.	385-440
Staffordshire plaques, ea.	93-107

See also **Icons** and **Stained Glass Windows.**

Remington, Frederic

Remington, Frederic

Lived 1861-1909; painter, sculptor, illustrator; best known for his sketches and bronzes depicting the Wild West as it really was. His bronze statues were cast by the Roman Bronze Works, New York; also by Henry-Bonnard Bronze Company, New York. They were marked "Copyright by Frederic Remington." His sketches bring high prices. You can't buy a bronze for under $75,000. "The Cheyenne," 23¾" high, is illustrated here.

313

Reverse Paintings on Glass

Reverse Paintings on Glass

This type of painting was done on the back of the glass in reverse so the writing could be read. Popular during the early and mid-1800s, some of the English and Scotch paintings were considered rare today. Just about every subject was used: women, children, and prominent people being the most popular. Average price $60-160.

"White House on the Potomac,"
gilded frame, 12¼"×10¾",
c. early 1800s (ill.) . . . . $ 67- 78

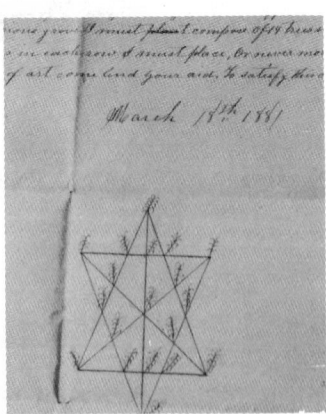

Riddles and Puzzles

Riddles and Puzzles

"What has four wheels and flies?" The old riddles and puzzles (see illustration) are finding their way into collectors' hands. The illustrated puzzle was hand-drawn in ink around 1875. They're worth just about what you're willing to pay for them.

Ridgway Pottery

Ridgway Pottery

John and William Ridgway operated their pottery at Hanley, England, from 1814 until 1830. Their "The Beauties of America" series is world-famous. William Ridgway operated at Hanley from 1830 until 1854. Ridgway Potteries, Limited is still in business. They use scenes and borders of another potter.

Bowl, 10", Capitol, Washington . $110-135
Bowl, 10", Pennsylvania
   Hospital, Philadelphia 140-150
Bowl, Racing the Mail, 8½" dia. .   67- 77
Gravy, tureen, Bank, Savannah . 150-165
Mug, Eloping, 5" high 46- 52
Plate, 8", Library, Philadelphia . . 185-194
Plate, 6¼", Athenaeum, Boston . 173-183
Platter, Maidenhair Fern,
   8½" long 47- 56
Soup tureen tray, Deaf and
   Dumb Asylum, Hartford 145-170
Vegetable dish, 11" , Hospital,
   Boston 142-162

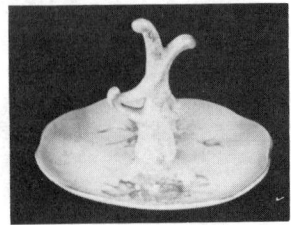

Ring Trees

Ring Trees

Made of glass, metal, or porcelain, these small, treelike objects held one's rings for safekeeping while one bathed or slept. They were popular during the mid-Victorian era.

Cut glass, clear base, blue stem . . $ 45- 52

314

Parian ware, in shape of upraised
hand 52- 60
Porcelain, decorated, American,
2½" high (ill.) 14- 19
Porcelain, 3-branch, Germany . . . 15- 20
Sterling silver in shape of 4-
branched tree, 3" high 31- 41
Just about every porcelain maker, here and
abroad, made them.

Rockingham-Bennington Pottery

This is sometimes called Bennington Ware
because it was made there in the mid-1800s.
The original was made in the Staffordshire
District before 1800. It was heavy, with a
brown glaze. Actually, it was made by many
potteries in the Ohio River Valley, and theirs
was considered as good as that made in Bennington. See **Bennington Pottery**.

Bedpan . . . .$ 67- 77
Bottle, monk 140-150
Bowl, chocolate glaze, tan
ground, 9" dia. 78- 88
Coffeepot, brown glaze, 10" dia. . 68- 78
Compote, blue flower decor 88-109
Creamer, cow, black, gold, glazed,
6¼" long 90-110
Cup/saucer, green/gold, flowers . . 63- 72
Cuspidor, brown glaze, flower
decor 84- 93
Flask, brown glaze, acorns,
leaves, 7½" high 72- 82
Footwarmer 100-112
Inkwell, monk's head, 3" high . . . 96-107
Pitcher, birds in swamp, 1850s,
England, brown glaze 137-150
Plate, light brown, 9¼" dia. 53- 63
Spill holder, brown glaze 58- 70
Teapot, white, orange, gold,
glazed, 7" high 120-140
Toby jug, brown glaze, England,
1850s 132-140
Tureen, covered, brown glaze,
acorn finial on cover 225-260
Vase, white, multicolored flowers,
8" high 58- 67

Rogers Statuary

John Rogers, an American born in 1829,
studied sculpting in Europe and worked in
plaster of paris to achieve some of his finest
works. He put on the market more than 80
different subjects during the mid and late
Victorian period, his pieces being reproduced
more than 100,000 times! Highly collectible.

Rogers Statuary

Balcony . . . .$ 550- 600
Bath 520- 550
Henry Ward Beecher 500- 530
Bubbles 535- 555
Bushwacker 470- 490
Camp Life 560- 600
Campfire 570- 600
Charity Patient 580- 610
Checker Players 650- 680
Chess 675- 710
Coming to the Parson 650- 700
Council of War (hands in any
of 3 positions) 1,200-1,400
Elder's Daughter 540- 580
Favored Scholar 610- 650
Fetching the Doctor 710- 730
First Love 480- 520
Fugitive Story 810- 825
Going for the Cows (ill.) 520- 540
Hide and Seek 710- 735
Home Guard 750- 800
John Alden and Priscilla 710- 750
Mail Day 710- 725
Miles Standish 410- 430
Matter of Opinion 600- 670
Mock Trial 740- 760
One More Shot 680- 710
Referee 650- 710
School Days 740- 780
Taking the Oath—Drawing
Rations 735- 810
Traveling Magician 480- 510
Washington 1,100-1,300
We Boys (head up or down) . . 495- 550
Weighing the Baby 780- 810
Wounded Scout 985-1,100
Wrestler 1,200-1,300

Rookwood

Founded in Cincinnati, Ohio, in 1880 by
Mrs. Maria Longworth Storer, it was
America's first art pottery. Tiger Eye, Iris,
Vellum, and Ombroso matt glazes are some

(continued)

Rookwood

of the various glazes used over the 80-year period. The famous reversed R and P, uniformly adopted in 1886, appears on every piece. In 1887 a flame point was placed above the monogram and one point was added each year until 1900. In 1901 Roman numerals showed each ensuing year. Any similarity between the Rookwood produced in Ohio and that produced in Starkville, Mississippi, is purely coincidental. Kataro Shirayamadani, Albert R. Valentien, Matt A. Daly, Laura F. Fry, William Purcell McDonald, and Artus Van Briggle are some of the many famous artists who worked for Rookwood. Rookwood was Mrs. Storer's father's estate outside Cincinnati, so named because of the many rooks (crows) in the area.

Ashtray, blue "rooks," 4″ dia., 1915	$ 45-	55
Ashtray, brown "rooks," 4½″ dia., 1912	60-	75
Ashtray, elk's head, B.P.O.E., 6″ dia., 1917	62-	70
Basket, pink/green matt finish, 11″ high, dated 1911	88-	100
Bookends, ships at sea, signed McDonald, dated 1925	190-	210
Bookends, white horses, 7¼″×6″, 1919, pr.	160-	170
Bowl, cherry blossoms, 3″ high, 1907, Iris ware	150-	160
Bowl, green matt finish, dated 1920	61-	71
Candleholder, pink, 10″ high, dated 1914	88-	97
Candlestick, tulip shape, 8¾″ high, matt glaze, signed C.S.	155-	175
Cigar humidor, Indian head, 9″ high, unsigned, 1932	170-	190
Chocolate pot, water lily motif, 9″ high, 1904, initialed M.M.	190-	220
Creamer, daisies, initialed C.S., 1898	200-	250
Electrolier, tulip shape, 14″ high, 1905, unsigned, matt glaze	270-	300
Ewer, brown/tan, flowers, vellum finish, signed Kataro Shirayamadani (he was Japanese, probably Rookwood's greatest decorator), dated 1897		3,700+
Ewer, Japanese flower, 5½″ high, unsigned, 1904	270-	320
Flower frog, green/blue, 1925, unsigned	70-	80
Jug, handled, grape design, 6″ high, 1905, initialed M.M.	375-	420
Lamp, pinecone decoration, Iris ware, 24″ high, 1904, unsigned	380-	420
Mug, grape design, 4¾″ high, 1905	170-	190
Pitcher, green, floral, signed Reed, dated 1893	650-	750
Plate, 9½″ dia., dragonflies, 1904, matt glaze, unsigned	160-	180
Sugar bowl, clover design, 4″ high, unsigned, matt glaze	170-	190
Tea caddy, poppy design, 5¼″ high, unsigned, Iris ware	170-	195
Teapot, 7½″ high, Tiger Eye glaze, initialed O.G.R., 1893	300-	400
Vase, blue, vellum finish, original store label, signed LNL, 1918	450-	510
Vase, brown/tan, 7″ high, initialed C.S., 1897	510-	575
Vase, brown, vellum finish, signed Carrie Steinle, dated 1901	495-	535
Vern, fern fronds, 6½″ high, 1893, Tiger Eye glaze, unsigned	360-	440
Vase, green, matt finish, 1932 (ill.)	92-	115
Vase, Japanese iris, 10″ high, 1907	310-	400
Vase, light green, 7″ high, 1924, unsigned	145-	180
Vase, matt glaze, green/ blue, 1935, 6″ high, unsigned (ill.)	80-	90

Vase, night-blooming
cereus, 13″ high, initialed
S.S. 440- 510
Vase, pinecone design, on
teakwood base, 12″ high,
1908 . . . .   450- 560
Vase, wild carrot, 6¼″ high,
1904 . . . .   380- 440

Rorstrand Faience

Rorstrand Faience

The company was founded in 1726 at Great
Rorstrand, near Stockholm, Sweden. Designs
in the early 1900s took on an Art Nouveau
style. The firm is still in business. It's mentioned here because it's beginning to show up
in the better shops. It's expensive and you
should know what you're doing if you decide
to collect it. See **Collectors' Plates**

Vase (ill.) $495-625

Rose Bowls

These are crimped and pinched-edge bowls
used for holding dried rose petals. Decorative only, their rose-scented aroma helped
freshen the air in the parlor or dining room.
Mid-1800s, of every type glass. Being reproduced.

Amberina, Honeycomb pat-
tern, 6″ dia. $325-365
Amethyst glass, enameled
flowers   160-170
Bristol glass, enameled flowers . . 135-145
Cranberry, white enamel decor . . 100-115
Mt. Washington and Wheeling
Peachblow 525-575

New England Peachblow, acid
finish   740-760
Overshot, fan design   165-185
Satin glass, flower decor, gold
trim   185-200
Spanish Lace, blue, 4½″ dia. 70- 75
Tiffin glass, black, poppies 55- 64
Vasa Murrhina, pink, red, flecks
of mica   135-145
Vaseline, 3″ dia. 75- 90

Rose Canton
See **Rose Medallion China**.

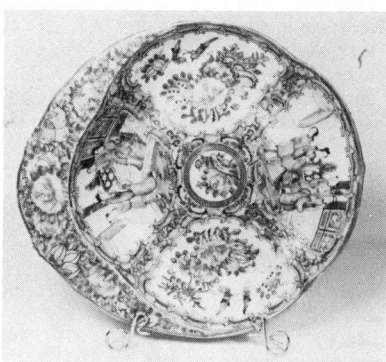

Rose Medallion China

Rose Medallion China

A product of China, it was decorated in
Canton and exported to every country in the
world. It gets its name from the glazed
pieces having figures of people alternating
with panels of pink flowers, butterflies, and
birds. If all the panels are filled with flowers
only, it's called Rose Canton. This ware has
been produced and reproduced for hundreds
of years. Watch out!

Basket, people, roses, but-
terflies, 4½″ dia. . . . . $ 580- 670
Bowl, people, roses, birds,
butterflies 245- 275
Box, covered, usual design,
2½″ high 125- 140
Bulb or crocus pot . . . .   1,800+
Candleholders, people,
flowers, 11½″ high, pr. 700- 800
Canister, set of 3, 3″, 4″, 5″,
signed "China" 250- 325
Compote, typical design of
birds, flowers, etc., 8″ high .   170- 190
Creamer and sugar, covered . .   165- 190
Cup/saucer, thorn handle 92- 107
Cuspidor, typical scenes 485- 545

317

(continued)

Dish, flowers, figures, 10"
dia. (ill.) 175- 210
Jardinieres, teakwood stand,
8¾" high, pr.   900-1,100
Mug, rose floral band, birds,
flowers, etc. 170- 195
Plate, 7" dia. 90- 110
Plate, 12" dia. 180- 220
Platter, 19th century, typical
scenes, 16" dia. 340- 380
Powder box, roses, people,
green ground 120- 145
Shaving mug   80-   90
Sugar bowl, berry handles,
people and flowers 320- 370
Tea set, in lined wicker caddy
for traveling, 2 cups 445- 510
Tea set: teapot, creamer,
sugar, all 800- 900
Teapot, usual scenery, China .   275- 325
Tureen, typical scenes,
11½" long 380- 450
(Tureen of early 1800s,
on stand, would be worth
$1,600.)
Urn, typical decorations, 16"
high 420- 485
Vase, 9¾" high, on teakwood
stands, 19th century, pr. . .   370- 445
Vase, roses, scenes, people,
birds, etc. 295- 340
Washstand set, Chinese
enameled, mid-1800s,
usual design 590- 675

Rosenthal China

Rosenthal China

Established in Selb, Bavaria, by P. Rosenthal in the 1880s, the firm specialized in figure groups, dinner sets and other pieces. It was considered a fine hard-paste porcelain, and it's expensive when found today.

Bowl, berry, pink flowers,
gold rim, scalloped, footed . $ 78-   87
Box, lady's face on lid, gold
border on cover, 5" high . . .   80-   90
Candlesticks, white, gold trim,
pr. 80- 100
Centerpiece with female
figure, white, beige, gray,
signed "K. Himmelstoss"
and Rosenthal, 17" high
(ill.)   2,100-2,500
Chocolate pot, 6 cups/saucers,
pinecones, trees, beige
ground 220- 240
Chocolate set, demitasse, blue
and gold, service for 6 . . . . .   295- 320
Compote, white ground,
flowers, handles, gold trim,
8" high   60-   70
Creamer/sugar, orchard scene,
gold trim   62-   72
Cup/saucer, pink roses, blue
ground   66-   76
Figurine, dancer, white and
gold, 9" high 145- 155
Fish set, carp, seaweed edge
around plates, 10" dia. 190- 220
Pitcher, white, pink roses,
gold trim, 6" high   56-   67
Plate, blue ground, roses,
hand-painted, artist-
signed   70-   80
Platter, fish scene, 1900,
hand-painted   82-   92
Sugar, pink and gold 80- 100
Tazza (shallow, ornamental
cup or vase, sometimes with
pedestal)   87-   96
Tea set, teapot, creamer,
sugar, yellow/red roses 89- 110
Vase, pink flowers, gold trim,
8½" high   88-   97

Roseville Pottery

Roseville, Ohio, 1892, this pottery firm was making stoneware jars, cuspidors and flowerpots. In 1898 the firm moved to Zanesville but didn't make art pottery until 1900. No art pottery was ever made at Roseville. Their first art line was called Rozane. Some of the marks used were "RPCo."; "Rozane—RPCo" beneath; "Rozane Ware Royal"; "Rozane Ware Mara"; paper "Roseville Pottery Co." labels were also used. This pottery was comparable to Weller. It never reached the quality level of Rookwood.

Roseville Pottery

Ashtray, red, blue handles, old
RV mark . . . . $ 37- 46
Bank, piggy, 4" high, unsigned . . 43- 53
Basket, 6½" high, Bittersweet,
Roseville, U.S.A. in relief 47- 56
Basket, pinecone pattern, script
signature 51- 60
Bookends, pinecone pattern,
script signature, pr. 52- 61
Bowl, Donatello pattern
(cherubs), cream color, beige,
green 58- 68
Bowl, roses, pansies, blue/green,
script signature 52- 61
Candleholder, floral pattern, 10"
high, script signature 42- 50
Cornucopia, Mock Orange, 5½"
high, Roseville, U.S.A. in
relief 46- 60
Cup, 3½" high, clover motif,
Juvenile line, unsigned 36- 44
Jardiniere, 9" high, Cameo line,
unsigned 69- 80
Jardiniere, pinecone pattern, twig
handles, script signature 61- 70
Letter holder, 3½" high, brown,
flowers, Rozane Ware Royal . . 71- 80
Mostique jardiniere, 9½" high,
unsigned 83- 92
Tankard, Della Robbia line, 10½"
high, unsigned 140-170
Tankard, 11" high, monk, brown,
Rozane Ware 171-190
Tankard, 10½" high, signed "V.
Adams," Rozane Ware Royal . 169-182
Teapot, creamer, sugar, flower
decor, script signature, all 70- 84
Teapot, 4¼" high, Mayfair, Rose-
ville, U.S.A. in relief 35- 44
Urn, 8½" high, Rosecraft Vintage
line, "R" containing small "v" . 60- 70

Vase, Aztec, 8" high 64- 74
Vase, Bittersweet, 6¼" high,
Roseville, U.S.A. in relief 54- 55
Vase, bud, yellow/green/blue,
script signature 62- 72
Vase, double bud, 6" high, Floren-
tine, "R" containing small
"v" 58- 68
Vase, Carnelian line, 10½" high,
blue "R" stamped on bottom . . 60- 70
Vase, 12" high, flowers, Azurine,
no mark (probably had paper
label) 62- 71
Vase, 6" high, Dahlrose line,
unsigned 50- 60
Vase, 13½" high, Della Robbia
line, Rozane Ware 78- 87
Vase, Donatello, 15" high 70- 80
Vase, Egypto, 11½" high, Rozane
Ware Egypto 82- 91
Vase, 19¼" high, dogs hunting,
Rozane R.P.Co. 98-115
Vase, 8" high, Florentine line,
"R" containing small "v" 54- 66
Vase, 14" high, Indian chief
brown/red, Rozane Ware inside
circle 135-160
Vase, 13" high, metallic lustre
line, Rozane Ware Mara 140-158
Vase, 9" high, Woodland,
"Fujiyama" rubber stamped
on bottom 92-107
Vase, 11½" high, Woodland line,
floral designs, Rozane Ware . . . 80- 90
Vase, Rozane Ware, 12" high
(ill.) 135-160
Wall pocket, 10" high, Donatello
line 60- 70

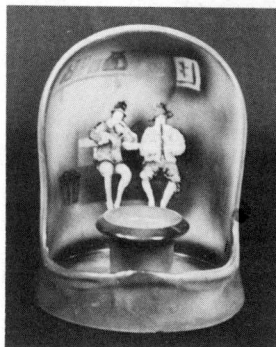

Royal Bayreuth

Royal Bayreuth

This type of novelty ware was made in Germany for many years. The tapestry type porcelain is collectible today.

319

(continued)

Ashtray, clown $130-150

Ashtray, monkeys playing cards,
   black mark 74- 83

Berry set, dish, 6 saucers, grapes,
   leaves 142-156

Bowl, Little Jack Horner, 5¾"
   dia. 58- 69

Bowl, lobster-claw handles, pink/
   red/purple 140-160

Box, Jack Be Nimble on lid,
   colors 72- 81

Candlesticks, devil playing cards,
   pr.   95-110

Chamberstick, green, musicians,
   4¾" high (ill.), considered rare . 260-290

Creamer and sugar, Fishermen
   pattern 82- 96

Creamer, bear 130-150

Creamer, clown 160-190

Creamer, crab 82- 94

Cup, demitasse, devil and dice . . .   70- 80

Cup/saucer, demitasse, poppy
   decor 150-162

Dresser dish, pink florals, greens,
   7" long 50- 60

Gravy boat, tomato, leaf
   underplate 160-180

Hair receiver, Little Bo-Peep,
   light blue 76- 84

Humidor, tomato color, lidded,
   7" high 110-130

Inkwell, boy in tree, 4" dia.   99-110

Match holder, clown, black mark . 130-150

Mug, Little Miss Muffet, 3¼"
   high 109-110

Mustard jar, devil and cards   97-112

Pin tray, Santa Claus decor 140-160

Pitcher, animal decor, blue mark,
   4" high 100-130

Plate, feeding, Sunbonnet Baby . 150-170

Plate, flower basket, pink/blue,
   set of 8 130-140

Powder jar, pink/blue   99-118

Salt, open, lobster motif 47- 57

String holder, hanging, poppy
   decor 172-191

Sugar/creamer/pitcher, devil and
   cards 230-260

Tea set, strawberry, 3-pc. 285-310

Teapot, creamer, sugar, tomato
   color 162-180

Toothpick holder, deer head   92-107

Tray, dresser, flower decor,
   8" wide 82- 92

Vase, Dutch scene, 6" high 86- 93

Vase, peasants, blue 102-114

Royal Bayreuth Tapestry

fabric tightly stretched over the surface. It was then decorated and glazed. Royal Bayreuth specialized in this in the late 19th century. Prices of this porcelain would be about 75% higher than similar pieces in previously listed **Royal Bayreuth.**

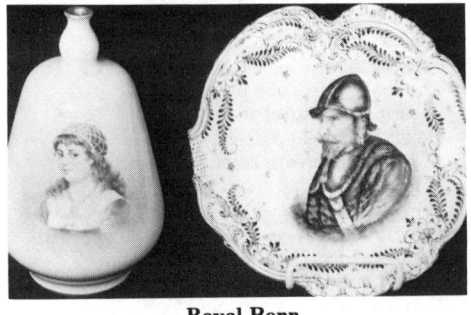

Royal Bonn

Royal Bonn

Established in Bonn, Germany, in the last half of 18th century by Clemers August, most of what you find today is ornately decorated with flowers, sometimes with portraits. It was a fine-paste porcelain. Some pieces were marked with a castle.

Bowl, brown glaze, flowers, 10"
   dia. . . . . $ 64- 72

Celery tray, flower motif 74- 84

Clock, colored flowers, 11½" high 350-425

Cologne bottle, tapestry-like
   surface, flowers, handled 80- 90

Compote, ships at sea, 8" high . . .   70- 88

Cracker jar, floral, gold trim 160-177

Plate, pink flowers, green ground,
   12" dia. 70- 82

Plate, guardsman, leaf rim (ill.) . .   85- 92

Vase, Delft blue, white, windmill
   scene, 8" high 107-112

Vase, floral, blue ground, handles,
   12½" high   92-114

Royal Bayreuth Tapestry

This type porcelain, made about 1890, was created by covering porcelain with a piece of

Vase, green ground, rose/yellow
flowers, pr. 180-210
Vase, peasant girl, 8″ high (ill.) . . 75- 85

Royal Canadian Mounted Police

Royal Canadian Mounted Police

Originally called the Northwest Mounted
Police, this constabulary was organized in
1873 to bring law and order to the Canadian
west and especially to prevent Indian dis-
orders. "The Mounties always get their
man!" threw fear into more than one person,
Nelson Eddy notwithstanding.

Buffalo hide winter coat,
c. 1900s $350-400
Buffalo hide winter gloves, elk
hide gauntlets, c. 1900s 50- 60
Coffee mug, c. 1940s (ill.) 7- 10
Photo of Nelson Eddy in RCMP
uniform, signed 40- 45
RCMP brass coat buttons, 6 in
set 25- 30
"Riders of the Plains" sheet
music, c. 1920s 10- 15

Royal Copenhagen Porcelain

Established in 1772, this firm has been in
business ever since, manufacturing fine porcelain. Their Christmas plates are world-
famous. See Christmas Plates.

Bottle, wine, castle scene . . . . $ 47-   56
Bowl, sculptured figure of
mermaid, 6″ 98- 107
Coffeepot, blue/white 192- 228
Cruet, blue/white, stopper . . .   120- 140
Cup/saucer, blue/white,
basketweave, 1924 mark,
set of 8   80-   90

Dinner service, six 8-pc. place
settings 950-1,200
Figurine, bear, 7″ high, deep
blue, 1928 . . . .   98- 115
Inkwell   70-   84
Mug, large, 1968   74-   81
Plate, brown/blue, Iris pattern   58-   67
Plate, mermaid in wintertime,
pr.   60-   69
Platter, blue and white, 10″
long   83-   92
Rooster, 1925, 6″ high, pr. . . .   178- 210
Toby jug, John Peel   70-   80
Tray, green and gold, 11″
long   55-   64
Vase, bluebirds and flowers . .   120- 140
Vase, blue/white, 1934, slender
neck 130- 145
Vase, flowers, blue/white,
dated 110- 112

Royal Doulton Figurines

Royal Doulton Figurines

The Royal Doulton figurines sought by collectors were produced at the Doulton
Burslem factory, Staffordshire, England.
Early prices date from c. 1909. Figures were
produced in both soft and hard-paste porcelain. Prices will vary according to production
numbers on backstamps.

A'Courting, HN#2004 . . . . $500-545
Angela, HN#1204   410-435
Autumn Breezes, green,
HN#1913   375-425
Balloon Seller, HN#583   365-435
Biddy, HN#1513   275-350
Bridget, HN#2070   260-335
Butterfly Lady, HN#720   520-585
Carpet Seller, HN#1464   245-285
Charley's Aunt, HN#35   450-475
Clockmaker, HN#2279   160-190
Curly Knob, HN#1627   345-390

(continued)

Dorcas, HN#1558	295-345
Enchantment	235-260
Eugene, HN#1521	395-455
Faraway, HN#2133	185-255
Flora, HN#2349	195-265
Forty Winks, HN#1974	230-275
Giselle, HN#2140	365-445
Granny's Heritage, HN#2031	390-485
Harlequin, HN#2186	170-220
Huntsman, HN#2492	130-165
Invitation, HN#2170	110-140
Janet, blue, HN#1538	235-275
Jovial Monk, HN#2144	100-135
Kate Hardcastle, HN#2028	385-440
Lady Bettie, HN#1967	320-365
Lavinia, HN#1955	260-295
Mantilla, HN#2712	240-280
Marietta, HN#1341	375-445
Master Sweep, HN#2205	440-485
Midsummer Noon, HN#2033	270-325
Miss Muffet, red, HN#1936	170-225
Old Mother Hubbard, HN#2314	180-245
Paisley Shawl, 8½", HN#1392	300-365
Parson's Daughter, HN#2018	240-275
Pearly Boy, HN#1482	270-335
Regency Beau, HN#1972	575-675
Rosebud, HN#1983	325-375
Sairey Gamp, HN#556 (ill.)	450-535
Spring Flowers, HN#1807	265-295
Sweet Anne, HN#1318	220-265
Sweeting, HN#1935	135-175
Town Crier, HN#2119	180-240
Victorian Lady, HN#728	495-600
Wardrobe Mistress, HN#2145	425-485
Windflower, HN#1939	285-345

Biscuit jar, horses, white body, applied flowers, Lambeth	$ 450-	520
Bottle, Dewars Scotch	82-	92
Bowl and pitcher, cobalt, gold trim	180-	192
Bowl, Robin Hood	77-	86
Candlestick, castles, Crown and Lion mark	54-	63
Cheese dish, blue/yellow, white ground, 6½" high	90-	100
Cup/saucer, demitasse	39-	47
Humidor, barrel-headed, green, fruit decor	72-	82
Jug, grapes, brown glaze, marked	49-	57
Mug, blue medallions, cobalt	70-	80
Pitcher, 6" high, "Morrisian" (ill.)	56-	66
Plate, Admiral Nelson, fleet at Spithead	66-	74
Toby mug, 6" high	84-	93
Vase, blue, Dutch Girl, 5" high	49-	58
Vase, cobalt, Arabian heads form handles, 8½" high	99-	110
Vase, dog and horse, blue/ olive/green glazes, 14" high, Hannah Barlow's sgraffito decoration	2,200-2,700	
Vase, mottled blue/pink, birds	72-	81

Just about all the jugs have been reproduced, so be careful.

Royal Doulton Pottery

Royal Doulton Pottery

This is the same **Doulton Pottery** mentioned earlier in this Guide. After 1901 the word Royal was added. Scenes from daily English life identify this pottery. It's still being made.

Royal Dux

Royal Dux

Made in Bohemia, this porcelain was imported into the U.S. around 1900, mostly for sale in gift shops. It was considered inexpensive then, not so today.

Basket, blue basketweave pattern, satin ground, 4½" dia. . . . $150-170

Bowl, girl with long hair, green/
  orchid flowers, handles 140-160
Figurine, camel, rider, 17½"
  high 430-480
Figurine, flapper, white/blue, gold
  decoration, 13½" high, c. 1920
  (ill.) 520-572
Figurine, hound in lying position
  gold matt, 14" long 140-162
Figurine, lady holding water jug,
  Austria, 18" high, pr......... 180-190
Planter, boy playing flute, 7"
  high 240-270
Planter, Grecian woman, ivory,
  on gold base, 11½" high...... 235-265
Vase, applied flowers, Austria,
  15" high 110-124
Vase, applied flowers, peaches,
  apples, 12½" high 210-260
Vase, floral, leaves, pink ground,
  17¼" high 140-160
Vase, pink/green, 19½" high 170-180

Royal Flemish Glass

A product of the Mt. Washington Glass
Company, 1889, it's identified by the heavy
gold enameled lines dividing the surface of
the glass into separate sections. Various
decorations are found on the matt finish
body. The pieces were colored in shades of
gold, beige, and brown.

Bowl, tan/pink/light green,
  mustard panels, alternating
  w/frosted and gilted, raised
  coin and rampant lion
  motifs, 6" across $2,200-2,500
Cookie jar, gold coin medal-
  lions, silver top and
  handles 2,400-2,700
Pitcher, satin glass finish,
  russet tan, enameled gold
  decor 2,400-2,700
Planter, opaque enamel in
  russet, tan/brown, gold
  decor, gold lion in
  medallion.............. 1,750-2,100
Rose jar, green medallions,
  steeple top............. 1,800-2,200
Vase, russet, tan and brown,
  enameled gold decor 1,900-2,400
Vase, stick type, medallion
  design, 11" high, initialed
  R.F. on bottom 2,400-2,750

Royal Rudolstadt

Established in 1720 at Thuringia, Germany. Later the factory was moved to

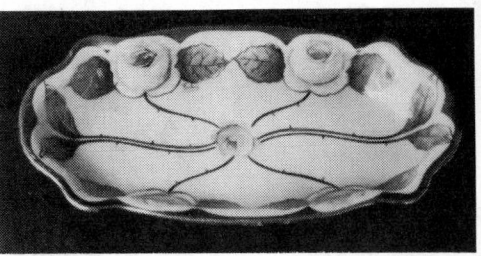

Royal Rudolstadt

Rudolstadt. Most of what you find in shops
today is of the late 19th century. The marks
are R for the early years, RW with crown on
top for the later years. Pieces marked Germany were made after 1890. It's beautiful
china with a Dresden-like coloring, often deli-
cately decorated with flowers, sometimes
faces of famous people such as Beethoven.

Basket, floral decor, gold handle,
  old mark $101-118
Bowl, tiger lilies, footed 165-210
Bowl, winter scene, horse, sleigh . 165-180
Butter dish, burnt orange/green,
  covered 155-170
Cheese dish, bridal roses, floral .. 98-112
Compote, enameled flowers, gold
  trim..................... 85- 92
Dish, shell-shaped beige ground,
  daisies and violets, multi-
  colored, 8½" dia. 90-108
Hatpin holder, bluebird decor ... 80- 90
Nappie, leaf-shaped 70- 77
Pitcher, flower decor, serpentine
  handle................... 89-108
Plate, fruit, gold band, 8½" dia. .. 70- 77
Plate, green ground, white roses,
  8" dia.................... 79- 90
Tray, pin, oval, pink flowers,
  6" long (ill.) 32- 36
Vase, multicolor floral, claw feet
  and handles in gold, 6" high ... 150-165
Vase, Psyche, open handles, tan/
  brown ground, ruby neck 240-270

Royal Vienna

The factory was founded in 1719 and
thrived when taken under royal patronage.
This was a Meissen-type ware noted for its
brilliant colors and artistic excellence. It was
most collectible even in the 1800s. One of its
distinguishing marks is the Beehive. What
you find in shops today has been produced by
other factories, some of which are still making it.

323

(continued)

Royal Vienna

Basket, blue body, handles,
applied leaves and fruit ...$ 240- 270
Compote, red, cobalt, Beehive
mark 160- 190
Cracker jar, dancing girls,
floral decor 270- 300
Ewer, cream ground, floral
sprays, 10" high 140- 160
Jar, lady dancing, cupids,
cranberry, Beehive mark in
red 140- 162
Plate, rose, gold, Palette mark,
8" dia. 150- 170
Plate, portrait, gold border,
signed Wagner, Beehive
mark in red 210- 220
Plate, white/black, signed
Riener, 1750 mark, set of
12 2,600-2,800
Salt dip, ornate feet, beaded
gold, Beehive mark 52- 61
Statuette, 8½" high (ill) 475- 575
Stein, monk, brown ground,
Beehive mark 560- 640
Teapot, white, fruit decor,
hand-painted, Beehive
mark 135- 170
Tray, green, gold trim 170- 192
Urn, Queen Louise, ormolu
finial, 14" high, pr. 370- 420
Vase, medallion center, blue,
red, Beehive mark, pr...... 295- 320
Vase, pink ground, painted
scene, figure in center, 12"
high 400- 442
Vase, handled, Queen Louise,
wife of Frederick Wilhelm
III, King of Prussia, 13"
high 1,350-1,700

Royal Worcester Porcelain

Royal Worcester Porcelain

This was a company within a company. See
Worcester Porcelain for details. The Royal
Worcester Porcelain Company, Limited, was
formed in 1862 and is still in business. Important to know your marks or you'll end up
buying new for old.

Basket, beige, green leaves, 6½"
dia. $143-188
Bone dish, flower decor 48- 60
Bottle, perfume, roses, flowers .. 84-100
Cake stand, flowers, gold trim,
8½" high 185-210
Candle snuffer, nun, 6½" 110-128
Chocolate mug, floral enameled .. 42- 51
Chocolate pot, cream back-
ground, after 1891 252-261
Creamer, floral decor, large
leaf in relief near handle 170-180
Cup, boullion, 4½" dia. (ill.) 15- 24
Ewer, green/gold lion, 10½" high 197-220
Figurine, Sunday's Child, F.
Doughty, 4¾" high 92-107
Flower holder, horn-shaped,
early 1900s 110-120
Mug, blue/white, Dr. Wall,
Crescent mark 340-360
Pitcher, 9" high, horn-shaped,
cream background 170-190
Plate, floral scene, raised shell
edge, 8¼" dia. 72- 81
Plate, floral center, leaf border,
9" dia. 120-140
Sugar shaker, signed 98-107
Tea caddy, gold/blue spatter 172-190
Tea set (teapot, sugar and
creamer), floral decor 420-450
Thimble, flowers, signed 62- 72
Vase, floral decor, applied
handles 320-370
Vase, shell design, gilting, 8½"
high 260-320

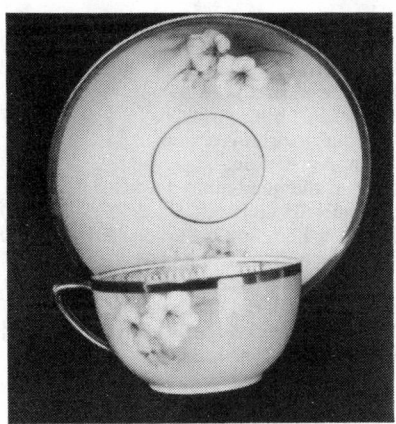

RS Germany

RS Germany

This is the same porcelain as RS Prussia. The name Germany was simply substituted for Prussia in 1891. Because of the demand for RS Prussia, especially the red star, dishonest dealers are removing the RS Germany and replacing it with the RS Prussia mark. It's a decal, 140 to the sheet, but the lettering is too modernistic. If in doubt, scrape vigorously with your fingernail.

Basket, roses, handles . . . . $	45- 60
Bowl, brown/green ground, flowers, 9¼" dia.	67- 80
Bowl, floral decor, 9½" across . . .	78- 88
Box, covered, roses, green mark .	48- 57
Candlestick, flared top, green lilies, 6" high	60- 70
Celery vase, pink roses, gold, open handles	60- 68
Cheese dish, flowers, bisque finish	110-120
Chocolate pot, white ground, brown at top, roses, 6 cups	196-220
Creamer and sugar, pink roses . . .	90-110
Cup/saucer (ill.)	60- 70
Dish, yellow, hand-painted, artist signed	50- 57
Hatpin holder, yellow floral, gold, marked	49- 58
Hatpin holder, white lilies	46- 54
Inkwell, covered, hand-painted . .	29- 42
Jam jar, lidded, flowers, green mark	50- 61
Nappie (dish with a handle), beige, apples, green mark	98-112
Plate, roses, gold edge, 8½" dia. .	50- 60
Relish dish, green ground, flowers	26- 27
Salt dip, rose decor, footed, marked	19- 28

Sauce, has tray, apricot roses, gold border, blue mark	49- 51
Sugar, covered, blue/pastel, flower decor	59- 62
Teapot, poppies, gold trim, green mark	42- 52
Toothpick holder, flowers, gold trim	42- 51
Tray, orange poppy, marked, 3¾" dia.	44- 48
Vase, green, pink roses, 6" high . .	58- 69
Vase, iris, 5" high	59- 71

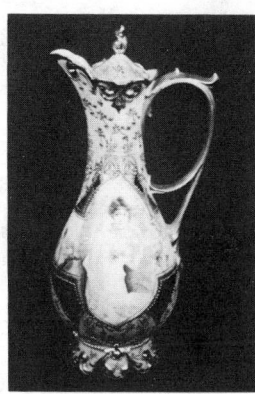

RS Prussia China

RS Prussia China

This porcelain made by Reinhold Schlegemilch's firm in the Prussian district of Erfurt, Germany, is similar to Haviland. It was made in the last half of the 19th century and is identified by the RS in a wreath and a red (or green) star. Red star is more collectible today. See **RS Germany**. The word Germany was substituted for Prussia in 1891.

Basket, pink/red roses, blue to white bottom . . . . $	275- 325
Berry set, 6-pc., water lilies, green/gold trim	495- 525
Bowl, berry, green shading to blue and white, roses, red mark	152- 181
Cake plate, red mark	175- 220
Celery, swans, embossed loop ends, 9½" dia.	170- 190
Chocolate pot, Autumn, Tiffany coloring, 10" high, red mark	1,150-1,400
Chocolate pot, 6 cups, floral, roses, white to green	400- 500
Compote, green, roses, gilt hand-painted, green mark . .	170- 198

(continued)

Creamer and sugar, colored
flowers, blended floral
decor, red mark 240- 320
Cup/saucer, demitasse, set of
6, red mark 375- 475
Cup/saucer, flower decor,
green/white   67-   78
Dresser set (tray, 2 colored
dishes), pink floral, green
mark 310- 400
Hair receiver, castle scene, red
mark 110- 140
Hatpin holder, bluebirds 163- 181
Manicure set: tray, buffer
holder, jars, red mark 240- 260
Muffineer, white, pink roses
on pearlized base, 4" high . .   185- 210
Mug, shaving, floral, pink,
green, red mark 150- 181
Mustard jar, green decor,
green sprays 90- 115
Pitcher, milk, garden scene,
swans on pool, red mark . . .   340- 380
Plate, tan, green, yellow,
floral, red mark 140- 170
Relish, brown decor, gold
trim 90- 112

Rubina Verde Glass

Rubina Verde Glass

Hobbs, Brockunier and Company, Wheeling, West Virginia, around 1890. Shading from yellow-green to cranberry, it's now considered Art Glass and brings a good price when found. Alas, being reproduced.

Bowl, crimped top, enameled,
ITP pattern, 3" high, c. 1880s
(ill.) $110-128
Bowl, vine pattern, applied shell
feet   140-150
Cologne bottle, red shading,
clear stopper, 4½" high   110-127
Celery, 6¼"   130-150
Creamer, melon-ribbed, 9" high . .   225-265

Cruet, daisy, fern, opalescent,
stopper, clear handle   280-320
Decanter, cut, cranberry, 9" high   175-198
Epergne, clear to opalescent,
2-pc., 12" high   247-277
Perfume, swirl, matching
stopper, 6½" high 77- 86
Pitcher, diamond-quilted, reeded
handle, 6" high   280-320
Tumbler, ITP, flowers, enameled .   110-130
Tumbler, quilted, 4" high   170-190
Vase, double tree trunk, 7" high .   70- 81
Vase, hobnail, red shading to
green, scalloped top, 7½" high   220-224
Vase, white enamel daisies,
gold leaves, pr.   365-440

Ruby Glass

Ruby Glass

This was a flashed glass, usually of the souvenir type. Deep red in color, it was made from the late 1880s until World War II. Some people confuse it with red Carnival.

Berry bowl, Saxon pattern, 12
smaller bowls . . . .$ 52- 62
Butter dish, covered, Button
Arches 81- 90
Celery, Dakota (Baby Thumb-
print) 48- 56
Cologne bottle, threaded stopper,
8" high 62- 72
Compote, Thumbprint pattern,
7½" high 44- 52
Cordial, Iowa State Fair 38- 47
Creamer, sugar, butter, spoon-
holder, gold intaglio
carnations   101-112
Decanter, clear stopper 39- 47
Goblet, diamond design, set of 12,
all   160-175
Ice bucket, metal bail handle 34- 42

Lamp, signed Glow Lamp, Inc. . .	31- 44
Mug, souvenir, St. Louis Exposition, 1904, "Saddie" . . .	34- 42
Pitcher, Atlantic City, 1908, To the Fairest	38- 47
Spoonholder, cherubs, 5½" high .	40- 50
Toothpick holder, Bettie	37- 46
Toothpick holder, Button Arches	35- 47
Tumbler, JHS, King's Crown . . .	31- 40
Tumbler, Reading, Pa.	27- 36
Tumbler, Thumbprint pattern, 4" high	29- 38
Vase, floral sprays, urn shape, 14" high (ill.)	66- 73
Vase, fluted, disc stem, 8" high . .	57- 66

Russell, Charles Marion

Living from 1865 to 1926, he was one of the greatest writers and painters of things having to do with the Wild West. He always signed his paintings "CM Russell" with a tiny buffalo skull. His works are extremely collectible today. The buffalo skull is called a "remarque" (personal "signature" of the artist). Look for them on many paintings.

Sadirons

Sadirons

The old handle types were heated on a stove. They're used as doorstops or bookends today.

Average price . . . . $	19- 27
Gasoline iron (ill.), early 1900s . . .	17- 27

Salopian Ware

Made in England at Salop in 1772, this decorated pottery was by Thomas Turner who took over the works in that year. In 1780 he opened a warehouse in London and marked his wares with an S or Salopian impressed or painted under the glaze. His Willow pattern is highly collectible. After he

Salopian Ware

retired in 1799, the firm was sold and moved across the river by the new owners, John Rose and Company. The factory still operates, under a new name—Coalport.

Bowl, blue/white, 11" dia. . . .	$365- 425
Creamer, House pattern . . .	440- 470
Cup/saucer, blue/white, Deer pattern, handleless .	325- 360
Cup/saucer, Early Cow pattern (ill.)	340- 378
Cup/saucer, late, Bird pattern (ill.)	320- 340
Jug, mask spout, 12½" high	925-1,100
Plate, farm scene, 6½" dia. . .	330- 350
Saucer, birds, cottage motif, 5" dia.	172- 192
Saucer, fowl, fishing scene, 5" dia.	174- 186
Tea set, blue/white, 6 cups and saucers, covered teapot, sugar and creamer, some pieces marked Caughley	1,900+
Teapot, House pattern	550- 625

Salt Glaze

Salt Glaze

Though the Staffordshire District, England, was considered the center of salt

(continued)

glazed pottery, some of the finest was made by the United States Pottery Company, Bennington, Vermont, 1853-1858. See **Parian Ware.**

Butter, covered	$248-278
Creamer, hand thrown, red clay, 5″ high (ill.)	52- 63
Crock, hand thrown, cobalt leaves, signed "R.C.R.– Philadelphia" (ill.)	115-140
Jug, wide-necked, bulbous, pewter lid	200-240
Mug, blue, applied handle, stoneware	85- 99
Pitcher, 4 countries of Great Britain, pewter lid, registry mark	188-210
Pitcher, Niagara Falls design, U.S. Pottery Co.	220-240
Platter, white, 8½″ long	130-151
Tea set, apostle figure, 3-pc., American	885-970
Teapot, wild roses, U.S. Pottery Co.	170-181

Salts

Salts

Open salts, popular from the 18th century on in America, stayed in vogue until the shaker type appeared on the market in the 1860s. Novelties in pressed glass are collectible today, such as those in the shape of birds and animals. You'll find specific prices for specific types listed in this Guide.

Bird salt, apple green glass	$ 81- 90
Bird salt, clear glass	54- 62
Bird salt, pattern glass	18- 28
Bird salt, vaseline glass	72- 80
Gold, white, Austrian (ill.)	8- 10
Noritake (ill.)	9- 13
Swan salt, cut glass bowl, sterling silver body and wings (wings fold back when not in use)	74- 83

Samplers

Made from the mid-1700s until they fell

Samplers

from style in the early 1900s, samplers were made of cloth, usually, and contained homey messages such as Love Thy Neighbor, the alphabet, etc. Dates are given in listing.

Early 1800s, Jane Foulis Standrews, alphabet, bird/ flowers, blue/green/black (ill.)	$155-178
1806, alphabet, 9″×12″, framed	140-170
1812, Love Thy Neighbor, alphabet around border, frame	192-220
1815, alphabet and numbers, Hannah L. Maywood, framed	185-220
1818, religious verses, birds in corners, walnut frame	210-240
1819, memorial to War of 1812, child's name, frame	228-278
1847, church, flower border, Ruth Ann Mills, framed	225-260
1866, name of soldier killed at Atlanta, framed	195-225
1869, Home Is Where the Heart Is, flowers, etc., no frame	170-180
1873, Child's poem, on linen, birds, flowers, walnut frame	165-192

Sandwich Glass

Sandwich Glass

The Boston and Sandwich Glass Company was founded by Deming Jarves in 1825 at Sandwich, Massachusetts, and operated until around 1888. Many fine types of glass were made there, including pressed, cut, and blown. See specific pieces listed in **Pattern**

328

Glass Section. Look out for you-know-what!

Basket, cranberry, clear handle,
6½" dia. $310-330
Candlesticks, miniature (ill.) 90-110
Cologne, jade green to white,
Moorish overlay design, 7"
high 160-180
Dish, lacy, Hearts design 74- 84
Ewer, pink/white, clear thorn
handle, 13" high 340-375
Lamp, amethyst, 9" high 440-500
Lamp, whale oil, Star and Buckle,
8½" high 285-320
Plate, Beehive, 9¾" dia. 120-140
Plate, Leaf and Scroll, 6" dia. 60- 70
Pitcher, bladder, (hole in side for
ice to cool liquid), frosted
cranberry 420-447
Pitcher, icicle, cranberry overlay . 425-470
Pitcher, overshot 230-240
Salt, eagle, opalescent 170-190
Salt, fleur-de-lis (ill.) 160-180

Sarreguemines China

Sarreguemines China

This factory operated both in Germany and France. It was first established in the 1770s in Germany by Utzchneider and Company, later at Degoin, France, where they made chinaware sets, cameoware and other pieces comparable to Wedgwood in quality. Florals, cherubs, and picnic scenes are a few of the many themes used. Usually signed Sarreguemines.

Bowl, fruit, fruit decor, 10" dia. . . $ 58- 72
Creamer, green glaze, man's
head, 7" high, signed (ill.) 88-101
Ewer, butterflies, gold decor 52- 61
Jam jar, covered, dark yellow,
molded apple on cover 42- 60
Pitcher, cream, green/yellow,
5" high marked 72- 81
Pitcher, hunting scenes, 10" high 97-118
Pitcher, roses, leaves in relief,
green/rose, 8½" high 99-112

Plate, flower decor, reticulated
edge, marked, 4½" dia. 34- 43
Toby jug, 6½" high, typical 120-150
Vase, blue, green/yellow
geometric designs, 12" high . . . 92-107
Wine jug, cherubs, trees, 11"
high 82- 96

Satin Glass

Satin Glass

Frederick Shirley of the Mt. Washington Glass Company was issued the first patent to make this beautiful glass on June 29, 1886. Seven days later, Joseph Webb of the Phoenix Glass Company was issued his patent on July 6. It would seem both gentlemen had gotten their ideas from one Benjamin Richardson who outlined the method of making Satin Glass in 1858. In any event, this is a satin-finished glass, first blown into a mold, then treated in various ways to achieve the beautiful satin finish. It's been heavily reproduced since World War II, with thousands of pieces flooding the country. Do know your dealer of this glass.

Basket, swirl ribbed, peach/white,
thorn handle $262-290
Bottle, cologne, deep blue, MOP,
6" high 170-182
Bowl, raised Poppies and Leaves,
blue/black, 5" dia. 172-182
Box, 6" square, pink/blue floral
decor 197-225
Candleholder, black/green,
quilted base, 9" high 60- 70
Cologne bottle, blue, enamel
decor, cut stopper, 7" high 152-170
Compote, green, MOP, floral
decor 365-425

(continued)

Cracker jar, Swirled Rose
pattern, MOP, 4½" dia...... 162-172
Cracker jar, 7½" high, Venetian
Swag, quadruple-plate lid,
enameled floral, signed M.W... 174-182
Rose bowl, blue and white stripes,
Stevens and Williams 220-250
Salt/peppers, enameled floral
decor 147-155
Sugar shaker, pink/white 144-164
Tumbler, Diamond Quilted,
raspberry 138-149
Tumbler, Herringbone pattern,
white lining, 4" high......... 132-140
Vase, Diamond Quilted, white
to pink, 7" high............. 288-325
Vase, tri-cornered, Diamond
Quilted, enameled flowers and
leaves, MOP, 6" high (ill.) 260-280

Satsuma Ware

Satsuma Ware

Glazed pottery (faience), cream ground,
Japanese, decorated with raised enamel
figures, scenes, flowers, etc. A feudal lord
brought Korean potters to Japan around
1600, settling them on the Island of Kysuhu.
Their wares were undecorated until around
1750. By early 1800, the repetitive and
geometric patterns were introduced. Figural
Satsuma Ware was made primarily for export, around 1850. There are four important
periods: Edo, c. 1615-1868; Meiji, c. 1869 to
1912-14; Taisho, 1912-14 to 1926-28; Showa,
1926-28 to present. Satsuma-style Ware,
from around 1900 on, was mass-produced.
It's what you find the most of in shops today.

Bottle, Edo period, yellow
ground, cherry blossoms,
8½" high $975-1,150
Bottle, Meiji period, Phoenix
birds, dragons, 9¼" high .. 225- 250
Bowl, Showa period, Arhats
(elderly men) and Phoenix
birds 235- 265
Bowl, Taisho period, square,
floral motif 164- 180
Box, Taisho period, dragon,
Diaper (repetitive) pattern,
3"×5" 95- 120
Box, Taisho period, Ebisu
(abundance-of-food god),
2½"×4" 110- 125
Brush pot, Showa period,
Fukurokuju (longevity god),
2½" high 95- 115
Buttons, Taisho period,
dragon on each, ¾" dia.,
6 in set, all 90- 115
Cup/saucer, Meiji period,
Arhats and clouds........ 85- 95
Cup/saucer, Taisho period,
Hotei (contentment god),
garden scene 60- 70
Cup/saucer, Showa period,
Kame (tortoise), Diaper
pattern 45- 55
Cup/saucer, Showa period,
Phoenix birds, yellow
ground................ 45- 55
Figurine, Showa period,
Bishamon (glory god), 3½"
high 27- 32
Figurine, Showa period,
Ebisu, 3½" high 27- 36
Figurine, Showa period,
Fukurokuju, 3½" high 27- 36
Figurine, Showa period, Hotei,
3½" high 27- 36
Figurine, Jurojin (longevity
god), 3½" high 27- 36
Figurine, Showa period,
elephant, 3" high........ 19- 27
Jar, covered, Edo period,
Phoenix birds, dragons,
7" high 425- 455
Jar, covered, Taisho period,
Arhats, black ground, 6"
high 135- 150
Juice set, Taisho period,
Arhats; elephant juice
pitcher w/Mahoot finial, 6
matching tumblers, all 160- 195
Pitcher, Meiji period, Arhats,
garden motif, 7¼" high ... 450- 475
Pitcher, Taisho period,
Phoenix birds, clouds, 6¼"
high 185- 220

Pitcher, Showa period, ladies
in garden, blue ground, 7″
high 60- 70
Planter, Taisho period,
elephant, sitting, multi-
colors, 6″ high 50- 60
Tea set, Taisho period, 21 pcs.
(6 cups, 6 saucers, 3
teapots, 6 cookie plates),
Arhats, clouds, dragon
finials, all 385- 575
Tea set, Showa period, 33 pcs.,
Arhats and Kwannon,
dragon finials, usual
Satsuma-style decorations
overall 650- 725
Teapot, Taisho period,
elephant-shaped, pagoda
finial, 7½″ high 75- 85
Teapot, Showa period,
elephant-shaped, Kwannon
finial, 6¼″ high 40- 48
Vase, Edo period, Arhats,
clouds, 15″ high 1,200-1,350
Vase, Meiji period, Awata
(gray-cream), Kannon,
8¼″ high 740- 800
Vase, Meiji period, Kara Shi
Shi-with-Tama (pear or
jewel ball) finial, dragon
handles, 19¼″ high 775- 825
Vase, Meiji period, Phoenix
birds/dragons, yellow
ground, 9″ high 725- 775
Vase, Taisho period, Kabuki
dancers, 16¼″ high 265- 310
Vase, Taisho period, peonies,
lavender ground, Kara Shi
Shi (lion-dog) handles,
11½″ high 195- 245
Vase, Taisho period, warrior
motif, figural dragon
handles, 23″ high (ill.) 550- 600
Vase, Showa period, Phoenix
birds, clouds, blue/green
ground, 16″ high 165- 195

Scales

They have been used for centuries to weigh
anything of value. Brass and iron scales are
the most common.

Apothecary, brass pans, iron
base $130-150
Apothecary, iron, porcelain 54- 63
Balance, hand-wrought iron
hooks, 24″ long 68- 77
Beam, hanging type 142-152
Candy, brass pans 91-108

Scales

Chemist, wood case, glass
windows 125-140
Counter, American Cutlery (ill.) . . 52- 64
Dayton 34- 43
Drugstore, walnut base, marble
top 122-140
Egg weigher, fits in pocket 42- 51
Gold dust, wooden box for
traveling, all 9 weights 84- 92
Hanging, 2 pans, brass, 12
weights, marked pound 72- 81
Ice, big dial face, brass hand,
30″ top to bottom 52- 70
Jeweler, brass pans, drawer 110-130
Platform, Fairbanks, Pat'd 1879 . 140-172
Platform, iron, 12″×15″ 74- 84
Postal, 6 weights, wood base,
American, 1879 date 115-138
Store, goods weighing type,
marble base 100-130

Schneider

This is a French glass, identified by its
mottled colors and fine craftsmanship.
Mid-1800s until just before World War I.

Bowl, topaz, acid cut, signed,
14″ high $195-220
Bowl-vase, colors fused in glass,
7″ high, signed 220-240
Compote, orange/blue glass,
9½″ high, signed 270-290
Finger bowl and plate, Art Deco,
smoked glass 170-188
Lamp, wall, red/white shading,
5½″ wide signed 180-190
Pitcher, varicolored roses,
twisted handle, signed 270-285
Tazza, orange, amethyst,
bubble effect, 7″ diameter,
signed 178-198

(continued)

Urn, apricot to clear, 10 ribs,
15" high 740-830
Vase, black blotches, 8" high,
signed, also marked Ovingtons,
France 220-270
Vase, blue/red mottled, 10" high,
signed 270-310
Vase, yellow ground, lacy enamel,
pinchbottle shape, signed 300-325

Schoenhut Toys

Albert Schoenhut established his firm in
Philadelphia in 1872 to make toys and
pianos. His biggest success was his
Humpty-Dumpty Circus, introduced in 1903.
His multijointed animals in vivid colors are
much sought after today. The firm is still in
business.

Animals

Alligator, glass eyes . . . . $	250-	275
Bear, brown, glass eyes	250-	275
Bear, brown, smaller, painted eyes	140-	165
Buffalo, carved ruff	275-	325
Buffalo, cloth ruff, glass eyes .	295-	325
Camel, double hump, large (ill.)	225-	265
Camel, double hump, small . . .	190-	225
Camel, single hump, decal eyes	230-	265
Camel, single hump, glass eyes	245-	275
Deer, glass eyes	290-	325
Donkey, large, glass eyes	125-	150
Elephant, large, blanket, glass eyes	225-	250
Elephant, large, painted eyes (ill.)	150-	175

Giraffe, large, painted eyes (ill.)	220-	245
Giraffe, smaller, painted eyes .	220-	240
Goat, glass eyes	130-	160
Goose, painted eyes	220-	240
Hippo, painted eyes	200-	225
Lamp, glass eyes	215-	235
Leopard, glass eyes, open mouth, painted teeth	245-	270
Poodle, carved ruff	200-	225
Poodle, cloth ruff, glass eyes .	235-	265
Tiger, painted eyes	165-	185

Blocks

Auto Build, 5-in-1	130-	140
Little Tots, original box	95-	115

Circus

Humpty Dumpty, original box, original poster, first introduced in 1902; circus items made until 1926; complete circus, including booklet "Illustrations of Schoenhut's Marvelous Toy Circus. Copright 1902," 18"×44" tent, many animals and performers, all in good to very good condition, all		3,400-3,975

(Note: Animals w/glass
eyes, performers w/bisque
heads bring much higher
prices.)

Circus Personnel

Acrobat, gent	155-	170
Acrobat, lady, bisque head . . .	240-	275
Clown, large, cotton suit	95-	115
Clown, large, silk suit	110-	130
Delvan Humpty Dumpty figures, ea.	25-	35+

(The Delvan Company
reproduced the original
circus c. 1950.)

Schoenhut Toys

Sconces

Lion tamer, bisque head	250-	280
Lion tamer, wooden head	190-	220
Ring master, bisque head	275-	300
Ring master, wooden head . . .	150-	170
Strong man, bisque head	290-	315

Comic Characters

Barney Google	215-	235
Felix the Cat, large	135-	155
Felix the Cat, small	90-	115

Games

Elfy Blocks, 9 pcs.	78-	88
Locomotive, Modlwood	125-	150
Metalophone w/wooden hammer	90-	115
Naval War, original box	130-	145
"Ole" Million Face	120-	140
Spirit of Hollywood camera . .	75-	90

Pianos/Stools

Baby Grand	235-	265
Stool, double	160-	180
Stool, single	75-	90
Upright, large	170-	180
Upright, medium	150-	170
Upright, small	130-	145

Rolly Dollys

Baby, large	200-	235
Clown	165-	185
Clown and donkey	210-	235
Drummer Boy, small	120-	145
Negro Billikin, small	140-	155

Sconces

Lighting devices that fastened on the wall, they came in all shapes, usually made of ornate brass and primarily made to hold candles. Many people have them electrified.

Brass, 4-arm, French, flowers in glass, pr.	$360-420
Brass, 2-arm, French, figural design, pr.	310-340
Brass, 2-arm, eagle design, outstretched wings hold candles . .	320-360
Glass, 4-arm, cut, hanging prisms, American	298-330
Iron, 3-arm, painted, floral designs	120-142
Tin (Toleware), candle type, early 1800s, pr.	225-245
Wood and gesso eagle, carved and gilded, late 18th century, American (ill.)	800-900

Scrimshaw

These are objects carved from the teeth of whales or the tusks of walrus. This type of carving was a hobby popular with sailors to pass the time during the 1800-1900 period.

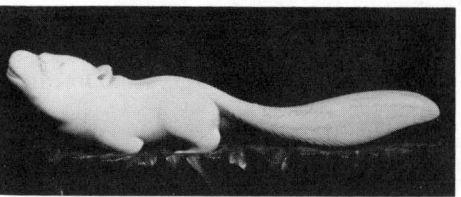

Scrimshaw

They would rub ink in the carving to make it stand out. Extremely collectible today, they're being reproduced in New England.

Beaver, 4¼" long (ill.) . . . . $	145-	170
Bust of man, 3" high	155-	180
Cane, 38" high, brass tip at bottom	180-	195
Carpenter's square, teakwood handle, 1850s	240-	280
Corset stays, 8, home scenes, 1840s	180-	210
Crochet hook, floral design . . .	44-	62
Mother, child on swing, walrus tusk carved, 11" long	290-	340
Napkin ring, striped cat	98-112	
Naval battle scenes, square rigged ship, 1840s	710-780	
Naval scene, Union and Rebel flags	300-348	
Powder horn, man's name, date 1793, Boston Harbor .	1,100-1,300	
Punch, lady's name	62-	73
Sailing ship, cuff links, early 20th century	140-170	
Walrus tusk cribbage board, 1800s, 14" long	1,900-2,300	
Whale tooth, eagle and flag, 5½" long	650-	700
Whale tooth, whaling scene, 18th century, 5"	800-	950
Yardstick	150-	195

Scroddled Ware

Manufactured in Bennington, Vermont, at the Fenton Pottery, it was made by varying the amounts of a coloring agent in each batch of clay. It was all stirred together, this time with a larger amount of the usual cream-colored clay. The finished mixture was then pressed into a mold. After being fired, a clear coat of glaze was applied. Considered rare, you can still find it if you know what to look for.

Cuspidor, Diamond pattern, feldspar glaze, gray/blue	$210-240
Pitcher, Diamond pattern, 11" high, reddish-brown	290-340

(continued)

Teapot, brown/tan, feldspar
glaze 270-310
Washbowl and pitcher, dark
brown, both 515-570
Probably other pieces.

Scuttle Mugs

This is just another shaving mug, but the shape is so different we thought you'd like to see one. Age group is same as other shaving mugs. Repros!

Cream-colored, floral decor,
Germany . . . . $ 42- 51
Floral and gold flowers, Thomas
in script, Austria 42- 51
Pink roses, Haviland 54- 62
Union, Patent September 20,
1870 . . . . 41- 52
White ironstone, country scene,
Germany 34- 42

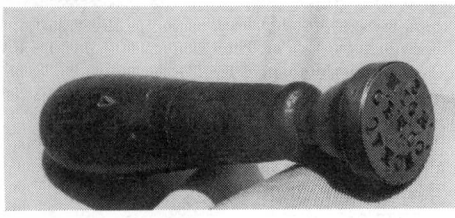

Sealing Wax Seals

Sealing Wax Seals

They've been used for centuries to seal letters, documents, etc. 17th century French seals, solid gold, are especially collectible. Look for signet rings and seals that fastened to gold watch chains.

Gold watch chain type seal,
1800s . . . . $ 64- 72
Hand seal (ill.) 27- 35
Signet ring seal (usually coat-of-
arms in 14k gold) 375-425

Seals

By pressing down on the handle, you could impress the firm's name in the paper. The seal was usually made in lead, the holder of cast iron painted black and trimmed in red or green. Much in use in late 19th century and until World War I when notary publics came into popularity. Used today by collectors as paperweights.

Indicative price, in good
condition . . . . $ 28- 39

Seine Balls

You find these floating up on the salt water beaches. Used for holding seines (nets), when they break loose they float for thousands of miles. Blown glass balls in green, blue, amber, they're collectible for those decorating a wall or den. They are mentioned here only because you see so many turning up in shops.

3" to 5" dia., colored . . . . $ 37- 46
6" and larger, colored 44- 51

Service Medals

Service Medals

We're not talking about military but those medals and ribbons that were given to civilians during World Wars I and II for meritorious service. Also lapel pins.

Lapel pin, same as above (ill.) . $1.50-2.50
Ribbon, Corps of Engineers,
World War II (ill.) 1.50-2.50

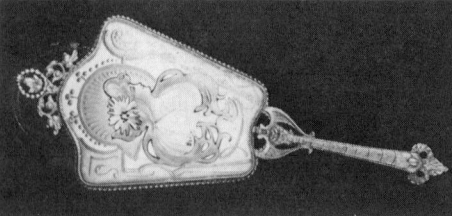

Sevres

Sevres

Madame Pompadour persuaded the factory to move from Vincennes to Sevres, France, around 1750. King Louis XV sanctioned the works, and some of the finest china the world has ever seen was made during that period. Biscuit and soft-paste porcelain were also made. Early pieces are scarce and expensive. Please, know your dealer.

Basket, blue/white, 13½"
oval, signed . . . . $ 950-1,100

Bowl, flower decor, ormolu
handles and feet, 7½" high . 525- 625
Centerpiece, Art Nouveau,
8"×4" 310- 400
Clock, 2 urns to match, signed
and dated 1756 2,575-2,700
Coffee jar and saucer, blue/
gold, 18th century........ 400- 438
Creamer and sugar, yellow/
red roses, gold trim, signed
Bavaria 180- 220
Cup/saucer, heavily enameled,
19th century 250- 290
Figurine, Bacchus under tree . 170- 210
Fruit cooler, roses, flowers,
gold, metal liner, 1780s 1,650-1,775
Lamp, dated 1754, rare
(demand receipt when you
buy), pr................. 3,100-3,400
Mirror, portrait, plaque of
Sarah Bernhardt, brass
frame, beveled glass, 6¼"
long (ill.) 140- 175
Pitcher, red rose, gold trim,
marked Bavaria 160- 180
Plate, blue, gold trim decor,
scalloped edges, 6" dia..... 190- 220
Plate, blue/lavender ground,
hand-painted, 1890s 158- 170
Statuette mantlepiece set of 4,
bisque, cherub dancers 275- 320
Tea service, 4-pc., dated 1769 . 560- 680
Teapot, light blue, portrait
medallion, gold handle 175- 240
Urn, enameled top, multi-
colors, 12" high, pr........ 500- 600
Vase, landscape, castle scene,
43" high, signed 1,400-1,800

Sewing Accessories

The delicate art of sewing by hand is
almost a thing of the past. Those items used
in the 18th, 19th, and early 20th centuries are
now collectible.

Cardboard thread winder, 8-
pointed star, c. 1820 ...... $ 25- 30
Chintz sewing bag, complete
w/needles, c. 1840 .... 40- 50
Dog-shaped "bird" (rare) ... 140-150
Iron buttonhole cutter, c. 1820 45- 50
Ivory/cloth tape measure,
English, 3" high, c. 1750 ... 60- 70
Ivory beeswax holder, to wax
thread, c. 1830s 40- 45
Ivory fish, 1½" long, for
winding thread, English,
c. 1750 .... 20- 30
Moroccan leather sewing box,
brass feet, hinges, pulls,
English, satin cushions, 3
compartments, c. 1730 (ill.) . 550-600
Leather needle box, "By
Appointment to her
Majesty—".............. 35- 45
Sewing bird, brass, 1 cushion.. 45- 50
Sewing bird, brass, 2 cushion.. 65- 75
Thimble, Acanthus design,
silver, c. 1850 .... 40- 45
Thimble, ½" high, Meissen,
made by the Herold work-
shop, early 18th century,
sold at auction in London by
Christie's in 1969 .... 4,700+
Thimble, porcelain, Meissen,
hand-painted, c. 1840s 95-110

Shades, Glass

Sewing Accessories

Shades, Glass

Banquet lamps, more popularly known as
Gone With the Wind lamps, produced the
first attractive shades. With kerosene, then
electricity, glass lampshades really came into

(continued)

their own. A few of the firms who specialized in making glass shades were Dietz, 1874 on; Dithridge, 1896; Douglas, 1871; Bartlett, 1871. Today one finds just the shades in many shops. Turned upside-down, they make attractive vases, candleholders, etc. See specific glass companies in this Guide for specific prices.

Frosted shade (ill.) . . . .$ 8-12
White shade, Greek key (ill.)   8-12

Shaker Collectibles

Ann Lee, also known as Mother Ann or "Ann the Word," founded the Shaker movement in 1774, arriving from England with her husband and seven followers. Their name is derived from a particular dance used in their religion. The first Shaker community was at Watervliet, New York, established in 1787. It lasted until 1938. There are two Shaker communities still in operation, one at Canterbury, New Hampshire, founded in 1793, and Sabbathday Lake, Maine, established also in 1793. The items made by these remarkable people are highly collectible today. Some are being reproduced.

Shakespeare

Shakespeare

Anything to do with this English poet and dramatist is being collected today. Don't expect to find an original manuscript, but there are many and varied items around, especially in England where the Bard of Avon lived.

Lithographs, 8"×11", various
scenes at Stratford, ea. . . . .$ 4- 6

Mug, Shakespeare's face, 4¼"
high 12-17
Plaque, Shakespeare's profile,
9" high (ill.) 18-24
Plate, French, "Shakespeare's
House, Stratford-on-Avon,"
7" dia. 35-44
Program from Stratford Theater,
1912   8-11

Shaving Mugs

Shaving Mugs

Popular around the time of the Civil War, they came into their own when a rash, called Barber's Itch, swept this country in the late 1800s. After that, men demanded their own mugs, usually with their names and/or occupations painted on them. They were made of porcelain, glass, silver plate. Scuttle mugs were also a fad of the day.

Fraternal:
A.O.H. (Ancient Order of
Hibernians) . . . .$ 68- 78
A.O.U.W. (Ancient Order of
United Workmen) 77- 86
B. of L.F. (Brotherhood of Loyal
Firemen) 75- 85
B.P.O.E. (Benevolent Protective
Order of Elks) 75- 84
F.O.E. (Fraternal Order of
Eagles) 72- 81
I.A.S. (Italian-American Society)   69- 78
K. of C. (Knights of Columbus) . . 78- 88
K. of P. (Knights of Pythias) 72- 82
L.O.O.M. (Loyal Order Of
Moose) 64- 74
K.O.L. (Knights of Labor) 65- 75
Masonic, square and compass . . . 75- 85
W.O.W. (Woodmen of the
World) with leaf 62- 72
Miscellaneous
American Eagle 82- 95
American flag, early 72- 82
Automobile, early 180-210
Automobile, 1920s 120-140
Barnyard 45- 55
Bicycle and rider, early 180-200

Birds, any type except American
   eagle 45- 55
Chicken...................... 40- 50
Deer's Head 51- 61
Donkey...................... 50- 60
Elephant..................... 55- 65
Flag, any nation except USA.... 42- 52
Flag, sword and cannon 72- 85
Grapes, bunches of 40- 50

Occupational

Accordion, initialed........... 162-174
Anvil and hammer 140-150
Auctioneer's emblem 107-117
Baggage car 160-180
Baker's emblem (2 lions and
   pretzel) 152-162
Barbershop................... 141-151
Baseball and bats 140-150
Beer brewer's emblem 107-117
Beer wagon, horses, and driver .. 170-180
Blacksmith shoeing horse 130-142
Boilermaker at work 141-150
Bookbinder................... 153-163
Bookkeeper.................. 120-130
Bottle blower at work 150-160
Bricklayer at work 127-136
Brush maker's store 121-130
Buggy maker 154-162
Bull's head and tools 122-131
Butcher chopping meat 121-130
Butcher dressing a steer 119-127
Caboose 110-120
Camera with stand 175-182
Carpenter at work 120-130
Chairmaker at work 121-130
Cigar store 131-140
Clerk at desk 109-118
Coal miner with tools 140-150
Dentist drawing teeth 227-231
Doctor attending patient 261-280
Druggist working............. 151-160
Electric streetcar 130-140
Express wagon, 2 horses 140-150
Fire engine with 2 horses ...... 225+
Flint glassblowers at work...... 240-270
Furniture store............... 128-137
Hardware store 131-140
Harnessmaker at work 161-170
Hatter....................... 152-167
Hearse, horses, and driver 170-180
Hook and ladder, 2 horses ... 210-240
Horse shoer at work 130-140
Hose cart 145-160
Lager beer wagon 134-144
Letter carrier in uniform 137-141
Locomotive and tender 155-170
Machinist's calipers 122-131
Mail wagon, horse, and driver ... 128-142
Man shearing sheep 112-122
Marble cutter 139-147
Mattress maker at work 118-127

Miller dressing burr 121-130
Miner with pick and shovel 150-170
Molder at work............... 122-131
Musicians 120-129
Nailer at work............... 109-120
Oil derrick and scenery 170-180
Omnibus with horses 160-170
Painter at work 128-134
Paperhanger at work 137-142
Porter carrying trunk 121-132
Printer at case 140-150
Prizefighter 375-450
Razor and shears 132-141
Restaurant and bar 131-140
Saddler at work 127-140
Saloon No. 1, bartender and
   customer................... 145-155
Saloon No. 2, bartender and 4
   customers 162-172
Saloonkeeper's emblem 142-151
Sawmill...................... 152-162
Sheriff with felon 151-161
Sign painter at work 122-131
Steam engine 138-147
Steamship 151-160
Stonecutter at work 121-131
Switchmen's emblem 120-140
Tailor at work............... 129-139
Taxi driver 141-150
Telegraph key and hand....... 130-141
Tinner at work 140-150
Tobacconist 129-140
Tugboat 222-247
Wheelwright................. 121-127
Window glass blower 160-180
Wine maker 141-151
Wine taster.................. 152-167
Woodcarver working 140-160
Workmen's emblem 121-130

Sheet Music

The nostalgia boom has renewed the interest in old sheet music. Some of the titles are hilarious. Pre-WWI sheet music is especially sought after. Patriotic, ethnic, ragtime, romance—Irving Berlin, George M. Cohan, Al Jolson, Rudy Vallee, Frederick V. Bowers(?)—all collectible.

1880s to 1914, average price in
   good condition .... $ 8-16
WWI, patriotic, average price in
   good condition 7-12
1920 to 1939, average price in
   good condition 4- 7

Obviously, there are exceptions to these price ranges. If you like it, buy it.

Shell Work

Shells brought home from the seashore or purchased in kits at stores were used to make these bouquets. Usually found under a glass dome or behind glass in a frame, the work is collectible today.

Shell, bouquet, 8″ high, in glass
  enclosed gilt frame . . . . $ 30- 37
Shell, seashore scene, 16″×20″
  in gold frame 40- 47

Ship Models

Ship Models

Models of ships have been found in the tombs of Egyptian kings. Old models are highly collectible, some bringing huge prices.

Chinese junk, bamboo and
  mother-of-pearl, early 19th
  century (ill.) $290-350
New Bedford whaler, carved
  from ivory, inlaid abalone
  shell, 13″ long, late 1800s . . . . .   2,400+
Old Ironsides, miniature, in quart
  bottle, ivory, 5½″ long . . . . . .   3,100+
Scale model of French frigate,
  bone, 18th century, all original   2,650+
3-masted schooner, hand-carved,
  33″ long, dated 1894   695-850

Siderolith Ware

Made in Bohemia by many firms, it was earthenware molded in relief and decorated with bright colors. Schiller and Son made it after 1851. Their imitations of Wedgwood confused many people then and still do today. Usually signed S and G. Don't confuse it with Shore and Goulding, England.

Prices 50-60% lower than Wedgwood—see.

Silhouettes

"Man reduced to his simplest form" is the easiest way to explain them. Supposedly named for an 18th century Frenchman, these are outline pictures. The most famous

Silhouettes

American ones were cut by Charles Peale, 1800 to 1810. Either cut from black and mounted on white, or white (Peale) mounted on black. If you find one signed August Edouart, you've found a jewel.

Costume ball (ill.) . . . .$ 40- 50
Girl and boy in matching gold
  leaf/walnut frames, mid-1800s,
  pr. 110-120
Horse-drawn carriage in gold
  leaf frame 51- 60
Lady in bonnet, in gold leaf
  frame 128-150
Lincoln (probably done from
  photograph) 72- 81
Washington, profile, in walnut
  frame 71- 80

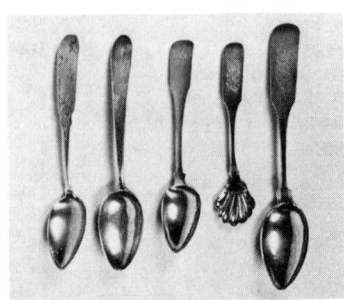

Silver

Silver

See **Silver Definitions** for information on specific types. page 623.

Coin

Butter dish, engraved floral
  scene, Bailey and Co., 1845 . . .$750-900
Butter knives, scroll/shell design,
  Bailey and Co., 1847 200-250
Child's knife, fork, and spoon,
  Gray and Libby, Boston, 1847,
  all 300-400

Silver

Silver

Silver

Ladle, mustard, initialed JR,
  marked Pure Coin 44- 58
Ladle, punch, marked Pure Coin,
  1850 220-250
Spoon, coffin handle, Edmond
  Milne, Philadelphia, 1757 (ill.) . 200-325
Spoon, gold washed bowl (ill.) ... 66- 76
Spoon, Samuel Williamson,
  Philadelphia 1794 (ill.) 220-240
Spoon, Wm. Mannerback,
  Reading, Pa., 1825 (ill.) 200-300
Teaspoon, signed Miksch,
  Bethlehem (ill.) 225-248

Plated EPNS, EPWM, American
Basket, 9″ diameter, EPNS,
  1900s 30- 50
Butter dish, EPNS, flower
  pattern, 6″ diameter, early
  1900s 36- 47
Candlestick, 3-branch, silver
  plate, grape design, 18½″
  high (ill.) 90-110
Candlesticks, triple plate, Victor
  Silver Co., late 1800s, pr. 49- 58

Triple Plate
Butter Dishes
Revolving, plain, engine,
  medallion, chased or
  engraved, Meriden Silver
  Plate Co., c. 1868 .... 64- 75
Cake Baskets
Grecian chased, Meriden Silver
  Plate Co., c. 1870 .... 80- 90
Medallion and chased, engraved,
  Meriden Silver Plate Co.,
  c. 1869 .... 77- 86
Medallion and chased, plain,
  Meriden Silver Plate Co.,
  c. 1868 .... 71- 81
Caster Sets
Beefsteak pattern, chased caster,
  6 bottles, c. 1888 110-150
Befitting pattern, plain caster,
  5 bottles, c. 1888 96-130
Decide pattern, chased caster,
  5 bottles, c. 1889 106-140

Silver

Decipher pattern, plain caster,
  5 bottles, c. 1888 100-170
Wince pattern, fancy gilt, 6
  bottles, Derby Silver Co.,
  c. 1885 135-162
Windlass pattern, w/bell handle,
  6 bottles, Derby Silver Co.,
  c. 1885 172-190
Celery Stands
Grecian chased, w/white glass,
  Meriden Silver Plate Co.,
  c. 1870 .... 52- 72
Medallion and chased, w/white
  glass, Meriden Silver Plate
  Co., c. 1875 .... 51- 60
Cups
Engine, plated or gilt, Meriden
  Silver Plate Co., c. 1869 ...... 41- 54
Grecian or damask, engraved or
  plain, Meriden Silver Plate
  Co., c. 1869 .... 37- 47
Goblets
Engine, plated or gilt, Meriden
  Silver Plate Co., c. 1874 ...... 41- 51
Plain, plated or gilt, Meriden
  Silver Plate Co., c. 1867,
  ea. 40- 50
Ice Pitchers
Grecian pattern, engine turned,
  Meriden Silver Plate Co., c.
  1887 94-112
Medallion pattern, Meriden Silver
  Plate Co., c. 1885 97-112
Paneled chased, Meriden Silver
  Plate Co., c. 1887 99-110
Syrup Cups and Plates
Damask chased, with plate,
  Meriden Silver Plate Co.,
  c. 1869 .... 67- 77
Grecian chased, without plate,
  Meriden Silver Plate Co.,
  c. 1875 .... 61- 71
Plain, with plate, Meriden Silver
  Plate Co., c. 1868 .... 52- 62

(continued)

Teapots
  Flowers, signed "Meriden,"
    8½" high (ill.) 97-107

Quadruple Plate
Cake Baskets
  Debris pattern, etched, dated
    1800s 140-150
  Decade pattern, satin chased,
    c. 1889 117-127
  Decamp, chased, 1880 130-140
Cups
  Crumb brush, satin engraved,
    c. 1889 . . . . 22- 31
  Crumb tray, satin engraved,
    c. 1889 . . . . 41- 50
  Elfin pattern, hand-chased,
    c. 1888 . . . . 47- 67
  Florentine pattern, gold-lined,
    c. 1887 . . . . 46- 56
  Pied Piper of Hamelin, gold-
    lined, c. 1889 . . . . 52- 70
  Rose pattern, engraved handle,
    c. 1895 . . . . 48- 58
Napkin Rings
  Barefoot boy, 3" high, hand-
    engraved, c. 1900 . . . . 40- 70
  "Best Wishes," chick and
    wishbone, c. 1880 . . . . 41- 51
  Carved man and dog, 3" high,
    1905, satin finish, engraved . . . 42- 52
  Deficit pattern, hammered and
    applied gilt, c. 1889 . . . . 34- 43
  "Father," hand-engraved, 3" dia.,
    c. 1890 . . . . 29- 37
Peppers
  Decorous pattern, c. 1888 . . . . . . 30- 40
  Decorum pattern, c. 1892 . . . . 30- 40
  Decoy, c. 1889 . . . . 27- 37
  Decree, gold-lined, c. 1889 . . . . . . 31- 40
Pickle Casters
  Behave pattern, blue, red or
    canary bottle, c. 1889 . . . . 86- 94
  Deduce pattern, red bottle, c.
    1890 . . . . 74- 83
  Napkin ring and pepper, Defence
    pattern, c. 1890 96-108
  Tea caddy, Defaming pattern,
    satin bright cut, c. 1889 78-110
Salts
  Declivity pattern, owl, c. 1889 . . . 47- 56
  Devotion, cut glass, c. 1890 . . . . . 40- 50
  Decolor pattern, cut glass, c. 1888 42- 52
Tea Servers
  Teapot, on warming stand, 3
    pieces, 14" high, signed
    "Pairpoint Manufacturing
    Company" (ill.) 74- 97
Toothpick Holders
  Boy Riding Turtle, Umbrella,
    all plate, c. 1888 . . . . 82- 91

Card receiver, a non-tarnishable,
  c. 1888 . . . . 51- 70
Deplore pattern, oxidized boots,
  c. 1888 . . . . 31- 40
Jewel casket, "Old Oaken
  Bucket," opens by turning
  crank, c. 1890 92-107
Manicure set, 7 pieces in plush
  case, hammered old silver,
  c. 1889 120-131
Porcupine, plain or gilt, c.1889 . . . 39- 47
Vases
  Bleed pattern, non-tarnishable,
    c. 1888 . . . . 67- 77
  Decorated porcelain, farm scene,
    c. 1892 . . . . 71- 78
  Glass container, "Girl with
    butterfly net," silver and gold,
    c. 1888 92-107
  Valley pattern, Derby Silver
    Co., 1883 . . . . 86- 93
  Value pattern, Derby Silver
    Co., 1883 90-110

Sterling Silver, American
Miscellaneous
  Blotter, flowers in repousee,
    c. 1870s 230-260
  Candleholder, embossed roses
    and scrolls, "Gorham
    Sterling," 1¾" high 250-270
  Desk set, inkwells and calendar,
    c. 1880 340-370
  Indian Chief, 4" wide, c. 1910 295-380
  Instand, cut glass bottles,
    "Cupids," in repousee, c. 1875 . 375-420
  Nude in Pond, 4½" wide, c. 1890 . 350-400
  Paper knife, Art Nouveau, c. 1895 320-380
  Stamp box, "Dog" on top, c. 1880 95-112
  Thermometer, repousee frame,
    still works, c. 1895 195-240
Bookmarks
  Eraser, Indian head in relief,
    c. 1890 97-107
  Gentleman's cane, mushroom
    cap, engraved, c. 1875 140-160
  Indian head, 4½" long, signed
    "Tiffany," 1896 150-170
  Lobster-shaped, 6" long, c. 1880 . 120-140
  Penholder, repousee, 8" long,
    c. 1875 120-130
  Roman goddess, 4" long, c. 1885 . 110-120
  Shaving brush, Art Nouveau,
    c. 1900 140-160
  Shaving mug, "Boxer" engraved
    on side, c. 1890 295-310
Pocket Flasks
  Bar jigger, Imp thumbing nose,
    c. 1880 140-170
  Button box in shape of collar,
    marked "Collar," c. 1875 190-210

Chatelaine, 3-chain, inlaid
diamond, c. 1870 270-290
Cut crystal, Art Nouveau,
"Lady," c. 1895 240-260
Cut crystal, Indian Chief in
relief, c. 1890 220-240
Glove cologne, repousee, 3" long,
c. 1870 190-220
Liquor label, "Whiskey," c.
1890 110-140
Nudes in relief, c. 1880 220-240

Sterling Silver, Foreign
French

Bonbon dish, gadroon edging,
3½" high 275-320
Dish, 1810, embossed flowers . . . 240-280
Salt cellar, reeded border, set
of 4 550-625

Irish

Cup, harp decor, mid-1800s 300-400
Master salt, footed, with spoon . . 320-400

Italian

Table bell, late 1800s, coat-of-
arms, 5" high 210-240

Russian

Beaker, late 1700s 385-425
Candlestick, 12" high, pr. 385-425
Mug, late 1800s 450-525
Napkin ring, etched flower
decor 195-220

Swedish

Creamer, flowers and foliage
decor, early 1800s 360-390
Tea set (pot, creamer, sugar,
waste bowl, tray), 1800s . . . . . . 5,100+

Silver Deposit Glass

Popular since the late 1800s, it's simply silver deposited on the glass, usually by electro-depositing, a method involving electricity, flux, and silver anodes. It's still being made today.

Bonbon dish, footed, 6½" dia. . . . $ 67- 78
Bottle, cologne, green, 4" high . . . 62- 74
Bowl, 7", 8", 9", clear glass 110-140
Bowl, 10" dia., cobalt 140-180
Bud vase, 6½" high, marked
Sterling 220-270
Cologne bottle with stopper, 4"
high, marked Sterling 300-370
Compote, green, 7½" high 60- 70
Cruet, 7" high, cut glass stopper,
marked Sterling 210-270
Decanter, 9½" high, cut glass
stopper, EPNS 123-140
Mustard jar, 4" high 60- 70
Perfume bottle, 4" high, cut glass
stopper, marked Sterling 220-240
Plate, green, sterling silver 84- 92

Toothpick holders, 2", 3" high . . . 41- 50
Vase, bud, flared top, 8" high . . . 56- 72
Vase, 6", 8" high 62- 70
Vase, 9½" high, marked Sterling 210-240

Silver Lustre Ware

Silver Lustre Ware

Produced in large quantities between the early 1800s and 1840, in Staffordshire, England, it went out of style in the 1850s when electroplating of metal items came into vogue.

Bowl, festoon and shell decor $110-155
Coffeepot, 10½" high 375-450
Candleholder, ribbed design,
11½" high 92-112
Creamer, fine ribbed design,
4½" high to top of handle 160-180
Creamer, dolphin handle 150-170
Footed teapot, 8½" high 310-340
Goblet, 4" high 90-112
Goblet, 5" high 72- 84
Pitcher, Leaf pattern, 4½" high
(ill.) 78- 89
Pitcher, white quilted body,
silver lustre at top 300-360
Sugar bowl, ribbed design 145-170
Teapot, 5½" high 265-320
Toby jug 290-340

Silver Resist Ware

Silver Resist Ware

This ware gets its name from the fact that the drawings or patterns resist the lustering

341

(continued)

solutions, and when fired in the kiln the entire surface of the piece, except for the pattern, is glazed. Similar to Silver Lustre except the pattern appears on the surface.

Creamer	$172-190
Cup/saucer, berry and leaf	107-118
Jug, 5″ high	170-180
Pitcher, 6¼″ high	260-280
Pitcher, canary ground, floral motif, 7″ high	270-310
Teapot, 5½″ high	220-228
Teapot, 6″ high (ill.)	210-220

Silveria

Silveria

This glass was produced by Stevens and Williams, Brierly Hills, England, about 1900. Its inventor, John Northwood II, gave it its name, and it was made by sandwiching silver foil between two layers of transparent crystal or colored glass. Drippings of transparent glass cover the outer layer of the glass. Two Frenchmen arrived at the formula in the late 1870s, but Northwood is generally credited with the manufacture of the glass. It's interesting to note that Northwood's son came to America and is given credit (?) for creating Taffeta glass, better known, worldwide, as Carnival glass. Some pieces of Silveria are signed "England" while others may have the familiar "S & W" in script, with or without a fleur-de-lis on a ground pontil. Scarce, but a treasure when found.

Vase, applied green handles,
  pink/yellow/green drip-
  pings, 5″ high, c. 1900,
  signed "S & W" (ill.) $1,500-1,700

Slag Glass

See specific items in **Pattern Glass Section**.

Slag Glass

Bowl, footed, purple, embossed
  design, 4″ high (ill.) . . . . $ 72- 82
Salt, fish-shaped, purple (ill.) 60- 80

Slides, Chain

Slides, Chain

These objects helped adjust the length of the watch hanging around the lady's neck. Gold or gold-plated, sometimes ornately set with precious stones, they're hard to find today because so many have been made into bracelets.

14k gold, inlaid pearl on each
  side, late 1800s $250-280
10k gold, imitation diamond 48- 59
18k gold, small ruby, initials 250-300
Keep in mind that 10k gold or less was usually used with imitation stones. The same applies to gold-plated.

Slipware

Made in Europe and the U.S. for many years, it's a ceramic decorated by applying slip (clay reduced to a liquid batter) to the surface of the piece being made.

Bowl, gray, 7″ dia. . . . . $ 71- 80
Jug, figures in brown, 6″ high . . . 78- 88
Pitcher, lustre striping, floral
  band, Staffordshire, 13″ high . 110-130
Plate brown/cream color, 10″
  dia. 142-160
Plate, red/brown, Pennsylvania
  Dutch motif, 9″ dia. 50- 60

342

Platter, brown, cream color,
ornate decor, oval, 14″ dia. ... 150-160
Pot, bean, red, glazed inside,
9″ high 92-107

Slot Machines

Slot Machines

The One-armed Bandit rides again! Now, more collectible than ever, coin-operated slots are bringing brisk prices, coast-to-coast. Remember when Fiorello LaGuardia, New York City's comic-reading mayor, personally smashed several hundred with his trusty fire ax? Some states have laws concerning slot machines, so check before you give a check.

Caille Superior Nude Front,
restored $3,200-3,500
Caille Victoria, center pull,
restored 7,200-7,700
Jennings Lightups, 10¢,
rebuilt 1,500-1,750
Jennings Silver Chief
Sportsmen, 10¢, rebuilt 1,350-1,500
Jennings Standard Chief, 5¢,
rebuilt 1,350-1,500
Mills Cherry Front, 25¢, fully
restored 1,600-1,875
Mills Chrome Twenty One,
10¢(ill.) 1,850-2,250
Mills Dewey, 5¢, excellent
condition 8,000-8,450
Mills Diamond Front, 25¢,
fully restored 1,600-1,875
Mills Four Column FOK
Vender, 5¢, fully restored .. 1,850-2,275
Mills H.T., 5¢, restored 1,400-1,600
Mills Lion Front, 5¢ 1,850-2,250
Pace Comet, 5¢, restored 1,875-2,250

Pace Fancy Front, 1¢, restored 1,975-2,400
Pace Four Star, 25¢, mint
condition 1,500-1,750
Q. T. Fire Bird w/gumball
side vender, 1¢, fully
restored 2,250-2,475

Smith Brothers

Alfred and Harry Smith established the decorating department at the Mt. Washington Glass Company in 1871. They were known for their excellence in enameling on bisque or opal glass. They established their own firm in 1875 in New Bedford, Massachusetts, and made the famous Smith Vase in the late 1800s until it was cheaply copied and sold in dime stores by the hundreds.

Biscuit jar, daisies, blue shading,
silver top, signed $340-370
Bowl, covered, signed 242-270
Cream bowl, white daisies,
beaded top 199-240
Creamer/sugar, blue flowers,
silver collar, white 190-220
Cracker jar, Burmese color, gold
florals, silver bail 440-470
Plate, Santa Maria, 1880s, 10″
dia., signed 550-580
Sugar shaker, ribbed, opaque,
white, flowers, silver top,
9″ high 110-128
Toothpick, flower decor, 3″ high,
signed 99-112
Vase, bird decor, enameled,
signed 260-290
Vase, Burmese pink, yellow,
fruits, acid cut 310-340

Smoking Accessories

Smoking Accessories

Box, cigar, inlaid M.O.P. top,
rosewood, 12″×10½″ .... $ 74- 83
Box, cigar, mahogany, brass
fittings, 14″×11″ (ill.) 70- 80
Cutters, cigar—see

Snuff Bottles

Snuffboxes

Soapstone

Snuff Bottles

Usually intricately carved on the outer surface, they were made of glass, porcelain, jade, coral, etc. They were carried originally by Orientals in the 18th century. The habit of taking snuff, thought to be a medical cure-all, spread to Europe in the mid-1800s, probably even earlier. Snuff bottles were usually carried by women.

Agate, carved, woman on
bridge, stopper, Ch'ien Lung
mark .... $ 550+
Glass, blue painting on inside,
2¼" high 42- 52
Jade, stopper (ill.) 285-310
Lapis lazuli, garden scene, coral
stopper 183-192
Mother-of-pearl, 19th century ... 104-114
Opal, fish scene, coral stopper ... 410-450
Peking enamel, women in
garden 195-220
Rock crystal, quartz stopper 188-210

Snuffboxes

Made from metal, usually gold or silver, intricately carved, sometimes inlaid with precious gems, carried by men during the same period as snuff bottles.

Chinese, gold-on-steel, hinged
lid, footed $221-240
Cloisonne, blue enamel, flowers,
with lid 192-240
Glass, green/blue enamel, floral
decor.................... 99-108
Sterling silver, initialed, lid 170-180
Tortoiseshell, primitive figures,
Chinese, early 1800s 347-420
Wood, inlaid silver, 4-leaf clover
on lid (ill.) 62- 71

Soapstone

Call it steatite, if you want to get technical.

Also sometimes called potstone. Usually attributed to China, most of what you find in shops today was found in the Delaware River area and New England and was carved there.

Ashtray .... $ 19- 27
Bed warmer, wire handle 38- 47
Bookends, brown/black, pr. 40- 50
Candleholder, carved, fruit,
brown/white, 3" high 31- 40
Figurine, elephant, 3½" high 44- 47
Figurines, Chinese couple,
4" high, pr. (ill.) 48- 57
Toothpick, fruit decor, 4" high .. 32- 41
Vase, brown/black, carved leaves,
8" high 47- 56
Vase, floral, neutral to black/
brown, 5" high 60- 71

Songbooks

Anyone remember Blind Lemon Jefferson, Ida Cox, the Jubilee singers, or Charlie Jackson? All greats in their own right, long, long ago. Songbooks of the blues, folk songs, hymnals, all are collectible.

Folk Songs of the American
Negro, 1907 .... $ 9-14
The Paramount Book of Blues,
1924 17-25
Revival Songs, published in
Dallas, Tex., in 1929 .... 4- 6

Souvenir and Commemorative Plates

Don't confuse these with the better quality early Staffordshire plates, popular in the mid-1800s. The souvenir plates came into vogue about the time of the Philadelphia Centennial in 1876 and stayed popular until the 1930s.

Souvenir Spoons

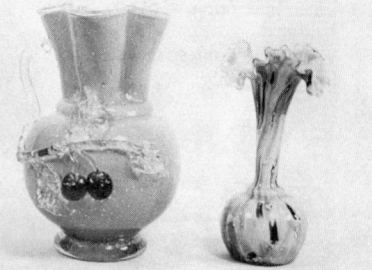

Spangle Glass

Alaska Yukon Pacific Exposition,
1909 . . . . $ 39- 52
Ashbury Park Amusement Park,
New Jersey, blue 42- 51
Capital Island, Maine, sailing
ships, 9″ dia. 42- 51
Carolinas, Pinehurst, North
Carolina, 9″ dia. 40- 50
Faneuil Hall, Boston, 8″ dia. 40- 50
Israel, Independence, 7″ dia. 40- 60
Mackinac Island, 1907 (ill.) 30- 40
West Virginia Centennial, red/
blue, 10″ dia. 42- 52

Souvenir Spoons

Made as mementos for fairs and other
events, they enjoyed their greatest popularity in the late 1800s. They covered every conceivable subject and were usually made of
a silver-plated material or sterling silver.
Reproductions in almost every category.

Actress, Norma Talmadge . . . . . . $ 23- 31
Atlanta, Ga., bale of cotton 18- 27
Atlantic City, N.J., steel pier,
1904 . . . . 13- 27
Brooklyn Bridge, 1883 . . . . 14- 27
Colorado state seal, Denver,
engraved in bowl of spoon 19- 27
Indianapolis, 1909 . . . . 14- 23
Louisiana Purchase Exposition,
1903, sterling silver 133-140
Mt. Vernon, Va., sterling silver . . 131-150
Pan-American Exposition, 1901 . 33- 42
Saratoga, N.Y., demitasse,
sterling silver 131-141
William Shakespeare, England . . 33- 42
World's Fair, 1904 . . . . 34- 44

Spangle Glass

Mica or other metallic flakes were imbedded between two layers of glass. Many
firms made it in the late 1800s. Don't confuse it with Spatter (End-of-Day) glass. Poor
repros being made.

Basket, blue/pink, mica, fluted
rim, clear handle $118-124
Basket, green/yellow, mica, thorn
handle, 7¼″ dia. 160-172
Bowl, blue, mica, 7″ dia. 85- 92
Bowl, cased pink/yellow, 6½″
dia. 85- 94
Cookie jar, usual marking, silver-
plated top and holder, 6″ high . 78- 82
Paperweight, blue flowers, gold
mica flakes 142-154
Pitcher, blue, mica, cased,
miniature, 4½″ high 130-150
Sugar/creamer, green, cased,
mica flakes 78- 89
Vase, cream lined, white/pink,
spangles, 8″ high 82- 94
Vase, pink, silver flecks, red
cherries, applied clear handle,
"Stevens and Williams" (ill.) . . 108-119
Vase, ruffled, spatter and
spangle, 6½″ high (ill.) 91-110
Vase, yellow ground, peach, mica,
cased pair, 6″ high 86- 92

Spanish Lace Glass

The opalescent designs of flowers and
foliage identify this glass, popular in the late
1800s.

Barber bottle, cranberry, 9″
high . . . . $ 71- 81
Basket, blue/pink, ruffled,
scalloped, silver holder 97-108
Bowl, blue/pink, ruffled lip 140-160
Bride's basket, blue, ruffled 160-170
Epergne, cranberry, 14″ high . . . 275-300
Finger bowl, opalescent swirls . . . 60- 80
Lamp, cranberry, Fenton Glass
Works 160-180
Pitcher, vaseline, original tin
top 152-160
Rose bowl, vaseline glass 72- 81
Salt shaker, opalescent ruby,
4″ high 41- 51
Spooner, vaseline 79- 82
Toothpick, blue swirls, 3″ high . . 60- 70

(continued)

Vase, blue opalescent, 8½"
high 66- 73
Vase, blue opalescent, ruffled
top, 6½" high 69- 79

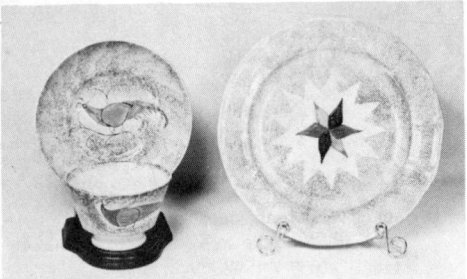

Spatter

Spatter

This is not a ware but a type of decoration used by potters worldwide. That made by Staffordshire potters, 1820-1850, interests collectors most. Much of it is ironstone. Adams made a lot in both the regular Staffordshire, 1830s, and in ironstone in the 1840s. Most platters are octagonal. Plates are smooth rim or sided. The most popular pattern is Schoolhouse; Peacock is second. The most colorful is called Rainbow. Most popular colors were yellow, green, purple, pink, and blue. G. Adams and Son, Alcock, Cotton and Barlow, Davenport, J and G Heath, Powell and Bishop, Wedgwood (blue rim type) are just a few of the many firms who used this type decoration.

Bowl, blue, Peacock pattern, 6½"
dia. $240-280
Creamer, blue, Schoolhouse
pattern, 6" high 185-199
Cup and saucer, blue, Peafowl
pattern 240-270
Cup/saucer, Peafowl (ill.) 240-260
Pitcher, red and blue, School-
house pattern, 7" high 270-290
Plate, red, Peacock pattern, 9"
dia. 310-350
Plate, red/green background,
Schoolhouse pattern, 9½" dia.. 375-420
Plate, Star pattern, 8¼" dia.
(ill.) 220-270

Spatter Glass

It's doubtful that this glass was ever formally called End-of-Day. Legend has it that

Spatter Glass

at nightfall the glassblowers used what was left over to make whimsies for friends and family. There's too much of it on the market. Though it was commercially made, it never achieved any great popularity when made in the late 1800s by many firms. Being reproduced.

Basket, multicolored, clear
handled .... $ 79- 87
Bowl, cased, typical spatter
colors, rigaree feet 64- 74
Creamer, 4" high 32- 42
Cup/saucer, blue ground, usual
colors 41- 50
Ewer, tortoise/opalescent
background, 8" high 57- 67
Jug, milk, yellow/blue spatter,
6" high 39- 49
Pitcher, blue/yellow/brown, clear
handle, 3" high 67- 77
Pitcher, yellow/red/blue/green,
7½" high 97-128
Slipper (souvenir or whimsey
item), green, white/red 42- 51
Toothpick, pink/green/brown,
4" high 47- 52
Tumbler, diagonal ribbing, 4¾"
high 61- 70
Tumbler, 5" high 29- 39
Tumbler, yellow/brown/green ... 29- 31
Vase, blue/red/green, 11" high ... 50- 60
Vase, red/bronze/green, 7½" high 60- 70
Vase, yellow, green (ill.) 50- 60

Spinning Wheels

Who made and used the first one is not really known. We do know that there are two basic types of wheels, the flax wheel and the wool wheel. Basically, the spinning mechanism on a wool wheel is a metal spike, usually called a spindle. The spinning mechanism on the flax wheel is the bobbin and flyer.

Spinning Wheels

American two-handed flax wheel,
c. 1850s $275-325
Appalachian area wool wheel,
c. 1840s 275-350
Connecticut double flyer wheel,
c. 1840s 250-275
European flax wheel, c. 1840s
(ill.) 275-300
New England wool wheel,
c. 1840s 325-350
New York two-handed wheel,
stamped A. Webster, c. early
19th century 295-345
Pennsylvania wool wheel,
c. 1830s 350-375
Shaker "SR AL" wool wheel,
c. 1830s 375-400
Shaker wool wheel, stamped
F.W., c. 1840s 375-400

Spongeware

Spongeware

Similar to Spatter, the designs were applied to the ware by daubing the color. Dealers call it Spatterware, or lump the two together. Any knowledgeable person can tell the two apart.

Bowl and pitcher, American
made $270-290
Bowl, blue, 8" diameter 61- 72

Bowl, green or cream ground,
10" dia. (ill.) 49- 62
Butter crock, covered, blue,
18" high 142-150
Cup/saucer, multicolored, marked
Adams 76- 79
Cuspidor, blue, blue bands 42- 54
Pitcher, blue decoration on buff
ground, 6½" high (ill.) 57- 67
Pitcher, blue, New England, 8"
high 81- 92
Plate, blue, 8½" dia. 50- 60
Spittoon, blue, 3" high 62- 70
Vegetable dish, blue, 5" dia. 54- 61

Spoonholders

Spoonholders

You'll find hundreds of these in pattern and cut glass. Pewter, quadruple plate, porcelain—just about every material was used. The one shown here is triple plate, c. 1890, $35-45, not including the spoons. The most famous is Jumbo—see in **Pattern Glass Section**, this Price Guide.

Spoons

Sterling silver spoons are especially collectible. The maker and year decide the price. Prices given are for sterling only. Spoons are classified by maker, with pattern and type specified. Keep in mind what sterling silver has done in 1980.

Durgin
Bead, fruit spoon, gold bowl $170-180
Bead, table or teaspoon, 5½" 179-182
Gorham
Blythe Spirit, sugar spoon 140-160
Cambridge, soup, teaspoon 122-131

347

(continued)

Hundreds of other makers and patterns. Find a reliable dealer if you're interested in collecting silver, especially sterling. Also, see **Silver, Souvenir Spoons.**

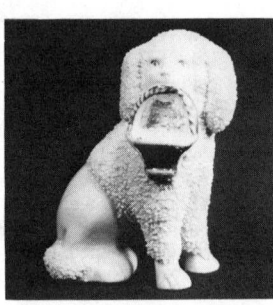

Staffordshire Figurines

Staffordshire Figurines and Figures

Boy and girl under tree, 5½"
high .... $ 93-110
Cinderella, marked, 4" high 42- 51
Dog, miniature, glazed white,
3" high (ill.) 27- 36
Dog, white lustre, seated, 14"
high 79- 87
Greyhound chasing rabbit, 11"
high 47- 52
Horse, rider, groom holding
bridle, 1785, 11" high 75- 81
Lover in a bower, 15" high 59- 60
Man and lion, 8" high 79- 80
Old woman and pipe, 1770,
4½" high 440-510
Red Riding Hood, wolf, etc.,
7½" high 97-108
White cow, boy herder, 7" high .. 190-220

Sports

Photo Courtesy Hake's Americana & Collectibles

Sports Collectibles

The older the better—a few items bringing high prices today are listed below.

Autographs actually signed by
the player (Autopens—signatures signed by a machine—have
little or no value.) ....$ 8-11
Blankets, cloth fabric inserts,
found in early 1900 tobacco
packages................... 14-27

Staffordshire Items

Staffordshire Items

Box, boy riding Newfound-
land dog, cover . . . . $ 50- 60
Cheese dish, blue/white,
Fenton, England 53- 70
Creamer and sugar, Stag
pattern, blue, white 49- 58
Cup/saucer, light blue,
Challinor, handleless 47- 57
Hen dish, white bisque top,
colored head, basket-
weave base 142-160
Ice pail, ribbed, lion mask
handles, cylindrical, pr. 420-470
Inkwell, masks on side, claw
feet, cobalt bands 140-160
Jug, brown/yellow, willow,
Pagoda, Porto Bello,
5" high 90-110
Match holder, boots,
striker, pr. 42- 67
Mug, Bacchus head, beard,
pointed ears, 1800 151-171
Needle case, enamel, blue/
green, red garlands 140-160
Pitcher, apple green, 12"
high 62- 71
Plate, Avon cottage, blue,
set of 6, 10" dia. 43- 44
Plate, Mayflower, 10" dia.
(ill.) 43- 46
Platter, Lambton Hall,
castle scene, blue 99-107
Quill holder, tree trunk, 2
white dogs 64- 72
Tea service, strawberry
lustre, 1825, 24 pcs. . . . . 1,350+
Toby jug, black/green,
lustre trim, 10" high 190-220
Urn, Nottingham stone-
ware, 1775, 6" high, pr. 221-240
Thousands of reproductions.

Stained Glass Windows

Louis Comfort Tiffany made some of the
most beautiful. The more valuable come
from Europe, but be on the lookout for old
churches, old houses, even old railroad sta-
tions being torn down.

Church window, all glass perfect,
3'×6' $750-950
Railroad station window,
Southern, 2½'×6' 460-520
Window, green/blue, glass prisms,
beveled glass, 6'×4' 525-670
Windows, each side front door,
Victorian house, late 1800s,
pr. 525-598

Stamps

There are more common stamps to be
found than rare ones. Also, rarity doesn't
necessarily mean you will sell it for a lot of
money. If no one wants it, rarity is of little
value market-wise. Consult a reliable dealer
if you think you have a valuable stamp.

Stangl Pottery

Stangl Pottery

J. Martin Stangl was superintendent of the
technical division of the Fulper Pottery Company as early as 1911. In 1930, Stangl acquired the Fulper firm. After 1935 emphasis
was shifted from artware to dinnerware, produced under the Stangl name. In late 1955
the corporate title was formally changed to
the Stangl Pottery Company. The pottery
was made as late as 1972, the year of Stangl's
death. "MS" is sometimes found on certain
pieces though not all were signed. The
Stangl birds are the most collectible.

Bluebird, signed . . . . $ 41- 50
Bowl, white, flower shape, 8" dia.   18- 27

349

(continued)

Cardinal on stump	54- 62
Hummingbird, signed "STANGL POTTERY COMPANY" (ill.) .	54- 66
Oriole, signed as above	48- 59
Rooster, signed as above	64- 72

Statuary, Ivory

Hong Kong ivory, seen more and more in shops today, is actually bone from a horse's leg. Don't be fooled. See **Ivory**

Buddha	$ 47- 56
Camel	45- 53
Elephant	72- 81
Maid and maiden, Chinese, (ill.)	485-590
Man and woman in garden, 11½" high	1,150+

Statuary, Porcelain

Bisque, porcelain, plaster of paris (see **Rogers Statuary**), Parian Ware, Majolica (European and American). See specific categories.

Nude, feeding fawn, Hutchenreuther, Bavaria, 12" across (ill.)	$420-440

Steins

The Westerwald area of Germany in the 17th century made the finest steins ever made. Mettlach also made fine steins, as did Dresden at Meissen, Germany. Also, see **Mettlach**. Another repro item.

½ liter, flower motif, forest scene, pewter lid	$320-370
½ liter, green/buff, Liberal Arts Palace, St. Louis Exposition, 1904	340-370
½ liter, roses, castle scene, porcelain, pewter lid	320-370
1 liter, etched decor, porcelain lined, pewter lid	360-410
1 liter, musicians, barmaid, drinking scene, pewter lid	350-420
2 liter, blue and buff, pewter cap, 17" high	410-500
3 liter, brewery wagon and horse, advertising item, 1890s	192-210
Bardolph and Falstaff, #614, Germany, 9½" high, pewter cap, 1½ liter (ill.)	180-210
Character steins, plain	160-172
Crystal deer, forest, hunters, pewter cap, 11½" high	290-370
Etched and art glass	220-260
Family crest, pewter lid, dated 1863, Germany	230-280
Fraternal, glass or pottery	175-188
Geschut, #1102, ½ liter	265-300
HR, etched	210-250
Hand-painted glass	150-170
Hunt scene, wild boars, pewter lid, 3 liter, 16" high	275-285
Lithophane bottom, nude, pewter top, Germany, 10" high, new . .	115-145
Musterschutz, Bismarck, multi-colored	375-500
Musterschutz characters	240-270
Occupational porcelains	170-185
Pewter, scene in relief	200-240
Plain crystal	140-170
Pottery, scene in relief	110-140
Schultz and Dooley, Utica club beer, advertising item, 1900s . .	102-140
Stoneware, 3 liter, pewter cap, 16" high	172-182

Stereoscopes and Cards

These viewers came into use in the U.S. around 1850. They were invented in England a few years before. The picture is taken with

Statuary, Ivory

Statuary, Porcelain

Steins

Stereoscopes and Cards

a dual lens camera, then reproduced as two pictures. Seen through the viewer, the pictures blend into one 3-dimensional view. Every subject known to man was put on the cards.

Single cards, any subject, average (rare)	$1.50- 30
Stereoscope and 12 cards	120-140
Stereoscope and 300 cards	325+
Stereoscope card, Philadelphia actress (ill.)	1.50- 2
Stereoscope, hand viewer, brass-mounted, 1896, 24 cards	140-170
Stereoscope, sliding adjuster, wooden, 36 cards	140-170
Stereoscope, sliding adjuster, 75 cards in box, Civil War scenes	325-360
Stereoscope, table model, walnut stand, Saturnscope, 1892, 12 cards	220-240

Steuben Glass

Steuben Glass

Frederick Carder founded the firm in Corning, New York, in 1903. In the field of decorative arts few men contributed more. In 1918 the huge Corning Glass Works assumed con-

Steuben Glass

trol of the Steuben Glass Company. Mr. Carder stayed with Steuben until 1933, acting as art director. He continued working in his own laboratory until he closed it in 1953 at the age of 90. He passed away in 1963 at the age of 100. Few men of his genius will pass this way again.

Acid Cutback

Black and alabaster vase, 7" high	$815- 915
Black and amethyst, 12" high	800- 900
Rosaline and alabaster, vase, 4½" high	670- 720

Aurene

Bowl, blue, signed Aurene under glaze, 8" dia.	410- 420
Candlesticks, twisted stem, gold, 10" high, pr.	420- 450
Compote, gold, Aurene under glaze, 6" high	380- 410
Decanter with tray and 6 liquor glasses, signed	800- 900
Goblet, gold, red-gold interior, signed Steuben on bottom	240- 270
Gold Aurene and alabaster vase, 8½" high	1,450+
Perfume, blue, Aurene underglaze, numbered, pr.	280- 310
Salt, gold, Aurene under-glaze, pedestal type, 1½" high	180- 198
Vase, blue, acid cut, 12" high	765- 840
Vase, blue, iridescent, 9" high in silver holder	250- 270
Vase, blue, ribbed, Aurene underglaze, 5½" high	250- 280
Vase, red (rare)	2,975+

Calcite

Candlesticks, gold Aurene, pr.	275- 295

(continued)

Sherbet with plate, blue
Aurene (rare in some
colors) 360- 380
Vase, footed, blue Aurene
(rare in some colors) 560- 590

Diatreta
Not shown, extremely rare
and seldom found.

Ivory
Vase, 7" high, paper label 265- 300
Vase, 6½" high, paper label ... 245- 270

Ivrene
Vase, 5" high, paper label ..... 600+
Vase, 12" high, lightly incised
script Steuben signature ... 800- 900

Jade
Bowl, yellow, 3" high,
Steuben signature 380- 410
Candlesticks, blue jade and
alabaster, 12" high, pr. ..... 785+
Goblet, green jade and
alabaster, 5½" high (ill.) 128- 136
Perfume, blue, 6" high,
script Steuben 370- 420
Vase, blue, not signed 300- 375

Rosaline
Bowl, finger, with plate,
paper label 400- 440
Perfume, alabaster foot,
stopper, paper label 400- 450
Sherbet with plate, paper
label 240- 270
Vase, alabaster disc foot,
7½" high, no signature
or label 165- 195

Topaz
Carbon yellow bowl, 11"
dia., paper label 195- 220
Topaz yellow vase, 6½"
high, no label 160- 190

Verre de Soie
Basket, paper label 220- 240
Bowl, rose, paper label 199- 270
Compote 280- 310
Perfume, cut flowers and
leaves, sterling cap (ill.) 160- 185
Perfume, cut floral design,
plunger type, brass fix-
tures, high pedestal base
(ill.) 160- 190
Vase, bud, 6" high, paper
label 210- 260
Vase, Jack-in-the Pulpit, 6"
high, paper label 190- 240

Stevengraphs

Thomas Stevens established his firm in 1854 at Coventry, England. He produced his first bookmarks in 1862, his first Steven-

Stevengraphs

graph in 1874. He originated the name Stevengraph; his bookmarks should be called Stevens Bookmarks. The bookmarks were originally sold pinned to a paper backing bearing his name and trademark. Longer than wide, they are mitered at one end and finished with a tassel. His Stevengraphs are miniature silk pictures and matted. His name was never woven into the Stevengraph. His name is woven into the bookmarks at a mitered corner.

Bookmarks
Birthday Blessings .... $ 84- 97
Centennial, George Washington . 160-185
Home Sweet Home 170-182
The Lady Godiva Procession 160-177
Many Happy Returns of the Day 93-107

Stevengraphs
Clifton Suspension Bridge, Stg.
140 410-450
The Death of Nelson, Stg. 152 ... 285-340
Iroquois, Stg. 162 600-700
The Lady Godiva Procession,
Stg. 150 281-330
The Last Lap, Stg. 176 277-312
Madonna and Child, Stg. 87 710-900
The Old Tyne Bridge, Stg. 144 .. 820-870
Triumph, 1879 (ill.) 135-145

Stevens and Williams

Their factory has been at Brierley Hill, Staffordshire, England, for years. Some of the world's finest glass has been made by this firm.

Basket, clear to green, floral,
crystal motif, 6" dia. $300-400
Bowl, swirls, camphor to cranberry, metal holder 450-600
Ewer, blue satin, enameled bird,
coralene stem 325-415
Jam dishes, Rubina, pair set in
footed silver holder 260-350
Rose bowl, cranberry threading,
blue interior, footed 400-450

Tazza, Rosaline baluster stem,
 9″ across 475-572
Vase, enameled iris, acid-cut
 green ground, cameo type, 9″
 high 475-500
Vase, peach color, enameled
 floral, blown 320-350
Vase, white satin, enameled floral,
 rainbow lining, 9″ high 410-470

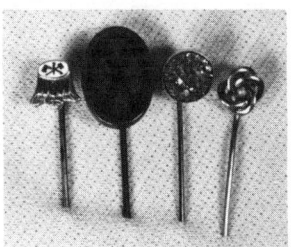

Stickpins

Stickpins

Today they're collectible because scarf pins are back in style. Diamond Jim Brady wore one that was $5,000 worth of diamonds. Most of what you find in shops today are in the $6 to $10 range. One exception is the Tennessee River pearl, worth $50 to $500. See **Tennessee River Pearls**. Of course, if it's marked 14k or 18k, it's worth much more. Generally, $6 to $10 for gold filled, $20 to $25 for 14k; with authenticated diamonds, rubies, etc., much more. Get it in writing! Also, see **Jewelry**.

Anthracite diamond, 10k stem
 (ill.) . . . . $ 18- 23
Australian opal, 14k white gold . . 75- 90
Brass-plated, initial (ill.) 7- 12
Emerald, 18k gold 70- 80
Pearl, genuine, 14k mounting . . . 68- 70
Pearls, seed type, 10k stems 12- 17
Ruby, genuine, 18k 70- 78
Ruby, imitation, 10k setting 12- 17
Sapphire, genuine, 14k 65- 73
Sapphire, imitation, 10k 13- 19
Silver-plated, initial (ill.) 8- 11
Sterling silver, initials 19- 26
Turquoise, coin silver stem 28- 35

Stiegel-type Glass

"Baron" Henry Stiegel made what is referred to as Stiegel glass at the American Flint Glass Works, Manheim, Pennsylvania, around 1765. Few authorities will positively identify it.

Stiegel-type Glass

Case bottled, etched designs, pr. . . $380-460
Flip glass, painted decorations . . 220-250
Glass, 2 etched birds in sunburst
 (ill.) 142-160
Glass, 2 lovebirds and a heart
 (ill.) 400-460
Glass, fluted sides (ill.) 140-165
Ink bottles, clear etched designs,
 pewter cap 165-180
Mug, strap handle, etched tulip,
 6½″ high (ill.) 170-185
Tumbler, floral designs 138-147
Wine, etched designs, 4½″ high . 140-155

Stoneware

Stoneware

For centuries potteries worldwide have made items to hold fluids, herbs, and the like. Though usually crude earthenware, some have been made of salt-glazed ware, basalt, and other formulations.

Bottle, Pennsylvania, early 1800s $ 45- 60
Bowls, every size 58- 67
Canteen, round, to be carried over
 arm in field, European (ill.) 90-120
Churn, lug handles, blue stencil,
 Hamilton & Jones, 19″ high . . . 88- 97
Crocks, every size, those
 inscribed worth more 79- 89
Jar, blue stencil H & J, Greens-
 boro, Pa., 12¼″ high 62- 72
Jug, sorghum, whiskey, syrup,
 water (ill.) 51- 61

(continued)

Milk pitcher, 8" high, mid-1800s . 58- 68
Mug, impressed and blued band
top, blue band bottom, 5¼"
high 54- 64
Pudding mold, flower design
inside 47- 57
Stein, blue/gray, figures,
Germany 55- 65

Store Items

Store Items

Adding machine, American,
1900s .... $ 52- 62
Can, Arbuckle Tea, painted tin . . 20- 24
Card, advertising Hood's Pills . . . 11- 21
Cash register, hand-crank;
National, 1900 785-950
Cheese cutter, counter type 87- 97
Chewing gum machine, coin-
operated 285-320
Cigar box, dated 1855 .... 8- 12
Cigar cutter 47- 57
Cigarette slot machine, penny . . . 226-238
Cracker box, square, tin, 7" 8- 12
Dispenser, wrapping paper 28- 37
High-button shoe sign, iron,
hung over cobbler's shop 157-167
Ice tongs, store 67- 77
Lunch box, Union Leader
tobacco, tin 10- 13
Machine for dispensing gum, 1¢
each with Fortune card, 1900s . 300-382
Sausage stuffer 47- 52
Spool cabinet, 3-drawer, walnut
(ill.) 275-325
Spool cabinet, J. and P. Coats,
5 drawers, brass, knobs,
O.N.T.* 485-565
*O.N.T. means "Our New Thread"

"Stradivarious" Violins

No you do not own a Stadivarius. According to authorities, there are few unlisted
violins made by this genius, Antonio
Stradivari, Italian, 1644-1737. Fakes?
Thousands! Over 2,000 in East Tennessee
alone. Most fakes were made in the late
1800s. Some labeled, some not, all guaranteed. There are few genuine Strads for sale.
Good fakes, with or without labels, bring
anywhere from $150 to 175.

Stretch Glass

Stretch Glass

An iridescent glass whose surface looks like
onionskin. Unknowing collectors buy it for
Steuben's Verre de Soie or Tiffany. Made in
the 1930s by Imperial.

Ashtray, blue iridescence,
Imperial .... $ 34- 41
Bowl, 8½" dia., light blue 42- 48
Bowl, reticulated 9¼" dia.,
pedestal base, light green 42- 47
Candlesticks, pair, amethyst,
9½" high (ill.) 44- 52
Compote, 7½" dia., pedestal
type, blue 41- 48
Plate, 9" dia., white 31- 40
Vase, peacock blue, 8¼" high . . . 38- 41
Being reproduced.

String Holders

The hanging type and the beehive type
were the most common. Used in grocery
stores and homes, 1800s to 1900s. Near-
perfect reproductions on the market today.

Counter type, pyramid cone ..... $ 30- 39
Glass beehive (scarce) 170-185
Iron beehive 42- 51
Iron, hanging-type, 4½" high
(ill.) 35- 42

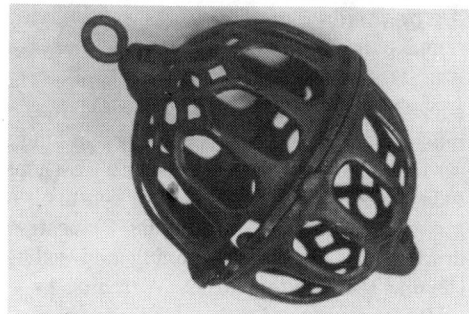

String Holders

Pottery, many shapes, coneshaped 27- 36
Sandwich Glass, overlay, red/
white.................... 100-112

Sunbonnet Baby Collectibles

Sunbonnet Baby Collectibles

These cute figures were originated by Bertha Corbett in the early 1900s. Cards, prints, and porcelain were decorated with the Sunbonnet figures. Royal Bayreuth China Company made many items in children's dishes.

Card, Tuesday (ill.) .... $ 15- 20
Card, Fourth of July (ill.) 15- 20
Card, Friday, (ill.) 15- 20
Card, Saturday, Ullman's 15- 20
Creamer, babies cleaning house,
Royal Bayreuth 160-170
Mug, babies sweeping floor,
Royal Bayreuth 118-126
Nappy, "Washing," 5" dia. 175-190
Pitcher, 5" high, babies eating
supper, Royal Bayreuth 162-172
Picture, babies gardening, framed 88- 98
Picture, babies sewing, framed .. 87- 92
Plate, "Ironing," signed R.B.,
7⅝" dia. 150-160
Platter, signed KT & K, 7¼" 82- 92
Postcard, set of 7, doing some-
thing different on each 70- 80
Sugar bowl, babies setting table,
Royal Bayreuth 159-166

Tea tile, babies serving guests,
Royal Bayreuth 150-162
Tray, "Washing," 7¼"×10",
signed R.B................ 228-258
Vase, babies playing in yard,
Royal Bayreuth 160-170
Vase, "Mending," 6¼" high 285-310

Sunderland Lustre

Sunderland Lustre

Marbled or spotted decorations shading from pink to purple describes this fine ware. Gold compound applied over a white body created many shades of pink lustering. Many potteries made it, the better known firms being Wedgwood, Enoch Wood, and Adams.

Bowl, "Sailor's Departure," 10"
dia. $420-460
Box, black transfer, Old English
scene, unattached lid 122-138
Button jar, purple lustre, pin-
cushion on lid, 1820s 135-155
Cake plate, cottage scene 168-180
Creamer, raised floral figures.... 130-155
Cup/saucer, c. 1880............ 110-128
Jug, coat-of-arms, scenic, 6" high 260-295
Mug, bridge over river, late 1700s 170-198
Pitcher, ship scene, ocean, 5½"
high 265-285
Plaque, "For man dieth," 6½"×
8" (ill.) 140-150
Plaque, "Prepare to Meet Thy
God," 9"×8" 158-170
Shaving mug, soldiers in bar-
racks, late 1800s........... 152-162
Salt shaker, 4" high 94-107
Teapot, black/pink, 6¼" high ... 240-280

Sundials

By the position of the shadow of a pointer (gnomon), cast by the sun on the face of a dial marked in hours, one could tell the time of day. Pocket-size sundials were also used in the late 1700s and early 1800s. Full-sized sundials were popular in gardens in the 1920s. Look for one at an old home being

(continued)

torn down. The early ones are collectible to-day.

Brass, unmarked	$165-185
Pewter, unmarked	160-180
Pocket, ivory, 18th century	175-220
Pocket, silver dial, silver engraved case	130-142

Swansea Porcelain

This pottery/porcelain was made at Swansea, Glamorganshire, Wales, about 1764, until the late 1800s. The wicker-bordered Swansea plates—birds, flowers, landscapes—are especially collectible today. The most reliable mark is an impressed SWANSEA, with or without crossed tridents. Know your dealer, please.

Cup and saucer, Willow pattern	$ 78- 92
Plate, wicker bordered, 8″	120-130
Platter, Willow pattern, 22″	142-162
Saucer, Willow pattern, 3½″	91-107

Taffeta

See **Carnival Glass.**

Tape Measures

Look for these in Grandma's sewing box, old sewing machine drawers. When you're cleaning out that attic or basement, don't ever throw away a box without looking through it carefully. Tape measures were made of tin, ivory, bone, wood. The other types were silk with hand-lettered numbers.

Bone, thimble-shaped, 24″, late 1800s	$ 15- 24
Ivory, in shape of ship, late 1800s	27- 31
Porcelain, hand-painted, Germany, late 1800s	16- 22
Wood, 18″, primitive, mid-1800s	12- 18

Tapestries

Tapestries

There are tapestries and there are "tapestries." Some hanging in the Louvre, the ancient royal palace now converted into a museum in Paris, France, are worth a king's ransom. Most of what you find in shops today are late 18th or mid-19th century. A great many dealers are stripping "tapestry" drapes; that is removing lining and selling them as genuine tapestries. Watch out!

Castle scene, pond, fish, birds, French, 80″×90″	$1,600-1,900
Court of Louis XIV, France	290- 350
Court scene, French, 4′×6′	270- 310
Deer and birds, scarlet on ivory, c. 1910 (ill.)	55- 70
English court, pastoral scene, 3′×3½′	198- 272
Ladies on horseback, gentlemen companions, French, 3′×6′	245- 265
Shepherd, shepherdess, sheep, original, France, 70″×95″	3,400+
Troubadour serenading ladies	80- 90

Taxidermy

Stuffed animals, birds, fish, some good, some bad, are collectible. Any, in good condition, make nice items for a den.

Average price, birds, animals, fish, in good condition	$ 70- 85

Tea Leaf Lustre

This inexpensive type of lustre was produced both in England and America, using gold lustre decorations on late ironstone china. Sometimes called Lustre Band with Sprig.

Bone dish	$ 26- 34
Bowls, vegetable, 16″ dia.	56- 65
Butter dish, covered	61- 70
Butter pat, Wedgwood	10- 14
Cake plate, Meakin	47- 57
Coffeepot, Wedgwood, 9″ high	82- 92
Creamer	43- 52
Cup/saucers, coffee, handleless	37- 49
Pitchers, milk, water	61- 70
Plates, 8″, 9″, 9½″ soup, 10″	28- 37
Platters, 12″, 13″, 14″, 16″, 16½″ long	48- 57
Sauce	46- 54
Soap dish, removable insert	50- 60
Sugar bowl	58- 69
Tea service, pot, creamer, sugar, 6 cups, 6 plates, all	310-400

Tea Sets

Tea Sets

Usually a teapot, creamer, sugar, and 6 cups/saucers; sometimes with a tray to match. Made by the earliest pottery factories in Europe. Price is dependent on maker, date, and condition of set, number of pieces. See specific types and prices elsewhere in this Guide.

Flowers on cream ground,
Limoges, France, teapot,
covered sugar, creamer, 6 cups,
6 luncheon plates (ill.), all $320-360
Grasshopper, bamboo handles,
English, mid-1800s 270-310

Telephones

Telephones

The first one was patented in 1876 by Alexander Graham Bell. The wood case wall type is the most common. European types, Dutch, and French are more expensive. Good reproductions are on the market today.

Desk type, dial, American, 1930s $ 50- 64
Dutch, cradle type, ivory mouth-
piece 142-162
French, cradle type, lacquered
box 152-170
German, cradle type, 8″ high,
marked Kjabhavend Telefon-
Aktieselskab (ill.) 164-174
Wall type, American, oak box,
crank, mouthpiece 210-239

Tennessee River Pearls

This is a member of the mussel family. In the late 1800s they were found in mussels,

"farmed" from the rivers. The shell of the mussel was used for "pearl" buttons. On occasion an odd-shaped pearl was found. Worthless then, today they bring high prices, some upwards of $500. Found primarily in Southern shops.

Teplitz

This porcelain was mass-produced in the late 1800s in Germany, usually in vase form. Originally priced in shops from 25¢ to $3; prices have soared.

Basket, floral decor, twisted
handle, 6½″ high $124-136
Bowl, 5-legged pedestal, black/
green mottling 87- 97
Ewer, cream background, gilded
Art Nouveau lizard handle,
gold sunrise, bird, raised gold
feathers (ill.) 112-132
Jardiniere, 4-handled, cream/
maroon banding 180-210
Mug, Indian chief, blue back-
ground, 4½″ high 67- 77
Vases, all types and colors,
typical price 92-107
Wall plaque 255-270

Teplitz   Terra-Cotta

Terra-Cotta

Used for making pottery, figurines, and other ornamental objects, it's a brown-red clay usually found in river banks. The Chinese have been using it for thousands of years.

Chinese farmer, 7″ high . . . . $ 45- 50
Chinese merchant at counting
table, 8″ high, 10½″ dia. 65- 75
German tea set, 4-pc. 150-175
Italian jewelry box, 4″ wide 55- 65
Italian peasant on donkey, 6¼″
high (ill.) 75- 85

Thermometers

These instruments for measuring temperature consist of three principal types: (1) **Fahrenheit,** the freezing point of water is 32 degrees and the boiling point 212 degrees; (2) **Centigrade,** the freezing point is 0 degrees and the boiling point 100 degrees; (3) **Reaumur,** the freezing point is 0 degrees and the boiling point 80 degrees. Now you know! The earlier types are being collected and bring brisk prices.

Thimbles

The Greeks and the Egyptians, from the earliest times, used this sewing tool. Tailor's thimbles, open thimbles, some say the word is derived from "thumbpbell." Whatever, these small objects are collectible and come in every material from stone to gold to glass to porcelain to aluminum to plastic. What you'll pay for a specific type depends on the material, scarcity, and demand.

Threaded Glass

Threaded Glass

Supposedly made at Sandwich, the glass threading around the object was put on by hand, later by machine. Attributed to Nicholus Lutz, probably more than one person made it to keep up with demand in the mid-1800s. All colors were used, including cranberry. Another repro item.

Atomizer, red/blue	$ 62-72
Basket	98-107
Biscuit jar, cranberry/clear	140-150
Bowl, 5″ high, applied white feet .	162-180
Decanter, blue on clear, 11½″	
high	86- 95
Jam jar, silver-plated lid and bail .	110-130
Pitcher, 12″ high, cranberry,	
floral decor, clear handle (ill.) . .	172-182

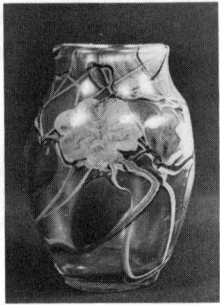

Tiffany Glass

Tiffany Glass

Louis Comfort Tiffany was an artist, an interior decorator, and a genius at making art glass in many forms. Today, all his creations are world-famous and highly sought after. His Favrile trademark was registered in 1894. In 1896 a permanent numbering system was instituted, as follows: A to N prefix, 1896-1900; O to Z prefix, 1901-1905; A to N prefix, 1906-1912; O to Z prefix, 1913 to 1920. Numbers only, before 1896. Early pieces were not signed, having only fragile paper labels. All numbers were acid-signed as were the signatures, "Louis C. Tiffany," "L.C. Tiffany," and the initials "L.C.T." Most lamp bases were stamped "Tiffany Furnaces." Look out for forgeries.

Ashtrays
Gold Dore, nest of 4, all		
signed . . . . $	435-	485
Zodiac, symbol in center,		
signed	155-	170

Blotter Ends
Sea Horse, 12″ high,		
stamped Tiffany Studios,		
pr.	110-	145
Spanish pattern, 12″ high,		
stamped Tiffany Studios,		
pr.	185-	235
Zodiac, 12″ high, stamped		
Tiffany & Co., pr.	210-	255

Bonbons
Blue iridescent, signed		
L.C.T. Favrile	350-	385
Gold iridescent, signed as		
above	325-	345

Bookends
American Indian pattern,		
signed Tiffany Studios,		
pr.	345-	385
Buddha, 6″ high, as above,		
pr.	295-	340
Owl's head, as above, pr. . .	320-	365

Bowls

Blue iridescent, floral vine, signed L.C.T., 7" high ... 1,375- 1,675
Blue iridescent, ribbed, signed L.C. Tiffany, 10" dia. 1,650- 1,975
Blue iridescent, scalloped rim, signed L.C. Tiffany, 5½" high 445- 480
Gold iridescent, crystal stem, green/white base, 7" dia. 235- 260
Gold iridescent, fluted edge, signed, 5" dia. 225- 245
Gold iridescent, scalloped edge, signed L.C. Tiffany, 8¼" dia. 440- 495

Boxes

Blue iridescent, ribbed panels, signed L.C.T. 625- 675
Gold iridescent, hexagon, Gold Dore, signed 415- 445

Candlesticks

Blue iridescent, twisted stem, 14¼" high, signed . 2,750- 3,550
Gold iridescent, Favrile/ bronze, 8" high, signed L.C. Tiffany, pr. 3,100- 3,395
Gold iridescent, Favrile/ bronze, 15" high, signed . 8,750- 9,200

Chalices

Gold iridescent, pink high-lights, signed L.C.T., pr. (ill.) 765- 850
Paperweight base, signed L.C.T. 465- 518

Champagnes

Gold iridescent, grape design, 6¼" high, signed L.C.T. 245- 265
Gold iridescent, hollow stem, 7½" high, signed .. 395- 435
Lavender pastel, 8" high, signed 370- 420

Compotes

Gold iridescent, pedestal base, 8" high, signed L.C.T. 475- 525
Gold iridescent, wafer stem, 7½" high, signed L.C. Tiffany 395- 445
Gold/blue iridescent, 5" high, signed L.C. Tiffany 675- 740
Green iridescent, 8" high, signed 495- 570

Dishes

Gold iridescent, Favrile, scalloped edge, 4" dia. .. 275- 315
Nut, blue iridescent, signed, 4¼" dia. 410- 435

Goblets

Flower form, pink, 5¾" high, signed 340- 380
Gold iridescent, hollow stem, intaglio, 6¼" high, signed 255- 269
Gold iridescent, swirl stem, 7" high, signed L.C.T. 330- 365
Gold luster, iridescent on amber, 7" high, signed .. 435- 470

Lamps

Floor, Dragonfly, 22" dia., signed Louis C. Tiffany on shade, Tiffany Studios on base 34,000-37,000
Lily, 5-light, shades and base signed 3,875- 4,400
Lily, 12-light, floor, 4' 8¼" high, all pcs. signed 19,500-20,600
Table, Arrowroot, 20" dia. shade, both shade and base signed 19,700-21,400
Table, Daffodils, shade 20" dia., all pcs. signed 24,800-25,975
Table, Peony Wisteria shade, all pcs. signed ... 73,000+

Pitchers

Blue iridescent, 3" high, signed L.C.T. 1,700-1,875
Gold iridescent, etched grapes, 7" high, signed L.C. Tiffany 1,150- 1,300
Green iridescent, tea, applied leaves, 7½" high 925- 975

Plates

Gold opalescent, Feather design, 11" dia., signed .. 295- 345
Pastel blue, yellows, signed L.C.T. Favrile 285- 325
Purple iridescent, 6" dia., signed 245- 260

Salts

Amber, ruffled edge, 4 feet, 3½" dia., signed L.C.T... 290- 320
Blue iridescent, ruffled edge, 2¾" dia., signed... 180- 195
Gold iridescent, twisted pulls, 2" dia., signed L.C.T. 165- 180
Rainbow iridescent, ruffled edge, 2½" dia., signed L.C.T. 140- 165

Shades

Gold Drape, brown ground, 8½" dia., signed 425- 564
Gold iridescent, tan ground, 6½" dia., signed 350- 415
Purple opalescent, green feathers, 7" dia., signed . 395- 450

(continued)

Sherberts

Blue iridescent, pinched sides, 2¼″ dia.	320-	360
Gold iridescent, 3″ dia., signed L.C.T.	265-	290
Gold iridescent, 2½″ dia., set of 6, all signed, all . . .	1,275-	1,450

Toothpicks

Gold iridescent, blue feathers, 3½″ high, signed	575-	675
Gold iridescent, green feathers, 2¼″ high, signed	650-	725

Tumblers

Amber, paperweight base, signed L.C.T. and numbered	610-	675
Blue iridescent, Twist pattern, 5¼″ high, signed . .	750-	800
Clear, green feathers, 6″ high, signed L.C.T. and numbered	240-	285

Vases

Amber iridescent, signed . .	1,350-	1,575
Blue iridescent, scalloped top, fluted stem, 9″ high, signed L.C. Tiffany and numbered	2,350-	2,500
Bud, blue iridescent, feather design, 8½″ high, signed	750-	875
Flower form, ribbed, gold interior, 7½″ high, signed	2,475-	2,675
Multi-colored, paperweight base, 5½″ high, signed L.C. Tiffany and numbered 375 T (ill.)	4,900-	5,650

Tiffin Glass

One of the prettiest wares made by the Tiffin Glass Company, Tiffin, Ohio, was their Black Satin glass. It was also made by the U.S. Glass Company, Pittsburgh, late 1800s. All prices listed are for Black Satin.

Basket, 10″ high . . . . $	61-	70
Bottle, perfume, brass plunger . .	39-	51
Bowl, 4″ high, 7″ dia. at top	41-	52
Compote, crystal stem, 7″ high . .	42-	51
Tumbler	16-	27
Urn, 5½″ high	47-	57
Vase, 7″ high, flower decor in gold trim	52-	62
Vase, 6½″ high, gold decoration around top	52-	62
Wine set, 6 wines and decanter, all	99-108	

Tiles

Decorative tiles have been used for floors, benches, fireplaces, for centuries; table tiles for the same length of time. Made in every country in the world.

Blue/gold, flower decor, Austria . $	16-	25
Delft, sailing scene, in frame	24-	33
Fireplace type, floral decor, 6″×6″	19-	27
Mercer tile, Moravian Pottery & Tile Works, Doylestown, Pa., octagonal, brown glaze	21-	31
Mercer tile, octagonal, blue glaze, cutout grape design	23-	32
Mercer tile, octagonal, "Rain," terra-cotta, 6½″ high	52-	62

Tin Containers

Tin Containers

Bennett, Sloan & Co., clove can, pull off lid, 3½″×2¼″ . . . . . . $	7-	9
Bleecker & Simmons, tea can, hinged lid, 2″×4″	7-	9
Chase & Sanborn, Orange Pekoe tea can, screw lid, 4½″×3¾″ . . .	6-	9
Chicago Fire Appliance Co., Eclipse fire extinguisher, snap in lid, 22″×6½″	17-	22
Conant, Patrick & Co., Milk Maid brand coffee, in cream pail with pull-off top, 7¼″×13″	33-	42
Co-Operative Mfg. Co., Bull Dog brand fire extinguisher, snap in lid, 22″×6½″	18-	26
Eureka Powders Works (gun), circular tin, screw cap, 4¾″×10″	25-	35
Hazard Powder Co. (gun), circular tin, screw cap, 7½″×19½″ . . .	38-	60
Huntley & Palmers biscuit tin, log chest, hinged lid, 4¼″×7″ .	46-	55
Huntley & Palmer biscuit tin, stack of Worcester plates, circular, hinged lid, 2″×26½″ . . .	85-100	
Kings Great Western Powder Co. (gun), screw cap, 7¾″×6″	22-	30
Larus & Bros. Co. Hand Bag Cut Plug, hinged lid, 6″×4½″	32-	44

Mayo's Tobacco Co. Brownie,
Roly-Poly tin, pull-off lid,
7″×19″ 245-365
Mayo's Tobacco Co., Negro
mammy, Roly-Poly tin, pull-off
lid, 7″×19″ 255-365
United States Tobacco Co., North
Pole Cut Plug, pull-off lid,
5″×6″ 47- 57
Savings bank, hinged lid, key,
5″×8″ (ill.) 12- 17

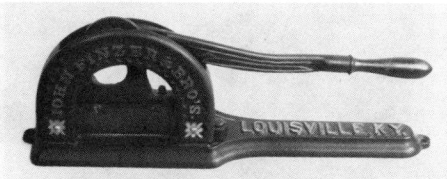

Tobacco Cutters

Tobacco Cutters

Before the advent of cigarettes, plug tobacco and snuff were the thing along with foul-smelling cigars. Plug tobacco came in bars and had to be cut. The cutter was used for this purpose.

Black Beauty .... $ 46- 56
Brown Mule, iron 42- 51
Climax Plug 38- 47
Imp Thumbing Nose, iron 78- 87
John Finzer & Bro's, Louisville,
Ky., iron, gilded letters (ill.) ... 42- 52
Ordinary types, iron 38- 47
R.J.R.T. Co. (R. J. Reynolds
Tobacco Co.), iron 52- 61

Tobacco Jars, Containers

Tobacco Jars, Containers

Usually made of porcelain, wood, or metal with a lid, they were used as humidors for cigars or pipe tobacco. In vogue in the mid-1800s.

Black boy, straw hat $108-118
Bulldog, Bristol glass 77- 87
Dutch scene, glazed pottery, pipe
finial on lid (ill.) 82- 92

Elephant toe, ivory handle on lid,
10″ high (ill.) 70- 80
Human skull, white, black bones . 125-150
Indian chief, Majolica 150-180
Kitten holding friends, porcelain . 110-122
Lion's head, 7″ high 64- 72
Mayo's Roly Poly, litho-on-tin, fat
man w/pipe 245-355
Monkey's head, Majolica 110-122
Owl, Majolica, 7½″ high 67- 77
Pig with broom 111-127
Pirate, Staffordshire 167-220
Rookwood, brown tan, 1909 160-180
Royal Bayreuth, tapestry ware,
pasture scene 140-160
Sea captain, Majolica, pipe in
mouth 150-180

Toby Jugs

Supposedly taken from Sterne's *Tristam Shandy,* Uncle Toby was a popular shape for ale mugs in the early 1800s. The better ones came from England, in every color. Hundreds of fakes are on the market, especially from Japan.

Cat, 9″ high $160-175
Creamer, Delft type, blue/white . . 190-235
Creamer, Rockingham-type glaze,
man with tricornered hat, 6″
high 140-160
Jug, Napoleon, 10″ high 275-310
Jug, Santa Claus, 8″ high 120-160
Jug, Staffordshire, 1850s, old
gentleman holding jug 410-445
Jug, Staffordshire, 1850s, squat,
embossed figure 460-520
Jug, Toby Philpot, Pratt ware,
11″ high 750-900
Jug, George Washington head,
American made (N.J.), prob-
ably Trenton 558-610
Jug, Ralph Wood, seated man
with tricorn hat 410-460
Jug, identical to above, except
marked Japan 64- 74

Toleware (Tin)

This is a misnomer as "tole" originally meant items made of sheet iron and then decorated. Popular use has caused "tole" to be known as decorated tin items, especially those coming from the Pennsylvania Dutch country in the mid-1800s. Scarce today because so much was thrown away when it became dented. Being reproduced.

Candle box with loop for
hanging $190-210

(continued)

Coffeepot, black, orange, red, green decor, 12″ high	250-265
Coffeepot, blue/yellow, 6″ high	220-275
Creamer, 6″ high, initialed M.B.	230-260
Deed box, original stenciling, black, green, red decor	310-340
Document box, handled black, gold floral stenciling, red/yellow striping, 3″×3¼″ (ill.)	100-125
Document box, handled, stenciled	260-280
Food warmer, stenciled flowers	160-180
Jug, typical colors, 5″ high	440-500
Lantern, processional type, cross on staff, original stenciling	230-345
Muffineer, fruit/flowers, 4¼″ high	140-160
Pitcher, red/yellow, hinged lid, 7″ high	178-195
Syrup pitcher, green/black, red flowers, 5½″ high	170-190
Tea canister, red/green, 6″ high	130-150
Tray, black, gold stenciled flowers, leaves and borders, red/green/yellow (ill.)	92-107
Tray, red, pink, white flowers, original paint	285-320

Toothpick Holders

Toothpick Holders

In the 1800s it was considered polite to pick one's teeth after eating. The holders were made of every type of material, usually glass or a pot metal, silver-plated, with the toothpicks being made from wood slivers or shaved quills from birds' feathers. Wealthy gentlemen carried gold toothpicks, usually attached to their watch chains.

Baby's bootie, clear glass	$ 22- 31
Boot, star on heel, blue glass	27- 37
Butterfly, glass	28- 37
Canoe, green glass	24- 33
Carnival glass, marigold, kittens	54- 63
Chick-in-egg	62- 72
Chicken on wishbone, quadruple plate No. 346	27- 37
Chicks eating grain, wicker basket pattern, clear glass	48- 58

Dog with hat, light blue glass	34- 44
Glass, Diamond Fan, 2″ high	12- 16
Glass, flint (ill.)	15- 25
Horse and cart, clear glass	34- 42
Lizard holding container on back, clear glass	48- 64
Monkey on log, blue	32- 42
Ribbed, opal glass	38- 47
Saddle on barrel, frosted base, glass	44- 52
Seashell, amber glass	32- 41

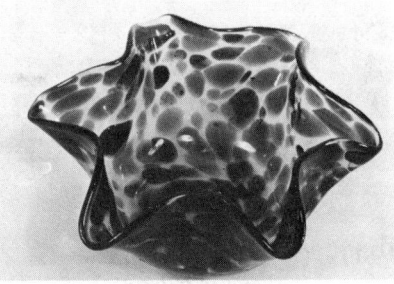

Tortoiseshell Glass

Tortoiseshell Glass

A German chemist developed this glassware in imitation of tortoiseshell. The process involved blowing several bulbs of different shades of brown glass. These were broken into fragments, etc., then rolled among fragments of brown glass. It's a scarce glass and was made by the Sandwich Glass Company and a few firms in Germany.

Basket, gold enamel rim	$192-220
Bowl, 8″ dia.	70- 80
Box, jewelry, three-tiered	220-245
Finger bowl, ruffled, metallic flecks throughout, 6″ dia., Sandwich (ill.)	110-130
Rose bowl, enameled flowers	82- 92
Vase, silver rim, 9″ high	70- 80

Touraine Pattern China

The Alcock family made this semivitreous paste porcelain in England in the mid-1800s, using dark blue decorations and a faint gold band around the border.

Butter dish, covered	$ 29- 38
Cheese dish, covered	41- 50
Creamer	29- 38
Cup/saucer	34- 42
Pitcher, milk	41- 51
Plates, 6½″, 8¼″, 10″, 11½″ dia.	32- 40
Platter, 12″ long	42- 52
Teapot, 6 cups/saucers, all	170-188

Toys

Carved from wood, stone, cast from iron, machine-pressed, soldered, the very old, and the not-so-old—all highly collectible today. See **Banks, Mechanical** and **Banks, Still**.

Airplane, by Marx, tin mechanical windup, 1940s ....$ 35- 47
Amos 'n' Andy Fresh Air Taxicab, tin mechanical windup, 1930s 340- 400
Amos 'n' Andy radio script, "Amos' Wedding," 1935.... 110- 135
Amos walking toy, tin mechanical windup, 1930s 138- 158
Andy walking toy, tin mechanical windup, 1930s 145- 165
Animated cow, 1920s, moving the tail made it "moo." 46- 56
Are-E-Go-Round, tin mechanical windup, Reeves, Milford, Conn., early 1900s, patent applied for 190- 230
Baby carriage, go-cart sleeper, sateen parasol, wire wheels, 1900s 127- 141
Baby carriage, tin, cloth top 2½' long, 1920s 72- 82
Baby Grand piano, Schoenhut, tin, 1900s............... 250- 270
Balky mule, tin mechanical windup, 1920s, by Lehmann, 72- 81
Bear-on-a-ball, composition, mechanical windup, 1940s .. 51- 60
Bellringers, cast iron and brass, 7" long, 1892 .... 101- 115
Blocks, lithograph on cardboard, alphabet, mid 1800s, set 64- 74
Boat, tin, steam-operated, 1900 560- 610
Brake, four seat, iron, Pratt & Litchford, Conn., 28" long, 1906, iron............... 9,000+

Charlie McCarthy Radio
Photo courtesy Hake's Americana & Collectibles

Buckboard, cast iron, Wilkens, 1895, 14" long 250- 275
Bus, cast iron, Arcade Mfg. Co., 1920s 180- 210
Buster Brown in Cart, 7½" long, 1900s 172- 182
Busy Bee seesaw, tin mechanical, sand operated, litho, 1920s 61- 71
Cab, No. 662, iron, Hubley, late 1800s, 9¾" long 132- 142
Calliope, cast iron, Hubley, 1920s, 16" long 210- 240
Cannon, wooden, 1900s....... 41- 51
Cannon, "Big Bang" type, 3" barrel, 1930s, carbide type .. 51- 61
Car, VW, cast iron, 1950s 34- 45
Carousel, tin mechanical windup, bisque-headed dolls, 1880s .... 2,450+
Casey Jones, rider type, metal, late 1930s 190- 210
Cash register, tin, "Benjamin Franklin," by Kamkap, 1930s 72- 82
Cat with ball, tin mechanical windup, U.S. Zone, Germany, 1940s 23- 33
Chalkware hearth cat, early 1900s 60- 70
Charlie Chaplin squeeze toy, Germany, 1920s 245- 255
Charlie McCarthy radio by Majestic, c. 1930s, price if radio works (ill.) 70- 80
Chicken in a basket, tin mechanical windup, 5½" high, 1920s 72- 81
Chimes, wooden Trinity, lithograph on wood, 8 buttons, late 1800s 120- 150
Clown and monkey, celluloid/tin mechanical windup, 1930s .. 62- 74
Columbia tin pull toy steamboat, late 1800s 355- 385
Crapshooter, by Cragston, tin windup, 1930s 57- 67
Dog-and-cat fight, bell toy, cast iron, 1890s, 9" long 150- 160
Double-decker, friction toy, 1930, 13" long 125- 155
Drum, lithograph decorated, w/sticks, early 1900s 52- 61
Figure on horse, wooden, clockwork mechanism, 1900s 92- 107
Galloping horse and buggy, tin mechanical clockwork, 1882, 18" long 270- 320
Girl-with-doll-on-sled bell toy, cast iron, Daisy, 1893, 9" long 130- 140

(continued)

Howdy Doody
Photo courtesy Hake's Americana & Collectibles

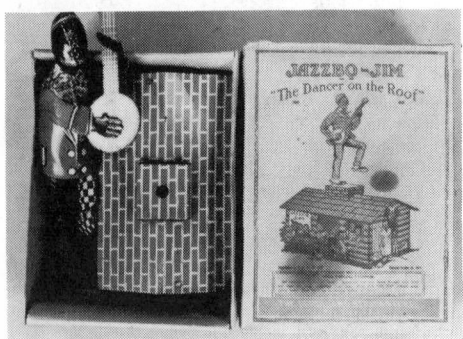

Jazzbo Jim
Photo courtesy Hake's Americana & Collectibles

Joe Penner
Photo courtesy Hake's Americana & Collectibles

Greyhound bus, cast iron, 1930s, 9" long	68-	79
Gyroscope, pot metal, complete with instructions, 1930s	41-	51
Hanson, No. 661, iron, Hubley, late 1800s, 9¼" long	140-	180
Harmonica, Original Emmet Richter, tin/wood, 1920s	27-	37
Horse, wooden, pull toy, 1900s .	285-	325
Hose reel, cast iron, Hubley, 20" long, 1900s	400-	450
Howdy Doody tumbling toy, tin windup, c. 1950s (ill.)	40-	50
Ice skates, wood/iron, hand-forged, 1880s	61-	72
Irish mail velocipede, 1910	545-	635
Jazzbo Jim, tin windup, Straus, c. 1921; dances on tin roof when activated; in original box (ill.)	150-	175
Joe Penner, tin windup, lithographed, Marx, early 1930s; walks, carrying Goo Goo, his duck, hat and cigar move up and down; carrying basket of ducks with "Wanna buy a duck? Sincerely Joe Penner," on large tag (ill.) . . .	175-	230
Jumbo on wheels, stuffed, 1882, 9" long	360-	390
Kid Sampson, tin mechanical windup, B & R trademark, 1921	240-	280
Little Daisy sweeper, made by Bissell for give-aways, 28½" long, 1920s	62-	71
The Lone Ranger popgun, c. 1930s (ill.)	10-	15
Magic Lantern Kit, complete—tickets, brass lantern, 12 slides, in original box, late 1800s	150-	175
Mansion of Happiness game, Parker Bros., 1885	58-	68
Matchbox fighter planes, 6 in set, 1940s, ea.	5-	9
Mercedes, tin mechanical windup, early 1900s	410-	470
Merry-go-round, clock-work toy, Althof Bergman, New York, late 1800s	710-	735
Merry-go-round ring, cast iron, 1890s, ea.	23-	34
Mickey Mouse Band pull toy, Fisher Price, beats drum when toy is pulled (ill.)	60-	70
Monkey, tin mechanical windup, mohair coat, Japan, 1920s	42-	51
Monkey cage, revolving, iron, Hubley, 21½" long	240-	270

Moody's new racer, by Moody
& Co., Chicago, 1870, child-
size velocipede 550- 650
Moon Mullins (and Kayo) Rail-
road Handcar, by Marx,
deluxe model 560- 610
Moon Mullins (and Kayo) Rail-
road Handcar, by Marx,
regular model 310- 340
Motorboat, tin mechanical
windup, 1920s 70- 80
Motorcycle, cast iron, 6" long,
1920s 52- 61
Naughty Boy, tin mechanical
windup by Lehmann, 1910 . . 290- 320
Noah's Ark animals, hand-
carved, 2" to 3" high, late
1800s, ea. 17- 22
Noah's Ark, wooden pull toy,
lithographed paper on wood,
early 1900s 91- 107
"Oh Boy" bus, No. 105, 1920s . 74- 83
Overland Circus, animals in
cage, iron, 1920 . . . . 240- 270
Pail, wood handle, lithograph
on tin, 1920s 18- 24
Phaeton, cast iron, 1901, 11"
long, pony type 182- 192
Piano, upright, Schoenhut,
wood, w/stool, 1900s 250- 275
Plate, alphabet, ceramic, 2½"
dia., Germany, late 1800s . . . 72- 90
Plate, Buster Brown, ceramic,
2½" dia., Germany, 1900s . . 38- 47
Popeye and the Parrot Cages,
Marx, tin mechanical
windup, 1930s 140- 160
Projector, hand-operated, con-
cave mirror at rear, 6" high,
1920s 92- 107
Roller skates, hard rubber
wheels, child's, 1950s 24- 34
San Francisco Streetcar No. 41,
tin, 1900s 260- 285
Sewing machine, child's size,
early 1900s 54- 64
Singing bird, tin mechanical
windup, 4" high, Germany,
1950s 52- 61
Sled, wood/metal, child's hand-
painted, 1920s, 33" long 60- 70
Soldier, tin mechanical windup,
1910 . . . . 150- 170
Speedboy 4, tin mechanical
windup, 1920s 81- 91
Steam engine, horizontal,
heated electrically, by
Weeden, early 1900s 275- 320
Steamroller, tin, Buddy L, rider
type, 1930s, 12½" high 105- 119

Stereoptican (steroscope),
Buckeye Stereoptican Co.,
Cleveland, 1900s 98- 118
Streetcar, tin, friction, doors
open and close, c. 1920s 162- 190
Stove, Hubley, No. 893S, 4¾"
high, cast iron, 1900s 86- 96
Sulky, cast iron, Hubley type
pull toy, 8½" long, early
1900s 240- 270
Superman Fighting Airplane,
tin mechanical windup, litho,
Marx, 1940 . . . . 250- 270
Tally Ho, iron, 1893, 18" long . . 495- 520
Taxi, cast iron, by Arcade,
painted, 5" long, 1928 . . . . . . 180- 196
Teddy bear, miniature by Steiff,
1920s, 2½" high 72- 84
Temple toy, India, brass
mid-19th century, Bankura
bronze 150- 170
Tin Lizzie, 1920s, friction type . 140- 160
Toonerville Trolley, tin mechan-
ical windup, made by Nifty,
1922, 6¾" high 510- 540
Toy soldier, friction type, 1920s 61- 71
Traffic B squad car, tin mechan-
ical windup, Marx, 1930s . . . 140- 190
Train, cardboard puzzle, Milton-
Bradley, early 1900s 49- 58

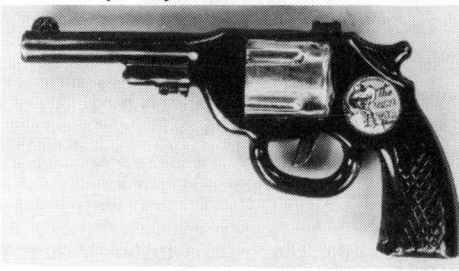

Lone Ranger Popgun
Photo courtesy Hake's Americana & Collectibles

Mickey Mouse Band
Photo courtesy Hake's Americana & Collectibles

365

(continued)

Train, lithograph on wood, 3-pc., 1850s	220-	240
Train, miniature, tin, lithographed, 6½" long, 4-pc., late 1800s	275-	300
Train, tin, lithographed, mid-1800s, 7" long	238-	268
Truck, metal Buddy "L", 1920s	170-	190
Truck, tin, Metalcraft Corp., St. Louis, 1930	160-	185
Tricycle, Tom Thumb, metal, wooden hubs, spokes, 1910	250-	290
Tut, Tut, tin mechanical wind-up by Lehmann, 1904	310-	385
Walking-on-hands clown, by Chien, 1920s	62-	70
Waterloo game, Parker Bros., 1895	52-	60
Wells Fargo stage-coach, Tootsietoy, 1920s	51-	61
Wheelbarrow, tin, 29" long, 1920s	52-	62
Wheelbarrow, wooden, 1920s, 18" long	15-	24

Tramp Art

Tramp Art

Supposedly, the tramps (hoboes), during the depression years, carved boxes, birdcages, chests, etc., to pass the time. The art was known before the 1930s and is still being practiced.

Birdcage, green trim	$260-280
Box, porcelain knobs, hinged lid	120-150
Magazine rack, wall type, 24" high	125-145
Rack, wall type, inlaid wood designs, 11" high (ill.)	92-107

Trevais Glass

In 1907 the Boston and Sandwich Glass Factory was reopened by the Alton Manufacturing Company. One of the items they made was Trevais ware, a glass to compete with Tiffany. It was quite good but the life of the

Trevais Glass

company was short. This glass is occasionally found on Cape Cod and is expensive. It's mentioned only because it was associated with one of the world's great glass manufacturers.

Vase, gourd shape, green with silver pearlized effect, orange liner, silver floral and leaf overlay, 9" high (ill.) . . . . $1,300+
Most pieces are in the $1,000 to $1,600 range.

Trivets

Trivets

Old wrought-iron types of the 1830s were equipped with tall legs for use over a fire or with a ring to hold a pot. A 3-legged trivet was called a spider; 6-legged, a cat. Those with short legs were used to hold hot dishes. What you find in shops today are cast iron and were used to hold a sadiron (flat iron). Beware of reproductions flooding the market.

Crisscross	$ 21-	30
Diamond T, iron	24-	33
Eastern Star	29-	38
Fox and Grapes, brass	47-	57
Heart, iron (ill.)	27-	37
Horseshoe shape, Good Luck, iron	34-	44
Jenny Lind, iron	37-	46
Order of the Cincinnatus, iron	38-	49
Order of Odd Fellows, iron	32-	42
Snake and Eagle Head, iron	27-	37
Sunflower	19-	27

Turtle, iron 38- 47
George Washington, iron (brass
 100% higher) 34- 43

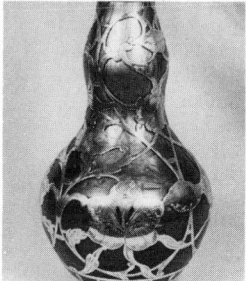

Tucker China

Tucker China

Made only from 1825 to 1838 in Philadelphia, this rare china is believed to be the first porcelain made commercially in America. It is similar to Sevres. William Tucker made the first. In 1828, Thomas Hulne joined the firm. Judge Joseph Hemphill and William's brother, Joseph, took over the firm in 1832 when William died. In 1837 the Judge withdrew from the firm, and Joseph Tucker continued for one more year. All pieces were hand-decorated and rare.

Bowl, delicate florals, 3″ high
 (ill.). . . . .$ 165- 220
Cup/saucer, tea, no handle,
 floral pattern 385- 450
Dish, oval, covered 850- 950
Dish, round, covered 675- 770
Pitcher, floral pattern 525- 625
Plate, 6¾″ dia., landscapes of
 Philadelphia, set of 6 . . . . . . 1,400+
Plate, 7¼″, 8¼″ dia., set of 6 . 450- 550
Platter, floral pattern . . . . 1,300+
Urn, 3½″ high, floral pattern,
 gold decoration on base,
 pr. 1,700-2,200
Urn, 10¼″ high, floral pattern, gold painted base,
 handled, pr. . . . . 2,600+

Tumblers

Tumblers

Lots of repros around.

Cobalt, pressed (ill.) . . . .$ 28- 37
Cut, 3¾″ high (ill.) 41- 50
Cranberry, ITP (ill.) 46- 56
Decorated cranberry 42- 50
European Mary Gregory 22- 30
Geneva pattern custard glass . . . 92-107
Herringbone satin glass 142-152
Hobnail in Square 27- 35
New England Peachblow 460-520

Val St. Lambert

Val St. Lambert

Founded in the late 1700s, this Belgian firm made a cameo glass which featured cased glass bodies lavishly cut with the lapidary wheel and acid-engraved. They also made other types of glass.

Biscuit jar, blue/green floral,
 silver cover, signed $420-500
Bottle, perfume, frosted crystal
 cut to yellow, silver stopper,
 6½″ high 250-320
Bowl, crystal/cranberry, 11½″
 dia. 180-192
Box, blue/rose poppies, 4″ square,
 signed 272-290
Cologne bottle, blue/red flowers,
 frosted ground, signed 225-255
Dish, blue, clear ground, 5″ dia.,
 signed 240-260
Jewelry box, pink flowers, frosted
 ground, hinged lid, signed 310-330
Plate, game bird, 8″ dia., signed . 120-132
Tray, dresser, etched crystal,
 clear/green, 6″ long 115-125
Vase, blue/purple, frosted
 ground, signed (ill.) 485-575
Vase, red-to-clear, signed 360-420

Valentines

In early Christian times and based on a pagan feast called Lupercalia, churches adopted February 14, the day of the martyrdom of Bishop Valentine in 270 A.D., as Valentine's Day. The first written valentines

367

(continued)

Valentines

in America date back to the late 1600s, but they really didn't get started until the mid-1700s. Lithographed valentines date from the 1840s. The lace-paper type is credited to Esther Howland, 1840s. Fun to collect today.

Assortment, 1920s-1930s (ill.) . . . . .$ 1- 2
Lacy type, mid-1800s 4- 8
What you're willing to pay is about what they're worth.

Vallerystahl Glass

This French/German glass has been made for years at Vallerystahl, Lorraine, France. After the Franco-Prussian War the area became part of Germany. Returned to France in 1918, the factory was destroyed by Allied bombers in World War II. What you find in shops today is from the mid-1800s to about 1915.

Bottle, perfume, blue, swirl
ribbed, gold star decor $120-140
Box, covered, blue milk glass,
3½"×4" 72- 82
Candlestick, carved frosted glass   125-160
Compote, fluted top, milk glass . .   94-109
Covered dish, swan, milk glass . . 110-130
Dish, covered, cow motif 76- 86
Goblet, footed, blue, signed 52- 62
Jam jar, Grape and Leaf 68- 78
Plate, Thistle pattern, 6" dia.,
signed 79- 87
Salt dip, Ram's Head, white 51- 61
Tumbler, cobalt, 4" high 47- 56

Van Briggle Pottery

Artus Van Briggle worked at Rookwood Pottery in the late 1800s, then moved to Colorado Springs for his health. The company is still in business. Van Briggle's work at Rookwood was far superior to anything he ever made in Colorado. He died in 1904.

Bookends, maroon/green, pr. . . . .$ 92-120

Bowl, blue, 1924, paper label 48- 58
Bowl, Persian Rose, dated 1918 in
bottom, 3" dia. 52- 62
Candleholder, red/brown 52- 61
Candlesticks, Persian Rose, 3¾"
high, Pat. #733, signed 48- 58
Creamer, blue, Grecian Key 50- 60
Figurine, Indian maiden,
turquoise 130-152
Lamp, Art Deco style, figural
lady, Oriental, 10½" high,
monogram mark 67- 77
Pitcher, maroon, 5" high, 1932 . .   64- 72
Planter, oval shape, green/blue,
incised signature 48- 58
Plaque, Indian maiden, blue,
signed 74- 83
Tulip bowl, turquoise, 8½" long,
3" high, signed 52- 61
Tulip flower frog, 20 holes, signed   28- 40
Vase, floral decor, Colorado
Springs mark 58- 67
Vase, plum color, handled, incised
signature, 1934 . . . .   54- 62
Vase, red/green, Greek Key, 6"
high (ill.) 52- 61
Vase, turquoise, daffodils, 9½"
high, signed 79- 84
Vase, turquoise, 2½" high, scal-
loped rim, signed 41- 50

Van Briggle Pottery   **Vasa Murrhina Glass**

Vasa Murrhina Glass

Made by the Vasa Murrhina Art Glass Company, Sandwich, Massachusetts, in 1884, this was a glass in which the body was transparent, showing imbedded pieces of colored glass and mica flakes. Another repro item.

Art glass basket, pink and white
swirls, silver mica, clear handle $140-166
Bowl, multicolored, mica flecks . . 142-152
Bride's basket, tan/gold flecks,
white casing 220-260
Creamer, rainbow, cased, 5" high   80- 90

Decanter, cranberry, gold flecks,
ribbed handle 177-188
Fairy lamp, green/blue mottling . 250-300
Lamp, amber, mica flakes, 9"
high 188-220
Tumbler, blue/white, silver mica
flecks 99-108
Vase, pink/blue, silver flecks, 8"
high 132-142
Vase, blue/pink, silver flecks,
ruffled, 8" high 132-142
Vase, clear, red and silver flecks,
3¾" high (ill.) 72- 82

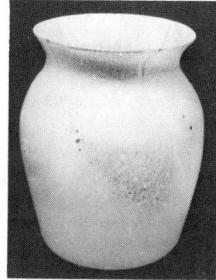

Vasart Glass

Vasart Glass

Made in Scotland by the Streathearn Glass Company, this is a fairly new art glass. "Vasart" is usually engraved on the base.

Basket, blue/yellow, loop handle,
6" high, signed . . . .$ 87- 97
Bowl, yellow on base, speckled at
top, 4" dia., signed 72- 81
Mug, handled, green/blue, signed   54- 64
Tumbler, blue/white, striped,
signed 52- 61
Vase, Cluthra type, apricot to
clam broth, 9" high, signed (ill.) 280-325

Vaseline Glass

A greenish-yellow glass that looks like petroleum jelly. A product of the 1870s, it's still being made today.

Basket, 5" high . . . .$ 32- 41
Berry set, Wildflower, clear, 7-pc. 84- 93
Bowl, embossed flowers, footed . . 51- 60
Butter dish, covered, Diamond
Quilted 54- 63
Cake stand, opaline swirl 61- 71
Candleholder, twisted stem, 11"
high 34- 43
Compote, dolphin stem, opales-
cent rim 81- 90
Cruet, Argonaut, original stopper 160-170
Dish, candy, covered 21- 32
Mug, kitten pattern 31- 40
Perfume bottle with stopper (ill.) . 41- 50

Pitcher, Maple Leaf 77- 86
Salt/pepper, Diamond Quilted, pr. 31- 40
Spooner, Alaska 77- 86
Teaberry gum stand 58- 67
Toothpick holder, flower decor,
ribbed, footed 27- 37
Tumbler, Wreath and Shell
pattern, opalescent 66- 74
Vase, swirl, 6" high 51- 61
Wine, clear stem and foot 24- 35

Vaseline Glass   **Venetian Glass**

Venetian Glass

A lot of people confuse it with Carnival because of its iridescence. It isn't and was first made 700 years before Carnival on an island near Venice, Italy. The factory was government-owned and continued until the early 1900s. It was usually colored, fragile, and very thin.

Basket, swirled blue/pink threads,
handled . . . .$ 48- 58
Bowl, ruffled edge, blue/gold
threads, 4" dia. 42- 51
Candlesticks, yellow with cobalt
edging, applied pink and white
violets, green leaves, 10½"
high, pr. (ill.) 90-100
Candy dish, typical Venetian,
6" dia. 52- 61
Compote, Dolphin, early 1800s . . 180-196
Cup/saucer, pink, lacy 55- 64
Epergne, pink/blue opalescent,
23" high 142-158
Goblet, blue/gold threads, 8"
high, clear stem 44- 53
Paperweight, twisted red/blue
threads 79- 92
Vase, blue swirl design, 7½" high,
fluted top 77- 87

Verlys Glass

This is a French glass, made there in the 1930s. It is also made in America. It's either

(continued)

blown or molded, the American glass signed with a diamond-point-scratched name. The French has a molded signature. Bringing brisk prices today.

Ashtray, doves, French signature	$ 42- 56
Bowl, blue acorns, signed, French	135-170
Bowl, Daisy pattern, 6-sided, American	86- 96
Box hinged, flower decor, American	74- 84
Plate, fish swimming, clear and frosted, 5" dia. (ill.)	56- 70
Tray, child with animal in relief, American	84- 94
Vase, flowers in relief, 7" high, American	95-108
Vase, frosted lovebirds, 5" high, French	110-120
Vase, lovebirds, flowers	97-125

Verlys Glass	Villeroy and Boch

Villeroy and Boch

This firm of potters began in Luxembourg around 1875. Later known as Boch and Buschmann, besides making the world-famous Mettlach steins (see **Mettlach**), the firm also made plaques, cider sets, breadboards, and garden tiles.

Bowl, punch, floral decor	$110-130
Butter dish, covered, design in heavy relief	81- 91
Compote, creamware, 9" high	75- 85
Cup/saucer, Dresden pattern	30- 40
Mug, advertising Detroit beer company, 5" high	27- 37
Pitcher, gravy, tray attached, flower decor	40- 50
Plaque, ocean liner at sea, 11" dia.	77- 87
Plate, 9½" dia., windmill, cows in field	40- 50
Plate, 10" dia., Dresden pattern	57- 67
Stein, American eagle, pewter top, 9" high (ill.)	490-520
Teapot with 6 cups/saucers, flower decor	110-130

Vase, 8" high, garden scene	52- 60
Vase, 11½" high, ancient German castle	67- 77

Walking Sticks (Canes)

They were considered stylish in Europe during the late 17th century. Usually they were made of rattan; later some had concealed guns, swords, liquor flasks. In the 1800s wealthy gentlemen had canes with 14k gold heads, some inlaid with diamonds.

Gold-headed, insert tube for ¼ pint whiskey	$275- 340
Silver-plated head, Malacca type	57- 67
Sterling-silver head, Malacca type	250- 325
Sword concealed in handle, Malacca type, English, 18th century	325- 415
Two-shot pistol concealed in handle, Malacca type	875-1,000
Walking stick, carved burl head, thorn wood	38- 47

Warwick China

Warwick China

Made in Wheeling, West Virginia, 1887. It's comparable to Weller and Roseville pottery, same price range.

Indicative piece, plate, 12¼" dia., signed Laport (ill.)	$ 19- 27

Wash Sets

A water pitcher and large bowl, usually with toothbrush holder, soap holder, and a smaller pitcher for hot water, were called a wash set. They were used before the days of indoor plumbing. Some were "run-of-the-mill," some were ironstone, others were made by Haviland. Highly collectible today. Many "new" sets on market today.

Haviland, complete 7-pc. set, yellow/pink flowers, signed	$290-350

Wash Sets

Ironstone, Mason's Patent, bowl
and pitcher, smaller pitcher ... 170-210
Meakin, floral decor, bowl and
pitcher 180-225
Pink lustre bowl and pitcher,
Sailor's Farewell, 1840s (ill.) ... 475-550
Weller pottery bowl, pitcher,
toothbrush holder, soap dish .. 195-230

Washboards

They are mentioned here because those
from the early 1900s made of wood, brass, or
glass are being collected for use in the kitchen
and den as bulletin boards.

Average price, in good condition ... $12-23

George Washington

George Washington

Little can be said about this great American that hasn't already been said. Anything
to do with our first president is most collectible.

Bust, Wedgwood, black basalt,
13½" high, dated 1872 ...... $ 1,700
Campaign stool, mahogany,
c. 1775 15,500
Cream ladle, Sheffield plate,
c. 1874 2,300
Salt cellars, Sheffield plate,
c. 1780, pr. 2,900
Statuette, English porcelain, 11"
high (ill.) 750

Watch Chains and Fobs

Some are very ornate; all had the same purpose.

Chains

Curb, 3-strand, 14k, hand-
engraved slide .... $ 900-1,000
14k gold, double strand, locket
inset w/diamonds, pen/pen-
cil holder, c. 1875 1,400-1,500
14k gold, single strand, 12"
long 675- 750
Onyx charm, gold-filled, 8"
long 35- 45
Rope, 2-strand, gold-filled, 11"
long 45- 55
10k gold, single strand, 10"
long 95- 125
Woven hair vest guard, gold-
filled mountings, 8½" long . 35- 45

Fobs

A.M.P. Co., Chicago (milk
products), silver, c. 1905 ... 35- 45
Banigan rubbers (footwear),
bronze, c. 1910 .... 18- 23
Best on Earth (Wells' shoes),
silver, c. 1909 .... 35- 45
Chicago Tailoring Co., bronze,
c. 1900s 9- 14
Commercial Travelers, Utica,
N.Y., multi-color enamel,
c. 1920 .... 8- 11
Deutsches Haus, a German-
American club in Rochester,
N.Y., bronze, c. 1916 ...... 6- 9
FOE—Liberty, Truth, Justice,
Equality—bronze, c. 1918 .. 5- 9
Iceman's Convention, silver,
c. 1920 .... 25- 33
Joy silver streak (drilling co.),
silver, c. 1950s 25- 33
LeRoi pneumatic air tools
(drilling co.), bronze,
c. 1950s 9- 14
LeTourneau, certified operator
(driver's name, etc.), bronze,
c. 1930s 24- 33
Lincoln (Lincoln story contest,
awarded by Pittsburgh
Press), bronze, c. 1922 ..... 6- 9

(continued)

Patriotic 1917 victory ("V"
17), bronze, c. 1917 . . . . . . 4.50- 7
. U.S. Navy, sailor, bronze,
c. 1918 . . . . 6- 9

Watches

Watches

The Europeans were far ahead of us when it came to making watches. We got around to making them in the 1830s. Until then every one we used was imported from Europe. Keyless watches came into being around 1700; with a second hand, around 1780; radium dials, around 1898; the wristwatch, around World War I. Any Elgin, Hamilton, or Waltham numbered under 1,000 is collectible today. Abbreviations used are as follows: DS—double sunk dial; GF—gold filled; HC—hunter case; LS—lever set; OF—open face; RR—railroad; S#—serial number; SW—stem wind; WGF—white gold filled; YGF—yellow gold filled.

Ball (Webb C. Ball Co., Cleveland, Ohio)
Official Standard, 21 jewels, LS,
YGF OF case, c. late 1890s . . . $ 57- 67
Official Standard, 17 jewels, YGF
case, OF, c. 1890s 62- 72
Official Standard, 19 jewels, 10k
YGF case, OF, c. 1910 . . . . 66- 75

Columbus (Columbus Watch Co., Columbus, Ohio)
Champion, OF, transparent back,
YGF, c. 1895 . . . . 34- 44
Coin silver, keywind, OF, en-
graved case, c. 1890s 95-120
17 jewels, swingout OF case,
Roman dial, nickel silver case . 98-110

Elgin
Coin silver, HC, keywind, 15
jewels 85-100
Father Time, YGF, OF, 21 jewels 98-115
Keystone, silveroid OF case 54- 63
Model 349, 21 jewels, LS, coin
silver OF case 95-125

Veritas, 21 jewels, LS, YGF OF
case 140-150
Veritas, 21 jewels, OF silveroid
case 97-110
Wheeler, 15 jewels, keywind, coin
silver HC 95-115
Wheeler, 17 jewels, silveroid OF
case 44- 54

Hamilton (Hamilton Watch Co., Lancaster, Pa.)
Model 924, YGP OF case, 17
jewels, nickel case 68- 78
Model 935, 17 jewels, DS, HC . . . 65- 75
Model 937, 17 jewels, OF, trans-
parent back case 105-125
Model 940, coin silver HC, 21
jewels 120-145
Model 940, 21 jewels, LS, YGF
OF 73- 83
Model 940, 21 jewels, RR, OF
case 58- 68

Illinois (Illinois Watch Co., Springfield, Ill.)
Bunn Special, 24 jewels, LS,
silveroid OF case 110-125
Bunn Special, 24 ruby jewels, LS,
YGF OF case 245-260
Coin silver, keywind, HC, 15
jewels 84- 94
Columbia, keywind, 15 jewels,
silveroid OF case 44- 54
Hoyt model, keywind, OF silver
case 85- 95
Santa Fe Special, 21 jewels, LS,
YGF OF case 120-140

Ingersoll (Robert H. Ingersoll, Trenton, N.J., and Waterbury, Conn.)
American Pride, back wind,
c. 1891 . . . . 38- 48
Ingersoll Trenton, yellow OF 12- 16
Ingersoll Trenton, 19 jewels, OF,
YGF, Windsor patented case . . 54- 64
Midget, OF 18- 27
Reliance, OF, 7 jewels, white base
metal 18- 27
Yankee, back keywind, paper dial 24- 34

New York Standard (New York Standard Watch Co., Jersey City, N.J.)
Columbia, 7 jewels, OF case 19- 28
15 jewels, YGF OF case (ill.) 45- 55
Keystone, 15 jewels, white nickel
OF case 14- 17
New Era, 7 jewels, RR, silveroid
OF case 44- 55
Perfection, 15 jewels, 14k YGF
OF case 18- 28

Seth Thomas (Seth Thomas Watch Co., Thomaston, Conn.)
Alaska, swing out-cup OF case . . 68- 78
Bay State Imperial, coin silver
OF case, enamel dial 58- 68
Centennial, 7 jewels, YGF OF
case, engine turned case 44- 54

Coin silver HC, Series 2 model,
cut-out movement 110-130
Wadsworth, 15 jewels, OF case,
enamel dial 70- 80

Swiss

Agassiz, 21 jewels, 18k gold OF
case, high grade 145-165
Agassiz, 21 jewels, HC, multi-
color gold, original velvet box . 375-425
Bulova, 17 jewels, YGF OF, 8
adjustments 120-135
Hebdomas, YGF OF case, visible
balance, 8-day 68- 78
Hebdomas, OF case, exposed
escapement, multi-color dial,
8-day 60- 70
Longnes, 17 jewels, 14k YGF OF,
10-sided case 94-110
Longines, 17 jewels, YGF OF
case, blue Arabic numerals . . . 74- 84
Tiffany, Movado round OF 14k
YGF, 8-day 60- 70
Tiffany, 17 jewels, 18k YGF OF,
double gold back covers 195-220

Waterford Glass

Waterford Glass

This fine glass was first made in Ireland in
1729. The chandeliers are world-famous. A
flint-type glass, it was dark in color before the
1830s. Then the formula was improved and
the color became whiter and more brilliant.
They shut down in 1852 and didn't reopen for
100 years. Now back in production, the glass
they're making is marvelous.

Celery, Diamond Point Fan . . . . . $ 48- 60
Cracker jar, etched, silver lid 122-140
Cruet, cut stopper, 11½" high,
old mark, pr. 190-225
Goblet, large (ill.) 142-160
Knife rest, signed Waterford 110-140
Lustres, 13" high, cut prisms, pr. 610-620
Mustard jar, contemporary, 3½"
high 28- 37

Pitcher, ornate silver lid, 11" high 195-220
Salt, new 14- 19
Souvenir-type wines, Queen Eliza-
beth II Coronation, ea. 44- 52
Toothpick 14- 19
Tumbler, cut 70- 80
Urn, cut, square base, 10" high . . 315-355
Vase, Diamond Cut, square base . 225-270

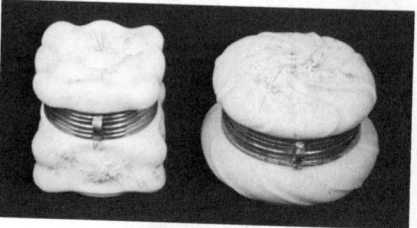

Wave Crest Ware

Wave Crest Ware

The C.F. Monroe Company, Meriden, Connecticut, bought its blanks abroad and also
from the Pairpoint Manufacturing Company,
c. late 1890s. Reminiscent of Crown Milano,
all pieces were formed from opaque white
glass, blown into shape in full-size molds.
Five backmarks were used to identify Wave
Crest: Black Mark—Wave Crest Trade
Mark; Red Banner Mark—"Wave Crest" on
pennant, The C.F.M. Co.; Kelva—Kelva
Trade Mark; Nakara—Nakara C.F.M. Co.;
paper labels—Wave Crest Ware, Pat. Applied
For.

Box, blownout, enameled
flowers, brass collar (ill.) . . . $ 610- 685
Box, crown mold, "Collars and
Cuffs" in Burmese painted
coloring, Nakara, 5½" high,
7½" dia. 2,100-2,375
Box, crown mold, cream
ground, flower motif (ill.) . . 525- 600
Box, embossed rococo, Black
mark, Christmas trees on
sides, Cupid on lid, 4" dia. . . 740- 810
Box, hexagonal, Nakara,
blownout rose on 6-sided
base, 4" dia. 515- 585
Box, oval, Nakara, florals,
white beading on blue
ground, 5½" dia. 550- 625
Box, pomade, Red Banner
mark, embossed rococo,
1¾" high 600- 650
Box, round, Nakara, Gibson
girl on lid, lavender ground,
8" dia. 2,000-2,350

373

(continued)

Box, round, Nakara, white
beading on pink ground,
2½" dia. 485- 550
Box, watch, Black mark,
double shell, florals on
glossy white finish, 3" dia. .   395- 445
Humidor, "Cigars", Nakara,
green on green, 6" high 565- 610
Humidor, Indian chief on side,
browns, 7" high 585- 625
Humidor, Nakara, elk's head
w/B.P.O.E., 7½" high 725- 800
Jar, biscuit, C.F.M. Co., lilacs
on shiny finish, silver-plated
trim, 8" high 415- 485
Jar, biscuit, Egg Crate (Puffy),
clovers on 4 sides, plated
trim, 8" high 525- 575
Tray, jewel, handled, Bishop's
Hat blank, 5½" high 520- 565
Tray, trinket, Nakara,
Bishop's Hat blank, 4½"
high 520- 565
Vase, Kelva, florals, brass
ormolu feet, 7¼" high 520- 575
Vase, Red Banner mark,
maiden riding butterfly,
ormolu handles and feet,
13½" high   2,450-2,600
Vase, Red Banner mark, white
florals, mauve cartouches
around entire piece, brass
handles and feet, 14" high .   2,000-2,300

Weather Vanes

They were usually in the shape of birds,
animals, racing sulkies, ships. Scarce today,
the old ones are being stolen in New England
from atop old barns and homes.

Angel Gabriel, remounted
on iron bracket . . . . $17,000+
Automobile, early brass, on
orb 2,000- 2,400
Bear, copper, gilded w/gold
leaf 1,100- 1,250
Cigar, on orb, copper w/gold
leaf 850- 925
Cow, copper, made by J.W.
Fiske, c. 1893 . . . .   1,400- 1,650
Deer running, hollow
copper, N.E.S.W. on orb,
directional arrow 1,100- 1,300
Dexter with jockey, copper
w/gold leaf 1,650- 1,800
Eagle, spread wings, hollow
copper, complete 1,700- 1,900
Fish, on orb, brass, 3' long .   975- 1,100
Fish, 30" long, made by
J.W. Fiske, c. 1898 . . . . .   1,150- 1,350

Hackney stallion, copper
w/gold leaf, 48" long,
c. 1893 . . . .   2,400- 2,600
Hog, tin, on orb 725- 825
Horse over hurdle, 30" long,
J.W. Fiske 1,750- 1,950
Indian, with bow and arrow,
"Mashamoquet" . . . .   27,000+
Owl, on broom, 3' long,
copper w/gold leaf 1,100- 1,375
Peacock, copper, on ball,
complete   10,300-10,500
Pigeon on ball, w/arrow,
copper, w/gold leaf,
complete 995- 1,250
Rooster and arrow, com-
plete, J.W. Fiske 775- 875
Rooster on milk glass light-
ning ball, complete 975- 1,250
Sulky driver, complete with
horse 1,750- 2,300
Tiffany scroll, 6' long,
complete 975- 1,100
Wagon and scroll banneret,
4' 6" long, copper w/gold
leaf 750- 850
Wagon wheel and arrow, 7'
long, copper w/gold leaf .   800- 875

Webb Glass

Thomas Webb and Sons operated their factory at Stourbridge, England, and made
some of the finest glass the world has ever
known. Poor imitations are being made.

Bowl, cameo, cranberry/white
carving, signed Thomas
Webb $1,200-1,375
Fairy lamp, Burmese glass,
scalloped top, signed Webb   375- 425
Fairy lamp, Sociable, Burmese
glass, 11" high, 3 decorated
Fairy size shades, 3 Bur-
mese shade holders, 3 small
flower holders, 1 larger
flower holder, 1 connecting
piece, all in a brass frame,
signed Thomas Webb   1,300-1,500
Match holder, rose to yellow,
3" high 275- 295
Pitcher, blue/white, cameo
carved leaves, 9½" high . . .   750- 850
Pitcher, rose to yellow, cameo
carved, flowers, 11¼" high,
signed 765- 875
Perfume bottle, acid finish,
rose to yellow, signed 550- 600
Perfume bottle, brown/white,
cameo carved leaves, signed   600- 625

Perfume bottle, pink/white,
cameo carved, sterling
silver cap 575- 625
Rose bowl, pink to yellow,
fluted lip, 3″ high, signed . .   325- 350
Rose bowl, yellow/white, 2¾″
high, signed 350- 375
Tumbler, rose to yellow, cameo
carved flowers, signed 275- 325
Vase, blue ground, 12″ high,
signed 475- 525
Vase, pink opalescent, enam-
eled flowers, 13″ high 325- 355
Vase, pink to yellow, ruffled
top, 10½″ high 375- 400
Vase, yellow to white, cameo
carved flowers, 11¼″ high,
signed   975-1,000

Wedgwood

Wedgwood

Josiah Wedgwood founded the first pottery at Burslem, England, around 1759. Jasperware is the best known product. Basalt,
Creamware and Terra-Cotta are other well-
known types. Jasperware was made in over
25 colors, blue and white being the most
popular over the years. Wedgwood's history
is equally as confusing as that of Haviland.

Ashtray, Jasperware, blue/
white . . . .$ 87-   96
Biscuit barrel, hunting scene,
c. 1860, 9½″ high 245- 265
Biscuit barrel, village scene,
silver metal top, 10″ high . .   225- 260
Biscuit jar, Jasperware,
brown/white, 10″ high,
silver metal lid 235- 255
Biscuit jar, Jasperware, pink/
white, hunting scene, 8¾″
high 240- 260
Biscuit jar, pottery, blue/
yellow/green, flowers, 9½″
high 165- 195

Bowl, basalt, 4″ dia. 175- 200
Bowl, Fairyland luster, pixies
and elves, 2½″ high 585- 625
Bowl, Jasperware, green/
white, Grecian scenes, 3″
dia. 165- 185
Bowl, Jasperware, lavender/
white, floral decor, 2½″ dia.   180- 210
Box, basalt, hinged lid, 4¾″
square 135- 160
Box, Jasperware, blue/white,
hinged lid, late   60-   70
Box, red, flower decor, 5″
square   85-   95
Bust, Lincoln, basalt, 9″ high.   150- 185
Bust, Shakespeare, basalt,
13¼″ high 750- 825
Candlesticks, Jasperware,
brown/white, floral decor,
8½″ high 210- 235
Candlesticks, Jasperware,
Classic design, blue, 6″
high, pr. 190- 220
Candlesticks, Jasperware,
Grecian maidens, 8¼″ high,
pr.   235- 265
Compote, creamware, green/
white, dancing ladies, 6¼″
high 225- 255
Compote, Jasperware, blue/
white, court scene, 7″ high .   185- 225
Creamer, basalt, flower decor,
4″ high 140- 165
Creamer, Blue Willow design,
4″ high   75-   85
Creamer, caneware, blue
ground, leaves, 3¼″ high . .   165- 180
Cup/saucer, demitasse, basalt,
after 1900   20-   25
Cups/saucers, basalt, set of
12, ... 1,600-1,750
Cups/saucers, caneware,
Oriental scene, set of 6, all .   700- 775
Decanter, Jasperware, red/
white, Grecian dancers,
stopper, 12″ high 245- 275
Dish, cheese, Jasperware,
Grecian design, 6″ dia. 125- 140
Dish, relish, Jasperware, blue/
white, 5½″ dia. 140- 155
Hair receiver, basalt 155- 170
Hair receiver, Jasperware,
blue/white 145- 160
Humidor, seashell finial,
coral/shell decor, 6½″ high .   160- 180
Jardiniere, dark blue, floral
decor, 7″ high 375- 425
Jardiniere, Grecian ladies,
green/white, 7½″ high 265- 300
Jug, Jasperware, brown/white,
tavern scene, 6½″ high 185- 210

(continued)

Jug, Jasperware, green/white, dancing ladies, 6" high	165-	180
Medallion, basalt, Roman statesman, 3¼" dia.	145-	165
Pitcher, blue/white, 6¼" high .	175-	200
Pitcher, crimson, 5" high	155-	175
Pitcher, green/white, 7" high .	170-	190
Plate, Ivanhoe, Friar Tuck, 10" dia.	73-	83
Plate, pink/white, 9" dia.	75-	85
Plates, blue/white, 10" dia., set of 6, all	250-	275
Sugar bowl, blue/white, 4¼" high	75-	85
Tea set, Jasperware, blue/ white, 4-pc., all	465-	510
Tea set, Jasperware, yellow/ white, 3-pc.	325-	345
Teapot, basalt, classical figures, 5" high	145-	160
Teapot, Majolica, seashell finial, 6" high (ill.)	145-	160
Tiles, calendar, 1900-1909, ea.	48-	54
Tray, blue/white, medallion center, 6" wide	85-	100
Tray, Jasperware, handled, Grecian maidens, 11" dia...	110-	135
Urn, basalt, 9" high	145-	160
Urn, Jasperware, green/white, 5¼" high	235-	265
Vase, basalt, cherubs, 7½" high	165-	180
Vase, Fairylnd luster, hummingbirds, 7¼" high......	675-	725
Vase, Jasperware, blue/white, dancing nudes, 7" high	180-	210
Vase, Queensware, blue, fruit decor, 7½" high	55-	65

Weights

The kind used on grocers' and apothecaries' scales make fine paperweights, decorative background for planters, etc. They're not expensive by today's standards.

Druggist's set of 12, brass, in mahogany box	$ 31-	40
Grain scale type, slot in side, 1 lb. to 5 lb., set of 6	42-	52
Grocer's type, set of 8, ¼ oz. to 2 lb., iron.................	19-	32

Weller Pottery

In 1872 Sam Weller made Bluebird pottery on his Fultonham, Ohio, farm; in 1882 he moved to Zanesville. In 1890 he produced glazed ware, cuspidors, umbrella stands, and jardinieres. In 1895 he organized the Lonhuda Faience Company with William A.

Weller Pottery

Long. Pieces made were marked with an "L" and "F" and an impressed shield. Weller got rid of Long in 1896, changing the name of the pottery to Louwelsa, a combination of letters from his and his daughter's names. Many kinds of pottery were made by Weller including Sicard, Thurada, Eosian, Floretta, Aurelian, Dickens Ware, and LaSa. Weller competed with Roseville and Rookwood. His quality matched Roseville's, but other than Sicard and LaSa, he never matched the Rookwood quality. The factory closed in 1949.

Basket, hanging, fruit decor, 9" dia.	$ 72- 81
Bowl, flowers, blue/pink, artist-signed	72- 78
Candlestick, Louwelsa mark, brown/green, 9" high	92-110
Clock case, flowers, green leaves, Louwelsa, 7" high (clockworks, Seth Thomas, 1870s)	385-450
Decanter, handled, flower decor, 10" high	82- 92
Mug, Etna, blue/red decor	74- 84
Pitcher, ivory ground, multi-colored panels, kingfisher decor, 8" high (ill.)	31- 41
Spittoon, floral decor on brown glaze	77- 86
Tankard, Dickens Ware, handled, 6½" high	210-230
Umbrella stand, Louwelsa, brown/flowers, 19" high	290-340
Vase, blue/pink flowers, signed McLaughlin, 11½" high......	107-118
Vase, dogwood flowers, pink/blue, incised Weller	67- 77
Vase, lavender flowers, white background, 10" high	84- 93
Vase, 6" high, signed Sicard	455-500
Vase, 7" high, signed Weller, LaSa	160-182

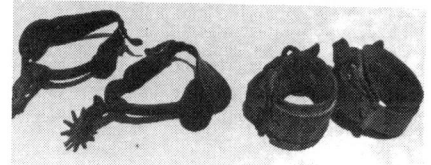

Western Frontier Items

Western Frontier Items

For less than 40 years the Wild West was really wild. Anything to do with this period of American history is collectible today.

Branding irons—see
Buckle, brass, stagecoach,
  stamped Tiffany, old . . . .$ 40- 48
Buckle, silver, copper initials 27- 38
  Also see **Belt Buckles**
Colt revolver, Wells Fargo,
  marked WF and Company,
  5-shot 575-675
Hobbles (leg tethers) 42- 50
Knife, Bowie type, with leather
  scabbard, 1860s 450-525
Lariat made from woven
  horsehair 72- 89
Saddle, silver inlaid, tooled
  leather, rodeo prize, 1926 . . . . . 4,000+
Spurs, rowel type, probably
  Mexican silver 62- 71
Spurs, rowel type, Mexican,
  cast iron (ill.) 48- 58

Wheeling Peachblow

Wheeling Peachblow

Hobbs, Brockunier and Company, Wheeling, West Virginia, made this fine ware, simulating the coloring of the original Morgan Peach Blow vase which was supposedly sold at auction (the original from the collection of a Chinese gentleman named Wang Ye) for some $18,000 in the late 1800s. The Wheeling type is red-rose at the top, shading to a bright yellow at the bottom. The rare vases, glossy or acid finish, on a gargoyle stand, are priceless today. Being reproduced.

377

Butter dish . . . . $1,600+
Cruet, glossy, with stopper,
  6¾" high 1,000-1,300
Morgan vase on gargoyle
  stand, glossy finish 15½" . . 2,000+
Pitcher, acid finish 1,750-1,950
Pitcher, rose to yellow, white
  liner, 5" high (ill.) 850-1,100
Rose bowl 725- 900
Tumbler, glossy finish, rose to
  yellow, 3½" high (ill.) 325- 450
Water set, glossy finish,
  pitcher/6 tumblers 4,400-4,800

Whieldon

Whieldon

Thomas Whieldon started his first factory at Fenton Low in 1719. Josiah Wedgwood was in business with him from 1754 until 1759. Whieldon made Agate Ware, a deep cream-colored earthenware of the Astbury type, decorated with a mottled lead glaze stained brown, blue and yellow, green, grayish-black. Whieldon stayed in business until 1795. His pieces are highly collectible.

Creamer, flower pattern, lid
  attached by metal chain, 1750s $450-560
Mug, flower pattern, 1760s (ill.) . . 320-370
Plate, Tortoiseshell ware, 18th
  century 260-310
Plate, mottled browns, 1750s 160-180
Pitcher, flower patterns, 1760s
  (ill.) 450-485

Whisk Brooms

Here we're talking about the porcelain-type body, usually a "doll" type. The doll was used either as a top for a pincushion or a whisk broom. The whisk is usually straw or grass.

Bisque baby, molded/painted
  hair, 6¼" high . . . .$ 65- 75
Bisque, molded/painted hair, 8"
  tall overall 55- 65

(continued)

China, Austria, #8034, molded
features, 7″ high 70- 80
China, Germany, molded/painted
hair, features, 7″ high 43- 52
China, Germany, molded/painted,
lady with hat (ill.) 45- 55
China, Japan, molded/painted
hair, features, 8″ high 65- 70

Whisk Brooms   **Whiskey Sample Glasses**

Whiskey Sample Glasses

In the late 1800s and early 1900s, salesmen and drummers carried these little shot glasses to impress the customer that their product was best.

Big 6 Gin shot glass, 1 oz. . . . . . . $ 18- 27
Calvert, 2¼″ high (ill.) 9- 18
Dilley's No. 5 Pure Rye shot
glass, 2 oz. 16- 27
Habenero Piza Tabasco, ½ oz. . . . 9- 21
Hanover Rye, Cincinnati, Ohio,
shot glass, 2 oz. 18- 27
Hayner Distilling Co., Dayton,
Ohio, and St. Louis, 3 oz. 17- 26
Vino Chinato bitters/wine shot
glass, 1 oz. 12- 24

Wicker Furniture

Wicker Furniture

Staging a big comeback after years of neglect, that old porch furniture is very "in"

again. Particularly popular are birdcages and ferneries. Prices of all pieces will vary considerably depending on condition, materials used, and whether wicker is handwoven or machine-loomed. New pieces are flooding the market, so watch out!

Baby carriage, handwoven
willow $260-320
Birdcage with stand, handwoven   165-198
Child's highchair, handwoven
willow 172-194
Chair, c. 1880s (ill.) 166-176
Chair, large fireside, handwoven
cane 270-290
Chair, large fireside, loomed,
man-made fibers 155-170
Chair, rocker, loomed, man-made
fibers 142-152
Desk and chair, loomed, man-
made fibers 310-370
Fernery, depending on materials,
condition, etc. 170-180
Lamp, floor, 72″ high 250-285
Love seat, photographer's prop,
40″ across (ill.) 365-420
Phonograph cabinet, floor, hand-
woven willow 385-425
Settee, depending on materials,
condition, etc. 240-280
Sofa, 76″ wide 420-450
Table, round top, 36″ dia. 195-240

Willow Ware

Willow Ware

This was first made in England in 1772, in America about 1880. It was made in every quality, from Spode and Minton to the 5¢ and 10¢ store variety. Chinese legend says two

378

escaping lovers were turned into doves. Found in light and dark blue, also in pink and green. Red is rare. Lots of scenes other than the dove bit were used. Maker, year, and quality dictate prices here.

Butter dish, covered, Ridgway . . $	62- 77
Butter pat	8- 12
Butter tray, 6" dia.	15- 24
Cereal bowl, Meakin	18- 26
Cup/saucer, Allertons	27- 31
Egg cup, Buffalo pottery	19- 27
Pitcher, red, Ridgway	74- 84
Plates, 8", 8½", 10" dia., made in Ohio, each (ill.)	24- 33
Platter, 12½"	47- 57
Sugar bowl, covered, Ridgway . .	58- 67
Teapot, Doulton	110-120
Tureen, gravy, covered	180-220

Witch Balls

From the early 1820s until the late 1890s these glass globes, usually placed in a stand or hung in the window, were supposed to prevent disease or ward off evil spirits. Wiping daily removed whatever evil was lurking in the neighborhood. Highly collectible today. Don't confuse them with the heavier glass balls used to float fishing nets.

Witch ball . . . . $	55- 70

Witch Canes

It's doubtful if these served the same purpose as Witch Balls (see). Probably the product of the whimsy maker. Whatever, they're beautifully made and fragile. Valuable when found.

Glass, twisted thread, crook handle, 5½" long	$475-575
Glass, Latticinio type, bulb on end, 5" long	410-462

Wood Carvings

Carrying on probably the oldest form of art, whittlers have been around since the days of the Romans. European woodcarvers, especially the German and French, decorated many of the finest palaces in the world. What we find today usually was carved in the mid-1800s.

Angel heads (probably from a church), c. early 1800s, pr. . $	280- 320
Buddha, lacquered, late 18th century	145- 175

Wood Carvings

Drunk under lamp post, 10" high; removable head is a bottle opener, lamp a corkscrew	24-	33
Duck, outspread wings, handpainted, c. 1880s	190-	230
Eagle, outstretched wings over flag shield, c. mid-1800s	575-	675
Hunter with dog, European, c. early 19th century	240-	265
Mother with child, Italian, 7" high (ill.)	45-	55
Sailing ship, in oval walnut frame, New England, c. 1850s	220-	245
"Sinister" eagle (looking to left), stern shield for ship . .	1,100-1,300	
Swiss couple, 5" high, early 20th century, pr.	48-	60

Wood, Enoch and Sons

Wood, Enoch and Sons

About 1784 Enoch Wood established his factory at Burslem, England. Later his sons joined him and they exported a large quantity of ceramics to the U.S. From 1819 until the 1840s the firm produced more marked American historical views than any other Staffordshire firm.

(continued)

Jug, Sunderland Lustre, impressed mark (ill.) $400-500
Plate, 7½" dia., dark blue, Pass in the Catskill Mountains . . . 180-225
Plate, 8¾" dia., dark blue, The Capitol, Washington 170-196
Plate, soup, dark blue, City of Albany, 10" dia. 160-182
Platter, dark blue, Highlands, Hudson River 470-550
Platter, dark blue, Military Academy, West Point, 9¼"×12" 585-645
Platter, dark blue, Niagara from the American side, 15" long . . . 370-395

Woodenware

Woodenware

Today, these wooden items used in the home in the last half of the 19th century are collectible. Dough bowls are scarce.

Bootjack, cherry, dated 1830 . . . . $ 87-100
Bowl, maple burl, 4" dia. 52- 62
Breadboard, maple, 11" dia. 60- 70
Breadboard, pine 54- 64
Broom, 1-pc., oak splint 64- 71
Bucket, oak, for well 32- 42
Butter molds—see
Butter paddle 32- 42
Calf yoke, with bow 160-180
Candle box, pine, sliding top, 16" long 74- 84
Candy scoop, poplar, 5" long 26- 36
Canteen, round 110-120
Cheese ladder, cherry 62- 72
Churn, barrel, with crank 74- 83
Churn, bucket type 84- 92
Churn, complete with dasher and lid 182-192
Cider funnel, poplar, 5½" long . . . 29- 38
Cookie board, Carved Daisy pattern, walnut, 6"×8" 54- 63
Cranberry picker, maple, child's size 110-130
Cream skimmer, pine, handled . . . 52- 62
Cup, burl walnut, handled 70- 80
Cutting board, walnut 28- 37

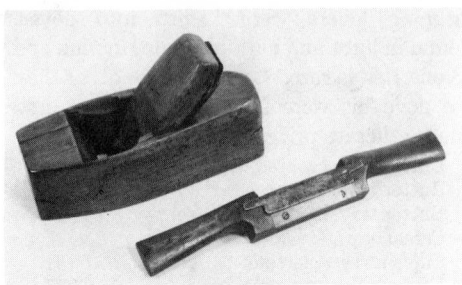

Woodenware

Darning knob, maple, 8" long . . . 33- 42
Dough bowl, maple, hand-carved . 92-125
Egg carrier, 1 doz., wooden dividers 48- 56
Flour scoop 42- 52
Knife tray, 2-compartment w/handle, cherry 61- 71
Ladle, 14" long 48- 58
Lemon squeezer (ill.) 32- 42
Letter box, cherry, hinged lid . . . 81- 90
Oak keg, staved and hooped with hickory bands 88- 97
Ox yoke, large, with bows 220-250
Pickle bucket, original lid 70- 80
Pie crimper, walnut wheel 62- 72
Piggin, staved and hooped 78- 92
Plane, maple, 7" long, signed L. Cook (ill.) 41- 51
Potato masher, pine, 9" long 20- 27
Rolling pin, pine, 15" long, solid . 24- 33
Sap bucket, hickory bands 52- 61
Scriber, maple, 5½" long (ill.) 27- 36
Shoulder yoke, pine 101-109
Spoke shaver, maple, brass insert and handle (ill.) 44- 54
Spoon rack, pine, 8 carved slots, 16" high 220-240
Spoon rack, walnut, 6 carved slots, hanging type 195-210
Stirrup, pine (great for holding paper napkins) 21- 31
Sugar bucket 52- 61
Towel rack, cherry, removable roll 53- 62
Vise, used for holding leather, wood, etc. 108-118
Wooden box, Shaker type, "T.F." initials in top 188-199
Wooden grain or gunpowder shovel 240-320
Yarn winder, maple 99-140

Worcester Porcelain

This was Tonquin, originally titled in 1751 Worcester Tonquin Manufacture. Dr. John

Worcester Porcelain

Wall (and partners) founded the firm at Worcester, England. The Dr. Wall or First Period ended in 1783; then Thomas Flight purchased all assets. In 1793, Martin Barr came in as a partner. Flight and Barr changed in 1807 to Flight, Barr and Barr. Name changed again in 1813. In 1840 Chamberlin and Company consolidated with the parent company. The firm was sold in 1852 to Kerr and Binn which is still in existence. What you find of the early Worcester is from the 1870-1900 period. Royal Worcester entered the picture in 1862. It's confusing, so if you don't know what you're about, learn. Find a reliable dealer or collect something else. Reproductions of the Dr. Wall period are in shops today, having been reproduced over 60 years ago. No one agrees on what Worcester porcelain should or will bring. The well-known price guides are from $200 to $500 apart on the **same** item. Let me say that experience only will teach the new collector. The experienced collector will spend little time reading my remarks. I can't even say, "Know your dealer," as few dealers can honestly tell the real from the unreal.

World Expositions and Fairs

The first exhibition opened at the Crystal Palace in London in 1851. The first World's Fair opened at the Crystal Palace in New York City in 1853. The first exposition opened in Philadelphia in 1876. Mementos of these great events are highly collectible today, the older the better. What you find in shops is from the late 1800s in the form of spoons, glass mugs, toothpick holders, in metal or glass. These items stayed in vogue until the Sesquicentennial Exposition in Philadelphia, 1926.

Arlington Mills woven advertising
  display, Columbus, 12″×18″ . . .$94-110
Bottle, milk glass, New York
  World's Fair, 1939 . . . . 18- 28
Creamer, Chicago Exposition, 1893 22- 30
Discovery of America medal 23- 33
Elongated (rolled-out) dime 23- 30
Elongated (rolled-out) penny 8- 10
Handkerchief, panorama of
  fairgrounds 14- 19
Holy Bible, souvenir of Exposition 30- 40
Match holder, New York World's
  Fair, 1939 . . . . 14- 18
Plate, St. Louis Exposition, 1904 . . 18- 28
Photo album, red velvet cover,
  color pages of buildings 63- 72
Spoon, Chicago Exposition, 1893 . 23- 33
Umbrella, paper, New York
  World's Fair, 1939 . . . . 17- 25

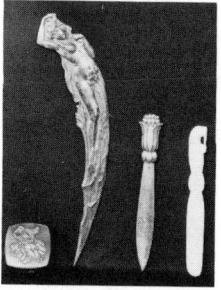

Writing Accessories

Writing Accessories

The pieces illustrated are all sterling silver (see **Sterling Silver**). Many writing sets were made of plated materials, metal-over-glass (see **Tiffany**). As a complete set or individually, these accessories are collectible, especially if you find a piece stamped Tiffany Studios, New York.

Letter opener, Art Nouveau lady,
  brass, 10″ long (ill.) $47- 54
Letter opener, Eskimo, 6¾″ long
  (ill.) 85- 95

381

(continued)

Letter opener, sterling silver, 6¼″
long (ill.) 48- 58
Stamp box, Japan, bronze/brass,
1¾″ high (ill.) 63- 73

Zanesville Art Pottery

Zanesville Art Pottery

David Schmidt organized the Zanesville Roofing Tile Company in 1896 and changed the name to the Zanesville Art Pottery Company in 1900. Cobalt blue jardinieres were produced and also a line of utensils for baking and cooking purposes. Around 1904, art pottery, a luster type, was introduced. Their most famous pottery was called La Moro. It looks like Weller's Louwelsa. They also produced a matt-ground ware. In 1920, after a series of fires, the firm was sold to Sam Weller of Weller pottery fame.

Bowl, brown-and-white lined, 6″
dia., early .... $ 74- 83

Bowl, enameled flowers on a
crackled ground, 10″ dia. 140-168
Casserole, brown-and-white lined,
9½″ dia., early 110-120
Coffeepot, pink floral, early 92-107
Jardiniere, brown and gold glazes,
9″ high (ill.) 121-131
Vase, 9½″ high, floral decor on
dark brown, La Moro 140-160
Vase, 7″ high, flowers, high glaze,
La Moro 172-190
Vase, 6″ high, wild rose decor,
La Moro 92-112

Zsolnay Porcelain

In the 1850s the factory was established at Funfkirchen, Hungary, by Vilmos Zsolnay to make soft-paste porcelains, usually enameled in many colors and highly glazed.

Bowl, harbor, blue, gold, signed .. $185-210
Dish, castle, gold, green, iridized,
4½″ dia. 92-109
Pitcher, floral decor, multi-
colored, 7″ high, signed 160-180
Tea set (teapot, creamer, sugar,
6 cups/saucers), signed 192-212
Vase, blue, green, gold, reticu-
lated at top, 6½″ high, signed . 275-310
Vase, enameled, 10″ high, signed . 245-285

Section of Pattern Glass
Alphabetical by Pattern Name

The discovery of a mechanical means for producing press-molded glass articles was probably the most significant contribution made by American craftsmen to the glass industry's development in the 19th century. That it would prove to be of great national importance is now an accepted fact from an historical point of view.

The unfortunate fire of December 17, 1836, which destroyed much of the Patent Office and its records, left the patent records for the first half of the 19th century somewhat incomplete; therefore the controversy of who was first, in Pattern Glass, and with what, still rages.

Generally, Joseph Magouun's patent for a manually operated glass press (December 6, 1845); Frederick McKee and Charles Ballinger's patent for a steam-operated glass press (March 29, 1864); William King's patent for a revolving block-type press and Henry Leasure's patent for an air-cooled glass press (March 5, 1872) are usually accepted as milestones in the industry. Certainly, there were others, such as Hiram Dillaway's patent for a glass mold (August 21, 1841) in which ten glass stoppers for decanters or cruets could be pressed in one operation. Equally important was Daniel Ripley's patent (October 20, 1868) for a mold that pressed two or more articles of glass in one operation.

There are three methods of pressing glass: (1) Block Molding, the simplest; (2) Split Molding, where the mold is made up of two or more parts; and (3) Font Molding whereby each article is made absolutely identical in form and dimension.

For those who could not afford expensive, hand-cut pieces, pressed glass, which gave way to Pattern Glass with a clear, rather that a stippled background, conferred a great benefit of beauty and utility. This inexpensive glass for everybody revolutionized the glass industry in America.

Guide to Pattern Glass
with Duplicate Names

Acme—see Butterfly with Spray
Acorn—see Willow Oak
Alexis—see Priscilla
Amberette—see Klondike
Andes—see Beaded Tulip
Arched Fans—see Caprice
Arctic—see Polar Bear
Ashland—see Snowdrop
Atlanta—see Clear Lion's Head
Austrian—see Fine Cut Medallion

Baby Thumbprint—see Dakota
Ball—see Notched Bar
Banded Prism Bar—see Doyle's 400
Beaded Bull's Eye and Drape—see Alabama
Beaded Mirror—see Beaded Medallion
Bean—see Egg in Sand
Bearded Man—see Queen Anne
Bearded Prophet—see Bearded Head
Beatty Rib—see Ribbed Opal
Berkley—see Blocked Arches
Big Block—see Henrietta
Blazing Pinwheels—see Shoshone
Blazing Star—see Pinwheels
Block and Pleat—see Persian
Block with Stars—see Hanover
Blockade—see Diamond Block with Fans
Bluebird—see Bird and Strawberry
Boswell—see Seashell
Bosworth—see Star Band
Brilliant—see Stars and Stripes
Broughton—see Pattee Cross
Bryce—see Ribbon Candy
Bullet—see Atlas
Buttressed Loop—see Buttressed Arch

Cable with Ring and Star—see Cable
   with Ring
California—see Beaded Grape
Cameo—see Classic Medallion, also see Ceres
Candlewick—see Banded Raindrop
Cannonball—see Atlas
Centennial—see Liberty Bell
Centennial Shield—see American Shield
Chain Lightning—see Lightning
Challinor's No. 313—see Challinor's Tree
   of Life
Challinor's Thumbprint—see Barrelled
   Thumbprint

Clear Lily—see Daisy and Button with
   Narcissus
Clear Panels with Cord Band—see Rope
   Bands
Colossus—see Lacy Spiral
Columbia—see Heart with Thumbprint
Columbian—see Coin
Column Block—see Panel and Star
Coral—see Fishscale
Crescent and Fan—see Starred Scroll
Cross Roads—see Ashman
Crow-Foot—see Yale
Crown Jewels—see Chandelier
Crystal Anniversary—see Crystal Wedding
Crystal Ball—see Atlas
Cut Log—see Cat's-eye and Block, also
   see Ethol

Daisy—see Thousand Eye
Daisy in Oval Panels—see Bull's Eye and Fan
Daisy in Panel—see Two Panel
Daisy in Square—see Two Panel
Deer and Doe—see Deer and Pine Tree
Derby—see Pleat and Panel
Dewey—see Spanish-American
Diamond (Lippman)—see Flat Diamond
Diamond and Concave—see Diamond
   Thumbprint
Diamond Bar—see Lattice
Diamond Horseshoe—see Aurora
Dinner Bell—see Cottage
Dogwood—see Art Novo
Doll's Eye—see Memphis
Double Arch—see Interlocking Crescents
Double Loop—see Ribbon Candy
Double Pear—see Gypsy
Double Red Block—see Hexagon Block
Draped Top—see Victoria
Duquesne—see Wheat and Barley
Dynast—see Radiant

Egyptian—see Parthenon
Elite—see Pillow and Sunburst
English Hobnail Cross—see Klondike
Enigma—see Wyoming
Excelsior—see Ruby Thumprint, also see
   Giant Bull's-Eye

Fancy Diamonds—see Three-in-One
Figure Eight—see Ribbon Candy

384

Fine Cut Bar—see Panama
Finecut and Blazing Star—see Pinwheels
Finecut and Feather—see Cottage
Finger Print—see Almond Thumbprint
Fisheye—see Torpedo
Flamingo—see Frosted Stork
Flat Panel—see Pleating
Flora—see Opposing Pyramids
Floral Diamonds—see Shoshone
Florida—see Herringbone, also see Emerald
    Green Herringbone
Flower Flange—see Dewey
Flowered Scroll—see Duncan 2000
Fluted Diamond Point—see Panelled
    Sawtooth
Flying Robin—see Hummingbird
Forest Ware—see Ivy-in-Snow
45 Colonis—see Colonis
Frosted Banded Portland—see Barred Oval
Frosted Fleur-de-Lis—see Stippled
    Fleur-de-Lis
Frosted Flower—see Twinkle Star
Frosted Magnolia—see Water Lily
Frosted Waffle—see Hidalgo

Galloway—see Virginia
Gem—see Nailhead
Georgia—see Peacock Feather
Gloria—see Pattee Cross
Goddess of Liberty—see Ceres, also see Act
Golden Agate—see Holly Amber
Good Luck—see Horseshoe
Guardian Angel—see Cupid and Venus

Hand—see Pennsylvania
Hartley—see Panelled Diamond Cut and Fan
Hearts and Spades—see Mediallion
Hinoto—see Diamond Point with Panels
Honeycomb—see New York
Hops and Barley—see Wheat and Barley
Hops Band—see Maple

Iceberg—see Polar Bear
Ida—see Sheraton
Indian Tree—see Barley
Indiana—see Cord Drapery
Indiana Swirl—see Feather
Inverted Prism—see Masonic
Inverted Thumbprint with Daisy Band—see
    Honeycomb with Flower Rim
Irish Column—see Broken Column

Japanese—see Grace
Jersey Swirl—see Swirl
Jewel Band—see Scalloped Tape
Job's Tears—see Art

Kamomi—see Balder
Kansas—see Jewel with Dewdrop
King's Crown—see Ruby Thumbprint
Lace—see Drapery
Lacy Medallion—see Princess Feather
Large Thumbprint—Ashburton
Late Sawtooth—see Cobb
Lawrence—see Bull's Eye
Leaf—see Maple Leaf
Lily—see Sunflower
Lion's Leg—see Alaska
Lippman—see Flat Diamond
Locust—see Grasshopper with Insect
London—see Picket
Long Spear—see Grasshopper with Insect
Loop—see Pillar
Loop and Jewel—see New England Pineapple,
    also see Jewel and Festoon
Loop with Pillar—see Michigan
Loop with Stippled Panels—see Texas
Looped Cord—see Beaded Chain

Magic—see Rosette
Maltese—see Jacob's Ladder
Maple—see Panelled Grape
"The Martyrs' Mug"—see Assassination Mug
Maryland Pear—see Gypsy
Mikado—see Daisy and Thumbprint,
    Cross Bar
Mitred Diamond Points—see Mitred Bars
Moon and Star with Waffle—see Jeweled
    Moon and Star

N.P.L.—see Pressed Leaf
Nautilus—see Argonaut Shell
Neptune—see Queen Anne
New Century—see Delaware
New Grand—see Grand
New Jersey—see Loops and Drops
North Pole—see Polar Bear
Notched Rib—see Broken Column
No. 11—see Thousand Eye

Oak Leaf—see Willow Oak
Oaken Bucket—see Pail
Oats and Barley—see Wheat and Barley
O'Hara—see Loop
Old Acorn—see Chestnut Oak
Old Man of the Mountain—see Bearded Head
Oregon—see Beaded Loop
Orion—see Cathedral
Owl in Fan—see Parrot

Panel with Diamond Point—see Late
    Diamond Point Band
Panelled Agave—see Cactus

Panelled Daisy and Button—see Queen
Panelled Diamond and Fine Cut—see Carmen
Panelled Flower, Stippled—see Maine
Peerless—see Lady Hamilton
Pennsylvania—see Pavonia
Pert—see Ribbed Forget-Me-Not
Pillar and Bull's Eye—see Thistle
Pioneer—see Westward Ho
Plain Sunburst—see Diamond Sunburst
Pointed Panel—see Queen
Pointed Thumbprint—see Almond
  Thumbprint
Portland Petal—see Loop
Potted Plant—see Flower Pot
Prayer Rug—see Horseshoe
Pretty Band—see Flower and Quill
Pride—see Beveled Star
Prism and Diamond Band—see Diamond Band
Prism Arc—see X-Log
Pygmy—see Torpedo
Question Mark—see Oval Loop
Quixote—see Harvard
Ray—see Lutz
Regal—see Panelled Forget-Me-Not
Rib—see U.S. Rib
Ribbed Leaf—see Bellflower
Ribbed Pineapple—see Prism and
  Flattened Sawtooth
Ripple Band—see Ripple
Roanoke—see Sawtooth
Rochelle—see Princess Feather
Romeo—see Block and Fan
Royal—see Sprig
Royal Crystal—see Harvard
Sampson—see Teardrop and Tassel
Sandwich Loop—see Hairpin
Santa Claus—see Queen Anne
Sawtooth Band—see Amazon
Scalloped Daisy Red Top—see Button Arches
Scalloped Diamond Point—see Late Diamond
  Point Band
Scalloped Loop—see Yoked Loop
Sedan—see Panelled Star and Button
Shell and Scroll—see Garland and Roses
Shield in Red, White and Blue—see
  Bullet Emblem
Shields—see Tape Measure
Single and Double Vine—see Bellflower
The Sisters—see Three Faces
Smocking Bands—see Double Beetle Band
Spades—see Medallion
Spanish Coin—see Coin
Sprig—see Ribbed Palm, also see Barley

Square—see Shell and Tassel
Square and Dot—see Spirea Band
Squared Dot—see Spirea Band
Star Galaxy—see Effulgent Star
Star in Honeycomb—see Laverne
Stemless Daisy—see Cosmos
Stippled Scroll—see Scroll
Stippled Star—see Willow Oak
Strawberry—see Fairfax Strawberry
Striped Dewdrop—see Panelled Dewdrop
Sultan—see Curtain
Sun and Star—see Priscilla
Sunburst Medallion—see Daisy Medallion
Sunburst Rosette—see Frosted Medallion
Swirl—see Jersey Swirl

Tall Baby Thumbprint—see Challinor
  Thumbprint
Teardrops and Diamond Block—see Art
Teepee—see Wigwam
Texas—see Loop with Stippled Panels
Theatrical—see Actress
Thistle—see Willow Oak
Three Stories—see Persian
Thumbprint—see Argus
Thumbprint Band—see Dakota
Tidal—see Florida Palm
Tippecanoe—see Westward Ho
Tooth and Claw—see Esther
Trilby—see Valentine
Triple Bar—see Scalloped Prism
Tulip—see Tulip with Sawtooth
Tulip Petals—see Church Windows
Twin Pear—see Gypsy

U.S.—see Coin

Valencia Waffle—see Block and Star
Victor—see Shell and Jewel, also see Shoshone
Viking—see Bearded Head
Virginia—see Banded Portland

Washboard—see Adonis
Water Lily—see Frosted Magnolia, also see
  Rose Point Band
Winged Scroll—see Ivorina Verde, also see
  Louis XV
Winona—see Barred Hobnail
Wisconsin—see Beaded Dewdrop
Wreath—see Willow Oak

Zipper—see Cobb

Aberdeen

Aberdeen

Maker unknown, c. early 1870s, clear, non-flint.

Butter dish, covered $37-48
Compote, open 22-27
Creamer 31-41
Egg cup 18-27
Goblet (ill.) 19-29
Pitcher, water 48-60
Sauce, flat 14-19
Sugar bowl, open, covered 29-50

Acanthus Scroll

Maker and date unknown, clear, possibly color, possibly engraved.

Butter dish, covered $28-39
Cake stand 22-32
Creamer 31-36
Goblet 19-29
Pitcher 35-47
Spoonholder 18-29
Sugar bowl, covered 27-40

If color, if engraved, 50 percent higher than clear prices listed.

Acorn

Maker and date unknown, probably c. 1870s. Don't confuse it with Hobbs' opaque colors, c. 1890, or Beaumont's crystal colors, c. late 1890s.

Butter dish, covered, acorn finial $37-47
Celery 29-42
Egg cup 27-38
Compote
  a. Covered, acorn finial 62-72
  b. Open 50-63
Creamer 44-55
Goblet 35-46
Pitcher 63-76
Sugar bowl
  a. Covered, acorn finial 47-59
  b. Open 37-48

Probably other pieces. Goblet being reproduced.

Actress

Actress

(Theatrical; Goddess of Liberty): La Belle Glass Company, Bridgeport, Ohio, about 1872; probably Crystal Glass Company, same town, 1879. Clear; clear and frosted prices given. 20 percent less for clear.

Bowl, footed, 6″ .... $ 50- 60

 (continued)

Butter dish, covered 74- 85
Cake stand 110-130
Candlesticks, pr. 185-220
Celery "Pinafore" 160-180
Cheese dish, covered, scene from
  "The Lone Fisherman" 187-215
Compote
  a. Covered, clear, 8" high
     standard 138-165
  b. Covered, low standard.... 120-155
Creamer 70- 80
Goblet, clear, footed 84-120
Honey dish, covered 70- 85
Marmalade jar, w/cover 67- 78
Pickle dish, "Love's Request" .. 45- 58
Pitcher
  a. Milk (ill.) 174-195
  b. Water 178-200
Platter
  a. Scene from "Pinafore".... 125-165
  b. "Miss Nielson" 98-140
Relish dish 36- 45
Sauce
  a. Flat 20- 29
  b. Footed 28- 39
Salt/Pepper, pr. 62- 75
Spoonholder, clear or frosted .. 62- 76
Sugar bowl 78- 94
Tray, bread, "Give Us This
  Day" 75- 95

Pickle jar is being reproduced; possibly
other pieces.

Adonis

McKee & Bros., Pittsburgh, 1897. Crystal, canary, blue, green, others.

Celery
  a. Oval $22-34
  b. Tall 25-38
Compote, stemmed
  a. Covered 60-70
  b. Open 43-53
Dish, round
  a. 1½" 11-15
  b. 4" 17-25
  c. 8" 34-45
Jelly, footed, 4½" high 32-38
Molasses can, pewter top 40-52
Pitcher
  a. 1 quart (ill.) 48-61
  b. 1 gallon 67-78
Plate, 10" 16-26

Tumbler 19-30
Color, 50 percent higher than clear
prices listed.

Adonis   Alabama

Alabama

(Beaded Bull's Eye and Drape): U.S. Glass Company, Pittsburgh, 1898. First of the extensive "States" series made by above company. Clear, probably in colors with gilt trim.

Butter dish, covered $36-47
Cake stand 42-54
Celery 23-35
Compote
  a. Covered 31-43
  b. Open, 5" 27-37
Creamer 28-37
Goblet 23-40
Honey dish, covered 10-16
Nappie, handled.............. 19-24
Pitcher
  a. Milk (ill.) 49-64
  b. Syrup 38-52
  c. Water 49-62
Relish dish, oblong 19-28
Spoonholder 23-33
Sugar bowl, covered 34-55
Tumbler 19-29

Alaska

(Lion's Leg): Northwood Glass Company, 1897. Opalescent, pearl blue, pearl yellow, pearl flint, green.

Berry set
  a. Bowl, berry, op. blue ....$ 82- 95
  b. Bowl, berry, vaseline 44- 57
Butter dish, covered, op. blue ..187-235

Alaska

Creamer, green (ill.) 60- 73
Sugar, creamer, square, pr., pearl
   blue 285-310
Jewel tray 45- 60
Pitcher, water, decorated 260-310
Rose bowl, op. blue, vaseline,
   or emerald on stand, round
   pedestal foot 78-90
Spoonholder, emerald green ... .57- 67

Probably other pieces.

Alligator Scales

Alligator Scales

Maker unknown, c. 1870s, clear, flint.

Goblet (ill.) $29-40
Other pieces?

Almond

Maker and date unknown, clear, non-flint.

Decanter $20-30
Goblet (ill.) 19-32
Salt, footed..................... 13-22
Wine 12-19

Probably other pieces

Almond

Almond Thumbprint

(Pointed Thumbprint; Finger Print): Bryce Bros., Pittsburgh, 1890. Clear, colors.

Butter dish, covered, cable
   edge $89-110
Celery vase 68- 80
Creamer 69- 82
Compote, covered
  a. High standard, 4¾", 7",
     10" 69- 93
  b. Low standard........... 56- 66
Egg cup 34- 43
Goblet, several styles 54- 65
Pitcher, water (ill.) 115-135
Sugar bowl, covered 68- 80
Tumbler 43- 52

Probably other pieces. Color, 150 percent higher than clear prices listed.

Almond Thumbprint

Amazon
Amazon

(Sawtooth Band): Bryce Brothers, Pittsburgh, Pennsylvania, c. 1890, crystal, plain and engraved. Reissued by U.S. Glass Company after 1891. Set consisted of 65 pieces!

Bowl, waste	$31-40
Butter dish, covered	44-53
Cake stand	44-52
Compote, 6¾" high	47-58
Creamer	34-43
Goblet (ill.)	24-34
Pitcher, water, milk	54-65
Salt/Pepper, pr.	30-43
Sugar bowl, open, covered	37-46
Wine	24-34

American Shield

(Centennial Shield): Maker unknown, probably made for 1876 Centennial. Clear, non-flint.

Butter dish, covered	$159-190
Creamer	120-148
Spoonholder	115-142
Sugar bowl, covered	158-182

Only known pieces.

Angora

Maker unknown, c. late 1880s, clear, non-flint.

Butter dish, covered	$35-49
Creamer	26-35
Goblet	27-40
Spoonholder	22-32
Sugar bowl, covered	29-40

Probably other pieces.

Anheuser Busch

"A" ale glass possibly LaBelle Glass Company, Bridgeport, Ohio, c. 1880, clear, non-flint.

Ale glass	$26-42

Anthemion

Anthemion

Model Flint Glass Company, Findlay, Ohio, 1890. Crystal glass only; possibly emerald green, others.

Bowl, berry, 7"	$26-38
Butter dish	45-57
Cake plate, high standard, 9¼" high	38-49
Celery	22-34
Creamer	27-40
Marmalade jar	19-30
Pitcher	
a. Milk (ill.)	60-70
b. Water	59-67
Plate, 10"	20-30
Relish dish	14-23
Sauce, flat	12-22
Spoonholder	28-38
Sugar bowl	40-46
Tumbler	28-37

Anvil

Toothpick (or match holder, anvil-shaped), Windsor Glass Company, Pittsburgh, Pennsylvania, c. 1887.

Clear	$42-52
Canary	45-58
Amber	63-75
Blue	53-64

Apollo

Apollo

Adams & Company, Pittsburgh, 1875; also, McKee Bros., same city, 1894. Etched and frosted. Prices are for Plain. Etched, 20 percent more.

Bowl, 9½" d.	$17-26
Butter dish, covered	48-58
Cake stand	39-49
Celery, frosted (ill.)	25-33
Cheese dish	23-32
Compote	
a. Covered, high standard	50-60
b. Open, low standard	28-36
Creamer	35-45
Egg cup	16-24
Goblet	24-33
Pickle	11-20
Pitcher, water	45-56
Pitcher, syrup	26-35
Sauce	
a. Flat	11-18
b. Footed	14-22
Spoonholder	25-34
Sugar bowl, open and covered	38-47
Tray, water	40-48
Tumbler	24-34
Wine	19-28

Apple Blossom

Northwood Glass Company, Indiana, Pennsylvania, c. 1896, decorated milk glass.

Butter dish, covered	$67- 82
Cake stand	56- 66
Compote	61- 72
Creamer	45- 56
Goblet	39- 43
Pitcher, syrup	95-120
Sugar bowl, covered	83- 94
Sugar shaker	69- 86
Tumbler	47- 56

Probably other pieces.

Aquarium

Aquarium

Maker and date unknown. The water pitcher is occasionally seen. Probably tumbler to match.

Water pitcher (ill.)	$140-160
Tumbler	29- 42

Probably other pieces.

Arabesque

Arabesque

Bakewell, Pears & Company, Pittsburgh, before 1864. Clear.

Butter dish	$54-63
Celery	34-44
Compote	
a. Covered, 6" and 8", high standard	52-63
b. Covered, 6" and 8", low standard	42-53

(continued)

Arch and Forget-Me-Not Bands

Maker unknown, 1880s.

Probably other pieces.

Arched Grape

Arch and Fern
with Snake Medallion

Arch and Fern
with Snake Medallion

Sandwich Glass, mid-1800s. This is
NOT Pressed Glass. It is blown 3-mold;
just that, blown into a mold, not plunger-
pressed. It is shown as a comparison only.

Arched Grape

Sandwich Glass, 1870s. Clear glass.

Probably other pieces.

Arched Leaf

Arch and Forget-Me-Not Bands

Arched Leaf

Maker unknown, c 1870s, clear, flint, non-flint.

Goblet	$19-28
Plate, 7", 10"	19-33
Salt, footed	20-30
Sugar bowl (base ill.)	41-52

Flint, 50 percent higher than non-flint prices listed.

Arched Ovals

United States Glass Company, c. 1900, clear, flashed with red; cranberry-flashed ("rose"), emerald green.

Goblet	$26-35
Toothpick holder	23-32
Tumbler	27-35
Wine	22-33

"Rose" and emerald green, 25 percent higher than clear, flashed with red prices listed. Probably other pieces.

Argonaut Shell (Nautilus)

Argonaut Shell (Nautilus)

Northwood Glass Company, about 1900. Custard, colors, clear, opalescent. Custard decorated in dark green and gold.

Berry set	Custard	Color
a. Large bowl	$165-180	$100-115
b. Small bowl	52- 65	37- 47
Compote	120-130	75- 85
Salt/Pepper, pr.	160-170	86- 96
Butter dish, covered	190-215	87- 97
Sugar bowl, covered	325+	76- 85
Pitcher, water	360+	150-170
Tumbler	90-100	44- 49

Probably other pieces. Custard bowl being reproduced.

Argus

Argus

(Thumbprint): Bakewell, Pears & Company, 1870. Crystal, colors (rare).

Ale glass, 7½"	$130-150
Butter dish	84- 97
Celery vase, 2 types	67- 84
Champagne	63- 73
Cordial	30- 40
Creamer, applied handle	61- 73
Decanter, pint, quart	76- 97
Goblet	42- 52
Mug, applied handle (scarce)	77- 90
Sauce	26- 35
Spoonholder	49- 60
Sugar bowl, covered	74- 86
Tumbler, footed jelly, water	46- 56
Tumbler, whiskey, handled	38- 47
Wine	38- 48

Arrowhead in Oval

(continued)

Arrowhead in Oval

Higbee Glass Company, c. 1890, clear, non-flint; all pieces marked with "bee" trademark.

Cup, punch .... $ 9-17
Goblet (ill.) 19-25
Wine 14-23

Undoubtedly other pieces.

Art

Art

(Job's Tears, Teardrops and Diamond Block): Adams & Company, Pittsburgh, 1870s. Clear.

Basket, fruit .... $ 73- 83
Bowl, berry, 8" 33- 43
Butter dish, covered 52- 61
Cake stand, 10" 54- 64
Compote
  a. Covered, footed, 7" 63- 72
  b. Open, footed, 7½" 46- 53
Cracker jar 40- 50
Creamer 41- 51
Cruet 28- 38
Dish, banana 120-140
Goblet 42- 54
Mug 27- 37
Pitcher, water (ill.) 64- 75
Relish 19- 28
Sauce, footed, flat 13- 21
Spoonholder 24- 33
Sugar bowl, covered and open 43- 53
Tumbler 21- 31
Wine 22- 32

Art Novo

Art Novo

(Dogwood): Co-Operative Flint Glass Company, Beaver Falls, Pennsylvania, 1905. Clear.

Butter dish $23-32
Creamer 18-27
Lamp, miniature (ill.) 26-36
Spoonholder 17-26
Sugar bowl 23-33

Probably other pieces.

Artichoke

Artichoke

Probably Dalzell, Gillmore and Leighton, Findlay, Ohio, 1890s. Crystal, opaque white, also with the figure work in satin finish, colors.

Bowls $12-17
Butter dish 44-55
Cake stand 42-60
Compotes
  a. Covered, high standard 45-60
  b. Open, high standard 22-30
Creamer 25-32

Cruet	16-22
Goblet	12-17
Pitcher (ill.)....................	26-36
Sauces	6-12
Spoonholder	20-27
Sugar bowl, covered	24-34

Probably other pieces. Opaque white, colors, 50 percent higher than clear prices listed.

Ashburton

Ashburton

(Large Thumbprint): New England Glass Company, Cambridge, Massachusetts, 1855. Clear. Also made at Sandwich; also McKee Bros., 1850s.

Ale glass, 5″ high, flint	.....$	77- 87
Bitters bottle		52- 62
Butter dish		120-155
Celery		
a. Plain top................		73- 86
b. Scalloped top		110-120
Cordial, 4½″ high		66- 73
Creamer, (rare)		185-210
Decanters, 7 types		67-145
Egg cups, 2 types, flint		35- 44
Goblet		
a. Flaring sides, flint,		
barrel (ill.)		76- 90

b. Straight sides, lady's	57- 67
Lamp	80- 89
Lemonade glass	47- 60
Mugs, 2 types	56- 66
Sauce, 2 sizes	23- 31
Spoonholder	38- 50
Sugar bowl, covered	116-132
Toddy jar, covered, 2 sizes	
(rare).....................	240-265
Tumbler	
a. Jelly....................	30- 43
b. Water	40- 53
c. Whiskey, handled	88-100
Wine bottle, with tumble-up ..	148-168
Wine, straight stem or barrel ..	49- 59

Cordial, goblet (flaring sides), quart jug, lemonade glass, sugar bowl, wine being reproduced. Possibly other pieces.

Ashburton with Grape Band

Ashburton with Grape Band

Maker and date unknown.

Tumbler (ill.)	$26-36

No other pieces known to this writer.

Ashman

Maker unknown, c. mid-1880s, clear, etched.

Butter dish, covered	$34-47
Cake stand	35-45
Celery	37-48
Compote	
a. Covered, 6″ to 12″	45-56
b. Open, 6″ to 12″	24-36
Creamer	27-35
Goblet	24-33
Pitcher......................	42-54
Spoonholder	19-28
Sugar bowl, covered	32-42

Probably other pieces.

Assassination Mug

Assassination Mug

(Also called "The Martyrs' Mug"): Garfield on one side, Lincoln on other. Obviously made after 1881, the year Garfield was assassinated. By whom this mug was made is not known. Clear glass.

Mug, 2¼" high (ill.) $57-70

Atlas

Atlas

(Cannon Ball, Bullet): Adams & Company, Pittsburgh, 1889. Clear, vari-colors, ruby flashed.

Bowls, open $18-32
Butter dish, covered 32-42
Cake stand, 10" high, clear 44-53
Creamer, covered, applied handle. 30-43
Goblet 24-33
Pitcher, water................. 36-47

Sauce, footed 18-26
Spoonholder 19-27
Sugar bowl, covered 33-43
Wine......................... 24-30
Probably other pieces.

Atlas

Atlas

(Crystal Ball): Bryce Bros., Mt. Pleasant, Pennsylvania. 1889. Clear; sometimes flashed with red, gold.

Bowls, covered, flat $18-28
Butter dish, covered 40-50
Cake stand, 10" high, clear 28-38
Creamer 30-39
Goblet (scarce) 27-36
Sauce, footed 12-18
Pitcher, water, 2 types 42-52
Spoonholder, flat or footed base .. 27-37
Sugar bowl, covered 29-40
Wine, clear 28-37

Probably no other pieces. Red, gold, 75 percent more than clear prices listed.

Aurora

(Diamond Horseshoe): The Brilliant Glass Works, Brilliant, Ohio, c. 1888, clear, panels sometimes engraved. Pattern produced by Greensburg Glass Company, c. 1889, when Brilliant got into financial difficulties.

Butter dish, covered $38-47
Cake stand 33-45

Compote
  a. Covered 35-42
  b. Open 19-27
Cordial 18-26
Creamer 27-37
Goblet 27-35
Pitcher, water 38-47
Salt/Pepper, pr. 16-29
Spoonholder 18-26
Sugar bowl, open 26-35

Prices are Greensburg. Many other pieces.

Bakewell Block

Bakewell, Pears & Company, Pittsburgh, c. early 1850s, clear, flint.

Butter dish, covered $180-195
Celery 90-100
Champagne................. 92-105
Creamer 168-178
Decanter 127-140
Goblet 105-122
Spoonholder 64- 74
Sugar bowl, covered 82- 96
Tumbler, bar, whiskey 83- 94

Probably other pieces.

Balder

Balder

(Kamoni; Pennsylvania): U.S. Glass Company, Pittsburgh, through early 1900s. Clear, colored or gilt tops.

Bowl, gilt trim $44-54
Butter dish, covered 44-53
Creamer, small, gold trim 18-29
Goblet 21-33
Pitcher, syrup (ill.) 34-44
Spoonholder, w/ruby flashed top .. 30-40
Sugar bowl, covered 34-45

Tumbler, water or whiskey 21-32
Wine........................ 29-33
Probably other pieces.

Ball and Bar

Ball and Bar

Westmoreland Glass Company, Grapeville, Pennsylvania, 1896. Clear.

Butter dish $38-48
Creamer 32-44
Pitcher (ill.).................. 57-69
Spoonholder 31-41
Sugar bowl 37-47

Probably other pieces.

Balloon

397

(continued)

Balloon

Made in lower Ohio Valley in early 1850s. Clear.

Creamer $170-190
Goblet 69- 80
Pitcher (ill.) 268-295
Sugar bowl 178-195

Probably a few other pieces but considered extremely rare today.

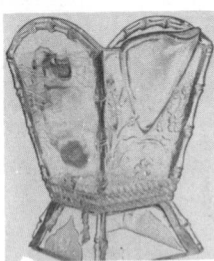

Bamboo

Bamboo

La Belle Glass Company, Bridgeport, Ohio, 1883. Plain and engraved crystal glass.

Butter dish $40-54
Celery 22-31
Compotes, 7", 8", 9", covered 39-55
Creamer 28-38
Dish, 7", 8", 9", oblong 19-29
Pitcher, water 39-51
Sauce, 4" 10-16
Salt/Pepper, pr. 29-38
Spoonholder (ill.) 17-27
Sugar bowl, covered 34-43
Tumbler 23-32

Banded Buckle

Sandwich glass, mid-1850s; other factories, Pittsburgh, 1870s. Clear glass.

Bowls, open $14-23
Butter dish 41-52
Compote
  a. Open, low standard 44-53
  b. Covered, low standard 37-47
Cordial 27-34
Creamer 34-44
Egg cup 21-30
Goblet (ill.) 23-32
Pitcher, water 48-58

Banded Buckle

Salt, footed 9-15
Spoonholder 17-26
Sugar bowl 32-43
Tumbler 20-29

Probably other pieces.

Banded Fleur-de-Lis

Banded Fleur-de-Lis

Imperial Glass Company, Bellaire, Ohio, 1890s. Clear.

Butter dish $33-43
Creamer 22-33
Pitcher (ill.) 37-47
Spoonholder 19-28
Sugar bowl 28-38

Probably many other pieces.

Banded Icicle

Bakewell, Pears & Company, 1870s. Clear.

Butter dish $39-52
Compote
  a. Covered, 6", 8", high
    standard 50-61
  b. Open, 8", low standard 31-43

Banded Icicle

Creamer 33-41
Goblet 22-26
Pitcher (ill.) 62-72
Sauce 14-21
Spoonholder 20-27
Sugar bowl 39-52

Probably other pieces.

Banded Portland (Virginia)

Banded Portland (Virginia)

U.S. Glass Company, 1901. Crystal and rose flashed.

Bottle, water $35-45
Butter dish, covered 23-33
Celery 22-32
Compote
  a. Covered 34-45
  b. Covered, jelly 26-36
Cruets 14-20
Dish, sardine 18-22
Jar, jam 23-32
Pitcher, syrup (ill.) 36-46
Relish boat 14-23

Salt/Pepper, pr. 20-27
Sugar
  a. Bowl, covered 24-33
  b. Shaker 28-34
Toothpick holder 23-28
Tumbler 18-27
Wine 29-36

Probably other pieces. 50 percent higher for colors than for clear prices listed.

Banded Raindrops

Banded Raindrops

(Candlewick): Clear, rare in amber, opalescent blue and milk glass. These pieces 100 percent more than clear pieces listed.

Butter dish $39-48
Celery 22-31
Compote, 7", covered 29-41
Creamer 22-32
Cup and saucer 19-28
Goblet 20-28
Pitcher, water (ill.) 44-56
Plates, 7½" and 8¾" 19-26
Relish 13-22
Sauce 10-19
Spoonholder 18-27
Sugar bowl 36-46
Wine 23-34

Banner Butter Dish

Probable Bryce, Walker and Company, made for Centennial, 1876. Clear, blue and amber. A rare pattern!

Butter dish (ill.)
  a. Clear $125-168
  b. Blue 165-240
  c. Amber 265-475

(continued)

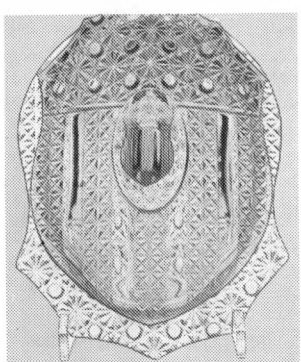
Banner Butter Dish

Barberry

Barley

Barberry

Boston & Sandwich Glass Company, Sandwich, Massachusetts, 1860s. Later reproduced by several companies in Pittsburgh area, 1880s. Clear and colors; amber and blue, 50 percent and 70 percent more.

Bowl, covered, 8″ $35-45
Butter dish 57-67
Cake plate 40-53
Celery 38-47
Compote, covered, high and
low standard 42-63
Cordial 33-40
Creamer 49-59
Egg cup, oval berries 37-50
Goblet, oval berries 30-40
Pickle 15-23
Pitcher, water, applied
handle (ill.) 78-91
Plate, 6″ deep 32-41
Salt, footed, 6″ 23-33
Sauce, flat and footed 14-23
Spoonholder 24-34
Sugar bowl, covered 61-70
Syrup jug, pewter top 65-73
Wine 21-32

Barley

(Sprig; Indian Tree): Late 1870s. Clear, any piece in color, rare; 50 percent more than clear.

Butter dish, covered $34-44
Cake stand, 9″, 9¼″, 9½″, 9⅝″ 34-45
Celery 23-32
Compote, covered and open 23-50
Cordial 17-23
Creamer, open 18-27
Dish, oval 14-22
Goblet· 25-34
Jam jar, with lid 55-65
Pickle 18-27
Pitcher, water, 2 types 40-50
Plate, 6″ 52-62
Platter, oval 32-40
Sauces, footed, 4″, 5″ 12-19
Spoonholder 21-31
Sugar bowl, covered and open . . 20-39
Wine 24-33

Barred Forget-Me-Not

Barred Forget-Me-Not

Canton Glass Company, Canton, Ohio, 1883. Clear, canary, vaseline amber, blue, apple green.

Butter dish $42-52
Cake plates
a. 9″, closed handles 35-45
b. Extra large, on stand 45-54
Compote
a. Covered, on high foot 43-54
b. Covered, low foot, 8″ 54-65
c. Open, small, on high foot . . 43-54
Cordial 15-22
Creamer 30-39
Goblet 25-35

Pickle dish, square handles...... 19-28
Pitcher (ill.).................... 43-52
Spoonholder 24-35
Sugar bowl, square handles 31-40
Wine........................ 24-34

Probably other pieces. Canary, 30 percent, blue, 60 percent, apple green, 100 percent higher than clear prices listed.

Barred Hobnail

Barred Hobnail

(Winona): Brilliant Glass Works, Brilliant, Ohio, 1888. Clear, opalescent, varicolored.

Bowls $13-23
Butter dish, covered 29-39
Creamer 23-32
Goblet 22-31
Pitcher, water, ½ gallon (ill.) 39-50
Salt shaker 12-17
Sauce, flat 12-16
Spoonholder 12-19
Sugar bowl, covered 30-41

Probably other pieces.

Barred Oval

Barred Oval

(Frosted Banded Portland): George Duncan & Sons, Pittsburgh, Pennsylvania, c. 1890, clear, frosted or color flashed. Reissued after 1891 by U.S. Glass Company.

Bottle, water $32-41
Butter dish, covered 30-40
Celery 24-33
Compote, open 22-29
Creamer 22-31
Goblet 21-30
Pitcher, water................. 48-60
Plate, small.................. 22-30
Sugar bowl, covered (ill.) 43-52

Frosted or color flashed, 50 percent higher than clear prices listed.

Barred Star

(Spartan): Gillinder & Company, Pittsburgh, c. early 1880s, clear, non-flint.

Butter dish, covered $29-39
Cake stand 31-40
Celery 22-31
Compote, covered 27-39
Creamer 32-39
Pitcher...................... 38-48
Salt/Pepper, pr. 12-21
Spoonholder 18-27
Sugar bowl, covered 32-41

Probably other pieces.

Barrel Excelsior

Sandwich, early; later, McKee Bros. Pittsburgh, 1850s and 1860s. Clear.

Ale glass .... $ 38- 52
Butter dish, covered, early 85-105
Celery
  a. Plain top............... 46- 55
  b. Scalloped top 75- 85
Decanters, pint, quart, 3 pints,
  early 73- 80
Goblets, flaring and
  straight sides 36- 44
Lamp, early 120-145
Mug 44- 55

(continued)

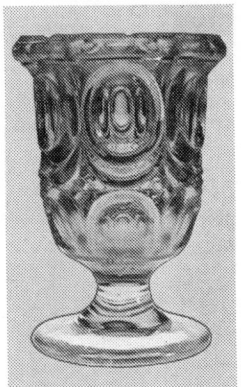

Barrel Excelsior

Spoonholder (ill.)	42- 51
Sugar bowl, covered, early	150-180
Tumbler, water, whiskey	37- 47
Wine bottle, with tumble-up, early	135-165

Probably other pieces.

Barrelled Thumbprint
(Challinor's Thumbprint)

Barrelled Thumbprint (Challinor's Thumbprint)

Challinor, Taylor, Ltd., Tarentum, Pennsylvania, 1880s.

Butter dish	$43-54
Celery	33-43
Creamer	40-48
Goblet	44-56
Pitcher (ill.)................	61-71
Spoonholder	32-40
Sugar bowl	42-52
Wine	29-39

Probably other pieces.

Basket Weave

Basket Weave

Mid-1880s. Clear, amber, blue, canary, milk white, apple green.

Bowl	
a. Berry	$ 35- 44
b. Covered, flat	35- 45
c. Large, finger	25- 33
Butter dish	38- 48
Cake plate................	35- 49
Compote, covered...........	46- 56
Cordial	28- 38
Creamer................	31- 43
Cup and saucer	29- 37
Egg cup, double	19- 29
Goblet...................	24- 34
Lamp	29- 40
Mug	22- 35
Pickle	18- 28
Pitcher	
a. Syrup, metal top, clear	45- 55
b. Water (ill.)	53- 65
Plate, sheaf or wheat handles ..	118-155
Salt	9- 19
Sauce, round, flat............	10- 16
Salt/Pepper, pr.	33- 42
Spoonholder	20- 29
Sugar bowl	36- 46
Tray, round, 12″ dia.	35- 44

Probably other pieces. Goblet and water pitcher being reproduced. Color pieces 50 to 100 percent higher than clear pieces listed.

Basket Weave with Frosted Le

A design of the 1880s, it was made by many companies in many patterns. Clear, canary, yellow, blue, green.

Basket Weave with Frosted Leaf

Bowl, berry $18-27
Cake plate 36-45
Compote, covered 35-44
Cordial 15-22
Egg cup, double 18-24
Cups/saucers 14-20
Goblet 17-26
Pitcher, water (ill.) 48-56
Saucedish, round, flat 10-16
Syrup, metal top 23-31
Tray, water 24-34

Prices are for clear. Canary, yellow, green, 40 percent more; blue, 100 percent more. Probably other pieces.

Bead and Scroll

Bead and Scroll

Maker and date unknown.

Berry bowl, 8″ $17-26
Butter dish, covered 24-34

Compote, jelly 21-31
Creamer 31-41
Goblet 17-26
Pitcher, water (ill.) 35-44
Saucedish, flat 11-17
Spoonholder 26-36
Sugar bowl, covered 31-41
Tumbler 19-28

Probably other pieces.

Bead Column

Bead Column

Maker and date unknown.

Butter dish, covered $26-37
Creamer 19-28
Pitcher (ill.).................... 33-44
Spoonholder 19-29
Sugar bowl 21-31

Possibly other pieces were made.

Beaded Acorn Medallion

The Boston Silver-Glass Company, East Cambridge, Massachusetts, c. 1869, clear, non-flint.

Butter dish, covered $53-63
Creamer 54-64
Goblet 35-44
Pitcher 59-70
Spoonholder 24-33
Sugar bowl, covered 54-64
Wine 22-32

Probably other pieces.

Beaded Arch Panels

Maker and date unknown.

Goblet $19-28
Mug, handled (ill.).............. 27-37

Probably other pieces.

(continued)

Beaded Arch Panels

Beaded Band

Beaded Band

Maker unknown, c. 1884, clear, color (rare).

Butter dish, covered $36-44
Compote, open 27-36
Creamer 27-36
Jug, syrup 42-51
Pitcher, water 51-61
Spoonholder 27-37
Sugar bowl, open, covered
(base ill.) 27-37
Wine 23-33

If color, 100 percent higher than clear prices listed.

Beaded Chain

(Looped Cord): Maker unknown, c. 1870s, clear, non-flint.

Butter dish, covered $45-54

Celery 33-42
Creamer 37-45
Goblet 29-37
Pitcher, water 44-53
Plate, 6″ 29-39
Sauce, flat 16-27
Spoonholder 28-37
Sugar bowl, covered 37-46

Probably other pieces.

Beaded Dart Band

Beaded Dart Band

Possibly McKee Bros., Pittsburgh, 1880s. Clear, colors.

Butter dish $27-36
Celery holder 10-13
Compote 24-33
Creamer 21-31
Goblet 14-23
Pickle caster with fork (ill.) 60-70
Spoonholder 10-16
Sugar bowl, covered 22-31

Probably other pieces.

Beaded Dewdrop

(Wisconsin): U.S. Glass Company, Gas City, Indiana, 1898.

Bottles, oil, vinegar $17- 25
Bowl
a. Covered, oblong, 6″, 8″ 24- 33
b. Covered, round, 7″, 8″ 26- 35
Butter dish, large, small,
covered 59- 67
Celery vase 33- 43
Celery tray 22- 32
Compote
a. Covered, 6″, 7″, 8″ 56- 64
b. Open, 8½″, 9½″, 10½″ 44- 53

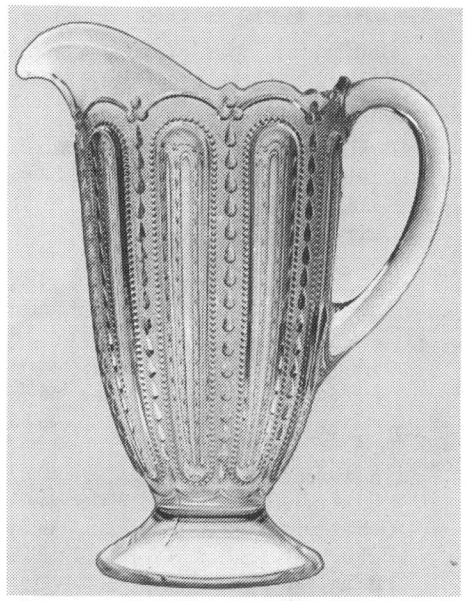

Beaded Dewdrop

Condiment set, 4-piece in holder .	90-105
Creamer, individual and large . .	30- 48
Cruet	29- 37
Dish		
a. Candy	23- 31
b. Oval, handled, covered, 6″	54- 64
c. Oval, handled, open, 6″	21- 36
d. Sweetmeat	31- 40
Goblet.	50- 59
Mug, large	46- 55
Pitcher		
a. 3 pints	52- 62
b. 1 quart (ill.)	70- 80
Sauce, flat and handled	11- 14
Salt/Pepper, short, tall, pr.	45- 54
Spoonholder	29- 38
Sugar bowl, large and small,		
covered	32- 64
Syrup jug, with cover	57- 67
Toothpick holder	54- 63
Tumbler	42- 50
Wine	41- 51

Beaded Ellipse

Cambridge Glass Company, Cambridge, Ohio, late 1890s. After 1906, all products permanently marked "Near-Cut" on inside base. Clear.

Butter dish	$34-43
Creamer	22-31

Beaded Ellipse

Compotes	40-50
Goblet	23-33
Pitcher		
a. Milk	37-46
b. Water (ill.)	38-52
Spoonholder	17-25
Sugar bowl	32-41
Wine	15-25

Probably other pieces.

Beaded Fan

Beaded Fan

Maker unknown, 1875-1880. Clear.

Butter dish	$36-45
Celery vase	22-31
Compote	32-40
Creamer	31-41
Pitcher (ill.)	31-40
Spoonholder	23-32
Sugar bowl		
a. Covered	37-47
b. Open	19-27

Probably other pieces.

Beaded Fine-Cut   Beaded Flange

Beaded Fine-Cut

Maker and date unknown. Clear, possibly in colors.

Butter dish $24-33
Creamer 22-32
Goblet 24-36
Pitcher (ill.)................... 39-48
Spoonholder 19-28
Sugar bowl 26-35

Probably other pieces.

Beaded Flange

Fostoria Glass Company, 1891. Crystal and colors.

Butter dish $24-34
Creamer 30-39
Goblet 23-35
Pickle dish 19-29
Spoonholder 21-30
Sugar bowl 32-42

Probably other pieces. Colors, 50 percent higher than clear prices listed.

Beaded Grape

Beaded Grape

(California): U.S. Glass Company, Pittsburgh, 1880s. Clear and emerald green.

Bowl, rectangular $20-30
Butter dish, covered 56-65
Cake plate on stand 61-71
Celery tray, oblong 34-46
Compote
  a. High foot, 7″, 8″, 9″ 72-85
  b. Small, 4″ high (rare) 80-90
  c. Shallow, on standard 56-65
Cordial 44-55
Creamer 55-65
Cruet 46-55
Dish
  a. Oblong, deep 40-52
  b. Square, 5¼″, 6¼″, 7¼″, 8¼″.. 44-55
Goblet, green (ill.) 46-54
Pickle 19-27
Pitcher, water
  a. Round, several sizes 52-70
  b. Square, several sizes 50-65
Platter, oblong (rare) 68-95
Plate, square, 8½″ 27-37
Sauce, 3½″, 4″, 4½″ 16-29
Salt/Pepper, metal tops, pr...... 40-50
Spoonholder 35-44
Sugar bowl, covered 50-60
Toothpick holder 29-38
Tumbler, water 35-45
Vase, 6″ 40-52

Probably other pieces. Green pieces 50 percent higher than clear prices listed. Almost EVERY piece being reproduced!

Beaded Grape Medallion

Boston Silver-Glass Company, East Cambridge, Massachusetts, late 1860s. Clear.

Butter dish ....$ 56- 67
Celery vase 62- 73
Compote, covered, high, low,
  oval 72- 90
Creamer, applied handle 96-118
Egg cup 35- 45
Goblet 37- 46
Pitcher, water (ill.) 105-128
Salt, footed, oval and round, flat 25- 35
Spoonholder 37- 47
Sugar bowl 69- 80

Probably other pieces.

Beaded GrapeMedallion

Cordial	20-30
Creamer	27-36
Dish, oval, 7½", 9½", 10½"	14-22
Goblet	36-45
Mug, handled	29-38
Pickle dish, boat shape	22-32
Pitcher	
a. Milk (ill.)	38-50
b. Syrup	39-49
c. Water, ½ gallon	50-60
Saucedishes, 2 types	17-26
Shakers	
a. Salt/Pepper, pr.	39-48
b. Sugar	34-44
Spoonholder, footed and flat	22-45
Sugar bowl	
a. Covered	34-44
b. Open	37-46
Tray, bread	41-51
Tumbler	32-42
Vase, toothpick holder	25-35
Wine	31-40

Beaded Loop

Beaded Loop

(Oregon): U.S. Glass Company, 1906-08. Clear, ruby-flashed.

Bowl, berry, covered	$24-34
Butter dish, 2 types	44-56
Cake stand, 6", 9½"	45-55
Celery	40-50
Compote	
a. Large, covered	40-50
b. Open, jelly	33-43

Beaded Medallion

Beaded Medallion

(Beaded Mirror): Sandwich Glass, late 1860s, or early 1870s. Clear only.

Butter dish, covered	$63-75
Compote, covered	50-60
Creamer	55-64
Egg cup	33-44
Goblet	40-50
Pitcher (ill.)	80-95
Relish dish	26-35
Salt dish, footed	30-39
Sauce, flat and footed	15-23
Spoonholder	36-45
Sugar bowl, covered	40-50

Probably other pieces.

Beaded Oval and Scroll

Beaded Oval and Scroll

(Dot): Bryce Bros., Pittsburgh, late 1870s. Clear.

Bowl, 6½" $25-35
Butter dish, covered 45-54
Cake stand 32-42
Compote
  a. High standard, covered 42-53
  b. High standard, open 40-50
Cordial 18-28
Creamer 32-41
Dish, oval 19-27
Goblet 33-45
Pickle dish 28-36
Pitcher, water (ill.) 56-65
Sauce 14-22
Salt/Pepper, pr. 25-35
Spoonholder 42-53
Sugar bowl
  a. Covered 55-65
  b. Open 40-48

Beaded Panels

Beaded Panels

Crystal Glass Company, Pittsburgh, Pennsylvania, 1877. Crystal.

Butter dish $27-36
Compote 32-41
Creamer 24-34
Egg cup 18-29
Goblet 17-27
Honey dish 12-19
Pitcher, water (ill.) 30-40
Salt/Pepper, pr. 18-29
Sauce 12-19
Spoonholder 19-27
Sugar bowl 34-44
Tumbler 22-32
Wine 15-28

Probably other pieces.

Beaded Panels
(maker unknown)

Beaded Panels

Maker unknown, late 1880s. Clear, non-flint.

Goblet $17-24
Spoonholder 14-20

Undoubtedly other pieces.

Beaded Swirl and Disc

Beaded Swirl and Disc

Maker and date unknown.

Butter dish, covered $30-38
Cake stand 26-32
Celery 20-28

Compote, covered 34-42
Creamer, covered 25-33
Cruet 14-23
Pitcher
  a. Milk (ill.) 41-50
  b. Syrup 26-35
  c. Water 47-54
Salt/Pepper, pr. 19-25
Sugar bowl, covered 32-41

Probably other pieces, possibly in colors.

Beaded Tulip

Beaded Tulip

(Andes): McKee Brothers, Pittsburgh, c. 1894, clear, non-flint; possibly, blue.

Bowl, oblong $35-45
Butter dish, covered 46-56
Cake stand, 9″ high 53-63
Creamer 30-39
Goblet (ill.) 39-48
Pickle, oval 23-33
Pitcher, water, milk 48-63
Spoonholder 23-33
Sugar bowl, covered 44-53
Tray, water 43-53
Wine........................ 37-46

Tray, water, blue, 100 percent higher than tray, water, clear, listed.

Bearded Head

(Viking; Bearded Prophet; Old Man of The Mountain): Hobbs, Brockunier & Company, Wheeling, West Virginia, 1876. Clear. The bearded head is that of a Roman Warrior, NOT a Viking.

Bearded Head

Bowl, covered, large $55-65
Butter dish, covered 57-67
Celery 30-42
Compote, covered, 7″, 8″ 56-74
Creamer, 3 heads 40-50
Pickle dish 23-33
Pitcher, water (ill.) 50-75
Platter 43-52
Relish, footed 32-42
Salt 27-36
Sauce 23-33
Spoonholder 25-35
Sugar bowl, covered 48-58

Goblets and tumblers were not made. This pattern apparently was reproduced before World War II. In what pieces it is not known. Careful!

The Bedford

409

(continued)

Bedford, The

Fostoria Glass Company, Moundsville, West Virginia, 1901-1905. Clear. Over 60 pieces were made in this popular pattern. Non-flint.

Butter dish	$34-43
Celery vase	17-26
Creamer	31-40
Goblet	27-36
Pitcher (ill.)	42-51
Spoonholder	18-27
Sugar bowl	35-44
Tumbler	26-34

Many other pieces.

Bellflower

Bellflower

(Ribbed Leaf): Sandwich Glass Company, 1840s; McKee Bros., Pittsburgh, 1868; others. Clear, cobalt blue, amber, opaque. Amber considered rarest. Blue next. One could write an entire book on Bellflower. There are many qualities and types—this must be taken into consideration when giving a price on a particular piece. A silvery-looking "lace glass" would probably be Sandwich; the dull-looking glass, some of it with worn designs, would be the lesser glass, probably made after the Civil War. Prices given here are for what one generally finds in shops today. If you can authenticate a piece as being genuine Sandwich, it's worth at least 150 percent more than the prices given here. Know your dealer, please!

Bowl
   a. Berry, flat, scalloped $116-148
   b. Round, 6″, 8″ edge   110-135

   c. Deep, oval   98-125
   d. Flat, scallop and point
      edge   125-138
Butter dish, covered
   a. Beaded edge   85- 95
   b. Rayed edge   88-100
   c. Scalloped edge   105-120
Cake stand (rare), if found   1,400+
Caster sets, 5 bottles (rare)   450+
Celery vase (rare)   275+
Compotes, any and all, 6 types 32- 65
Creamer, Double or Single
   Vine   118-138
Decanter, 3 types (rare)   138-150
Egg cup (rare in colors)   30- 42
Goblets, 6 types   28- 50
Honey dish, 3″, 3¼″, 2½″   20- 32
Lamps, 3 types   135-180
Mug, handled, small (rare)   230-240
Pitcher
   a. Milk, Double Vine (rare) 750+
   b. Syrup, 10-sided (rare)   900+
   c. Water, 2 sizes   80- 95
Plate, 6″ (rare)   80-100
Salt
   a. Covered, footed (rare)   155-170
   b. Open, footed   44- 57
Sauce   18- 28
Spoonholder
   a. Double Vine   62- 72
   b. Single Vine   52- 65
Sugar bowl
   a. Double Vine, covered   98-115
   b. Single Vine, covered   88-115
   c. Octagonal (rare)   450+
Tumbler, footed, fine rib   150-160
Whiskey — small tumbler
   (rare)   180-195
Wine, Single Vine   75- 85

Belted Worchester

410

Belted Worchester

Maker unknown, c. late 1850s, clear, flint.

Champagne $40-50
Cordial 30-40
Goblet (ill.) 32-44
Sugar bowl, covered 50-62
Whiskey, handled, ... 30-38
Wine 26-35

Another member of the "Worchester" family. Probably other pieces.

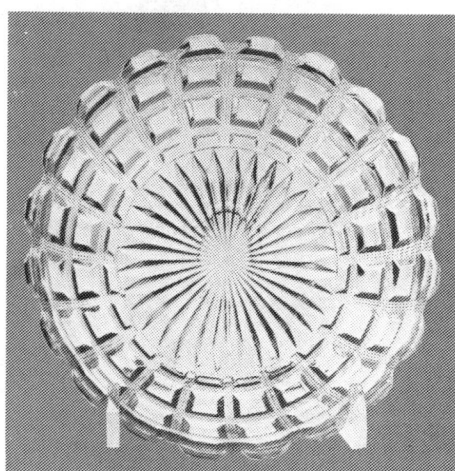
Berlin

Berlin

Adams & Company, Pittsburgh, 1874, Clear.

Butter dish $30-40
Compote
  a. Covered 46-55
  b. Open 34-44
Creamer 24-36
Dish, oval 17-26
Egg cup 19-28
Honey dish 17-26
Pickle dish 15-25
Pitcher
  a. Milk 55-65
  b. Water 55-65
Plate (ill.), 7" deep 23-33
Salt/Pepper, pr. 24-33
Sauce 17-26
Spoonholder 20-30
Sugar bowl 35-45
Tumbler 30-40
Wine 29-39

Berry Cluster

Berry Cluster

Maker unknown, 1880s. Clear.

Butter dish $42-47
Celery vase 19-27
Creamer 35-46
Goblet 20-29
Pitcher, water (ill.) 52-59
Spoonholder 19-28
Sugar bowl
  a. Covered 36-45
  b. Open 15-25

Probably other pieces.

Bethlehem Star

Bethlehem Star

Maker unknown, 1880s, clear, non-flint.

Butter dish $24-32
Celery 14-21
Creamer 17-26
Goblet 15-23
Pitcher (ill.) 32-41
Sauce 7-11

(continued)

Spoonholder 12-20
Sugar bowl 18-26
Probably other pieces.

Beveled Diagonal Block

Beveled Diagonal Block

Challinor, Taylor & Company, 1880s. Clear. Also by Bryce Bros., 1888. Nonflint.

Butter dish $36-43
Compote 35-44
Creamer 36-44
Cake stand 40-47
Celery vase 28-36
Cordial 12-21
Goblet 22-30
Marmalade jar 19-27
Pitcher, water 32-40
Plate 13-21
Salt/Pepper, pr. 18-27
Spoonholder (ill.) 21-30
Sugar bowl 32-40
Tumbler 20-28
Wine 18-27

Probably other pieces.

Beveled Star

(Pride): Model Flint Glass Company, Findlay, Ohio, 1890, called this pattern Pride. Clear, emerald green, cobalt, amber.

Butter dish, covered $46-54
Celery 22-30
Compote, covered, high standard . 51-64
Creamer 28-37
Goblet 25-34
Pitcher, water (ill.) 47-55

Beveled Star

Salt/Pepper, pr. 25-34
Spoonholder 30-38
Sugar bowl 32-40

Probably other pieces. Emerald green, cobalt, 50 percent higher; amber, 100 percent higher than clear prices listed.

Bicycle Girl

Bicycle Girl

Dalzell, Gilmore and Leighton, Findlay, Ohio, 1880s; later by National Glass Company, Greentown, Indiana.

Pitcher, water, clear (ill.) $355-365
Possibly tumbler to match 140-150

Bigler

Boston & Sandwich Glass Company, Sandwich, Massachusetts, c. 1850s, clear, flint.

Bowl $68- 78
Celery 80- 90
Champagne 90-105
Cordial 89- 98
Decanter, bar type 67- 77

Bigler

Goblet, (ill.)	48- 57
Mug, handled	71- 81
Tumbler.....................	59- 69
Wine	56- 66

Possibly creamer and sugar bowl (rare).

Birch Leaf

Birch Leaf

Maker unknown, c. 1870s, clear, milk glass, flint.

Butter dish, covered, on pedestal (ill.)	$64-73
Creamer	31-40
Egg cup	22-30
Goblet	22-31
Salt, master, footed	15-19
Spoonholder	22-31
Sugar bowl, covered	63-71

Milk glass, 100 percent higher than clear prices listed. Probably other pieces.

Bird and Strawberry

Bird and Strawberry

(Bluebird): 1890s, berries, birds, leaves, colored, clear. Non-flint.

Bowl, footed, berry, round	$48- 57
Butter dish, covered	45- 53
Cake stand, 9″ diameter	46- 53
Compote, open, 2 sizes	70- 85
Creamer, w/color	42- 51
Goblet.......................	22- 31
Pitcher (ill.)	50- 60
Relish, heart-shaped	20- 26
Sauce, clear	17- 25
Spoonholder	20- 28
Sugar bowl, covered	54- 63
Tumbler.....................	20- 25
Wine	30- 36

Probably other pieces.

Bird Napkin Ring

Bird Napkin Ring

With salt (in bird's back) and pepper. Sandwich Glass; considered scarce. There

413   (continued)

is a pair of these at the Houston Museum, Chattanooga, Tennessee.

Bird napkin ring w/Salt/Pepper,
pr. (ill.) ....$350 +

Bird on Nest Mug
Challinor & Taylor, Ltd., Tarentum, Pennsylvania, 1880s.

Mug $57-67

Bird on Nest Mug

Birds and Harp Mug

Birds and Harp Mug
A novelty drinking mug for children in the late 1800s.

Mug $42-51

Birds at Fountain

Birds at Fountain
Early 1880s. Clear, opaque.

Bowl	$22-30
Butter dish	42-51
Cake stand	43-53
Compote, covered, 8″	57-66

Creamer	31-40
Goblet	44-52
Mug (ill.)	23-31
Spoonholder	17-26
Sugar bowl, covered	28-36

Probably other pieces.

Blackberry

Blackberry
William Leighton, Jr., Wheeling, West Virginia, 1870. Clear, milk, white.

Butter dish, covered ....$	69- 79
Celery vase (rare)	80- 90
Champagne..................	47- 57
Compote	
a. Covered, high foot........	90-100
b. Covered, low foot	80- 90
Creamer	63- 73
Dish, oval, 8¼″ x 5½″ (rare) ..	64- 74
Egg cup, double and single	45- 58
Goblet, (rare)	48- 58
Honey dish	21- 30
Pitcher, water (rare) (ill.)	165-175
Salt, footed, 2 styles	32- 42
Sauce, flat	19- 27
Spoonholder	57- 67
Sugar bowl, open	70- 80
Syrup	46- 55
Tumbler	32- 42

Milk glass, 80-90 percent higher than clear prices listed. Being reproduced in butter dish, celery vase, creamer, egg cup (single), goblet, water pitcher, sugar bowl. Possibly others. Careful!

Blaze
New England Glass Company, East Cambridge, Massachusetts, c. 1869, clear, flint.

Butter dish, covered ....$	64-73
Celery	65-73
Compote, covered, low standard,	

7″, 8″	68-82
Creamer	75-85
Goblet	40-48
Plate, 6″, 7″	27-36
Sauce, 4″, 5″	17-25
Spoonholder	34-42
Sugar bowl, covered	60-70
Tumbler	38-46
Wine	53-62

Possibly other pieces.

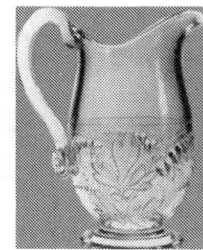

Bleeding Heart

Bleeding Heart

Sandwich Glass Company, 1860-1875, other companies later. Clear, opaque.

Bowl, waste	$35- 45
Butter dish	60- 69
Cake plate on stand, 9½″ high	72- 82
Compote	
a. Covered, high foot	67- 77
b. Covered, low foot	56- 66
c. Oval, covered	57- 66
Cordial	33- 42
Creamer, applied handle	56- 65
Dish, oval, large	32- 42
Egg cups	
a. Barrel shape	38- 46
b. Straight side	33- 43
Goblet	
a. Plain and knob stem	40- 49
b. Thin, design low on bowl	
(ill.)	39- 47
Mug, handled	33- 43
Pickle dish, oval	30- 40
Pitcher, water, (ill.)	93-103
Plates (rare)	73- 82
Platter, oval	74- 83
Salt, oval and round, footed	32- 42
Sauces, 3 types	12- 34
Spoonholder	37- 46
Sugar bowl	69- 80
Tumbler	
a. Footed	37- 46
b. Water	26- 35
Wine	68- 80

Block and Circle

Block and Circle

Maker and date unknown. Clear, non-flint.

Goblet	$17-25
Lamp, miniature	23-33
Pitcher, water (ill.)	41-50
Tumblers to match	16-24

Possibly other pieces.

Block and Fan

Block and Fan

(Romeo): Richards & Hartley Glass Company, Tarentum, Pennsylvania, 1880s. Clear, clear with red flashing.

Bowl, berry, 8″ dia.	$25-35
Butter dish	42-50
Cake stand, 10″ dia.	37-46
Celery	23-33
Compote	40-47
Cordial	17-25
Creamer	27-35
Cruet (ill.)	26-42
Goblet	49-58
Lamp	38-48
Jam jar	30-40
Pitcher, water, pedestal base	41-50
Plate, large	25-35
Sauce, flat and footed	8-18
Salt/Pepper, pr.	46-55
Spoonholder	25-35

(continued)

Sugar, covered and open 40-50
Tumbler 29-36
Wine........................ 40-48

Red flashing 90 percent higher than clear prices given.

Block and Honeycomb

Block and Honeycomb

McKee & Bros., Pittsburgh, 1874. Clear, non-flint.

Butter bowl.................... $38-47
Goblet 24-33
Pitcher (ill.).................. 65-73
Sugar bowl 42-51

Probably other pieces.

Block and Palm

Probably Beaver Falls Co-Operative Glass Company, Beaver Falls, Pennsylvania, c. 1890, clear, milk glass, non-flint.

Butter dish, covered $39-49
Cake stand 38-47
Celery 27-37
Creamer 42-52
Goblet 26-35
Pitcher, water................. 42-52
Salt/Pepper, pr. 30-39
Sauce, flat 11-16
Spoonholder 21-30
Sugar bowl, covered 35-43

Milk glass, 100 percent higher than clear prices listed. Probably other pieces.

Block and Rib

Block and Rib

Maker and date unknown. Chalk white glass, also clear.

Butter dish, covered $33-42
Celery holder 19-28
Creamer 19-28
Goblet 19-25
Pitcher, water (ill.) 35-44
Spoonholder 21-30
Sugar bowl, covered 30-39

Probably other pieces.

Block and Star

Block and Star

(Valencia Waffle): 1885-1895. Clear, canary, blue, amber.

Butter dish, covered $24-33
Celery 22-31
Compote
  a. Covered 32-41
  b. Open 20-28

416

Creamer 19-28
Goblet (ill.) 21-30
Sauce
  a. Flat 13-20
  b. Footed 15-22
Spoonholder 22-32
Sugar
  a. Covered 30-40
  b. Open 21-29
Relish 14-21
Wine........................ 20-28

Probably other pieces. Color, 60 percent more than clear prices listed.

Block and Sunburst

Block and Sunburst

George Duncan and Sons, Pittsburgh, 1880. Clear, ruby flashed, non-flint.

Butter dish $40-48
Compote 42-51
Cream tankard 37-46
Goblet 21-30
Mug 24-32
Pitcher, water (ill.) 66-74
Sauce 16-25
Spoonholder 25-33
Sugar bowl 35-42
Tumbler 29-37
Wine........................ 21-31

Probably other pieces.

Block and Thumbprint

Possibly Union Glass Company, Somerville, Massachusetts, c. 1860s, clear, flint and non-flint.

Butter dish, covered $33-42
Celery (ill.) 26-35
Compote, covered 34-44
Creamer 31-40

Block and Thumbprint

Spoonholder 24-33
Sugar bowl, covered 30-40
Tumbler, footed 32-42

Flint, 40 percent higher than non-flint prices listed. Probably other pieces.

Blockade

Blockade

Challinor, Taylor, Ltd., Tarentum, Pennsylvania, 1885, clear only.

Butter dish, covered (stemmed) ..$24-33
Celery (stemmed) 26-36
Compotes, covered, 6″, 7″, 8″, 9″,
  flared or straight 21-31
Creamer (stemmed) 17-28
Goblet (ill.) 25-35
Pitcher, qt., ½ gal. 44-53
Sugar bowl, covered (stemmed) .. 37-47
Tumbler 22-31

Many other pieces. Lower half of stem is hollow.

Blocked Arches

Blocked Arches

(Berkley): U.S. Glass Company, c. 1893, clear, non-flint, possibly stained ruby.

Bowl, finger	$20-29
Creamer	34-42
Cup/saucer	20-27
Goblet	24-33
Jug, syrup	42-51
Shaker, salt	14-19
Spoonholder	14-22
Sugar bowl (base ill.)	36-44
Tumbler	20-25
Wine	20-27

If stained ruby, 50 percent higher than clear prices listed. Other pieces.

Bosc Pear

Bosc Pear

Maker unknown, 1920s. Clear, flashed purple pears, gold flashed leaves, non-flint.

Butter dish, covered	$36-46
Celery	24-33
Creamer	42-51
Pitcher, water (ill.)	44-54
Spoonholder	27-35
Sugar bowl	28-37
Tumbler	17-26

Probably other pieces.

Bow-Tie

The Thompson Glass Company, Uniontown, Pennsylvania, c. 1886, clear, non-flint.

Bowl, fruit, 10″	$68-78
Butter dish, covered	74-83
Creamer	52-62
Goblet	52-61
Pitcher, water	72-82
Spoonholder	34-42
Sugar bowl, covered	72-80

Firm only in business for three years. Possibly other pieces.

Boxed Star

Boxed Star

Maker unknown, 1890s, clear, non-flint.

Butter dish	$22-31
Creamer	14-22
Pitcher, water (ill.)	31-40
Spoonholder	18-26
Sugar bowl	23-32
Tumbler	20-27

Probably other pieces.

Bradford Grape

Bradford Grape

Maker unknown, c. 1850s or 1860s, clear, flint.

Butter dish, covered .... $ 92-101
Champagne.................. 64- 73
Cordial.................... 63- 72
Creamer 94-103
Goblet (ill.) 71- 80
Pitcher, water 184-193
Spoonholder 47- 56
Sugar bowl, covered 92-101
Tumbler (rare) 108-117
Wine...................... 72- 81
Possibly other pieces.

Branched Tree

Branched Tree

Probably National Glass Company, Greentown, Indiana, 1890s, non-flint.

Butter dish $44-53
Celery 24-33
Compote, covered, high, low
   standard 42-51
Creamer 29-37

Goblet 24-32
Pitcher, water (ill.) 70-80
Spoonholder 23-32
Sugar bowl 38-47
Probably others.

Brickwork

Brickwork

Probably National Glass Company Greentown, Indiana, around 1900. Clear and caramel slag, non-flint.

Butter dish $37-45
Celery 20-28
Creamer 26-34
Goblet 35-44
Pitcher, water (ill.) 42-52
Salt/Pepper, pr. 20-28
Spoonholder 22-31
Sugar bowl, covered 34-43
Caramel slag, 70 percent higher than clear prices listed.

Brilliant

Brilliant

Possibly McKee Brothers, Pittsburgh, c. 1870s, clear, flint.

Goblet (ill.) $54-63
There should be other pieces.

Bringing Home the Cows

Bringing Home the Cows

Dalzell, Gilmore and Leighton Company, 1870s. Clear.

Butter dish, covered $170-187
Creamer 125-138
Pitcher, milk (ill.) 290-315
Spoonholder 92-108
Sugar bowl, covered 158-167
Probably other pieces.

Britannic

Britannic

McKee Bros., Pittsburgh, 1893. Clear crystal with ruby stain. Popular after Columbian Exposition of 1893.

Butter dish, covered $37-46
Compote
  a. Covered 52-61
  b. Open 44-52
Cake stand, small, large 43-52
Creamer 30-40
Cruet 22-31
Cups, custard 14-22
Goblet 19-28
Pitcher (ill.).................. 37-47
Salt/Pepper, pr. 19-28
Spoonholder 24-34
Sugar bowl, covered 42-52
Tumbler 32-42
Wine...................... 22-34

Red flashing, 65 percent higher; amber flashing, 45 percent higher than clear prices listed.

Broken Column

Broken Column

(Irish Column, Notched Rib): U.S. Glass Company, 1892, before that by Columbia Glass Company, Findlay, Ohio, 1891. Clear, clear with ruby-stained depressions.

Banana dish $75- 85
Basket, handled 92-101
Bowl
  a. 8½" diameter 40- 48
  b. Covered, various sizes 39- 47
Butter dish, covered 44- 54
Cake stand, large 54- 64
Celery...................... 38- 47
Compote
  a. Covered, high standard.... 55- 65
  b. Open, high standard 38- 47
Celery tray 37- 47
Creamer..................... 36- 44
Cruet 38- 46
Custard cup 22- 30
Finger bowl 19- 29
Goblet, lady's 42- 52
Pickle caster, complete 83- 93
Pitcher, water (ill.) 57- 67
Plate, 7" (rare) 45- 54
Sauce, flat.................... 15- 24
Salt/Pepper, pr. 39- 48
Spoonholder 22- 31
Sugar
  a. Bowl, open 37- 46
  b. Shaker (rare) 38- 47
Syrup jug 54- 63
Tumbler, plain 34- 43
Water bottle 42- 52
Wine 47- 56
Goblet is being reproduced. Ruby-stained depression pieces 150 percent higher than clear prices listed.

Brooklyn

Brooklyn

Maker unknown, c. late 1860s, early 1870s, clear, flint. Possibly a Bakewell, Pears product.

Compote
a. Covered $64-73
b. Open 34-44
Creamer 52-61
Decanter 51-60
Goblet (ill.) 44-53
Pitcher, water 71-80
Sugar bowl, covered 68-74
Probably other pieces.

Buck and Doe

Maker and date unknown.
Goblet $150-170

Buckingham

Buckingham

U.S. Glass Company, 1906. Clear, cranberry and green, non-flint.

Bowl, 8¼" dia. (ill.) $54-63
Butter dish, covered 47-56
Celery 23-32
Compote
a. Covered 42-52
b. Open 30-39
Creamer 42-51
Goblet 27-36
Pitcher, water 60-69
Spoonholder 20-30
Sugar bowl, covered 46-55
Tumbler 21-30
Probably other pieces. Color, 25 percent higher than clear prices listed.

Buckle   Buckle

Sandwich Glass, early 1870s; also Gillinder & Sons, Philadelphia, same period. Clear, sapphire blue (rare). Flint and non-flint.

Bowl, wire basket container .. $ 50- 60
Butter dish, covered, flat 59- 69
Champagne................. 78- 87
Compote, open, low standard .. 70- 80
Cordial.................... 68- 78
Creamer, applied handles,
pedestal foot 90-100
Egg cup 22- 31
Goblets, 2 types 40- 55
Pickle dish, large, oval 26- 35
Pitcher, water 185-220
Salt dip
a. Footed 18- 27
b. Oval, flat (rare)......... 30- 40
Saucedish, 4" 11- 20
Spoonholder, scalloped rim 40- 48
Sugar bowl, covered, flint 46- 55
Tumbler 43- 53
Color, 80 percent more than clear prices listed. Flint, 50 percent higher than non-flint prices listed.

Buckle with Diamond Band

Maker unknown, c. 1880s, clear, non-flint.

Butter dish, covered $43-52
Creamer 35-42
Goblet 34-41
Pitcher, water................. 37-46
Spoonholder 24-33
Sugar bowl, covered 43-51
Probably other pieces.

Buckle with Star

Buckle with Star

(Orient): Bryce, Walker & Company, Pittsburgh, Pennsylvania, c. 1875, clear, non-flint.

Bowls, oval, round $19-27
Butter dish, covered 39-48
Celery 34-42
Compote, covered 56-64
Creamer (ill.) 39-48
Goblet 33-42
Pitcher....................... 49-59
Relish, oval 14-22
Sauce, flat 10-17
Spoonholder 24-33
Sugar bowl, covered 32-42
Wine........................ 21-31
Probably other pieces.

Bulldog with Hat Toothpick

A scarce novelty from Sandwich. Supposedly clear only, but the Houston Museum, Chattanooga, Tennessee, has one in amber and one in blue! Being reproduced in all colors.

Bulldog with Hat Toothpick

Clear .... $ 78- 95
Amber 160-170
Blue 150-160
Also made by Belmont Glass Co., Bellaire, Ohio, c. 1885.

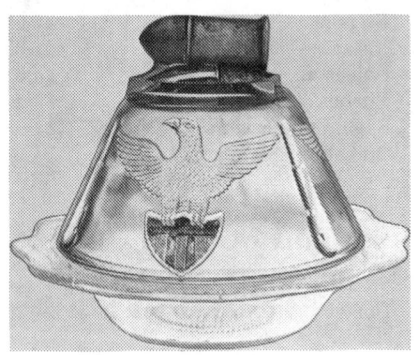

Bullet Emblem

Bullet Emblem

(Shield in red, white and blue): Clear, Spanish-American War souvenir, made in 1898.

Butter, covered (ill.) $255-270
Creamer 167-176
Spoonholder 125-134
Sugar bowl, covered 210-220
Possibly other pieces.

Bull's Eye

Bull's Eye and Daisy

Bull's Eye

(Lawrence): New England Glass Company; also Sandwich. Clear, milk-white, other colors (rare).

Bitters bottle	$110-120
Butter dish	145-160
Caster bottle	30- 40
Celery vase	71- 81
Champagne	88- 97
Cologne bottle	89-108
Compote	
a. Open, large, high standard	92-108
b. Open, low standard	77- 86
Cordials, 2 styles	44- 54
Creamer	120-135
Cruet	52- 62
Decanter	
a. Bar lip, pint and quart	57- 67
b. Usual type, pint and quart	52- 62
Egg cup, covered (rare)	150-159
Goblet, knob and plain stem	65- 75
Jar, covered, small	64- 74
Lamp	72- 82
Pickle dish, oval	41- 50
Salt	
a. Footed	22- 29
b. Footed, oblong, covered (rare)	42- 52
Spoonholder (ill.)	49- 58
Sugar bowl	105-115
Tumbler, water	88-110
Water bottle with tumble-up	64- 74

Colored pieces, 50 percent higher than clear prices listed.

Bull's Eye and Daisy

Maker unknown, c. 1890s, clear, clear with bull's eyes in red, purple, green, gilt rims, non-flint.

Butter dish, covered	$44-53
Creamer	41-50
Goblet	24-32
Pitcher, water	47-57
Salt shaker	17-26
Spoonholder	21-30
Sugar bowl, handled (ill.)	24-34
Tumbler	17-26
Wine	16-25

Colors, 80-100 percent higher than clear prices listed.

Bull's Eye and Fan

Bull's Eye and Fan

(Daisies in Oval Panels): Mid-1890s. Clear; sometimes combined with color.

Bowl	$ 9-17
Butter dish, covered	22-32
Creamer	37-44
Goblet	17-26
Pitcher, water (ill.)	42-51
Sauce, flat	14-22
Spoonholder	15-24
Sugar	
a. Covered	26-36
b. Open	18-27

Probably other pieces. Pieces with colored dots in eyes, 20 percent higher than clear prices listed.

Bull's Eye and Prism

Bull's Eye and Prism

Maker unknown, c. late 1840s, early 1850s, clear, flint.

Goblet (ill.) $110-120
Other pieces unknown.

Bull's Eye and Spear Head

Bull's Eye and Spear Head

Dalzell, Gilmore & Leighton, Findlay, Ohio, c. late 1870s, clear, non-flint.

Bottle, caster	$22-31
Butter dish, covered	51-60
Compote	
a. Covered	21-30
b. Open	54-63
Creamer	35-44
Decanter (ill.)	41-50
Goblet	40-47
Lamp, night	31-40
Spoonholder	31-40
Sugar bowl, covered	55-65
Wine (ill.)...................	33-42

Probably other pieces.

Bull's Eye with Fleur-de-Lis

Bull's Eye with Fleur-de-Lis

Boston & Sandwich Glass Company, mid-1800s; probably Union Glass Company, Somerville, Massachusetts, 1860s. Clear and amber. Flint only.

Ale glass (rare)	$140-175
Butter dish, covered	180-200
Celery	94-112
Compote	
a. Open, high standard	110-120
b. Open, low standard	105-115
Creamer (rare)	240-265
Decanter	
a. Pint	87-106
b. Quart	145-165
Goblet	75- 87
Lamp	
a. Glass only	70- 80
b. Glass bowl, brass stem, marble base	145-168
Pitcher, water (rare) (ill.)	280-300
Salt, footed	58- 68
Sugar bowl	140-150

Amber, 60 percent higher than clear prices listed.

Butterfly

424

Butterfly

Bakewell, Pears & Company, Pittsburgh, 1895-1905. Clear or clear with frosted handles, non-flint.

Butter dish, covered	$48-56
Celery	23-29
Creamer	34-42
Mustard, covered, handled	17-25
Pickle dish	17-24
Pitcher, water (ill.)	56-64
Relish dish, oval	18-24
Salt/Pepper, pr.	21-30
Sugar bowl, covered	54-62

Probably other pieces.

Butterfly and Grape

Butterfly and Grape

Fenton Art Glass Company, Williamstown, West Virginia, early 1920s, "Golden Iridescent" only. Non-flint.

Bowl, berry	$50-58
Butter dish, covered	57-66
Creamer	42-51
Pitcher, water, jug, not footed	50-59
Spoonholder	24-32
Sugar bowl, covered, footed	52-61
Tumbler	18-26

Butterfly with Spray

Butterfly with Spray

(Acme): Bryce, Higbee and Company, Pittsburgh, early 1800s. Clear. Non-flint.

Butter dish, covered	$46-54
Celery	16-25
Compote, covered, high, low standard	34-46
Creamer	26-35
Goblet	24-33
Mug (ill.)	28-38
Pitcher, water	47-54
Spoonholder	26-34
Sugar bowl, covered	41-50
Tumbler	16-24

Probably many other pieces

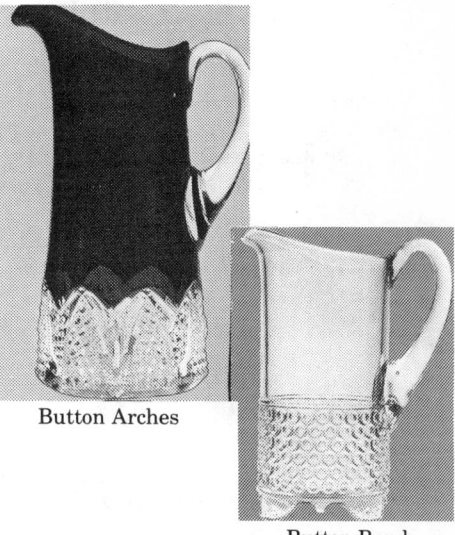

Button Arches

Button Band

Button Arches

(Scalloped Daisy, Red Top): Duncan & Miller Glass Company, Washington, Pennsylvania, 1897. Clear, clear with red top.

Bowl, 8"	$21-28
Cake stand	30-36
Compote, jelly	15-21
Creamer	22-30
Cruet	24-33
Goblet	19-27
Mug	24-32
Pitcher, water (ill.)	36-43
Salt/Pepper, pr.	24-29
Spoonholder	18-27

(continued)

Sugar bowl, covered 30-37
Toothpick holder 32-38
Tumbler 22-29
Wine 17-26
Probably other pieces. "Red top" pieces 35 percent more than clear prices listed. Reproduced in butter dish, wine, creamer and goblet.

Button Band

Early 1880s. Clear, non-flint.
Bowl $18-25
Butter dish 29-37
Cake stand 40-47
Compote, open 41-50
Creamer 26-29
Goblet 19-27
Pitcher, water (ill.) 32-39
Sugar bowl, covered 34-36
Tumbler 19-26
Wine 19-25
Probably other pieces.

Buttressed Arch

Buttressed Arch

(Buttressed Loop): Possibly Adams Glass Company, Pittsburgh, mid-1880s. Clear. Non-flint.
Butter dish, covered $34-43
Celery vase 23-29
Creamer 26-34
Goblet 20-27
Pitcher, water (ill.) 46-54
Sauce 13-19
Spoonholder 18-25
Sugar bowl, covered 31-40
Probably other pieces.

Cabbage Leaf

Cabbage Leaf

Maker unknown, 1870s and 1880s. Clear amber, heavily stippled and frosted, opalescent.
Butter dish, covered . . . .$ 85- 94
Celery 62- 72
Compote, covered,
  high standard 100-120
Creamer 52- 62
Pickle dish, large leaf shape . . 35- 45
Pitcher, water (ill.) 80- 90
Plate, rabbit head in center . . 49- 56
Spoonholder 37- 47
Sugar bowl, covered 82- 92
Stippled and frosted pieces 20 percent more; amber 50 percent more than clear prices listed. Tumbler not known but probably made. BEWARE! Every pattern has been reproduced in almost every color — even goblets!

Cabbage Rose

Cabbage Rose

Central Glass Company, Wheeling, West Virginia, 1880s; possibly at Sandwich earlier. Clear. Non-flint.

Butter dish ....$	72- 82
Cake plate on standard, 11" ..	69- 78
Celery	53- 63
Compotes, 6", 7", 8", 9"	64- 84
Cordial......................	40- 50
Creamer	64- 74
Egg cup	37- 46
Goblet	47- 57
Pickle dish	23- 32
Pitcher	
a. Quart (ill.)	65- 75
b. Three pints (rare)........	112-123
Salt, footed	25- 34
Saucedish, 4", 5"	11- 20
Spoonholder	42- 52
Sugar bowl, open	32- 40
Sugar bowl, with lid	64- 74
Tumbler, water	46- 55
Wine (rare)	49- 58

Goblet being reproduced.

Cable

Cable

Possibly Sandwich Glass of the 1850s, clear, flint; rare in opaque, blue opaque, green opaque, silver-stained panels.

Butter dish, covered ....$	95-105
Compote, open	49- 56
Creamer (rare)	400-450
Egg cup	44- 53
Goblet	66- 75
Lamp, marble base	97-118
Pitcher, water (rare).........	375-450
Spoonholder (ill.)	55- 64
Sugar bowl, covered	94-106
Tumbler, footed	168-185

Colors, 120-140 percent higher than clear prices listed.

Cable with Ring

Cable with Ring

Sandwich Glass Company, 1860s. Clear only. Flint.

Butter dish ....$	58- 70
Compote, open, 8¼"	60- 69
Creamer	60- 68
Honey dish	18- 24
Lamp	80- 90
Pitcher (ill.)	92-107
Sauce, flat	11- 16
Sugar bowl, covered	80- 88

No goblet or tumbler known.

Cactus

Cactus

(Panelled Agave): Indiana Tumbler & Goblet (National) Company, 1903. Crystal, chocolate (caramel slag). Non-flint.

Berry bowl ....$	90-100
Butter dish	126-134
Butter dish, stemmed	230-240
Celery tray	57- 65
Compote	
a. Large	170-179
b. Medium	132-140
c. Small	96-105
Cracker jar	122-130
Creamer	81- 90
Cruet	97-105
Mug	67- 73
Mustard jar.................	124-129
Pitcher, water (ill.)	188-197

(continued)

Relish dish 77- 86
Salt/Pepper, pr. 64- 73
Spoonholder 69- 74
Sugar bowl 85- 93
Syrup, Dewey or metal lid 83- 92
Toothpick 52- 61
Tumbler, water and lemonade   63- 72
Prices listed are for chocolate. Being
reproduced — careful!

Canadian

Canadian

Burlington Glass Works, Canada,
1870s. Clear.

Butter dish, covered $57-67
Celery 43-52
Compote
  a. Covered, 6", 7", 8" 58-74
  b. Open, high and low
    standard 38-47
Cordial 25-33
Creamer 45-54
Goblet 43-53
Jam jar, covered 38-47
Pitcher, milk and water
  a. Large (ill.) 71-80
  b. Small 58-68
Plate, 6", 8", 10" 32-42
Sauce, flat and footed, 4" 13-19
Spoonholder 37-44
Sugar bowl, covered 57-66
Wine........................ 38-47

Cane

Sandwich Glass Company, 1875-1885.
Also Gillinder Glass Company and

Cane

McKee Glass Company, same period.
Clear, amber, apple green, blue, yellow.

Bowl, berry, 3-panel, footed $26-36
Bowl, finger.................... 22-27
Butter dish 44-54
Creamer 29-38
Goblet 26-34
Jam jar...................... 32-39
Pickle dish, oval............... 18-24
Pitcher, water (ill.) 37-45
Sauce
  a. Covered 9-16
  b. Flat 10-17
Salt/Pepper, pr. 35-44
Spoonholder 25-34
Sugar bowl 44-52
Toddy plate 23-33
Tray, water 38-43
Tumbler, water 24-32
Green, common. Amber and blue, 60
percent higher than clear prices listed.

Cane Column

Mid-1800s. Clear, canary, amber, blue.
Non-flint.

Butter dish, covered $37-45
Creamer 34-43
Goblet 27-35
Pitcher (ill.).................. 41-50
Sauce, flat 17-25
Spoonholder 22-29
Sugar bowl
  a. Covered 35-42
  b. Open 21-30
Wine........................ 22-26

Cane Column

Probably other pieces. Colored pieces, 80 to 100 percent higher than clear prices listed.

Cane Insert

Cane Insert

Tarentum Glass Company, Tarentum, Pennsylvania, 1898-1906, clear, clear with gold gilt, emerald green with gold gilt, pink with gold gilt, custard, pea green custard. Non-flint.

Butter dish, covered	$40-48
Cake stand	41-50
Compote	31-39
Creamer (ill.)	27-36
Goblet	29-37
Pitcher, water	54-63
Sugar bowl, covered	31-40

Made in a full line of ware. Gold gilt, custard, 75 percent higher than clear prices listed.

Cane Medallion

Cane Medallion

Westmoreland Glass Company, Grapeville, Pennsylvania, 1896. Clear, opaque. Non-flint.

Bowl, berry, oblong, oval	$16-24
Butter dish	24-33
Creamer (ill.)	25-32
Pickle	11-18
Pitcher, water	40-48
Spoonholder	22-29
Sugar bowl, covered	33-43
Toothpick	22-27
Tumbler	18-26

Probably other pieces.

Cape Cod

Probably Sandwich, c. 1870s, clear, non-flint.

Bowl, handled		$32-42
Butter dish, covered		56-65
Celery		34-42
Compote		
a. Covered, 6″, 7″, 8″		56-72
b. Open, 6″, 7″, 8″		34-49
Creamer		33-42
Goblet		41-49
Jar, jam		46-54
Pitcher, water		58-67
Spoonholder		32-42
Sugar bowl, covered		57-66
Wine		37-46

Probably other pieces.

Capitol Building

Souvenir glass of the 1920s. Different buildings on different pieces.

Dessert plate	$20-27
Goblet (ill.)	34-42
Sherbet	34-39
Tumbler	31-40
Wine	24-32

Capitol Building

Caprice

Caprice

(Arched Fans): Possibly Cambridge Glass Company, Cambridge, Massachusetts, c. early 1900s, clear, frosted, blue, gold, non-flint.

Goblet (ill.) $20-26
Plate, 14½" 37-45
Salt dip........................ 11-18
Sauce 9-17
Wine......................... 15-21

Colors, 80 percent higher. Clear, frosted, 20 percent higher than clear prices listed. Probably other pieces.

Caramel Strigil

Caramel Strigil

Probably Indiana Tumbler and Goblet Company, before 1903, when the factory burned. McKee Bros. made an identical pattern in 1897, calling it "Nelly," only in clear glass. In 1900, both firms joined National Glass Company, so either firm could have made this pattern.

Tankard, cream (ill.) $145-170
Probably other pieces made.

Cardinal Bird

Cardinal Bird

Probably Ohio Flint Glass Company, Lancaster, late 1870s. This company was the ancestor of the Anchor-Hocking Glass Company. Clear.

Butter dish, covered .... $ 58- 68
Creamer 43- 53

Goblet 45- 55
Pitcher, water 118-132
Sauce
  a. Flat, round 18- 28
  b. Footed, 4", 5½" 21- 31
Spoonholder (ill.) 32- 41
Sugar bowl, covered 61- 71
Possibly other pieces were made.

Carmen

(Panelled Diamond and Fine-Cut): Fostoria Glass Company, Moundsville, West Virginia, c. 1896, clear, clear flashed with yellow, non-flint.

Bowls, berry, 7", 8" $15-24
Butter dish, covered 34-43
Cake stand 32-41
Celery 18-26
Compote
  a. High standard, 7", 8" 32-47
  b. Low standard 19-28
Creamer 30-37
Cruet, oil 19-27
Goblet 22-30
Pitcher, water, tankard 31-40
Spoonholder 19-28
Sugar bowl, open 22-30
Wine 19-27
Yellow flashing, 20 percent higher than clear prices listed.

Cat on a Hamper

Cat on a Hamper

Indiana Tumbler & Goblet (National) Company, Greentown, Indiana, before 1903. Chocolate, amber, blue, green, clear. Two types made, short and tall. Prices listed, same for both.

Chocolate $170-180
Amber 133-142
Blue 180-190
Green 127-140
Clear 101-112

Extremely rare when top of hamper is in red, as shown in photo. It is believed no museum except the Houston has this type hamper. Rare!

Catawba Grape

Catawba Grape

Fairly new glass. Clear, also colors. Lots of it around.

Goblet $17-25
Wine (ill.) 13-24

Cathedral

431

(continued)

Cathedral

(Orion): Bryce Bros., Pittsburgh, late 1880s. Crystal, amber, vaseline, blue amethyst.

Bowl, berry, 5″, 6″, 7″, 8″ $30-46
Butter dish 61-71
Cake plate on stand 44-52
Compote
  a. Covered, large, high
     standard 57-65
  b. Open, low standard 33-42
Creamer 45-52
Dish, round, footed 18-23
Egg cup 28-36
Goblet 40-49
Pitcher, water, 3 quart 60-69
Saucedish
  a. Flat, 4″ 13-20
  b. Footed, 4″, 4½″ 16-24
Spoonholder 29-36
Sugar bowl, covered 52-62
Tumbler, water 30-40
Wine glass 33-42
Vaseline and amber, 45 percent; blue, 90 percent; amethyst, 125 percent higher than clear.

Cat's Eye and Block

(Cut Log): Westmoreland Specialty Company, c. 1896, clear, sometimes in camphor glass. non-flint.

Butter dish, covered $58-67
Cake stand 62-71
Celery 54-62
Creamer, 3″, 5″ 19-28
Goblet 27-36
Pitcher, water 44-53
Sugar bowl, covered 51-60
Tumbler 24-32
Wine 34-42
Camphor, 50 percent higher than clear prices listed.

Celtic Cross

Duncan, Miller Glass Company, Pittsburgh, Pennsylvania, c. 1888, clear, etched, non-flint.

Butter dish, covered $44-51
Compote, covered 33-41

Creamer 32-40
Goblet 22-30
Spoonholder 26-35
Sugar bowl, covered 38-47
Etched, same price. Probably other pieces.

Centennial Beer Mug

Centennial Beer Mug

This was made by M. Daniel Connolly, or designed by him.

Beer mug $44-50

Centennial Beer Mug

Centennial Beer Mug

Hobbs, Brockunier & Company, designed for Philadelphia Centennial, 1876.

Butter dish $64-74
Centennial mug (ill.) 39-48

Ceres

Ceres

(Cameo, Goddess of Liberty): Possibly Indiana Tumbler & Goblet Company, 1898-1900. Crystal, opaque white, opaque turquoise, clear, amber, purple-black opaque.

Butter dish $39-47
Candy jar, covered 22-29
Compote, open, low standard 37-46
Creamer .... : 22-30
Mug, handled 30-37
Pitcher, water 40-49
Spoonholder (ill.) 19-27
Sugar bowl, covered 36-42
Probably other pieces. Colored pieces, 50 percent higher than clear prices listed.

Chain

Chain

Fort Pitt Glass Works, Pittsburgh, Pa., c. early 1880s, clear, non-flint.

Butter dish, covered $46-56
Compote, covered 40-50
Cordial 28-37
Creamer 19-26
Goblet 22-31
Spoonholder 19-27
Sugar bowl (base ill.) 44-52
Wine 27-36
Probably other pieces.

Chain

Chain

Possibly Sandwich, early. The creamer shown here is almost identical with one made by R. B. Curling & Sons, Fort Pitt. This glassworks was located in Pittsburgh.

Butter dish $52-62
Creamer, cheaper version 42-52
Goblet, cheaper version 18-26
Pitcher, water (ill.) 39-47
Platter 18-21
Spoonholder 26-29
Sugar bowl 40-48
Wine 21-28

Chain and Shield

Late 1870s. Clear. Non-flint.

Butter, covered $33-42
Creamer 27-36
Goblet 15-23
Pitcher (ill.) 29-37
Platter, oval 28-39

(continued)

Chain and Shield

Sauce, flat	12-17
Spoonholder	18-26
Sugar, covered	29-36

Undoubtedly other pieces.

Chain with Star

Chain with Star

Possibly A. J. Beatty & Company, Steubenville, Ohio, 1880s. Clear.

Bowl, footed, small and large	$19-27
Butter dish, covered	41-51
Cake stand	35-43
Compote, covered, high and low standard	46-56
Creamer	43-52
Dish, oval	15-22
Goblet	20-29
Pickle dish	12-17
Pitcher, water (ill.)	47-57
Plate, 7", 9", 10", 12"	25-44
Plate, bread, handled	36-44

Sauce, flat and footed	11-16
Salt/Pepper, pr.	20-27
Spoonholder	27-36
Sugar bowl, open	24-33
Wine	23-32

Challinor Thumbprint

(Tall Baby Thumbprint): Challinor, Taylor & Company, Ltd., Tarentum, Pennsylvania, c. 1880s, clear, non-flint.

Bottle, water	$29-40
Bowl	24-33
Butter dish, covered	34-32
Creamer	27-31
Goblet	22-31
Spoonholder	22-30
Sugar bowl, covered	31-40
Tumbler	24-32

Other pieces.

Challinor's Tree of Life

Challinor's Tree of Life

(Challinor's No. 313): Challinor, Taylor, Ltd., Tarentum, Pennsylvania, 1885-1893, opal, olive green, roseblush pink, turquoise blue, yellow. Pieces were plain or hand-decorated in colors. Non-flint.

Butter dish, covered	$44-52
Can, molasses	19-27
Creamer	21-30
Dish, diamond-shaped	11-20
Jar, cracker (ill.)	48-60
Salt/Pepper, pr.	22-31
Spoonholder	23-31
Sugar bowl, covered	42-50

Hand-decorated pieces, 75 percent higher than plain prices listed.

Chandelier

Chandelier

(Crown Jewels): O'Hara Glass Company, Ltd., 1880s, non-flint.

Bowl, finger $17-26
Celery 38-47
Compote
  a. Covered 79-88
  b. Open 45-53
Creamer, clear or etched 43-52
Pitcher, water (ill.) 77-87
Salt, footed 15-23
Sauce, flat 14-22
Spoonholder 33-39
Sugar
  a. Covered 56-66
  b. Open 32-40

Probably other pieces.

Checkerboard

Westmoreland Glass Company, Grapeville, Pennsylvania, c. 1900, clear, non-flint.

Bowls
  a. Large $24-32
  b. Small 14-21
Butter dish, covered 31-41
Celery 22-31
Cheese dish 24-33
Creamer 25-34
Cruet 20-29
Goblet 18-27
Pitcher, milk 31-40
Salt/Pepper, pr. 20-28
Spoonholder 17-26
Sugar bowl, covered 26-35
Tumbler, iced tea 13-22
Wine 13-22

Kemple Glass Company, East Palestine, Ohio, reproducing some pieces in milk glass.

Cherry

Cherry

Bakewell, Pears & Company, Pittsburgh, Pennsylvania, c. 1870, clear, opal, flint.

Butter dish, covered $56-64
Compote
  a. Covered, high standard 56-65
  b. Open, high and low
    standard 42-51
Creamer 41-51
Goblet (ill.) 30-33
Sauce 14-23
Spoonholder 24-34
Sugar bowl, covered 52-63
Wine 15-24

Opal, 50 percent higher than clear prices listed. Being reproduced in most pieces. Know the original or leave it alone!

Cherry and Fig

Possibly Sandwich, 1880s. Clear. Usual pieces; prices could be compared with those of Circled Scroll.

Cherry Lattice

Northwood Glass Company, 1890s, 1900s. Clear. Non-flint.

Berry set
  a. Large bowl $42-50
  b. Small bowl 13-18
Butter dish, covered 42-50
Compote 33-40
Creamer (ill.) 48-56
Spoonholder 40-50
Sugar bowl, covered 51-60

Possibly other patterns.

Cherry and Fig

Cherry Lattice

Chestnut Oak

Chestnut Oak

(Old Acorn): Possibly Sandwich, early 1870s. Clear.

Butter, covered	$33-40
Celery	17-25
Compote	
a. Covered	34-40
b. Open	23-31
Egg cup	14-19
Goblet	18-27
Pitcher, water	36-44
Sauce, flat	15-25
Spoonholder	19-27
Sugar	
a. Covered	44-52
b. Open	20-30

Chrysanthemum Sprig

Chrysanthemum Sprig

Northwood Glass Company, 1890s. Custard. Non-flint.

Banana boat	$165-180
Berry set	
a. Large bowl	140-150
b. Small bowl	62- 70
Butter dish, covered (ill.)	147-167
Creamer	77- 84
Salt/Pepper, pr.	101-112
Pitcher, water	170-178
Spoonholder	74- 84
Sugar bowl, covered	99-112
Tumbler, water (rare in blue)	52- 61

Probably others. Rare in blue. 100 percent higher than custard prices listed.

Church Windows

(Tulip Petals): U.S. Glass Company, c. 1903, clear, non-flint. They called it "No. 15,082." Previous maker is not known, nor is date known.

Butter dish, covered $46-55
Cake stand 22-31
Celery 19-26
Compote, jelly, covered 38-47
Creamer 24-33
Dish, sardine 18-24
Goblet 17-25
Pitcher, ½ gal. 39-47
Spoonholder 16-24
Sugar bowl
  a. Covered 50-59
  b. Open 32-42

Many other pieces.

Circled Scroll

Circled Scroll

1880s, 1890s. Clear, canary, green, blue, with opalescent edge and trim. Non-flint.

Bowl, berry
  a. Covered $30-40
  b. Open 19-27
Creamer 43-51
Pitcher, water (ill.) 64-72
Sauce, clear.................. 15-22
Sugar
  a. Covered 44-51
  b. Open 24-32
Tumbler 29-37

Probably other pieces. Colored pieces, 50 percent higher than clear prices listed.

Circular Saw

Circular Saw

Maker and date unknown. Clear, some have gilt trim. Non-flint.

Bowl
  a. Berry $19-27
  b. Punch 46-54
Butter dish, covered 29-37
Cracker jar 19-27
Creamer (ill.) 28-34
Saucedish 15-24
Spoonholder 21-30
Sugar bowl, covered 28-37
Tumbler 19-28

Probably other pieces.

Classic

Classic

Gillinder & Sons, 1880s, open and closed feet. Clear, frosted.

Bowl, footed 6¼" dia. ....$ 37- 49
Butter dish, covered, log feet .. 270-290
Celery vase, 6 log feet 228-237
Compote
  a. Covered, open feet 155-170
  b. Open, 6" standard........ 105-115
Creamer 112-120
Goblet 182-192

(continued)

Pitcher
  a. Collared base 260-280
  b. Open, log feet (ill.) 300-320
Plate
  a. President Cleveland 140-155
  b. Blaine, Hendricks, Logan . 150-164
  c. Warrior 155-165
Sauce, open, log feet 38- 44
Spoonholder, open, log feet 92-101
Sugar bowl, covered, very
  large 158-168

Footed type brings 25 percent more than collared base type.

Classic Medallion

Classic Medallion

(Cameo): Another good clear, non-flint glass of the 1880s, non-flint.

Butter dish, covered $30-39
Celery vase 21-30
Compote
  a. Covered 41-50
  b. Open 30-40
Creamer 27-30
Pitcher, water (ill.) 42-51
Spoonholder 22-29
Sugar bowl
  a. Covered 31-42
  b. Open 20-29

Probably other pieces.

Clear Diagonal Band

Late 1880s. Clear, non-flint.
Butter dish $41-50
Celery vase 25-34
Compote
  a. Covered, high standard 43-52
  b. Covered, low standard 32-41

Clear Diagonal Band

Cordial 16-25
Creamer 28-37
Goblet 25-34
Marmalade jar, covered 28-37
Pitcher, water (ill.) 34-44
Platter, "Excelsior" 43-52
Sauces, flat and footed 8-14
Salt/Pepper, pr. 19-28
Spoonholder 19-26
Sugar bowl
  a. Covered 41-50
  b. Open 20-28
Wine 18-26

Probably other pieces.

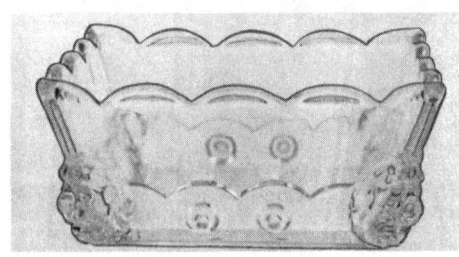

Clear Lion's Head

Clear Lion's Head

(Atlanta): Fostoria Glass Company, Moundsville, West Virginia, 1895. Plain, etched and engraved, non-flint.

Bowl, berry (ill.) $24-33
Butter dish, covered 37-42
Cake stand, large, square 34-40
Compote
  a. Covered, 5", square stem 44-54
  b. Open, 5", square stem 24-33
Creamer 36-42
Goblet 22-30
Jam jar 18-27
Pickle dish 16-24
Salt 11-16
Sauce, flat 13-18

Spoonholder	14-23
Sugar bowl, covered	32-40
Sugar bowl, open	30-40
Toothpick holder	14-19

Clear Stork

Clear Stork

Possibly Mosaic Glass Company, Fostoria, Ohio, 1890-91, non-flint.

Butter dish	$42-50
Compote	60-68
Creamer	39-49
Goblet	33-42
Pitcher, water (ill.)	72-80
Spoonholder	27-34
Sugar bowl, covered	46-55
Tumbler	21-29

Probably other pieces. Frosted Stork prices 60 percent higher than clear prices listed.

Clio

Clio

Challinor, Taylor, Ltd., Tarentum, Pennsylvania, 1885-1891, clear, amber, blue, non-flint.

Butter dish, covered	$31-40
Celery	17-24
Compote, covered (ill.)	26-35
Goblet	19-27
Pitcher, qt., ½ gal.	40-50
Spoonholder	17-26
Sugar bowl, covered	34-44

Probably other pieces.

Coach Bowl

Coach Bowl

McKee & Bros., 1886. Crystal, amber, canary, blue (draft tongue in photo broken off). Also being reproduced in milk glass, amber, purple, blue, other colors.

Coach Bowl (ill.)	$160-185

In colors, 50 percent higher.

Coarse Cut and Block

Coarse Cut and Block

Model Flint Glass Company, Findlay, Ohio, 1880s. Clear, non-flint.

Butter dish	$22-31

(continued)

Celery 17-24
Compote
   a. Covered, high standard 31-40
   b. Open, low standard 19-27
Creamer 24-32
Goblet 14-22
Pitcher, water (ill.) 29-38
Spoonholder 14-21
Sugar bowl, covered 33-40

Probably other pieces.

Cobb

Cobb

(Late Sawtooth; Zipper): Richards & Hartley, Tarentum, Pennsylvania, 1888. Clear. Non-flint.

Butter dish, covered $35-43
Compote, covered 42-51
Creamer
   a. High..................... 26-34
   b. Low 22-30
Goblet 16-22
Pitcher (ill.)................... 38-47
Salt/Pepper, pr. 16-24
Spoonholder 21-30
Sugar bowl 30-40
Tumbler 14-22

Probably other pieces.

Coin

Coin

(Columbian; Spanish, Coin): Made by one of the factories mentioned in Coin, U.S., where they used Spanish coins and possibly some English coins, same date, 1892. Spanish coins are bronzed. Never as collectible as U.S. coins.

Bowl
   a. Berry, 10" $108-115
   b. Finger 66- 75
Butter dish, covered (ill.) 133-150
Cake stand 55- 65
Compote
   a. Covered, 6", 7", 8" 85-125
   b. Open, 7", 8", 10" 65- 75
Creamer 75- 84
Goblet 64- 73
Pitcher, water 72- 82
Salt/Pepper, pr. 60- 70
Sugar bowl, covered 69- 79
Toothpick holder 32- 40
Tumbler 37- 46

Being reproduced. Know your seller!

Coin

Coin

(U.S.): Central Glass Company and Hobbs, Brockunier, Wheeling, West Virginia, for a few months in 1892. Space doesn't allow us to tell all about this glass. Because real coins were used, the Treasury Department made the company stop after only a few months' production. Terribly scarce today. 5¢ piece, 10¢, 25¢, 50¢ and the silver dollar. Clear, frosted, sometimes silvered or gilded. Prices given for indicative pieces. Being skillfully reproduced. Careful! Demand a receipt!

Bowl, berry
a. 25¢ $250-265
b. $1.00 292-310
Bread platter, frosted coins.... 295-330
Butter dish
a. $1.00 560-570
b. 50¢ 495-520
Cake stand
a. $1.00, frosted 460-470
b. 50¢ 430-440
Celery, 50¢ 330-340
Celery, 25¢ 250-260
Compote, covered
a. 50¢, 8″ dia. 560-570
b. 25¢ (ill.) 475-485
c. $1.00, frosted, finial 640-660
Creamer, 25¢ 368-390
Goblet
a. $1.00 362-372
b. 10¢ 340-355
Mug, $1.00 225-245
Pitcher
a. Milk, 50¢............... 465-500
b. Water, $1.00 575-590
Sugar bowl
a. Covered, 50¢, finial 560-600
b. Covered, 25¢, finial 500-550
Toothpick holder, $1.00 160-175
Tumbler
a. $1.00 on base (rare) 250-260
b. 10¢ 235-245
Wine, one-half dime (rare) 330-340

The toothpick holder was reproduced in Indiana a few years ago before the government stopped it. A few reached the market. Now, bread tray (50¢) and tumbler ($1.00 on base) are being reproduced.

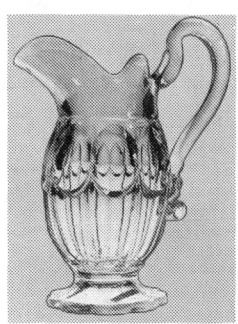

Colonial

Colonial

Sandwich Glass, 1850-1860. Clear, opal or other colors, rare.

Ale glass, tall, footed........... $60-70
Celery glass 62-70
Champagne................... 60-70
Egg cup 16-24
Goblet, knob stem 39-44
Pitcher (ill.)................... 64-73
Spill holder 37-46
Sugar bowl 78-92

Possibly other pieces. Colors, 150 percent higher than clear prices listed.

Colonis

Colonis

(45 Colonis): U.S. Glass Company, 1913. Clear, non-flint.

Butter dish $29-37
Cake stand, 8″ 27-35
Celery vase 20-27
Compote
a. Covered, high standard 31-39
b. Open, low standard 26-34
Cordial 19-29
Creamer 24-36
Dish, oval.................... 14-22
Egg cup 17-23
Goblet 21-30
Pitcher
a. Milk (ill.) 37-46
b. Water 37-42
Sauce 14-21
Spoonholder 17-23
Sugar bowl, covered 36-42
Tray 24-33
Tumbler 20-30

Colorado

Columbia

Colorado

U.S. Glass Company, 1897, another of their "States" series. Crystal glass, both plain, engraved, and crystal with ruby stain. Also green and deep blue with gold decorations. Also amethyst — rare in this color.

Banana bowl	$32-42
Bowl, berry, 6"	14-23
Butter dish, covered	56-66
Cheese dish, low, footed	40-50
Creamer, individual and large ..	25-39
Dish	
a. Crimped edge, 4", 8"	19-27
b. Flared edge, 4", 8"	19-26
Pitcher, water (ill.)	68-83
Salt/Pepper, pr.	24-34
Spoonholder	27-39
Sugar bowl	
a. Individual	27-37
b. Large, covered	54-64
Toothpick holder	24-34
Tumbler	22-32

Ruby, 20 percent; blue, 55 percent; green, 100 percent; amethyst, 200 percent higher than clear prices listed.

Columbia

U.S. Glass Company, 1907. Clear. Probably others earlier, non-flint.

Bowl, 7", 8", 9", 10"	$22-36
Butter dish, covered	27-36
Celery tray	17-24
Creamer (ill.)	21-30
Custard cup...................	17-25
Dish	13-20
a. Olive	18-26
b. Sundae	25-34

Pitcher, water.................	31-40
Relish bowl	14-22
Salt/Pepper, pr.	18-25
Spoonholder	19-27
Sugar bowl, covered	24-30
Tumbler	18-27

At least 125 different pieces were made in this pattern.

Comet

Comet

Sandwich Glass, c. late 1840s, clear, flint. Don't confuse this rare glass with McKee Brothers' glass of the same name, c. 1887.

Goblet (ill.)	$ 84- 97
Pitcher, water	390-425
Tumbler, whiskey, water......	133-146

Possibly other pieces.

Concaved Almond

Concaved Almond

Maker unknown, used for souvenir purposes in 1890s, a style created at the Chicago Exposition in 1893. Emerald green, ruby stain.

Goblet $26-32
Pitcher, water (ill.) 44-53
Toothpick..................... 22-31

Probably other pieces. Colors, 50 percent higher than clear prices listed.

Connecticut

U.S. Glass Company, c. 1898, clear, non-flint.

Bowls, 4", 6", 8" $13-23
Butter dish, covered 26-36
Cake stand, 10" 44-53
Celery tray 14-23
Creamer 20-29
Pitcher, tankard, 3 types 32-41
Salt/Pepper, pr. 17-27
Tumbler 13-21
Wine 17-26

Many other pieces.

Continental

A. H. Heisey Company, Newark, Ohio, 1903. Not all pieces marked with "Diamond H."

Butter dish
   a. Covered $36-42
   b. Covered, footed 40-52
Creamer
   a. Flat 30-39
   b. Footed 34-53

Continental

Pitcher, water (ill.) 77-84
Spoonholder
   a. Flat 30-40
   b. Footed 33-42
Sugar bowl
   a. Covered 43-49
   b. Covered, footed 52-60

Prices are for signed pieces.

Continental Bread Tray

Continental Bread Tray

Another in the series of historical plates sold at the Philadelphia Exposition in 1876. Clear only. Atterbury and Company, Pittsburgh.

Plate, 13" by 9" (ill.) $110-125

Coolidge Drape

Coolidge Drape

Maker unknown, 1880. Clear and cobalt (blue) in several sizes. Lamp famous because this was pattern of lamp in room in which Coolidge took presidential oath after Harding's sudden death.

Any size in clear .... $ 94-108
Any size in cobalt 160-175

Cord and Tassel

Cord and Tassel

Central Glass Company, 1872. Clear.

Bowl, oval	$16-26
Butter dish, covered	44-54
Cake stand, high standard	38-47
Celery	35-45
Compote, high standard	77-87
Cordial	24-34
Creamer, applied handle	45-54
Egg cup	27-36
Goblet	33-43
Lamp, applied handle	64-74
Mug	17-26
Pitcher, water (ill.)	60-70
Sauce	12-20
Spoonholder	32-41
Sugar bowl, covered	45-55
Wine	27-36

Probably other pieces.

Cord Drapery

Cord Drapery

(Indiana): Indiana Tumbler & Goblet (National) Company, Greentown, Indiana, 1900. Clear, amber, blue, green, chocolate, opal.

Berry bowl	$18-25
Butter dish, clear	22-34
Cake plate	24-34
Compote	
a. Stemmed, large	50-60
b. Stemmed, covered, jelly	34-44
c. Stemmed, fluted	52-62

Creamer	17-26
Goblet	17-32
Pitcher, water (ill.)	80-90
Spoonholder	15-22
Salt/Pepper, pr.	12-19
Tumbler	14-21

Chocolate, 400 percent higher; other colors, 300 percent higher than clear prices listed.

Cordova

Cordova

O'Hara Glass Company, Pittsburgh, 1890. Clear, non-flint.

Bowl	
a. Covered	$17-26
b. Finger	14-19
c. Open	16-25
Butter dish	28-38
Cake stand	32-42
Celery	24-32
Compote, covered and open,	
high standard	33-42
Creamer	25-34
Cruet	21-30
Inkwell (rare)	65-75
Pitcher	
a. Syrup (ill.)	30-38
b. Water	42-51
Spoonholder	19-28
Sugar bowl	31-41
Tumbler	19-28

Probably made in other pieces.

Coreopsis

Possibly, Dalzell, Gilmore & Leighton Company, Findlay, Ohio, c. 1888, white opaque.

Butter dish, covered	$82-97
Creamer	67-82
Spoonholder	48-62
Sugar bowl, covered	82-94

Probably other pieces.

Cornucopia

Cornucopia

Maker unknown, 1885-1890. Clear, fine fruit group on reverse side.

Butter dish, covered $29-46
Celery 16-27
Compote, covered 32-39
Creamer 16-27
Goblet 14-24
Pitcher, water (ill.) 43-60
Spoonholder 14-24
Sugar bowl, covered 29-42

Probably other pieces.

Cosmos

Cosmos

(Stemless Daisy): Probably Dithridge & Son, New Brighton, Pennsylvania, 1900. Opaque.

Butter dish, open and covered
  (ill.) $220-240
Caster set; salt/pepper,
  mustard 240-260
Creamer 135-144
Lamps
  a. Large, round with shade.. 192-210
  b. Miniature with shade 145-155
  c. Miniature, base only 120-130
Lemonade pitcher with 6 mugs. 750-800
Pitcher, water, 8¾″ high 250-265

Salt/Pepper, pr. 115-125
Spoonholder 93-102
Sugar bowl, covered 190-205
Tumbler 70- 80

Probably other pieces.

Cottage

Cottage

(Dinner Bell; Fine Cut Band): Adams & Company, Pittsburgh, 1874. Clear, dark green (rare), amber.

Butter dish, covered $31-41
Cake stand, 9″ high 34-43
Celery vase 23-32
Compote, covered and open,
  high standard 31-41
Creamer 23-32
Cruet, w/stopper.............. 28-37
Fruit bowl, high standard 31-40
Goblet 20-28
Pitcher, pint, quart, half
  gallon, amber 37-47
Plate, 6″, 7″, 8″, 9″ 18-25
Salt/Pepper, pr. 23-31
Spoonholder 20-29
Sugar bowl, covered 32-41
Tray, water 24-33
Tumbler 19-27
Wine...................... 17-26

Probably other pieces made. Colors 70 percent higher than clear prices listed. Dark green considered rare.

Cow

Maker unknown, c. 1870s, clear, non-flint.

Butter dish, covered, 6″ long $85-94

Cradled Prisms

Probably Challinor, Taylor, Ltd., c. late 1880s, clear, non-flint.

Butter dish, covered $32-41
Creamer, footed 24-32
Spoonholder 15-24
Sugar bowl, covered 26-35

Probably other pieces.

Croesus

Croesus

Riverside Glass Works, Wellsville, West Virginia, 1897. Crystal, emerald, royal purple (amethyst), gold trim.

Bowl, berry . . . . $ 70- 80
Butter dish 110-120
Celery 67- 76
Creamer, regular 67- 78
Cruet 79- 89
Pickle dish 32- 38
Pitcher, water (ill.) 100-115
Salt/Pepper, pr. 48- 56
Spoonholder 45- 55
Sugar bowl 92-107
Toothpick holder 43- 52
Tumbler 34- 42

Emerald green, 125 percent; amethyst, 250 percent higher than clear prices listed. Entire table set being reproduced in Japan.

Crossed Block

Possibly Hartley & Richards, late 1800s. Clear, non-flint.

Butter dish, covered $41-50
Creamer (ill.) 28-37

Crossed Block

Spoonholder 19-28
Sugar bowl, covered 41-50

Probably other pieces.

Crossed Fern

Atterbury & Company, Pittsburgh, Pennsylvania, c. 1876, clear, opal, turquoise, non-flint.

Bowl, collared $14-22
Butter dish, covered 27-36
Compote, covered 29-38
Creamer 14-22
Pitcher 31-40
Spoonholder 17-25
Sugar bowl, covered 21-30
Tumbler 14-23

Opal, turquoise, 40 percent higher than clear prices listed.

Crossed Ferns with Ball and Claw

Atterbury & Company, c. 1876, clear, opal, turquoise, non-flint. Same prices as "Crossed Fern" — see.

Crossed Shield

Crossed Shield

Fostoria Glass Company's No. 1303, late 1890s. Clear, non-flint.

Butter dish, covered $30-39
Creamer 31-40
Compotes, several sizes 27-46
Cordial 15-24
Decanter 44-53
Egg cup 16-25
Goblet 17-26
Pitcher, water, (ill.) 47-56
Spoonholder 16-25
Sugar bowl, covered 25-34
Tumbler 19-27

Probably other pieces.

Crystal

McKee Brothers, Pittsburgh, c. 1859, clear, flint.

Ale glass $37- 47
Bowl, covered 55- 65
Celery....................... 52- 61
Compote, covered, high standard 59- 69
Creamer..................... 67- 75
Decanter, qt.................. 62- 72
Egg cup 32- 42
Goblet....................... 37- 46
Pitcher, water 89-100
Spoonholder 38- 46
Sugar bowl, covered 78- 88

Other pieces.

Crystal Wedding

Crystal Wedding

(Crystal Anniversary): Adams Glass Company, early 1880s. Clear, amber, canary, blue, non-flint.

Banana stand $58-67
Butter dish, covered 42-51

Cake stand, high standard 68-78
Celery 32-41
Compote
  a. Open, low standard 39-48
  b. Covered, high standard (ill.) . 77-87
  c. Covered, low standard 58-68
Creamer, clear 35-44
Goblet 32-41
Pitcher 56-65
Salt/Pepper, pr. 32-41
Spoonholder 29-37
Sugar bowl, covered 43-53
Tumbler 23-33

Probably other pieces. Goblet and compote being reproduced. Colors 100 percent more than clear prices listed.

Cube with Fan

U.S. Glass Company, c. 1900, clear, non-flint.

Bowl, finger...................$16-24
Celery 18-25
Dish, jelly 14-21
Goblet 16-22
Plates, 5", 7½"................. 13-23
Sugar bowl, covered 25-34
Tumbler 14-21

Many other pieces.

Cupid and Venus

Cupid and Venus

(Guardian Angel): Richard & Hartley Glass Company, Pittsburgh (Birmingham), Pennsylvania, 1875-1884. Clear, yellow, amber, non-flint.

(continued)

Butter dish $66-75
Cake plate, 11" 46-54
Celery 45-55
Champagne................... 58-67
Compote
  a. Covered, high and low
    standard 57-71
  b. Open, high standard 46-56
Creamer, footed 45-53
Jam jar, covered (ill.) 54-64
Mug, 2", 2½", 3½" 33-48
Pickle caster 65-75
Pitcher, large and small 58-67
Plate, bread, 10½" 34-43
Plate, bread, handles 35-44
Sauce
  a. Flat, round 10-14
  b. Footed, 3½", 4", 5" 8-14
Spoonholder 36-45
Sugar bowl, covered 62-69
Wine (scarce) 24-85

Probably other pieces. Color, 40 percent higher than clear prices listed.

Currant

Currant

Sandwich glass, 1870s. Later, Campbell, Jones & Company, Pittsburgh, 1870s. Crystal.

Butter dish $61-70
Cake plate on stand, 2 types 65-74
Celery vase 45-54
Compote
  a. Covered 8", high foot 60-68
  b. Covered, 8", 9", low foot 56-65
Cordial 34-40
Creamer 54-63
Dish, oval, 6" x 9", 5" x 7" 22-31
Egg cup 22-30
Goblets, 5½", 6" 32-44
Pitcher, water (ill.) 66-75
Spoonholder 29-38
Sugar bowl, covered 56-64

Tumbler, footed 32-39
Wine 34-42
Probably other pieces.

Currier and Ives

Currier and Ives

Bellaire Goblet Company, Findlay, Ohio, 1880s. Clear, rare in colors — amber, blue. Non-flint.

Butter dish, covered $55-64
Cordial 24-32
Creamer 29-36
Cup and saucer 33-43
Goblet, knob stem 25-34
Lamp, No. 2, complete w/burner
  and chimney 34-44
Pitcher, large and small 38-48
Salt/Pepper, pr. 43-52
Spoonholder 23-32
Sugar bowl, covered 47-57
Tray, "Balky Mule on RR
  Tracks" 57-66
Wine 20-30

Probably other pieces. Color, 250 percent higher than clear prices listed.

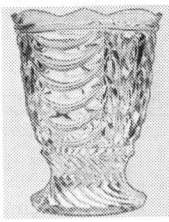
Curtain

Curtain

(Sultan): Bryce Bros., Pittsburgh, 1875-1885. Clear, non-flint.

Bowl, covered, 6", 7", 8" $20-34
Bowl, open, 6", 7", 8" 17-29

Butter dish 48-57
Cake plate on stand 34-43
Celery boat 32-40
Compote
  a. Covered, high standard,
    6″, 7″, 8″ 45-54
  b. Open, high standard,
    7″, 8″, 10″ 39-48
Creamer 40-47
Goblet 31-39
Mug, large 21-30
Pitcher, quart, half gallon 54-64
Salt/Pepper, pr. 29-37
Spoonholder (ill.) 31-40
Sugar bowl 41-46
Tumbler 25-33

Probably other pieces.

Curtain Tieback

Maker unknown, c. mid-1880s, clear, non-flint. Two types of feet.

Bowl, berry, 7″ square $12-21
Butter dish, covered 24-32
Celery 13-21
Creamer 16-24
Goblet 18-26
Pitcher, water................. 32-40
Spoonholder 12-19
Sugar bowl, open 16-24
Tumbler 14-22
Wine....................... 13-21

Other pieces.

Dahlia

Dahlia

Canton Glass Company, Canton, Ohio, 1880s. Clear, amber, vaseline, blue, green. Amber and yellow are scarce.

Butter dish $48-57
Cake plate on stand 34-39
Champagne................... 47-56
Compote, large, covered, high
  standard 58-67
Cordial 32-42
Creamer 26-35
Egg cup, double (rare) 50-58
Goblet, etched (scarce) 45-54
Mug, handled, 2 sizes 35-45
Pitcher, water, milk (ill.) 42-51
Platter, grape handles, oval 34-44
Spoonholder 29-36
Sugar bowl, open 27-36
Wine........................ 39-47

Colors 30-50 percent higher than clear prices listed. Amber, yellow, 150 percent higher.

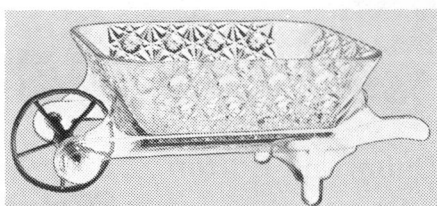
Daisy and Button

Daisy and Button

Gillinder and Sons, Philadelphia, 1876, in time for the Centennial; also, Hobbs, Brockunier and Company, Wheeling, West Virginia. Souvenir items were extremely popular at the Fair. This D & B wheelbarrow with metal wheel is rare today. It can be seen at the Houston Museum.

No single glass pattern has been or is being reproduced more than Daisy and Button in all its variations. Collect it if you like it but not because you think you're getting a bargain. KNOW YOUR DEALER!

Daisy and Button

Daisy and Button

One of the rarest pieces ever made is this "Helmet" covered butter dish. Don't look for it in shops. You can see this one at the Houston Museum in Chattanooga.

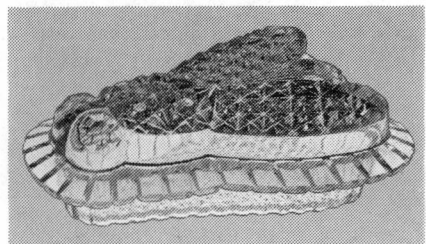

Daisy and Button

Daisy and Button

Another rarity in the D & B pattern is the "Bee" covered dish. I honestly believe that every original D & B pattern is being reproduced today. Be so terribly careful when you buy. Make sure your dealer is an authority before you buy! This "Bee" is at the Houston Museum.

Daisy and Button

Daisy and Button

This is a rare blue creamer with clear handle. Probably Hobbs, Brockunier and Company. We're showing you four different D & B pieces to show you how many, many different pieces were made. Enjoy looking. But save your money!

Daisy and Button,
Oval Medallion

Daisy and Button, Oval Medallion

One of the most popular patterns ever produced in this country.

Usual D & B prices. But, do be careful!

Daisy and Button, Oxford

Daisy and Button, Oxford

Sandwich, early. Clear and colored.

Clear shoe $45-52
Amber, canary shoe 45-52
Blue shoe 61-70

What one sees today in shops are reproductions. Watch it!

Daisy and Button, Panelled

Here again another of the D & B patterns. Too many reproductions to take a chance on this or any other D & B pat-

Daisy and Button, Panelled

tern. This pattern is rare in two colors —
amber and clear — but don't worry about
finding it outside of in a museum such as
the Houston Museum in Chattanooga,
Tennessee. Save your money.

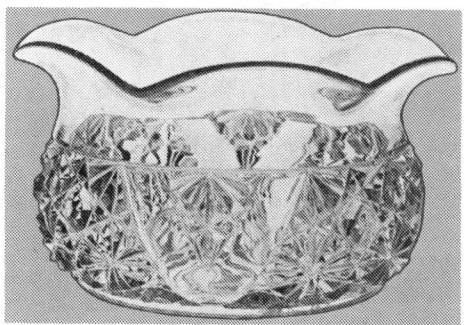

Daisy and Button "V"

Daisy and Button "V"

A. J. Beatty & Company, 1886-1887,
Clear.

Just as many patterns reproduced in
this "V" as in D & B. Not worth discuss-
ing. You're buying new unless you're
an expert.

Daisy and Button with Narcissus

(Clear Lily): Another D & B, maker unknown, late 1880s. Clear. Sometimes
flashed with gold, non-flint.

Butter dish	$25-33
Celery	18-26
Compote, open	24-33
Creamer	20-29
Decanter	40-50
Goblet	14-22

Daisy and Button with Narcissus

Pickle dish	11-18
Pitcher, water (ill.)	36-44
Sauce, 4″	13-22
Salt/Pepper, pr.	14-22
Spoonholder	15-23
Sugar bowl, covered	22-31
Tumbler	17-24
Wine	12-21

Probably other pieces. Wine being
reproduced, also bowls and vases.

Daisy and Button with Prisms

Daisy and Button with Prisms

It sounds like a broken record but save
your breath on these D & B patterns with
variations such as below. Just about
every genuine piece has been reproduced
and they're good. Buy it for what it is —
new — and enjoy it as such. But don't put
your money into it unless you know it
yourself. Few dealers can tell you
whether it's old.

Daisy and Thumbprint Cross-Bar

Daisy and Thumbprint Cross-Bar

(Mikado): Richards and Hartley Flint Glass Company, 1888. Clear, yellow, amber, light and dark, blue. Non-flint.

Bowl, flat, 6″, 8″ $14-22
Butter dish, flat, footed 32-40
Catsup bottle 21-30
Compote
  a. Covered, 7″, 8″ 36-49
  b. Open, 7″, 8″ 22-34
Creamer, regular (ill.) 20-30
Cruet 20-30
Goblet 20-29
Lamps, 4 sizes................. 24-57
Pitcher, quart, half gallon 35-46
Salt/Pepper, pr. 16-24
Spoonholder 18-27
Sugar bowl, covered 28-36
Tumbler 14-22
Wine........................ 14-21

Probably other pieces. Amber, yellow, 40 percent higher; blue, 100 percent higher than clear prices listed.

Daisy in Diamond

O'Hara Glass Company, Pittsburgh, 1886. Crystal, amber, rose, blue, non-flint.

Butter dish, covered $24-33
Celery 16-22
Creamer 20-29
Egg cup 12-19
Goblet 13-22
Pitcher, water (ill.) 28-37
Spoonholder 16-23
Sugar bowl, covered 22-31
Tumbler 16-24

Probably other pieces. Colors, 100-125 percent higher than clear prices listed.

Daisy in Diamond

Daisy Medallion

Daisy Medallion

(Sunburst Medallion): Maker unknown, 1880s. Clear, non-flint.

Butter dish, covered $20-29
Cake stand 17-26
Compote 18-27
Creamer 16-24
Pitcher 24-32
Spoonholder (ill.) 14-22
Sugar bowl, covered 20-29

Probably other pieces.

Daisy Whorl

Maker unknown, 1870s. Clear, also in colors.

Butter dish, covered $23-31
Compote
  a. Covered 26-34
  b. Open 18-26

Daisy Whorl

Goblet	16-24
Pitcher, water (ill.)	36-44
Spoonholder	12-20
Sugar bowl	
a. Covered	28-36
b. Open	18-27

Probably other pieces. Colors 50-75 percent higher than clear prices listed.

Dakota

Dakota

(Baby Thumbprint; Thumbprint Band): Doyle & Company, Pittsburgh, 1890s. Clear, red-flashed, non-flint.

Bowl, berry	$30-36
Butter dish, covered, etched	52-58
Cake stand, 10″	46-56
Celery, flat base	44-52
Compote, covered, 5″, 6″, 7″, 8″	46-62
Creamer, pedestal base	36-44
Goblet, etched	34-44
Pitcher, water, etched (ill.)	77-86
Salt/Pepper, pr.	33-42
Spoonholder	35-44
Sugar bowl, covered, etched	47-57
Tray, water, 13″	46-55
Tumbler	35-43
Wine	30-40

Probably other pieces. Red-flashed, 50 percent higher than clear.

Dancing Goat

Possibly, LaBelle Glass Company, Bridgeport, Ohio, c. 1878, clear, non-flint.

Ale glass	$52-61

Dart

Maker unknown, c. 1880, clear, non-flint.

Butter dish, covered	$22-31
Creamer	19-27
Goblet	12-21
Sauce	8-12
Spoonholder	13-22
Sugar bowl, covered	22-31

Other pieces.

Deer and Oak Tree

Deer and Oak Tree

Dalzell, Gilmore & Leighton, Findlay, Ohio; also, Indiana Tumbler & Goblet (National) Company, Greentown, Indiana. National took over both factories in 1889.

Pitcher, water (ill.)	$142-160

Chocolate color, 150 percent higher than clear price listed.

Deer and Pine Tree

(Deer and Doe): Sandwich glass, 1860s. Clear, blue, amber, green, yellow, non-flint.

Bowl, waste, green	$64- 73
Butter dish, covered, clear	70- 79
Cake plate on standard, clear	75- 84
Celery, clear	55- 63

(continued)

Deer and Pine Tree

Compote, covered, oblong, large	95-108
Creamer, clear	55- 65
Goblet, clear	45- 53
Jam jar	48- 55
Pickle dish, oblong, deep	26- 34
Pitcher, large and small, clear	62- 84
Plate, bread, amber	54- 63
Plate, bread, clear	41- 50
Plate, bread, green	52- 61
Platter, 13¼" x 8", clear	55- 63
Sauce, flat and footed	14- 22
Spoonholder, clear	46- 52
Sugar bowl, covered, clear	56- 64
Tray, large, 11" x 15", handled	82- 92

Probably other pieces.
Colors, 60 percent higher than clear prices listed.

Delaware

Delaware

(New Century): U.S. Glass Company, 1899. Crystal glass with rose stain ·and gilt trim; also, green glass with gilt trim; amethyst (rare), non-flint.

Bowl, round, fluted, boat-shaped, banana	$44-54
Butter dish	81-91
Celery	28-38
Creamer	38-47
Cruet	44-53
Pitcher, water (ill.)	65-78

Spoonholder	54-63
Sugar bowl, covered	69-82
Toothpick holder	23-33
Tumbler	33-42

Probably other pieces. Colors, 100 to 150 percent higher than clear prices listed. Amethyst, rare, 400 percent higher.

Dewdrop and Flowers

Dewdrop and Flowers

Probably originated at Sandwich; late 1870s, early 1880s. Clear.

Butter dish, covered	$27-36
Compote	
a. Covered	38-48
b. Open	22-31
Creamer	22-31
Goblet	19-29
Pitcher, milk (ill.)	36-44
Spoonholder	10-17
Sugar bowl	
a. Covered	25-32
b. Open	18-27
Wine	14-21

Dewdrop and Raindrop

Dewdrop and Raindrop

Kokomo Glass Manufacturing Company, Kokomo, Indiana, 1900-1905. Clear, clear/gilded, clear/ruby, non-flint.

Bowl, berry $14-23
Butter dish 28-36
Cordial, set of 6, each 20-27
Creamer 26-35
Cup, sherbet 12-20
Goblet 22-31
Pitcher, water (ill.) 38-44
Sauce 12-17
Salt/Pepper, pr. 21-30
Spoonholder 16-24
Sugar bowl 27-34
Tumbler 17-24
Wine 19-27

Cordial, goblet, sherbet cup and wine
being reproduced.

Dewdrop in Points

Dewdrop in Points

Greensburg Glass Company, Greensburg, Pennsylvania, probably 1875-1885.
Clear, non-flint.

Butter, covered $34-43
Cake stand, large 39-48
Compote
  a. Covered 63-73
  b. Open 47-56
Creamer, covered 40-49
Goblet 31-39
Pickle dish, oval 14-20
Pitcher (ill.) 70-80
Plate, bread 21-28
Sauce, footed 14-17
Spoonholder 27-36
Sugar bowl, covered 40-49

Probably other pieces.

Dewdrop with Star

Dewdrop with Star

Campbell, Jones & Company, Pittsburgh, 1877. Clear, non-flint.

Butter dish, covered, star base . . $60-70
Cake plate on standard 60-69
Celery, star in base 49-58
Compote
  a. Covered, high and low
    standard 72-87
  b. Covered, footed, 6″, 7″,
    star base 60-70
Creamer, star base 42-51
Goblet 40-48
Pickle dish 22-29
Pitcher, water (ill.) 82-92
Plates, 4½″ thru 11″ 19-32
Sauce, flat and footed 12-19
Spoonholder 29-38
Sugar bowl, covered, star base . . 47-55
Tumbler 27-36

Probably other pieces. The 7¼″ plate
and salt and probably footed sauces are
being reproduced.

Dewey

Dewey

(Flower Flange): Indiana Tumbler &
Goblet Company, 1898. Crystal, canary,
green, amber, blue, chocolate.

Bowl, berry $17-26
Butter dish, covered (ill.) 42-51

(continued)

Creamer 31-40
Cruet 43-51
Mug 38-47
Pitcher, water, 9½″ high 50-58
Salt/Pepper, pr. 34-42
Serpentine tray 29-37
Spoonholder 23-32
Sugar bowl 39-47
Tumbler 25-33

Other pieces were made. Chocolate, 300 percent higher; other colors, 70 percent higher than clear prices listed.

Diagonal Band

Diagonal Band

A pattern of the 1800s; clear. Apple green, scarce.

Prices almost identical with Diagonal Band with Fan, except apple green 100 percent higher than clear prices listed.

Diagonal Band with Fan

Diagonal Band with Fan

Maker unknown. Clear, 1880s.

Butter dish $38-47
Celery vase 23-32
Compote, high and low foot 29-39
Cordial 12-20
Creamer 28-37
Goblet 24-29
Pitcher, milk, 8″ (ill.) 40-49
Plate, 6″, 7″, 8″ 12-24
Sauce, footed, 4″, 4½″ 11-20
Salt/Pepper, pr. 28-38
Spoonholder 24-33
Sugar bowl 37-46
Wine 17-25

Probably other pieces.

Diamond and Sunburst

Diamond and Sunburst

Maker unknown, late 1860s. Clear. Non-flint.

Butter dish, covered $27-37
Cake stand 26-35
Celery vase 20-28
Compote
  a. Covered 32-41
  b. Open 17-26
Creamer, applied handle 24-33
Decanter 32-41
Egg cup 16-24
Goblet 23-32
Pitcher, water (ill.) 40-49
Spoonholder 21-29
Sugar bowl, covered 34-43
Tumbler 21-30

Probably other pieces.

Diamond Band

(Prism and Diamond Band): Central Glass Company, Wheeling, West Virginia, c. 1870, clear, non-flint.

Butter dish, covered $37-45
Celery 16-24
Compote, small, footed 32-40
Creamer 30-39
Dish, shallow 7-16
Goblet 17-26
Pitcher, water 30-40
Spoonholder 14-22
Sugar bowl, covered 34-41
Wine 16-23

Other pieces.

Diamond Block with Fans

(Blockade): Challinor, Taylor, Ltd., c. 1880s, clear, non-flint. It was their "No. 309." The pattern may have been continued by U.S. Glass Company after 1891.

Bowl, waste $16-24
Butter dish, covered 38-46
Celery 20-29
Creamer 24-33
Goblet 23-32
Pitcher, water 38-46
Spoonholder 16-24
Sugar bowl, covered 39-47

Many other pieces.

Diamond Mirror

Diamond Mirror

Maker unknown, late 1880s. Clear. Non-flint.

Butter dish, covered $26-35
Celery 14-22
Creamer 14-23
Spoonholder (ill.) 17-24
Sugar bowl
  a. Covered 26-35
  b. Open 17-26

Probably other pieces.

Diamond Point

Diamond Point

Sandwich glass, 1830; Bryce, Richards & Co., Pittsburgh, c. 1854; others, c. 1880s. Clear, rare in colors. Flint.

Ale glass $42- 50
Butter dish 86- 96
Celery 69- 78
Compote
  a. Covered, 6″, 7″, 8″, high
    and low standard 90-135
  b. Open, 6″, 7″, 8″, high and
    low standard 52- 61
Creamer, footed, scalloped 87- 97
Egg cup (rare in color) 42- 52
Goblet, large and small 55- 70
Pitcher, half pint, pint, quart . . 60-140
Plates, 3″ thru 8″ 22- 58
Spoonholder 59- 68
Sugar bowl, covered 95-120
Tumbler, jelly, water, whiskey . . 40- 89

Probably other pieces.
Color, 400 percent higher, opaque, 150 percent higher than clear prices listed.

Diamond Point Discs

(continued)

Diamond Point Discs

Probably made at Findlay, Ohio, late 1880s. Clear. Non-flint.

Butter dish, covered	$24-32
Cake stand	29-36
Celery	14-22
Compote	
a. Covered, 7″, 8″, high standard	30-38
b. Covered, 7″, 9″, colored base	35-48
Creamer	18-26
Goblet	16-24
Pitcher	40-47
Salt/Pepper, pr.	12-21
Spoonholder	18-26
Sugar bowl, covered	30-38

Probably other pieces.

Diamond Quilted

Butter dish, covered	$44-53
Creamer	29-37
Goblet	27-37
Pitcher, water	40-49
Sauce, footed (ill.)	11-16
Spoonholder	28-36
Sugar bowl, covered	34-39
Tray, water	31-39
Tumbler	17-24

Canary, 100 percent; light blue, 150 percent; light, dark amethyst, 200 percent higher than clear prices listed. Probably many other pieces.

Diamond Point with Panels

Diamond Point with Panels

(Hinoto): Boston and Sandwich Glass Company, 1850s. Clear, flint.

Celery	$108-117
Champagne	65- 74
Goblet	74- 82
Pitcher (ill.)	136-145
Salt, footed	40- 47
Spoonholder	42- 50
Sugar bowl	77- 84

Diamond Quilted

Maker unknown, c. 1880s, clear, many colors, non-flint.

Diamond Rosettes

Diamond Rosettes

Several Pittsburgh factories, 1870s until early 1900s. Clear, sometimes found in color — yellow, blue, light green. Non-flint.

Butter dish, covered	$28-37
Bowl	15-24
Celery holder	17-26
Compote	28-36
Compote, covered	41-50
Creamer	22-31
Goblet (ill.)	17-26
Pitcher, water	39-48
Spoonholder	15-24
Sugar bowl	
a. Covered	24-33
b. Open	13-21

Tumbler 15-24

Probably many other pieces. Color, 50 percent higher than clear prices listed.

Diamond Sunburst

(Plain Sunburst): Bryce, Walker & Company, Pittsburgh, c. 1860s, clear, non-flint.

Butter dish, covered $34-44
Cake stand 29-38
Celery 27-36
Compote, covered, high standard . 46-55
Creamer 29-37
Goblet 29-37
Lamp 29-38
Pitcher, milk 33-43
Spoonholder 21-31
Sugar bowl, covered 40-50
Tumbler 19-29
Wine 18-27

Probably other pieces.

Diamond Thumbprint

Diamond Thumbprint

(Diamond and Concave): Sandwich glass; McKee & Bros., 1850s. Clear, green-tinted, amethyst (due to improper mixing of metal), and yellow (rare), flint.

Bowl, waste.................$ 94-105
Butter dish, covered 155-165
Cake stand, 2 sizes 230-260
Celery 210-220
Champagne.................. 240-260
Decanter, original stopper 145-155
Goblet (rare) 370-400
Pitcher, water (ill.) 340-365
Spoonholder 80- 90
Sugar bowl, 2 styles 168-188
Wine jug, places for holding glasses, set .... 500+

This glass is extremely rare.

Diapered Flower

Diapered Flower

Probably Westmoreland Glass Company, 1890s. Opaque blue. Sandwich made it earlier. It was a container for mustard or other condiments. Non-flint.

Mustard jar (ill.) $49-57

Probably other pieces.

Dickinson

Dickinson

Sandwich glass, 1860s. Clear. Flint.

Butter dish, covered $44- 53
Compote	
a. Covered.................. 72- 81
b. Open (ill.) 52- 61
Creamer..................... 92-110
Goblet....................... 87- 96
Sauce, flat 19- 28
Spoonholder 56- 64
Sugar	
a. Covered.................. 47- 57
b. Open 30- 39
Pitcher, water 79- 89
Wine 24- 32

Possibly other pieces.

Divided Block with Sunburst

Divided Block with Sunburst

(Variant): U.S. Glass Company, after 1891. Crystal, plain and with ruby stain. Non-flint.

Butter dish, covered	$32-40
Celery vase	12-20
Compote, covered, high or low standard	24-33
Creamer	18-27
Goblet	15-24
Pitcher, water (ill.)	33-42
Salt/Pepper, pr.	12-21
Spoonholder	16-24
Sugar bowl, covered	28-36
Tumbler	15-24

Probably other pieces.

Divided Hearts

Boston & Sandwich Glass Company, c. early 1860s, clear, flint.

Butter dish, covered	$127-136
Compote	
a. Covered	115-128
b. Open	98-112
Creamer	106-114
Egg cup	65- 74
Goblet	86- 94
Lamp, marble base	115-125
Sugar bowl, covered	128-137

Possibly other pieces.

Dog

Possibly Sandwich, c. 1870s, clear, non-flint.

Compote, covered, low	$72-81
Compote, covered, high	86-94

"Dog and Child" Mug

"Dog and Child" Mug

Indiana Tumbler & Goblet Company, (National), Greentown, Indiana, 1902. Chocolate, Nile green. Non-flint.

Chocolate	$215-225
Nile green	232-242

Rare!

Dog Hunting

Dog Hunting

One of a series of animal designs put out by National Glass Company, Greentown, Indiana, before the plant was destroyed by fire in 1903. Non-flint.

Pitcher, water (ill.)	$200-220
Probably tumbler to match	77- 84

Dolphin

Dolphin

Sandwich, 1850s; McKee Bros., 1868; Bakewell, Pears & Company, 1868. Clear. Don't confuse it with Greentown's Dolphin covered dish.

Butter dish, covered	$160-170
Compote, high standard	90-100
Creamer	110-120
Goblet	110-120
Pitcher, water (ill.)	165-180
Spoonholder	82- 91
Sugar bowl, covered	115-130

Possibly other pieces.

"Dolphin"

"Dolphin"

Covered dish, Indiana Tumbler & Goblet Company, 1899. Clear, chocolate, blue. Non-flint.

Clear	$118-127
Blue	256-264
Chocolate	180-190

Double Beetle Band

Double Beetle Band

(Smocking Bands): Columbia Glass Company, Findlay, Ohio, 1880s. Clear, yellow, amber, blue. Non-flint.

Butter dish, covered	$29-38
Creamer	24-33
Goblet	19-27
Pitcher (ill.)	42-51
Sauce, footed, flat	14-23
Spoonholder	14-22
Sugar bowl	
a. Covered	28-36
b. Open	19-26

Probably other pieces. Yellow, 50 percent higher; amber and blue, 100 percent higher than clear prices listed.

Double Dahlia and Lens

Possibly an early Northwood or Fenton pattern of the late 1880s or early 1890s. The background is stippled on each panel, the flowers are stained purple, foliage green, on crystal background. Scrolls at top and over lip are in bright gold. At least in table set and probably other pieces. Non-flint.

461

(continued)

Double Dahlia and Lens

Butter dish, covered	$47-56
Creamer (ill.)	37-46
Spoonholder	29-38
Sugar bowl, covered	42-51

Double Donut

Double Donut

Findlay, Ohio, 1880s. Clear. Non-flint.

Butter dish	$24-33
Cake stand	24-32
Celery	17-25
Compote, open, low standard	32-41
Creamer	17-26
Goblet	17-26
Pitcher (ill.)	35-44
Salt/Pepper, pr.	15-24
Spoonholder	16-25
Sugar bowl	24-33

Probably other pieces.

Double Greek Key

This is Canadian glass, made by the Burlington Glass Works, Hamilton,

Double Greek Key

Ontario, 1880s. Clear, stippled, opaque white, blue.

Butter dish, covered	$94-104
Compote, covered	62- 72
Creamer	36- 45
Pitcher (ill.)	84- 94
Spoonholder	30- 38
Sugar bowl, covered	55- 65
Tassi (small compote), 6″	44- 53
Tumbler	38- 47

Probably other pieces. Don't overlook Canadian glass. Most of it is well made and most collectible. Color 50 percent more than clear prices listed.

Double Ribbon

Double Ribbon

Made by many factories in the 1870s. Frosted and clear, flint.

Butter dish	$45-53
Compote	
a. Covered, high foot	52-61
b. Open, high foot	32-40
Creamer	34-43

Egg cup 25-33
Goblet 38-46
Pickle dish 16-23
Pitcher (ill.) 49-58
Platter, bread, frosted 36-44
Sauce, footed, 4½" 13-21
Spoonholder 32-39
Sugar bowl, covered 33-42

Probably other pieces.

Double Spear

Double Spear

Maker unknown, 1880s. Clear, non-flint.

Butter dish, covered $31-41
Celery 24-29
Compote, covered, high standard . 44-53
Creamer 29-36
Dish, oval, deep 14-21
Goblet 22-31
Pickle dish 14-22
Pitcher, water (ill.) 47-54
Sauce 14-20
Spoonholder 22-29
Sugar bowl, covered 29-38

Probably other pieces.

Draped Fan

Doyle & Company, Pittsburgh, c. 1880s, clear, non-flint; pattern reissued by U.S. Glass Company in 1890s.

Butter dish, covered $33-42
Cake stand 33-42
Celery 16-25
Compote
  a. Covered 26-35
  b. Open 16-24
Creamer 24-33
Goblet 18-26

Pitcher, water 35-43
Spoonholder 21-30
Sugar bowl, covered 33-43

Many other pieces.

Drapery

Drapery

(Lace): Sandwich, early and later; Doyle & Company, Pittsburgh, 1870. Clear, non-flint.

Butter dish, covered $51-60
Compote, covered 42-51
Creamer, applied handle 39-49
Dish, oval..................... 16-24
Goblet 32-41
Pitcher (ill.) 49-58
Plate, 6" 22-31
Saucedish, flat, 4" 9-14
Spoonholder 32-40
Sugar bowl, covered 43-53

Probably other pieces.

Drapery

Drapery

Northwood & Company, late 1890s.

	Marigold	Vivid	Pastel
Pitcher (ill.)	$92-103	$138-147	$180-190
Rose bowl	41- 50	54- 63	71- 80
Vase, 4", 5",			
10" high			
flared top ..	24- 33	34- 42	44- 53

Drinking Scene on Mug

Drinking Scene on Mug

Indiana Tumbler & Goblet (National) Company, late 1890s. Non-flint.

Chocolate	$ 63- 73
White milk	32- 41
Blue milk	37- 46
Nile green	43- 52
Clear	21- 30
Amber	108-116

With lip, regular size, 100 percent higher; large steins, 350 to 400 percent higher.

Drum

Drum

Bryce, Higbee & Company, Pittsburgh, 1880s. Clear, and milk glass. Finials are tiny cannon.

Butter dish, covered, cannon finial (ill.)	$59-68
Creamer (ill.)	52-61
Mustard jar, covered, cannon finial	64-73
Spoonholder (ill.)	55-64
Sugar bowl, covered, cannon finial (ill.)	61-71

Possibly a few other pieces.

Duncan 2000

(Flowered Scroll): George Duncan's Sons & Company, Washington, Pennsylvania, c. 1893, clear; sometimes flowered scroll is colored amber. Non-flint.

Butter dish, covered	$30-39
Creamer	32-41
Pitcher, milk	34-43
Spoonholder	14-23
Sugar bowl, covered	30-40
Tumbler	16-25

Amber flowered scroll, 50 percent higher than clear prices listed. Possibly other pieces.

E Pluribus Unum

E Pluribus Unum

Gillinder & Sons, Philadelphia, Pennsylvania, mid-1800s. Clear. Non-flint.

Mug, handled	$71-80
Pickle dish	36-45
Platter (ill.)	87-96

Ear of Corn

Ear of Corn

Challinor, Taylor & Company, Tarentum, Pennsylvania, c. 1885. Clear, colored, opal. Non-flint.

Butter dish, covered	$51-60
Creamer, souvenir-type, green, "corn" in burnished gold	74-83

Creamer, standard size, clear,
colored, opal 51-61
Vase, clear-to-opal, 7″ high (ill.).. 72-82
Probably other table pieces.

Early Moon and Star

Early Moon and Star

New England Glass Company, 1840s.
Clear, canary, probably other colors.

Creamer	$160-170
Lamp, whale oil	185-194
Spoonholder (ill.)	75- 84
Sugar bowl, covered	174-183

Possibly other pieces. This is an extremely rare pattern.

Early Panelled Grape Band

Early Panelled Grape Band

Maker unknown, 1870s. Clear. Non-flint.

Butter dish, covered	$32-41
Celery	21-31

Creamer	26-35
Egg cup	19-28
Goblet (ill.)	31-40
Pitcher, water	43-53
Spoonholder	21-31
Sugar bowl, (ill.)	32-41

Probably other pieces.

Effulgent Star

Effulgent Star

(Star Galaxy): Central Glass Company,
Wheeling, West Virginia, 1880. Crystal
and colored glass.

Butter dish, covered	$49-56
Cake stand	51-60
Celery	24-29
Creamer	34-43
Goblet	41-50
Pitcher, water (ill.)	64-73
Spoonholder	22-31
Sugar bowl, covered	41-50
Tumbler	17-24

Probably other pieces.

Egg in Sand

Egg in Sand

(Bean): Maker unknown, 1880s. Clear
and amber, non-flint.

(continued)

Butter dish $46-55
Cake stand 45-55
Compote 51-60
Cordial 17-26
Creamer 26-36
Goblet 34-44
Pitcher, water (ill.) 47-57
Sauce 9-15
Salt/Pepper, pr. 33-43
Spoonholder 27-37
Sugar bowl 38-48
Tray, bread 32-41
Tumbler 20-28
Wine 24-33

Probably other pieces. Amber is 80 percent higher than clear prices listed.

Elk Medallion

Elk Medallion

Maker and date unknown. The elk is shown in three different panels; the piece is acid etched.

Goblet (ill.) $34-43

Ellipse

Ellipse

Richards & Hartley Flint Glass Company, Pittsburgh; later, Tarentum, Pennsylvania, 1875-1893. Clear only. Standard pieces made. Only goblet made after 1888.

Butter dish, covered $31-40
Celery 16-24
Creamer 14-22
Goblet (ill). 14-22
Pitcher, water 47-56
Salt/Pepper, pr. 11-20
Spoonholder 14-22
Sugar bowl, covered 26-35
Tumbler 14-23

Emerald Green Herringbone

Emerald Green Herringbone

(Florida): U.S. Glass Company, 1880s. Clear, emerald green. Non-flint.

Bowl, berry, large, deep $34-43
Butter dish 40-49
Celery 19-28
Compote, open, high foot 39-47
Creamer (ill.) 22-30
Goblet 20-29
Pitcher, water 46-54
Plates, square, 7¼", 9¼" 14-25
Salt/Pepper, pr. 29-36
Spoonholder 26-34
Sugar bowl 33-42
Tumbler, water 21-30
Wine 15-23

Probably other pieces. Emerald green, 200 percent higher than clear prices listed. Goblet is being reproduced, especially in green. Probably in clear, amber, and blue. Watch it!

English

English

Westmoreland Glass Company, 1896. Clear, opal ware. Non-flint.

Butter dish $32-42
Celery 20-29
Compote 24-33
Creamer 21-30
Goblet 18-27
Pitcher, water (ill.) 38-46
Salt/Pepper, pr. 18-27
Spoonholder 20-28
Sugar bowl, covered 26-36
Tumbler 18-27

Probably other pieces. Opal ware is 65 percent higher than clear prices listed.

Esther

(Tooth and Claw): Riverside Glass Company, Wellsburgh, West Virginia, c. 1896, clear, emerald green, non-flint.

Compote
  a. Covered $45-54
  b. Open 34-44
Creamer 70-78
Cruet 55-64
Goblet 39-48
Relish 20-28
Spoonholder 34-43
Sugar bowl
  a. Covered 49-58
  b. Open 24-33
Toothpick holder 34-43

Emerald green, 100 percent higher than clear prices listed. Other pieces.

Etched Grape

Etched Grape

U.S. Glass Company, 1900-1905. Clear, emerald green, with and without acid-etch, with vineyard design. Non-flint.

Butter dish $24-33
Celery vase 17-26
Creamer 18-27
Goblet 23-32
Pitcher, water (ill.) 41-50
Tumbler 15-24

Probably other pieces. Emerald green is 50 percent higher than clear prices listed.

Ethol

Ethol

(Cat's Eye and Block; Cut Log): Greensburg Glass Company, Greensburg, Pennsylvania, c. 1885, clear, non-flint.

Bowls, round, oblong $16-23
Butter dish, covered 39-48
Creamer 27-36
Goblet (ill.) 22-30
Pitcher, milk 38-47

 (continued)

Sugar bowl, covered 34-43
Tumbler 14-23
Wine 17-26

Probably other pieces. Don't confuse this pattern with that made by Westmoreland Specialty Company.

Etruscan

Bakewell, Pears & Company, Pittsburgh, c. 1874, clear, flint.

Butter dish, covered $68- 78
Cake stand 86- 96
Compote
  a. Covered, high standard.... 98-108
  b. Covered, low standard 73- 83
Creamer..................... 50- 60
Egg cup 28- 35
Goblet...................... 42- 51
Sauce 13- 22
Spoonholder 42- 50
Sugar bowl, covered 60- 70
Tumbler..................... 24- 32

Eugenie

McKee & Brothers, Pittsburgh, c. 1850s, clear, flint.

Butter dish, covered .... $ 81- 90
Celery 79- 88
Compote, covered, on standard . 110-120
Creamer (rare) 225-235
Egg cup 49- 56
Goblet 56- 63
Spoonholder 70- 80
Sugar bowl, covered, dolphin
  finial (rare) 185-210
Tumbler 48- 57
Wine....................... 51- 60

Probably other pieces.

Excelsior

Sandwich, 1850s; McKee Bros., 1868; C. Ihmsen and Company, 1851; others. Clear.

Ale glass .... $ 60- 72
Bitters bottle 52- 60
Butter dish 110-118
Candlesticks, pr. 260-275
Compote
  a. Covered, low foot 133-143
  b. Open, high foot 92-101
Creamer, 2 styles 108-117
Decanter, small, pint, quart .. 64- 73

Excelsior

Egg cup, double and single 43- 60
Goblet, barrel, Maltese Cross .. 56- 64
Pitcher
  a. Milk (rare), Sandwich .. 250+
  b. Syrup 136-145
  c. Water (rare) (ill.),
    Sandwich 340-365
Spoonholder 82- 91
Sugar bowl, 2 styles 89-140
Tumbler, footed, jelly, water .. 40- 60
Whale oil lamp w/Maltese
  Cross, Sandwich 150-165
Wine...................... 46- 54

Excelsior Variant

Excelsior Variant

(Excelsior with Double Ringed Stem): Probably McKee and Bros., 1868. Clear. Non-flint.

Butter dish $41- 50

Celery
a. Plain top 30- 37
b. Scalloped top 42- 51
Cordial 18- 26
Creamer (scarce) 96-106
Goblet..................... 24- 32
Spoonholder (ill.) 29- 38
Sugar bowl, covered 43- 51

Probably other pieces.

Eye-Winker

(Crystal Ball): Maker unknown, c. 1889, clear; possibly made by one of several factories in Findlay, Ohio. This pattern is not "Diamond Point Discs." Non-flint.

Butter dish, covered $56-65
Cake stand 68-78
Compote, open, scalloped edge .. 27-36
Creamer 35-44
Dish, banana 69-78
Lamp 57-67
Pitcher, syrup................ 72-82
Plate, scalloped edge, 8½" 26-34
Sauce, flat 10-14
Spoonholder 22-30
Sugar bowl
a. Covered 56-64
b. Open 24-33

Butter dish, creamer, lamp, pitcher, sauce, covered sugar bowl, toothpick holder and tumbler being reproduced.

Faceted Flower

Faceted Flower

Maker unknown, probably Midwest, late 1800s. Clear. Non-flint.

Butter dish, covered $33-42
Celery 15-24
Creamer 17-27
Goblet 15-25
Pitcher, water (ill.) 33-43

Spoonholder 16-25
Sugar bowl, covered 54-63
Tray, water 27-35

Probably other pieces.

Fairfax Strawberry

Fairfax Strawberry

(Strawberry): Clear and milk glass, late 1860s, some made at Sandwich. Also made at Bryce, Walker and Company, 1870. Non-flint.

Butter dish $100-120
Compote, covered, 8",high, low 135-165
Creamer 93-108
Egg cup 45- 58
Goblet (ill.) 70- 80
Honey dish 35- 45
Pitcher
a. Syrup 72- 82
b. Water 138-150
Sauce 32- 42
Spoonholder 62- 71
Sugar bowl 82- 96

Probably other pieces. Prices listed are for milk glass. Clear, 50 percent less. Egg cup, goblet, probably other pieces being reproduced, both in clear and milk glass. Careful!

Falling Leaves

Maker and date unknown. Otherwise ordinary glass, this pattern is unusual because the leaves are embossed on the **inside** of the body. So far, no mold-maker has figured out how it was done. Can anyone tell us? Apparently the usual pieces were made. Non-flint.

Berry bowl (ill.) $29-39
Butter dish, covered 41-50
Creamer 27-36

469

(continued)

Spoonholder 20-28
Sugar bowl, covered 33-40
Probably other pieces.

Falling Leaves

Fan

Fan

Northwood Glass Company, late 1880s. Blue with opalescent trim; made in Custard glass and Carnival glass. Non-flint.

| | Carnival Colors | |
	Custard	Marigold
Berry set		
a. Large bowl	$100-109	
b. Small bowl	30- 40	$30-40
Butter dish, covered	65- 73	
Creamer (ill.)	52- 61	
Spoonholder	50- 58	
Sugar bowl, covered	66- 69	

Probably other occasional pieces made in Marigold, Vivid, Pastel.

Fan and Star

Challinor, Taylor, Ltd., c. 1880s, clear, opaque white, decorated with enamelled flowers in different colors, non-flint.

Bowl $10-17
Butter dish, covered 20-27
Celery 16-24

Compote, covered 20-27
Goblet 14-22
Pitcher, water................ 24-32
Sauce 7-12
Spoonholder 12-17
Sugar bowl, covered 24-33

Opaque white, 100 percent higher than clear prices listed.

Fancy Diamonds

Fancy Diamonds

Maker unknown, late 1880s, early 1890s. Clear. Non-flint.

Bowl $13-21
Butter dish, covered 24-32
Creamer 23-32
Goblet 20-27
Pitcher (ill.)................. 38-44
Spoonholder 14-22
Sugar bowl, covered 28-35
Wine 12-18

Probably other pieces.

Fan with Diamond

Fan with Diamond

Maker unknown, late 1870s. Clear, non-flint.

Butter dish	$41-50
Compote	
a. Covered, high foot	49-58
b. Covered, low foot	41-50
Cordial	19-27
Creamer	33-42
Dish, oval, 9″ x 6¾″	13-22
Egg cup	17-25
Goblet (ill.)	26-34
Pickle dish	13-21
Pitcher, water	39-49
Sauce, flat, 4″	13-20
Spoonholder	25-34
Sugar bowl, open	20-27

Probably other pieces.

Feather

Feather

(Finecut and Feather; Indiana Swirl): McKee Glass Co., 1890s. Clear and green, rare in amber, red, chocolate.

Bowl, 7½″, 8½″	$22-31
Butter dish, covered	40-49
Cake stand, 8½″, 11″ (rare)	39-48
Celery	35-43
Compote, high standard	50-60
Cordial	19-26
Creamer	34-44
Cruet	32-41
Goblet	25-33
Pitcher, water (ill.)	40-48
Plate, 10″	24-32
Spoonholder	25-33
Sugar bowl	33-42
Toothpick holder	29-36
Tumbler	36-44
Wine	23-31

Probably other pieces. Green, 250 percent, amber, red, chocolate, 400 percent higher than clear prices listed.

Feather Duster

Feather Duster

U.S. Glass Company, 1880s. Clear and emerald green. Non-flint

Bowl, berry	$16-21
Butter dish	25-34
Compote, covered, 6″ high	34-40
Creamer	21-27
Egg cup	14-20
Goblet	19-27
Pitcher, water (ill.)	35-42
Spoonholder	14-22
Sugar bowl	30-36
Tumbler	14-22

Probably other pieces. Emerald green, 80 percent higher than clear prices listed.

Feather with Quatrefoil Center

Feather with Quatrefoil Center

Sandwich Glass Company, probably c. 1850s or 1860s, clear, flint.

Center plate, 9¼″ (ill.) $140-150

Fern Garland

McKee Glass Company, Jeannette, Pennsylvania, c. 1894, clear, non-flint, pieces marked "Pres-Cut."

(continued)

Butter dish, covered $27-36
Celery 12-19
Compote
  a. High standard 24-32
  b. Low standard 14-22
Creamer 18-24
Goblet 19-24
Pitcher 36-46
Spoonholder 14-22
Sugar bowl, covered 21-31
Tray, celery 12-19
Vase, violets 13-19

Probably other pieces.

Fern Sprig

Bellaire Goblet Company, Bellaire, Ohio, and Findlay, Ohio, c. 1800s, clear, non-flint. Pattern reissued after 1891 by U.S. Glass Company. Non-flint.

Butter dish, covered $35-42
Creamer 34-42
Goblet 21-30
Spoonholder 16-23
Sugar bowl, covered 35-42

Should be many more pieces.

Festoon

Festoon

Portland Glass Co., Portland, Maine, 1860s, non-flint.

Bowl, berry, 9″, 10″, finger $14-29
Butter dish, covered 45-53
Cake plate on stand, 9″, 10″, dia. . . . 39-47
Celery 26-34
Compote, high foot 46-54
Creamer 31-40
Pickle jar 35-39
Pitcher, water (ill.) 57-67
Plate, 7″, 8″, 9″ 38-49
Spoonholder 25-33

Sugar bowl, covered 56-64
Tumbler 30-39
Wine 19-26

Probably other pieces.

File

File

Columbia Glass Company, Findlay, Ohio, 1890-1907. Clear. Non-flint.

Butter dish $25-34
Celery 12-20
Creamer 25-33
Goblet 18-26
Lamp, tall 44-51
Pitcher (ill.) 47-57
Spoonholder 22-29
Sugar bowl 31-40
Tumbler 16-25

Probably other pieces.

Fine Cut

Fine Cut

Bryce Bros., Pittsburgh, 1870s. Crystal, blue, amber, yellow.

Bowl, finger, small $23-32
Butter dish, covered 45-54
Compote, covered 42-51

Creamer 30-38
Dish, oblong, deep 18-27
Goblet 29-37
Pitcher, water (ill.) 44-52
Plates, 6¼", 7¼", 10¼" 22-35
Saucedish 11-16
Spoonholder 34-39
Sugar bowl, covered 36-44
Toothpick holder 17-25
Tray, bread, water 38-46

Probably other pieces. Amber, yellow, 35 percent, blue, 70 percent higher than clear prices listed.

Fine Cut and Block

Fine Cut and Block

King Glass Company, Pittsburgh, 1880s. Clear, amber, sapphire blue, clear with color blocks.

Butter dish, covered $38-46
Cake stand
  a. Large 35-42
  b. Small 22-31
Compote, jelly 23-30
Creamer 54-62
Goblet, buttermilk 22-31
Lamp, handled, flat 25-32
Pitcher, water (ill.) 39-49
Spoonholder 24-32
Sugar bowl 37-44
Tumbler 18-26

Probably other pieces. Colors, 60 percent higher; colored blocks, 125 percent higher than clear prices listed.

Fine Cut and Panel

Probably Bryce Bros., Pittsburgh, 1880s; reissued by U.S. Glass Company in early 1890s. Clear and color, non-flint.

Butter dish, covered $37-44
Celery 27-34
Compote, open, high standard .. 35-42

Fine Cut and Panel

Creamer 29-37
Goblet 31-40
Pitcher (ill.) 41-50
Sauce 13-20
Salt/Pepper, pr. 23-33
Spoonholder 29-34
Sugar bowl, open 26-34
Tumbler 19-26
Wine 23-29

Probably other pieces. Amber, yellow, 50 percent, blue, 100 percent higher than clear prices listed.

Fine Cut and Rib

Fine Cut and Rib

Maker unknown, late 1880s. Clear.

Butter dish, covered $30-37
Celery vase 16-25
Creamer 22-31
Goblet 16-24
Pitcher, water (ill.) 32-41
Spoonholder 20-30
Sugar bowl, covered 27-36
Tumbler 14-23

Fine Cut Medallion

Fine Cut Medallion

(Austrian): Indiana Tumbler and Goblet Company, Greentown, Indiana, 1897-1898. Clear, canary, chocolate, green. Non-flint.

Banana dish	$45-53
Bowl, berry	20-29
Butter dish	40-47
Compote	
a. Jelly	24-32
b. Open, large	30-35
Creamer	18-26
Goblet	25-33
Pitcher, water (ill.)	48-53
Punch cup	10-15
Rectangular bowl	40-47
Rose bowl	
a. Large	42-50
b. Small	39-47
Spoonholder	27-36
Tumbler	30-39

The miniatures in chocolate are rare and expensive. Chocolate, 350 to 450 percent higher than clear; other colors are 300 percent higher than clear.

Fishscale

Fishscale

(Coral): Bryce Bros., Pittsburgh, 1880s. Clear, non-flint.

Bowl, 6″, 7″, 8″, open $24-36

Butter dish	42-51
Cake plate on stand, 9″, 10″, 11″	39-53
Celery vase	29-37
Compote	
a. Covered, high standard, 6″, 7″, 8″	56-76
b. Open, high standard, 4″, 7″, 8″, 9″, 10″	27-40
Creamer	36-44
Goblet	34-41
Pickle dish	20-26
Pitcher, quart and half gallon	38-52
Plate, round, 7″, 8″	20-29
Sauce, flared, footed, 4″	16-26
Spoonholder	24-32
Sugar bowl	46-54
Tumbler	24-32

Probably other pieces.

Flared Top Hairpin

Same prices as "Hairpin" — see .

Flared Top Belted Worchester

Maker unknown, c. 1850s, clear, flint.

Cordial	$26-32
Goblet	19-26
Sugar bowl, covered	34-42
Tumbler	16-23
Whiskey, handled	20-27
Wine	17-26

Possibly other pieces.

Flat Diamond

Flat Diamond

(Diamond, Lippman): Richards & Hartley Glass Company, Tarentum, Pennsylvania, 1885-1893, clear only, non-flint.

Butter dish, covered $54-63
Creamer 34-43
Goblet (ill.) 26-36
Spoonholder 25-34
Sugar bowl, covered 36-44
Tumbler 22-30

Should be other pieces.

Flattened Diamond and Sunburst

Flattened Diamond and Sunburst

Maker unknown, 1800s. Clear, colors. Non-flint.

Butter dish, miniature $16-23
Celery 12-19
Creamer, miniature 20-27
Goblet 14-23
Pitcher (ill.)................... 33-39
Saucedish, 4", 5" 12-20
Spoonholder 18-24
Sugar bowl, covered 22-29
Probably other pieces. Color is 60 percent higher than clear prices listed.

Flattened Sawtooth

George Duncan & Sons, Pittsburgh, c. 1880, clear, flint.

Bowl
  a. Finger $37-43
  b. Flat, 10" 66-75
Celery 54-64
Compote, covered 58-68
Creamer 42-49
Goblet 45-54
Pitcher 82-90

Spoonholder 50-59
Sugar bowl, covered 54-63
Wine........................ 27-34
Probably other pieces.

Fleur-de-Lis and Tassel

U.S. Glass Company, c. 1892, clear, opal, green with gilt decoration, non-flint.

Bottle, water $30-39
Butter dish, covered 34-43
Cake stand 24-32
Celery 17-25
Compote, covered 30-40
Creamer 26-35
Pitcher, milk 54-63
Pot, mustard 16-24
Spoonholder 14-22
Sugar bowl, covered 26-36
Tumbler 14-23
Wine........................ 14-20

Colors, 40 percent higher than clear prices listed.

Flickering Flame

Flickering Flame

Westmoreland Glass Company, 1896. Clear, some stained with ruby color. Non-flint.

Creamer (ill.) $28-38
Sugar, covered 31-40
Possibly others in this pattern.

Floral Oval

Maker and date unknown. Non-flint.

Plate, 7¼" square $28-37
Pitcher (ill.)................... 51-60
Wine........................ 17-25
Probably usual pieces.

Floral Oval

Flower and Quill

Florida Palm

(Tidal): Greensburg Glass Company, Greensburg, Pennsylvania, c. early 1900s, clear, non-flint.

Bowls, berry, 7", 8", 9" $13-26
Cake stand 20-30
Celery 17-24
Creamer 24-32
Goblet 18-25
Spoonholder 16-23
Sugar bowl, covered 24-32

Probably other pieces.

Flower and Quill

(Pretty Band): Possibly McKee Bros., 1880s. Clear. Non-flint.

Butter dish, covered $33-41
Celery, footed 20-29
Creamer 21-27
Nappy, flange handle, 4" 12-18
Pickle caster 40-47
Pitcher, water (ill.) 34-43
Plate, large, square 19-28
Spoonholder 21-30
Sugar bowl, covered 27-36

Probably other pieces.

Flower Band

Maker unknown, c. 1870s, clear, non-flint; possibly frosted.

Butter dish, covered .... $ 64- 73
Celery 35- 43
Compote, covered 135-145
Creamer 62- 70
Goblet 62- 72
Pitcher, milk 79- 88
Spoonholder 44- 53
Sugar bowl
  a. Open 42- 51
  b. Covered 73- 82

If it was made in frosted, 40 percent higher than clear prices listed.

Flower Pot

Flower Pot

(Potted Plant): Possibly Adams Glass Company, 1800s. Clear, non-flint.

Butter dish, covered $55-63

476

Cake stand, 10½" dia.	54-64
Compote, covered	49-58
Creamer	39-49
Goblet	33-40
Pitcher, milk (ill.)	39-49
Sauce, open, on standard	13-20
Spoonholder	31-40
Sugar bowl, covered	52-60
Tray, bread	45-54
Tumbler	18-27

Flower with Cane

Flower with Cane

Maker unknown, 1895-1905, flower stained pea-green with gilt center. Upper part also gilded. Ruby probably also used; flower also in other than green. Non-flint.

Creamer	$31-40
Pitcher (ill.)	42-50
Sugar bowl, covered	22-31

Probably other pieces. Colors don't affect prices listed.

Flute

Flute

Many factories made this clear glass, 1850s and 1860s. It went by many names: Bessimer Flute; Sexton Flute; Reed Stem Flute; Sandwich Flute; Duchess Flute. Prices listed are basic prices and not specific to any one pattern. All non-flint.

Ale glass	$25-34
Bitters bottle (6 and 8 flute)	32-44
Bowl, scalloped	26-34
Candlesticks, pr. (6 flute, no sockets), pr.	47-56
Creamer	39-48
Decanter, quart size	50-58
Goblet	28-36
Lamp	55-64
Mug	34-42
Tumbler, half pint, jelly, one gill, half gill (toy), each	26-34
Wine	19-27

Many other pieces.

Flute and Cane

Flute and Cane

Maker unknown, late 1870s. Clear. Non-flint.

Butter dish	$29-37
Celery vase	14-22
Creamer	18-27
Goblet	14-24
Pitcher	
a. Milk	30-38
b. Tankard (ill.)	37-45
Spoonholder	15-24
Sugar bowl, covered	21-27
Tumbler	14-23

Probably other pieces.

Fluted Scrolls

Fluted Scrolls

Northwood Glass Company, late 1880s. Clear, amber, sapphire blue, custard.

Bowl, footed	$22-29
Creamer	43-52
Epergne	62-71
Pitcher, water (ill.)	55-62
Sugar bowl, covered	44-52
Tumbler	27-34

Possibly other table pieces to match. Amber, sapphire, custard, 100 percent higher than clear prices listed.

Flying Birds

Maker unknown, c. 1870, clear, non-flint.

Goblet	$58-66

There should be other pieces.

Flying Swan

Flying Swan

By Westmoreland Specialty Company, Grapeville, Pennsylvania, 1890s. Clear, slag. Non-flint.

Butter dish	$ 37- 44
Celery	18- 24
Creamer	21- 30
Pitcher (ill.), slag	118-130
Spoonholder	19- 27
Sugar bowl, covered	37- 46
Toothpick holder	20- 30
Vase	24- 32

Probably other pieces. Colors, 75 percent higher than clear prices listed.

Forget-Me-Not-in-Scroll

Forget-Me-Not-in-Scroll

Maker unknown, c. 1870s, clear, non-flint.

Butter dish, covered	$26-33
Creamer	24-33
Goblet (ill.)	20-27
Pitcher	34-43
Spoonholder	16-23
Sugar bowl, covered	27-36

Probably other pieces.

Fostoria's Number 952

Fostoria Glass Company, Fostoria, Ohio, late 1800s. Clear. Non-flint.

Pitcher, water	$37-46
Tumbler to match	19-27

Probably other pieces, including four-piece table set.

Fostoria's Number 952

Four Petal

Four Petal

Bryce, McKee & Company or McKee & Brothers, c. 1850s, clear, blue, flint.

Compote, open, 6″ high $52-61
Creamer 78-87
Sugar bowl, open (ill.) 54-64

Only known pieces. Should be others. Blue, 50 percent higher than clear prices listed.

The Fox and the Crow

Fox and the Crow, The

Indiana Tumbler & Goblet (National) Company, late 1890s. Non-flint.

Pitcher, water, clear (ill.) $140-160
Probably tumbler to match.

Framed Blocks

Framed Circles

Framed Blocks

A member of the "Block-and-Thumb-print" family, c. 1870s, clear, flint, non-flint.

Goblet $44-52
Wine (ill.) 37-42

Flint, 40 percent higher than clear prices listed. Should be other pieces.

Framed Circles

Maker unknown, c. 1840s, clear, flint.

Goblet $42-51
Wine (ill.) 42-51

Probably other pieces.

479

Framed Ovals

Framed Ovals

Possibly Sandwich, c. 1840s, clear, gilt trimmed, flint. Could also be New England Glass Company, same era.

Brandy (or Pony Ale),
    footed (ill.) $82-90

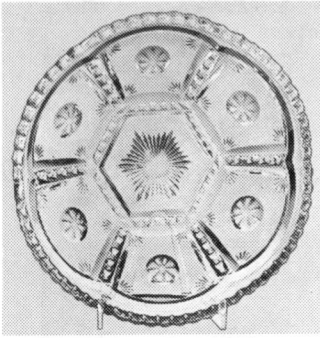

Frost Crystal

Frost Crystal

Tarentum Glass Company, Tarentum, Pennsylvania, 1906. Clear. Non-flint.

Butter dish $30-37
Celery boat 17-26
Creamer 14-21
Custard cup................... 12-20
Plate (ill.)................... 21-30
Spoonholder 22-31
Sugar bowl, open 34-42

Probably other pieces.

Frosted Block

Indiana Glass Company, Dunkirk, Indiana, 1913. Clear, amber, yellow, blue, green, pink; also, vaseline with opalescent border. This is a "new" glass. It compares to "Oatmeal glass." It comes in many pieces. If you like it, buy it.

Frosted Block

Berry bowl $11-14
Butter dish, covered 22-30
Celery 12-19
Compote, jelly................. 18-26
Creamer 16-24
Pitcher, water (ill.) 24-32
Salt/Pepper, pr. 13-20
Spoonholder 14-20
Sugar bowl, covered 21-30
Other pieces.

Frosted Circle

Frosted Circle

Bryce Bros., 1870s, U.S. Glass Company, after 1891. Clear. Non-flint.

Bowl, covered and open, 7", 8" .. $35-44
Butter dish, covered 51-60
Cake stand, 8", 9", 10",
    (10½" with pedestal) 55-75
Celery 30-36
Compote, covered, open, 7", 8".... 70-80
Creamer 47-55
Goblet 39-46
Pickle jar 32-39
Pitcher, water (ill.) 71-80
Plates, 4", 5", 7", 9" 19-29

Salt/Pepper, pr. 56-64
Spoonholder 31-39
Sugar bowl 49-58
Tumblers, 2 types 25-37
Wine 39-47

Probably other pieces. Goblet being reproduced.

Frosted Fruits

Frosted Fruits

Maker unknown, 1880-1890s. Clear and frosted. Non-flint.

Butter dish $52-60
Celery 22-30
Creamer 32-40
Goblet 29-37
Pitcher, water (ill.) 70-80
Sauce 14-21
Sugar bowl 42-50
Tumbler 30-38

Probably other pieces. Frosted is 40 percent higher than clear prices listed.

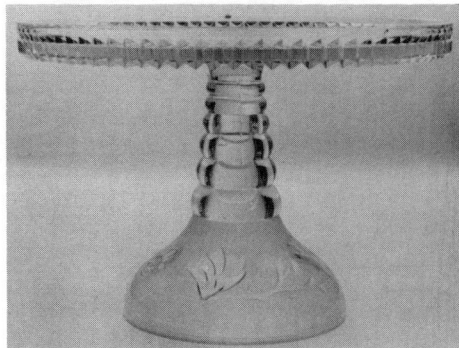
Frosted Magnolia

Frosted Magnolia

(Water Lily): Dalzell, Gilmore & Leighton, West Virginia factory, or Findley, Ohio, late 1800s. Frosted and clear. Non-flint.

Butter dish, covered $32-40
Cake stand (ill.) 42-47
Creamer 38-47
Goblet 52-60
Sauce, flat, deep, large 16-24
Sugar bowl, covered 34-41
Syrup jug 48-52

Probably other pieces.

Frosted Medallion

Frosted Medallion

(Sunburst Rosette): Maker unknown, late 1880s. Clear. Non-flint.

Bowl, oval $12-18
Butter bowl, covered 26-34
Creamer 21-27
Compote
  a. Covered 33-41
  b. Open 17-24
Goblet 17-24
Pitcher, syrup (ill.) 26-34
Spoonholder 14-20
Sugar bowl, covered 24-32
Tumbler 14-21

Probably other pieces.

Frosted Ribbon

Frosted Ribbon

Bakewell, Pears and Company; also George Duncan and Sons, 1878s. Non-flint.

(continued)

Ale glass $26-33
Bitters bottle 35-43
Bowl, waste 41-50
Butter dish 36-44
Celery 32-40
Compote
  a. Covered, high standard 40-49
  b. Covered, low standard 35-44
  c. Open, Dolphin standard 78-86
Creamer 36-45
Egg cup 26-34
Goblet 29-37
Pitcher, water, quart, and
  ½ gallon 35-43
Spoonholder 26-34
Sugar bowl 39-48
Tumbler 27-35
Wine 24-32

Probably other pieces. Goblet being reproduced.

Frosted Stork

Frosted Stork

(Flamingo): Crystal Glass Company, Bridgeport, Ohio, 1879. Non-flint.

Bowl, waste .... $ 47- 56
Butter dish 71- 80
Creamer 82- 90
Goblet 59- 66
Jam jar 61- 70
Pitcher, water (ill.) 134-143
Plate, 9″ 47- 54
Sauce 18- 24
Spoonholder 59- 66
Sugar bowl, covered, with finial 89-100
Tray, large 82- 92

Probably other pieces. This is a rare pattern.

Fuchsia

Sandwich, early; possibly Hobbs, Brockunier & Company, 1865. Clear. Non-flint.

Fuchsia

Butter dish, covered $42-51
Cake stand 31-40
Celery vase 21-30
Compote, open 40-47
Creamer 30-37
Goblet 29-36
Pitcher (ill.) 52-60
Plate, 8″, 10″ 37-49
Spoonholder 25-33
Sugar bowl 55-63
Tumbler 20-30

Possibly other pieces.

Gaelic

Gaelic

Maker and date unknown, possibly 1890-1905 period. Undoubtedly, one of the glass companies absorbed by the giant U.S. Glass Company. This water pitcher has a gold band at top and green leaves. Non-flint.

Bowl, oval, 9″ $14-20
Pitcher, water (ill.) 52-61
Punch cup 10-16

Relish dish, 7¼" 11-14
Probably tumbler to match 21-28

Garden of Eden

Garden of Eden

(Lotus): Probably McKee & Bros., 1865.
Clear. Non-flint.

Butter dish, covered $54-60
Cake stand 40-48
Creamer 28-32
Goblet, plain, and serpent head .. 50-64
Mug, handled 27-35
Pickle dish, oval............... 12-19
Pitcher (ill.)................... 54-63
Platter 34-42
Platter, bread 30-39
Sugar bowl, covered 29-37
Tray, bread 16-27

Probably other pieces.

Garfield Drape

Garfield Drape

Adams & Company, Pittsburgh, 1880s.
Clear. One of the Garfield Memorial
plates was produced by Campbell, Jones
& Company, in 1881. Clear, non-flint.

Bowl $29-38
Butter dish 69-77
Cake plate on stand 61-70
Celery 44-53

Compote, covered, high and
   low standard 54-72
Creamer 56-64
Goblet 36-44
Honey dish 18-24
Pickle dish, oval............... 24-32
Pitcher, water, milk 56-70
Plate
  a. "We Mourn Our Nation's
    Loss" (ill.) 85-93
  b. "Memorial," 11"........... 58-66
Sauce, footed and round 14-19
Spoonholder 29-37
Sugar bowl, covered 56-64

Probably other pieces.

Garland of Roses

Garland of Roses

Maker unknown, 1880. Clear, vaseline.
Non-flint.

Butter dish $16-23
Celery 11-14
Creamer (ill.) 15-23
Egg cup 11-18
Salt, open footed............... 9-16
Spoonholder 14-22
Sugar bowl, covered 22-31

Probably other pieces. Vaseline, 50 percent higher than clear prices listed.

Garter Band

Maker unknown, c. late 1880s, clear,
non-flint.

Butter dish, covered $24-33
Celery 21-30
Goblet 12-19
Sugar bowl, covered 22-30
Wine 14-21

Probably other pieces.

Geneva

Geneva

(Shell and Scroll): Northwood Glass Company, 1900. Clear, custard, with ruby or green decorations. Non-flint.

Bowls, 3 scroll feet	$44-52
Butter dish, covered	48-51
Creamer, covered	47-54
Pitcher, syrup	57-62
Salt/Pepper, pr.	51-60
Spoonholder	32-40
Sugar bowl, open, covered	54-63
Tumbler, footed, plain (ill.)	47-52

Probably other pieces. Custard, 150 percent higher than clear prices listed.

George Peabody

George Peabody

A hero in the War of 1812, a great philanthropist, honored both in England and America. (1795-1869).

Mug, English registry mark	$80-90
Bowl, English registry mark	84-93
Creamer, English registry mark (ill.)	71-80

Considered rare today.

Giant Bull's Eye

Giant Bull's Eye

(Excelsior): Belmont Glass Company, Bellaire, Ohio, 1880s. Clear. Non-flint.

Butter dish, covered	$34-40
Celery	20-27
Creamer	26-34
Goblet	24-31
Pitcher, water (ill.)	64-72
Spoonholder	25-33
Sugar bowl, covered	27-33

Probably other pieces. Possibly in color.

Giant Sawtooth

Maker unknown, 1830. Clear. Flint.

Goblet	$ 67- 77
Lamp, whale oil (ill.)	188-210
Spill holder	46- 54
Tumbler	52- 61

Probably other pieces.

Giant Sawtooth

Girl with Flower

Plate, 6″, blue (ill.) $38-47
Sauce, clear 31-40

Probably other pieces. Colors, 50 percent higher than clear.

Gibson Girl

Gibson Girl

Maker unknown, early 1900s. Clear, non-flint.

Butter dish	$70- 80
Creamer	54- 64
Pitcher, water (ill.)	89-100
Plate, 10″	68- 78
Spoonholder	52- 60
Sugar bowl, covered	60- 69
Tumbler	38- 46

Possibly other pieces.

Girl with Flower

Maker unknown, 1870s. Clear, green, blue. Non-flint.

Gladstone "For the Million"

Gladstone "For the Million"

This pattern honors William Ewart Gladstone, four times Prime Minister of England; (1809-1898).

Bowl, 8½″ dia.	$ 67- 77
Creamer (ill.)	240-250
Mug, amethyst	70- 80
Plate, aqua	55- 65

Of English make, fairly rare, but found on occasion. This is an unusual piece as the words are reversed — backwards. Possibly the only one in the world! Houston Museum.

Goat's Head

Hobbs, Brockunier & Company, Wheeling, West Virginia, c. 1878, clear, non-flint.

Butter dish, covered $49-58
Celery 42-51
Creamer 47-53
Compote, 6″ 67-73
Sugar bowl
   a. Open 38-47
   b. Covered 41-50

Probably other pieces.

Gooseberry

Gooseberry

Sandwich glass, 1870s. Clear, opaque white, non-flint.

Butter dish, covered $45-53
Cake stand, 9½″ dia. 40-49
Compote
   a. Covered, high foot, large 55-64
   b. Covered, high foot, 6″ 40-50
Creamer 39-47
Goblet 31-40
Honey dish 13-19
Lemonade glass 27-36
Pickle dish 11-17
Pitcher, water, syrup 58-71
Saucedish 11-17
Spoonholder 25-32
Sugar bowl 39-46
Tumbler, applied handle 27-34

Probably other pieces. Opaque white, 65 percent higher than clear prices listed. Being reproduced.

Gothic

McKee & Brothers, 1850s. Clear, flint.

Butter dish . . . .$ 81- 90
Cake stand 56- 64

Gothic

Caster bottle, each 22- 30
Champagne (rare) 82- 92
Compote
   a. Covered, on standard 160-168
   b. Open, footed 89- 96
Cordial 60- 69
Creamer 92-100
Egg cup 35- 43
Goblets, 2 styles 64- 73
Pitcher (ill.) 71- 80
Plate (rare) 50- 58
Sauce 19- 27
Spoonholder 55- 64
Sugar bowl 82- 90
Tumbler 49- 57
Wine (rare) 92-100

Probably other pieces.

Gothic Arch and Panels

Gothic Arch and Panels

Make and date unknown, clear, flint.

Butter dish, covered $56-63
Jar, horseradish 37-44
Paperweight 32-41
Sauce, footed 22-31
Spoonholder 38-47
Sugar bowl (base ill.) 56-66

Should be other pieces.

Grace

Grace

(Japanese): Richards & Hartley Flint Glass Company, Pittsburgh, Pennsylvania, 1870s. Pattern was discontinued prior to the company's removal to Tarentum in 1884. Scene is different on each individual table piece, though top and bottom horizontal borders are the same.

Butter dish, covered $44-53
Compote 29-37
Creamer 24-32
Goblet 29-34
Spoonholder 22-32
Sugar bowl, covered 47-56

Possibly other pieces.

Grand

Grape and Festoon

Grand

(New Grand): Bryce, Higbee & Company, 1885. Clear. Non-flint.

Butter dish, covered $35-44
Cake stand 32-40
Celery 21-28
Compote 42-51
Creamer 24-29
Goblet 21-30
Pitcher, water 34-41
Sauce 18-26
Spoonholder (ill.) 21-30
Sugar bowl, covered 36-42
Tumbler 31-41
Wine 29-38

Probably other pieces.

Grape and Festoon

Sandwich, early; they probably produced the clear leaf. Doyle & Company, Pittsburgh, 1870s, stippled leaf; probably other factories. Non-flint.

Butter dish $62-69
Celery 48-54
Compote, covered, high and
low standard 58-64
Cordial 27-34
Creamer, 2 styles 40-58
Egg cup, 2 styles 16-29
Goblet, 2 styles 37-49
Pickle dish, oval 16-21
Pitcher, water (ill.) 58-66
Plate, 6" 27-36
Saucedish, flat, 4" 14-23
Spoonholder 28-38
Sugar bowl, acorn knob 54-63
Wine 18-26

Probably other pieces.

Grape and Festoon with Shield

Possibly produced by Doyle & Company, 1860s. Clear, blue, other colors. Non-flint.

Butter dish $27-33
Celery 12-19
Compote, covered, high and
low standard 47-59
Creamer 27-34

(continued)

Grape and Festoon with Shield

Egg cup 12-21
Goblet 19-24
Mug, blue.................... 16-23
Pitcher, water (ill.) 47-56
Saucedish, flat, 4″, 6″ 11-24
Spoonholder 20-26
Sugar bowl 31-40

Probably other pieces.

Grape Band

Grape Band

Bryce, Walker & Company, Pittsburgh, Pennsylvania, c. 1869, clear, non-flint.

Butter dish, covered $39-47
Compote 45-53
Creamer 29-38
Goblet (ill.) 22-30
Pitcher, water................. 55-63

Spoonholder 22-30
Sugar bowl, covered 39-47
Wine........................ 20-27

Made in flint at an earlier date, late 1850s. 50 percent higher than non-flint prices listed.

Grape Bunch

Grape Bunch

Sandwich, c. 1870s, clear, non-flint.

Butter dish, covered $36-42
Compote 30-36
Creamer 27-32
Egg cup 21-31
Goblet (ill.) 21-30
Pitcher, water................. 34-40
Spoonholder 24-32
Sugar bowl, covered 30-38

Probably other pieces.

Grape Jug

This is one of the late fruit patterns, made in the late 1890s and early 1900s and should not be considered as Early American glass. Nevertheless, it's collectible today. Clear.

Grape jug (ill.) $28-37

Brings higher price because collectors buy it as a pitcher.

Grape Jug

Grape with Thumbprint

Grape with Thumbprint

Maker unknown, 1890s. Clear, non-flint.

Berry dish, covered	$58-68
Butter dish	40-48
Celery vase	17-24
Creamer	40-47
Goblet	27-34
Pitcher, water (ill.)	56-63
Spoonholder	28-37
Sugar bowl, covered	41-50
Syrup jug, several sizes	36-47
Toothpick holder	15-22
Tumbler	19-26

Probably other pieces.

Grape with Overlapping Foliage

Grape with Overlapping Foliage

Probably Sandwich, early. Later, other factories in Pittsburgh area, 1880s. Clear and milk-white.

Butter dish	$31-39
Celery vase	22-31
Creamer	30-40
Goblet	28-37
Pitcher	32-41
Spoonholder	24-32
Sugar bowl	30-37

Probably other pieces. Milk-white, 50 percent higher than clear prices listed.

Grape with Vine

Grape with Vine

Maker unknown, 1890s. Original pieces, red paint and gilt. Non-flint.

Butter dish	$27-34
Celery	18-26
Creamer	21-26
Goblet	27-32
Honey dish	14-21
Pitcher, water (ill.)	34-44

Grasshopper with Insect

Grasshopper with Insect

(Locust: Long Spear): Possibly Belmont Glass Works, Bellaire, Ohio, early 1880s. Clear and color.

Butter dish	$56-65
Celery vase	32-40
Compote, covered	61-70
Creamer	32-41
Goblet	65-72
Pickle dish, oval	19-26
Pitcher, water (ill.)	62-70
Sauce	14-22
Spoonholder	28-36
Sugar bowl, covered	49-56

Probably other pieces. Goblet being reproduced.

Grasshopper, with or without Insect

Grasshopper, with or without Insect

When grasshopper is present, he's climbing up side, directly above floral motif. With insect, 100 percent higher in price. Clear. Non-flint.

Bowl, covered	$27-36
Butter, covered	31-40
Compote, covered	34-42
Pitcher (ill.)	43-50
Plate, large	26-34
Sauce, flat	22-30
Spoonholder	21-29
Sugar, covered	33-41

Probably other pieces. Goblet being reproduced.

Greensburg's 130

Greensburg's 130

Greensburg Glass Company, Greensburg, Pennsylvania, late 1880s. Plain and engraved crystal. Non-flint.

Butter dish	$31-39
Celery dish	16-24
Creamer	22-30
Goblet	24-32
Honey dish	17-24
Pitcher, water, milk (ill.)	34-42
Sauce	14-20
Spoonholder	16-24
Sugar bowl, covered	33-42

Other pieces. Engraved crystal, 25 percent higher than plain prices listed.

Gridley Pitcher

A. J. Beatty & Sons, Dunkirk, Indiana, 1898. Clear.

Gridley pitcher	$140-149

Highly collectible today.

Gridley Pitcher

Hairpin

(Sandwich Loop): Sandwich, c. 1850s, clear, milk glass, flint.

Celery ....$ 65- 73
Champagne................. 52- 60
Compote, covered, low standard 62- 70
Egg cup 34- 42
Goblet 40- 49
Pitcher.................... 120-135
Spoonholder 39- 46
Sugar bowl	
a. Open 40- 48
b. Covered 64- 73
Tumbler 40- 48

Milk glass, 100 percent higher than clear prices listed.

Hairpin with Rayed Base

Same prices as "Hairpin" — see.

(Wm.) Haley's Glass Basket

(Wm.) Haley's Glass Basket

Two dates appear in the bottom: July 21, 1874, and April 5, 1881. Where it was made is not known.

Basket $72-82
Wine......................... 42-51

Other pieces.

Hamilton

Hamilton

Sandwich, early 1860s. Clear, flint.

Butter dish, covered ....$ 80- 89
Caster set, in standard........ 135-142
Celery 68- 76
Compote, covered 120-130
Creamer, applied or pressed	
handle 79- 86
Decanter, w/stopper 62- 70
Egg cup 36- 44
Goblet (ill.) 45- 53
Pitcher	
a. Syrup, metal top 72- 80
b. Water 155-163
Saucedish, 4″, 5″ 18- 26
Spoonholder, 2 styles 38- 46

(continued)

Sugar bowl, covered 70- 80
Tumbler, water, whiskey 82- 91
Wine 58- 66

Probably other pieces.

Hamilton with Leaf

Hamilton with Leaf

Sandwich, 1870s. Clear and frosted. Other factories, 1890s on. Sandwich prices shown.

Butter dish $118-126
Celery vase 114-121
Compote, open, high and
 low standard 90-100
Cordial 96-105
Creamer 82- 91
Egg cup 46- 54
Goblet 62- 70
Lamp, two sizes 92-101
Pitcher (ill.) 102-109
Salt, footed 54- 63
Spoonholder 65- 74
Sugar bowl 88- 94
Tumbler, water 63- 72
Wine 40- 49

Possibly other pieces.

Hand

(Pennsylvania): O'Hara Glass Company, Ltd., 1880. Clear.

Bowl, 7″, 8″, 9″, 10″ $24-35
Butter dish 55-63
Cake plate on stand, 10″ 42-49
Celery vase 36-44
Compote
 a. Covered, high foot 54-62
 b. Open 36-44

Hand

Creamer 44-53
Goblet 35-43
Honey dish 14-20
Jam jar 41-50
Pickle dish 19-26
Pitcher, water (ill.) 62-71
Platter, 8″ x 10½″ 32-41
Saucedish, flat, 4″ 13-20
Spoonholder 31-40
Sugar bowl 47-54

Probably other pieces.

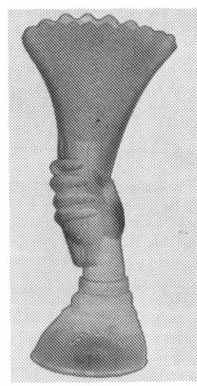

Hand Vase

Hand Vase

Gillinder and Sons, Philadelphia, Pa., for Centennial 1876. Clear and frosted.

Hand vase (ill.) $90-107

Highly collectible by "Hand" collectors.

Hanging Basket

Possibly Mosaic Glass Company, Fostoria, Ohio, 1890s. Clear, colors. Nonflint.

Butter dish .... $ 54- 64
Compote 46- 54

Hanging Basket

Creamer	34- 42
Goblet	22- 31
Pitcher (ill.)	117-124
Spoonholder	38- 47
Sugar bowl, covered	51- 60
Tumbler	30- 39

Colors, 50 percent higher than clear prices listed.

Hanover

(Block with Stars): Richards & Hartley Glass Company, Tarentum, Pennsylvania, c. 1888, clear, non-flint.

Butter dish, covered	$31-40
Cake stand	29-37
Celery	30-40
Compote	
a. Open	21-29
b. Covered	32-40
Creamer	20-27
Goblet	16-23
Pitcher, water	34-43
Spoonholder	14-20
Sugar bowl, covered	32-40
Tumbler	16-23
Wine	12-19

Probably other pieces.

Harp

Bryce Bros., Pittsburgh, 1840s or 1850s. Clear, green, other colors.

Butter dish, two sizes	$130-145
Compote, covered, low standard	172-180
Dish, covered, low foot	140-150
Goblet (rare)	
a. Flared sides	475-550
b. Straight sides	350-400

Harp

Lamps, whale oil	
a. Handled, double wick with snuffers	160-170
b. Larger, on glass standard	135-144
Saucedish	48- 57
Spill holder (ill.)	64- 73
Spoonholder	69- 78

Possibly other pieces.

Hartford

Hartford

Fostoria Glass Company, 1900s. Clear, yellow, amber, possibly green. Non-flint.

Bowl, 4½″, 5½″, 6″, 7″, 8″, 9″	$23-40
Butter dish, covered	36-45
Celery vase	27-36
Creamer (ill.)	24-33
Sauce, 4½″	20-28
Salt/Pepper, pr.	21-30
Spoonholder	20-29
Sugar bowl, covered, footed, plain base	32-41
Syrup jug	22-31
Tumbler	19-27

Possibly other pieces.

Harvard

Harvard

(Quixote): Tarentum Glass Company, Tarentum, Pennsylvania, 1898-1912, clear, custard, emerald green, pea green, ruby-stained. Non-flint.

Bowl, finger	$11-19
Butter dish, covered	31-40
Compote	24-33
Cup, punch	11-14
Goblet	20-24
Pitcher, water	50-59
Plate, 10½"	18-27
Sugar bowl, covered	30-39
Wine (ill.)	19-27

Many other pieces. Colors 100 percent higher than clear prices listed.

Heart

Heart and Waffle

Heart

Sandwich, very early. Clear. One of many Sandwich pieces at the Houston Museum, Chattanooga. It's shown here because it's Pressed Glass and still around.

Heart and Waffle

Probably Sandwich, mid-1850. Clear.
Lamp (ill.) $192-214

Heart Band

Heart Band

McKee Glass Company, 1897. Crystal glass with ruby stain. Non-flint.

Butter dish, covered	$40-50
Celery	23-29
Compote	37-44
Creamer	24-32
Goblet	23-31
Pitcher, water (ill.)	50-59
Spoonholder	30-37
Sugar bowl, covered	37-44
Tumbler	21-30

Probably other pieces.

Heart Stem

Heart Stem

Maker unknown, late 1880s or 1890s. Clear.

Butter dish	$42-51
Celery	26-34
Compote, covered, 7" high	47-56
Creamer (ill.)	41-50
Goblet	28-36
Pitcher	44-53
Spoonholder	27-36
Sugar bowl	42-51
Tumbler	21-30

Probably other pieces.

Heart with Thumbprint

Heart with Thumbprint

(Columbia): Sandwich, early; Tarentum Glass Company, 1898. Crystal, sometimes gold rims. Natural and green custard.

Bowl, berry, 9"	$27-37
Butter dish, covered	46-52
Celery vase	46-52
Creamer, individual, regular	50-60
Cruet with stopper	46-52
Goblet	39-47
Pitcher	54-62
Salt, master (ill.)	27-37
Sauce	14-21
Spoonholder	26-34
Sugar bowl	
a. Covered	46-51
b. Individual	30-40
Tumbler	32-42
Vases, 10", pr.	40-47
Wine	29-37

Probably other pieces.

Heavy Drape

Fostoria Glass Company, 1904. Clear. Non-flint.

Bowl, berry, flat and footed	$18-28
Butter dish, covered	32-40
Celery	18-26
Compote, covered and open	34-40
Creamer	17-24
Egg cup	14-22

Heavy Drape

Goblet	21-30
Pitcher, milk, water (ill.)	54-59
Salt/Pepper, pr.	22-29
Spoonholder	20-27
Sugar bowl, covered	26-32
Tumbler	22-30
Wine	17-23

Probably other pieces as there were some 50 pieces comprising the set.

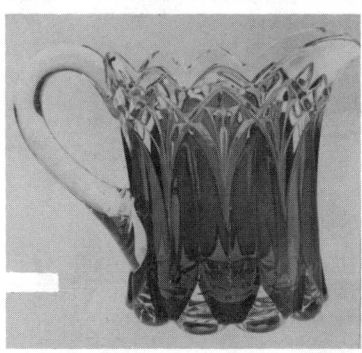

Heavy Gothic

Heavy Gothic

U.S. Glass Company, 1892. Clear, clear stained with ruby. Non-flint.

Butter dish	$32-40
Compote	36-42
Creamer	21-30
Egg cup	14-22
Goblet	22-30
Pitcher (ill.)	47-51
Spoonholder	24-29
Sugar bowl, two types	32-39
Tumbler	24-31
Wine	20-27

Probably other pieces. Ruby stained has no effect on prices listed.

Heavy Jewel

Heavy Jewel

Fostoria Glass Company, 1900s. Clear. Non-flint.

Butter dish	$21-30
Celery	18-27
Compote, covered and open	32-40
Creamer	20-26
Goblet	18-24
Pitcher (ill.)	31-40
Spoonholder	20-26
Sugar bowl	
a. Covered	21-30
b. Open	20-24
Tumbler	18-24

Henrietta

Henrietta

(Big Block): Adams and Company, 1874. Also Columbia Glass Company, 1889. Clear, blocks flashed in red. Non-flint.

Bowl, berry	$11-14
Butter dish	21-27

Celery	16-22
Compote	26-33
Creamer	22-30
Goblet	17-26
Pitcher, water (ill.)	37-43
Spoonholder	24-32
Sugar bowl	24-32
Tumbler	20-30

Probably other pieces. Red flashing, 60 percent higher than clear prices listed.

Heron

Heron

Another of the animal (and bird) series put out by Indiana Tumbler & Goblet (National) Company, late 1890s. Clear and chocolate.

Pitcher, water	
a. Chocolate	$248-260
b. Clear (ill.)	118-132

Probably tumblers to match.

Herringbone

Herringbone

Indiana Tumbler & Goblet (National) Company, late 1890s. Non-flint.

	Amber	Green	Clear
Butter dish, covered		$90-110	$42-52
Cake stand		60- 70	46-55
Cordial	$80-90	67- 77	38-47
Creamer		80- 90	22-31
Pitcher (ill.)		92-100	51-60
Salt/Pepper, pr.		50- 60	31-40
Spoonholder		42- 52	36-42
Sugar bowl		55- 64	32-42
Wine	72-82	50- 60	33-43

Chocolate

Mug (ill.) $70-80

Probably other pieces.

Herringbone

Herringbone

(Florida): U.S. Glass Company, 1890s. Clear and colors. Non-flint.

Berry set, 5 pc., all	$62-70
Bowl, 7½", 9" dia.	18-27
Butter dish	52-60
Compote	49-52
Creamer	43-51
Goblet (ill.)	31-40
Pickle dish	19-27
Pitcher, water	50-60
Sauce	18-26
Salt/Pepper, pr.	30-38
Spoonholder	31-40
Sugar bowl, covered	42-51

Probably other pieces. Color 50 percent more than clear prices listed.

Hexagon Block

Hexagon Block

(Double Red Block): Maker unknown, early 1890s. Clear, clear flashed in color; possibly amber. Non-flint.

Butter dish, covered	$45-53
Celery vase	31-40
Creamer	31-39
Pitcher (ill.)	57-64
Sauce	18-27
Spoonholder	25-32
Sugar	
a. Covered	41-50
b. Open	26-32
Tumbler	24-33
Wine	22-32

Probably other pieces. Flashed colors, 40 percent higher than clear prices listed.

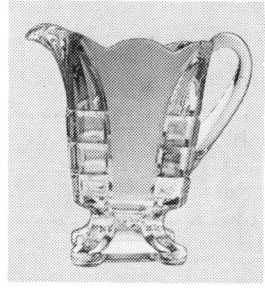

Hidalgo

Hidalgo

(Frosted Waffle): Adams & Company, Pittsburgh, 1880. Crystal, plain and engraved; also frosted.

Bowl, large, small	$23-29
Butter dish	32-41
Celery	26-34
Compote, covered, open, high or low standard	37-49
Cup and saucer	13-21
Goblet	17-24
Pitcher, milk (ill.)	41-50

(continued)

Sauce, flat and footed 12-20
Salt/Pepper, pr. 14-22
Spoonholder 18-26
Sugar bowl, covered 36-42
Tumbler 21-30

Probably other pieces. Frosted, 15 percent higher than clear prices listed.

Hobbs Diamond and Sunburst

Hobbs Diamond and Sunburst

Hobbs, Brockunier & Company, 1880s. Clear. Non-flint.

Butter dish, covered $27-34
Cake stand 26-32
Compote
  a. Covered 31-40
  b. Open 26-33
Creamer, applied handle 27-36
Egg cup 14-22
Goblet 21-31
Pitcher (ill.).................. 44-52
Sauce, flat 11-20
Spoonholder 20-27
Sugar bowl, covered 37-42
Tumbler 20-24

Probably other pieces.

Hobnail

Hobnail

So many companies made a "Hobnail" pattern, including New Brighton Glass Company, A. J. Beatty Company, McKee & Brothers, Gillinder Brothers, others. It came in clear and colors and is heavily reproduced today in just about every color.

Some of the **many** pieces made were berry bowls, perfume bottles, creamers, celerys, cordials, bone dishes, mugs, pitchers, salts (ill.), glass shades, spoonholders, sugar bowls, toothpick holders, trays, tumblers, vases, wines.

Hobnail Band

Hobnail Band

One of the Hobnail group, around 1890. Clear, non-flint.

Butter dish $34-43
Creamer 23-30
Goblet 18-25
Pitcher, water (ill.) 36-43
Spoonholder 19-26
Sugar bowl 28-35
Tumbler 9-14

Many other pieces.

Hobnail in Big Diamonds

Challinor, Taylor & Company, 1888. Clear.

Butter dish, covered $36-42
Creamer 24-32
Pitcher (ill.)................... 40-50

Hobnail in Big Diamonds

Spoonholder 22-27
Sugar
  a. Covered 34-42
  b. Open 24-33

Probably other pieces. Hobnail in Diamond same, except hobs are confined inside bars and do not cover the pieces.

Holly

Holly

Sandwich glass, late 1860s, early 1870s. Clear. Non-flint. Others made this pattern in custard.

Butter dish	$110-118
Cake stand	80- 88
Compote, covered, high or low standard	115-122
Creamer	70- 80
Egg cup	48- 57
Goblet (rare) (ill.)	70- 79
Pitcher, water	90- 99
Sauce	18- 26
Spoonholder	50- 58
Sugar bowl	90- 99

Tumbler, footed	47- 56
Wine	48- 56

Probably other pieces.

Holly Amber

Holly Amber

(Golden Agate): Indiana Tumbler & Goblet (National) Company, January to June, 1903 only. Holly amber and clear.

Butter dish (ill.)	$1,375-1,550
Candy dish, covered	500- 550
Compote	
a. Covered, large	1,600-1,700
b. Covered, small	1,150-1,350
Cruet	1,350-1,475
Parfait	600- 650
Pitcher, water	2,350-2,550
Salt/Pepper, pr.	920-1,100
Spoonholder	575- 615
Sugar bowl	580- 625
Tumbler	550- 625

Other pieces made. Clear, 20 to 50 percent of the amber prices listed. Butter dish, covered compote, jelly compote, creamer, cruet, 7½" plate, toothpick, and tumbler being reproduced. A **highly overrated** glass!

Holly-Band

 (continued)

Holly-Band

Maker unknown, 1870s. Clear. Non-flint.

Butter dish	$31-40
Celery	18-24
Compote	22-30
Creamer	22-28
Pitcher, applied handle	62-70
Spoonholder (ill.)	22-30
Sugar bowl	31-40
Tumbler	18-24

Probably other pieces.

Home

Home

Pioneer Glass Company, Pittsburgh, late 1880s; later reproduced by McKee Bros. in 1894. Clear, upper and lower bands sometimes decorated in ruby color. Non-flint.

Butter dish, covered	$37-46
Celery	22-31
Creamer	24-32
Goblet	18-26
Pitcher, water (ill.)	42-50
Spoonholder	21-31
Sugar bowl, covered	33-42
Tumbler	16-24

Probably other pieces. Ruby color has little or no effect on clear prices listed.

Honeycomb with Flower Rim

Honeycomb with Flower Rim

(Inverted Thumbprint with Daisy Band): Greentown, Indiana, around 1903. Clear, blue, green, custard. Non-flint.

Butter, covered	$24-33
Celery	16-24
Compote	
a. Covered	37-42
b. Open	24-33
Creamer	22-31
Pitcher (ill.)	42-51
Sauce, footed	9-14
Sugar bowl	
a. Covered	28-37
b. Open	31-40
Tumbler	21-30

Other pieces. Blue and custard, 90 percent; amber, 65 percent; others, 20 percent higher than clear prices listed.

Horn of Plenty

Horn of Plenty

Sandwich glass, early 1830s; Bryce, McKee, Pittsburgh, 1850s. Opalescent white, canary, clear, flint.

Butter dish	
a. Conventional knob, 6″ dia.	$140-150
b. Washington's head (rare)	525-625
Celery	115-123
Compote	
a. Covered, oblong, on standard	165-175
b. Open, low standard	110-120
c. Oval, on standard	310-328
Creamer, large	160-169
Decanter, pint, quart, ½ gallon	133-146

Egg cup 54- 62
Goblet 80- 88
Lamp, all glass 175-185
Mug, applied handle, 3" 153-160
Pitcher, water, milk (ill.) 320-340
Spoonholder 54- 59
Sugar bowl, 2 types 122-138
Tumbler, whiskey 92-100
Wine...................... 120-130

Probably other pieces. Canary, amber, blue, 85 percent higher than clear prices listed. Amber goblet and tumbler being reproduced.

Horsehead's Medallion

Horsehead's Medallion

Portland Glass Company, Portland, 1870s. Clear; rare in milk-white. Non-flint.

Celery ....$ 77- 84
Compote
  a. Covered 120-130
  b. Open 97-105
Creamer 78- 87
Spoonholder (ill.) 48- 56
Sugar bowl
  a. Covered 76- 84
  b. Open 64- 73

Probably other pieces. Milk-white, 100 percent higher than clear prices listed.

Horseshoe Stem

Maker unknown, 1880s. Clear. Non-flint.

Cake stand ....$ 54- 63
Compote
  a. Covered 57- 64
  b. Open 48- 56

Horseshoe Stem

Creamer 41- 50
Goblet 42- 51
Pitcher (ill.) 115-124
Sauce 27- 36
Sugar
  a. Covered 55- 64
  b. Open 38- 46
Tumbler 37- 46

Probably other pieces.

Hour Glass

Maker unknown, c. 1880s, clear, yellow, amber, blue, non-flint.

Butter dish, covered $33-42
Creamer 31-40
Dish, sauce, large 21-30
Goblet 29-32
Pitcher, water................. 28-38
Spoonholder 22-31
Sugar bowl, covered 26-36

Yellow, 65 percent; amber, blue, 100 percent higher than clear prices listed.

Huber

Huber

Several firms made this pattern — Sandwich, New England Glass Company, also Bakewell, Pears & Company, probably others, 1860s, and earlier. Clear, flint. Sandwich prices listed.

501

(continued)

Bitters bottle $40-48
Bowl, covered, 6″, 7″ 31-42
Butter dish 57-65
Celery (ill.) 32-41
Compote, covered, high and
   low standard, 7″, 10″ 71-80
Creamer, scalloped rim 50-59
Decanter
   a. Bar lip, pint, quart 43-56
   b. With stopper, pint, quart .. 55-69
Egg cup, handled 37-46
Goblet, hotel, large, small 27-47
Jug, quart, 3 pints 29-38
Mug, beer, pony beer........... 26-47
Pitcher, water, 2 styles.......... 58-67
Plate, 6″, 7″ 18-27
Salt, celery dip, footed 9-25
Spoonholder 23-32
Sugar bowl, covered 47-57
Tumbler, gill, one-half pint, large
   and small, taper bar 18-28
Wine........................ 18-25

Hummingbird

Hummingbird

(Flying Robin): Maker unknown, late 1880s. Clear, canary, amber, blue, non-flint.

Butter dish $56-65
Celery 40-49
Creamer, footed 40-48
Goblet 35-43
Pickle dish 10-17
Pitcher, milk, water, 8″
   high (ill.) 58-68
Sauce 12-22
Spoonholder 30-38
Sugar bowl 49-56
Tray, water 54-62
Tumbler 29-38

Canary, 40 percent; amber and blue, 75 percent higher than clear prices listed.

Hundred Leaved Rose

Hundred Leaved Rose

Possibly Model Flint Glass Company, Findlay, Ohio, 1890s. Clear, frosted, stippled. Non-flint.

Bowl $17-26
Butter dish, covered 37-46
Creamer 32-41
Pitcher (ill.)................... 44-52
Sauce, flat 14-23
Spoonholder 24-33
Sugar bowl
   a. Covered 44-51
   b. Open 27-37

Probably others. Frosted and stippled, 40 percent higher than clear prices listed.

Imperial

Imperial Glass Company, Bellaire, Ohio, c. 1901, clear, non-flint.

Butter dish, covered $39-48
Cake stand 32-41
Celery tray 16-24
Compote 29-37
Creamer 39-47
Goblet 29-39
Pitcher, milk, water 44-51
Salt/Pepper, pr. 24-29
Spoonholder 19-27
Sugar bowl, covered 32-41
Tumbler 32-42
Wine........................ 29-37

Probably other pieces.

In Remembrance Platter

A memorial platter issued after Garfield's assassination in 1881. Garfield shares a place with Lincoln and Wash-

In Remembrance Platter

ington. Clear only. Non-flint.

Platter (ill.) $140-150

Intaglio

Intaglio

Northwood Glass Company, 1910. Clear, custard, colors. Non-flint.

	Color	Custard
Berry set		
a. Large bowl	$64- 74	$120-140
b. Small bowl	31- 40	61- 71
Butter, covered	64- 72	172-179
Compote, jelly		141-152
Cruet		133-142
Sugar, covered	70- 80	101-112
Creamer	58- 68	80- 90
Pitcher (ill.)	76- 79	222-230
Spoonholder	60- 70	78- 88
Pitcher, water	90-100	174-177
Salt/Pepper, pr. . . .		160-170
Tumbler, water	42- 51	84- 96

Interlocked Hearts

Interlocked Hearts

Possibly Northwood Glass Company, Indiana, Pennsylvania, late 1890s, early 1900s. Non-flint.

Creamer	$27-36
Goblet	23-32
Pitcher, water (ill.)	40-50
Tumbler	16-24
Wine	20-29

Probably other pieces.

Interlocking Crescents

(Double Arch): The King Glass Company, Pittsburgh, Pennsylvania, c. late 1880s, clear, non-flint.

Butter dish, covered	$32-42
Creamer	34-41
Goblet	25-34
Spoonholder	17-26
Sugar bowl, covered	34-43

Only known pieces.

Iron Kettle

Adams & Company, 1874; Challinor Taylor & Company, 1885. Clear, colors. Non-flint.

Butter dish, covered	$38-48
Creamer (ill.)	28-37

(continued)

Iron Kettle

Spoonholder 21-30
Sugar bowl, covered 41-50

Probably other pieces. Colors 60 percent
higher than clear prices listed.

Ivorina Verde

Ivorina Verde

A. H. Heisey Company, Newark, Ohio, 1899. Opaque white with green trim (custard). Non-flint.

Butter dish, covered $107-115
Bowls 86- 93
Celery 62- 72
Creamer 81- 90
Cruet 60- 70
Pitcher, water 125-140
Spoonholder 48- 57
Sugar bowl, covered (ill.) 92-101

Probably other pieces.

Ivy-in-Snow

(Forest Ware): Cooperative Flint Glass Company, Beaver Falls, Pennsylvania, late 1880s. Clear, foliage stained red, gold leaf.

Butter dish, flat $54-63

Ivy-in-Snow

Cake stand, square 42-49
Celery 49-57
Compote, covered, small, medium,
    large, high standard 62-71
Creamer 37-44
Cup and saucer 21-30
Goblet 27-36
Jam jar..................... 29-36
Pitcher, water (ill.) 54-64
Sauce, flat, round, 4", 6" 19-29
Spoonholder 19-27
Sugar bowl 42-52
Tumbler 28-36
Wine........................ 24-33

Probably other pieces. Butter dish, cake stand, celery, creamer, goblet, pitcher, sugar bowl being reproduced.

Jacob's Coat

Jacob's Coat

Maker unknown, 1800s. Clear, amber, non-flint.

Bowl, berry $29-36
Butter dish, covered 41-50
Celery 29-38
Creamer 30-40
Goblet 33-40
Pickle dish 16-23
Pitcher (ill.)................. 51-60
Saucedish 8-14
Spoonholder 22-30
Sugar bowl, covered 32-41

Probably other pieces. Amber, 50 percent higher than clear prices listed.

504

Jacob's Ladder

Jacob's Ladder

(Maltese): Bryce Bros., Pittsburgh, 1870s. Clear, amber, yellow; colors scarce. Non-flint.

Bowl, 6″ dia. ....$	24- 32
Butter dish, covered, Maltese	
Cross finial	56- 64
Cake plate on stand	40- 48
Celery	35- 43
Compote, covered, open, large	
standard	37- 47
Creamer, footed	46- 54
Cruet, Maltese Cross stopper ..	52- 60
Dish, oval	16- 23
Dolphin compote (rare)	240-260
Goblet, knob stem	59- 68
Mug	28- 36
Pitcher, water (ill.)	130-140
Sauce	
a. Flat, round, footed, 3½″	
4″, 5″	12- 18
b. Footed, 4½″	14- 19
Spoonholder	29- 37
Sugar bowl, covered, Maltese	
Cross finial	61- 70
Tumbler, handled	52- 61
Wine......................	33- 41

Probably other pieces. Colors, 150 percent higher than clear prices listed.

Jardiniere

Maker unknown, c. 1887, clear, non-flint.

Butter dish, covered ....$	25-33
Creamer	22-31
Spoonholder	20-30
Sugar bowl, covered	28-36

Possibly other pieces.

Jefferson's Number 251

Jefferson's Number 251

Jefferson Glass Company, Steubenville, Ohio, 1904. Plain, colored and opalescent. Non-flint.

Berry bowls, 8″, 6″, 4½″ .....$	16- 27
Butter dish, covered	31- 40
Condiment set	36- 42
Creamer	20- 27
Cruet, handled (ill.)	30- 36
Jug, ½ gal.	27- 37
Salt/Pepper, pr.	17- 26
Spoonholder	22- 31
Sugar bowl, covered	30- 40
Toothpick, blue, opalescent	
(rare)	128-135

Probably other pieces. Colors and opalescent 60 percent higher than clear prices listed.

Jefferson's Number 271

Jefferson's Number 271

Jefferson Glass Company, Follansbee, West Virginia, 1907. Crystal, blue, green,

(continued)

also gold trimmed, with gold rims. Non-flint.

Butter dish, blue	$40-47
Creamer	25-34
Jug, one-half gallon	33-40
Nappy, 4″ and 8″	18-26
Pitcher, water, green	52-61
Spoonholder	20-30
Sugar bowl, covered	47-52
Tumbler (ill.)	29-32

Probably others.

Jersey

Jersey

McKee Bros., 1894. Clear. Non-flint.

Butter dish, covered	$31-40
Compote	
a. High standard	38-47
b. Low standard	36-45
Celery	24-32
Creamer	22-31
Goblet	24-33
Pitcher, ½ gal., small	40-50
Spoonholder	22-31
Sugar bowl, covered	37-42
Tumbler	22-32

Probably other pieces.

Jersey Swirl

Jersey Swirl

(Swirl): Windsor Glass Company, Pittsburgh, Pennsylvania, 1887. Clear and color: canary, amber, blue. Non-flint.

Butter dish, covered	$52-61
Compote	
a. Covered	42-52
b. Open	31-40
Creamer	34-42
Goblet	
a. Buttermilk (ill.)	32-42
b. Regular size	33-44
Pitcher, water, buttermilk	52-60
Plate, bread	27-31
Sauce	18-24
Salt dip	15-22
Sugar bowl	
a. Covered	47-56
b. Open	24-34
Tumbler	31-40
Wine	24-27

Canary, 40 percent; blue or amber, 60 percent higher than crystal prices listed. Being reproduced in goblets, covered compotes, nappies, plates (2 sizes), salt dips and sauces.

Jewel and Dewdrop

Jewel and Dewdrop

(Kansas): Cooperative Flint Glass Company, 1870s; reproduced by U.S. Glass Company, in 1907 as Kansas pattern. Clear and opalescent. Non-flint.

Bowl, berry, 6″, 7″, 8½″	$22-37
Butter dish	56-64
Cake stand, 8″, 9″, 10″	42-60
Celery	38-46
Compote	
a. Covered, high standard,	
deep bowl	50-59

b. Open, high standard 40-49
Creamer 28-36
Goblet (rare) 36-43
Pitcher, water (ill.) 39-47
Salt/Pepper, pr. 58-64
Spoonholder (rare)............. 40-50
Sugar bowl 44-53
Syrup 60-68
Toothpick holder 36-44
Tumbler 28-36
Wine........................ 36-43

Probably other pieces.

Jewel and Festoon

Jewel and Festoon

(Loop and Jewel): Maker unknown, Ohio, late 1880s. Clear. Non-flint.

Bowls, several sizes $21-34
Butter dish, covered 34-42
Creamer 29-37
Goblet 28-39
Pitcher (ill.).................... 55-65
Relish dish 18-26
Salt/Pepper, pr. 19-26
Sherbet cup................... 17-26
Spoonholder 27-36
Sugar bowl, covered 36-47

Probably other pieces. Tumbler being reproduced.

Jeweled Heart

Northwood Glass Company, 1900s. Clear, colored, Carnival. Non-flint.

	Clear	Color
Butter	$62-72	$120-130
Cruet, clear, colored		
(ill.)		42- 51
Lamp	51-60	82- 92

Pitcher..............	40-50	100-115
Pitcher,		
Carnival		172-182
Syrup	37-46	50- 60
Tumbler,		
Carnival		53- 64

Probably other pieces. Toothpick, goblet, creamer and sugar being reproduced.

Jeweled Heart

Jeweled Moon and Star

Jeweled Moon and Star

(Moon and Star with Waffle): Maker unknown, Ohio, 1880s. Clear and frosted moons, blue or red; amber and blue; red and amber. Non-flint.

Bowl, relish, oval $19-28
Butter dish, covered 36-45
Compote
a. Covered 40-50
b. Open 39-47
Goblet 42-51
Pitcher, water (ill.) 57-63
Sugar bowl, covered 41-50
Tray, water 38-47
Tumbler 29-39
Wine........................ 30-32

Probably other pieces.

Jubilee

Jubilee

McKee Glass Company, 1894. Clear. Non-flint.

Celery vase	$24-33
Compote	
a. Covered	27-32
b. Open	20-27
Creamer	21-28
Goblet	31-40
Pickle dish	14-21
Pitcher, water (ill.)	36-42
Salt/Pepper, pr.	16-24
Spoonholder	22-27
Sugar bowl	30-40
Tumbler	20-29

Probably other pieces.

Jumbo

Photo: Mr. and Mrs. A.M. Zinkeler, Chattanooga, Tenn.

Jumbo

Canton Glass Company, Canton, Ohio, 1883. Clear, Also made by Aetna Glass Co., Bellaire, Ohio, same period. Non-flint.

Butter dish		
a. Round		$330-350
b. Oblong (rare)		400-425
Caster set, 3 bottles		340-365
Compote, covered		320-345
Creamer		250-265
Cup and saucer		148-165
Dish, covered, frosted		160-175
Goblet (rare)		600+
Spoonholder		140-150
Spoon rack (rare) (ill.)		700+
Sugar bowl, covered		295-320

Possibly other pieces. The spoon rack is one of the rarest pieces of pattern glass in America today. Prices are for Canton pieces.

King's Curtain

King's Curtain

Maker unknown, 1880s. Clear. Non-flint.

Butter dish, covered	$42-51
Cake stand	43-51
Creamer	26-34
Goblet	26-34
Pitcher, water (ill.)	33-42
Plate	19-27
Salt shaker	18-27
Saucedish, flat	14-22
Spoonholder	24-33
Sugar bowl	
a. Covered	27-36
b. Open	26-33

Probably other pieces.

King's 500

(Parrot): King, Son & Company, Pittsburgh, 1891. Clear, transparent blue, possibly other colors. Non-flint.

Bowl, berry, blue	$37-42
Butter, coverd, cobalt, gold eyes	70-78
Cruet, blue (ill.)	58-63

King's 500

Photo: Mr. and Mrs. A.M. Zinkeler, Chattanooga, Tenn.

Probably the usual patterns, the usual prices for a glass of this date. The cruet shown is in a beautiful blue.

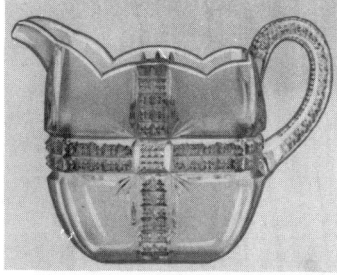

Klondike

Klondike

(Amberette; English Hobnail Cross): A. J. Beatty Company, Findlay Ohio, 1870s. Other companies, 1880s. Clear or frosted with color — amber, lilac/gold. Non-flint.

Bowl, 6" sq.	$125-145
Butter dish, covered	300-320
Compote, covered, 8"	220-240
Creamer (ill.)	130-140
Pitcher, square, tankard	550-600
Salt/Pepper, pr.	240-260
Sauce, footed, flat, others	80- 90
Spoonholder	175-185
Sugar bowl	
a. Covered	298-320
b. Open	130-145
Syrup	240-250
Toothpick holder, 2 types	220-240

Tray, square, 5½", 7", 8½"	150-160
Tumbler	185-200
Vase, bud, 8½" high	340-360

Many other pieces. Colors 50 percent higher than clear prices shown.

Knights of Labor

Knights of Labor

Bakewell, Pears & Company, Pittsburgh, 1879. Clear, canary, amber, blue. Non-flint.

Plate, bread (ill.)	$87-95
Mug	46-55

Colors, 65 percent higher than clear prices listed.

Krom

Krom

Maker unknown, c. 1830s, clear, flint.

Goblet (ill.)	$64-74
Whiskey, several sizes	27-36

Lacy Dewdrop

Co-Operative Flint Glass Company, Beaver Falls, Pennsylvania, c. 1890, clear, milk glass, non-flint. Possibly other colors.

Bowl, berry $22-31
Butter dish, covered 37-44
Creamer 33-42
Goblet 37-45
Mug 21-31
Pitcher, water 41-49
Spoonholder 21-30
Sugar bowl
  a. Open 19-27
  b. Covered 42-50
Tumbler 15-19

Milk glass, 30 percent higher than clear prices listed. Probably other pieces.

Lacy Medallion

Lacy Medallion

U.S. Glass Company, 1890s. Souvenir-type, gilded in opaque white, sometimes with flowers painted on sides. Non-flint.

Cup $31-40
Mug (ill.) 44-52
Toothpick 27-36
Tumbler 22-31
Wine 32-40

Other pieces.

Lacy Spiral

Lacy Spiral

(Colossus): Maker unknown, late 1880s. Clear. Non-flint.

Butter dish, covered $37-46
Compote
  a. Covered 44-53
  b. Jelly, open 29-36
  c. Open 30-34
Creamer 32-40
Pitcher, water (ill.) 48-54
Spoonholder 27-36
Sugar bowl, covered 41-52
Relish dish 20-27

Probably other pieces.

Lady Hamilton
Photo: Mrs. Paul Brown, Chattanooga, Tenn.

Lady Hamilton

(Peerless): Richards & Hartley Flint Glass Company, Pittsburgh, 1875. Clear.

Celery vase 47-56
Compotes (22 different types
  were made) 22-96
Creamer, low and high stem 39-47
Goblet 38-47
Mustard jar 40-50
Spoonholder 26-36
Sugar bowl 57-66
Tumbler 39-47

"Lafayet"

Boat-shaped saltcellar: This is a rare piece because it's one of the few, if not the **only** piece of glass signed at the Boston & Sandwich Glass Company, Sandwich, Massachusetts.

"Lafayet"

No price given because there are few, if any, available today. Shown only because Sandwich made some of the finest glass the world has ever known.

Large Stippled Chain

Large Stippled Chain

Probably Gillinder & Sons, 1870s. Clear. Non-flint.

Creamer $39-47
Goblet 30-40
Pitcher (ill.) 54-63
Sugar bowl
   a. Covered 42-51
   b. Open 31-40

Probably other pieces.

Late Crystal

Richard & Hartley Company, 1888; also, McKee Bros., 1894, and U.S. Glass Company, 1898. Clear. Non-flint.

Late Crystal

Celery $18-24
Compote
   a. Covered, low and high foot .. 36-44
   b. Open, low foot only 25-33
Creamer 20-30
Egg cup 12-19
Goblet 22-30
Pitcher, water (ill.) 30-40
Salt/Pepper, pr. 16-24
Sauce, flat and footed 11-20
Spoonholder 18-27
Sugar bowl 32-41
Tumbler 20-30

Probably other pieces.

Late Diamond Point Band

Late Diamond Point Band

(Scalloped Diamond Point, Panel with Diamond Point): Central Glass Company, Wheeling. West Virginia, 1870s. Nonflint.

(continued)

Bowl, round, oval $14-22
Butter dish, covered 23-31
Cake stand, small, large 26-34
Cheese dish, covered 30-40
Creamer 21-31
Goblet 20-28
Pitcher (ill.) 40-47
Sugar bowl, covered, open 26-34

Probably other pieces.

Late Panelled Grape

Late Panelled Grape

Another of the "Grape" patterns, late 1890s. Clear. Non-flint.
Bowl, berry $14-20
Butter dish, covered 22-31
Creamer (ill.) 24-33
Dish, covered 17-24
Goblet 16-22
Pitcher, milk, water 31-40
Wine 16-24

Goblet being reproduced.

Late Panelled Grape, Variant

Late Panelled Grape, Variant

Maker unknown, 1890s. Clear, probably premium glass at grocery stores. Non-flint.
Bowl, berry $11-16
Butter dish, covered 18-22
Creamer (ill.) 16-21
Goblet 14-23
Pitcher
  a. Milk 24-32
  b. Syrup 21-30
  c. Water 20-27
Wine 12-17

Probably other pieces.

Late Swan, Opaque

Late Swan, Opaque

Westmoreland Specialty Company, Grapeville, Pennsylvania, 1891-1892. Opaque white and opaque turquoise. Non-flint.
Sugar bowl, covered
  a. Opaque white $82-91
  b. Opaque turquoise (ill.) 79-89

Probably other pieces.

Late Thistle

Pittsburgh, late 1890s. Clear. Non-flint.
Butter dish, covered $41-50
Cake stand, small 32-40
Compote
  a. Covered 44-51
  b. Open 32-41
Honey dish, covered 31-40
Pitcher, milk (ill.) 55-62
Sugar bowl 42-50
Tumbler 33-41

Probably other pieces.

Late Thistle

Lattice

Lattice

(Diamond Bar): King, Son & Company, Pittsburgh, Pennsylvania. 1880. Clear, non-flint.

Butter dish	$49-58
Cake stand	56-64
Celery	34-42
Compote, covered, high standard	47-54
Cordial	22-29
Creamer	36-43
Egg cup	20-26
Goblet	30-39
Pitcher, water (ill.)	52-61
Plate, 6½", 7¼", 10", 12"	12-28
Platter, clear, "Waste not, want not"	39-48

Salt/Pepper, pr.	23-32
Sauce, flat, footed	10-17
Spoonholder	24-32
Sugar bowl	36-44
Wine	19-27

Probably others.

Leaf and Flower

Leaf Bracket

Leaf and Flower

Hobbs, Brockunier & Co., Wheeling, West Virginia. A Wheeling West Virginia product made in the 1890s. Clear, clear and frosted with amber or green flowers. Red has been reported.

Bowl, finger or waste	$17-26
Butter dish, covered	41-50
Caster set	44-53
Creamer	26-35
Creamer, amber stained flowers	51-60
Pitcher, water (ill.)	44-51
Sauce, flat	17-21
Tray, celery	20-32

Probably other pieces. Clear and frosted, 30 percent higher; amber, green, 70 percent higher; red, 100 percent higher than clear prices listed.

Leaf Bracket

Indiana Tumbler & Goblet (National) Company, Greentown, Indiana, 1900. Crystal, opal, chocolate, Nile green. Non-flint.

Berry bowl	$ 47- 54
Butter dish	72- 81
Celery tray	46- 54
Creamer	54- 62
Cruet (ill.)	108-117
Salt/Pepper, pr.	52- 61

(continued)

Spoonholder	52- 61
Tumbler	41- 50

Probably other pieces. Chocolate, 80 percent higher; opal and Nile green, 30 percent higher than clear prices listed.

Pitcher	46-54
Relish, oval	19-24
Sauce, flat, footed	16-24
Spoonholder	18-29
Sugar bowl, covered	47-57

Probably other pieces.

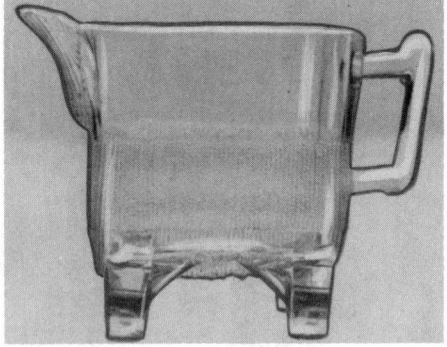

Legged Trough

Legged Trough

Maker and date unknown. How many pieces (creamer, sugar, tumbler, etc.) were made is unknown to this writer. It must have taken some doing to remove it from the mold! Knowers — **write!**

Lens and Star

O'Hara Glass Company, Pittsburgh, Pennsylvania, c. 1886, clear, non-flint.

Bowl, waste	18-24
Butter dish, covered	26-34
Celery	16-22
Creamer	27-36
Pitcher, water	32-41
Spoonholder	22-31
Sugar bowl, covered	34-43
Tray, handled	34-44
Tumbler	18-26

Probably other pieces.

Leverne

(Star in Honeycomb): Maker unknown, c. early 1870s, clear, non-flint.

Butter dish, covered	$37-42
Celery	26-35
Compote	
a. Open	27-34
b. Covered	42-51
Goblet	24-33

Liberty Bell

Liberty Bell

(Centennial): Gillinder & Company, Philadelphia. Made for 1876 Centennial. Rare in milk glass. Non-flint.

Butter dish, covered	$157-167
Celery	98-110
Child's table set (4 pc.)	160-170
Compote, open, 6", 8"	115-124
Creamer	
a. Plain handle	87- 96
b. Reeded handle	157-166
Goblet	63- 72
Pitcher, water	630-650
Plate, 6", 8", 10"	85-135
Platter, 9¼" x 13", Independence signers' names on border (ill.)	260-280
Salt	
a. Celery dip, master salt	38- 46
b. Shaker top, bell-shaped	82- 91
Salt/Pepper, pr.	225-245
Spoonholder, pedestal base	105-115
Sugar bowl, covered	140-150
Sugar bowl, open	84- 94

Probably other pieces. Milk glass, 150 percent higher than clear prices listed.

Liberty Bell Novelty Bank

This bell was made for the St. Louis Exposition in 1903.

Liberty Bell Novelty Bank

Liberty Bell bank (ill.) $44-54

Others were made and it gets confusing. If you like them, buy them.

Lightning

Lightning

(Chain Lightning): Tiffin Glass Company, Gas City, Indiana, 1890s. It was called Chain Lightning in the factory by the men. Clear. Non-flint.

Bowls, several styles	$17-32
Butter, covered	36-44
Celery vase	27-38
Compote	
a. Covered	41-47
b. Open	28-37
Creamer (ill.)	29-34
Goblet	26-34
Pitcher, water	41-50
Spoonholder	30-40

Probably others.

Lily-of-the-Valley

Lily-of-the-Valley

Sandwich, 1870s. Clear, etched. Non-flint.

Butter dish, footed, on three feet	$62-71
Celery	54-63
Compote, covered, high standard .	84-93
Cordial	48-57
Creamer, on three feet	47-56
Cruet, tall stopper	61-70
Dish, oval....................	34-40
Goblet	37-46
Pitcher, milk (scarce), (ill.)	80-90
Sauce, flat	20-28
Spoonholder, on three feet	40-49
Sugar bowl, on three feet........	62-71
Wine (scarce)	46-54

Probably other pieces.

Lincoln Drape

Lincoln Drape

Sandwich, late 1860s. Clear, milk-white, sapphire blue (both rare). Flint.

Butter dish	$110-120
Celery	93-103
Compote	
a. Open, low standard	70- 79
b. Covered	88- 98

(continued)

Creamer	133-143
Decanter	94-107
Egg cup	56- 66
Goblet, w/tassel (ill.)	82- 91
Pitcher, water	345-360
Plate, 6"	57- 64
Spoonholder	66- 75
Sugar bowl, open	58- 66
Tumbler	40- 49

Probably other pieces. Colors, 45 to 75 percent higher than clear prices listed.

Lined Band Round Thumbprint

Lined Band Round Thumbprint

Maker unknown, c. 1860, clear, flint.

Champagne	$42-51
Compote, open	38-46
Goblet (ill.)	25-34
Tumbler, footed	19-27
Wine	31-40

Probably other pieces.

Lion

Lion

(Atlanta): Gillinder & Sons, Philadelphia, 1870s. Clear and frosted, milk glass.

Bread plate, frosted	$ 66- 75
Butter dish, 2 styles	90-115
Celery, etched	108-116
Compote	
a. Covered, large, high standard	130-140
b. Covered, low, 5", collared	110-120
Creamer, frosted lion on base	72- 80
Goblet	67- 75
Paperweight, milk glass, lions reclining	148-160
Pitcher	
a. Milk	340-380
b. Syrup, metal top	240-260
c. Water	210-230
Sauce, footed, small medium, large	18- 23
Spoonholder	57- 66
Sugar bowl, rampant lion finial (ill.)	95-110
Tumbler	90-108
Wine, frosted	140-162

Probably other pieces. Butter dish, celery, cordial, egg cup, goblet, water pitcher, sauce, etc., being reproduced. Don't buy it for genuine!

Lion and Baboon

Lion and Baboon

Maker unknown, a humorous design of the 1880s. Clear.

Butter dish, covered	$ 61- 70
Creamer	74- 79
Compote, covered	85- 92
Miniature 4-piece table set	115-132
Pitcher (ill.)	88- 97
Spoonholder	34- 42
Sugar bowl, covered	59- 62

Probably other pieces.

Lion's Head

Lion's Head

Miniature set possibly Gillinder & Sons, c. 1870s, clear, non-flint.

5-piece table set (ill.) $280-310

Little Owl

Little Owl

Bryce, Higbee & Company, Pittsburgh, mid-1880s. This is part of a "Menagerie Toy Set," which includes "Bear" covered sugar, "Fish" spoonholder, "Turtle" butter dish. Crystal, old gold, blue and white opaque, amber, other colors. You see too few of these to price them. Don't buy one of these as Sandwich, especially the owl.

Little River

Possibly Sandwich, 1870s. Clear, possibly colors.

Pickle caster $77-86
Pickle jar (ill.)................ 46-54

The scene shown in photo (windmill) is unknown to collectors. Probably other pieces.

Little River

Log Cabin

Log Cabin

Central Glass Company, Wheeling, West Virginia, 1875. Clear, non-flint.

Butter dish $195-215
Compote, covered, on
stand (ill.).................. 230-240
Creamer 120-130
Mustard 68- 80
Pitcher, water 235-250
Sauce 39- 48
Spoonholder 108-119
Sugar bowl (rare), covered 160-170

Probably other pieces.

Loganberry and Grape

Loganberry and Grape

Dalzell, Gilmore & Leighton, mid-1880s. Clear. Non-flint.

Butter dish, covered	$36-45
Celery	24-33
Creamer	36-45
Goblet	22-31
Pitcher, water (ill.)	40-50
Tumbler	21-30

Probably other pieces.

Long Maple Leaf

Long Maple Leaf

Possibly, Westmoreland Specialty Company, late 1800s. Clear. Non-flint.

Butter dish, covered	$32-41
Celery	17-22
Creamer	26-29
Goblet	16-23
Mug with cap	21-28

Pitcher, water (ill.)	50-59
Salt/Pepper, pr.	20-27
Spoonholder	17-26
Sugar bowl, covered	33-39

Probably other pieces.

Loop

Loop

(O'Hara): O'Hara Glass Company, Pittsburgh, late 1850s or 1860s. Also made by Gillinder & Sons, 1860s, and by Portland Glass Co., Portland, Maine, 1870s. They called it Portland Petal.

Butter dish, covered	$42-51
Cake stand	44-53
Celery	24-32
Compote	
a. Covered, high standard	60-70
b. Open	34-40
Creamer, 6″ high	34-43
Egg cup	19-27
Goblet, 3 styles	22-37
Pitcher, water, applied	
handle (ill.)	60-70
Spoonholder	24-33
Sugar bowl	
a. Covered	41-50
b. Open	31-40
Wine	32-40

Probably other pieces.

Loop and Dart

Loop and Dart

Sandwich, early; Richards & Hartley, Portland Glass Company, Portland, Maine, 1860s. Clear.

Butter dish, covered, round
  ornaments $52-61
Celery vase, diamond band 50-57
Compote, 8″, low foot............ 38-47
Cordial....................... 36-44
Creamer, diamond ornaments .. 78-87
Egg cup, round ornaments 25-34
Goblet, buttermilk.............. 35-44
Pitcher, water (ill.) 72-81
Plate, 6″ (rare) 73-83
Salt, footed 32-41
Spoonholder, round ornaments .. 29-36
Sugar bowl, covered 51-60
Tumbler, footed, water 32-40
Wine........................ 23-31

Probably other pieces.

Loop and Dart with Round Ornaments

Loop and Dart with Round Ornaments

Portland Glass Company, Portland, Maine, c. 1869, clear, non-flint, flint.

Butter dish, covered $52-61
Butter patty 16-24
Compote, covered 65-74
Creamer 78-87
Egg cup 25-34
Goblet (ill.) 35-44
Pitcher, water.................. 72-81
Spoonholder 29-36

Sugar bowl
  a. Covered 51-60
  b. Open 25-33

Flint, 25 percent higher than non-flint prices listed. Sauce being reproduced.

Loop and Moose Eye

Loop and Moose Eye

Maker unknown, c. 1870s, clear, flint.

Creamer $27-36
Decanter 37-44
Goblet (ill.) 29-37
Spoonholder 22-30
Sugar bowl, covered 39-44

Probably other pieces.

Loop with Dewdrops

Loop with Dewdrops

Earlier maker unknown; reproduced by U.S. Glass Company, 1892. Non-flint.

Bowl, 5″, 6″, 7″, 8″ $12-23
Butter dish, covered 39-47
Cake plate on stand, 9″, 10″ 47-53
Celery vase 30-39
Compote
  a. Covered, 5″, 6″, 7″, 8″,
    high foot 39-54

(continued)

b. Open, 5", 6", 7", 8",
  high foot 22-31
Creamer 36-41
Dish, oval, 7", 8", 9" 20-34
Goblet, knobbed stem 34-43
Mug, with cap 24-32
Pitcher, ½ gal. (ill.) 40-49
Salt/Pepper, pr. 29-38
Spoonholder 27-34
Sugar bowl, covered 36-45
Tumbler 21-28
Wine 29-34

Probably other pieces.

Loop with Stippled Panels

Loop with Stippled Panels

(Texas): U.S. Glass Company, 1900 and 1907. Crystal, crystal with gilded top, ruby in the body. Non-flint.
Bowl, berry, 7½", 8½", 9½",
  flat, footed $16-39
Butter dish 27-34
Cake stand, footed, 10", high
  and low standard 40-50
Celery 19-27
Creamer 22-31
Cruet, faceted stopper 31-41
Goblet 27-37
Pitcher, three pints (ill.) 33-42
Salt/Pepper, pr., large, small 26-34
Spoonholder 17-26
Sugar bowl, small 27-35
Toothpick holder 14-22
Tumbler 14-20
Wine 20-29

Probably other pieces. Colors, same price.

Loops and Drops

Loops and Drops

(New Jersey): Maker unknown, c. 1890s, clear, ruby-flashed, non-flint.
Butter dish, covered (ill.) $56-64
Creamer 44-53
Goblet 34-42
Spoonholder 30-40
Sugar bowl, covered 51-62

Ruby-flashed, 50 percent higher than clear prices listed. Probably other pieces.

Louis XV

Louis XV

(Winged Scroll): Northwood Glass Company, Indiana, Pennsylvania, 1898. Custard, "Ivory and Gold," green, other colors. Non-flint.

	Color	Custard
Berry set		
a. Large bowl	$92-107	$155-170
b. Small bowl	50- 60	88- 98
Butter dish, covered	88- 98	180-192

Compote		115-125
Creamer	78- 87	105-110
Cruet	84- 92	155-165
Pitcher, water	99-110	150-160
Salt/Pepper, pr.	62- 72	130-140
Spoonholder	79- 88	105-115
Sugar bowl, covered		
(ill.)	75- 84	112-132
Tumbler, water	59- 68	70- 80

Louisiana Purchase Exposition

Louisiana Purchase Exposition

The World's Fair held in St. Louis, Missouri, 1904, to commemorate the centennial of the Louisiana Purchase 100 years before. Plates and iced tea (or beverage) glasses were popular souvenirs. Crystal, crystal with frosted center, milk-glass.

Beverage glass	$37-46
Plate	33-42
Tumbler (ill.)	31-40

Probably other pieces.

Lutz

Lutz

McKee Bros., Jeannette, Pennsylvania, 1894. Clear. Non-flint.

Goblet	$31-40
Mustard jar	26-31
Pickle jar	26-35
Pitcher, water (ill.)	49-58

Probably other pieces.

William McKinley Campaign Items

William McKinley Campaign Items

Most were made by McKee & Bros. in 1896. Non-flint.

Bread plate, "His Will Be Done"	
(ill.)	$78-88
Goblet, bust	44-53
Gold tray	82-91
Mug (cup), covered	37-46
Plate, "Protection and Plenty" ..	57-67
Tumbler, clear	37-47
Tumbler, frosted	44-52

Other pieces.

Madison

Madison

Maker and date unknown, clear, flint.

Compote, covered	$72- 81

(continued)

Creamer 94-102
Goblet 42- 52
Spoonholder 44- 52
Sugar bowl (base ill.) 90-100

Should be other pieces.

Magnet and Grape, Frosted Leaf

Magnet and Grape, Frosted Leaf

Sandwich glass, early. Clear glass with frosted leaf.

Butter dish $120-140
Celery 188-196
Champagne 115-130
Compote, open (scarce),
   several types 120-130
Cordial 96-105
Creamer 110-118
Decanter with matching stoppers
  a. Pint 80- 90
  b. Quart 97-107
Goblet
  a. Knob stem (ill.) 80- 90
  b. Plain stem 64- 73
  c. Variant, large American
    shield 240-260
Salt, footed 48- 57
Saucedish, 4″ 32- 41
Spoonholder 49- 58
Sugar bowl, covered 100-110
Tumbler, water, whiskey 64- 73
Wine jug, two styles (rare) 70- 80

Creamer, goblet, covered sugar bowl being reproduced.

Magnet and Grape, Stippled Leaf

Sandwich glass, 1870s. Clear glass with stippled leaf, non-flint.

Magnet and Grape, Stippled Leaf
Butter dish, acorn knob $48-56
Compote, open 32-39
Cordial 32-41
Creamer 50-59
Goblet, knob stem 49-58
Pitcher (ill.) 82-92
Salt, footed 19-26
Saucedish, 4″ 8-13
Spoonholder 30-38
Sugar bowl 27-35
Tumbler 28-36

Maine

Maine

(Panelled Flower, Stippled): U.S. Glass Company, Pittsburgh, early1890s. Clear, emerald green.

Bowl, 6″, 7″, 8″ $24-38
Creamer 24-32
Dish, relish 15-20
Mug, handled 24-32
Pitcher (ill.) 46-54
Sauce, flat 12-20
Spoonholder 21-29
Sugar bowl, covered 33-41
Toothpick holder 21-28

Tumbler 24-33

Probably other pieces. Green, 100 percent higher than clear prices listed.

Maize

Maize

Libbey & Son Company, Toledo, Ohio, 1889. White opaque, yellow, clear, custard.

Bowl
  a. Berry, 9″ $165-174
  b. Finger, 5″ 120-130
Celery vase 140-150
Creamer 170-179
Decanter, pint, quart 112-122
Pitcher
  a. Syrup (ill.) 128-142
  b. Water 280-290
Spoonholder 105-112
Sugar bowl 280-300
Toothpick holder 150-165
Tumbler 110-120

Probably other pieces. Clear, yellow, custard, 30 percent higher than white opaque prices listed. Being reproduced in many sizes and shapes. Careful here!

Manhattan

Manhattan

U.S. Glass Company, 1902. Clear, gilt in the sunken circles, red-flashed, amber. Non-flint.

Bowl, berry, 7″, 8″, 8½″, 9½″,
  10″, 11″, 12½″ ....$ 25- 37
Bowl, punch, large, cups 135-150
Butter dish 47- 57
Cake stand 52- 60
Celery vase, tall.............. 37- 46
Compote, 9½″, 10½″ 44- 52
Creamer, individual, large 24- 33
Pitcher, syrup (ill.) 42- 51
Plate, 5″, 9½″, 11″, 12″ 22- 32
Sauce, 5″, footed; 4½″, flat 18- 27
Spoonholder 21- 31
Sugar bowl
  a. Covered 50- 58
  b. Open, individual 21- 29
Tumbler, iced tea, water 22- 30
Water bottle 31- 40

Probably other pieces. Red-flashed 25 percent higher than clear. Amber 50 percent higher. Being reproduced in bowls, creamer and sugar, goblets, iced teas, plates, sherbets and wines.

Manhattan

Manhattan

Tarentum Glass Company, Tarentum, Pennsylvania, 1895, clear only. Non-flint.

  Butter dish, covered (ill.) $27-32
  Cake stand 24-32
  Celery 14-21
  Creamer 12-20
  Pitcher, water................. 28-37
  Spoonholder 14-24
  Sugar bowl, covered 27-36
  Wine 14-24

All standard pieces made.

Maple

(Hops Band): King, Son & Company, Pittsburgh, Pennsylvania, c. 1870s, clear.

Butter dish, covered	$31-39
Cake stand, large	40-48
Celery	32-41
Compote, covered	37-46
Creamer	24-33
Egg cup	24-32
Goblet	22-30
Pitcher	36-44
Salt, footed	22-31
Spoonholder	17-19
Sugar bowl	
a. Open	16-26
b. Covered	30-39

Probably other pieces.

Maple Leaf

Maple Leaf

Northwood Glass Company, 1890s. Custard, Carnival, non-flint.

Berry set	
a. Large bowl, stemmed, Custard	$115-126
b. Small bowl, stemmed, Custard	47- 56
Butter dish, covered, Custard	95-104
(same item, Carnival marigold)	62- 71
(same item, Carnival vivid)	93-102
Creamer, Custard	74- 82
(same item, Carnival marigold)	35- 45
(same item, Carnival vivid)	61- 70
Ice cream set, Carnival	
a. Large bowl, stemmed, marigold	44- 52
(same in Carnival vivid)	91- 98
b. Small bowl, stemmed, marigold	17- 26
(same in Carnival vivid)	30- 40
Pitcher, Custard	169-178
(same item, Carnival marigold)	64- 69
(same item, Carnival vivid) (ill.)	135-144
Spoonholder, Custard	92-101
(same item, Carnival marigold)	46- 55
(same item, Carnival vivid)	64- 73
Sugar bowl, covered, Custard	94-103
(same item, Carnival marigold)	34- 42
(same item, Carnival vivid)	60- 70
Tumbler, Custard	81- 90
(same item, Carnival marigold)	32- 41
(same item, Carnival vivid)	34- 43

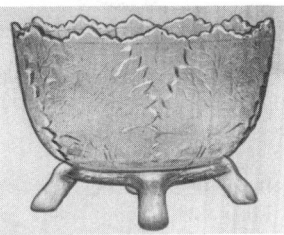

Maple Leaf

Maple Leaf

(Leaf): Gillinder & Sons, Greensburg Pennsylvania, late 1880s; they called it Leaf. Clear, canary, amber, vaseline, blue, sapphire, other colors. Non-flint.

Butter dish	$52-60
Celery vase	35-43
Compote	
a. Covered, high standard	81-90
b. Round, open, footed	55-63
Goblet	43-53
Pitcher, large	59-67
Plate, 10″, 10½″, Grant Peace	39-47
Sauce, 5″, 6″, footed	13-20
Spoonholder	24-32
Sugar bowl (ill.)	38-43
Tumbler	24-32

Probably other pieces. Colors, 40 to 60 percent higher than clear prices listed. Being heavily reproduced in various sizes and colors.

Marquisette

Co-Operative Flint Glass Company, Beaver Falls, Pennsylvania, c. early 1880s, clear, flint.

Butter dish, covered	$50-60
Celery	40-48

Compote
a. Open 24-33
b. Covered 50-60
Creamer 44-52
Goblet 27-35
Spoonholder 32-42
Sugar bowl
a. Open 37-42
b. Covered 42-52
Wine......................... 21-30

Probably other pieces.

Marsh Fern

Riverside Glass Works, Wellsburg, West Virginia, c. 1889, clear, non-flint. This was their "No. 327."

Bowl $25-34
Compote, high standard 31-40
Creamer, tankard 32-41
Goblet 27-36
Spoonholder 21-30
Sugar bowl, covered 37-42

Other pieces.

Marsh Pink

Marsh Pink

Maker unknown, Ohio, 1880s. Clear, rare pieces in amber. Non-flint.

Bowl, open and covered $31-39
Butter dish, covered 34-39
Cake stand, small 42-50
Compote, covered 42-48
Jam jar...................... 33-39
Pitcher (ill.)................... 42-51
Spoonholder 30-40
Sugar bowl, covered 34-39

Probably other pieces. Amber 150 percent higher than clear prices listed.

Maryland

Maryland

U.S. Glass Company, one of their "States" series. Clear, with gold. Non-flint.

Bowl $22-29
Butter dish, covered 39-42
Compote, open 35-42
Custard 18-26
Creamer 27-34
Cruet 21-30
Honey dish 14-20
Goblet 29-37
Pitcher, water, with
gold (ill.) 41-50
Plate, bread.................. 19-27
Sauce 17-25
Spoonholder 30-31
Sugar bowl, covered 28-34
Tumbler 24-28
Wine......................... 29-34

Mascotte

Ripley & Company, Pittsburgh, c. 1884, clear, plain or engraved. Reissued by U.S. Glass Company after 1891. Non-flint.

Butter dish
a. Plain $50-59
b. Horseshoe-shaped, marked
"Maud S." (rare) 85-95
Celery, etched................. 37-45
Compote
a. Open 38-47
b. Covered 75-83
Dish 18-24
Goblet, etched................. 33-41
Sugar bowl, covered 40-47
Tumbler 19-27
Wine......................... 23-31

Other pieces. Ripley prices listed.

Masonic

(Inverted Prism): McKee Glass Company, Jeannette, Pennsylvania, c. 1894, clear, non-flint.

Bowl, berry	$28-36
Butter dish, covered	44-52
Cake stand, high standard	40-49
Creamer	37-45
Pitcher, water	54-63
Spoonholder	18-26
Sugar bowl, covered	42-50
Tumbler	22-30

Probably other pieces.

Massachusetts

Massachusetts

U.S. Glass Company, 1898. Clear. Non-flint.

Butter dish, covered	$32-40
Cruet	20-26
Dish, candy	18-27
Creamer	30-37
Pitcher	51-61
Plate, 8″	30-39
Shot glass	18-26
Table lamp	50-59
"Teapot" (intended as rum jug) (ill.)	68-73
Water carafe	40-47

Probably other pieces.

Medallion

(Spades, Hearts and Spades): Maker unknown, 1880s. Clear, yellow, amber, blue, apple green. Non-flint.

Butter dish	$41-50
Cake stand	32-40
Celery vase	30-38

Medallion

Compote, covered, high standard	46-53
Creamer	30-38
Goblet	29-37
Mug	22-30
Pitcher, water (ill.)	54-62
Sauce, flat, footed	12-17
Spoonholder	23-32
Sugar bowl	35-43
Tumbler	22-29
Wine	25-33

Probably other pieces. Yellow, amber, blue, 100 percent; apple green, 150 percent higher than clear prices listed.

Melrose

Greensburg Glass Company, Greensburg, Pennsylvania, c. 1890s, clear, plain or etched, non-flint.

Butter dish, covered	$42-51
Cake stand	37-44
Celery	30-39
Compote, covered, high standard, 6″, 8″	47-51
Creamer, tankard	31-42
Goblet	22-31
Mug	18-27
Pitcher	
a. Quart	21-30
b. ½ gal.	32-40
Spoonholder	22-31
Sugar bowl, covered	33-42
Tumbler	16-22
Wine	18-26

Etched, 20 percent higher than clear prices listed. Other pieces.

Memphis

Memphis

(Doll's Eye): Northwood Glass Company, 1908-1910, clear, colors, Carnival.

Berry set (clear, colors only)
  a. Large bowl . . . . $ 31- 40
  b. Small bowl 17- 26
Butter dish, covered (clear,
  colors only) 42- 51
Fruit bowl & base 56- 62
Pitcher
  a. Syrup 51- 60
  b. Water 145-151
Punch set
  a. Bowl & base 52- 61
  b. Cup 17- 26
Spoonholder (clear, colors
  only) 41- 50
Sugar bowl, covered (clear,
  colors only) 40- 50

Colors, 50-75 percent; Carnival, 60 percent higher than clear prices listed. Probably other pieces.

Mephistopheles

Mephistopheles

Germany; also made in this country, late 1800s. Clear, frosted.

Ale glass, "Germany" $31-40
Goblet 39-47
Mug (ill.) 43-53
Pitcher, applied handle 53-59

Probably other pieces made.

Michigan

Michigan

(Loop with Pillar): U.S. Glass Company, c. 1893, clear, gilted, some pieces with painted decorations. Non-flint.

Bowl, berry, 7½″, 8½″, 10″ $29-39
Butter dish, covered
  a. Large 34-43
  b. Small 42-50
Creamer
  a. Individual 22-31
  b. Large 31-40
Cruet 28-36
Goblet (ill.) 31-40
Pitcher, tankard 37-46
Salt/Pepper, pr. 33-40
Spoonholder 23-31
Sugar bowl, covered 34-44
Tumbler 32-40
Wine 28-37

Minerva

Sandwich glass, 1870s. Clear. Non-flint.

Butter dish, covered . . . . $ 86- 94
Cake plate, on standard, 13″ . . 105-112
Compote, high and low
  standard 67- 92
Creamer 52- 61

Minerva

Goblet	80- 90
Marmalade jar, w/lid	72- 81
Pitcher, water	108-116
Plate, small, closed handles, 9"	51- 60
Platter, "Give Us This Day" ..	70- 78
Sauce, flat round, footed round	19- 28
Spoonholder	34- 39
Sugar bowl, covered (ill.)	64- 74

Probably other pieces.

Minnesota

U.S. Glass Company, c. 1898, clear, green with gold decoration. Non-flint.

Bowl
a. Berry, round, 6", 7", 8" $31-40
b. Flared edge, 4½", 7½", 8½", 9½" 28-48
Butter dish, covered 46-54
Celery tray, 10", 13" 28-38
Compote
a. Round, 6", 7", 8" 54-73
b. Square, 6", 7", 8" 51-70
Creamer 33-41
Goblet 22-31
Pitcher, water 47-54
Sugar bowl, covered 42-51
Tumbler 18-25

Green with gold decoration, 25 percent higher than clear prices listed.

Mirror

McKee Brothers, Pittsburgh, Pennsylvania, c. 1870s, clear, flint.

Ale...........................$20-24
Champagne................... 27-36
Compote, 6" 51-60
Cordial 28-32
Goblet 25-31

Mirror

Jar, pickle	26-34
Spoonholder	11-18
Tumbler (ill.)	27-34
Wine	35-43

Probably other pieces.

Missouri

Missouri

U.S. Glass Company, after 1891. Clear, blue, emerald green, canary, amethyst.

Butter dish, covered $39-47
Celery 21-30
Compote, high and low standard 32-41
Creamer 32-42
Goblet 28-37
Pitcher, pint, ½ gallon (ill.) 37-44
Spoonholder 21-31
Sugar bowl, covered 36-46
Tumbler 21-30

Probably other pieces. Blue, green, 50 percent higher; canary, amethyst, 100 percent higher than clear prices listed.

Mitred Bars

(Mitred Diamond Points): Bryce Brothers, Pittsburgh, c. 1885, clear, non-flint.

Bowl, oval	$18-27
Butter dish, covered	31-40
Cake stand	22-29
Celery	22-30
Creamer, covered	31-40
Goblet	27-37
Spoonholder	21-31
Sugar bowl, covered	34-44
Wine	18-24

Other pieces.

Monkey

Monkey

George A. Duncan and Sons, Pittsburgh, 1880s. Clear and opalescent. Nonflint.

Bowl, waste	$108-116
Butter dish, covered	158-167
Celery	53- 62
Creamer	105-110
Jar, pickle	57- 64
Mug, 2 styles	71- 82
Pitcher (ill.)	228-240
Spoonholder	92-101
Sugar	
a. Covered	160-168
b. Open	82- 91
Toothpick holder	63- 72
Tumbler	72- 81

Probably other pieces. Opalescent, 80 percent higher than clear prices listed. Spoonholder and toothpick holder being reproduced.

Monroe

Maker unknown, made well before the Civil War. Clear and brilliant. Extremely rare in lamp. Shown here because too many patterns remain unidentified as to maker, etc. If you know, write to the Houston Museum, Chattanooga, Tennessee.

Lamp (rare) (ill.) ....$600+

Monroe

Moon and Star

Moon and Star

(Star and Punty): Sandwich, 1870s; Palace, Pioneer Glass Company, 1892; Wilson Glass Company, 1890, same name. Imperial, Cooperative Flint Glass Company, 1890s. Mold sold to Phoenix Glass Company, 1937. Many reproductions on market today. Clear, some

(continued)

pieces with color added, also milk glass.

Bowl, berry, 6″, 12½″	$ 20-	40
Butter dish, covered	58-	67
Cake stand, 6″ dia.	52-	61
Celery	38-	47
Compote, covered, 7″, 8″, 10″,		
high standard	48-	85
Creamer	55-	63
Goblet, clear, frosted.........	39-	47
Pitcher, water (ill.)	115-125	
Sugar bowl, covered, jeweled ..	59-	69
Tumbler, footed, flint	51-	60
Wine......................	31-	39

EVERY item being reproduced. Careful!

Morning Glory

Morning Glory

Sandwich, c. 1860s, clear, flint.

Compote, open	$180-190
Creamer (rare)	295+
Egg cup	140-150
Goblet (ill.)	260-270
Wine.......................	140-150

Goblet and wine being reproduced in clear and in color.

Nail

Bryce Bros., Pittsburgh, 1885. Crystal glass with ruby stain, etched.

Bowl, footed...................	$12-17
Butter, covered	21-30
Creamer	22-31
Goblet	27-36
Pitcher, water (ill.)	58-66
Sauce, footed	14-23
Salt/Pepper, pr................	13-21

Nail

Spoonholder	14-22
Sugar bowl	
a. Covered	26-35
b. Open	13-20
Tumbler	15-25

Probably other pieces. With ruby stain, 100 percent higher than clear prices listed.

Nailhead

Nailhead

(Gem): Sandwich, early; later, Bryce, Higbee & Co., Pittsburgh. Clear orange in the grooves, clear aquamarine. Non-flint.

Butter dish	$46-54
Cake stand, 4″ high	34-39
Celery	32-39
Compote, covered, open,	
scalloped	38-53
Cordial	29-37
Creamer	30-40
Goblet	26-34
Pitcher, water (ill.)	59-68

Plate, round, 9″, square, 7″ 19-26
Saucedish 9-16
Salt/Pepper, pr. 30-38
Spoonholder 24-32
Sugar bowl, covered, scalloped .. 34-42
Tumbler 21-29
Wine........................ 18-27

Probably other pieces. Colors, 50 percent higher than clear prices listed.

New England Pineapple

New England Pineapple

(Loop and Jewel): Boston & Sandwich Glass Company, c. 1860s, clear, flint. Colored pieces considered rare.

Butter dish, covered	$120-130
Champagne..................	106-115
Compote, open	74- 84
Creamer	175-184
Decanter, with or without stopper	90-138
Goblet (ill.)	47- 54
Sauce	17- 25
Spoonholder	44- 52
Sugar bowl, covered	89-115
Tumbler, water	80- 88

Other pieces. Goblet and wine being reproduced.

New York (Honeycomb)

Many firms made this pattern, among them, Bakewell, Pears & Company, 1860s on. Early in clear; later in yellow, blue, amber, green, opalescent.

Bowl, 6″, 7″, 8″, 9″, 10″	$24-36
Butter dish	37-47

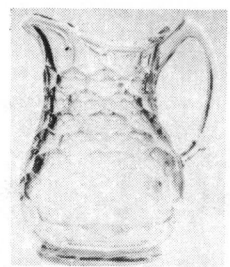

New York (Honeycomb)

Caster bottle	15-23
Celery, Laredo, flint	48-56
Creamer	38-47
Decanter, pint, quart	42-53
Goblet	33-42
Jug, one-half pint, pint, quart, 3 pints	29-42
Pitcher, water (ill.)	55-64
Salt/Pepper, pr.	30-39
Spoonholder	26-36
Sugar bowl	38-48
Tumbler, one-half pint, one-third pint, footed	28-42
Wine........................	30-38

Many other pieces. Colors, 40 to 60 percent higher than clear prices listed.

Niagara

Fostoria Glass Company, Fostoria, Ohio, c. 1900, clear, non-flint.

Bowl, berry	$17-25
Butter dish, covered	29-38
Creamer	20-29
Pitcher	
a. Tankard	22-31
b. Water	36-45
Spoonholder	13-20
Sugar bowl, covered	26-34
Tumbler	14-21

Other pieces.

Notched Bar

(Ball): McKee & Brothers, Jeannette, Pennsylvania, c. 1894, clear, non-flint.

Bottle, castor	$36-44
Butter dish, covered	61-70
Creamer	52-61
Cruet	40-50
Jar, jam	68-73
Spoonholder	26-36

531

(continued)

Sugar bowl, covered 55-62
Wine 32-39
Probably other pieces.

Nova Scotia Grape and Vine

Nova Scotia Grape and Vine

Nova Scotia, Canada, late 1880s. Non-flint.

Pitcher, water (ill.) $38-47
Tumbler to match 16-25

Probably other pieces.

Nursery Tales

A product of Pennsylvania, 1880s. Each piece shows different characters from old nursery tales. Clear and opal glass. Non-flint.

Child's 4-piece set (butter
  dish, creamer, spoonholder,
  sugar bowl), miniature
  Clear $145-154
Punch set with 6 cups,
  miniature
  Clear 190-210
Sauce 44- 53

Opal, 100 percent more than clear prices listed.

Octagonal Beehive Deep Dish

Sandwich, early. Clear glass only, it is 9¼-inch in diameter and was used to hold a compote.

Beehive dish (ill.) $160-170
Compote to match
  (extremely rare) ....500+

Odd Fellow

Probably Adams & Company, Pittsburgh, early 1880s. Clear. This firm spe-

Octagonal Beehive Deep Dish

Odd Fellow

cialized in selling their wares in Central and South America. If traveling there, look for Adams, if you know their patterns. Much has been found "South of the border." Non-flint.

Butter dish, covered $41-50
Cake stand, 8″, 9″, 10″ 38-49
Celery 23-32
Creamer 29-37
Goblet, knob and round
  stem (ill.) 27-37
Pitcher, large, small 44-53
Spoonholder 24-32
Sugar bowl 35-43

Many other pieces, some being reproduced, such as horseshoe-handled platter.

O'Hara Diamond

U.S. Glass Company, c. 1891, 1892, clear, plain, flashed with ruby stain. Non-flint.

Bowl, 8″ $17-24

Celery 19-26
Creamer 25-32
Cup/saucer, custard 14-21
Goblet 22-31
Pitcher, tankard............... 37-46
Spoonholder 22-30
Sugar bowl, covered 25-33
Tray, piecrust edge 21-30

Ruby stain, 40 percent higher than clear prices listed.

One-Hundred-and-One

One-Hundred-and-One

Probably Bellaire Goblet Company, Findlay, Ohio, late 1870s. Clear, non-flint.

Butter dish $65-75
Celery 54-63
Compote, covered, high foot, 8″ .. 63-72
Creamer 39-47
Goblet 40-50
Lamp, handled, flat 82-92
Pickle, oval, tapered 26-36
Plate
  a. 7″, 8″, 9″, 10″, 11″ 20-51
  b. Bread, round, 11″, "Give
    us this day" 63-72
Sauce, flat, 4″ 12-20
Salt/Pepper, pr. 36-43
Spoonholder 45-53
Sugar bowl 50-60
Relish dish, oval, deep 17-24

Probably other pieces.

Opposing Pyramids

(Flora): Green Glass Company, Pittsburgh, 1889. Clear. Non-flint.

Butter dish, covered $32-40
Creamer 27-36
Goblet (ill.) 26-33
Pitcher, water................. 42-51
Sugar bowl, covered 34-43

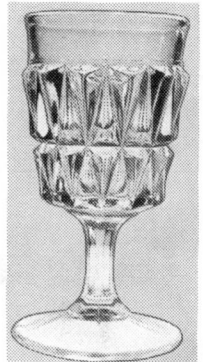

Opposing Pyramids

Tumbler 28-35
Wine........................ 19-25

Probably other pieces.

Optic

U.S. Glass Company, c. 1892, clear, often ruby stained or engraved or both. Non-flint.

Bowl, berry $14-22
Butter dish, covered 27-35
Celery 17-22
Creamer 23-31
Goblet 14-21
Pitcher, water................. 34-43
Spoonholder 17-24
Sugar bowl, covered 25-33
Toothpick holder 14-20

Ruby stained and/or engraved, 20 percent higher than clear prices listed.

Oregon

Richards & Hartley Flint Glass Company, Tarentum, Pennsylvania, c. 1888, clear, clear, flashed with ruby blocks, non-flint.

Butter dish, covered $38-47
Celery 22-31
Compote, covered 40-48
Creamer 35-43
Goblet 27-35
Pitcher, water................. 47-54
Sauce, footed 18-26
Spoonholder 26-35
Sugar bowl, covered 37-46

Ruby blocks, 50 percent higher than clear prices listed.

Oriental

Oriental

Probably La Belle Glass Works, Bridgeport, Ohio, 1875-1880. Clear. Non-flint.

Butter dish, covered	$30-37
Celery	28-34
Compote, covered	31-40
Creamer	27-35
Goblet	19-27
Pitcher	35-40
Spoonholder	19-27
Sugar bowl	
a. Covered (ill.)	34-42
b. Open	24-32
Tumbler	12-19

Probably other pieces.

Orion Inverted Thumbprint

Orion Inverted Thumbprint

Canton Glass Company, Canton, Ohio, 1894. Clear, amber, blue, green, milk-white, yellow, black. Non-flint.

Butter dish, covered	$31-40
Celery	19-26
Compote	
a. Covered	27-34
b. Open	24-32
Creamer	21-30
Pitcher, water (ill.)	34-42
Sauce, footed	16-25

Spoonholder	20-28
Sugar bowl	
a. Covered	30-38
b. Open	16-24

Probably other pieces. Milk-white, 25 percent; yellow, 45 percent; amber, green, 65 percent; blue, 100 percent higher than prices listed for clear.

Oval Loop

(Question Mark): Richards & Hartley Flint Glass Company, Pittsburgh, Pennsylvania, c. 1880, clear, non-flint.

Bowls, round, oval	$21-30
Butter dish, covered	36-45
Celery	19-27
Compote, covered	40-48
Creamer	18-26
Goblet	19-27
Pitcher	37-44
Shaker, sugar	24-32
Spoonholder	20-28
Sugar bowl, covered	30-39
Tumbler	24-33
Wine	20-27

Other pieces.

Oval Miter

McKee & Brothers, Pittsburgh, c. 1865, clear, flint.

Butter dish, covered	$51-64
Compote	
a. Open, 6″, 8″	44-54
b. Covered, high standard	65-72
Goblet	42-51
Sauce, flat	15-24
Spoonholder	31-40
Sugar bowl	
a. Open	52-61
b. Covered	53-61

Probably other pieces.

Oval Panels

Maker unknown, c. late 1880s, non-flint.

Goblet	
Clear	$20-28
Amber	23-31
Yellow	25-34
Blue	30-40

Other pieces?

Owl and Possum

Owl and Possum

Maker unknown, 1880s. Clear. Non-flint.

Goblet (ill.) $67- 76
Pitcher, water 96-105
Sauce, footed................. 30- 37

Probably other pieces.

Paling

Paling

Maker unknown, c. 1880s, clear, non-flint.

Butter dish, covered $27-34
Creamer (ill.) 21-30
Goblet 20-27
Spoonholder 17-24
Sugar bowl, covered 25-33

Other pieces.

Palm Beach

U.S. Glass Company, C. 1895, yellow, blue, non-flint.

Butter dish, covered $140-150
Creamer 61- 70
Pitcher, water 161-170
Sauce 30- 37
Spoonholder 62- 72
Sugar bowl, covered 140-148
Tumbler 60- 70

Blue, 20 percent higher than yellow prices listed.

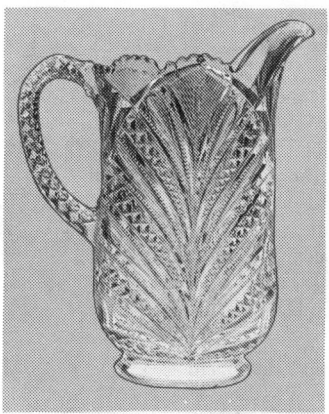

Palm Leaf Fan

Palm Leaf Fan

Maker unknown, early 1890s. Clear.

Bowl, large $23-31
Butter dish, covered 30-38
Cake stand, large 31-40
Celery vase 21-28
Compote
  a. Covered 32-41
  b. Open 27-35
Creamer 21-30
Pitcher, water (ill.) 36-44
Sugar, covered 32-41
Wine........................ 17-26

Probably other pieces.

Palmette

Maker unknown, c. 1870s, clear, non-flint.

Butter dish, covered $54-63
Cake stand 41-50
Celery 33-42

(continued)

Palmette

Compote
  a. Covered, low standard 45-54
  b. Open, 8″ high 28-36
Creamer (with applied handle,
  rare) 53-62
Goblet 27-35
Pitcher (with applied handle,
  rare) 82-92
Salt, master (ill.) 20-29
Spoonholder 30-39
Sugar bowl, covered 39-48
Tumbler, water, footed 30-40
Wine 30-40

Probably other pieces.

Panama

Panama

(Fine Cut Bar): U.S. Glass Company, c. 1890s, clear, non-flint.
  Butter dish, covered $24-33
  Compote, covered 26-35
  Cordial 14-21
  Creamer 17-25
  Decanter 26-34
  Goblet 22-31

Salt/Pepper, pr. 16-25
Spoonholder 17-26
Sugar bowl, covered 31-40
Tumbler 14-22
Wine (ill.) 19-28

Many other pieces.

Panel and Cane

Panel and Cane

Maker unknown, 1890s. Clear. Non-flint.
  Butter dish, covered $30-35
  Celery vase 18-24
  Goblet 18-25
  Pitcher (ill.) 33-42
  Spoonholder 14-22
  Sugar bowl, covered 23-33

Probably other pieces.

Panel and Star

(Column Block): O'Hara Glass Company, Ltd., Pittsburgh, Pennsylvania, c. 1880, clear, non-flint.
  Butter dish, covered $36-45
  Celery 19-27
  Creamer 20-28
  Goblet 21-30
  Jar, pickle 16-24
  Pitcher 37-46
  Sauce, footed 14-21
  Shaker, salt................... 18-27
  Spoonholder 16-24
  Sugar bowl, covered 23-33

Other pieces.

Panelled Acorn Band

Sandwich, early; other factories later. Clear, opaque. Sandwich prices listed.

Panelled Acorn Band

Butter dish, covered $78-88
Compote
  a. Covered 74-82
  b. Open 54-61
Celery vase 72-80
Creamer, applied handle 51-60
Egg cup 26-34
Goblet 29-37
Pitcher (ill.)................... 76-84
Sauce, flat, footed 21-24
Spoonholder 20-28
Sugar bowl, covered 61-70

Probably other pieces. Goblet being reproduced.

Panelled Cable

Panelled Cable

Sandwich made a Cable pattern in the 1860s to commemorate the laying of the Atlantic Cable. There's a certain similarity between the Sandwich product and Panelled Cable, except this was made much later, probably in the 1890s period. Sandwich closed its doors in 1888. Another of those "Who-where-when" patterns.

Panelled Cane

Panelled Cane

(Cane Column): Possibly A. H. Heisey, Newark, Ohio, c. 1897, clear, canary, amber, blue, non-flint.

Butter dish, covered $25-34
Creamer 27-36
Goblet (ill.) 19-28
Sauce, flat 7-14
Spoonholder 15-22
Sugar bowl, open 18-26
Wine 14-21

Canary, 75 percent; amber, 85 percent; blue, 100 percent higher than clear prices listed.

Panelled Cherry

Panelled Cherry

Northwood Glass Company, 1880s. "N" sometimes found in bottom. Clear, cherries red, leaves gold. Non-flint.

(continued)

Butter dish, covered	...........$74-79
Compote, covered, low standard	... 72-81
Creamer	... 40-48
Goblet	... 32-41
Pitcher	
a. Syrup	... 60-70
b. Water (ill.)	... 70-78
Sauce, flat, footed	... 17-24
Spoonholder	... 33-41
Sugar bowl, covered	... 62-70
Tumbler	... 22-31

Panelled Daisy

Panelled Daisy

(Brazil): Bryce Brothers, Pittsburgh, Pennsylvania, c. 1888, clear, non-flint; amber, rare.

Bowl, waste	...$26-35
Butter dish, covered, footed	... 14-54
Cake stand, 8″, 9″, 10″, 11″, high standard	... 46-60
Creamer (rare)	... 52-61
Goblet	... 36-44
Pitcher	
a. Water	... 63-72
b. Syrup	... 53-61
Plate, 7″ square (ill.)	... 24-29
Salt/Pepper, pr.	... 40-48
Spoonholder	... 30-37
Sugar bowl, covered	... 51-60

Amber, 300 percent higher than clear prices listed. Goblet being reproduced.

Panelled Dewdrop

(Striped Dewdrop): Campbell, Jones & Company, Pittsburgh, Pennsylvania, c. 1878, clear, non-flint. Two types: plain base; rows of dewdrops on base.

Panelled Dewdrop

Butter dish, covered	...........$56-65
Celery	... 33-41
Cordial	... 18-26
Creamer	... 41-50
Goblet	... 35-45
Pitcher, water	... 54-62
Sauce	... 7-13
Spoonholder (ill.)	... 34-44
Sugar bowl, covered	... 44-53

Other pieces. Rows of dewdrops on base, 20 percent higher than plain base prices listed.

Panelled Diamond Cut and Fan

Panelled Diamond Cut and Fan

(Hartley): Richards & Hartley, late 1800s. Clear, amber, blue, canary. Non-flint.

Bowl $16-25
Butter dish, covered 32-41
Cake stand 39-47
Celery 18-25
Compote
  a. Covered 42-50
  b. Open 24-32
Creamer 27-36
Goblet (ill.) 20-27
Pitcher, water 38-42
Sauce, flat 11-20
Spoonholder 17-25
Sugar bowl
  a. Covered 26-35
  b. Open 14-22
Wine 13-21

Probably other pieces. Colors, 100 percent higher than clear prices listed.

Panelled Forget-Me-Not

Panelled Forget-Me-Not

(Regal) Bryce Bros., Pittsburgh, 1870s. Clear, amber, yellow, blue, green. Amethyst, rare.

Bowl, covered $44-52
Butter dish, covered 45-53
Cake plate on standard 38-46
Celery 34-42
Compote, covered, high
  standard, 8″ high 57-64
Cordial 30-38
Creamer 27-37
Goblet 34-42
Jam jar 38-46
Pickle dish, oval 17-25
Pitcher, two sizes 38-48
Sauce, flat, round, footed 12-20
Spoonholder 28-37
Sugar bowl, covered 39-46

Probably other pieces. Colors, 40-50 percent higher than clear prices listed. Amethyst, 175 percent higher.

Panelled Grape (Number 507)

Panelled Grape
(Number 507)

Kokomo Glass Manufacturing Company, Kokomo, Indiana, 1904. Clear, colors, rare in milk glass. Westmoreland reproduced it in crystal and milk glass. Non-flint.

Bowl, round, covered $42-50
Butter dish 51-60
Compote, covered 42-51
Creamer 37-46
Pitcher, applied handle (ill.) 51-60
Sauce, footed and flat 12-20
Spoonholder 17-24
Sugar bowl
  a. Covered 31-40
  b. Open 18-25

Probably other pieces. Milk glass 60 percent higher than clear prices listed. All items made being reproduced.

Panelled Heather

(continued)

Panelled Heather

Maker unknown, early 1890s. Clear. Non-flint.

Butter dish	$30-37
Cake stand	32-40
Compote, covered	37-44
Creamer	26-32
Goblet	19-27
Pitcher	
a. Milk	38-46
b. Water (ill.)	32-41
Spoonholder	22-31
Sugar bowl, covered	32-40

Probably other pieces.

Panelled Hobnail

Panelled Hobnail

Bryce Bros., 1875-1885. Clear, amber, blue, opaque-white, vaseline, canary. Non-flint.

Butter dish, covered	$24-33
Compote	
a. Covered	24-31
b. Open	17-24
Creamer	22-31
Goblet	17-26
Pitcher (ill.)	28-37
Sugar bowl	
a. Covered	26-34
b. Open	14-22
Wine	15-24

Probably other pieces. Amber, canary, opaque-white, 60 percent higher; blue, green, 80 percent higher than clear prices listed.

Panelled Honeycomb

Bryce, Walker & Company, 1880. Clear. Non-flint.

Butter dish	$28-36
Celery	14-23

Panelled Honeycomb

Compote	27-34
Creamer	22-31
Goblet	20-27
Pitcher (ill.)	40-47
Spoonholder	16-24
Sugar bowl, covered	27-34

Probably other pieces.

Panelled Ivy

Panelled Ivy

Possibly Bryce Bros., late 1880s; later U.S. Glass Company. Clear, possibly colors. Non-flint.

Butter dish, covered	$27-36
Cake stand	24-33
Celery	16-22
Compote	
a. Covered	38-46
b. Open	24-32
Goblet	22-31
Pitcher (ill.)	32-41

Probably other pieces. If in color, at least 60 percent higher than clear prices listed.

Panelled Oak

Panelled Oak

Maker unknown, 1890s, early 1900s.
Clear. Non-flint.

Butter dish, covered	$30-37
Celery vase	18-23
Creamer	26-32
Goblet	21-30
Pitcher (ill.)	37-44
Spoonholder	20-28
Sugar bowl, covered	31-40
Tumbler	16-24

Probably other pieces.

Panelled Ovals

Maker unknown, c. 1860s, clear, flint.

Butter dish, covered	$60-68
Compote	
a. Open	24-33
b. Covered	50-60
Creamer	48-53
Egg cup	29-39
Goblet	40-48
Spoonholder	41-50
Sugar bowl	
a. Open	16-25
b. Covered	37-43

Other pieces.

Panelled Pleat

Robinson Glass Company, Zanesville,
Ohio, c. 1894, clear, non-flint.

Butter dish, covered	$21-30
Creamer	19-26
Goblet	17-25

Spoonholder	16-25
Sugar bowl, covered	24-33

Possibly other pieces.

Panelled Primula

Panelled Primula

Maker unknown, 1900s. Clear. Non-flint.

Butter dish, covered	$28-38
Cake stand	30-39
Celery vase	21-30
Compote	
a. Covered, high standard	38-46
b. Open, high and low standard	31-40
Creamer	17-26
Goblet	16-24
Pitcher, water (ill.)	32-41
Salt/Pepper, pr.	16-25
Spoonholder	15-24
Sugar bowl, covered	22-31
Tumbler	14-22

Panelled "S"

Panelled "S"

Maker unknown, 1880s. Clear. Non-flint.

Butter dish, covered	$32-41
Celery	21-30

541

(continued)

Compote 25-32
Creamer 27-35
Goblet (ill.) 24-32
Plate, 5", 6", 7½" 14-22
Pitcher, water 46-53
Spoonholder 32-41
Sugar bowl, covered 34-42

Probably other pieces.

Panelled Sawtooth

Panelled Sawtooth

(Fluted Diamond Point): Duncan & Miller Glass Company, Washington, Pennsylvania, 1880s. Clear. Non-flint.

Butter dish, covered $37-46
Cake stand 29-38
Celery 18-27
Goblet 22-31
Pitcher (ill.) 44-52
Spoonholder 14-22
Sugar
  a. Covered 30-38
  b. Open 24-32
Wine 14-23

Probably other pieces.

Panelled Star and Button

Panelled Star and Button

(Sedan): Maker unknown, late 1880s. Clear. Non-flint.

Butter dish, covered $21-30
Creamer 19-27
Goblet 21-30
Pitcher (ill.) 29-32
Spoonholder 21-30
Sugar bowl
  a. Covered 28-36
  b. Open 19-27
Wine 17-24

Probably other pieces.

Panelled Stippled Scroll

Panelled Stippled Scroll

Maker unknown, early 1900s. Clear, amber, blue. Non-flint.

Celery vase $14-20
Compote 26-34
Creamer 14-22
Goblet (ill.) 19-27
Pitcher, water 32-41
Spoonholder 16-22
Sugar bowl, covered 25-33
Tumbler 16-24

Probably other pieces. Color 40 percent more than clear prices listed.

Panelled Strawberry

Maker unknown, late 1890s. Clear, foliage and berries burnished gold; also, maroon to pink. Non-flint.

Butter dish $37-46
Celery 16-24
Creamer 24-32
Goblet 26-31

Panelled Strawberry

Pitcher (ill.)	49-58
Sauce, 5″, 6″, 6½″	18-27
Spoonholder	21-30
Sugar bowl, covered	31-40
Tumbler	16-25

Colors don't affect price.

Panelled Sunflower   Panelled Thistle

Panelled Sunflower

Maker unknown, 1880s. Clear, blue. Non-flint.

Butter dish	$27-36
Celery	18-27
Creamer	22-31
Goblet (ill.)	20-27
Spoonholder	16-24
Sugar bowl	23-31

Probably other pieces. Blue, 65 percent higher than clear prices listed.

Panelled Thistle

J. B. Higbee Glass Company, Bridgeville, Pennsylvania, 1910, possibly earlier. Clear. Non-flint.

Bowl, berry, 6½″, 7″, 8½″, 9″, footed	$27-40
Butter dish	45-54
Cake plate on stand, large, small	27-37
Celery, 11″	30-38
Compote, open, small, medium, large	19-33
Creamer, knob feet	32-41
Cruet	39-46
Dish, honey, oblong, oval, round	46-55
Goblet, two styles	38-47
Pickle dish, 7½″, 8¼″	17-23
Pitcher, two sizes	54-63
Plate, 7¼″, 8¼″, 9½″, 10¼″	26-35
Salt/Pepper, pr.	52-60
Spoonholder	24-32
Sugar bowl, 2 handles	41-50
Tumbler, water	26-34
Wine, two styles	28-36

Probably other pieces. With Bee mark 25 percent higher. Goblet, 7¼″ plate and salt being reproduced.

Panelled Wheat

Panelled Wheat

Hobbs, Brockunier & Company, Wheeling, West Virginia, 1871, crystal and milk glass.

(continued)

	Clear	Milk Glass
Butter dish, covered . .	$27-36	$ 36- 44
Compote		
a. Covered, footed . .	32-40	94-103
b. Open		39- 48
Creamer	17-24	37- 47
Goblet	16-24	84- 92
Pitcher, water, (ill.)		100-108
Sauce, flat	6- 8	14- 19
Spoonholder	10-14	20- 27
Sugar bowl		
a. Covered	28-37	36- 46
b. Open	12-18	19- 24

Possibly other pieces.

Pansy and Moss Rose

Pansy and Moss Rose

Maker and date unknown. Clear. Non-flint.

Prices comparable to Panelled Strawberry.

Parrot

Parrot

(Owl in Fan): Possibly Richards & Hartley, Tarentum, Pennsylvania, 1880s. Clear. Non-flint.

Bowl	$32-40
Celery	21-29
Goblet (ill.)	36-46
Wine (rare)	46-54

Doubtful if other pieces were made.

Parthenon

(Egyptian): Sandwich glass, c. 1870s, clear, flint.

Butter dish, covered	$45-54
Celery	32-41
Compote	
a. Open, high, low standard	36-45
b. Covered, high, low standard	44-52
Creamer	37-42
Goblet	35-42
Pitcher, water	50-60
Platter	
a. Figure of a woman	47-56
b. Salt Lake Temple	56-66
Spoonholder	27-36
Sugar bowl, covered	42-51

Possibly other pieces.

Pattee Cross

(Broughton; Gloria): Maker unknown, c. 1900. In 1912, Sears, Roebuck listed it in their catalog under the name "Gloria." Clear, green, non-flint.

Butter dish, covered	$25-33
Celery	16-22
Creamer	18-24
Goblet	13-21
Pitcher	30-37
Sugar bowl, covered	25-32

Green, 40 percent higher than clear prices listed. Prices of 1900 pieces listed. Probably other pieces.

Pavonia

(Pineapple Stem): Ripley & Company, Pittsburgh, 1885. Clear, red-flashed, etched. Non-flint.

Butter dish, covered, etched	$54-63

Pavonia

Cake stand, etched
   a. Large 54-60
   b. Small 41-50
Celery, etched................. 31-39
Compote
   a. Covered, high standard 60-68
   b. Open, high standard 50-59
Creamer, pedestal base, etched .. 37-46
Goblet, pineapple stemmed,
   etched 37-46
Pitcher, water, pineapple
   stemmed 56-64
Spoonholder, etched (ill.) 25-34
Sugar bowl 49-57
Tumbler, etched.............. 20-28
Wine, etched 35-42

Probably other pieces. Red-flashed 25 percent higher than clear.

Peacock Eye

Peacock Eye

An early Sandwich pattern, clear, flint. Don't confuse it with Peacock Feather (Georgia).
    Bowl, 8⅞" dia. (ill.) $168-175

Peacock Feather

Peacock Feather

(Georgia): Originally an old Sandwich pattern. In 1907, U.S. Glass Company made same pattern and called it Georgia as part of their "States" series. Clear, blue, amethyst, other colors.
    Bowl, berry $32-41
    Butter dish, covered 44-53
    Cake stand, 9", 10", 11" 45-63
    Celery boat 28-36
    Compote
       a. Shallow, high standard 28-37
       b. Covered, deep, high
          standard 45-54
    Creamer 34-43
    Dish, oval.................... 21-27
    Lamp, handles, oil, blue 80-89
    Pitcher, water (ill.) 64-72
    Salt/Pepper, pr. 44-52
    Spoonholder 27-34
    Sugar bowl, covered 44-53
    Tumbler 28-36

Probably other pieces. Colors 50 percent higher.

Peerless

Richards & Hartley Flint Glass Company, Pittsburgh, c. 1875, clear, non-flint.
    Bottle, caster $28-37
    Champagne................... 31-40
    Creamer, round, angular 35-44
    Egg cup 23-31

(continued)

Goblet 24-33
Jar, pickle 27-36
Pitcher, water, ½ gal. 46-53
Spoonholder 18-27
Sugar bowl, covered 42-50
Tumbler 26-34

Many other pieces. Twenty-two compotes alone!

Pendelton

Pendelton

Maker unknown, late 1860s, early 1870s. Clear. Non-flint.

Butter dish $32-39
Celery vase 21-30
Creamer 16-25
Goblet 20-21
Pitcher, syrup, metal cap
  (ill.) 36-45
Spoonholder 18-27
Sugar bowl, covered 27-36
Tumbler 17-26

Probably other pieces.

Pentagon

George Duncan & Sons, Pittsburgh, 1880. Clear. Non-flint.

Creamer, individual $29-38
Creamer, tankard type 31-40
Pitcher, water, tankard
  type (ill.) 47-55

Other pieces probably exist in this pattern.

Persian

(Three Stories; Block and Pleat): Bryce, Higbee & Company, Pittsburgh, Pennsylvania, c. 1885, clear, non-flint.

Bowls, oval, 8″, 9″, 10″ $15-29
Butter dish, covered 35-43
Celery 24-32

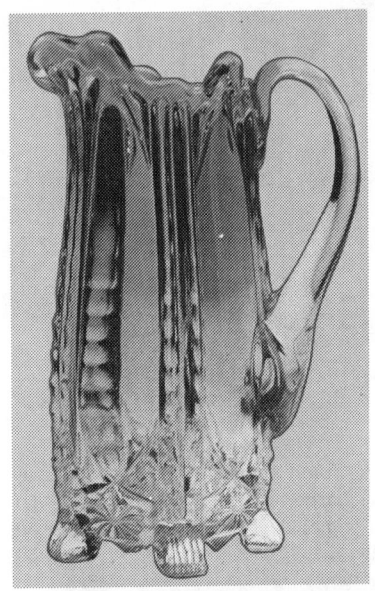

Pentagon

Persian

Creamer (ill.) 25-33
Goblet 21-30
Mug 24-32
Nappies, fruit, 6″, 7″, 8″ 11-26
Pitcher, ½ gal. 41-50
Sugar bowl, covered 37-46

Many other pieces.

Pert

(Ribbed Forget-Me-Not): Bryce Bros., 1880. Clear. Non-flint.

Butter dish, covered $30-38
Creamer (ill.) 26-29
Spoonholder 17-24
Sugar bowl, covered 24-32

Probably these pieces made for a whist table.

Pert

Petal and Loop

Petal and Loop

Sandwich, early; later produced by O'Hara Glass Company, Pittsburgh; they called it the "O'Hara" pattern (see Loop). The piece shown here is Sandwich; smaller petals and loop designs on base of standard.

Compote (ill.) $110-120
Dish, honey 34- 43

Philadelphia

New England Glass Company, c. 1860s, clear, flint.

Bowl, covered	$31-40
Celery	27-35
Egg cu p	24-33
Goblet	42-51
Spoonholder	25-34
Sugar bowl	
a. Open	19-27
b. Covered	34-42

Wine 28-36
Possibly other pieces.

Picket

Picket

(London): King Glass Company, Pittsburgh, late 1880s. Clear, stippled. Nonflint.

Butter dish, covered	$60-68
Celery vase	35-43
Compote	
a. Covered, 6", 8", high foot....	52-62
b. Open, high, low foot	37-45
Creamer	34-42
Goblet	37-45
Marmalade jar	33-42
Match holder	28-36
Pickle jar, with cover	37-47
Pitcher, water (ill.)	55-64
Salt, flat, oblong..............	13-20
Sauce	9-15
Spoonholder	23-32
Sugar bowl, covered	42-51
Tray for water set	48-56

Pigs in Corn

547

(continued)

Pigs in Corn

Maker unknown, 1875-1885. Clear, goblet only.

Goblet (ill.) $125-134

Pilgrim Bottle

Pilgrim Bottle

Variant; maker and date unknown. May come in colors or trimmed with ruby or gilt. Non-flint.

Bottle (ill.) $54-64

Pillar

Pillar

(Loop): Bakewell, Pears & Company, Pittsburgh, Pennsylvania, c. 1850s, clear, flint.

Ale (ill.) $42-51
Bottle, bar, 7" 36-44
Cordial 60-67
Creamer 62-71
Decanter, no stopper 47-51
Sauce, flat 14-20
Sugar bowl, covered 61-70

Should be other pieces.

Pillow and Sunburst

Pillow and Sunburst

(Elite): Westmoreland Specialty Company, 1891; again in 1896; again in 1917. Clear. Non-flint.

Butter dish, covered $28-35
Celery 18-27
Compote
  a. Covered 35-43
  b. Open 18-24
Creamer 24-32
Goblet 22-31
Pitcher, water (ill.) 40-48
Spoonholder 16-24
Sugar bowl 27-34

Probably other pieces.

Pillow Bands

Pillow Bands

Maker unknown. Clear and colors. Non-flint.

Berry bowl $16-24
Butter dish 29-37
Celery 18-27
Compote
  a. Covered 32-41
  b. Open 23-33
Creamer 16-24
Cruet, cobalt blue 37-46
Goblet 24-32
Pitcher (ill.) 32-41
Spoonholder 20-28
Sugar bowl, covered 26-35

Probably others. Colors 50 percent more than clear prices listed.

Pillow Encircled

Pillow Encircled

Maker unknown, early 1890s. Clear and ruby flashed. Non-flint.

Butter dish, covered $27-32
Compote
  a. Covered 35-42
  b. Open 26-34
Creamer 20-27
Dish, oval 10-14
Pitcher (ill.) 35-43
Sauce 11-14
Spoonholder 16-23
Sugar bowl
  a. Covered 24-32
  b. Open 14-22
Tumbler 14-23

Probably other pieces. Ruby flashing, 60 percent higher than clear prices listed.

Pineapple

Hobbs, Brockunier & Company, Wheeling, West Virginia, 1886. Clear, opalescent, colors. Non-flint.

Butter dish, covered $35-42

Pineapple

Celery 18-26
Pitcher (ill.) 42-51
Spoonholder 26-34
Sugar bowl
  a. Covered 30-37
  b. Open 18-26

Other pieces. Opalescent and colors, 50 percent higher than clear prices listed.

Pineapple and Fan

Pineapple and Fan

Adams & Company, Pittsburgh; later by U.S. Glass Company, 1891. Clear, color. Non-flint.

Bowl, berry, 8″, 9″ $17-24
Butter dish, covered 36-44
Cake stand 25-33
Celery, medium, tall 19-27
Creamer, individual, large 21-30
Mug 18-26
Pitcher
  a. Half gallon, ¾ gallon,
    tankard 52-61
  b. One quart, one pint,
    water 34-44
Sauce, 4″, 4½″ 13-21
Spoonholder, laydown type 28-36
Sugar bowl
  a. Individual, covered 27-36
  b. Large, covered 42-50
Tumbler, water 18-23

(continued)

Probably other pieces. Color, 50 percent higher than clear prices listed.

Pioneer's No. 15

Pioneer's No. 15

Pioneer Glass Company, Pittsburgh, Pennsylvania, c. 1890s, clear with ruby stain. Non-flint.

Butter dish covered	$20-30
Compote, covered	24-33
Creamer	18-26
Goblet	17-24
Pitcher, milk	34-43
Salt/Pepper, pr.	14-21
Spoonholder	16-23
Sugar bowl, covered	20-30
Tumbler (ill.)	16-25
Wine	13-22

Probably other pieces.

Pioneer's Victoria

Pioneer's Victoria

Pioneer Glass Company, 1885. Crystal glass with ruby stain. Some pieces are engraved.

Butter dish, covered	$27-36
Celery	18-26
Compote, high, low standards	24-33

Creamer	18-26
Egg cup	17-23
Goblet	16-23
Pitcher, water (ill.)	24-32
Sauce	16-24
Spoonholder	18-25
Sugar bowl	22-30

Probably other pieces. Ruby stain has no effect on price.

Plaid

Plaid

Maker unknown, rare pattern of the 1880s. Clear. Non-flint.

Celery	$29-38
Creamer	25-34
Goblet	24-33
Pitcher, water (ill.)	44-51
Sugar bowl, open	27-36

Possibly other pieces.

Plain Tulip

Possibly Sandwich, 1850s. Clear. Non-flint.

Celery		$17-26
Compote		
a. Covered, large, high standard		50-58
b. Open, large		37-43
Creamer		32-41
Goblet		24-32
Pitcher		
a. Syrup (ill.)		30-38
b. Water		46-53
Spoonholder		21-28
Sugar bowl		28-34
Tumbler		18-27
Wine		16-25

Probably other pieces.

Plain Tulip

Pleat and Panel

Pleat and Panel

(Derby): Bryce Bros., Pittsburgh, 1870s; they called it Derby; it is better known as Pleat and Panel today. Clear, amethyst, yellow, blue. Non-flint.

Butter dish, covered	$54-62
Cake plate, square, on standard	
9", 9¼"	44-52
Compote, covered and open	28-54
Creamer	38-46
Dish, oblong and square	19-25
Goblet, 2 types	24-32
Lamp, 9¼" high	39-48
Pickle dish	17-25
Pitcher, water (ill.)	54-63
Plate, square, 3½", 6", 7½", 8½"	19-37
Platter, closed, open handles	36-45
Salt/Pepper, pr.	43-51
Spoonholder	24-32
Sugar bowl, covered	45-53

Probably other pieces. Colors, 75 percent higher than clear prices listed. 7" plate, 7½" plate and goblet being reproduced.

Pleating

(Flat Panel): Bryce Brothers, Pittsburgh; Gillinder & Sons, Philadelphia, c. 1880s. Reissued by U.S. Glass Company, c. 1891, clear, flashed in red. Non-flint.

Butter dish, covered	$30-38
Cake stand	29-36
Celery	13-22
Compote	
a. Open	20-27
b. Covered	36-44
Creamer	24-32
Pitcher, water	29-39
Spoonholder	21-30
Sugar bowl, covered	34-43

Flashed in red, 60 percent higher than clear; Bryce Brothers prices listed.

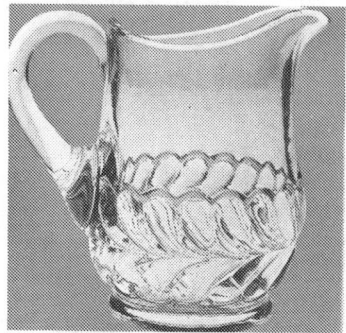

Plume

Plume

Adams Glass Company, 1874. Clear, red-flashed. Non-flint.

Bowl, berry, finger	$18-27
Butter dish, covered	45-53
Cake stand	38-47
Celery	29-38
Compote	
a. Covered	38-47
b. Open, scalloped top	29-38
Creamer	24-32
Goblet	37-45
Pickle	16-27
Pitcher, water (ill.)	51-60
Sauce	11-15
Spoonholder	24-32
Sugar bowl, covered	44-52
Tray, water	52-60
Tumbler	19-26

(continued)

Probably other pieces. Red-flashed 25 percent higher than clear prices listed. Goblet being reproduced.

Plume and Block

Plume and Block

Richards & Hartley Glass Company, Tarentum, Pennsylvania, 1885-1891, clear, clear with ruby stain. Non-flint.

Butter dish, covered	$30-37
Celery (ill.)	19-27
Compotes, 4″, 6″, 8″	25-32
Creamer	18-26
Pitcher, ½ gal., gal.	45-53
Spoonholder	18-26
Sugar bowl, covered	32-41

Possibly other pieces.

Plutec

Plutec

McKee Glass Company, Jeannette, Pennsylvania, c. early 1900s, clear, non-flint. All pieces marked "Prescut."

Bowl, nut	$18-27
Butter dish, covered	25-34
Cake stand	34-42
Compote, covered	26-36
Creamer	22-30
Dish, pickle	12-19
Goblet (ill.)	24-28
Pitcher, water	36-45
Spoonholder	22-30
Sugar bowl, covered	22-31

Many other pieces.

Pointed Cube

Pointed Cube

Maker unknown, c. 1880s, clear and frosted. Non-flint.

Decanter	$29-38
Tray, wine	22-30
Wine (ill.)	19-27

Frosted, 20 percent higher than clear prices listed. Probably other pieces.

Pointed Jewel

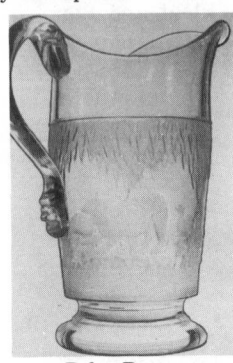

Polar Bear

Pointed Jewel

Columbia Glass Company, Findlay, Ohio, 1880s; later U.S. Glass Company,

1892. Clear. Non-flint.

Butter dish, covered $42-51
Creamer 22-28
Custard cup................... 11-14
Goblet 19-27
Pitcher (ill.)................... 34-39
Spoonholder 19-26
Sugar bowl 26-34
Tumbler 18-25
Wine........................ 17-26

Probably other pieces.

Polar Bear

(Iceberg; Arctic; North Pole): Crystal Glass Company, Bridgeport, Ohio, 1880s. Clear; partly frosted. Non-flint.

Bowl, waste................. $ 78- 87
Butter dish, clear 90-100
Creamer, clear 67- 75
Goblet
  a. Clear 95-104
  b. Frosted 107-115
Pickle dish 30- 37
Pitcher, water, frosted (ill.).... 190-200
Platter, oval, handled 95-104
Sauce 30- 39
Spoonholder 54- 63
Sugar bowl, covered 93-102
Tray, water, round, oval 160-170

Probably other pieces.

Popcorn

Popcorn

Sandwich, 1860s. Crystal only.

Butter dish $70-79
Cordial...................... 53-62
Creamer 57-65
Goblet, with and without ear 45-60
Pitcher, water (ill.) 80-89
Sauce 19-24
Spoonholder 30-38

Sugar bowl 64-72
Wine........................ 33-41

Probably other pieces.

Portland

Portland

Middle-west, 1880s. Clear and with gilt. Non-flint.

Bride's basket in frame $88-97
Butter dish, covered 42-51
Celery 26-34
Compote, covered, jelly......... 34-43
Creamer 38-42
Cruet (ill.) 26-35
Goblet 32-41
Jam jar...................... 24-32
Pitcher, water................. 47-56
Punch bowl 49-57
Spoonholder 22-27
Sugar bowl 36-44
Sugar shaker 43-49
Tumbler 26-29
Wine........................ 24-32

Many other pieces made.

Powder and Shot

Powder and Shot

Originally Sandwich; other makers unknown. Clear. Non-flint.

(continued)

Butter dish $87-95
Caster bottle 37-45
Celery 58-66
Compote, covered, high and
  low standard 58-90
Creamer 73-82
Egg cup 44-53
Goblet 48-56
Pitcher, water (ill.) 73-81
Sauce 18-25
Spoonholder 43-51
Sugar bowl 79-87
Tumbler 31-40

Pressed Diamond

Pressed Diamond

Central Glass Company, Wheeling, West Virginia. Clear, yellow, amber, blue (scarce). Non-flint.

Butter dish, covered $41-50
Celery 27-34
Creamer 24-32
Compote
  a. Covered 44-52
  b. Open 23-32
Goblet 24-32
Pitcher (ill.) 37-45
Spoonholder 17-26
Sugar bowl, covered 41-50
Tumbler 20-27

Probably other pieces. Yellow, 70 percent higher; amber, blue, 125 percent higher than clear prices listed.

Pressed Leaf

(N.P.L.): Sandwich, early; Central Glass Company, Wheeling, West Virginia, 1881; McKee Bros., Pittsburgh, 1868, called it N.P.L. Clear. Non-flint.

Bowl, open, high and low foot
  7″, 8″ $26-42

Pressed Leaf

Butter dish, covered 44-53
Cake plate on stand 62-72
Compote, covered, high, low
  standard, 6″, 7″, 8″ 55-64
Cordial 23-30
Creamer 49-57
Dish, oval, 5″, 6″, 8″, 9″ 23-33
Egg cup 21-30
Goblet 27-35
Lamp, applied handle 56-64
Pitcher, water (ill.) 81-90
Sauce 12-17
Spoonholder 29-36
Sugar bowl 56-63
Wine........................ 38-45

Probably other pieces.

Primrose

Primrose

Canton Glass Company, Canton, Ohio, 1880s. Crystal, amber, canary, blue, apple green, opaque-white, turquoise, purple slag, opaque-black. Apple green and yellow, rarest colors. Non-flint.

Bowl, berry, round, deep $24-32
Butter dish 45-53
Cake plate on standard 37-45
Compote, covered, 6", 7½", 8", 9" 28-48
Creamer 34-43
Goblet, plain, knob stem 27-36
Pickle dish 14-22
Pitcher, milk (ill.) 40-49
Plate, 4½", 6", 7", 8¾", cake...... 13-28
Sauce, footed, 4", 5½" 13-20
Spoonholder 21-29
Sugar bowl, covered 34-42

Probably other pieces. Yellow and amber 55 percent higher; blue, green, 80 percent higher than clear prices listed.

Princess Feather

Princess Feather

(Lacy Medallion; Rochelle): Sandwich called it Princess Feather; Bakewell, Pears, Blackwell & Company called it Rochelle. It was also called Lacy Medallion by U.S. Glass Company, late 1880s. Clear, opaque white. Non-flint.

Butter dish $71-80
Celery 40-49
Compote
a. Covered, 6", 7", high
   standard 61-69
b. Open, 8", low standard...... 40-47
Creamer 54-63
Egg cup 32-40
Goblet 34-42
Honey dish 14-22
Pitcher, half gallon (ill.) 70-80

Plate, 6", 7", 8", 9", cake 30-40
Spoonholder 28-37
Sugar bowl, open 30-39

Opaque white, 50 percent higher than clear.

Printed Hobnail

Printed Hobnail

Maker unknown, 1880s. Clear, amber, canary, blue, green, amethyst. Non-flint.

Butter dish $40-49
Celery vase 32-40
Creamer 25-33
Goblet 23-31
Mug, handled 18-25
Pitcher, water (ill.) 40-50
Saucedish, 4" 10-17
Spoonholder 24-32
Sugar bowl 36-44
Tray for water set 32-40
Tumbler 19-27
Wine........................ 18-26

Probably other pieces. Amber, canary 60 percent higher; blue, green, amethyst, at least 125 percent higher than clear prices listed.

Priscilla

(Alexis; Sun and Star): Dalzell, Gilmore & Leighton Company, Findlay, Ohio, 1890s. Clear, with red dots. Non-flint.

Bowl, square, 8", flat, 10½",
   rose........................$27-35
Butter dish, covered 53-61
Cake stand, 10" dia. 40-50
Celery 30-37

(continued)

Priscilla

Compote
a. Covered, 7" 60-69
b. 5" high.................... 20-27
c. Open, 7½" 38-44
Creamer 33-41
Goblet 26-34
Mug 16-23
Pitcher, water................ 85-93
Spoonholder 24-32
Sugar bowl, covered 32-41
Toothpick holder 28-36
Tumbler (ill.) 19-27
Wine........................ 28-36

Probably other pieces. With red dots 40 percent higher than clear prices listed. Being reproduced in volume.

Prism

Prism

Maker unknown, c. 1860s, flint and non-flint. Don't confuse it with "Prism and Flute" — their trade name was also "Prism," a non-flint product.

Champagne................... $36-43
Compote, open 40-47

Creamer 60-68
Decanter 47-56
Goblet (ill.) 40-47
Pitcher 72-81
Wine........................ 37-44

Non-flint, 50 percent lower than flint prices listed. Probably other pieces.

Prism and Flattened Sawtooth

Prism and Flattened Sawtooth

(Ribbed Pineapple): Maker unknown, 1850s. Clear.

Goblet (ill.) $52-62
Lamp 63-73
Spoonholder (or spill) 44-54
Sugar bowl, open 52-63

Probably other pieces.

Prism with Diamond Points

Possibly Sandwich Glass, early; or Midwest, c. 1860s, clear. Flint.

Butter dish, covered .... $ 80- 89
Compote, covered, knob stem .. 100-110
Cordial..................... 29- 37
Creamer 70- 80
Egg cup, double 48- 56
Goblet
a. Plain stem 50- 59
b. Knob stem 63- 72
Pitcher, 6½" high 105-112
Spoonholder 40- 48
Sugar bowl, covered 58- 66
Tumbler 44- 52
Wine...................... 53- 61

Psyche and Cupid

Possibly Hartley Glass Company, Tarentum, Pennsylvania, 1880s. Clear. Non-flint.

Butter dish $70-79
Celery 43-50
Compote, high, low standard 57-72

Psyche and Cupid

Creamer	37-47
Goblet	40-48
Jam jar	32-40
Pickle dish	23-30
Pitcher, water (ill.)	65-73
Sauce	12-18
Spoonholder	36-45
Sugar bowl	45-55
Wine	30-38

Probably other pieces.

Quartered Block

George Duncan's Sons & Company, Washington, Pennsylvania, c. 1894, clear, non-flint; possibly clear with colored top.

Butter dish, covered	$30-37
Cake plate, flat, high	25-34
Celery	20-24
Compote	
a. Low standard	23-32
b. High standard	31-40
Creamer, pt.	26-29
Dish, horseradish	19-27
Goblet	21-30
Spoonholder	16-25
Sugar bowl	
a. Open	17-26
b. Covered	32-42
Tub, ice	32-42

Many other pieces. If clear with colored top, 30 percent higher than clear prices listed.

Quatrefoil

Maker unknown, 1880s. Clear, apple green. Non-flint.

Bowl	$ 14- 22
Butter dish, covered	32- 40
Compote, covered	30- 37
Creamer	24- 30
Goblet (rare)	84- 92

Quatrefoil

Pitcher (ill.)	37- 46
Salt/Pepper, pr.	16- 25
Spoonholder	14- 22
Sugar bowl	
a. Covered	25- 33
b. Open	16- 24
Tumbler (some say it was never made)	110-150 +

Colors, 75 percent higher than clear prices listed.

Queen   Queen Anne

Queen

(Sunk, Pointed Panel; Panelled Daisy and Button): McKee Glass Company, Jeannette, Pennsylvania, 1894; other factories same period. Clear, yellow, amber, apple green, blue.

Butter dish, covered	$31-40
Compote	
a. Covered	34-43

(continued)

b. Open 20-28
Creamer 22-31
Goblet 21-30
Pitcher, water (ill.) 37-46
Sauce, oval 11-15
Spoonholder 17-24
Sugar bowl
  a. Covered 29-36
  b. Open 20-25
Tumbler 20-25

Probably other pieces. Yellow, 50 percent; amber, apple green, 60 percent; blue, 80 percent higher than clear prices listed.

Queen Anne

(Bearded Man; Santa Claus; Neptune): La Belle Glass Company, Bridgeport, Ohio, 1878. Clear, colors. Non-flint.

Butter dish $41-50
Celery 30-36
Compote, covered, 7″, 8″ 40-52
Creamer 31-40
Pitcher, water, syrup (ill.) 60-70
Sauce, footed, 4½″ 30-37
Spoonholder 26-33
Sugar bowl, open 30-40

Probably other pieces. Colors, 25 percent higher than clear prices listed.

Quilt and Flute

Quilt and Flute

Maker and date unknown. Clear. Probably made for use as a container for mustard. Non-flint.

Creamer (ill.) $17-24
Mustard jar 14-23
Sugar bowl 21-30

Possibly other pieces.

Quixote

Tarentum Glass Company, Tarentum, Pennsylvania, 1899. Non-flint.

Quixote

Butter dish $34-42
Celery 18-24
Goblet 20-27
Pitcher 40-47
Spoonholder (ill.) 17-25
Sugar bowl 24-33

Probably other pieces.

Racing Deer

Racing Deer

Probably Indiana Tumbler & Goblet Company, late 1890s. Clear, chocolate.

Pitcher, water - chocolate $220-230
Pitcher, water - clear (ill.) 92-101

Radiant

(Dynast): Maker unknown, c. late 1880s, clear, etched, non-flint.

Butter dish, covered $32-41
Cake plate 32-41

558

Celery	16-23
Compote	
a. Open	17-25
b. Covered	30-40
Creamer	27-37
Goblet	23-33
Pitcher, syrup	29-40
Salt/Pepper, pr.	27-36
Spoonholder	16-24
Sugar bowl, covered	32-41
Tumbler	18-27
Wine	16-24

Clear, etched, same price. Probably other pieces.

Rainbow

McKee & Brothers, Pittsburgh, c. 1894, "Rose pink," gold decorated. McKee was the first of the manufacturers to use a permanent trademark, "PRES-CUT" 1894, in the glass. Non-flint.

Butter dish, covered	$40-46
Carafe	36-44
Creamer	32-41
Goblet	30-37
Jar, cigar, gold or silver lid	28-36
Pitcher, water	70-78
Tumbler	19-26
Wine	23-33

Many other pieces.

Raindrop

Raindrop

Maker unknown, c. 1880s, clear, canary, amber, blue, light green (rare), non-flint.

Bowl (ill.)	$12-18
Butter dish, covered	31-39
Compote, open, high, low	
standard	24-33

Creamer	25-33
Egg cup, double	27-35
Pitcher, syrup	38-45
Sauce, flat, footed	10-18
Tray, large	40-48

Canary, 70 percent higher; amber, blue, 100 percent higher; light green, 150 percent higher than clear prices listed.

Raspberry

Raspberry

Maker unknown, late 1870s. Clear. Non-flint.

Butter dish, covered	$26-34
Celery	16-20
Compote	
a. Covered	30-38
b. Open	18-27
Creamer	17-24
Goblet	17-26
Pitcher, water (ill.)	41-50
Spoonholder	17-24
Sugar bowl, covered	32-41
Tumbler	16-23

Probably other pieces.

Ray

McKee Bros., 1894. Plain or engraved or ruby-stained or frosted on the plain parts. Non-flint.

Bowls, round, 6″, 7″	$20-26
Celery vase, tall	17-26
Dish, oblong, deep, 7″, 9″	18-24
Pitcher (ill.)	40-47
Plate, 6″	17-21

(continued)

Ray

Saucedish, round, 4″, 5″, footed .. 16-21
Sugar bowl
   a. Covered 32-40
   b. Open 20-27

Probably other pieces. Ruby-stained, 50 percent higher than clear prices listed.

Red Block

Red Block

Doyle & Company, reproduced by U.S. Glass Company, 1892 and later. Clear, blocks painted red. Non-flint.

Butter dish	$ 80- 89
Celery vase	50- 58
Creamer, large and individual	50- 66
Dish	
a. Cheese..................	80- 88
b. Oblong, 8″, 9″, 10″	30- 38
Goblet	48- 57
Pitcher, water (ill.)	100-110
Salt/Pepper, pr.	80- 89
Spoonholder, double handled ..	40- 48
Sugar bowl, covered	64- 73
Tumbler	34- 42
Wine bottle	55- 63
Wine glass	43- 51

Probably other pieces. Red, 25 percent higher than clear prices listed. Many reproductions.

The Regent

Regent, The

H. Northwood and Co., Wheeling, West Virginia, 1880s. Clear, blue-green, amethyst (extremely rare), decorated with gold; also in crystal. Clear prices given.

Bowl	$34- 42
Butter dish	60- 70
Compote....................	82- 91
Creamer....................	60- 70
Cruet set	77- 84
Pitcher, water (ill.)	92-107
Salt/Pepper, pr.	40- 48
Sherbet	32- 40
Spoonholder	50- 58
Sugar bowl	67- 73

Probably other pieces. Colors, 40 percent to 250 percent higher than clear prices given.

Reticulated Cord

Reticulated Cord

Maker unknown, 1880s. Clear; color scarce. Non-flint.

Butter dish, covered $29-37
Cake stand, large 36-43
Celery vase 22-31
Creamer 32-41
Pitcher, water (ill.) 40-47
Relish 11-16
Spoonholder 18-23
Sugar bowl
  a. Covered 34-40
  b. Open 28-34
Tumbler 16-27
Wine......................... 14-19

Probably other pieces. Color, 125 percent higher than clear prices listed.

Rexford

Rexford

Tarentum Glass Company, Tarentum, Pennsylvania, 1912-1918, clear glass only. Pieces were made with flared, straight, or belled edges. Non-flint.

Butter dish, covered $21-30
Cake stand, 9¾" 22-30
Celery 16-22
Creamer 16-23
Goblet 17-24
Pitcher 30-37
Spoonholder (ill.) 18-26
Sugar bowl, covered 24-29
Wine........................ 14-23

Many other pieces.

Ribbed Forget-Me-Not

Ribbed Forget-Me-Not

(Pert): Bryce, McKee & Company, 1880. Clear. Non-flint.

Butter dish, covered $27-34
Creamer 23-33
Cup, handled 12-17
Mustard jar with cover.......... 24-32
Pitcher (ill.)................... 38-46
Spoonholder 22-31
Sugar bowl, covered 34-42

Probably other pieces.

Ribbed Grape

Ribbed Grape

Maker unknown, possibly Sandwich, 1850s. Clear. Flint. If colors, rare.

Butter dish, covered ....$ 90-100
Celery vase 55- 63
Compote
  a. Covered, 6", high
    standard 160-170
  b. Open, low foot 70- 79
Cordial..................... 60- 72
Creamer 135-144
Goblet 55- 63
Pitcher (ill.) 185-195

561

(continued)

Spoonholder 40- 49
Sugar bowl, covered 91-100
Probably other pieces. If colors, 250 percent higher than clear prices listed.

Ribbed Opal

Ribbed Opal

(Beatty Rib): A. J. Beatty Glass Company, Steubenville, Ohio, 1888. Crystal, amber, blue, canary, three opalescent colors.

Creamer, large $37-46
Mug 28-34
Pitcher, water (ill.) 46-54
Relish 22-30
Sugar
  a. Bowl..................... 32-40
  b. Shaker.................. 33-41
Tumbler, 2 types 31-40
Wine........................ 22-31

Probably other pieces. Blue opalescent, 90 percent higher; yellow opalescent, 150 percent higher than clear prices listed.

Ribbed Palm

Ribbed Palm

(Sprig): McKee & Bros., Pittsburgh, 1868. Clear. Flint.

Butter dish .... $ 88- 97
Celery 80- 89

Compote, 7", 8", 10", high,
  low standard 60-130
Creamer 105-103
Dish, 6", 7", 8", 9", deep 42- 62
Goblet 42- 51
Lamp, three types 82-100
Pitcher, 9" high, applied
  handle (rare) (ill.) 165-180
Sauce, 4" 18- 26
Spoonholder 40- 48
Sugar bowl, covered 68- 76
Tumbler, whiskey 80- 89
Wine....................... 60- 69

Probably other pieces. Color, 100 percent higher than clear prices listed.

Ribbon

Bakewell, Pears & Company, Pittsburgh, c. 1870, clear, frosted, non-flint.

Butter dish, covered .... $ 63- 72
Compote
  a. Dolphin stem, scalloped .. 330-350
  b. Round, rectangular bowl .. 150-160
Creamer 50- 58
Dish, cheese, covered 100-108
Goblet 36- 44
Spoonholder 34- 43
Sugar bowl, covered 67- 76
Tray, water 105-112
Wine (rare) 92-102

Other pieces.

Ribbon Candy

Ribbon Candy

(Figure Eight; Double Loop; Bryce): Bryce Bros., 1880s; U.S. Glass Company, 1898. Clear. Non-flint.

Bowls, various $23-36
Butter dish, covered 39-47
Celery 24-32
Cruet 37-44

Cup/Saucer 22-30
Creamer 24-32
Honey dish 34-42
Pitcher, water (ill.) 60-69
Sugar bowl
   a. Covered 35-43
   b. Open 21-29
Tumbler 22-30

Probably other pieces.

Richmond

Richmond

Nickel Plate Glass Company, Fostoria, Ohio, 1889, early 1890s. Clear.

Butter dish $27-34
Celery 18-26
Creamer 21-30
Compote
   a. Covered 34-42
   b. Open 27-36
Creamer 27-34
Goblet 24-32
Pitcher, water (ill.) 41-50
Salt/Pepper, pr. 22-29
Spoonholder 20-30
Sugar bowl 37-46
Tumbler 22-31
Wine 21-30

Probably other pieces.

Richmond

Richards & Hartley Glass Company, Tarentum, Pennsylvania, 1885-1891, clear glass only. Non-flint.

Butter dish, covered $27-36
Celery (ill.) 14-22
Compotes, 4", 6", 7", 8" 15-34
Creamer 15-24
Goblet 16-25
Pitcher, qt., ½ gal. 34-39
Sugar shaker 19-26

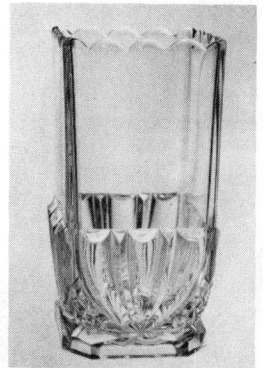

Richmond

Sugar bowl, covered 28-37
Tumbler 14-23
Wine 21-30

Probably other pieces.

Ringed Framed Ovals

Ringed Framed Ovals

An "Oval" pattern originating at Sandwich Glass Company in the 1840s; clear, vaseline, apple green, flint.

Goblet $71-80
Tumbler (ill.) 82-90

Vaseline, 25 percent; apple green, 40 percent higher than clear prices listed.

Ripple

(Ripple Band): Sandwich, last 1870s, clear, non-flint. Inferior as far as Sandwich glass is concerned.

Bowl, oval $16-24
Butter dish, covered 23-31
Compote
   a. Open 22-31
   b. Covered 30-38

(continued)

Creamer 24-32
Goblet....................... 17-24
Lamp 32-41
Salt, footed, oval.............. 12-19
Spoonholder 17-24
Sugar bowl, covered 38-46
Wine........................ 18-24

Probably other pieces.

Roanoke

Roanoke

Gillinder & Sons, Greensburg, Pennsylvania, 1885; later by U.S. Glass Company, 1898. Clear, amber, emerald green. Non-flint.

Butter dish, covered $22-30
Celery 14-21
Creamer (ill.) 16-23
Goblet 14-22
Spoonholder 17-26
Sugar bowl, covered 21-30
Tumbler 18-27
Water pitcher 32-40

Probably many other pieces. Colors, 100-150 percent higher than for clear prices listed.

Robin Hood

Robin Hood

Fostoria Glass Company, 1898. Clear. Non-flint.

Butter dish $22-31
Celery 20-27
Creamer (ill.) 18-26
Compote
  a. Covered 32-37
  b. Open 20-27
Goblet 18-27
Pitcher, water................. 29-39
Spoonholder 17-24
Sugar bowl 28-34
Tumbler 19-28

Probably other pieces.

Rock Crystal

McKee Glass Company, Jeannette, Pennsylvania, c. 1894, clear, colors, non-flint.

Butter dish, covered $26-36
Cake stand 22-31
Celery 18-27
Creamer 19-28
Cup, custard 13-19
Glass, sundae 11-14
Goblet 18-27
Pitcher...................... 26-33
Spoonholder 16-24
Sugar bowl, covered 24-33

Colors, 50 percent higher than clear prices listed. Many other pieces.

Roman Rosette

Roman Rosette

Bryce, Walker & Company, 1875. Reproduced by U.S. Glass Company, in 1892, again in 1898. Clear; few pieces in color; clear pieces sometimes decorated with ruby on vertical ribbing. Non-flint.

Bowl, 5″, 6″, 7″, 8″ $23-38
Butter dish, covered 51-60
Cake plate on stand, 9″, 10″
  (rare) 62-71
Caster set 77-85
Celery 34-42
Compote, covered, high, low
  standard, 5″, 6″, 7″, 8″ 46-62
Creamer, one pint 35-45
Goblet 30-39
Mug, large, medium 21-29
Pickle dish 24-29
Pitcher, syrup (ill.) 50-59
Sauce, flat, footed 12-20
Salt/Pepper, pr. 39-47
Spoonholder 26-35
Sugar bowl, covered 45-53
Tumbler 35-44
Wine 40-49

Probably other pieces. Goblet being reproduced. Red color, 25 percent higher than clear prices listed.

Rope Bands

Rope Bands

(Clear Panels with Cord Band): Possibly McKee & Son, Pittsburgh, late 1870s. Clear; color, scarce.

Cake stand, large $37-42
Celery 19-27
Compote, covered 37-44
Creamer (ill.) 22-31
Goblet 20-30
Platter 27-36
Sugar
  a. Covered 31-40
  b. Open 23-32
Tumbler 17-27

Probably other pieces. Color, 100 percent higher than prices listed.

Rose-in-Snow

Rose-in-Snow

Bryce Bros., Pittsburgh, 1870s. Clear, amber, blue, yellow. Non-flint.

Butter dish, round, square . . . . $ 57- 66
Compote, covered, high low
  standard 56- 64
Creamer, round, square 39- 47
Dish, oval, large, small 14- 26
Goblet 36- 44
Mug 32- 41
Pitcher, water (ill.) 110-118
Plate, 5″, 6″, 7¼″, 9″ (5″ rare) . . 17- 32
Sauce, flat, round, square 13- 20
Spoonholder, round, square 29- 38
Sugar bowl, round, square 43- 52
Tumbler, water 37- 45

Probably other pieces. Colors, 40-50 percent higher than clear prices listed. Pieces made in round and square shapes. Goblet, mug and 9″ plate being reproduced.

Rose Leaves

Rose Leaves

Maker unknown, c. 1880s, clear, non-flint.

Goblet (ill.) $24-32

Other pieces?

Rose Point Band

Rose Point Band

(Water Lily): Maker unknown early 1900s. Clear. Non-flint.

Butter dish $22-30
Celery 14-22
Creamer (ill.) 27-36
Goblet 20-28
Spoonholder 16-24
Sugar bowl, covered 30-38

Probably other pieces.

Rose Sprig

Campbell, Jones & Company, Pittsburgh, 1886. Clear, amber, yellow, blue. Non-flint.

Butter dish $37-46

Rose Sprig

Cake plate on stand	40-49
Celery vase	34-40
Creamer	35-43
Dish, three styles	22-34
Goblet	34-43
Mug, handled	28-38
Pitcher, water, two sizes (ill.)	49-57
Plate, 6½″, 10½″, square	27-38
Platter	35-44
Salt, sleigh	30-37
Spoonholder	24-32
Sugar bowl, covered	45-53
Tray, water	47-55
Tumbler	28-37

Probably other pieces. Colors, 40-50 percent higher than clear prices listed.

Rosette

Rosette

(Magic): Bryce Bros., Pittsburgh, called it Magic. Later produced by U.S. Glass Company, Tiffin, Ohio, who also called it Magic. Clear. Non-flint.

Butter dish, covered $36-44
Cake plates on stand, 9″, 10″, 11″ . 35-43
Celery 28-36
Compote
  a. Covered, high standard, 6″
    7″, 8″ 44-58
  b. Open, footed, 6″, 7″, 8″
    9″, 10″ 35-46

Creamer 26-33
Goblet 29-37
Pitcher, water,
    half gallon (ill.) 51-60
Plate, 7″, 9″, handled........... 28-41
Relish (fish shape)............. 27-35
Spoonholder 26-34
Sugar bowl, covered 32-41
Tumbler 24-28
Wine........................ 25-33
Probably other pieces.

Rosette with Pinwheels

Rosette with Pinwheels

Possibly U.S. Glass Company, after 1895. Clear. Non-flint.

Butter dish, covered $26-34
Celery 18-24
Creamer 20-27
Pitcher, water (ill.) 44-50
Spoonholder 20-27
Sugar bowl, covered 22-29
Probably other pieces.

Royal

Royal

Belmont Glass Company, Bellaire, Ohio, 1881. Clear. Non-flint.

Butter dish $32-41

Celery 17-24
Compote, covered 8″ high 30-40
Creamer 27-34
Goblet 19-27
Pitcher, water 36-44
Spoonholder 18-24
Sugar bowl, covered (ill.) 29-36
Tumbler 22-31
Probably other pieces.

Royal Crystal

Royal Crystal

Tarentum Glass Company, Tarentum, Pennsylvania, 1894. Clear, ruby flashed. Also known as Atlanta. Non-flint.

Butter dish, covered $41-48
Celery 19-27
Compote, open, 7¾″ 37-42
Creamer 21-28
Pitcher (ill.).................... 47-56
Sauce, flat 12-16
Spoonholder 21-28
Sugar bowl
    a. Covered 33-42
    b. Open 21-30

Probably other pieces. Red or amber flashing, 50 percent higher than clear prices listed.

Royal Ivy

(continued)

Royal Ivy

Northwood Glass Company, Martins Ferry, Ohio, 1889-1890. Clear, deep pink/clear; deep pink/clear, acid finished; pink/clear, amber mottled, non-flint.

Bowl, open, 7″	$ 50- 60
Butter dish, covered, clear to frosted	180-190
Creamer	100-115
Pitcher	
a. Syrup	65- 80
b. Water	180-190
Shakers	
a. Salt/Pepper, pr.	130-139
b. Sugar	120-130
Sugar bowl, covered	130-140
Toothpick holder	68- 75
Tumbler	68- 78

Probably other pieces. All color patterns at least 50 percent higher than clear prices listed.

Royal Oak

Royal Oak

Northwood Glass Company, Martins Ferry, Ohio, 1889-1890. Flint, deep pink/clear; deep pink/clear, acid finished; pink/clear, amber mottled. Non-flint.

Prices same as Royal Ivy, flint and colors.

Ruffled Edge Hobnail

Maker and date unknown. Non-flint.

Bowl, finger	$24-33
Butter dish, covered	28-34
Celery, opalescent (ill.)	16-24
Creamer	28-34
Sugar bowl, squat	36-44
Tumbler	18-27

Probably other pieces.

Ruffled Edge Hobnail

Ruffled Eye

Ruffled Eye

Indiana Tumbler & Goblet (National) Company, 1890s, this pattern is similar to Indiana's Dewey. Known to have been made in water pitcher. Non-flint.

Blue	$140-150
Amber	152-161
Green	130-139

Probably other pieces but not known to this writer.

S Repeat

Northwood Glass Company, then National Glass Company, Pittsburgh, 1903. Clear, colors: amethyst and gold; translucent sapphire; light green without gilt. Non-flint.

S Repeat

Butter dish $37-45
Celery 20-27
Compote, high, low standard 40-50
Creamer 27-35
Goblet 18-26
Pitcher, water 47-54
Salt/Pepper, pr. 24-32
Spoonholder 18-27
Sugar bowl, covered 42-51
Tumbler (ill.) 42-50

Probably other pieces. Colors, 50 percent higher than clear prices listed.

Saint Bernard

Fostoria Glass Company, Moundsville, West Virginia, c. 1894, clear, non-flint.

Bowl, berry $16-24
Compote, covered 32-40
Creamer 24-32
Goblet 16-24
Jar, jam, covered 30-38
Spoonholder 18-24
Sugar bowl, covered 24-31

Many other pieces.

Sandwich Block

Sandwich, early. Flint.

Piece shown in photo is blue perfume with stopper. Rare. No price available, but probably $475+.

Sandwich Block

Sandwich Covered Sugar

Sandwich Covered Sugar

Sandwich glass, early. Not pressed glass in the truest sense as it's blown-molded but nevertheless absolutely beautiful and still to be found. Flint.

Covered sugar (ill.) .... $600+

Sandwich Glass Sugar Bowl

Sandwich, later period, blue, amethyst. Flint.

Sugar bowl with lid $300-375
Probably creamer to match 260-290

569 (continued)

Sandwich Glass Sugar Bowl

Sandwich Star

b. Open, supported by 3
   dolphins, flint .... 700+
c. Amethyst, tall (rare),
   flint .... 900+
Cordial, flint .... 300+
Creamer, flint 290-310
Decanter, quart size 140-150
Goblet (rare), flint........... 370+
Pitcher, flint (ill.) .... 1,100+
Relish dish 60- 70
Spill holder 72- 81
Spoonholder 55- 63

Probably other pieces.

Sawtooth

Sawtooth

(Roanoke): New England Glass Company, and Sandwich, 1860s. Later called Roanoke and made by Ripley & Company, Pittsburgh, 1885. Also made by U.S. Glass Co. (Gillinder-merge). Non-flint.

Bowl, berry ....$ 49- 54
Butter dish 89- 98
Cake stand, 9″, 10″ 78- 94
Celery vase 67- 74
Compote
   a. Covered, 6″, 7″, 8″, 9″,
      10″, 11″ knob stem 114-123
   b. Open, 6″, 7″, 8″, 10″ 54- 63

Sandwich Spill

Sandwich Spill

Sandwich glass, early 1850s. Another example of magnificent glass. Flint.

Sandwich Star

Sandwich, early. Clear and amethyst (rare).

Compote
   a. Covered, high standard ..$270-300

Creamer 90- 98
Decanter, quart size 120-130
Egg cup 47- 55
Goblet 48- 56
Pitcher, water, ½ gal. (ill.) 103-112
Sauce, 4″, 5″ 17- 23
Spill holder, octagonal 36- 43
Spoonholder 40- 48
Sugar bowl 84- 93
Tumbler, footed, water 47- 55

Probably other pieces. Goblet, iced tea, sherbet and wine being reproduced in pink.

Sawtoothed Honeycomb

Sawtoothed Honeycomb

Steiner Glass Company, Buckhannon, West Virginia, 1906; again in 1908 by Union Stopper Company, Morgantown, West Virginia. Crystal; crystal with central honeycombs in ruby with rims in gold. Non-flint.

Celery $16-23
Creamer (ill.) 23-32
Goblet 19-26
Pitcher 44-56
Spoonholder 23-32
Sugar bowl, covered 35-43

Probably other pieces.

Saxon

Adams & Company, Pittsburgh, Pennsylvania, c. 1880, clear, plain and engraved, opal. Reissued after 1891 by the U.S. Glass Company. Non-flint.

Bowl, oval $27-35

Butter dish, covered 52-60
Creamer 32-40
Compote
  a. Open 18-26
  b. Covered 34-42
Goblet 24-32
Plate, 6″ 28-35
Spoonholder 22-30
Sugar bowl, covered 38-46
Tumbler 20-28

Other pieces.

Scalloped Diamond Point

Possibly Central Glass Company, Wheeling, West Virginia, c. 1870s, clear, non-flint.

Bowls, round, oval $14-23
Butter dish, covered 28-37
Cake stand, large, 10″ 30-39
Creamer 27-36
Dish, cheese 28-31
Sauce, flat, footed 11-16
Spoonholder 17-21
Sugar bowl, covered 30-40
Wine 22-31

Probably other pieces.

Scalloped Prism

(Triple Bar): Doyle & Company, Pittsburgh, c. early 1880s, clear, non-flint. Originally called "No. 84" by Doyle. Reissued by U.S. Glass Company in 1891.

Butter dish, covered $31-40
Goblet 18-27
Spoonholder 17-26
Sugar bowl, covered 32-41
Tumbler 14-21

Other pieces.

Scalloped Tape

571

(continued)

Scalloped Tape

(Jewel Band): Maker unknown, 1880s.
Clear, amber, canary, blue, apple green.

Butter dish, covered	$24-34
Cake stand	22-31
Celery	17-24
Creamer	19-27
Egg cup	11-16
Goblet	12-20
Pitcher, water (ill.)	31-40
Sauce	14-22
Sugar	
a. Covered	34-42
b. Open	26-34
Wine	12-27

Probably other pieces. All colored pieces at least 40 percent higher than clear prices listed.

Scarab

Scarab

Maker, date unknown, clear, flint.

Goblet (ill.)	$98-109

Other pieces? The goblet is beautiful!

Scroll

(Stippled Scroll): Maker unknown, 1880s. Clear. Non-flint.

Butter dish	$38-45
Celery	30-38
Compote, covered, high, low standard	27-40
Creamer	23-31
Egg cup	19-27
Goblet	22-29
Pitcher, tankard type	47-54
Spoonholder	20-28
Sugar bowl	38-46

Scroll and Daisy

Scroll and Daisy

Northwood Glass Company, Opaline and Carnival; usual Carnival colors. Non-flint.

Compote, candy or jelly	$40-48
Creamer (probably a mustard jar, with lid, originally) (ill.)	32-41

Colors, 50 percent higher than crystal, marigold prices listed.

Scroll with Acanthus

Scroll with Acanthus

Central Glass Company, Wheeling, West Virginia. Clear, sapphire blue, purple slag. This pattern also was made by Northwood, only in the Mosaic or slag type. The prices shown are Northwood, 1902. Non-flint.

Creamer (ill.)	$52-61
Compote, jelly, tall, stemmed	50-60

Sugar bowl, open 48-57
Apparently these were the only pieces made in this pattern.

Sugar bowl, covered 24-34
Probably other pieces.

Scroll with Flowers

Scroll with Flowers

Central Glass Company, late 1870s. Clear, later made by Northwood in apple green, amber and blue. Possibly other colors made. Prices listed are for Northwood. Non-flint.

Butter dish	$42-51
Cake plate, handled	46-54
Celery	38-46
Creamer	40-47
Egg cup, 2 handles	28-34
Goblet	33-43
Mustard, covered	41-50
Pitcher (ill.)...................	46-54
Salt/Pepper, pr.	36-44
Sugar bowl	52-61

Supposedly a rare pattern. Colors 50 percent higher than crystal/marigold prices listed. Probably other pieces.

Scroll with Star

Challinor, Taylor & Company, Tarentum, Pennsylvania, c. 1885, clear, non-flint.

Butter dish	$27-36
Cup	12-19
Creamer	18-27
Goblet	14-23
Sauce	12-19
Spoonholder	17-26

Scrolled Sunflower

Scrolled Sunflower

Another of those patterns lost on the back roads of time. Possibly Northwood who made several "Scroll" patterns. Shown for identification only. If you know, tell me.

?

?

Because that's just what it is! An absolutely beautiful pattern. Maker and date unknown and no prices available. Anyone know its name?

Seashell

(Boswell): Maker unknown, c. late 1870s, clear, non-flint.

Butter dish, covered	$28-36
Cake stand	22-30
Celery	14-21
Creamer	19-27
Goblet	24-28
Pitcher	27-36
Salt/Pepper, pr.	22-31
Spoonholder	22-31
Sugar bowl, covered	24-32

Probably other pieces.

Shell and Jewel

Butter dish, covered	$42-50
Cake stand	39-47
Compote, open, high foot	39-47
Creamer	29-37
Pitcher, water (ill.)	40-48
Spoonholder	23-30
Sugar bowl	34-43
Tumbler	19-26

No goblet made. Probably other pieces. Colors 100 percent higher than clear prices listed.

Seesaw

Seesaw

Probably Gillinder & Sons, c. 1870s.

Plate, 10″ dia. (ill.) $84-92

Serenade Plate

Indiana Tumbler & Goblet (National) Company, 1890s. Chocolate, white milk glass.

Serenade plate, large	$140+
Serenade plate, small	125+

Prices given are for chocolate; milk-white, 50-60 percent lower.

Shell and Jewel

(Victor): Westmoreland Glass Company, 1893, originally called it Victor. Better known today as Shell and Jewel. Clear, blue, green. Non-flint.

Shell and Tassel

Shell and Ribbing

Shell and Ribbing

This is blown, 3-mold glass, probably very early Sandwich. Not Pressed Glass but we thought you'd like to see one of the rarest types of glass in the world.

Shell and Tassel

(Square): George A. Duncan & Sons; Shell and Tassel, Round: 10 years later, 1890, Duncan & Heisey. On the Round, the finial on the covered pieces was a dog in a reclining position. Prices given are for both. Non-flint.

Berry set, 7 pcs. .... $ 90-105
Butter dish, round, covered,
   dog finial 76- 84
Cake stand, large, small 54- 63
Celery vase, round, square 50- 58
Compote
   a. Covered 56- 64
   b. Open, 4½", high standard . 53- 61
Creamer, round, square 34- 43
Goblet, 2 types 37- 46
Pitcher, round, square (ill.) 44- 53
Platter, bread 63- 72
Salt shaker 29- 38
Spoonholder, round, square.... 28- 37
Sugar bowl, round, square 87- 94
Vases, pr..................... 126-136

Probably other pieces. Colors, rare. 100 percent higher than prices listed for clear. Goblet being reproduced.

Sheraton

Sheraton

(Ida): Bryce, Higbee & Company, Pittsburgh, 1880s, called it Ida. Clear, amber, blue, green; and possibly yellow. Non-flint.

Bowl, berry $24-32
Butter dish 35-43
Compote, covered 34-43
Creamer 24-30
Goblet 24-30
Pitcher, water................. 27-35
Sauce, flat 13-19
Sugar bowl, covered 32-41
Tumbler 19-26
Wine......................... 17-24

Amber, blue, 100 percent higher than color prices listed. Probably other pieces.

Shimmering Star

Shimmering Star

Maker unknown, 1880s. Clear. Probably made at an earlier date also. Non-flint.

Butter dish, covered $32-41
Cake stand 31-32
Pitcher (ill.)................... 37-44
Sauce, flat 11-19
Spoonholder 20-21
Sugar bowl
   a. Covered 51-60
   b. Open 32-40
Tumbler 19-27

Probably other pieces.

Shoshone

Shoshone

(Victor; Blazing Pinwheels): U.S. Glass Co., c. 1895. Crystal, ruby-stained, emerald green. Non-flint.

Banana stand (ill.)............. $32-37
Butter dish, covered 34-39
Compote, covered and open,
   7", 8½" 30-45
Creamer, 3½", 5" high 28-34
Goblet 22-29
Mug 20-27
Pitcher, milk, several sizes 52-64
Spoonholder 21-29

(continued)

Sugar bowl 31-40

Colors 100 percent higher than clear prices listed.

Shrine

Make unknown, c. 1880s, clear, non-flint.

Bowl	$21-30
Butter dish, covered	44-53
Compote, jelly	24-32
Creamer	38-47
Goblet	18-27
Sauce	7-12
Spoonholder	19-24
Sugar bowl	
a. Open	27-37
b. Covered	41-50
Tumbler	24-32

Shuttle

Shuttle

Indiana Tumbler & Goblet (National) Company, 1900. Chocolate, clear, caramel. Non-flint.

	Chocolate	Clear
Cordial		$11-17
Creamer		28-33
Goblet		29-38
Mug (ill.)	$72-80	30-38
Pitcher, syrup..........	60-70	34-41
Punch cup	50-58	16-23
Salt/Pepper, pr.		26-34
Saucedish		12-19
Spoonholder	47-54	26-34
Tumbler	37-46	17-24
Wine.................	23-31	20-27

Caramel, 200 percent more than clear prices listed.

Singing Birds

Singing Birds

Northwood Glass Company, Wheeling, West Virginia, 1900s. Clear, Custard, Carnival, other. Non-flint.

Berry set		
a. Large bowl, marigold	....$	50- 60
Large bowl, vivid	....	67- 75
b. Small bowl, marigold	....	16- 24
Small bowl, vivid	....	27- 34
Butter dish, covered, clear	....	28- 31
Butter dish, covered, marigold		62- 71
Butter dish, covered, vivid	....	110-118
Creamer, clear (ill.)	....	40- 48
Creamer, marigold	....	40- 48
Creamer, vivid	....	60- 68
Mug, custard, marigold, vivid..		22- 31
Mug, color, non-iridescent	....	27- 36
Pitcher, marigold	....	70- 80
Pitcher, vivid	....	120-128
Sherbet (custard) (rare)	......	40- 47
Sugar bowl, covered, clear	....	37- 44
Sugar bowl, covered, marigold		51- 60
Sugar bowl, covered, vivid	....	67- 76
Spoonholder, clear...........		24- 32
Spoonholder, marigold		40- 50
Spoonholder, vivid...........		54- 63
Tumbler, marigold	....	24- 32
Tumbler, vivid	....	27- 36

Custard, Carnival, 100 percent higher than clear prices listed.

Single Rose

Probably Westmoreland Specialty Company, c. 1890-1900, clear, opaque white; sometimes colored, in rose and green, gilded. Non-flint.

Butter dish, covered	$43-51
Creamer	30-38
Pitcher, water.................	41-49
Spoonholder	18-24
Sugar bowl, covered	37-46

Opaque white, 25 percent; rose, 30 percent; green, gilded, 40 percent higher than clear prices listed. Possibly other pieces.

Siskyou

Siskyou

A member of the "Block" family, c. 1880s, clear, non-flint.

Same values as "Block and Fan" — see.

Slashed Swirl

Slashed Swirl

Riverside Glass Company, Wellsburg, West Virginia, 1891. Clear. Non-flint.

Butter dish, covered	$25-32
Celery	17-23
Compote	30-37
Creamer	16-24
Goblet	19-27
Pitcher, water (ill.)	36-41
Salt/Pepper, pr.	18-27
Sugar bowl	27-36

Tumbler	16-24
Wine	14-21

Probably other pieces.

Slewed Horseshoe

Slewed Horseshoe

Possibly Imperial Glass Company, Bellaire, Ohio, after 1906. Clear. Non-flint.

Butter dish	$23-31
Cake stand	25-32
Celery	22-31
Creamer	24-33
Compote	25-34
Goblet	20-27
Pitcher, syrup (ill.)	34-42
Spoonholder	13-21
Sugar bowl, covered	21-30
Tumbler	17-26

Probably other pieces.

Smocking

577

(continued)

Smocking

Sandwich Glass, 1840s. Clear. Flint.

Butter dish, covered	$ 85- 93
Compote, footed, open, 6″ high	68- 74
Creamer, applied handle (rare)	95-102
Goblet	66- 73
Lamp, 9″ high...............	130-138
Spill, holder	49- 58
Sugar bowl, covered (ill.)	84- 92

Probably other pieces.

Smooth Diamond

Smooth Diamond

Possibly McKee Bros., late 1880s. Clear. Non-flint.

Butter dish	$29-36
Compote	24-32
Creamer	21-30
Goblet	21-27
Pitcher, water (ill.)	40-48
Sugar bowl, covered	31-40
Tumbler	23-30

Probably other pieces.

Snail

George Duncan & Sons, Pittsburgh, c. 1880s, clear. After 1891, by U.S. Glass Company, who added ruby color to the plain bands, sometimes engraving through the color. Non-flint.

Bowls, berry, finger...........	$30- 42
Butter dish, covered	69- 77

Cake stand	77- 84
Celery......................	68- 76
Compote, covered.............	79- 87
Creamer, two sizes	31- 42
Goblet......................	43- 51
Pitcher, water	89-100
Spoonholder	31- 40
Sugar bowl	
a. Individual...............	23- 31
b. Large, covered	34- 42
Tumbler.....................	38- 46

Ruby colored bands, 100 percent higher than clear prices listed. Many other pieces.

Snakeskin with Dot

Snakeskin with Dot

Maker unknown, late 1870s. Clear, occasionally found in deep blue and in amber.

Celery vase	$17-26
Creamer	30-35
Goblet	19-27
Pitcher, water (ill.)	33-41
Plates, 4½″ to 7″	16-23
Sugar bowl, covered	31-40

Probably other pieces. Deep blue and amber, 50 percent higher than clear prices listed.

Snow Band

(Puffed Bands): Maker unknown, c. early 1880s, clear, blue, possibly other colors, non-flint.

Butter dish	$24-32

Compote
a. Open 16-23
b. Covered 27-34
Creamer 24-32
Goblet 13-21
Pitcher, water................. 30-37
Relish 14-22
Sauce, flat 10-14
Spoonholder 14-21
Sugar bowl, covered 27-34
Wine........................ 15-23

Blue, 40 percent higher than clear prices listed. Probably other pieces.

Snowdrop

(Ashland): Portland Glass Company, Portland, Maine, c. 1880s, clear. Non-flint.

Dish, ice cream, leaf-shaped $21-30
Goblet 19-24
Tray, ice cream 27-34

Should be other pieces.

Snowflake

Snowflake

Probably U.S. Glass Company, early 1900s. Clear. Non-flint.

Butter dish $30-36
Cake stand 34-42
Celery 17-23
Compote, covered, high, low
standard 22-32
Creamer 20-25
Goblet 21-30
Pitcher
a. Milk (ill.) 38-46
b. Water 40-47
Spoonholder 18-26
Sugar bowl, covered 30-32
Tumbler 17-23

Probably other pieces.

Southern Ivy

Southern Ivy

Maker unknown, mid-1800s. Clear. Non-flint.

Bowl, berry $18-24
Butter dish, covered 28-35
Creamer 27-34
Cruet, small 28-37
Egg cup 19-24
Pitcher, water (ill.) 38-46
Saucedish, 4″ 9-16
Spoonholder 20-28
Sugar bowl, covered 30-37
Tumbler, water 19-26

Probably other pieces made. No goblet made.

Spanish-American

Spanish-American

(Dewey): Bryce Bros., Pittsburgh. Clear, possibly colors, including milk white, 1890s. Non-flint.

Butter dish, covered $36-44
Celery 32-39
Compote 39-47
Creamer 27-34

579

(continued)

Pitcher (ill.) 45-53
Spoonholder 14-20
Sugar bowl 43-51
Tumbler 17-24

Probably other pieces. At one time given away as a baking powder premium. Tumbler more scarce than pitcher. Don't confuse this "Dewey" with another that's also known as Flower Flange.

Spearpoint Band

Spearpoint Band

Maker and date unknown. Clear with ruby stain. Non-flint.

Butter dish $21-28
Creamer 18-24
Pitcher, water (ill.) 34-42
Sugar bowl, covered 22-31

Probably other pieces.

Spiral and Maltese Cross

Maker unknown, c. early 1880s, clear, non-flint.

Butter dish, covered $28-36
Creamer 17-24
Spoonholder 16-23
Sugar bowl, covered 30-37

Should be other pieces. We're always glad to hear from collectors and dealers alike. Constructive criticism is always welcome; it helps us produce a better price guide for *you*.

Spiralled Ivy

Another of the "Ivy" patterns, mid-1880s. Clear. Non-flint.

Spiralled Ivy

Butter dish, covered $44-52
Creamer 33-41
Pitcher, water (ill.) 49-58
Sauce 9-15
Spoonholder 23-30
Sugar bowl, covered 34-42
Tumbler 20-27

Probably other pieces.

Spirea Band

Spirea Band

(Square and Dot; Squared Dot): Bryce, Higbee & Company, c. 1885. Non-flint.

Butter dish, covered $38-46
Cake stand 34-42
Celery 27-34
Compote
  a. Covered 45-53
  b. Open 34-42
Creamer 25-32
Goblet 20-28
Pitcher, water (ill.) 33-41
Platter 25-34
Salt/Pepper, pr. 29-37
Spoonholder 23-33
Sugar bowl, covered 29-36
Tumbler 19-27
Wine 20-29

Probably other pieces. Amber, canary, blue, 65 percent higher; green 100 percent higher than clear prices listed.

Sprig

Squared Star

Sprig

(Royal): Bryce, Higbee & Company, Pittsburgh, early 1880s. Clear, with and without sprig decoration. Non-flint.

Bowl, berry	$27-35
Butter dish	46-54
Cake stand	45-53
Celery	35-43
Compote	
a. Covered, high standard, 12″	51-61
b. Open, low standard	33-42
Creamer	39-47
Goblet	34-39
Pitcher, water (ill.)	51-60
Platter, oval	39-47
Sauce, flat, footed	12-20
Spoonholder	28-36
Sugar bowl, covered	41-50
Tumbler	22-30
Wine........................	28-36

Probably other pieces.

Squared Star

Maker unknown, 1890s. Clear. Non-flint.

Butter dish	$22-28
Creamer	20-25
Spoonholder (ill.)	24-34
Sugar bowl	37-46

Probably other pieces.

Squirrel

Squirrel

Indiana Tumbler & Goblet (National) Company, Greentown, Indiana, 1880s. Clear. Finials are squirrels. Non-flint.

Butter dish, covered, squirrel knob (ill.)	$108-116
Creamer	84- 93
Goblet (extremely rare)	450+
Pitcher, water	118-126
Sauce, footed, flat	36- 44
Sugar bowl	
a. Covered (ill.)	86- 93
b. Open	54- 62

Possibly other pieces. Chocolate (pitcher, water is known) would be 200 percent higher than clear prices listed.

Star and Dart

Star and Dart

Maker unknown, c. 1850s, clear, flint.

Butter dish, covered (ill.) $44-53
Creamer 30-39
Spoonholder 19-26
Sugar bowl, covered 39-47

Should be other pieces. A note to you nice people who have been kind enough to buy this *Price Guide.* IF you have information concerning **any** pattern, PLEASE, let's hear from you. IF you don't agree with the prices quoted, PLEASE, let's hear from you. IF you think the piece illustrated is a spoonholder rather than a celery (etc.), PLEASE let's hear from you. Constructive criticism is **always** welcome.

Star and Pillar

Star and Pillar

Possibly Nickel Plate Glass Company, 1891. Clear. Non-flint.

Butter dish, covered, also footed . . $40-45

Celery 20-27
Creamer 40-46
Goblet 21-30
Pitcher, water 60-68
Salt/Pepper, pr. 27-34
Spoonholder 28-37
Sugar bowl, covered 40-50
Tumbler 19-28
Wine 17-26

Probably other pieces.

Star and Punty

Star and Punty

Sandwich, early. One of the finest patterns ever made at Sandwich. Clear.

Cologne bottle $210-220
Creamer 218-227
Pitcher (ill.) . . . . 465+
Sugar bowl 260-270
Whale-oil lamp . . . . 550+

Relatively few pieces made. Possibly a few more, but doubtful.

Star Band

(Bosworth): A "new" glass as far as age goes; 1900s. Clear. Non-flint.

Butter dish $17-25
Celery 14-21
Compote 23-31
Creamer 22-30
Goblet 16-24
Pitcher (ill.) 27-36
Spoonholder 17-24

Star Band

Sugar bowl 18-27

Probably other pieces. As it gets older, it will probably become more collectible.

Star-in-Bull's-Eye

Star-in-Bull's-Eye

U.S. Glass Company, 1907, probably before. Clear, gold trim. Non-flint.

Bowl, berry $14-19
Butter dish 23-32
Cake stand 27-36
Celery vase 14-20
Compote
  a. Covered 34-40
  b. Open, 6" high.............. 27-34
Creamer (ill.) 16-25
Goblet 18-24
Pitcher, water.................. 34-42
Spoonholder 18-24
Sugar bowl, covered 32-38
Tumbler, gold band (ill.) 20-27

Probably other pieces.

Star in Honeycomb

Bryce Bros., Pittsburgh, late 1880s

Star in Honeycomb

Clear. Non-flint.

Butter dish, covered $31-40
Compote
  a. Covered 32-41
  b. Open 22-28
Cake stand 31-40
Creamer 22-28
Goblet 19-25
Pitcher (ill.).................... 28-34
Sauce, flat 12-16
Spoonholder 18-26
Sugar bowl, covered 40-50
Tumbler 22-28

Probably other pieces.

Star Pattern

(continued)

Star Pattern

Not specific name; given only for filing purposes. No one can find it in any book. 8-pointed stars. Not made by U.S. Glass Company. Anyone know?

Star Rosetted

Star Rosetted

McKee & Bros., Pittsburgh, 1875. Clear. Non-flint.

Butter dish	$41-50
Compote, open, high, low standard	36-64
Creamer	32-41
Goblet	26-34
Pitcher, water	47-56
Plate, 10″, "A Good Mother" (ill.)	45-54
Spoonholder	20-28
Sugar bowl	39-47

Probably other pieces.

Starlyte

Lancaster Glass Company, Lancaster, Ohio, 1910. Clear.

Butter dish	$19-25
Celery vase	14-21
Compote	27-33
Creamer	21-30
Goblet	17-19
Pitcher, water (ill.)	27-34
Spoonholder	17-24
Sugar bowl, covered	30-36

Probably other pieces.

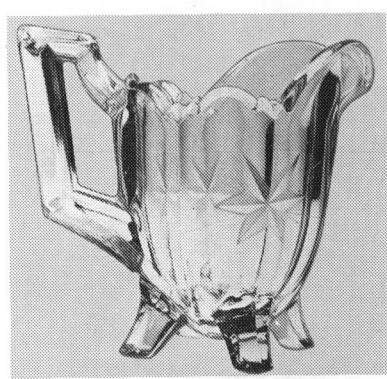

Starlyte

Starred Scroll

Starred Scroll

(Crescent and Fan): Maker unknown, c. early 1900s, clear, non-flint.

Butter dish, covered	$22-31
Celery	18-26
Jug, syrup (ill.)	26-33
Spoonholder	16-22
Sugar bowl, covered	22-31
Wine	12-19

Stars and Bars

Stars and Bars

(With Stippled Leaf): This is a clear

glass of the late 1870s, or early 1880s.
Most books show it without stippled leaf.

Butter dish	$20-27
Celery dish	16-24
Creamer	24-32
Dish, oval, 7″, 8″, 9″, 10″, 11″	14-24
Dollhouse set of creamer, butter dish, sugar, set	48-54
Goblet	17-24
Jam jar	16-22
Night lamp, small	24-32
Pitcher, milk (ill.)	37-44
Spoonholder	13-20
Sugar bowl, covered	24-32

Undoubtedly many more pieces.

Stars and Stripes

Stars and Stripes

(Brilliant): Called Brilliant in an 1899
Ward Catalog. Non-flint.

Butter dish	$30-36
Celery	16-22
Compote	22-30
Creamer	19-26
Goblet	19-26
Pitcher (ill.)	31-40
Spoonholder	18-25
Sugar bowl	23-32
Tumbler	16-22

Probably other pieces. Probably there
are milk glass pieces; if so, 50 percent
higher than clear prices listed.

States, The

U.S. Glass Company, 1905. Clear, some
pieces gold trimmed. Non-flint.

Butter dish, covered	$40-48
Celery	20-27

The States

Compote, 7″, open	31-40
Creamer	22-30
Dish, handled, round	14-20
Pitcher, water, gold trimmed (ill.)	46-54
Plate, large	18-23
Sugar bowl, covered	31-40
Toothpick holder	38-46
Tumbler	19-27

Probably other pieces. Gold trim doesn't
affect price of clear prices listed.

Stippled Band

(Panelled Stippled Bowl): Maker unknown, c. 1870s, clear, non-flint.

Butter dish, covered	$44-52
Celery	28-36
Creamer	34-42
Goblet	22-31
Pitcher	45-52
Spoonholder	21-29
Sugar bowl, covered	35-43
Tumbler	23-29

Other pieces.

Stippled Chain

Gillinder & Sons, 1870s. Non-flint.

Butter dish, covered	$49-58
Creamer	31-40
Goblet	24-32
Pickle dish	19-27
Pitcher, water (ill.)	47-55
Salt, footed	17-26
Sauce	9-16
Spoonholder	24-32
Sugar bowl, covered	39-46
Tumbler	17-24

Probably other pieces.

(continued)

Stippled Chain

Stippled Cherry

Stippled Cherry

Probably Lancaster Glass Company, 1880s. Clear. Non-flint.

Bowl, berry, 6″, 8″ $24-33
Butter dish 45-53
Celery 30-38
Creamer 31-40
Pitcher, water (ill.) 40-49
Plate, 6″, 9¼″, bread 20-36
Saucedish, 4″ 12-20
Spoonholder 19-27
Sugar bowl, covered 34-43
Tumbler, water 21-30

Probably other pieces.

Stippled Daisy

Maker unknown, 1880s. Non-flint.

Compote, open $40-49
Creamer 29-37
Relish, oval 13-21
Sauce, flat 11-20
Spoonholder 22-30
Sugar bowl
    a. Covered 34-42
    b. Open 22-30

Stippled Daisy

Tumbler (ill.) 20-28
Wine 19-25

Probably other pieces.

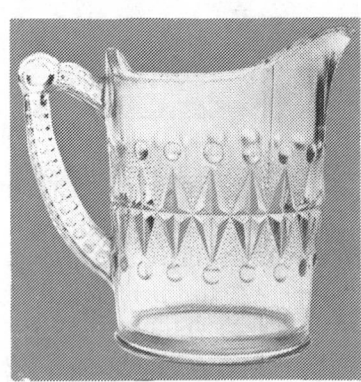

Stippled Dart and Balls

Stippled Dart and Balls

Another product of the 1890s. Clear. Non-flint.

Butter dish, covered $23-32
Creamer 16-23
Goblet 13-21
Pitcher (ill.) 31-40
Sugar bowl, covered 24-32
Tumbler 15-22
Wine 12-19

Probably other pieces.

Stippled Double Loop

Made in Pennsylvania in the late 1880s. Scarce and in demand. Non-flint.

Stippled Double Loop

Butter dish, covered	$31-40
Creamer	24-32
Goblet	23-30
Pitcher (ill.)	44-53
Spoonholder	21-30
Sugar bowl, covered	34-42
Tumbler	19-28

Stippled Fleur-de-Lis

Stippled Fleur-de-Lis

(Frosted Fleur-de-Lis): Maker unknown, c. late 1880s; clear, amber, blue, green, milk glass, non-flint.

Butter dish, covered	$35-43
Cake stand	24-32
Creamer (ill.)	27-36
Goblet	24-32
Spoonholder	21-30
Sugar bowl, covered	34-42

Amber, blue, milk glass, 40 percent higher; green, 60 percent higher than clear prices listed.

Stippled Forget-Me-Not

Stippled Forget-Me-Not

Bryce Bros., 1880s, also Model Flint Glass Company, after 1891. Clear, color, extremely rare (amber, opal). Non-flint.

Butter dish	$55-64
Cake plate on stand, large, small	40-56
Celery	48-56
Compote, covered, 6″, 7″, 8″	49-68
Creamer	40-47
Goblet	39-46
Mug	23-32
Pitcher, water (ill.)	55-63
Plate, baby center, 7″, star center, 7″, kitten center, 9″	34-48
Sauce, flat, footed	19-26
Spoonholder	40-50
Sugar bowl	52-59
Tumbler, bar, half pint, gill, footed	29-37
Wine	32-48

Amber, opal, 200 percent higher than clear pieces listed.

Stippled Fuchsia

Probably Sandwich, c. 1870s, clear and stippled, non-flint.

Butter dish, covered	$34-42
Compote	
a. Open	34-42
b. Covered	45-52
Creamer	39-44
Goblet	25-30
Pitcher	42-50
Spoonholder	22-31
Sugar bowl, covered	41-49

Probably other pieces.

Stippled Grape and Festoon

Stippled Grape and Festoon

Doyle & Company, Pittsburgh, 1870. Clear and stippled (this pattern with stippled background is the scarcest of the grape and festoon family). Non-flint.

Butter dish	$76- 84
Celery	44- 50
Compote, covered, low standard	66- 73
Cordial	32- 40
Creamer	49- 56
Egg cup	25- 32
Goblet	35- 43
Pitcher, water, applied handle (ill.)	91- 100
Spoonholder	35- 42
Sugar	
a. Open	38- 46
b. Covered	52- 61
Wine	29- 36

Probably other pieces.

Stippled Leaf and Flower

Stippled Leaf and Flower

Maker unknown, 1870s. Clear. Non-flint.

Butter dish, covered	$30-38

Creamer	27-35
Dish, sauce	11-15
Decanter, stopper	37-46
Goblet	22-30
Pitcher, water (ill.)	72-80
Spoonholder	18-26
Sugar	
a. Covered	42-51
b. Open	22-31
Tumbler	30-37

Probably other pieces.

Stippled Medallion

Stippled Medallion

Union Glass Company, Somerville, Massachusetts, late 1860s. Clear. Non-flint.

Butter, covered	$34-43
Celery	21-28
Creamer	27-36
Goblet (ill.)	22-31
Pitcher, water	37-46
Spoonholder	18-26
Sugar	
a. Covered	32-41
b. Open	24-32

Probably other pieces.

Stippled Peppers

Sandwich glass, 1870s. Clear. Non-flint.

Creamer	$36-44
Egg cup	23-31
Goblet	31-40
Pitcher, water	51-59
Salt, footed	17-25
Sauce	10-17
Spoonholder	28-35

Probably other pieces.

Stippled Peppers

Stippled Sandbur

Stippled Sandbur

(Stippled Star Variant): Maker unknown, early 1890s. Clear. Non-flint.

Bowl	$24-32
Butter, covered	34-41
Celery vase	22-30
Compote, covered	34-42
Creamer	23-31
Goblet	19-27
Sauce, flat	16-24
Spoonholder	18-27
Sugar bowl, covered	31-40
Wine	22-30

Probably other pieces.

Stippled Star

Gillinder & Sons, Greensburg, Pennsylvania, 1870s. Probably Sandwich, much
earlier. Non-flint.

Butter dish	$60-68
Celery	49-57
Compote, large, high standard	70-78

Stippled Star

Creamer (ill.)	46-53
Dish, oval, 8"	24-30
Egg cup	28-35
Goblet	34-42
Pickle dish	17-25
Pitcher, water (ill.)	70-81
Sauce, flat, 4", 6"	13-20
Spoonholder, 5½" high	40-47
Sugar bowl, covered	53-62
Tumbler	23-31

Probably other pieces. Creamer, goblet,
salt dip, sugar bowl and wine being
reproduced in clear (original) and new
colors.

Stippled Star Flower

Stippled Star Flower

(With the band, called Star Flower
Band): Maker unknown, late 1880s. Clear.
Non-flint.

Butter dish	$27-36
Celery	15-24
Creamer	17-24
Goblet (ill.)	20-27
Salt, footed	12-21
Spoonholder	16-24
Sugar bowl, covered	23-31
Tumbler	17-22
Wine	12-19

Other pieces.

Stove

Stove

Maker and date unknown, clear, colors.
A novelty of the late 1800s. Non-flint.

Clear (ill.) $115-135
Color, 125 percent higher than clear
price listed.

Strawberry

Strawberry

Sandwich Glass, 1850-1860. Clear,
opaque white (milk glass). Non-flint.

Butter dish, covered $67- 75
Compote, covered, 8″ high,
low standard 85- 92
Creamer...................... 54- 62
Egg cup 36- 44
Goblet....................... 45- 53
Honey dish 23- 32
Pickle dish 25- 33
Pitcher
a. Syrup.................... 49- 59
b. Water (ill.) 95-105
Salt, footed 29- 38
Saucedish, flat 22- 29
Spoonholder 44- 53
Sugar bowl 54- 63

Probably other pieces. Prices listed are
for milk glass. Clear, 85-100 percent less.
Egg cup and goblet being reproduced.

Strawberry Jar

Strawberry Jar

Don't confuse this with the Sandwich
Glass Strawberry. This was a container
for grocery products — mustard, etc.
Possibly made by Specialty Glass Com-
pany and Indiana Tumbler & Goblet
Company. Non-flint.

Strawberry jar (ill.) $30-39

Strigil

Strigil

Possibly McKee Bros., Pittsburgh, late
1880s. Clear. Non-flint.

Butter dish $27-35
Celery 20-27
Compote 33-41
Creamer 30-37
Egg cup 16-25

Goblet 19-26
Pitcher 40-47
Sauce 17-26
Spoonholder 17-27
Sugar bowl 34-42
Tumbler 18-27

Probably other pieces.

Strutting Peacock

Strutting Peacock

Possibly Westmoreland Glass Company, late 1880s. Clear, other colors. Non-flint.

Bottle, decanter type...........$35-43
Butter dish, covered 40-48
Creamer, covered 26-34
Goblet 30-39
Mug, 4″ high 14-22
Pitcher, half gallon (ill.) 58-63
Plates, 6″, 7″, 8″, 9″ 31-42
Spoonholder 20-27
Sugar bowl, covered 30-38
Tumbler, 4″ high 22-27

Probably other pieces. Blue, purple, green, 50 percent higher; opalescent white or white Carnival, 125 percent higher; reds, 125 percent higher than clear/marigold prices given.

Stylized Flower

Stylized Flower

Challinor, Taylor & Company, Tarentum, Pennsylvania, 1885. "Mosaic glass" in brown and other colors. Also, crystal and opal. Only six pieces known in this pattern.

Butter dish $42-51
Creamer 21-30
Pitcher
  a. Quart (ill.) 55-64
  b. ½ gallon 45-53
Spoonholder 21-30
Sugar bowl, covered 41-50

Opal, 50 percent higher than clear prices listed.

Summit, The

Thompson Glass Company, Uniontown, Pennsylvania, c. 1895, clear, flint.

Butter dish, covered $54-62
Celery 30-39
Creamer 39-46
Pitcher, large, tankard 65-75
Spoonholder 27-37
Sugar bowl, covered 49-57

Possibly other pieces.

Sunbeam

Sunbeam

McKee & Brothers, Jeannette, Pennsylvania, c. 1898, clear; later, emerald with gold decorations. Non-flint.

Bowl, berry $12-20
Celery 13-22
Compote, jelly (ill.) 14-22
Creamer, individual 12-19
Sauce 8-12
Sugar bowl, covered 23-31

 (continued)

Tumbler 17-24

Emerald with gold decorations, 50 percent higher than clear prices listed.

Sunburst

Sunburst

McKee & Bros., 1898. Clear. Non-flint.

Butter dish $45-53
Cake plate on standard,
  2 types 37-46
Celery 29-38
Compote, covered, low
  standard 44-53
Cordial 21-29
Creamer 35-42
Egg cup 24-32
Goblet 26-35
Pitcher, large, small 45-54
Plate, 6″, 7″, 11″ 24-34
Spoonholder 28-37
Sugar bowl 41-50
Wine 22-31

Probably other pieces.

Sunflower

Sunflower

(Lily); Atterbury & Company, Pittsburgh, 1881. Crystal, amber, blue, opal, mosaic glass.

Butter dish, covered $47-56
Creamer 32-41
Goblet 20-30
Nappy 27-36
Pitcher (ill.) 50-60
Spoonholder 22-31
Sugar bowl
  a. Covered 44-52
  b. Open 30-38

Probably other pieces. Amber, 50 percent higher; mosaic, 100 percent higher than clear prices listed.

Sunflower Container

Sunflower Container

Westmoreland Specialty Company or Specialty Glass Company. This is a creamer, originally made as a commercial jelly container.

Sunflower container (ill.) $27-35

Sunk Daisy

Co-Operative Flint Glass Company, Beaver Falls, Pennsylvania, 1898. Clear and green. Non-flint.

Butter dish, covered $27-36
Compote 30-38
Creamer 20-27
Goblet 18-26
Pitcher (ill.) 38-43

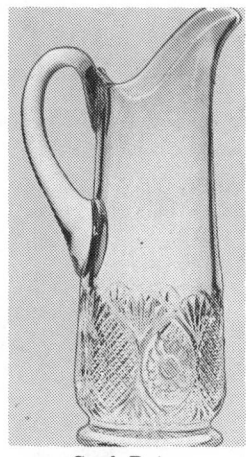

Sunk Daisy

Sugar bowl, covered 20-29
Wine 15-23

Probably other pieces. Green, 50 percent higher than clear prices listed.

Sunk Diamond and Lattice

Sunk Diamond and Lattice

Maker unknown, 1885-1890. Clear. Non-flint.

    Butter dish $27-35
    Celery vase 22-31
    Compote
      a. Covered 32-41
      b. Open 14-22
    Creamer 18-26
    Pitcher, water (ill.) 30-39
    Salt/Pepper, pr. 16-25
    Spoonholder 14-22
    Sugar bowl, covered 27-35
    Tumbler 17-24

Probably other pieces.

Sunk Honeycomb

Another of the many "Honeycomb" pat-

Sunk Honeycomb

terns; this one of the late 1880s. Clear as well as with a ruby top. Non-flint.

    Creamer, clear $30-37
    Cruet with stopper 27-35
    Decanter, 12½" high, original,
      stopper, ruby top 58-67
    Pitcher, water, ruby top 71-80
    Spooner, ruby top 34-42

Sunken Buttons

Sunken Buttons

Maker unknown, Ohio, late 1880s. Clear, canary, amber, blue. Non-flint.

    Butter dish, covered $27-36
    Compote
      a. Covered 31-40
      b. Open 27-35
    Creamer 24-32
    Goblet 23-32
    Pitcher, syrup (ill.) 32-40
    Platter 27-36
    Salt/Pepper, pr. 18-27

(continued)

Sugar bowl
  a. Covered 34-42
  b. Open 27-35
Wine 18-27

Probably other pieces. Canary, 50 percent higher; amber, blue, 125 percent higher than clear prices listed.

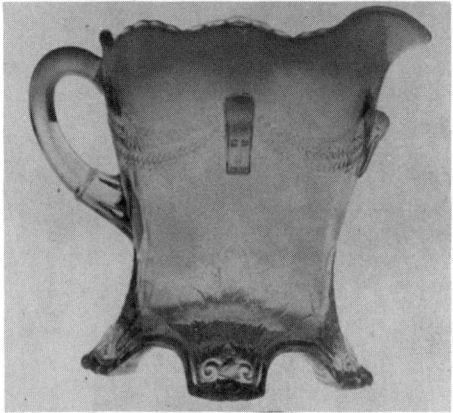

Swag with Brackets

Swag with Brackets

Jefferson Glass Company, Steubenville, Ohio, late 1800s. Crystal, sapphire with whitened rims, amethyst, opalescent white. Non-flint.

Butter dish, covered $43-52
Celery 19-27
Creamer 23-32
Pitcher, water (ill.) 42-50
Spoonholder 32-41
Sugar bowl, covered 34-39
Tumbler 18-27

Probably other pieces. Colors 90 percent higher than clear prices listed.

Swan

Maker unknown, 1880s. Clear, light amber, yellow, deep blue. Possibly Westmoreland. Non-flint.

Butter dish, covered, 5″ dia. ..$ 89- 98
Creamer 49- 57
Dish, oval, covered........... 43- 50
Goblet 63- 71
Marmalade jar, covered, swan
  finial 73- 82
Pitcher, water (ill.) 110-118
Sauce, footed, round, flat, 4″ .. 15- 22
Spoonholder 36- 43

Swan

Sugar bowl, covered 71- 80

Probably other pieces. Amber, yellow, 45 percent higher; blue, 65 percent higher than clear prices listed.

Swan with Tree

Swan with Tree

U.S. Glass Company, Gas City, Indiana, late 1880s. Clear. Non-flint.

Goblet $40-49
Pitcher, water (ill.) 53-63

At least these two pieces; possibly more.

Swirl

(Jersey Swirl): Windsor Glass Company, Pittsburgh, c. 1887, clear, amber, blue, yellow. Non-flint.

Butter dish, covered $45-53

Cake stand 41-50
Celery 29-36
Compote, covered 41-50
Creamer 34-32
Goblet
  a. Buttermilk, large 33-41
  b. Regular 30-38
Pitcher, water 44-52
Spoonholder 24-31
Sugar bowl, covered 42-50

Yellow, 30 percent; amber, blue, 50 percent higher than clear prices listed. Many repros in the colored glass; also in clear buttermilk goblet.

Swirl and Cable

Swirl and Cable

Possibly Sandwich, mid-1850s. Clear.

Creamer $37-46
Pitcher, milk (ill.) 61-69

Probably other pieces.

Swirl and Diamond

(America): Riverside Glass Works, Wellsburg, West Virginia, called it America. Also made by Riverside's successor, American Glass Company, Anderson, Indiana, in 1899. Crystal.

Bowl $17-27
Butter dish, covered 37-46
Creamer 22-31
Pitcher, water (ill.) 47-53
Sauce, flat 15-24
Spoonholder 17-26

Swirl and Diamond

Sugar bowl
  a. Covered 36-43
  b. Open 18-25

Probably other pieces.

Sydney

Sydney

Fostoria Glass Company, 1905, possibly earlier. Clear. Non-flint.

Butter dish, covered $32-40
Celery 16-27
Compote
  a. Covered 35-42
  b. Open 25-33
Creamer 20-29
Goblet 24-32
Molasses jug 16-24
Pickle dish, 6″, 8″, 9″ 12-27
Pitcher (ill.) 46-54
Salt shaker 13-22
Spoonholder 14-22
Sugar bowl, covered 34-39

Probably other pieces.

Syrup Jug with Applied Handle

Syrup Jug with Applied Handle

Maker and date unknown. Bird on lid, Britannia lid. Non-flint.

Syrup jug (ill.) $45-54

Anyone have information on it?

Tackle Block

Tackle Block

Maker unknown, c. 1840s, clear, flint.

Goblet (ill.) $57-64

Possibly other pieces.

Tall Argus

Maker unknown, 1850s. Clear. Flint.

Goblet ....$ 76- 84

Pitcher, water (ill.) 145-154

Possibly other pieces.

Tall Argus

Tape Measure

Tape Measure

(Shields): Portland Glass Company, early 1870s. Clear. Non-flint.

Butter dish $34-42

Goblet 22-31

Pitcher, water (ill.) 50-58

Sauce, flat 14-20

Probably other pieces.

Teardrop and Tassel

Teardrop and Tassel

(Sampson): Original name was Sampson, made by Indiana Tumbler & Goblet Company, 1890s. Better known today as Teardrop and Tassel. Clear, blue, amber, opaque white, green yellow. Non-flint.

Butter	Amber	White	Nile Green
dish	$110-120		$125-135
Creamer	65- 73	$ 40- 50	80- 89
Goblet			
(rare)	62- 70		
Pitcher (ill.) ..	500+	220-245	140-150
Relish tray	69- 77		
Spoon-			
holder........	54- 62	48- 58	
Sugar bowl,			
covered	64- 73	57- 67	105-110
Tumbler	48- 56		
Wine..........	68- 76	110-130	

	Blue	Green	Clear
Butter			
dish	$ 87- 95	$ 82- 92	$ 57- 65
Creamer	59- 67	52- 62	40- 47
Goblet	91-100	52- 62	66- 74
Pitcher,			
(ill.)	150-175	275+	72- 81
Relish			
tray..........	59- 69	52- 62	43- 51
Spoon-			
holder........	54- 62	52- 62	36- 44
Sugar			
bowl	83- 92	62- 72	58- 66
Tumbler	50- 58	29- 39	35- 43
Wine			
(rare)	105-112	54- 64	70- 79

Probably other pieces.

Teardrop and Thumbprint

Teardrop and Thumbprint

Ripley & Company, Pittsburgh; later, U.S. Glass Company, early 1900s. Plain or engraved, clear, blue; pattern on blue enameled on white. Non-flint.

Bowl	$16-25
Butter dish, covered	31-40
Cake stand	34-42
Celery	17-25
Creamer, covered	20-27
Compote, open	21-30
Goblet	18-27
Pitcher, water (ill.)	41-50
Sugar	
a. Covered	30-40
b. Open	20-27
Wine........................	16-25

Probably other pieces. Blue, 100 percent higher than clear prices listed.

Teasel

Teasel

Bryce Bros., Pittsburgh, 1870s. Clear.

Butter dish, covered	$31-40
Cake stand	21-30
Celery	12-17
Compote	21-29
Creamer	21-30
Cruet	16-25
Goblet (ill.)	19-27
Sauce, square footed	10-14
Spoonholder	13-21
Sugar bowl, covered	30-37

Probably many other pieces.

Tennessee

U.S. Glass Company, 1900. One of their "States" series. Clear. Non-flint.

(continued)

Tennessee

Butter dish	$44-52
Cake stand	46-55
Celery	20-29
Creamer	24-32
Goblet	26-34
Jam jar	21-30
Pitcher, water (ill.)	57-64
Relish, oval	21-30
Spoonholder	19-27
Sugar bowl, covered	31-40
Tumbler	22-30

Probably others.

Tennessee Mug

Tennessee Mug

So-called camphor glass, American flag, 16 stars on one side, Cherokee rose on other. Non-flint.

Mug (ill.) $28-36

Texas

(Loop with Stippled Panels): U.S. Glass Company, c. 1900, as "No. 15,067." In their 1907 catalog, given name of "Texas." Clear, clear with gilded top; also with ruby in the body. Non-flint.

Butter dish, covered	$46-54
Cake stand	55-63
Compote, open	28-37
Creamer	23-32
Goblet	29-39
Pitcher	41-50
Spoonholder	21-30
Sugar bowl, covered	29-37
Tumbler	17-27

Color, gilded top, 50 percent higher than clear prices listed. Other pieces.

Thistle

Thistle

(Pillar and Bull's Eye): Bakewell, Pears and Company, 1875. Non-flint.

Bowl, berry, covered	$34-42
Butter dish, covered	66-74
Cake plate on standard	58-66
Compote	
a. Covered, high standard	61-70
b. Open, low standard, 8"	35-43
Cordial	49-56
Creamer	60-68
Egg cup	33-40
Goblet	38-46
Pickle dish, tapered at one end	20-29
Pitcher (ill.)	62-70
Plate, 10¾" dia.	27-34
Sauce, flat, deep, 4"	17-24
Spoonholder	28-36
Sugar bowl, covered	55-63
Tumbler, footed, water	39-46

Wine 40-48
Probably other pieces.

Thousand Eye

Thousand Eye

(Daisy; No. 11): Richards & Hartley, 1888, called it Daisy; New Brighton Glass Company, New Brighton, Pennsylvania, 1889, also made it. It's also No. 11 in an old Adams Glass Company catalog. Clear and just about every color. Non-flint.

Bowl, banana $44-53
Bowl, berry, waste 35-43
Butter dish, knob, plain stem 55-63
Cake stand, knob, plain stem 52-61
Compote, covered 67-75
Creamer, knob, plain stem 44-52
Goblet, knob stem 41-50
Pitcher, large knob,
    plain stem (ill.) 68-76
Spoonholder, knob, plain stem . . 24-32
Sugar bowl, knob, plain stem 47-55
Tumbler, water 24-31

Many other pieces. Amber, yellow, blue, 40 percent higher; apple green, 60 percent higher than clear prices listed. Cruet, plain stem, goblet, hat (match holder), mug, 8″ sq. plate, tumbler and wine being reproduced.

Threading

(Threaded): Maker unknown, c, late 1870s, clear, non-flint.

Butter dish, covered $28-38
Compote
    a. Open 20-27
    b. Covered 35-44

Creamer 26-35
Spoonholder 27-35
Sugar bowl
    a. Open 16-25
    b. Covered 32-41
Probably other pieces.

Three Birds

Three Birds

Dalzell, Gilmore & Leighton Company, Findlay, Ohio, 1880s. Clear. Non-flint.

Pitcher, water (ill.) $54-63

Probably tumbler and other pieces to match.

Three Face

Three Face

(The Sisters): George A. Duncan's Sons, Pittsburgh, 1878. Clear and crystal-with-frosted-faces. Some pieces etched and engraved. Non-flint.

Butter dish $160-169

(continued)

Cake stand

   a. 8", 9½" 109-117

   b. Frosted base 135-143

Celery, pedestal base 106-114

Celery, scalloped top.......... 76- 84

Compote

   a. Covered, large 210-219

   b. Covered, 6", small....... 159-168

   c. Open, high standard 96-110

Creamer, 2 styles 109-116

Goblet 85- 93

Pitcher, milk, etched 254-263

Pitcher, water, ½ gal., rare (ill.) 295-305

Salt/Pepper, pr. 80- 87

Spoonholder 81- 90

Wine....................... 106-109

Probably other patterns. Butter dish, cake stand, champagne, 6½" covered compote, claret, creamer, goblet, lamp, sauce, salt/peppers, spoonholder, sugar bowl, wine, being reproduced. Advice is cheap. This advice won't cost you a thing: DON'T BUY IT! Some dealers sell the new for the same price as the old! ALL pieces being skillfully reproduced.

Three-in-One

Three-in-One

(Fancy Diamonds): Imperial Glass Company, Bellaire, Ohio, c, late 1880s, clear, non-flint.

   Bowl $24-32

   Butter dish, covered 43-50

   Creamer 28-36

   Goblet (ill.) 24-31

   Spoonholder 23-30

Sugar bowl

   a. Covered 32-41

   b. Open 27-35

Wine........................ 17-26

Probably other pieces.

Three Leaf Clover

Three Leaf Clover

Maker and date unknown. Any information on this lovely piece of flint glass would be deeply appreciated.

Three Panel

Three Panel

Hartley & Company, Tarentum, Pennsylvania, 1888. Clear, canary, amber, blue. Non-flint.

Bowl, 8½" $20-28
Butter dish, covered 42-50
Celery 29-35
Compote, open, 7", 8½", 9", 10",
   low standard 28-48
Creamer 29-36
Cruet 24-30
Goblet 28-36
Mug 20-29
Pitcher, water (ill.) 49-58
Sauce 14-20
Spoonholder 24-32
Sugar bowl 41-50
Tumbler 23-30

Probably other pieces. Colors, 60-100 percent higher than clear prices listed.

Tic-Tac-Toe

Tic-Tac-Toe

Maker unknown, c. late 1880s, clear, non-flint.

Goblet (ill.) $27-35
Salt, master, footed 11-16

Should be other pieces.

Tiebacks

Tiebacks

Boston & Sandwich Glass Company, c. 1850s, opalescent. They were used to hold the window curtains in place.

2" dia., pr. $47-56
3" dia., pr. (ill.) 56-64
4¼" dia., pr. 70-80

Tiny Lion

Tiny Lion

Maker unknown, Ohio, early 1880s. Clear; clear and frosted. Non-flint.

Butter dish, covered $38-46
Celery, 2 handles (ill.) 47-54
Compote 46-54
Creamer 30-38
Pitcher, water 52-61
Spoonholder 21-30
Sugar bowl
  a. Covered 37-46
  b. Open 30-36

Probably other pieces.

Tom Thumb — Humpty Dumpty Mug

Tom Thumb — Humpty Dumpty Mug

(Humpty Dumpty shown); maker unknown, a novelty of the 1880s. Clear only.

Mug (ill.) $48-57

Torpedo

Torpedo

(Pygmy, Fisheye): Thompson Glass Company, Uniontown, Pennsylvania, 1889. Clear. Non-flint.

Bowl
- a. Berry, 8" $33-40
- b. Rose, 4" (scarce)............ 45-53
- c. Open, 8", 8¼", 9", 9½",
    flared rim 39-46
- d. Waste, scalloped top 31-40

Butter dish, covered 81-90
Cake stand, 9", 10" 70-78
Compote
- a. Covered, jelly, 4" 58-66
- b. Open, jelly, flared rim 39-46
- c. Covered, 6", 8", 9" 60-68

Creamer, flat, footed, large
    and medium 43-51
Decanter 69-76
Goblet 54-62
Pitcher, syrup, (ill.) 61-70
Salt, individual 12-18
Sauce, 4½" footed honey, 3½"
    flat honey 14-26
Salt/Pepper, pr., 2¼" high,
    3" high 54-62
Spoonholder 34-41
Sugar bowl 54-62
Tumbler 43-50
Wine 32-40

Undoubtedly other pieces.

Tree of Life

Portland Glass Company, Portland, Maine, c. 1867. Clear, amber, blue, purple, canary, green and etched.

Bowl, flat, 8", 10", finger $22-40
Butter dish, hand/ball on cover ... 52-62

Tree of Life

Celery vase 40-47
Compote
- a. Open, 10", "Davis" 64-73
- b. Covered 81-90

Creamer 64-72
Goblet 48-57
Pitcher, water................. 65-75
Spoonholder 37-47
Sugar bowl, covered (ill.) 57-65
Tumbler, footed 34-42
Wine 41-52

Probably other pieces. Colors, 50-100 percent higher than clear prices listed. Some pieces came in a plated holder. No change in value. Some pieces signed "P.G. Co. Patent." Others, "Davis" (woven in design).

Tree of Life with Hand

Tree of Life with Hand

George A. Duncan's Sons, 1884. Clear blue. Probably other colors. Non-flint.

Bowl, finger .... $ 29- 36
Butter dish, covered 82- 91
Celery 44- 52
Compote, covered 120-129
Creamer 55- 63
Dish, berry 20- 27

Plate, berry 70- 77
Saucedish 18- 25
Sugar bowl
  a. Covered 72- 80
  b. Open 31- 40

Probably other pieces. No goblet seems to have been made in hand stem.

Tree of Life with Sprig

Tree of Life with Sprig

Portland, Glass Company, Portland, Maine, 1870s. Clear, possibly colors. Non-flint.

Butter dish $42-51
Celery 32-41
Creamer 30-38
Spoonholder 24-32
Sugar bowl, covered 37-46
Syrup jug, top missing (ill.) 31-40

Probably other pieces. Creamer has little wheels at base; other pieces don't. Don't let this confuse you.

Triangular Prism

Triangular Prism

Maker unknown, c. 1850s, clear, flint and non-flint.

Bowl, shallow $18-25
Butter dish, covered 43-52
Celery 32-41
Compote
  a. Low pedestal 19-28
  b. Tall pedestal 26-36
Cup, handled 14-20
Goblet, ladies' or gents' (ill.) 44-52
Salt, master, footed 21-30
Spoonholder 32-42
Sugar bowl, covered 44-51
Tumbler 18-27
Wine 34-39

Flint, 25 percent higher than clear prices listed. Probably other pieces.

Triple Triangle

Triple Triangle

Doyle & Company, Pittsburgh, Pennsylvania, c. 1885, clear and ruby-stained. Non-flint.

Butter dish, covered $35-44
Cup, punch 14-22
Creamer 25-33
Goblet (ill.) 44-51
Mug 30-40
Sugar bowl, covered 39-47
Wine 30-37

Ruby-stained, 25 percent higher than clear prices listed. Other pieces.

Troubadour Scene

Indiana Tumbler & Goblet (National)

(continued)

Troubadour Scene

Company, late 1890s. See colors with price.

Chocolate	$ 77- 86
White milk	43- 52
Blue milk	54- 62
Nile green	55- 63
Clear	43- 52
Amber (ill.)	135-143

With lip, regular size, 100 percent higher. Large steins, 350-400 percent higher.

Tulip with Sawtooth

Tulip with Sawtooth

(Tulip): Bryce, Richards and Company, Pittsburgh, c. 1854. Flint.

Butter dish	$133-140
Celery vase	78- 86
Compote	
a. Covered, large high standard	140-150
b. Covered, small, high standard	98-106
c. Open, large	106-114
d. Covered, low standard	74- 81
Creamer	89- 96
Decanter, quart	156-163
Goblet, knob stem, 7" high	49- 58
Jug	
a. Pint	94-102
b. Quart	134-139

Pitcher (ill.)	260-270
Spoonholder	54- 62
Sugar bowl	109-117
Tumbler, footed, water	41- 50
Wine (being reproduced)	43- 52

Probably other pieces.

Twin Teardrops

Twin Teardrops

Maker unknown, c. 1890s, clear, non-flint; possibly in emerald green.

Celery	$19-28
Compote, open (ill.)	29-38
Cruet	24-32
Dish, banana, flat	24-32
Plate, 7" square	19-27

If emerald green, 100 percent higher than clear prices listed. Should be other pieces.

Twinkle Star

Twinkle Star

(Frost Flower): U.S. Glass Company, 1901. Clear, clear and frosted. Six-pointed stars on **inside** of glass. Non-flint.

Butter dish, covered	$38-48

Celery 21-30
Creamer 31-39
Goblet 26-34
Pitcher, water (ill.) 53-62
Spoonholder 21-30
Sugar bowl, covered 28-36
Tumbler 23-32

Probably other pieces.

Two Band

Two Band

Maker unknown, c. late 1880s, clear, non-flint.

Butter dish, covered $30-38
Creamer (ill.) 26-34
Goblet 19-27
Spoonholder 24-32
Sugar bowl, covered 33-42
Also made in child's set:
Butter dish, covered 66-73
Creamer 54-59
Spoonholder 53-62
Sugar bowl, covered 71-80

Probably other pieces in adult size.

Two Panel

(Daisy in Panel; Daisy in Square): Richards & Hartley Flint Glass Company, Tarentum, Pennsylvania, c. 1880s; clear, apple green, amber, blue, canary. Non-flint.

Bowls, 3 sizes $24-32
Butter dish, covered 42-50
Celery 29-36
Compote
a. Covered, open, high
standard 34-41
b. Open, low standard 24-33

Two Panel

Creamer 31-40
Goblet (ill.) 25-33
Lamp 54-62
Mug, large 24-32
Pitcher 49-58
Spoonholder 29-37
Sugar bowl, covered 35-44

Apple green, 80 percent; canary, 60 percent; amber, blue, 50 percent higher than clear prices listed. Many other pieces. Goblet being reproduced, especially in color.

Umbilicated Sawtooth

Umbilicated Sawtooth

Another of the Sandwich patterns.
Bowl, 8″ $23-32
Butter dish, covered, on
pedestal (ill.) 48-54
Egg cup 27-36
Plate, 6″ 22-31
Salt, master, footed 16-25
Sauce 9-16
Tumbler 23-30
Wine 21-30

Probably other pieces.

Unique

Unique

Co-Operative Flint Glass Company, 1898. Clear. Non-flint.

Butter dish	$33-42
Celery vase	27-36
Creamer	31-40
Goblet	21-30
Pitcher	
a. Syrup metal cap (ill.)	27-35
b. Water	40-50
Spoonholder	21-30
Sugar bowl, covered	27-36
Tumbler	19-28

Probably other pieces.

U.S. Rib

U.S. Rib

(Rib): U.S. Glass Company, 1900. Green glass with gold rims; possibly crystal and other colors.

Butter dish	$54-63
Celery	34-39
Creamer (ill.)	42-50
Pitcher, water	67-75
Spoonholder	24-32
Sugar bowl, covered	44-52
Tumbler	30-39

Probably other pieces. Crystal 50 percent less than green prices listed.

Valentine

Valentine

(Trilby): U.S. Glass Company, Pittsburgh, late 1870s. Clear. Non-flint.

Butter dish	$ 52- 61
Celery	33- 39
Cologne bottle	28- 37
Creamer	26- 35
Goblet	31- 40
Match holder	21- 29
Pitcher, water (ill.)	140-150
Tumbler	37- 46

Victoria

Victoria

Bakewell, Pears & Company, early 1860s. Clear, canary, possibly other colors. Flint.

Bowl, 8½″ dia. (ill.)	$ 88- 97
Butter dish, low foot, 8″	110-116
Cake stand	
a. 9″	81- 90
b. 15″	143-151
Celery	33- 39

Dish, sweetmeat 66- 73
Compote
  a. Covered, 10" 132-140
  b. Open 57- 65
Creamer 89- 97
Sugar bowl (scarce) 167-174

Possibly other pieces. Colors, 140-170 percent higher than clear prices listed.

Victoria

(Draped Top): **Not** Bakewell, Pears but another pattern, made by Riverside Glass Works, Wellsburg, West Virginia, c. 1894, clear, with red, non-flint.

Butter dish, covered $30-40
Cake stand 33-43
Celery 20-28
Compote 26-36
Creamer 34-44
Goblet 19-29
Pitcher, water................. 38-48
Salt/Pepper, pr. 30-42
Spoonholder 20-29
Sugar bowl, covered 36-46

With red, 100 percent higher than clear prices listed.

Virginia

Virginia

(Galloway): U.S. Glass Company, 1901 Glassport, Indiana. Clear, red-flashed. Non-flint.

Butter dish, covered $44-52
Celery 30-37
Compote
  a. Covered, footed, 6", 7", 8" 50-64
  b. Open, footed, 6", 7", 8" 33-52
Creamer, individual, large 25-38
Goblet 29-37
Pitcher, water (ill.) 47-57

Sauce, flared, 4"; straight,
  4", 4½" 13-20
Spoonholder 28-37
Sugar bowl
  a. Covered, large 42-50
  b. Open, small 24-32
Tumbler 29-36
Wine........................ 33-41

Probably other pieces. There are several "Virginia" patterns; don't get them confused, price-wise. Red-flashed, 25 percent higher than clear prices listed.

Waffle

Waffle

Bryce, Walker & Company, Pittsburgh, Pennsylvania, 1860s. Flint.

Butter dish, covered $133-140
Celery, 9" high (ill.) 81- 90
Champagne goblet 110-117
Claret 46- 53
Compote
  a. Open, large, high
    standard 69- 76
  b. Open, small, high
    standard 56- 63
  c. Open, small, low
    standard 49- 56
Creamer, pint and quart
  (rare) 119-127
Decanter, pint and quart...... 100-109
Goblet, knob stem 59- 66
Pitcher, water (rare) 9½"
  high 109-117
Spoonholder 55- 63
Sugar bowl, covered 101-110
Tumbler, water 64- 72
Wine....................... 68- 74

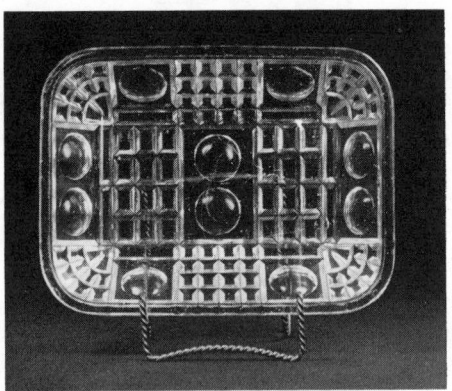
Waffle and Thumbprint

Waffle and Thumbprint

Possibly New England Glass Company or Sandwich, early; later, Ohio Valley, c. 1850s, 1860s, clear, flint and non-flint.

Bowl, rectangular (ill.)	$ 46- 53
Butter dish, covered	147-155
Cordial	87- 95
Creamer	133-140
Decanter	
a. Pint	90-105
b. Quart	128-136
Goblet	67- 75
Sugar bowl, covered	134-143

Non-flint, 50 percent lower than flint prices listed. Possibly other pieces.

Waffle with Fan Top

Waffle with Fan Top

Maker unknown, c. 1880s, clear, non-flint.

Goblet (ill.)	$29-37

Another member of the "Waffle" family. There should be other pieces.

Washboard

McKee & Brothers, Pittsburgh, c. 1897, clear, canary, blue, non-flint.

Bowls, round, oval	$17-29
Butter dish, covered	26-35
Cake stand, large	35-44
Creamer	29-38
Goblet	30-38
Pitcher	44-52
Sauce, flat	11-16
Spoonholder	21-30
Sugar bowl, covered	28-32

Colors, 35 percent higher than clear prices listed. Probably other pieces.

Washington

Washington

New England Glass Company, Cambridge, Massachusetts, c. early 1860s, clear, flint.

Butter dish, covered, on pedestal	$185-193
Celery	99-106
Compote, covered, tall	182-190
Cordial	135-144
Creamer	215-224
Egg cup	84- 92
Goblet	84- 94
Pitcher	
a. Syrup	130-139
b. Water	260-270
Sugar bowl (base ill.)	134-140
Tumbler	88- 97
Wine	106-114

Possibly other pieces.

Washington Centennial

Gillinder & Sons, Philadelphia, c. 1876, clear, non-flint.

Bowl, oval	$ 34- 43
Butter dish, covered	112-119
Celery	64- 70
Champagne	70- 79
Creamer	81- 90
Goblet	51- 60
Pitcher, water	109-117

Platters
a. Washington's head	160-175
b. "The Nation's birthplace"	142-151
c. Carpenter's Hall	135-144
Relish, flat, oval, marked "Centennial 1776-1876"	57- 65
Sugar bowl, covered	84- 94
Wine	59- 67

Probably other pieces.

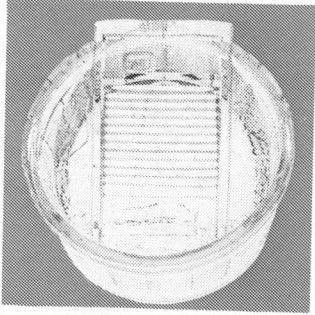

Washtub Soap Dish

Washtub Soap Dish

Maker and date unknown. A novelty item of the 1860s. Clear glass; also canary, amber, blue. Non-flint.

Washtub, clear	$45-54
Washtub, canary or amber	61-70
Washtub, blue (rare) (ill.)	77-85

Water Lily

(Frosted Magnolia): Dalzell, Gilmore & Leighton Company, Findlay, Ohio, c. 1890, clear, non-flint.

Butter dish, covered	$ 73- 83
Cake stand, large	75- 84
Creamer	62- 71
Goblet	74- 82
Pitcher, syrup	140-150
Sauce, flat	21- 29
Sugar bowl, covered	67- 74

Probably other pieces.

Waterfall

Waterfall

O'Hara Glass Company, Pittsburgh, 1880s. Clear, light blue, canary. Non-flint.

Butter dish	$38-47
Celery	25-32
Compote	42-51
Creamer	24-29
Goblet	27-36
Pitcher, water (ill.)	55-59
Spoonholder	26-34
Sugar bowl, covered	39-44

Probably other pieces. Colors, 50 percent higher than clear prices listed.

Waterlily and Cattails

Waterlily and Cattails

Northwood Glass Company, later Fenton, 1889. Clear, colored w/opalescence (blue, green Carnival glass). Lavender (rare). Northwood prices given. Non-flint.

Butter dish, covered	$47-55
Celery vase	25-32

(continued)

Creamer 34-42
Goblet 30-38
Pitcher, water (ill.) 47-54
Plate, 9″, 10″ 31-40
Spoonholder 31-40
Sugar bowl, covered 47-56
Tumbler 27-36

Probably other pieces. Sapphire and purple 100 percent higher than clear prices listed.

Way's Colonial

Way's Colonial

Maker unknown, c. 1840s, clear, flint. Possibly Central Glass Company, c. 1870s.

Sugar bowl, covered $61-70
Tumbler (ill.) 38-43
Whiskey, handled 39-47

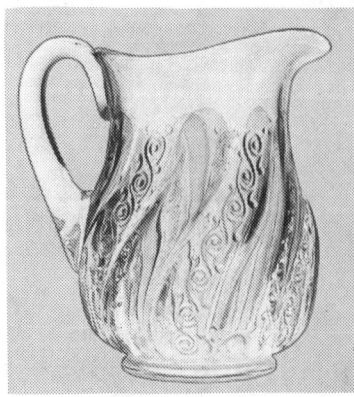
Wedding Bells

Wedding Bells

Fostoria Glass Company, Moundsville, West Virginia, 1900. Clear, amethyst gold, possibly green, pink flashed, flint.

Butter dish, covered $46-53
Celery 25-33
Creamer 35-43
Compote, covered, high, low
 foot......................... 39-47
Cruet, with stopper 38-46
Egg cup 22-29
Goblet 39-49
Pitcher, half gallon tankard (ill.) . 64-73
Spoonholder 28-38
Sugar bowl 38-47
Tumbler 24-33

Probably other pieces. Colors, 60 percent higher than clear prices listed.

Wedding Lamp

Wedding Lamp

On July 14, 1870, Daniel C. Ripley patented a mold for producing twin-fountain oil lamps, both by pressing and blowing. Extremely rare today, the one shown here is on display at the Houston Museum, Chattanooga, Tennessee.

Lamp (rare) (ill.) .... $650+

Wedding Ring

Wedding Ring

Maker unknown, 1870s. Clear. Flint.

Champagne	$24-32
Creamer	34-42
Decanter	34-39
Goblet	26-35
Pitcher, syrup (ill.)	39-52
Wine	22-29

Probably other pieces.

Westward Ho!

Westward Ho!

(Pioneer; Tippecanoe): Gillinder & Sons, Philadelphia, about 1879. It was originally called Pioneer; also Tippecanoe, this last name was never popular. Clear, frosted. Non-flint.

Butter dish, covered, standard	$175-183
Celery	133-140
Compote	
a. Covered, 6", high standard	233-244
b. Covered, 6", low standard	160-188
c. Oval, 9"	160-169
Creamer	112-121
Goblet, frosted	109-117
Jar, jam, covered (scarce)	185-189
Pitcher, milk	215-223
Pitcher, water (ill.)	210-218
Sauce, 4", footed	33-40
Spoonholder	92-100
Sugar bowl, covered	154-161
Wine	144-152

Probably other pieces. Butter dish, 6" compote, 9" compote, cordial, goblet, clear and frosted, water pitcher, sauce, wine being reproduced. Goblets originally clear or frosted. Being reproduced in amethyst, blue green, clear and frosted. Careful!

Wheat and Barley

Wheat and Barley

(Duquesne; Hops and Barley; Oats and Barley): Original trade name was Duquesne and it was made by Bryce Bros., Pittsburgh, late 1870s, early 1880s. Clear, amber, blue, yellow. Reproduced by U.S. Glass Company, 1889. Non-flint.

Butter dish, covered	$45-52
Cake stand, 8", 9", 10"	21-48
Compote	
a. Covered, 7", 8", high standard	42-49
b. Open, high standard	34-44
Creamer, plain and footed	25-34
Goblet	29-37
Pitcher	
a. Water (ill.)	35-43
b. Milk, syrup	40-48
Plate, 7", 9"	24-32
Sauce, footed, 4", flat	11-16
Salt/Pepper, pr.	34-42
Spoonholder	25-33
Sugar bowl, covered	36-44
Tumbler, footed, water	24-31

Probably other pieces. Canary, amber, 50 percent higher; blue, 65 percent higher than clear prices listed.

Wheat Sheaf

Maker unknown, late 1870s. Clear.

Butter dish	$31-40
Celery vase	24-31
Compote, low standard	36-44
Creamer	27-36
Goblet	22-30
Pitcher, water (ill.)	41-50
Spoonholder	24-32

(continued)

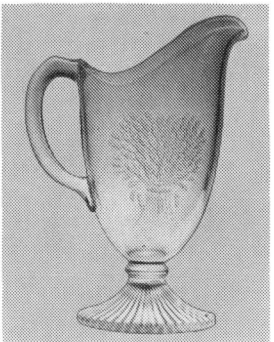

Wheat Sheaf

Sugar bowl 34-42
Tumbler 25-33

Probably other pieces.

Wheel in Band

Wheel in Band

Maker unknown, 1870s. Clear. Non-flint.

Butter dish, covered $32-41
Celery 20-29
Creamer 24-29
Goblet 23-31
Jam jar, covered 27-36
Pitcher, water (ill.) 40-50
Spoonholder 20-28
Sugar bowl, covered 31-40
Wine 21-29

Probably other pieces.

Whirled Sunburst in Circle

Maker and date unknown, 1890-1895. Clear.

Whirled Sunburst in Circle

Butter dish, covered $42-51
Creamer 32-41
Pitcher, water (ill.) 54-62
Spoonholder 21-31
Sugar bowl, covered 37-46

Probably other pieces.

Wigwam

(Teepee): Iowa Glass Company, Iowa City, Iowa, c. late 1880s, clear, non-flint.

Butter dish, covered $44-53
Creamer 31-40
Goblet 39-48
Spoonholder 31-40
Sugar bowl, covered 51-60

Probably other pieces.

Wild Bouquet

Wild Bouquet

Northwood Glass Company, 1902. Custard glass, gold trim, colors.

Bowl, berry, large ....$ 47- 57
Bowl, berry, small 24- 32
Butter dish, covered 36- 44

Compote 50- 58
Cruet 42- 52
Pitcher, water (ill.) 120-130
Tumbler 31- 40
Probably other pieces.

Wild Rose and Lady Lamp

Wild Rose and Lady Lamp

Riverside Glass Company, Wellsburg, West Virginia. The Millersburg Glass Company, Millersburg, Ohio, made nine of these lamps to honor the wives of the company officials. When Millersburg went out of business in 1914, Riverside Glass Company somehow obtained the Wild Rose and Lady lamp mold. Millersburg had the familiar wild rose and honeycomb on the outside of the lamp; Riverside has these on the underside. Also, Riverside had "Riverside Clinch on Collar" in raised letters on the outside at the base. All these lamps, both Millersburg and Riverside are highly collectible today.

    Lamp, Millersburg (rare) (ill.) . . $ 675+
    Lamp, Riverside 190-210

Wild Rose with Bow-Knot

Maker unknown, late 1880s. Clear, colors, frosted.
    Bowl $29-39
    Butter dish 32-41
    Creamer 28-39

Wild Rose with Bow-Knot

    Pitcher (ill.) 51-61
    Sauce 17-25
    Spoonholder 24-32
    Sugar bowl, covered 54-63
    Tumbler 32-41

Probably other pieces. Water pitcher had cover, meaning it was originally made as condiment holder — mustard, jelly, etc. Colors, 50 percent higher than clear prices listed.

Wild Rose with Scrolling

Wild Rose with Scrolling

Possibly Dithridge & Company, Pittsburgh, 1870s. Clear; possibly opaque white, other colors. It's almost as if this

 (continued)

miniature table set were made for the "wee people." Tiny and dainty.

Butter dish, covered (ill.) $65-75
Creamer 52-61
Spoonholder 31-40
Sugar bowl, covered 61-69

Probably other pieces.

Wildflower

Wildflower

Adams & Company, Pittsburgh, 1874; other factories later; reproduced by U.S. Glass Company, 1898. Clear, canary, amber, blue, green, amethyst, vaseline. Non-flint.

Butter dish, collared base,
covered $44-52
Cake stand, large, small 43-51
Celery 32-38
Compote
  a. 6″, 8″, covered, high
    standard 34-53
  b. 8″, low standard 31-40
  c. Open, high standard 27-34
Creamer 31-40
Goblet 31-39
Pitcher, water (ill.) 47-56
Sauce, flat, round, square 11-15
Salt/Pepper, pr. 43-50
Spoonholder 31-40
Sugar bowl, covered 41-50
Tumbler, water 24-32
Wine 39-45

Probably other pieces. Amber, yellow, blue, 50 percent higher; green, 100 percent higher than clear prices listed. Goblet, 10″ plate, round, flat sauce, tumbler, wine being reproduced.

Willow Oak

(Oak Leaf; Stippled Star; Acorn; Thistle; Wreath): Bryce Bros., Pittsburgh, made it in the 1880s and called it

Willow Oak

Wreath. It is also known by the other names listed here. Clear, amber, blue. Non-flint.

Bowl, waste, berry $34-42
Butter dish 56-64
Cake stand, 8½″ 34-43
Celery 34-41
Compote, covered, 7½″, 9″, high
  standard 49-58
Creamer 29-36
Goblet 31-40
Mug 31-39
Pitcher, large, (ill.) 47-56
Plates, 7″, 9″, closed handles 27-36
Salt/Pepper, pr. 44-51
Sauce, flat, footed, round 23-30
Spoonholder 29-36
Sugar bowl, covered 44-51
Tumbler 25-33

Probably other pieces. Amber, 50 percent higher; blue, 80 percent higher than clear prices listed.

Wiltec

Wiltec

McKee & Brothers, Pittsburgh, Pennsylvania, c. 1890s, clear, flint.

Butter dish, covered $41-50
Creamer 32-40
Spoonholder 24-32
Sugar bowl, covered (ill.) 35-44

Obviously other pieces.

Windflower

Windflower

Maker unknown, late 1870s. Clear. Non-flint.

Butter dish, flat, covered $57-63
Celery 35-41
Compote, covered, high, low
standard 71-80
Cordial 41-50
Creamer 39-47
Egg cup 27-34
Goblet 34-42
Pitcher, water (ill.) 52-61
Salt, footed 27-35
Sauce, 4″ 11-16
Spoonholder 26-33
Sugar bowl, covered 31-40
Tumbler, water 31-38
Wine 35-43

Probably other pieces.

Wooden Pail

(Oaken Bucket): Bryce Bros., 1880s. Clear, amber, blue, canary. Probably a container for candy, mustard, baking

Wooden Pail

powder, coffee. Bryce Bros. called it their "Bucket Set." Made in miniature and full size. Amethyst, rare! Non-flint.

Butter dish, covered $57-64
Creamer 41-50
Pitcher (ill.) 47-57
Spoonholder 24-29
Sugar bowl
a. Covered 44-51
b. Open 31-40

Undoubtedly other pieces. Miniature same price as large. Yellow, amber, 60 percent higher; blue, 85 percent higher; amethyst, 275 percent higher than clear prices listed.

Woodflower

Sandwich, 1870s. Clear and stippled.

Creamer $57-64
Goblet 57-62
Sugar bowl, covered 77-81

Probably other pieces.

Wreath and Shell

(continued)

Wreath and Shell

Albany, Indiana, Glass Company, late 1880s. Opaque colors.

Butter dish, covered $77-86
Rose bowl (ill.) 54-53
Tumbler 64-72

Probably many other pieces.

Wyoming

Wyoming

(Enigma): U.S. Glass Company, Gas City, Indiana, 1907. Crystal, colored glass, including mosaic glass. Non-flint.

Butter dish $31-40
Cake stand, 9″ 37-46
Creamer 24-28
Goblet 30-39
Pitcher, milk, water (ill.) 35-42
Spoonholder 22-31
Sugar bowl
  a. Covered 36-45
  b. Open 29-37
Tumbler 21-30
Wine 21-30

Probably other pieces.

X-Log

X-Log

(Prism Arc): Maker unknown, c. mid-1880s, clear, non-flint.

Bowl, vegetable, oval (ill.) $16-25
Butter dish, covered 31-40
Cake stand 37-45
Creamer 34-42
Goblet 21-30
Mug 19-27
Spoonholder 21-30
Sugar bowl, covered 31-39
Wine 22-29

Probably other pieces.

Yale

Yale

(Crow-Foot): McKee Glass Company, Jeannette, Pennsylvania, 1894. Clear, non-flint.

Butter dish, covered $35-44
Cake stand 33-42
Celery 25-34
Compote 40-49
Cordial 18-27
Creamer 26-35
Goblet 29-38
Pitcher
  a. Syrup 26-35
  b. Water (ill.) 41-50
Plate 25-34
Saucedish, 4″, 6″ 16-24
Salt/Pepper, pr. 29-37
Spoonholder 22-31
Sugar bowl, covered 34-44
Tumbler 20-28

Probably other pieces.

Yoked Loop

Yoked Loop

(Scalloped Loop): Maker unknown, c. 1860s, clear, flint.

Goblet $34-42
Sugar bowl
  a. Covered 47-56
  b. Open (ill.) 29-37

Should be other pieces.

York Colonial

York Colonial

Possibly Sandwich, c. 1850s, clear, flint; also opalescent, amethyst, blue. Later, Central Glass Company, c. 1870s, clear, non-flint.

Ale, footed $47- 53
Celery........................ 92-102
Compote, covered.............. 95-104
Creamer...................... 98-107
Goblet........................ 70- 80
Sugar bowl (base ill.) 54- 63
Tumbler...................... 37- 46

Colors (rare), 200 percent higher than clear prices listed. Central Glass pieces, 50 percent lower than Sandwich prices listed.

York Herringbone

York Herringbone

Maker unknown, late 1880s. Clear; clear with ruby stain. Souvenir pieces sold at 1893 World's Fair. Non-flint.

Celery $26-34
Creamer, green, individual
  (ill.) 48-58
Spoonholder 39-48

Probably other pieces.

Yuma Loop

(continued)

Yuma Loop

O'Hara Glass Company, late 1850s or early 1860s. Clear, flint. Contemporary of Loop (O'Hara). Same values.

Zipper Slash

Zigzag Band

Zigzag Band

Possibly Gillinder & Sons, 1870s. Clear.

Butter dish, covered	$37-46
Celery vase	23-31
Creamer	29-37
Goblet	25-34
Pitcher, water (ill.)	51-60
Spoonholder	20-29
Sugar bowl, covered	37-46
Tumbler	31-40

Probably other pieces.

Zipper Slash

George A. Duncan's Sons, Washington, Pennsylvania, 1893. Stained ruby-red above pattern; sometimes in yellow. Non-flint.

Butter, covered	$51-60
Creamer (ill.)	42-51
Spoonholder	31-40
Sugar bowl	57-66
Wine	32-40

Probably other pieces. Yellow, 50 percent higher; with souvenir marking, 50 percent less than clear prices listed.

Zipper

Richards & Hartley Glass Company, Tarentum, Pennsylvania, c. 1880s, clear, non-flint.

Butter dish, covered	$35-42
Celery	19-28
Compote	
a. Open	20-28
b. Covered	37-46
Jar, jam, covered	32-40
Pitcher, water	43-51
Sugar bowl	
a. Open	20-28
b. Covered	31-40

Probably other pieces.

Glass Companies

*These firms exhibited their wares at the Centennial Exhibition
in Philadelphia, Pennsylvania, in 1876.**

* Adams & Company, Pittsburgh, 1861; joined U.S. Glass Company in 1891 as Factory A.

Aetna Glass & Manufacturing Company, Bellaire, Ohio, 1880.

American Glass Company, Anderson, Indiana, 1889.

Anchor-Hocking Glass Company (see Ohio Flint Glass Company).

* Atterbury & Company, Pittsburgh, about 1858.

Bakewell & Company (also called Bakewell & Page), 1809.

Bakewell & Ensell, Pittsburgh, 1807.

Bakewell, Page & Bakewell, 1824.

* Bakewell, Pears & Company, 1836.

Bay State Glass Company, Cambridge, Massachusetts, about 1849.

Beatty, Alexander J. & Sons, Steubenville, Ohio, about 1850. Moved to Tiffin, Ohio in 1890.

Beatty-Brady Glass Company, Steubenville, then to Dunkirk, Indiana in 1898. Both taken over by the U.S. Glass Company; Factory S at Steubenville, and Factory T at Tiffin.

Beaumont Glass Company, Martins Ferry, Ohio, 1895. Sold to Hocking Glass in 1905.

Beaver Falls Co-Operative Glass Company, Beaver Falls, Pennsylvania, 1879.

Beaver Falls Glass Company, Beaver Falls, Pennsylvania, 1887.

Bellaire Goblet Company, Bellaire & Findlay, Ohio, 1878; merged with U.S. Glass Company in 1891. Both plants were moved to Tiffin, Ohio under the name Factory M.

Belmont Glass Company, Bellaire, Ohio, 1866.

* Boston & Sandwich Glass Company, Sandwich, Massachusetts, 1825.

Boston Silver-Glass Company, East Cambridge, Massachusetts, 1857.

Brilliant Glass Works, Brilliant, Ohio (originally called Novelty Glass Company), 1880.

Bryce, McKee & Company, Pittsburgh, 1850.

Bryce, Richards & Company, Pittsburgh, 1854.

Bryce, Walker & Company, Pittsburgh, 1865.

Bryce Bros., Pittsburgh, 1882. Taken over by U.S. Glass Company around 1889 and named Factory B.

Bryce Bros. again entered the business Hammondsville, Pennsylvania, 1896.

Bryce, Higbee & Company (also known as Homestead Glass Works), Pittsburgh, 1879.

J. B. Higbee Glass Company, Bridgeville, Pennsylvania, 1900.

* Excelsior Glass Works, Wheeling, West Virginia; moved to Martins Ferry, Ohio in 1879 under the name Buckeye Glass Company.

Campbell, Jones & Company, Pittsburgh, 1865.

Canton Glass Company, Canton, Ohio, 1883; factory moved to Marion, Indiana in 1894. In 1899 it joined with National Glass Company. In 1903 the factory site changed to Cambridge, Ohio. Another Canton Glass Company was founded in Marion, Indiana in 1904.

Jones, Cavitt & Company, Ltd., Pittsburgh, 1886.

* Central Glass Company, Wheeling, West Virginia, 1863. (Famous for their Coin pattern.) Joined U.S. Glass Company in 1891 as Factory O.

Challinor, Taylor, Ltd., Tarentum, Pennsylvania, 1884-1894.

Columbia Glass Company, Findlay, Ohio, 1886; incorporated into U.S. Glass Company in 1891 as Factory J.

Consolidated Lamp & Glass Company, Pittsburgh & Coraopolis, Pennsylvania, 1894.

Co-Operative Flint Glass Company, Beaver Falls, Pennsylvania, 1889.

* Crystal Glass Company, Pittsburgh, 1868; later moved to Bridgeport, Ohio, in 1882.

Craig & Ritchie, Wheeling, West Virginia, 1824 or 1826 — said to be the first plant in the U.S. for pressing glass. Before Sandwich on Cape Cod.

R. B. Curling & Sons (originally called Curling, Price & Company), Pittsburgh, 1827.

Dalzell, Gilmore & Leighton Company, Findlay, Ohio, 1888.

Diders, McGee, Brilliant, Ohio, date unknown.

Dithridge & Company, Pittsburgh, 1860s; also a factory at Martins Ferry, Ohio.

Doyle & Company, Pittsburgh, 1866; purchased by Phoenix Glass Company, Phillipsburgh, New Jersey in the early 1880s. In 1891, firm was purchased by U.S. Glass Company, known as Factory P.

Dugan Class Company, Indiana, Pennsylvania in 1892 (originally known as Indiana Glass Company).

* George Duncan & Sons, Pittsburgh, 1874; George A. Duncan & Sons, Washington, Pennsylvania, 1894; Duncan & Heisey Company, 1886-1889, Pittsburgh; Duncan & Miller Glass Company, Washington, Pennsylvania, 1870s — U.S. Glass Company's Factory D.

East Liverpool Glass Company, East Liverpool, Ohio, 1882.

Elson Glass Company, Martins Ferry, Ohio, 1882.

Enterprise Glass Works, Ravenna, Ohio, 1878.

Fenton Art Glass Company, Martins Ferry, Ohio, 1906; factory moved to present location in Williamstown, West Virginia, in 1906. The firm is still in business.

Findlay Flint Glass Company, Findlay, Ohio, 1888.

Fort Pitt Glass Works — better known as Dithridge & Company.

Fostoria Glass Company, Fostoria, Ohio, 1887; the factory was moved to Moundsville, West Virginia in 1891, and is still in operation today.

Franklin Flint Glass Company, Philadelphia, 1861.

Gillinder & Bennett, Philadelphia, 1863.

* Gillinder & Sons, Philadelphia, 1867; later sold to U.S. Glass Company and named Factory G.

Graham Glass Works, Brilliant, Ohio, 1895.

Greensburg Glass Company, Greensburg, Pennsylvania, 1889 (previously operated as Brilliant Glass Works, Brilliant, Ohio).

A. H. Heisey Glass Company, Newark, Ohio, 1895.

Hemingray Glass Company, Cincinnati, Ohio & Covington, Kentucky, founded in Cincinnati around 1848.

Hipkins Novelty Mold Shop, Martins Ferry, Ohio, 1884.

*Hobbs, Brockunier & Company, Wheeling, West Virginia, 1863; factory known as J. H Hobbs Glass Company. Taken over by U.S. Glass Company in 1891, calling their new acquisition Factory H.

Homestead Glass Works, Pittsburgh, 1879.

Huntington Glass Company, Huntington, West Virginia, 1891. Originally called Central City until incorporated as Huntington in 1909.

C. Ihmsen & Company, Pittsburgh, 1850s.

Imperial Glass Company, Bellaire, Ohio, 1901. Still in business today.

Indiana Glass Company, Dunkirk, Indiana, 1897. Joined National Glass Company merger in 1899.

Indiana Tumbler & Goblet Company, Greentown, Indiana, 1894. In 1899, firm merged with nineteen other factories to become National Glass Company.

Jefferson Glass Company, Steubenville, Ohio, 1901; moved to Follansbee, West Virginia in 1907.

Jenkins Glass Company, Greentown, Indiana, 1894.

Jersey Glass Company, Jersey City, New Jersey, 1825.

Jones, Cavitt & Company, Pittsburgh, 1884.

*Keystone Tumbler Works, Rochester, Pennsylvania, 1897.

King Glass Company, Pittsburgh, 1880. This firm was absorbed into the U.S. Glass Company in 1891, thereafter known as Factory K.

King, Son & Company, Pittsburgh, 1869.

Kokomo Glass Company, Kokomo, Indiana, 1899. It was destroyed by fire but rebuilt in 1906 as the D. C. Jenkins Glass Company.

*La Belle Glass Company, Bridgeport, Ohio, 1872.

Lancaster Glass Company, Lancaster, Ohio, 1915.

McKee & Brothers Glass Works, Pittsburgh, Pa., 1853-1888. Moved to Jeannette, Pa.; known as McKee-Jeannette Glass Works, 1889-1908. Called McKee Glass Co. from 1908-1951, when purchased by Thatcher Glass Mfg. Co. Now owned by Jeannette Glass Co.

Model Flint Glass Company, Findlay, Ohio, 1888.

Mosaic Glass Company, Fostoria, Ohio, 1887.

Muhleman Glass Works, LaBelle, Ohio, 1888.

National Glass Company, Bellaire, Ohio, 1877. Not **the** National Glass Company.

National Glass Company, Cambridge, Ohio, 1901 (also called Cambridge Glass Company).

New Brighton Glass Company, New Brighton, Pennsylvania, 1884. Originally known as American Ferroline Company.

* New England Glass Company, Cambridge, Massachusetts, early 1800s. Later New England Glass Works.

Nickel Plate Glass Company, Fostoria, Ohio, 1888. Joined the U.S. Glass Company in 1891, becoming their Factory N.

Northwood: Union Glass Works, Martins Ferry, Ohio, 1887; Elwood City, Pennsylvania, 1890; Indiana, Pennyslvania, 1895; Wheeling, West Virginia, 1901 (this factory is probably where he made most of his Carnival Glass.)

Novelty Glass Company, LaGrange, Ohio, 1880; later became U.S. Glass Company's Factory T.

* O'Hara Glass Company, 1848. Joined U.S. Glass Company in 1891 as Factory L.

Ohio Flint Glass Company, Lancaster, Ohio, 1899. Soon merged with the National Glass Company — out of these combines emerged today's giant Anchor-Hocking Glass Company.

Oriental Glass Company, Pittsburgh, early 1890s.

Phoenix Glass Company, Monaca, Pennsylvania, 1880.

Pioneer Glass Company, Pittsburgh, 1891.

Portland Glass Company, Portland, Maine, 1864.

* Richards & Hartley Glass Company, Tarentum, Pennsylvania, 1884-1893.

* Ripley & Company, Pittsburgh, 1866; joined U.S. Glass Company in 1891 as Factory F.

Riverside Glass Company, Wellsburgh, West Virginia, 1879.

Robinson Glass Company, Zanesville, Ohio, 1893.

* Rochester Tumbler Company, Rochester, Pennsylvania, 1872.

Steiner Glass Company, Buckhannon, West Virginia, 1870s.

Tarentum Glass Company, Tarentum, Pennsylvania, 1894-1918.

Thompson Glass Company, Uniontown, Pennsylvania, 1889.

* Union Glass Company, Somerville, Massachusetts, 1851.

U.S. Glass Company, 1891. (See Factories A-T).

Specialty Glass Company, East Liverpool, Ohio, 1889.

West Virginia Glass Company, Martins Ferry, Ohio, 1861.

Westmoreland Glass Company, during World War I.

Westmoreland Specialty Company, early 1890s.

Windsor Glass Company, Pittsburgh, 1887.

Whitla Glass Company, Beaver Falls, Pennsylvania, 1887. In 1890 the company reorganized as Valley Glass Company.

NOTE: There were probably many other glass companies, but as some stayed in business less than a year, and since many never published a catalog or advertised their products in newspapers, etc., the above list gives a fairly comprehensive list of the "better known" producers of pressed glass in the United States from 1824 until the early 1900s.

Silver Definitions

Coin

Made from melted American currency, usually before 1860, usually with 800 or 900 parts of silver. Coin silver spoons are fragile, often found in a repaired condition.

EPNS

Electroplate on nickel silver is nickel metal dipped in a silver solution as electricity is run through the piece.

EPWN

Electroplate on white metal—same process as above.

Plated

The base of plated silver is usually Britannia Ware, 10 parts tin, 1 part antimony. After shaping, the article was plated by an electrolytic method which placed a thin coating of silver over the base metal. Less silver was used than in Sheffield silver.

Sheffield Plate

This is a plated product produced by placing thin sheets of silver on either side of a heavy copper sheet. The basic standard was 8 pounds copper to 2 pounds silver. Dishonest silversmiths used much less silver. There was a heavy penalty if and when they were caught. Pieces you see today that show more copper than silver are examples of this cheaper method.

Silver Plate

Silver plate in England is the equal to our sterling in this country. Solid English silver was marked with the familiar hallmarks: Lion passant, leopard's head, king's (or queen's) head, plus maker's touchmark.

Sterling Silver

By law, it must contain 92.5 parts of pure silver, both here and in England. "Sterling" —Irish, after 1720 (rare), or American, after the 1860s.

Quadruple Plate

Four times dipped.

Triple Plate

Three times dipped.

African Silver

English plate after 1850, by Hills, Monke and Company.

Brazil Silver

Globe Nevada Silver Works, Birmingham, England; on a nickel silverware that was not silver plate.

German Silver

Silver-colored metal from nickel, copper and zinc.

Oregon Silver

Just another trade name used on silverplated English wares after the 1800s.

Siberian Silver

Silver on copper, English; Hayman and Company, late 1800s.

Please note: In 1980 the price of 925/1000 (sterling) silver shot to nearly $60 an ounce. That price has since dropped, but the manufacturers of sterling (flatware, holloware) have raised their prices 300 to 500 percent. This does not indicate the intrinsic (antique) value of the silver piece.

About the Editor

Robert W. Miller is a member of the Appraisers Association of America, the National Trust for Historic Preservation, the Audubon Society, the National Geographic Society and the Smithsonian Institution.

He's a recognized authority on antiques and does consultant work for museums, worldwide. Former editor of The *Antique Trader Weekly,* former host of his own television program on PBS, Mr. Miller is also a contributor of articles on antiques and collectibles to the magazine, *Better Homes and Gardens.*

When not lecturing in Europe or autographing his many books at antiques shows around America, Mr. Miller can usually be found driving one of his antique cars along the "world's most beautiful beaches" in Panama City Beach, Florida. He admits to being two years older than the 1924 Model T Ford Touring Car shown here.